FORENSIC SCIENCE
HANDBOOK VOLUME III

Richard Saferstein, Ph.D., Editor
Forensic Science Consultant

Prentice Hall

Upper Saddle River, New Jersey
Columbus, Ohio

Library of Congress Cataloging-in-Publication Data
(Revised for volume 3)

Forensic science handbook.

   Includes bibliographies and index.
   1. Criminal investigation—Addresses, essays, lectures.   I. Saferstein, Richard, 1941–
HV8073.F585   363.2'5   81-12036
ISBN 0-13-325390-2
     0-13-220715-X

Editor in Chief: Vernon R. Anthony
Acquisitions Editor: Tim Peyton
Editorial Assistant: Alicia Kelly
Director of Marketing: David Gesell
Marketing Manager: Adam Kloza
Senior Marketing Coordinator: Alicia Dysert
Project Manager: Wanda Rockwell
Creative Director: Jayne Conte

Pearson Education Ltd., London
Pearson Education Singapore Pte. Ltd.
Pearson Education Canada, Inc.
Pearson Education—Japan

Pearson Education Australia Pty. Limited
Pearson Education North Asia Ltd., Hong Kong
Pearson Educación de Mexico, S.A. de C.V.
Pearson Education Malaysia Pte. Ltd.

Prentice Hall
is an imprint of

www.pearsonhighered.com

ISBN-13: 978-0-13-220715-7
ISBN-10:   0-13-220715-X

To the memory of my friend
and fellow forensic scientist
Don Nittskoff.

CONTRIBUTING AUTHORS

Jack Ballantyne, Ph.D.
Associate Director for Research
National Center for
Forensic Science
University of Central Florida
Orlando, FL 32816-2366

Dr. Edward G. Bartick, Director
Forensic Science Program
Department of Chemistry and
Biochemisrty
Suffolk University
Beacon Hill
Boston, MA 02114-4280

David Benjamin, Ph.D.
77 Florence St.
Suite 107 N
Chestnut Hill, MA 02467-1918

Chesterene Cwiklik
Cwikik & Associates
2400 6th Ave. S
Suite 257
Seattle, WA 98134

Peter De Forest, D.Crim.
John Jay College
445 West 59th St.
New York, NY 10019

Kerstin M. Gleim
3635 Woodland Park Ave. North
Seattle, WA 98103

Erin K. Hanson, M.S.
University of Central Florida
National Center for Forensic
Science
Orlando, FL 32816

Lawrence Kobilinsky, Ph.D.
John Jay College/CUNY
899 Tenth Ave.
New York, NY 10019

Thomas Kupiec, Ph.D.
Analytical Research Labs
840 Research Parkway
Suite 546
Oklahoma City, OK 73104

Nicholas Petraco, M.S., D-ABC
New York City Police Department
(Retired)
Forensic Science Consultant
73 Ireland Place
Amityville, NY 11701

Nicholas D.K. Petraco, Ph.D.
John Jay College of Criminal
Justice, 445 West 59th St.
New York, NY 10019

Vishnu Raj, BDS, MSFS
Analytical Research Labs
840 Research Parkway
Suite 546
Oklahoma City, OK 73104

Edward Suzuki, Ph.D.
Washington State Patrol Crime
Laboratory
2203 Airport Way South
Suite 250
Seattle, WA 98134-2045

Arie Zeichner, Ph.D.
Nof Harim 19 B/2
Jerusalem 96190
Israel

CONTENTS

PREFACE

Like its predecessors, *Forensic Science Handbook, Volume III,* aims to describe theories and practices of forensic science to both practitioners and students of the subject. It is testimony to the ability of forensic science that its subject matter can barely be contained within three volumes of this series. The editor is extremely gratified with the wide circulation enjoyed by the first two volumes of the *Handbook,* and views their success as confirmation of his belief that in-depth reviews of pertinent forensic science topics can put the subject in a better perspective for both the practitioner and student. It's gratifying that many consider the handbooks to be the starting point for researching current forensic science methodology.

Forensic Science Handbook, Volume III, 2nd edition, aims to fill the voids of the first two books. The *Handbook* opens with an overview discussion aimed at developing a strategy to guide forensic analysts through processes needed to make scientifically and legally reliable decisions about the focus, priority, and sequence of examinations of laboratory physical evidence (Chapter 1). Given the intensity of research in the area of forensic DNA typing, it is not surprising that two chapters of this book are devoted to this topic. The reader first encounters an in-depth general treatment of the structure and chemistry of DNA with accompanying discussions of adjunct subjects such as polymerase chain reaction (Chapter 7), followed by a chapter detailing the subject of short-tandem repeats positioned on the Y chromosome (Chapter 8).

The spectrum of topics encompassing the field of forensic science is impressive and makes for a diverse collection of chapters bound within the covers of this volume. The advent of Fourier transform infrared analysis revitalized infrared spectroscopy as a vibrant forensic analytical tool. Dr. Edward Suzuki's chapter (Chapter 3) offers the reader an overview of infrared theory and its applications to forensic science analysis, followed by Dr. Ed Bartick's in-depth treatment (Chapter 4) of recent advances in the forensic science technology—infrared microspectrophotometry. One's grasp of the fundamentals of forensic toxicology will be expanded by Dr. David Benjamin's chapter (Chapter 5) covering the principles of analytical pharmacology. The abuse of prescribed drugs has seen a meteoritic rise in recent years. Understanding the consequences and implications of polydrug interactions is now fundamental to the knowledge base of the forensic toxicologist and is the subject of an in-depth chapter in the *Handbook.* Finally, the chapter by the Petracos and De Forest reemphasizes the traditional and daily practices employed by crime laboratories for the characterization of a wide variety of physical evidence.

Finally, I'm deeply grateful to all the contributors of this book as well as the first two volumes for the time and effort they gave to this series. They all deserve to share in the success of the *Forensic Science Handbooks.*

Richard Saferstein

1

■ ■ ■

Forensic Casework from Start to Finish

Chesterene L. Cwiklik
Pacific Coast Forensic Science Institute Inc., 2400 Sixth Avenue South #256, Seattle, WA 98134 and Cwiklik & Associates, Seattle, WA, 2400 Sixth Avenue South #257, Seattle, WA 98134

Kerstin M. Gleim
Pacific Coast Forensic Science Institute Inc., 2400 Sixth Avenue South #256, Seattle, WA 98134 and Emerald City Forensics, 4253 Woodland Park Avenue N., Seattle, WA 98103

INTRODUCTION

Science Applied to the Law

The word *forensic* refers to debate, and by extension, to the law. The forensic science practitioner is a scientist, engineer, physician, anthropologist, crime scene analyst, and other examiner who works in the context of the legal system.[a] It is not always a comfortable fit. The legal practitioner—a lawyer—is trained to approach truth by argument, whereas a scientist is trained to approach truth by testing.[1] The training of a lawyer involves forming and evaluating competing hypotheses in order to argue either side of a proposition, that is, either side of a statement to be tested. The training of a scientist is to form hypotheses to be tested via experiment to determine which, if any, hypothesis is true. Communications can be difficult unless this difference is acknowledged and bridged.

---

[a]*Scientist* is used in the rest of the text to designate scientists, engineers, physicians, anthropologists, toxicologists, crime scene analysts, and so on.

Another difficulty for the scientist is that in many countries, the judicial system is adversarial,[b] whereas science is collegial. The culture of the law is to fight the good fight so that justice prevails, whereas the culture of the scientist is to work within a community of colleagues to establish truth. The contribution of said colleagues may be acrimonious criticism, and the culture of either profession may be honored as much in the breach as in the practice, but it governs expectations, ethics, and what is considered good work.

In most jurisdictions, the criminal or civil defense is allowed to retain its own scientific expert to review, examine, or rebut work performed by a prosecution or plaintiff's expert, a practice that can be thought of as a quality assurance measure of the judicial system. Although each expert is expected to be impartial and not to be an advocate for either side, the scientist as well as the scientific work may be subjected not only to scrutiny, but also to attack by the opposing attorney.

By using a logical approach and reasoning tools, the forensic scientist and the forensic science laboratory can make the decisions that allow the most important work to be done, to be performed reliably, reported accurately, and to withstand scrutiny. That is the focus of this chapter.

Casework Decisions and the Analytical Plan

Forensic casework is a process involving a number of decisions and judgments regarding which items to examine, which samples to collect, which properties to test in a particular instance, which tests to perform, how initial results modify the testing plan, and with what testing the work can be considered complete. It is important that these decisions and judgments be based on sound criteria that are grounded in the case questions and structured on good scientific practice.

Good analytical decisions flow from an analytical plan. The scientist cannot form an analytical plan in an information vacuum, and must have enough background information about the case and the case issues to be able to form hypotheses. The background information includes what are presumed—but not always known—to be facts.

Investigators and lawyers typically must establish certain elements of the case, including what happened, whether there was a crime, who was the perpetrator, what sequence of events led to the actual crime, whether other people had a role, and whether a motive could be inferred. Once someone is charged with a crime or a lawsuit is levied, the lawyers involved form hypotheses about the case that are broader than those of the scientist. The hypotheses formed by a scientist, and the need for background information, are limited to those questions that can be addressed by physical evidence. Usually, the scientist does not need to know motive, or the overall personal history of a victim or suspect, but must know which activities or habits of those individuals may produce damage, staining, or debris.

For example, when bloodstains on a person's clothing are of interest, it is important to know that said person is an emergency medical technician (EMT).

---

[b]In some countries, the judicial system is based on the model of arbitration or conflict resolution.

Similarly, it is useful for the scientist to know competing accounts of what transpired to determine whether there is evidence that supports or casts doubt on either account. If it is suspected that more than one location was involved in a homicide or that an assault victim had recent sexual contact with more than one person, the scientist must be aware of this information to evaluate whether the necessary reference samples are available.

Background samples are equally important as background information. If a fiber found on a suspect's pants has characteristics like those of the fibers constituting a sweater worn by the victim, it is not potential evidence of contact unless one knows that the fiber is truly foreign. If that type of fiber is also found in the normal debris of the suspect's residence or workplace, it is not foreign to that person and cannot be used as evidence of contact with the sweater. The same reasoning applies to very small amounts of DNA, or to isolated particles of gunpowder residue that are not part of a pattern, as they may be part of background debris.

Relevant, Significant, and Specific

Scientific work is *relevant* if it addresses the case issues and *significant* if it can narrow down hypotheses. Work is *specific* if it can narrow down potential sources. Testing decisions should be governed first by potential significance, and only then by potential specificity.

CASE EXAMPLE 1

A vehicle struck a cyclist and the cyclist died after being thrown onto the roadway. The clothing of the cyclist was examined for transfer of automotive paint. Single-layer paint smears and multi-layer paint chips were observed. The most significant paint evidence is the smeared paint, as it can be linked to an impact. The multi-layer paint chips are more specific, as they narrow down a source vehicle, but are less significant, because paint chips from unrelated incidents can be transferred from the roadway. Once the smears have been examined, those paint chips with a top layer like that of the paint smears could narrow the source vehicle.

Responsibility, Accountability, and Control

The *responsibility* of the forensic scientist is to the evidence, but he or she is accountable to all the parties with a legitimate interest in the case, such as police and private investigators; agents of regulatory agencies, prosecuting and defense attorneys; suspects, defendants and victims of crime, the parties and attorneys in civil cases; juries; and the courts. They, as well as the citizenry and community at large, have a stake in rigorous and reliable scientific work being performed, work that the public, the law enforcement and legal communities, the courts, and individuals accused of crimes can be confident is useful, complete, and fair.

The scientist, although accountable, has only partial control of the work being done for several reasons, including those that follow. Thus, ongoing communication with investigators and other scientists working on the case is a critical component of doing good scientific work.

1. The crime laboratory scientist only sometimes collects samples from the relevant scene or related scenes (this is less true of forensic environmental scientists, engineers, and medical examiner personnel). Most evidence in criminal cases is collected by non-scientist evidence technicians or by the police themselves. When scientists respond to a scene, it is usually different scientists who later examine the items and the samples that were collected. In such circumstances, the scientist examining the evidence in the laboratory has not selected the sample, did not see the item or the sample in context, and is working with incomplete information.

2. Police and other investigators usually select which evidence is submitted to the crime laboratory for examination. It is of great benefit for at least one of the scientists working on a case to examine photographs of the scene, to discuss the case with the investigator, and discuss the items being submitted and the goals of examinations to be performed. Sometimes the detective or investigator requests specific tests or asks that specific items be examined. It may be that some of the requested work does not really address the case issues, and that the issues could be addressed by work that was not requested. The scientist can suggest additional items to be submitted, and suggest that other examinations not be performed, at least not at the outset.

3. The management of the laboratory (or equivalent institution) that designs and implements policies affecting which cases are handled, which evidence is accepted, how the work is assigned, how much work is assigned to an individual scientist, and how time and other resources are allocated to certain types of work.

4. Laboratory policy, external standards such as American Society of Testing Materials (ASTM) methods, and standards used by accrediting bodies all influence casework and may govern the specific testing that can be performed.

Doing the Right Thing and Doing It Right: Impact-Based Decisions

Good laboratory work means doing the right thing and doing it right. The work is germane, the analytical approach is sound, and work that could be exculpatory was performed if the right thing was done. If it was done right, the preliminary examinations are complete, the sample selection is appropriate, the data is accurate, the accuracy is known, the equipment is suitable, the person responsible for the analysis has adequate knowledge, and so on.

Impact-based decision making can be applied to such questions as whether laboratory work can make a difference (i.e., whether laboratory resources should be allocated to this work), whether particular evidence is relevant (i.e., whether it answers case questions), whether a particular result is significant (i.e., whether it narrows down hypotheses), and whether there is information that is germane but of limited significance, or simply does not address the case questions (i.e., can't exclude vs. can't tell). Impact-based reasoning underlies such questions as the following: Is there a small chance of getting results, but those results would be highly significant? Could examinations add little to what is known regarding a suspect's involvement, but still be potentially exculpatory? If a result confirms the case hypothesis, does it add much to what is already known? If the hypothesis were false, could this be demonstrated by the testing plan used? These questions are addressed by the conceptual tools that follow.

PRELIMINARY CASE ASSESSMENT

What We Know and What We Don't Know

A preliminary assessment should address the following: What are the questions of interest (i.e., the case issues), and which of these issues can be resolved by scientific testing.[2] The concerns of the person requesting laboratory services should be restated as testing issues. Not all issues are scientific, but they may have a bearing on the analytical plan.

CASE EXAMPLE 2

A woman was found in a rubble-strewn lot with a bleeding head injury and told investigating police that she was raped and hit on the head with a bottle by a man she described. A bottle was found at the scene. A transient matching the description was found two blocks away. That he was a transient affects assumptions about which deposits on his clothing and person would be recent, as he may have been wearing the same clothing for an extended time.[c]

The background information can be distilled into two simple lists: What we know, and what don't we know. The *What we don't know* list should form the basis for an analytical plan. It is not important at this stage to be certain that all the background information designated as *What we know* is reliable. Whether reliable or not it is really a *What we think we know* list—it forms the context for testing decisions. As testing progresses, the results can be reflected back to the initial information and help evaluate whether it is sound.

We know that the victim was found outside amidst rubble, that she was bleeding from a head wound, that a man who fits the victim's general description was found two blocks away, and that the man was a transient. *We also know* that a bottle was found.

We do not know what caused the victim's wound, whether the wound was inflicted by an assailant (it could also be self-inflicted or from a fall), or whether the bottle was used as a weapon. *We do not know* whether the victim was sexually assaulted; she sustained a head injury and may have been confused, and may even have had a seizure or small stroke. We do not really know whether a crime was committed. *We do not*

---

[c]Some of the details of the actual case have been changed for illustrative purposes.

know whether the suspect was an assailant, whether he stopped to help, or whether there is there any evidence that the suspect perpetrated an assault, and if he did, what type of assault. These are the things we want to find out. The *What we do not know* list forms the basis for hypothesis formation. We use this as an ongoing case example throughout the chapter, and follow up with more specific hypotheses later.

Framing the Case Questions: Who, What, When, Where, and How

The *What we know* and *What we don't know* lists need elaboration to be useful in forming an analytical plan. It is easy to elaborate by asking *Who, What, When, Where,* and *How*—the traditional questions asked by reporters, minus the *Why,* because motive cannot usually be addressed by scientific testing. For example: What happened? Was the victim assaulted? If yes, who did it? The suspect? Someone else? How did the victim get the head wound?

At this stage, if one asks only if the suspect did the deed, it is too narrow a focus. That is the proper question when the case is about to go to trial. At the investigative stage, the focus should be on getting information to answer those case questions that can affect the direction of the investigation, such as finding leads that help rule out suspects or that identify a perpetrator, any vehicles involved, and sites of interest other than the scene. A broader focus on the part of the forensic scientist helps the scientist keep an open mind, and lets the investigator investigate, rather than making decisions about scientific testing.

Hierarchy of Hypothesis-Forming Propositions: Origin, Activity, and Offense

Another tool that can be used in framing the case questions, and later in evaluating the results, is the hierarchy of propositions proposed by Cook, Evett, Jackson, and Jones (1998): *origin* (identification or source of material), *activity* (action), and *offense* (crime or civil offense).[3] Although developed for a crime-laboratory context, the hierarchy of propositions is a broadly useful tool and can be rephrased for use in environmental site testing as *materials, activities, and liability* (Ref. 4, p. 10). Not all of these levels of information are possible to provide in every instance, particularly the offense level, but each level should be addressed if the evidence permits.

In Case Example 2: If semen is found on the vaginal swabs, whose is it (*origin or source*)? Is there evidence of a struggle, such as damage to the victim's clothing or clumps of pulled hair (*activity*)? Was this an assault, an accident, or a self-inflicted injury (*offense*)?

CASE EXAMPLE 3

A man is found in his bed, dead from a near-contact gunshot wound to his head. A gun is found nearby. The immediate case question is whether it is homicide or suicide. The clothing, autopsy samples, gun from the scene, and scene photographs are examined in the laboratory. Source-level information (i.e., identification of materials) includes particles on the victim's hands, found to be gunshot residue; blood on the victim's sleeves, tested for DNA and attributed to the victim; and a bullet recovered from the victim, found to correspond with test bullets fired from a gun found beside the victim. Activity-level information includes blood spatter on the hands and one arm, determined to have spattered outward from the gunshot wound; the location of gunshot residue on the hand, found to be consistent with the victim's holding the gun; and the observation that the gun was found where it could have slid from the victim's hands. The offense level can be addressed in this case, as the evidence supports suicide.

CASE EXAMPLE 4

The body of a man found on a busy roadway had been run over by a vehicle. The clothing is submitted to the laboratory to search for any paint deposits that could provide information about a hit-and-run vehicle. Automotive paint smears are found on the shoulder of the victim's jacket, a location where paint is often found when a person is struck by a car and flipped over the hood. Comparison of paint reference standards suggested a make, model, and range of years of the source vehicle (*source*). However, the paint smear on the victim's jacket was deposited in the opposite direction from what would be expected had he slid across the hood, as the smear is observed as having an up-the-shoulder pattern instead of a downward pattern (*activity*). This laboratory finding leads police to investigate further. Subsequent investigation establishes that the victim was killed and then left in the roadway to draw attention away from murder (information regarding crime or *offense*).

CASE EXAMPLE 5

A woman's body is found in a motor home that had gone over a cliff on a mountain road, and her husband, who was not in the vehicle at the time, says that she missed a curve. The woman's daughters from a previous marriage are suspicious, and the daughters sue to prevent the husband from collecting on her life insurance policy and inheriting the woman's sizable estate. At the same time, the sheriff's office is conducting a criminal investigation. The life insurance policy naming the husband as sole beneficiary is submitted to the crime laboratory as well as to a private examiner for a questioned document examination. The signature is found to be superficially like that of the dead woman's, but is in fact non-genuine (*source*). The questioned document examination reveals a pressure-track guideline on the signed document not related to the visible signature. The defects of the signature include poor speed, hesitations, patching, tremor, and other traits of non-spontaneous writing. The husband's explanation for the guideline was that the first pen had run out of ink and he attributed the other odd features of the signature to a wobbly bar table. The excuses are not supported by the evidence. Hesitation marks and heavy grooved lines in the signature, made with a felt-tipped pen, indicate that it was a tracing, with the folds in the paper beneath showing through as the grooved lines in the writing (*activity*). The examination establishes that the signature on the document had been forged (*offense*).

In summary, the tools used at the outset are those for developing the questions to be answered: getting background information, sorting it into testable questions using a know-and-don't- know list, the traditional reporter questions (who, what when, where, and how), and the hierarchy of propositions for levels of information.

DEVELOPING AND ASSESSING CASE HYPOTHESES

Multiple Hypotheses at the Outset

The *What we don't know* and the *Who-What-When-Where-How* lists can be used to generate a number of possible explanations for the initial information. It is useful to generate multiple hypotheses at the outset, so that if one is disproved, the others are ready, and the scientist is less tempted to pursue a losing hypothesis simply because so much work has already been done.[4] It is important to consider even unlikely explanations if they are possible. The key at the hypothesis formation stage is *possibility,* not *likelihood.* The benefits of multiple hypotheses at the outset are several: preventing too narrow a focus, allowing for a clear next step, giving a basis for evaluating methods, promoting objectivity, preventing getting stuck on one track as testing progresses, and providing a basis for the degree of certainty in forming conclusions when testing is complete. Generally, the more that potential sources for a material have been narrowed down, the greater the degree of certainty of a conclusion. The more that hypotheses have been narrowed down, the greater the degree of certainty of an inference.

Hypothesis formation should incorporate a list of testable questions. Elements that cannot be addressed by laboratory work, such as whether the victim in Case Example 2 had a history of seizures, should be discussed with the person who requested the work, as they may have an impact on the significance of scientific findings. However, the analytical plan must focus on those issues that can be addressed by scientific testing, and the issues must be articulated clearly.

At this stage of Case Example 2, before any examinations have been performed, it is useful to list some possibilities or preliminary hypotheses. Preliminary hypotheses arise partly from the *What we do not know* list. Several possibilities that can be tested include the following:

1. The victim was assaulted by the suspect.
2. The victim was assaulted by someone else.
3. The victim fell and hit her head (perhaps she was dazed—not testable in the laboratory).
4. The suspect had no involvement in the incident.

These and other possibilities are sharpened into more formal hypotheses after some of the analytical results have been obtained.

DEVISING AN ANALYTICAL PLAN

Stage of the Case or the Project

In criminal cases, the stages of a case include an investigative stage (finding clues to what was done and who did it), the decision to file charges or complaints (where the focus shifts from a broad-based investigation to the activities of the parties being charged), and the probative (trial) stage (finding support that the accused actually did what they are accused of, or failing to find such support).[5] In environmental work, the stages of a project usually include a regulatory stage, a stage of assessing responsibility, and a remediation stage.[6] The case questions and work priorities differ with each stage. The stages in civil cases parallel those of criminal cases, except that the standard of proof (probative stage) is different. In criminal cases, proof must be developed beyond a reasonable doubt. In civil cases, the standard of proof is preponderance of evidence, and matters are often settled by negotiation rather than trial, but in either setting, the same tools are useful. The evaluative tools useful for the probative stage in either criminal or civil proceedings (formal mutually exclusive hypotheses and a thorough exploration of potentially exculpatory findings) are the underpinnings of rigorous scientific work of any type. These are discussed later in the chapter.

Tools for Deciding Where to Begin: Priorities and Impact

The scientist must decide which items or samples to examine, which examinations to perform, and in what order. The integrity of potential evidence is critical, and should that be in jeopardy, safeguarding access to the evidence and its integrity is urgent and must be done at the outset. Testing should begin by getting the most important information quickly, and is not complete until all relevant items or samples have been tested.

URGENT   Work should begin with what is *urgent* (i.e., materials that are labile or may degrade once collected or that might be otherwise lost). Items or samples that are urgent to examine may be of unknown importance and relevance, but immediate action is required because if something is not done quickly, any chance of gathering further information from that source may be jeopardized.

This consideration also affects collection of items. It may be that normal use would cause evidence to be lost—for example, if residues or body fluid deposits on a person would be lost by washing up. There may be attempts to destroy evidence, such as firearms or other weapons, bloody clothing, flammable liquids, and so on. Evidence at outdoor sites could be affected by weather or traffic, or because sites must be returned to the use of the owners. The urgent action may be sample collection or preservation rather than testing and might even be to contact the investigator to suggest that be done. In Case Example 2, urgent work includes talking with the investigator to find out if any shoeprints were photographed at the scene.

USEFUL   Within the set of items that are important to examine (potentially high impact) is a subset that is most likely to answer the main question. In other words, some items offer a better likelihood of obtaining useful results. These should be tested first. The information most needed at the beginning of an investigation is that which is needed to find a suspect, and once a suspect has been developed, to determine if the suspect can be the actual perpetrator.

In Case Example 2, the most useful items to examine first are the suspect's clothing, pubic combings, and penile swabs for any link to the assault (*Is it the right suspect?*), to examine the suspect's sexual assault kit swabs for any evidence of sexual activity (*Is he linked to the victim through sexual contact?*), and to examine the victim's sexual assault kit (*Was there sexual contact with the suspect or anyone else?*). These items could quickly establish a link between the suspect and the incident under investigation, even though it may not be sufficient to establish whether the suspect committed a crime.

IMPORTANT   After urgent samples are either tested or preserved for testing and the most useful initial tests have been performed, any other *important* (potentially high impact) items and samples should be tested next, including the items or examinations that have the potential to set the direction of the investigation. Testing them can eliminate possibilities that are not viable. This should be done at the outset so that time is used effectively.

Of nearly equal importance to finding or eliminating a link with a suspect is finding all the sites related to a crime. Sometimes the body of a homicide victim is found in a location remote from where the victim was killed. It is important to establish the actual crime scene, any vehicle used to transport the person or the body, and any intermediate sites. If evidence is received at this stage of the investigation, it may be necessary for the laboratory to provide information that aids the investigator to support or eliminate some of the possibilities quickly so that efforts can be focused most productively.[7]

RELEVANT (CRIME OBJECTS)   *Relevant items,* also referred to as *crime objects.*[8, 9] are those items that are an inherent part of the problem being investigated, and are the reference points for testing decisions, including when testing is complete. Crime objects in Case Example 2 include fresh blood on the victim and anything else that was clearly a part of the incident. Relevant items can have a high impact on the investigation even if testing yields unlikely results, and can change the course of the inquiry. The forensic scientist should usually ensure at least a cursory examination of the relevant items (crime objects), because any surprises here could make a big difference in a case.

SUSPECT OBJECTS   Another set of reference points is composed of those items or samples that characterize the suspect or suspects.[10] In environmental work, the corresponding set of reference points is made up of those items or samples that characterize the actors/agents/ potentially responsible parties (PRPs).[11] In Case Example 2, these include the clothing, reference samples of blood and hair, pubic combings, and penile swabs from the suspect. Unless the suspect is known to have been at the crime scene, suspect items are not an inherent part of the crime, and are significant only if a link is established. They form the reference points for a suspect and for whether there is a link.

CASE EXAMPLE 6

The body of a woman is found in her bed; she has been strangled with a sock tied around her neck. Entry appears to be through a window that was pried open in another room. The suspect is her upstairs neighbor. Crime objects include the ligature, formed with a sock probably from the victim's dirty-clothes basket; the victim's nightgown and watch; and samples taken at autopsy, including pubic combings, a hair found on her buttocks, tape lifts from her hands, and reference samples. Additional crime objects include a shoeprint on the ledge of the window that was pried open, as well as metal shavings and other debris from the window frame. Suspect objects includes a pair of pants found in his dirty laundry; his shoes and underwear; a sweatshirt found soaking in a plastic tub; and reference samples of blood, hair, and saliva. The hair on the victim's buttocks and foreign debris on the victim's person are analyzed and attributed to the suspect and his clothing. Because the suspect had been in the house before, only the crime objects were significant in evaluating transfer to his clothing. Carpet and furniture fibers on the suspect's shoes that correspond to reference samples from the victim's apartment are not significant (do not have the potential to answer the case questions) and not relevant (not an inherent part of the homicide).

IMPORTANT VERSUS RELEVANT   Other items at the site that are not an inherent part of the problem are potentially relevant, and are important to test because they have a potentially high impact on the investigation. Any involvement must be established rather than being inherent. For example, in Case Example 2, blood or blood-stained objects from the scene, other potential weapons, and any shoeprints are all important and should be examined, although it may not be known at the outset whether they are relevant to the incident under investigation.

In summary, deciding where to begin testing involves getting the most important information fast. The tools for deciding where to begin are evaluating what is *relevant* (inherent to the problem and can change the direction of the investigation), what is *important* (potentially high impact; relevance must be established), what is *useful* (has a high likelihood of getting useful results), and what is *urgent* (sample preservation and other immediate action). These tools are used in deciding which items to examine, which examinations to perform, and what can be left unexamined or untested.

Do urgent work first, and then do what is most useful. In the investigative stage of a case, detectives need to know whether they have the right suspect. If they do not find out quickly, they lose critical time. In Case Example 2, the suspect's clothing and penile swabs and the swabs from the victim are the most likely to yield information that either confirms or calls into question whether the current suspect is the actual perpetrator. Any evidence on the victim's clothing is next. However, the work cannot be considered complete for the probative stage until all the *relevant* items have been examined.

Modifying the Analytical Plan During the Testing Process

The results of the initial testing suggest the next steps. In Case Example 2, no semen was found on swabs from the victim and no DNA attributable to the victim was found on penile swabs from the suspect, but faint contact deposits of blood were found in the zippered fly area of the suspect's inner, middle, and outer trousers (he was wearing three pairs). The blood was tested and attributed to the victim. This is a clear link with the victim and the incident, but does not establish the suspect's role.

The point of an initial investigation is to form hypotheses that can be tested; the point of testing is to distinguish among hypotheses to eliminate the ones that are not true. It may be that testing results suggest additional hypotheses that are then evaluated. A good way to sort through this is to ask whether the evidence and results of testing would be different if one hypothesis rather than another hypothesis that it is being weighed against were true. To distinguish any two hypotheses, the evidence and results must be different for each. Otherwise they are not distinguishable with the tests performed so far. This concept is of interest to the courts and, under the rubric of falsifiability, is one of the criteria for deciding the admissibility of scientific evidence.[12] If the tests performed and proposed in the analytical plan cannot distinguish among the hypotheses, the testing plan should be modified and additional or different tests proposed.

In Case Example 2, it is likely that the blood on the pants was deposited while the suspect was opening or closing the fly of his pants, therefore must have had the victim's fresh blood on his hands. Was this because he assaulted her with the bottle? Or did he touch her after someone else assaulted her, perhaps in an attempt to help? The testing performed so far does not distinguish between these hypotheses. Of the original possibilities, one hypothesis is that the suspect was not involved in the incident. So far, this is the only hypothesis that can be eliminated.

Another tool in narrowing down hypotheses is to ask oneself what evidence is expected if a given hypothesis is true. If hypothesis *x* is true, one expects to find *y*. Finding *y* supports hypothesis *x*, and failing to find it suggests that hypothesis *x* should be reconsidered. In Case Example 2, if the bottle was used to strike the victim on the head with enough force to break the skin, one expects to find her blood and impacted hair on the bottle. Failing to find this does not disprove the hypothesis of the bottle as a weapon (blood could be wiped off and hairs could be dislodged), but raises questions about it. The scientist must then examine the evidence carefully for any other clues as to what may have transpired and should also ask police to search for other potential weapons.

In summary, the scientist, engineer, or other forensic practitioner narrows down the possibilities as test results come in. Specific steps that lead to defensible conclusions include the following:

1. Articulating alternative hypotheses that could explain the evidence and testing results.
2. Determining what tests can distinguish among the hypotheses, and what items must be tested (or further tested).

3. Looking for specific evidence that would be expected if a hypothesis is true.

4. Testing for that evidence if it has not yet been done.

These steps and the reasoning process should be documented in the bench notes. The record in the notes allows the scientist to recall which possibilities were considered and eliminated.

DEFENSIBLE CRITERIA FOR SAMPLING DECISIONS

Criteria for Sampling

Factors to consider when making decisions in sampling include the potential for source, activity, and offense information; significance to the case questions; the likelihood of getting useful results; the possibility of clear attribution; and groupings of materials. The likelihood of getting useful results rests on optimum sample type and condition; sufficient material for testing and retesting; and optimum accuracy, specificity, and attribution. Note that both significance and specificity are included in these factors, with specificity considered only after significance has been taken into account. *Attribution* refers to knowing which part of the material produces a specific result: background material or deposit, which component of a mixture, which layer or part of a mosaic, and so forth.

CASE EXAMPLE 7

Two men are arrested for a triple homicide of two young men and one young woman. A rabbit fur coat found near the body of the young woman exhibits numerous semen stains. The crime lab tests a sample from the center of one of these stains and finds DNA attributable to the victim and to both suspects. One of the suspects says that he was there but left before anything happened, and is adamant that he did not have sexual contact with the victim. Vaginal swabs from the victim include a semen fraction with DNA attributable to the other suspect only. The coat is reexamined, and additional samples are taken from the stain of interest, which, unlike the other deposits, is a noticeably asymmetrical stain (see Case Example 7 diagrams in Appendix A). Two additional samples are taken from the margins of the stain, and each yields a different result: One includes DNA attributable to a mixture of the victim's DNA and the other suspect. The second additional sample yields DNA attributable to the first suspect and to him alone. Numerous additional semen stains are found, several of which are tested, all yielding DNA attributable to the first suspect alone. When this is discussed with investigators, they already have indications from other items in the first suspect's bedroom that he likes to ejaculate into furry objects. There is no evidence to support this suspect's having sexual contact with the victim. The original sample taken by the crime lab is in an area of probable overlap and does not meet the criterion of clear attribution, as it is not possible to determine which component of the stain produced which result. (See Appendix A.)

The amount sampled must leave enough material for retesting, not only to repeat any tests, but also for any testing by opposing experts. In many jurisdictions, if there is not enough material for retesting, the scientist must notify the attorney he or she is working with so that they can notify the opposing attorney, as the latter may wish to have the testing witnessed by his or her own expert. It is also important to leave enough material for reexamination of activity level information, such as how a material was deposited. If an entire stain is extracted prior to DNA testing, even if there is ample extract for repeated DNA tests, it is no longer possible to reevaluate whether the material was spattered, dripped, deposited by direct contact, and so on.

Groupings of materials refers to overlapping stains, adhering or embedded trace evidence (it is important to know which, as debris embedded in a drying stain provides a timeline), adhering or embedded gunpowder, stains deposited on fresh damage, flammable liquid residues on a bloodstained item, a series of materials embedded on the nose of a bullet, and also includes mixtures. A mixture implies materials that have comingled so that the component parts are no longer separate. This is the situation with a mixture of alleles in DNA, but may not be true of other types of deposits where materials were deposited sequentially or can still be separated physically. It is best to test each material separately, if possible, and to take samples that allow such testing to be done. Samples should reflect not only each mixture, but also a clean area of each material (again, if possible). In the case of flammable liquids on a bloodstained item, the examiners in both disciplines should confer immediately about evidence preservation before either type of evidence is compromised.

In Case Example 2, faint deposits of blood were found in the fly area of the inner and outer pairs of pants worn by the suspect. The stain with the best chance for specific and unmixed results is the stain on the outer pants, but the stain on the inner pair of pants is more significant because it demonstrates that the genitals were exposed (*activity level information*). However, the inner pair of pants is encrusted with accumulated skin deposits as well as any residues of other body fluids, either his own or from previous sexual contact, and may yield a mixture of DNA. Both the more significant but contaminated stains on the inner pants and the cleaner potentially more specific stains on the outer pants should be sampled and tested. The stains on the middle pair of pants need not be as they could be grouped with the others by virtue of corresponding location and similar manner of deposit.

Types of Samples

Three types of samples are needed for most types of evidence analysis: evidence samples, samples that provide background information (controls), and standards or reference samples (comparison samples). The distinction among them may depend on the context. Is it background DNA, or evidence of the usual wearer? *Standards or reference samples* (comparison samples, or knowns) represent a person or object that is a possible source of an evidence sample. Their origin is known and is established by witnesses and documentation, such as chain of custody records or photographs of sample collection. *Evidence samples* (questioned samples or unknowns) are samples whose origin or whose link with the incident under investigation must be determined by testing. *Control samples* are run to make sure that a test is working properly so that a negative result is obtained when the material or property is absent and a positive result when it is there. One type of negative control, referred to as a *blank*, includes the sample matrix, but not the substance being tested for. Samples of background debris or background DNA sometimes fall into this category.

INTERPRETING THE RESULTS: DEFENSIBLE WORK, RECORDS, CONCLUSIONS, AND TESTIMONY

Deciding When You Are Done

Testing and analysis is complete when the case questions have been answered, or addressed as far as testing permits, when potentially exculpatory examinations have been performed, and when all relevant evidence items (crime objects) have been examined, at least cursorily. Once the hypotheses have been narrowed down and additional tests have been performed, the scientist can evaluate the hypotheses based on all the information available and perform any last few examinations. One should ask whether the results would be different if the hypothesis is wrong. If not, the tests are not adequate to the questions. If there are any relevant objects that have not yet been examined (i.e., crime objects or items that are reference points), this is the time to do so. An exploratory examination may be sufficient, and it is not necessary to test redundant samples from the same object or area. Finally, the scientist should resolve any findings that at first appear contradictory. If findings seem to point in two different directions, they may both be pointing in a third direction. See where the findings converge. That is the best explanation, even if others are possible. (See Diagram in Appendix B.)

CASE EXAMPLE 8

A young man and woman were accosted in the woods by three men. The young man was killed and the young woman raped. When three suspects are arrested, one of them admits to involvement in harassing the victims and to being a lookout, positioned some distance down a wooded path, while the other two were raping the victim. He says that he was unaware of the homicide and did not participate in the rape. DNA swabs of the victim's vaginal vault include a profile from the spermatozoa fraction that could be explained by a combination of the young man and all three suspects; however, it could also be explained by a combination of the young man who was murdered and two of the suspects, without including the one who claimed to be a lookout.

Pubic hair combings are obtained from both victims, but DNA testing of the hairs does not prove to be useful. The telogen—i.e., rest phase—roots are not suitable for nuclear DNA testing, and mitochondrial DNA (mDNA) testing cannot distinguish among the three suspects, who are maternal cousins. Should microscopic hair comparisons be performed? Microscopic examination is neither as specific nor as reliable as DNA testing in distinguishing among individuals. However, microscopic hair examination might be able to distinguish among the five individuals involved. Results from the less-specific microscopic comparison have the potential to distinguish between the two hypotheses, one of which includes the lookout as having had sexual contact with the young woman, and the other that does not—but only if the results are positive for hairs attributable to the lookout. If hairs attributable to the lookout are found, the hypothesis that he had no sexual contact with the young woman can be eliminated. If no such hairs are found, it is not possible to distinguish between the hypotheses.

The scientist should ensure that all potentially exculpatory examinations have been performed. This means searching for evidence that the principal hypothesis and assessment of responsibility may be wrong. Not every negative result invalidates the hypothesis; only those that may change the conclusions must be evaluated at this stage.

In Case Example 2, if none of the swabs from the victim include semen, and items from the suspect do not include vaginal fluid attributable to the victim, these test results fail to rule out digital rape, attempted rape, or sexual contact using a condom. There may be surprises. The victim's clothing can be examined for any evidence of semen spilled from a condom or any extravaginal ejaculate. Assuming that no condom was found at the scene or on the suspect's person, failure to find any such evidence on the clothing may lead us to question whether sexual contact occurred, as the suspect was apprehended shortly after the incident. However, a failure to find such evidence might also be expected if a sexual contact were digital or if no ejaculation occurred.

Levels of Information: Incorporating New Information into an Interpretation of Results

When evaluating the reliability of information available from scientific examinations, it is useful to consider the information that has been developed at the levels of data, results, conclusions, and interpretations. *Data* includes observations and measurements, including information about sampling. *Results* are the objective conclusions regarding tests and observations. *Conclusions* are the results referenced to scientific studies, and *interpretation* means relating results and conclusions to the issues under investigation. For example, a preliminary test for blood yields a certain color within a short time (*data*); this is a positive *result* for the presence of blood, and indicates that the material could be blood (*conclusion*) and may be worth testing further (*inference*). As new information is developed, whether scientific or historical, the data and results should not change unless a testing error has been made. Analytical conclusions should change only if the scientific research underlying the testing method has been demonstrated to be faulty. For example, neutron activation analysis (NAA) of corresponding trace elements in bullets had been used to reach conclusions that bullets were from the same batch, but more recent studies show such strong conclusions to be untenable.[13,14] Finally, the interpretation—relating results and conclusions to the issues—may change as new case information is developed so that the issues are reframed and reference points change.

CASE EXAMPLE 9

A 2-year-old child appeared in the hospital with injuries that his mother attributed to his falling down the steps from their second-floor rooms. Doctors alerted authorities to possible child abuse. Police, noting the cleanliness of the carpeted stairs and landing (the mother vacuumed daily), thought that if the child had really tumbled down the steps, there should be fresh deposits of hair. They took tapelifts of the stairs and landing, and no hairs attributable to the child were found among the debris, although they were found in debris vacuumed from the apartment itself. The absence of the child's hair supported suspicions that the injuries could not be accounted for by a fall, and the mother was charged with abuse of a child. A defense investigator later found out that while the child was in the hospital and before the tapelifts were collected, the child's grandmother vacuumed the stairs using a different vacuum cleaner and discarded the vacuumed debris. With this new background information, presented in court as a question to the scientist who was on the witness stand, the scientist (one of the authors) then gave the opinion that the absence of hair had no significance and did not address the case question.

It is scientifically and legally defensible to change an opinion about implications of scientific findings with new information about the case context. It is important that the scientist be clear about the levels of information, so that the integrity of the scientific work be intact even in the case of fraudulent, deceptive, or simply erroneous background information. Although interpretations may change, the data, results, and conclusions should survive intact. It is therefore important that not only observations and measurements but the process of reaching conclusions and interpretations also be documented. A good way to do this is through formal mutually exclusive hypotheses.

Formal Mutually Exclusive Hypotheses

A *clean experiment* means that the scientist knows what questions have and have not been answered. One can do this through formal mutually exclusive hypotheses. A detailed discussion is beyond the scope of this chapter, but several examples are presented here from Case Example 2:

1A. The suspect, and no one else, had sexual contact with the victim.
1B. Someone else, not the suspect, had sexual contact with the victim.
1C. There was no sexual contact with the victim during the incident under investigation.
1D. The suspect had sexual contact with the victim but did either not ejaculate into her or used a condom.
2A. The suspect had the victim's blood on his hands from hitting her on the head with a bottle.
2B. The suspect had the victim's blood on his hands from touching either her or the bottle shortly after someone else hit her on the head with a bottle.

Examinations showed no evidence of ejaculate in the victim, but unmixed semen attributable to the suspect was found on her clothing. This established sexual activity (i.e., that the suspect ejaculated on the victim), but not whether the contact was forcible. There was no damage to the clothing that might suggest a struggle. Blood attributable to the victim, found on the fly area of the suspect's pants, was probably deposited while the suspect was opening or closing the fly of his pants, indicating that he had the victim's fresh blood on his hands. There was no blood on her clothing attributable to anything other than dripping from the head wound, thus no suggestion of bleeding from an assailant. The blood deposit pattern on her pants indicated that it was deposited when the fly was open, implying that the events were contemporaneous. The bottle exhibited blood and hair, both attributable to the victim. The hair was crushed by impact, suggesting that the bottle was used as a weapon. The suspect's fingerprints were found on the bottle, but not in blood, so it was not determined whether he is the person who struck her with the bottle. However, the suspect is clearly linked with the victim, with sexual activity, and with the time of the head injury. If he did not hit her on the head himself, he would have to explain why he ejaculated on her rather than helping her.

EVALUATING ASSOCIATIVE EVIDENCE

ASSOCIATIVE EVIDENCE   *Associative evidence* includes objects, places, and persons and their effects that can be linked with other objects, persons, or places, usually by means of comparison with reference samples. The scientist must ask exactly what is being associated: an object with the person, an object with a location, an object with another object, and so on. If there is a transfer of evidence, was it direct or through an intermediary source?

CASE EXAMPLE 10

A hat is found in the residence of a suspect in a kidnapping. Most of the hairs in the hat are attributed to the victim, and several fibers on the hat correspond with carpet in the trunk of the suspect's car. This is proffered as evidence that the victim was in the trunk. However, no blood was shed, the victim's clothing retains little debris, and the car has been thoroughly cleaned, so it is not possible to cross-check for two-way transfer. The hat is linked with the victim through hairs, and with the trunk through carpet fibers (assuming that the corresponding fibers were from that carpet and not another of the same type), but there is no way to test whether the hat was in the trunk while the victim was wearing it. If the victim went willingly with the suspect as he claimed, she might have left her hat. Someone might have tossed it in the trunk and retrieved it later, or it might have touched another object that had been in the trunk, resulting in fiber transfer. The evidence does not distinguish between these hypotheses.

ALTERNATIVE EXPLANATIONS   There may be more than one explanation for information at any level. Example: A mixed deposit of sand grains coated with a glaze is tested chemically for the presence of blood and yields a negative result. The negative result may mean that the glaze is not blood, or it may mean that the test is inhibited by something such as heavy oil that does not allow the reagent to penetrate. It is useful to ask, if something is not what it at first appears to be, what else might it be? This does not require an identification of the material of interest, simply a sorting process that allows the scientist to decide whether the material should be sampled or tested differently, or whether one can stop work on that particular deposit and move on to the next task. If the material that yielded a negative test result looks like it could be something else, for example, wood stain rather than blood, one can move on.

DEGREES OF CERTAINTY   The degree of certainty of any finding depends on the level of information and quality of information.[15] For data and test results, this means *accuracy* (how well it corresponds to reality or a true value), *sensitivity* (whether small amounts can reliably be detected), and *specificity* (small number of false negatives, i.e., how far potential sources or values are narrowed down). For conclusions, this usually means specificity of potential sources; for inference, it means the degree of significance (how far hypotheses are narrowed down).

The Asymmetry of Positive and Negative Results

CASE EXAMPLE 11:

Someone broke into a house through the bathroom window and stood on a chair just inside the window once inside. Police who responded to the scene took a photograph of a shoeprint on the chair. The shoeprint is out of focus, and the soil that constituted the shoeprint is close in color to the chair. A suspect is arrested and his shoes collected. Does the shoeprint have any value as evidence? If the suspect's shoe cannot be excluded, the print as depicted is almost meaningless as associative evidence. When there are few characteristics to evaluate, or the values are broad, many shoes, including shoes with different tread designs, might produce prints that cannot be differentiated. However, if the shoeprints are different from those produced by the suspect's shoe, the evidence is useful exclusionary evidence. The shoeprint can have value as evidence, but only if it is exclusionary. In that case, it is highly significant.

A high potential value of a certain result does not mean that the result itself is likely. Because the print is of such poor quality, many shoes that did *not* cause the print would fail to be excluded. However, if a shoe could be excluded, the value would be high. An examiner might be tempted to conclude that the print has insufficient characteristics for an adequate comparison. The test (comparison with an out-of-focus print) is not very sensitive; that is, it does not have the capability to distinguish between a large number of different shoe soles that are potential sources of the print. However, if exclusion is possible and would be significant, albeit a "long shot," the test should be performed. Note that the interplay of specificity and sensitivity can be expressed graphically and can be viewed interactively online.[16]

Failure to Exclude versus No Information; Weak Exclusion versus No Information

Error can be introduced when limited information is confused with no information. Failure to exclude based on limited data is different from not being able to address the question because of a lack of data. There is also a difference between something that would be expected but is not there (which could exclude a hypothesis) and a simple absence of data, which provides no information.

CASE EXAMPLE 12

Failure to exclude: If the suspect in an assault is wearing a blue denim cotton shirt, and blue cotton fibers like those of his shirt were found on the white t-shirt of the victim, the blue cotton could have been transferred in the course of a struggle. That is just what would be expected had the assault occurred as reported. However, blue cotton of the type often used in denim is commonly found, and finding it on the victim's t-shirt means little. Contact with the suspect's t-shirt cannot be excluded. However, a finding of blue cotton cannot be used to suggest contact. There is some information here, but very little, and nothing that permits a significant association.

CASE EXAMPLE 13

Absence of material leading to exclusion: If the situation is a little different and there is no blue cotton on the white t-shirt (e.g., if the white t-shirt is new and being worn for the first time), the information is significant, because a transfer of blue cotton would be expected had contact occurred, and any debris would be expected to persist. Let us suppose this is confirmed by rubbing the blue denim shirt onto a reference fabric similar to that of the white t-shirt and finding that the blue cotton transfers. The absence of blue cotton on the white evidence t-shirt is significant evidence, strongly suggesting that the two garments were not in contact. Absence of material should be evaluated with respect to the context: whether there is other debris, and whether material would be expected had contact occurred.[17] In order to evaluate an absence of a material, it must be possible to distinguish between something with no transferred material, and something that had been recently cleaned or that would not support adhering debris.

CASE EXAMPLE 14

No information: In this example, instead of weak evidence, testing yields no information. Suppose that the suspect is wearing a black nylon jacket, but no black nylon fibers were found on the victim's clothing. Some nylon fabrics shed little and do not always result in much fiber transfer on contact, thus would not be expected as transfer on the victims' clothing even if the assault occurred as reported. Nor would it be expected if no assault occurred, or if someone other than the suspect were the assailant. The lack of black nylon fibers on the victim's clothing simply provides no information. One cannot address the question of whether the two items of clothing—and the persons wearing them—had been in contact. This is different from stating that one cannot eliminate that possibility. The latter statement in a scientific report or testimony implies that evidence was found and evaluated, and a possibility was included. When testing provides no information, the information status is essentially the same as if testing had not been performed.

CASE EXAMPLE 15

Weak exclusion: Someone broke into a residence through a small unlocked basement window, and a six-pack of beer was stolen. Police respond quickly and apprehend a man who was drinking the same brand of beer in a nearby alley. They collect several strands of hair from the window frame and submit them to the laboratory, where the hairs are compared microscopically and found to exhibit the same characteristics as hair reference samples from the suspect. Several blue acrylic fibers are found adhering to the evidence hair. There are also fibers adhering to the reference hair: black acrylic like the suspect's watch cap, not blue; the constituent fibers of his other clothing are of different types. The dissimilar adhering fibers suggest another source for the hair. Microscopic hair comparison does not permit unique attribution, nor would follow-up mitochondrial DNA testing. A weak exclusion means that credible doubts can be raised about a hypothesis, even if it cannot be excluded completely. In this case, the suspect cannot be excluded completely, because the hairs could have been deposited at a different time, or he could have been wearing another hat at the time of the break-in. These issues might be resolved by investigators.

In summary, if a correspondence of evidence leads to an association, it is important to be clear about exactly what is being associated. If there is a transfer of evidence, it is important to evaluate whether the transfer was direct or through an intermediary source. Because association and exclusion are not mirror images, the potential value of each must be evaluated separately. This is especially important in deciding whether it is of value to perform examinations. The strength of an exclusion depends on how well a specific hypothesis can be eliminated. The strength of an association depends on whether alternative hypotheses can be eliminated. The further the hypotheses can be narrowed down, the stronger the association.

COMMUNICATIONS: MAKING YOUR WORK UNDERSTANDABLE AND DEFENSIBLE

The purpose of most scientific analytical work is to provide information for other people to make decisions. It is incumbent on the scientist to understand the issues that the information is needed for, and the context in which the issues developed. This allows the scientist to formulate an analytical plan based on preliminary hypotheses (i.e. the possibilities developed from the information gathered prior to scientific testing, or prior to the current round of testing). It also allows the scientist and the investigator to work together more effectively.[18] Part of the function of laboratory work in testing is to prove objective and independent information that might not have been anticipated by police or the attorneys. Without background information that allows the scientist to form hypotheses, the effect of any prior bias or misinformation is increased.[19] Communication with the person requesting the work allows the scientific process to take place.

Note that bias arises from the information at hand.[20] Being *objective* means basing conclusions on facts, not on unstated assumptions or a preconception about what the outcome should be. Being *disinterested* means that one is impartial and has no stake in the outcome. The classical tools of the scientific method act as controls. However, *bias* can only be minimized, not completely eliminated, and arises not only from case information but also from one's experience and knowledge—the basis of the scientist's expertise. Bias is also introduced by the way our brains work and the way we make errors in judgment and reasoning. Further discussion of the sources and types of bias are beyond the scope of this chapter, but it should be noted that there is an accessible body of literature that treats this topic.[21, 22] An awareness of common cognitive errors can be helpful to scientists in devising ways to control for the biases; depriving the scientist of the background information does not accomplish this.

Communication during the testing process is equally important. Most of this communication is informal but should be no less rigorous than a written report. It is important that the scientist communicate not only the findings, but also their limitations. It is also important to promptly request access to a site to obtain additional samples when needed, or to request that they be obtained, or if not able to get such samples, to document the attempt and need to do so. Rigorous communication is a part of defensible work. This includes information communicated by way of telephone and email. When an investigator asks about a particular result, one should not say from mitochondrial DNA testing, "This hair is from the suspect" if the written conclusion and court testimony would be that the hair exhibits the same profile and could be from that person, any maternal relative, or less likely someone unrelated. Even informal communications should be documented to make a good record.

Finally, a written report and any testimony should include the basis for any conclusions and interpretations, with a record that includes the reasoning process for doing certain work and not other work. Whether the record is in the reports or the notes depends on the specific case, laboratory policy, and a number of other factors, but the important thing is to put it in writing in some part of the case file. Accurate work that is relevant, complete, grounded in the case issues, and rigorous—even in informal communications—should allow the scientific work to withstand scrutiny of other experts and of opposing counsel at trial.

RESOLVING TECHNICAL DISAGREEMENTS

Disagreements among forensic scientists may arise from questions raised during peer technical review, from second opinions, from conflicting opinions of outside experts, or from questions raised when the results of laboratory work do not agree with other information in the case. When disagreements or differences of opinion arise, it is important to resolve them methodically.

In the case of disagreement about *facts,* the parties who disagree or an impartial reviewer should look at the evidence itself and at the measuring conditions. For example, if one person reports a blue paint chip but another sees green, they may agree that the color reflects light of certain wavelengths or is like a certain paint chip reference or filter color.

When there are major differences in *opinion* among competent scientists, the differences are often based on untested assumptions. Untested assumptions can be uncovered and tested. If the testing cannot be done, all relevant hypotheses should be presented in the report. Another reason for differing opinions despite agreement on facts lies in the background knowledge against which results have been evaluated, and may not be a true disagreement. If the disagreement is about the *implications* of the data, it sometimes happens that one scientist has considered factors that the other scientist did not, or has different background information.

Sometimes an apparent disagreement is actually a different understanding of the questions being asked. Every person involved in the case understands it from a different perspective, resulting from different information, different experience, different knowledge, and different interests. Often these differences in perspective contribute to a fuller development of the case, but sometimes they lead to a different framing of the thing to be solved. If there is discussion in the early stages of the case, such a different framing can be averted or incorporated. However, some parties may not be privy to the discussion of others, or may become involved at a later stage. An awareness that framing occurs is crucial.[23]

Finally, sometimes a different framing can be a good thing. For example, if the "facts" of the case have been altered or falsified, or if evidence has been misidentified, contaminated, altered, or "planted," the forensic scientist would do well to reframe the questions being asked. In the case of a disagreement based on different framing, defining the framing can often resolve the points of dispute, and a good record allows this to happen.

CASE EXAMPLE 16

A man is involved in a fight with another man, gets beat up, and each of the men go back to their respective cars. The second man gets out of his car and the first man shoots him with a .25-caliber automatic pistol. The second man falls to the sidewalk.

Police are called. The second man says that he was running down the sidewalk away from the cars and was shot in the back of the leg. The first man says that he was sitting in his car after the fight cleaning up blood when he saw the second man coming at him. The first man got out a pistol he kept in the car and shot. He thought that he shot downward. He is not sure whether the second man turned around, and if so, whether before, during, or after the shot. Witnesses were not sure either. (*What we know.*)

The injured man goes to the hospital and is examined in the emergency room, where the attending physician reports a bullet wound to the leg with the entrance in back of the thigh and the exit in front. The first man is accused of assault with a firearm. Police take a photograph of the injury but it is sufficiently out of focus as to be unrecognizable. No other photographs are obtained. The clothing is not collected. The bullet is not found. The only evidence still available to examine is the wound itself, and the forensic scientist who is asked to evaluate the evidence receives permission to examine it.

The scientist is faced with several possibilities (*what we don't know* as foundation for hypotheses and testing plan): that the wound was a direct shot to the back, that the wound was a direct shot to the front, that the wound was from a ricochet to the back, and that the wound was from a ricochet to the front (*multiple hypotheses at the outset*). An entrance wound from a direct shot is typically a clean hole and the exit is typically more ragged. An entrance wound from a ricochet is frequently ragged. In addition, a ricochet from pavement or sidewalk would be expected to enter low and exit higher, whereas a direct shot from a vehicle to the lower leg would more likely enter high and exit lower. This depends somewhat on the angle of the leg, but is a good working premise.

Although it was now 6 months after the event, the scientist returns to the scene to search for the bullet, but it is not found (*attempt to ensure examination of crime objects*). Had the bullet been found, it could have been examined for the type of impact damage and for adhering debris that could have provided information about any ricochet, and perhaps about the path through the leg.

When the injury is examined, the healing wound in the front of the leg is smooth and round, but the wound in the back of the leg is ragged. This is more typical of a direct shot to the front of the leg, but could also be a ricochet shot to the back of the leg. Although it is not typical, it is nevertheless possible for a deformed bullet entering after ricochet to enter in a tumbling fashion, causing a larger and irregular entrance wound, and then during passage through tissue to stop tumbling and exit nose or base first, leaving a more rounded and smaller exit wound.

The front wound is higher than the back wound, potentially supporting either hypothesis; this depends on other factors. A direct shot to the front would have to be from a suitable height—a height expected if a person shoots while sitting in a vehicle. A ricochet to the back must be at a suitable angle—one possible within the constraints of the scene dimensions and the range of motion of the leg. (*If x is found, one expects y. Is y really there?*)

To distinguish between the hypotheses, a reconstruction is performed with the assistance of an anatomically correct mannequin in a computer program programmed with the height and weight of the injured person. The scientist also took direct measurements on the injured person of the distance of each wound from the heel, and the distance from wound to flex point of knee and hip. The range of distance between the car and the injured party is known from witness descriptions and physical constraints to be between 20 and 30 feet. With this information, the analysis corroborates the conclusion that the wound was from a direct downward shot to the front of the leg. Computer analysis shows that the injury trajectory could not be produced by a ricochet: the leg could not be placed at an angle that would allow a ricochet as steep as required to produce the observed injury, and the person could not be placed close enough. Thus, the hypothesis of a ricochet to the back of the leg is ruled out and with it the account of the injured man that he was shot while running away.

This leaves the question of the doctor's report that the entrance was to the back of the leg (*resolving technical disagreements*). When asked about the basis for his opinion, the attending physician said that he reported an entrance wound to the back of the leg because that is what the police officer told him. It was not a medical opinion.

Conclusions

Scientists and other forensic practitioners can use scientific reasoning tools and a logical framework for working with users of laboratory services to ascertain the case issues, then making clear, useful, defensible, scientifically sound, and legally reliable decisions about the focus, priority, and sequence of examinations and what the results mean. This provides a means for laboratory work to meet the needs of the users and the needs of the courts and justice system as a whole. These tools can be used in both the civil and criminal arenas to make decisions about casework, by laboratory management to allocate resources, and by attorneys evaluating and managing cases involving scientific work.

Acknowledgments

Portions of this material were presented by the authors at a workshop given to the Northwest Association of Forensic Scientists (NWAFS) at the 2002 fall meeting, by Ms. Gleim at the Spring 2001 meeting of the California Association of Criminalists and the Fall 2000 NWAFS meeting, and by Ms. Cwiklik at the American Academy of Forensic Sciences 2004 and 2006 annual meetings and the Washington Association of Criminal Defense Lawyers Spring 2003 seminar.

The authors thank Mrs. Mary Jarrett-Jackson, Mr. George Ishii, and Mr. Kay M. Sweeney for their insights on how to look at a case. Other colleagues too numerous to mention have influenced our thinking by dint of collegial work and discussion. Of particular mention are: Peter D. Barnett; Jan Bashinski (deceased); George K. Chan; Andrew Friedman (for discussions about the applications of conceptual tools to environmental casework); William R. Gresham, Ph.D.; Helen R. Griffin; Michael J. Grubb; George E. Johnston; Vanora Kean, Ph.D; Lynn D. McIntyre; Terry

Spear; and Jane M. Taupin. We recognize Peter DeForest, Dale Nute, Norah Rudin, and Keith Inman for contributing by way of publications, talks, and email lists to the discussion in the forensic science community about many of the topics we treat in this chapter. We thank Kim Duddy, Jennifer Iem, Linda D. McGarvey, Lynn McIntyre, and Kay M. Sweeney for discussing the ideas in this chapter, and Vanora Kean, Timothy Nishimura, and Kay Sweeney for three of the case examples. We are also grateful to our students and coworkers, especially Linda McGarvey, for their comments and willingness to explore this material. For wrangling over the nexus of science and the law, we thank attorneys Michael Schwartz, Terri Wood, and Chad Dold. For editing suggestions, we thank Rachel Greenberg. Ms. Cwiklik is also grateful to Charles J. Loner, Ph.D., and Chester A. Giza, Ph.D., undergraduate chemistry professors at Wheeling College, who insisted on rigorous work and thinking about experimental design.

References

1. R. L. Schwartz, "Teaching Physicians and Lawyers to Understand Each Other," *J. Leg. Med*, 2:2 (1981), p. 135. (The entire article, pp. 131–49, is of interest.)

2. P. R. DeForest, "Recapturing the Essence of Criminalistics," *Sci. Just.*, 39:3 (1999), 196–208. (See especially p. 199.)

3. R. Cook, I. W. Evett, G. Jackson, and P. I. Jones, "A Hierarchy of Propositions: Deciding Which Level to Address in Casework," *Sci. Just.*, 38:4 (1998), pp. 231–39.

4. J. R. Platt, "Strong Inference," *Science* 146:3642 (1964), 347–53.

5. S. S. Kind, "Crime Investigation and the Criminal Trial: A Three Chapter Paradigm of Evidence." J. Forensic Sci. Soc. 34:3 (1994), 155–64.

6. C. Cwiklik and K. M. Gleim. "Decision Tools for Forensic Casework Management: Proceedings of the National Groundwater Association Conference on Science and the Law. Chicago, July 6–7 (2006), pp. 67–81.

7. DeForest [ibid., p. 200].

8. D. A. Stoney, "Evaluation of Associative Evidence: Choosing the Relevant Question," *J. Forensic Sci. Soc.*, 24 (1984), pp. 473–82.

9. D. A. Stoney, "Fundamental Principles in the Evaluation of Associative Evidence," *Can. Soc. Forensic Sci. J.* (Special Edition: Abstracts of the 11th Meeting of the International Association of Forensic Sciences), 20:3 (1987), 280–82.

10. Stoney, "Fundamental Principles in the Evaluation of Associative Evidence" [ibid.].

11. Cwiklik and Gleim [ibid.].

12. *Daubert* v. *Merrell Dow Pharmaceuticals*, 509 U.S. 572 (1993).

13. Randich, Tobin, and Duerfeldt, cited in: *Forensic Analysis: Weighing Bullet Lead Evidence*. Washington, D.C.: National Academies Press, 2004. Report by the Committee on Scientific Assessment of Bullet Lead Elemental Composition Comparison, Board on Chemical Studies and Technology, Division of Earth and Life Studies, National Research Council of the National Academies.

14. R. Mejia, and I. Sample, "Chemical Matching of Bullets Fatally Flawed," *New Scientist*, 17 Apr (2002).

15. J. K. Taylor, *Quality Assurance of Chemical Measurements*, Chapter 1, "Introduction to Quality Assurance" Chelsea, MI: Lewis Publishers, 1987,

p. 1: "The quality of data is ordinarily evaluated on the basis of its uncertainty compared with end-use requirements. . . . The evaluation of data is thus a relative determination. What is high quality in one situation could be unacceptable in another."

16. L. Hopley, and J. van Schalkwyk, "The Magnificent ROC (Receiver Operating Characteristic Curve)," http://www.anaesthetist.com/mnm.stats.roc. Retrieved: November 4, 2006. (This Web site is updated regularly.)

17. C. Cwiklik, "An Evaluation of the Significance of Transfers of Debris: Criteria for Association and Exclusion," *J. Forensic Sci.*, 44:6 (1999), 1136–50.

18. DeForest [ibid., p. 199].

19. C. Cwiklik, "A Good Look at Blind Testing: Quality Assurance Systems and Bias," presented to the American Association of Forensic Sciences Meeting, Seattle, Washington, February 2006.

20. J. J. Nordby, "Can We Believe What We See If We See What We Believe— Expert Disagreement," *J. Forensic Sci.*, 37:4 (July 1992), pp. 1115–24.

21. T. Gilovich, *How We Know What Isn't So: The Fallibility of Human Reason in Everyday Life*. New York: The Free Press, 1991.

22. D. Kahneman, P. Slovic, and A. Tversky, *Judgment Under Uncertainty: Heuristics and Biases*. New York: Cambridge University Press, 1982.

23. J. J. Nordby, [ibid.]

Appendix A:

■■■

Overlapping Stains

RESULTS OF TESTING AND EVALUATION

a. An asymmetrical stain found on the lining of a rabbit-fur coat yielded DNA results attributable to the victim and both suspects. The sample was taken from the middle of the stain. Other stains on the lining, semen with no apparent admixture, were attributable to Suspect A only, and are probably direct ejaculate not drainage. Did the asymmetrical stain result from vaginal drainage of material from the victim, indicating that both suspects ejaculated into her? Or could the stain instead be made up of two superimposed deposits?

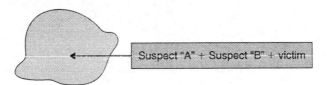

1a: DNA test results for asymmetrical stain.

b. Additional samples from the asymmetrical stain yielded two results: DNA attributable to Suspect A only in samples from two areas at the margins, and DNA attributable to Suspect B and the victim in another area.

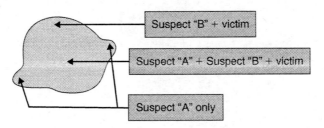

2a: Additional dna results.

We can deduce that the sample from the middle of the stain—that is, the area with DNA including profiles from both suspects—is from more than one partly superimposed stain.

a. We know that there is semen deposited by Suspect A only, and we know that there is a mixed deposit that includes DNA attributable to both the victim and to semen from Suspect B, but not to Suspect A.

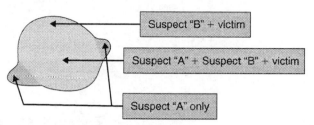

3a: Major hypothesis for co-deposits.

b. We cannot eliminate completely the possibility that the stain includes biological material originally deposited as a mixture of Suspect A and either the victim alone, or the victim and Suspect B. However, this would require that a co-deposited stain that includes the DNA of all three individuals just happened to be deposited roughly in the middle of the two other stains, and that one of the stains included the victim and Suspect B, but not Suspect A. The following two scenarios that can explain this option are possible, but somewhat weak. Although this hypothesis cannot be eliminated, the evidence does not specifically suggest it.

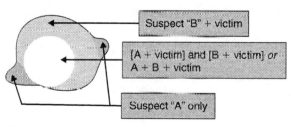

4a: Minor hypotheses for co-deposits.

Appendix B:

■■■

Convergence of Results

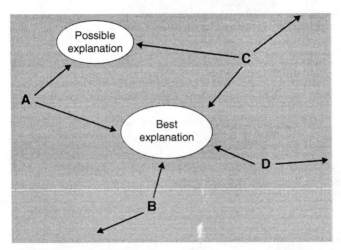

1b: Each data point or conclusion A, B, C, and D has more than one possible explanation, but the data converges on two explanations. The center oval represents the best explanation, and the upper oval represents another possible explanation. There may not be any data to contradict the latter, but the other explanation best fits all the facts. The less likely conclusion should be tested. For each hypothesis, ask: "what other observations would be expected if it were true? Are those observations, in fact, found?"

2

■ ■ ■

A Guide to the Analysis of Forensic Dust Specimens

Nicholas Petraco, M. S., D-ABC
New York City Police Department (Retired)
Forensic Science Consultant

Peter R. De Forest, D. Crim.
John Jay College of Criminal Justice,
The City University of New York

Nicholas D. K. Petraco, Ph.D.
John Jay College of Criminal Justice,
The City University of New York

The need for the increased utilization of trace evidence in the crime laboratory has been pointed out.[1,2] McCrone has estimated that considerably less than 1 percent of all the potential trace evidence in crimes is ever examined.[3] This phenomenon is peculiar indeed, considering the fact that trace evidence has been shown time and again to be a most valuable source of investigative information and proof. These data can be used to (1) help solve crimes; (2) associate the people, places, and things involved in the crime; (3) deduce the occupation(s) of the principal(s) involved in the crime; and (4) reconstruct the crime scene or the event itself.[4–22]

More than a century ago, Hans Gross speculated that dust is a representation of our environment in miniature. Gross further proposed that by recognizing the constituents composing a particular dust sample, one could estimate the surroundings from which the dust originated, and that this information could be used to help solve crimes.[4] This fact left the scientific investigator with a difficult challenge: the need to develop analytical methods that could be used to identify minute traces of the many different types of materials that occur in dust as trace evidence. McCrone and

31

Delly's work with Aroclor® 5442, polarized light microscopy, and *The Particle Atlas* series has certainly established an effective methodology for accomplishing the identification and characterization of all types of dust specimens.[23] Following their lead, some forensic scientists have developed schemes utilizing different mounting media for identifying some of the substances that occur as trace evidence. Graves published an excellent article on the characterization of the minerals in soil, in which he utilized a Cargille® oil having refractive index of 1.54.[24] Fong published a scheme for the identification of different synthetic fibers in a single mounting medium having a refractive index of 1.525.[25] Petraco describes a microscopic method for animal hair identification in Melt Mount® 1.539.[26,27]

Many of the theoretical principles and methods necessary for the collection, identification, examination, comparison, and evaluation of the various types of trace materials that occur in dust have already been presented in Volumes I and II of this Handbook series.[28–34] The primary goal of this chapter is to present a microscopic guide for the identification and characterization of the components of dust specimens mounted in a single refractive index medium, namely Melt Mount® 1.539. It is intended that this chapter provide the forensic microscopist with a reference that serves as an Introductory Guide to the examination of the trace materials commonly encountered in specimens of dust during routine forensic science casework. Emphasis is placed on the use of polarized light microscopy (PLM) and on those substances most often encountered by the authors in forensic dust specimens:

1. Human hair
2. Animal hair
3. Synthetic fibers
4. Mineral and glass particles, plaster chips, and other related materials
5. Miscellaneous substances: vegetable fibers and matter, starch grains, feathers, and so on

Many of the less traditional forms of trace evidential materials found in dust specimens have already been discussed by Palenik in Volume II[33] and thus are not covered in this chapter. However, serious readers should familiarize themselves with the identification of these substances because they will no doubt be encountered in their casework.

It is the authors' hope that this work will help guide the novice and experienced forensic examiner through the successful analysis of dust specimens, such as the one depicted in Figure 2-1. It is also the authors' wish that this effort will help foster the utilization of PLM and trace evidence in the crime laboratory.

OCCURRENCE, COLLECTION, AND PRESERVATION OF DUST SPECIMENS

Whereas dust traces can encompass an infinite number of different materials, the authors have found that two primary morphological forms compose most specimens of dust:

1. Fibrous materials
2. Particulate matter

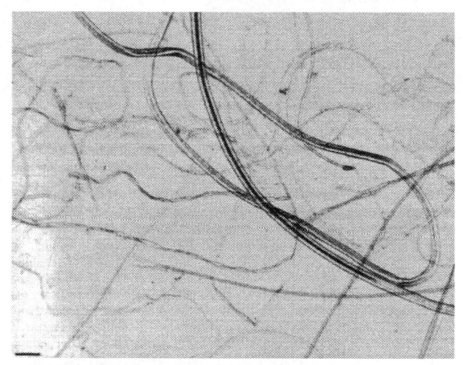

FIGURE 2-1 A specimen of questioned dust from a homicide investigation. The specimen is mounted in Melt Mount® 1.539 and contains the following trace materials: human hairs; animal hairs; synthetic fibers; vegetable fibers; duck and chicken feathers; glass, and mineral fragments. The black bar is equal to 100 μm.

The two primary morphological forms of materials composing dust specimens, and some of the substances that have been found occurring in dust are listed in Table 2-1.

When searching for dust specimens, one must realize that there is no limit to the places or things specimens of dust can be found in or on. Therefore, one must keep an open mind when searching for dust. Some of the more common items to examine for dust traces are items of the suspect's clothing, such as shoes, outer garments, and so on; the victim's clothing; the suspect's or victim's vehicle; any weapons or objects used to commit the crime; and so forth. It should be noted that the type of crime can often guide the examiner in collection efforts. Gaudette presents a comprehensive listing for fibers.[35] Many of his suggestions apply to the other elements found in dust, and for aggregate dust specimens as well.

Of paramount importance to the successful analysis of forensic dust specimens is the procedure employed in the collection and preservation of the various items of physical evidence to be examined. The associations made possible by dust traces are based primarily on the mutual exchange principle attributed to Dr. Edmond Locard by Nickolls.[36] If one is familiar with Locard's original work, one can see that all the basic elements of this hypothesis are clearly set forth.[37] Simply paraphrased, this

TABLE 2-1 Some of the different substances, both fibrous and particulate, that have been encountered in dust specimens during the authors' casework.

Morphological Form	Materials Encountered
Fibrous	Human hair and animal hair, synthetic fibers, mineral and glass fibers, vegetable fibers, natural fibers, feathers
Particulate	Mineral fragments; soils; glass chips; paint chips and smears; sawdust; wood splinters and chips; bark; twigs; leaf fragments; pollen; spores; paper; tobacco; starch grains; seeds; plant hairs; marijuana; spices; fragments of bricks, concrete, plaster and chalk; diatoms; metal flakes and shavings; rust fragments; crusts of blood; bone, skin and various tissues; insects and insect parts; clam shells, dry shrimp

principle postulates that whenever two people, places, or things interact, there is always a mutual cross-transfer of trace materials from one to the other.

The trace materials that are transferred during these contacts make the stated associations and deductions possible. Therefore, *accidental contact* between the items of physical evidence to be processed for trace evidential materials must be guarded against to prevent contamination. To eliminate this possibility, one must keep each item of physical evidence separate. This is easily accomplished by wrapping each item individually in paper, or by placing each in a separate paper container. Prior to wrapping the items should not be handled by the same individual or allowed to come into contact with common surfaces. Vacuum sweepings or tape liftings should also be packaged in separate paper containers. It is the authors' opinion that plastic containers should be avoided because they often possess an electrostatic charge that can attract foreign dust traces, causing contamination of the evidence, or repel potentially valuable dust traces. Another factor that is extremely important is whether the item(s) of physical evidence is wet or dry. If wet, the item(s) should be air dried prior to packaging. If dry, the item(s) can be packaged in paper as previously described. Here again, plastic containers should be avoided because they retain moisture, thereby encouraging microbial (bacterial or fungal) growth that may cause biological decomposition. Finally, one must keep in mind that dust traces, due to their nature, are easily lost. To prevent inadvertent loss, the paper packaging should be free of small holes or perforations.

Once received at the laboratory, the dust traces must be collected from each item of physical evidence. A comprehensive discussion of the collection procedures for the recovery of dust has already been given in this Handbook series.[38] Therefore, this section covers only the methodology normally used by the authors. It has been the authors' combined experience that a systematic approach is vital when retrieving dust traces, and that each item of physical evidence should be processed separately utilizing the following procedure.

The item to be examined should be removed from its container and laid out on a clean piece of paper that has been placed atop a well-illuminated examination table. The size of the paper is dictated by the size of the article being processed. Ideally, the room in which the examination takes place should be dust free (a clean-room). If this is not possible, the room should be kept as clean as possible, and be situated in a low-traffic area of the laboratory. Adequate table top space for laying out the items of physical evidence should be available. Each item of physical evidence is first observed visually, and then with a stereobinocular microscope. As pointed out by Palenik,[38] a boom stand is most useful for this purpose. In addition, a floor-type surgical operating microscope with a magnification range of 2× to 25× is an excellent device for scanning large objects for traces of dust. Various forms and techniques of illumination (oblique lighting, monochromatic laser light, ultraviolet light, xenon or quartz halogen lamps with fiber optics or gel cables, etc.) can aid in the visual location of dust traces. After location and documentation (sketching, photographing), all visible traces can be removed by hand with forceps or a needle.

Next, the item of physical evidence should be processed with some sort of transparent tape, as first suggested by Frei-Sulzer.[39] When using tape liftings to collect dust traces, the examiner should be aware that the position of the trace evidence on the item of physical evidence can be crucial to any reconstruction efforts. Therefore it is imperative to document the area(s) from which these traces are collected. Several studies and methods employing different approaches and adhesive materials have been published[13,16,40–42]; each has its own merits. The adhesive material and method to be used should be decided on by the individual examiner, depending on his or her own needs and resources. The authors use 1½-inch-wide transparent latent fingerprint lifting tape. The item to be processed is taped in segments or quadrants. For example, a pair of men's pants is taped as follows:

1. The upper or lower (U/L) front right leg
2. The U/L front left leg
3. The front top portion
4. The U/L rear right leg
5. The U/L rear left leg
6. The rear top portion

Inside areas such as pockets, cuffs, and interior legs are processed when necessary. Each tape lifting is marked for identification as to item and segment taped. The tape lifting is placed adhesive side down onto a clear Mylar® sheet to prevent contamination. After the taping process has been completed, the underlying paper should be checked for any trace material that may have fallen from the item being examined. This material should be collected and preserved for examination. The tape liftings are observed with a stereomicroscope to locate traces of dust. Contrasting color backgrounds made from pieces of oak tag are useful when screening tapes. All tape liftings should be stored in paper envelopes.

Finally, when necessary, the item can be vacuumed for dust traces. The vacuum sweepings trap described by Kirk can be used.[43] Another effective trace evidence vacuum trap has recently been described (see Figure 2-2).[44] This device is useful because

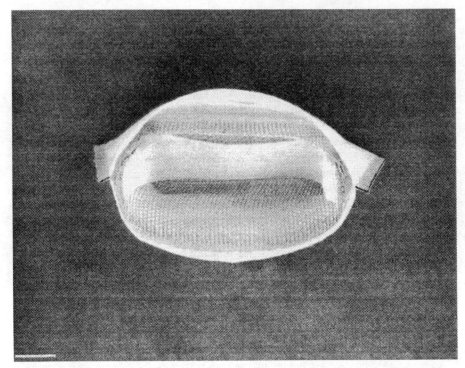

FIGURE 2-2   Trace evidence trap consisting of a vacuum filter bag, an aluminum basket, a piece of filter paper, and Velcro® strips. The white bar is equal to 25 mm.

it aids in the preliminary sorting of the trace materials often found in sweepings. It should be pointed out that although very efficient, vacuuming has many disadvantages; the primary one being that vacuuming often comingles the materials that were recently deposited (often the most important) with substances that were deposited long ago. In any case, vacuum sweepings should be used only when *absolutely necessary,* and only after visual and taping procedures have been previously conducted.[19,45,46] Once collected, the sweepings are preserved in paper containers (boxes or paper folds) for storage, until examination, or for future reference.

INITIAL EXAMINATION

All specimens of dust should be examined with a stereomicroscope for evaluation and sorting. A preliminary data sheet such as the one shown in Table 2-2 should be prepared for each dust specimen. If the specimen appears to be homogeneous, a representative sample is mounted on a microscope slide in Cargille's Melt Mount® with a refractive index (RI) of 1.539 for Na D line at 25°C. The dust specimen is then covered with a No. 1½ cover glass. The Melt Mount®, which must be heated to 60–70°C, can be applied with a glass rod, eyedropper, or in stick form.[47] The stick method is preferred by the authors. Prior to mounting, the specimen may be teased with two needles to loosen the

TABLE 2-2 Initial data sheet for the characterization and identification of the trace evidential materials commonly found in dust. This data is obtained visually and with a stereomicroscope.

Preliminary Data Sheet　　　Case No._____

I—Primary Morphology

　　Fibrous_____　　　Particulate_____　　　Both_____

II—Homogeneity

　　Homogeneous:　　Yes_____　　　No_____

　　　　Fibrous:　　　　Separate_____　　Clustered_____　　Both_____

　　　　Particulate:　　Separate_____　　Clustered_____　　Both_____

　　Heterogeneous:　　Yes_____　　No_____

　　Aggregate of both primary forms　　Yes_____　　No_____

　　　No. of possible fibrous types_____

　　　No. of possible particulate types_____

III—Initial Classification

　　Shape:_____　　Sketch:

　　If fibrous:

　　　Hair:　　Human_____　　Animal_____

　　　Synthetic fiber_____

　　　Vegetable fiber_____

　　　Other fiber_____

　　If particulate:

　　　Mineral grain_____ Glass chip _____

　　　Other particulate_____

---

fibers and debris composing the dust. A representative sample of a heterogeneous dust specimen can be mounted in the same manner. However, large particles that cannot be mounted should first be sorted for separate examination. After mounting, the specimen is examined with a polarized light microscope for characterization and identification. A review of forensic microscopy can be found in Volume I of this Handbook series.[28]

The authors have found Melt Mount® 1.539 to be a useful mountant for the identification of many of the materials commonly encountered in dust.[26,48] Melt Mount® 1.539 is a stable, solvent-free thermoplastic material. Once set, no changes in its optical properties have been observed to occur (to date). Its intermediate value of refractive index enables the microanalyst to observe internal morphological details that are necessary for characterization and identification purposes. When a change in relief (contrast) is required, it can be achieved simply by observing the specimen under plane polarized light while rotating the microscope's stage to change the specimen's orientation, or by heating the specimen on a hot stage. The degree of relief (shadowing) change between the specimen and the mountant depends on several important factors: whether the specimen is anisotropic with respect to its optical properties, the degree of birefringence within the specimen, and the value of the mounting medium's refractive index. If the substance is optically isotropic (possessing only one primary refractive index), there will be no apparent change in relief when the specimen's orientation is changed. Consequently, such specimens can be heated on a hot stage. If the specimen is optically anisotropic and at least one of its indices is higher or lower than that of Melt Mount® 1.539, there will be a change in relief when the specimen is rotated.

In the event that a fiber or particle must be isolated or recovered from the mounted dust specimen, the Melt Mount® preparation is gently heated on a hot plate, the cover glass is removed, and the item is retrieved with forceps or a fine needle while the preparation is observed with a stereomicroscope. The fiber or particle can be washed with xylene to removed excess mounting medium if it has been determined that the specimen is not soluble in xylene.

The data collected in Table 2-2 can be used for the initial classification of the material(s) composing the dust specimen and to guide the examiner to the appropriate identification procedure or scheme. Microscopic methods for the characterization and identification of the trace materials commonly found in dust specimens are presented in the following pages. The result obtained with these methods can be confirmed with other methods of analysis, such as Micro-FTIR, spindle stage methods, X-ray diffraction, SEM-EDXA, and so on. It is recommended that microscopists confirm their results whenever possible in order to build confidence in these microscopic methods and to further support their findings for court testimony.

CHARACTERIZATION AND IDENTIFICATION PROCEDURES

Human Hair

Human hair can occur in dust in several forms. First, complete hairs possessing an intact proximal (root) end, medial portion, and distal (tip) end, originating from various parts of the human body, are shed on a daily basis. These hairs can become airborne for short periods and eventually collect in the dust of a given environment or locality. Next, complete human hairs or hair fragments can accumulate in dust by normal grooming practices (such as brushing or combing) and by forcible means (such as pulling or cutting). Finally, hair that has been burned can become airborne and thus find its way into the dust of a given location. Such hair, if severely burned, is often rendered unsuitable for identification or comparison purposes, although it may have investigative value (see Figure 2-3).

If human hair stays in dust for a prolonged period of time, it can become broken or damaged by mechanical action, or decomposed by microbial or insect activity. Figure 2-4 shows a human hair that has been partially eaten. Chille et al. attribute this phenomenon to insect activity.[49] The significance of environmental exposure and its evidential interpretation has also been the subject of recent study.[50]

The identification and comparison of human hair is based on its physical morphology. A complete discussion of human hair examination is given in this Handbook series by Bisbing.[29] The identifying characteristics of human hair are readily observed when the hair is mounted in Melt Mount® 1.539.[48]

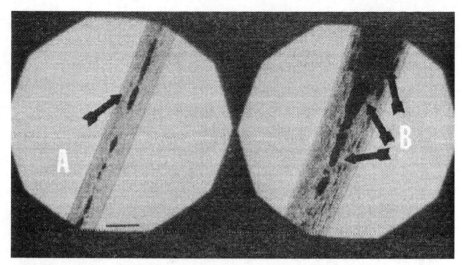

FIGURE 2-3 Burned human head hair found on the clothing of an arson suspect. The specimen in (A) is an intact portion of a head hair; the specimen in (B) is a burned portion of the same hair. Note the expansion of the cortex and the gaseous bubbles. The specimen is mounted in Melt Mount® 1.539. The black bar is equal to 50 μm. Burning of hair occurs at ≈300°C.

An excellent brief discussion of the differentiation of human hair from the hair of other mammals is given by Hicks.[51] Figure 2-5 depicts the three primary anatomical regions of hair used in species identification: the cuticle, the outermost layer of hair, which is composed of several layers of overlapping scales; the medulla, the central canal of the hair (either present or absent); and the cortex, the primary tissue

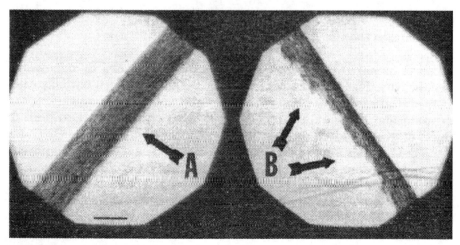

FIGURE 2-4 Two negroid head hairs from a specimen of dust obtained during a homicide investigation. The specimen in (A) is intact; the specimen in (B) is partially eaten by insects. The specimens are mounted in Melt Mount® 1.539. The black bar is equal to 50 μm.

composing the hair. The cortex contains the pigment granules, cortical fusi, and the other morphological features that make up hair. Figure 2-5 also shows a cast of the dominant scale pattern usually associated with hair of human origin. A procedure for the preparation of a temporary scale cast in Melt Mount® 1.539 has been published.[52] When necessary for identification purposes, a hair can be isolated from the dust specimen as previously described, cast in Melt Mount® 1.539, as detailed later, and then remounted in Melt Mount® 1.539 for further study.

The specimen to be cast is placed on a microscope slide that has a had thin layer of Melt Mount® 1.539 spread over most of its top surface. The slide containing the hair specimen is then heated on a hot plate (65–70°C) until the solid layer of Melt Mount® melts. The slide is then removed from the hot plate and allowed to cool until the Melt Mount® hardens. The hair that is now embedded in the Melt Mount® layer is peeled from the microscope slide. The resulting impression of the hair's scale pattern(s) can now be observed directly with a microscope at 100×.[52]

The human hairs that are usually encountered in dust specimens originate from the head or pubic regions of the body. However, hairs originating from other body areas such as the face, limbs, and so forth frequently occur. Therefore, examiners should familiarize themselves with the morphologies of all types of human hairs. Bisbing[53] and Hicks[54] list the various morphological characteristics used to determine the somatic origin of human hair. Figures 2-6 and 2-7 show the primary physical

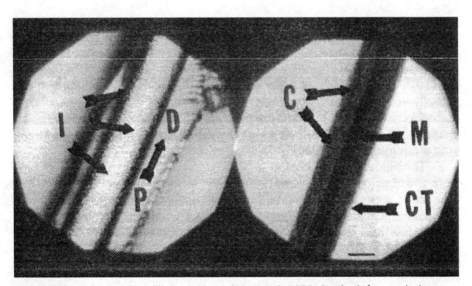

FIGURE 2-5   A human head hair cast in Melt Mount® 1.539. On the left, a typical imbricated scale pattern (I) common to hair of human origin is shown. The hair cast is shown from the proximal end (P) to the distal end (D). On the right, the three primary anatomical regions of a human hair: the cuticle (CT); the medulla (M); and the cortex (C), as they appear in Melt Mount® 1.539. The black bar is equal to 50 μm.

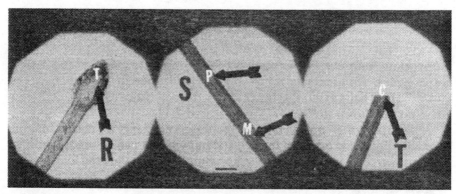

FIGURE 2-6   The morphological appearance of a shed human head hair showing the root (R), telogen (T) stage; the shaft (S), containing the pigment granules (P) and the medulla (M); and the tip (T), and cut (C). The specimen is mounted in Melt Mount® 1.539. The black bar is equal to 100 μm.

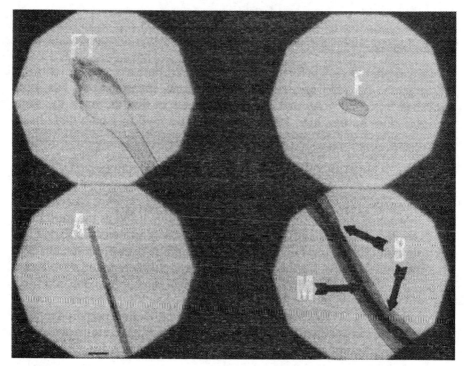

FIGURE 2-7   The morphological appearance of a typical shed human pubic hair: follicular root tag (FT), abraided tip (A), flat cross section (F), broad amorphous medulla (M), and buckling along shaft (B). The specimen is mounted in Melt Mount® 1.539. The black bar is equal to 100 μm.

characteristics used in the identification of human head and pubic hairs. It should be pointed out that these are just generalizations. Other configurations can and often do occur; for example, various important root morphologies are shown in Figure 2-8. A study of their forensic significance has also been published.[55] Other anatomical regions of human hair, such as the tip and shaft, can vary as well. Certainly more research is needed in this area.

The race of the person from whom a questioned hair originated can often be important in forensic investigations. Racial origin is made on the basis of morphological features. Hicks[54] and Bisbing[56] both present lists of these features. Head hairs exhibiting the primary characteristics used in racial determinations are shown in Figures 2-9, 2-10, and 2-11.

It is important to note that the observations necessary for determinations of somatic and racial origin of questioned human hair can be made while the hair is still mounted in the matrix dust specimen, without the need for isolating, demounting, or otherwise manipulating the dust preparation. The authors have successfully compared questioned and known hair specimens while the questioned hair was still mounted in the original Melt Mount® preparation.

Many protocols for the examination and comparison of human hair can be found in the literature.[57–67] Table 2-3 is a protocol for human hair examination used by the authors in their casework. A data sheet, such as the one shown in Table 2-4, makes the collection, tabulation, and interpretation of the data somewhat easier. The data recorded in Table 2-4 is used to help establish the somatic or racial origin of a questioned hair, as well as to show similarities or differences between questioned and known specimens.

Animal Hair

Animal hair often occurs in forensic dust specimens, both as complete hairs and as fragments. Its role as evidence in forensic investigations has been established.[2,13,17,26,68–75] Animal hair accumulates in dust in much the same manner as does human hair. Many domestic pets shed hair on a daily basis. Hair from grooming pets finds its way into the dust of a given location. Animal hair originating from articles of clothing and other textile materials made from animal hair or fur can become airborne and thus be incorporated into the dust of a given environment. A scheme to aid in the identification of the various species of animal hair that commonly occur in forensic science casework has been published.[26] This scheme utilizes Melt Mount® 1.539 as the mountant.

Complete animal guard hairs present in dust specimens are sorted out during the initial examination. These hairs should be examined visually and with a stereomicroscope. Each hair is sketched and measured, and its reflected light color(s) and color banding are noted. The data is recorded on a data sheet (see Table 2-5). After preliminary examination, the hair's scale pattern is cast in Melt Mount® 1.539.[52] Next, a wet mount of the guard hair is prepared in Melt Mount® 1.539. Occasionally it becomes necessary to cross section a guard hair for identification purposes. When this is required, and only if there is a large enough sample size, a cross section can be prepared in a few minutes with plastic microscope slides.[76] The specimen is then examined under plane polarized light with a polarized light microscope.

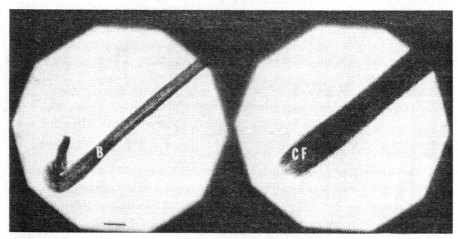

FIGURE 2-8   On the left, an anagen root from a known hair standard removed during autopsy. The specimen exhibits postmortem root banding (B). On the right, is a hair found with human skeletal remains; note the brushlike appearance of the root and cortical fibrils (CF). The specimens are mounted in Melt Mount® 1.539. The black bar is equal to 100 μm.

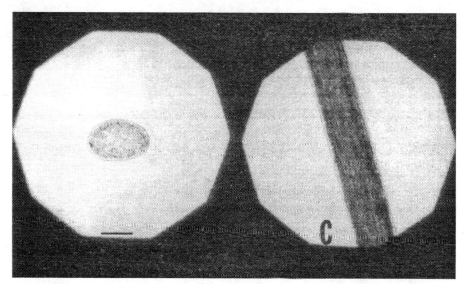

FIGURE 2-9   A typical caucasoid head hair (C). Note the oval cross section, the even shaft diameter, the medium cuticle margin and the even pigment granular distribution. The longitudinal view is mounted in Melt Mount® 1.539. The black bar is equal to 50 μm.

TABLE 2-3 Protocol for human hair examination and comparisons.

MACROSCOPIC CHARACTERISTICS (visual and stereomicroscopy)

I—Gross Features

1-Length (in cm)
a <1
b 1–5
c 1–10
d 1–20
e 1–30
f 1–50
g 10–30
h 15–50
i 30–50
j 10–100
k 50–100
l Other ranges

2-Reflected Light Color
a White (all hues)
b Blonde
c Lt. brown
d Brown
e Dark brown
f Red
g Black
h White & brown (all hues)
i White & black
j White & red
k White & blonde
l Lt. brown & brown
m Brown & dark brown
n Other color combination

3-Shaft Shape
a Straight
b Arched
c Wavy (2 or more arches)
d Curly or kinky (3 or more coils)
e Straight & arched
f Arched & wavy
g Other combination

4-Texture
a Fine
b Average
c Coarse

MICROSCOPIC CHARACTERISTICS (Light Microscope)

II—Cuticle

1-Margin
a Absent
b Present
c Both

2-Distribution
a Continuous
b Discontinuous
c Both
d Not applicable

3-Shape
a Smooth
b Serrated
c Looped
d Damaged
e Smooth & serrated
f Smooth & damaged
g Other
h Not applicable

4-Color
a Clear & colorless
b Clear & colored
c Pigmented
d Other
e Not applicable

5-Thickness
a Fine (<2 μm)
b Medium (2–4 μm)
c Thick (>4 μm)
d Not applicable

3-Transmitted Light Color Appearance
a Natural
b Artificial (treated)
c Both

III—Cortex

1-Shape of Distal End (Tip)
a Squared (Cut)
b Tapered to a point
c Abraded (Round)
d Split
e Fractured
f Frayed
g Angled
h Squared & tapered to a point
i Squared & abraded
j Squared & frayed
k Squared & other shape
l Other combinations

2-Transmitted Light Color
a Colorless (all hues)
b Blonde
c Lt. brown
d Brown
e Dark brown
f Red brown
g Red
h Black
i Colorless & brown
j Colorless & black
k Colorless & red
l Colorless & blonde
m Lt. brown & brown
n Brown & dark brown
o Browns (all hues)
p Other combinations

4-Color Distribution along Shaft
a Uniform color
b Variation in color
c Uniform & variation in color
d Other distribution
e Not applicable

44

5-Cross-Sectional Shape
a Oval
b Round
c Oblate
d Triangular
e Irregular
f Oval & round
g Oval & oblate
h Other combination

6-Pigment Shape
a Round
b Oval
c Other shape
d Clumpy aggregates
e Streaky aggregates
f Round & oval
g Other combination
h Not applicable

7-Pigment Distribution
a Uniform
b Uneven
c Random
d Toward medulla
e Toward cuticle
f Uniform & uneven
g Other distribution
h Not applicable

8-Pigment Density
a Light
b Medium
c Heavy
d Opaque
e Light & medium
f Medium & heavy
g Heavy & opaque
h Other
i Not applicable

9-Shaft Diameter Range
a Fine (25–80 μm)
b Medium (40–110 μm)
c Thick (80–140 μm)
d Other ranges

10-Shaft Diameter Variation
a No variation
b Slight (<10 μm)
c Medium (10–30 μm)
d Large (>30 μm)
e Other

11-Thickness Change along Shaft
a Gradual
b Abrupt
c Kinks
d Buckling
e Both
f Other

12-Cortical Fusi
a Absent
b Present
c Both

13-Cortical Fusi Distribution
a Near distal end (tip)
b Near proximal end (root)
c Medial portion (middle)
d Along shaft
e Random
f Other
g Not applicable

14-Root Structure
a Absent
b Present
c Both

15-Root Shape
a Bulbous
b Follicular tag
c Digested
d Bulbous & tag
e Bulbous & digested
f Root banding
g Other combination
h Not applicable

16-Proximal End (No Root)
a Broken end
b Cut end
c Other
d Not applicable

17-Growth Phase
a Telogen
b Catagen
c Anagen
d All growth phases
e Decomposition
f Skeletal
g Other
h Not applicable

18-Cortical Damage
a Chemical
b Mechanical
c Crushed
d Burnt
e Broken (fractured)
f Frayed
g Diseased
h Other
i None

19-Oddities
a Knotted
b Color banding
c Grapping
d Ovoid bodies
e Lice or eggs
f Other
g None

20-Foreign Substances
a Blood
b Other body fluid
c Tissue
d Fibers
e Starch
f Other
g None

IV—Medullary Structure

1-Medulla
a Absent
b Present
c Both

2-Amorphous/Opaque Configurations
a Amorphous/Opaque/continuous
b Discontinuous
c Sparse
d Not applicable

3-Amorphous/Translucent Configurations
a Amorphous/translucent/continuous
b Discontinuous
c Sparse
d Not applicable

4-Cellular/Opaque Configurations
a Cellular/opaque/continuous
b Discontinuous
c Sparse
d Not applicable

5-Cellular/Translucent Configurations
a Cellular/translucent/continuous
b Discontinuous
c Sparse
d Not applicable

6-Distribution
a Uniform
b Near root
c Near tip
d Medial
e Other
f Random
g Not applicable

7-Thickness
a Fine (< 10 μm)
b Medium (10–25 μm)
c Thick (> 25 μm)
d Not applicable

8-Medullary Index
a ≤0.3
b >0.3 – <0.5
c ≥0.5
d Not applicable

(Sources of data for Table 2-3: references originally compiled and prepared by N. Petraco.)

45

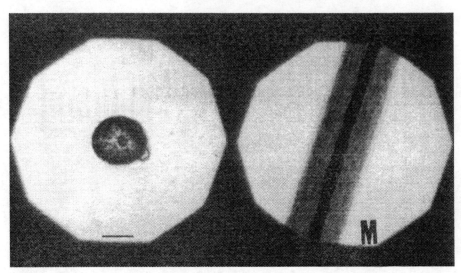

FIGURE 2-10 A typical mongoloid head hair (M). Note the circular cross section; the thick cuticle margin; the dense, streaky pigment distribution; and the even shaft diameter. The longitudinal view is mounted in Melt Mount® 1.539. The black bar is equal to 50 μm.

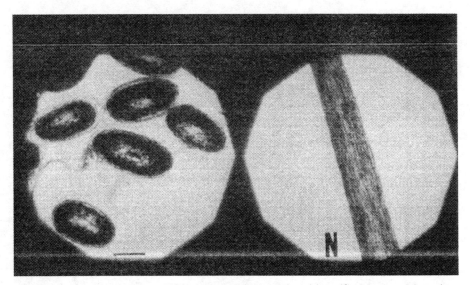

FIGURE 2-11 A typical negroid head hair (N). Note the oblate (flat) cross section, the thin cuticle margin, the shaft diameter variation, and the clumpy aggregates of pigment. The longitudinal view is mounted in Melt Mount® 1.539. The black bar is equal to 50 μm.

TABLE 2-4 Data sheet for human hair protocol shown in Table 2-3.

Human Hair Examination Data Sheet

Source_____ Known_____ Questioned_____
Person's Age_____ Sex_____ Race_____ Somatic Origin_____

Macroscopic Characteristics
  I—Gross Features
     1—Length   a b c d e f g h i j k l
     2—R.L. color   a b c d e f g h i j k l m n
     3—Shaft shape   a b c d e f g
     4—Texture   a b c

Microscopic Characteristics
  II—Cuticle
     1—Margin   a b c
     2—Distribution   a b c d
     3—Shape   a b c d e f g h
     4—Color   a b c d e
     5—Thickness   a b c d

  III—Cortex
     1—Tip shape   a b c d e f g h i j k l
     2—T.L. color   a b c d e f g h i j k l m n o p
     3—T.L. color appearance a b c
     4—Color distribution   a b c d e
     5—Cross-sectional shape a b c d e f g h
     6—Pigment granule shape a b c d e f g h
     7—Pigment distribution   a b c d e f g h
     8—Pigment density   a b c d e f g h i
     9—Shaft diameter range   a b c d
     10—Shaft dia. variation   a b c d e
     11—Thickness change/shaft a b c d e f
     12—Cortical fusi   a b c
     13—Cortical fusi dist.   a b c d e f g
     14—Root structure   a b c
     15—Root shape   a b c d e f g h
     16—Root end   a b c d
     17—Growth phase   a b c d e f g h
     18—Cortical damage   a b c d e f g h i
     19—Oddities   a b c d e f g
     20—Foreign substance   a b c d e f g

  IV—Medullary Structure
     1—Medulla   a b c
     2—Amorph./opaque config. a b c d
     3—Amorph./trans. contig. a b c d
     4—Cellular/opaque config. a b c d
     5—Cellular/trans. config.   a b c d
     6—Distribution   a b c d e f g
     7—Thickness   a b c d
     8—Medullary index   a b c d

Originally Prepared by N. Petraco

TABLE 2-5 A data sheet containing the information necessary for characterizing commonly occurring animal hair.

Animal Hair Data Sheet

Dominant scale pattern basal (base) region (Figures 2-12 and 2-13): _____

Scale pattern(s) along shaft (describe from root to tip): _____

Appearance of cuticle (scale) margin: _____

Cortex

    Shape of hair: Straight_____   Curly_____   Crimped_____   Other_____

    Length of shaft_____mm.   Sketch:

    Color: Single color_____   Bicolored_____   Multicolored_____

    If single: Reflected_____   Transmitted_____

    If bicolored or multicolored (describe from tip to root):

    Banding reflected:_____

    Banding transmitted:_____

    Pigment density and distribution: _____

      (e.g., heavy toward medulla)

    Shaft diameter in μm: Range_____   Ave._____   Maximum_____

    Root configuration: _____

    Cross-sectional shape: _____

    Miscellaneous: _____

    (e.g., ovoid bodies)

Medulla

    Medulla: Absent_____   Present_____

    Primary configuration (Figure 2-14): _____

    Medullary index (M.I.) = Medulla diameter/shaft diameter.

    M.I. = _____

    The scale cast is examined first. The dominant scale pattern in the basal region (near the root) of the hair is noted. Next, the scale pattern(s) from root to tip is scanned and noted. Figures 2-12 and 2-13 show examples of the six basic scale patterns. The wet mount is then examined to collect information concerning the specimen's transmitted light color, medullary configuration, and so on (see Table 2-5). Figure 2-14 depicts five primary medullary configurations. All the observations are recorded on the data sheet shown in Table 2-5. A review of hair morphology and terminology can be found in the literature.[74,75,77–82] The collected data should be compared with the data in Figure 2-15 for the preliminary identification of the family or species from which the questioned hair originated. In order to confirm the identification, the specimen is then compared with reference standards and data published in various articles, identification keys, manuals and atlases.[74,75,77–82]

    Often, animal guard hairs, under (fur) hairs, and fragments thereof can be tentatively identified as to species or family of origin on the basis of a few morphological characteristics without an elaborate identification scheme. The need and ability

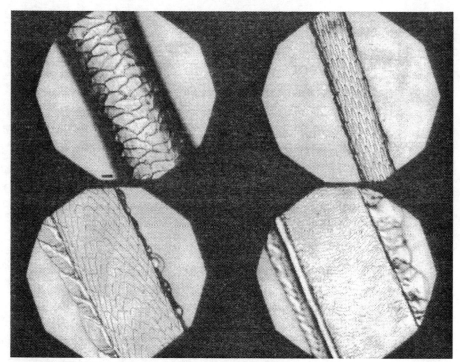

FIGURE 2-12 Four of six basic scale patterns: top left—Mosaic; top right—Pectinate; bottom left—Petal; bottom right—Imbricated. The black bar is equal to 20 μm. *Source:* Reprinted with permission from the publisher of N. Petraco, "A Microscopical Method to Aid in the Identification of Animal Hair," *The Microscope,* 35 (1987), pp. 85 and 86. Copyright 1987.

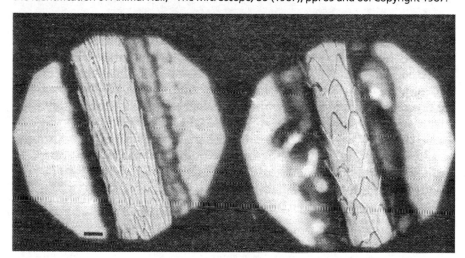

FIGURE 2-13 Two of six basic scale patterns: left—Chevron; right—Diamond petal. The black bar is equal to 20 μm. *Source:* Reprinted with permission from the publisher of N. Petraco, "A Microscopical Method to Aid in the Identification of Animal Hair," *The Microscope,* 35 (1987), pp. 85 and 86. Copyright 1987.

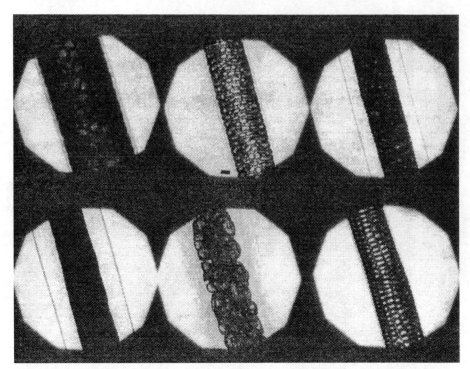

FIGURE 2-14 The five medullary configurations: top left—Wide Lattice; top center—Aeriform Lattice; top right—Fine Lattice; bottom left—Amorphous: bottom center—Globular; bottom right—Multiserial Ladder. The black bar is equal to 20 μm. *Source:* Reprinted with permission from the publisher of N. Petraco, "A Microscopical Method to Aid in the Identification of Animal Hair," *The Microscope,* 35 (1987), pp. 85 and 86. Copyright 1987.

to do this is useful when examining forensic dust specimens (see Figure 2-16). In order to identify these types of specimens accurately, one must have a thorough knowledge of animal hair morphology. This knowledge can be acquired by studying the morphology of hairs from known sources. Study specimens can be obtained commercially and from museum collections. It is advised that one acquire this background knowledge before attempting to identify hair and hair fragments.

Synthetic Fibers

Today, with the large production of synthetic fibers for all types of textile products, our environment is literally inundated with minute fragments of fibers. Dust specimens composed of synthetic fibers rolled together into balls are ubiquitous. These dust balls are formed from the wearing down of textile materials (rugs, mats, clothing, etc.), as well as the hair from animals and people, natural fibers, and other materials in our environment. Dust balls have been compared to soil samples and, like soil samples, often represent the environment(s) in which they are formed.[83] The synthetic fibers entangled in these dust specimens can be identified in the matrix specimen.

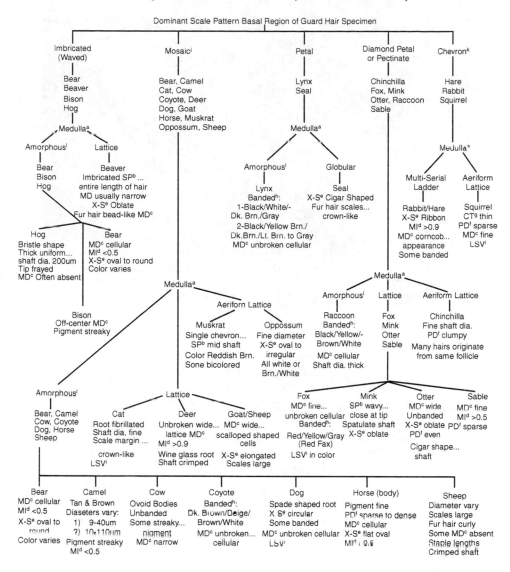

FIGURE 2-15 A flow chart for the preliminary identification of animal hairs found in forensic dust specimens. (Source of data: references 71–75 and 77–81.)

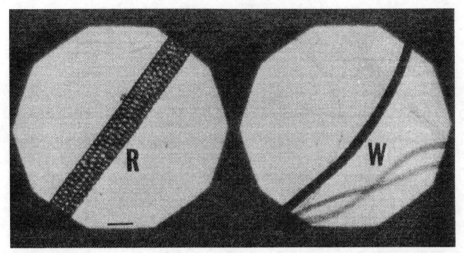

FIGURE 2-16 Questioned dust specimen found with the body of a kidnap/homicide victim. On the left, a fragment of rabbit guard hair (R). On the right, a fragment of wool (W) that has been dyed. The specimen is mounted in Melt Mount® 1.539. The black bar is equal to 50 μm.

The dust specimen is mounted on a microscope slide in Melt Mount® 1.539, as previously described (pp. 30–31). Prior to mounting, the specimen should be teased with two needles to loosen the fibers, hairs, and other debris. After mounting, the preparation is then observed under a polarized light microscope. The microscopist, on examining the dust preparation, observes a variety of fibers. At this point, examiners must use their eyes to single out the fiber in question and make a number of observations. Information concerning the fiber's morphology is collected first. Next, the relative refractive indices (RRIs) of the fiber's $n\|$ and $n\perp$ directions—as they compare with the mounting medium's RI (1.539)—are obtained by the Becke line method using plane polarized light. In the Becke line method, the fiber's elongated axis is made parallel to the vibrational (preferred) direction of the polarizer. The movement of the Becke line is noted when the microscope's focus is raised (the Becke line moves toward the medium of higher RI under these conditions). The fiber's elongated axis is then made perpendicular to the preferred direction of the polarizer and the movement of the Becke line is noted in this orientation; see Figure 2-17 for orientation of the fiber and Figure 2-18 for Becke line movement. The fiber is then observed between crossed polars. If the fiber is optically anisotropic, the amount of retardation the fiber exhibits is estimated using an interference chart and the appropriate compensator(s). The fiber's sign of elongation (SE) is determined at this stage of the examination. The fiber's estimated birefringence (EB) is computed using the collected data. Other comparative information about the fiber's appearance [delustering agent (Figure 2-19), twist, crimp (Figure 2-20), etc.] and optical properties [degree of relief (Figure 2-21), etc.] is collected. All data are recorded in the examiner's notes or on a fiber data sheet. A sample data sheet is shown in

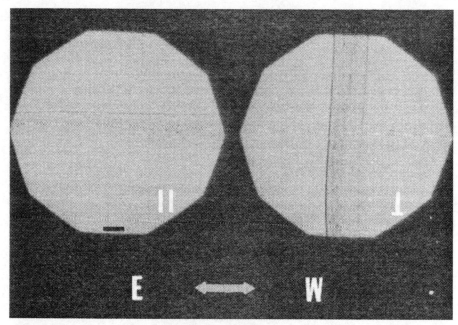

FIGURE 2-17   The olefin fiber specimen is oriented in the $n_\parallel$ (left) and $n_\perp$ (right) directions with respect to the East/West orientation of the polarizer. The fiber is mounted in Melt Mount® 1.539. The black scale is equal to 40 μm.

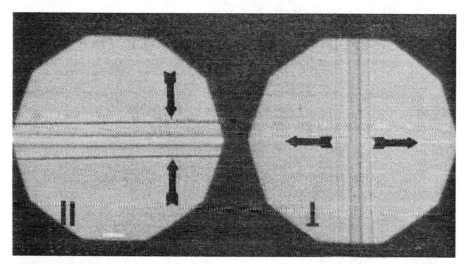

FIGURE 2-18   The Becke line (white halo) moves toward the medium of higher refractive index when the focus is raised. On the left, the Becke line moves toward the nylon fiber. On the right, the Becke line moves toward the mounting medium (Melt Mount® 1.539). The white bar is equal to 40 μm.

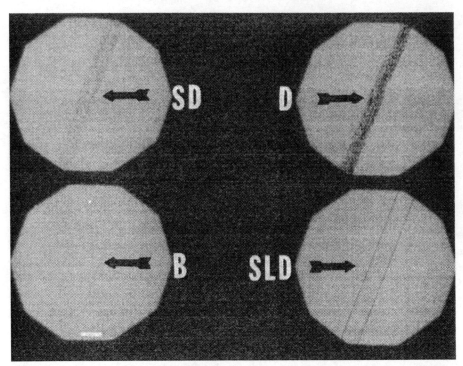

FIGURE 2-19 The appearance of fibers with and without delustering agent (TiO$_2$): no delustering agent, bright (B); semi-dull (SD); dull (D); and slightly dull (SLD). The specimens are mounted in Melt Mount® 1.539. The white bar is equal to 40 μm.

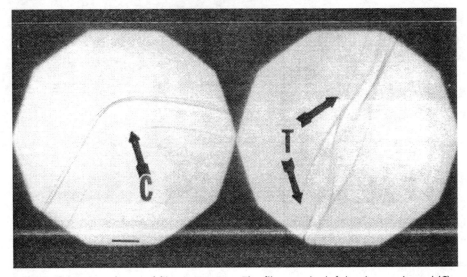

FIGURE 2-20 Two forms of fiber treatment. The fiber on the left has been crimped (C). The fiber on the right has been twisted (T). The specimens are mounted in Melt Mount® 1.539. The black bar is equal to 50 μm.

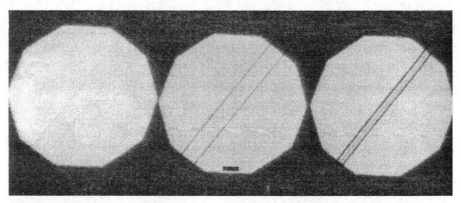

FIGURE 2-21 The various degrees of relief (shadowing) are exhibited left to right: low, medium and high relief. All specimens are mounted in Melt Mount® 1.539. The black bar is equal to 30 μm.

Table 2-6. The following is a list of the data necessary for the identification of an unknown fiber using Melt Mount® 1.539:

1. Fiber's morphology
   a. Longitudinal appearance—smooth, striated, etc.
   b. Cross-sectional shape
   c. Diameter or lobe thickness expressed in μm
2. Fiber's optical data
   a. Determine the relative refractive index (RRI)
      (Observe Becke line movement with polarized light.)
      1. Is n‖ above, below, or equal to 1.539?
      2. Is n⊥ above, below, or equal to 1.539?
   b. If anisotropic, estimate the fiber's retardation, using fixed or variable compensators. Refer to an interference chart.
   c. Calculate the fiber's birefringence using the following formula:

$$\text{Birefringence (Bi)} = \frac{\text{Retardation } (r)}{\text{Thickness } (t)} \frac{nm}{\mu m} \times 1000$$

$$\text{Bi} = (n‖ - n⊥)$$

   [Plot (t) and (r) on an interference chart and estimate the birefringence or calculate it from the data using the formula cited.]
   d. Determine whether the sign of elongation is positive or negative.
3. Additional comparative information
   a. Color—dyed or undyed?
   b. Delustering agent (TiO₂) present?
   c. Is the fiber crimped, twisted, other?
   d. Note the degree of relief.

TABLE 2-6 A data sheet with the information necessary for the classification of synthetic fibers. Circle or write in the appropriate data.

Synthetic Fiber Data Sheet

Fiber Morphology
    Longitudinal: Smooth_____   Striated_____   Irregular_____   Other_____
    Cross-sectional shape:_____
    Diameter or lobe(s) thickness in μm: _____
Optical Data
    Relative refractive indices—relative to medium (1.539)
        N parallel ($n\|$)   above_____   below_____   equal_____
        N perpendicular ($n\perp$)   above_____   below_____   equal_____
    Crossed polars: Isotropic_____   Anisotropic_____
    Estimated retardation in nanometers (nm): _____
      (interference colors)
    Estimated birefringence: _____
    Sign of elongation: Positive_____   Negative_____
Other Comparative Information
    Color:_____   Dyed_____   Undyed_____
    Delustering agent: Bright_____ Slightly dull_____ Semi-dull_____ Dull____
    Treatment: Crimped_____   Twisted_____   Other_____
    Degree of relief: Low_____   Medium_____   High_____
Other information:_____

To determine the generic classification of an unknown fiber, the collected data in Table 2-6 is compared with the information in Table 2-7 and Figure 2-22, to known published data, and to known standards. Each type of fiber in the dust specimen is identified in the same manner. If a comparison of a fiber is desired, the questioned fiber (in the matrix dust specimen) and the known fiber specimen(s) can be compared side by side on a comparison microscope composed of two polarized light microscopes that have been bridged together optically. Known fiber standards can be compared in the same manner.

Minerals, Glass, and Related Materials

Mineral grains form a large proportion of soil specimens. The identification and ratio of each mineral species as it occurs in soil samples has long been a subject of interest in the forensic science community.[1,12,14,24,32,37,91–98] An excellent paper by Graves[24] on soil classification, which is based on mounting aliquots of sieved soil specimens in Cargille® oil with a refractive index of 1.540 for the sodium D line at 25°C has set the standard for forensic soil mineralogical studies since its publication. McCrone's[98] work on soil comparisons and mineral identification also serves as an extremely valuable and informative source. Together, these two methods provide a sound and rational approach to the identification of mineral grains, glass chips, and the other related materials often encountered in forensic dust specimens. In this chapter, we adapt Graves' approach because of the close proximity in refractive index value of Cargille's® Melt Mount® 1.539 (–0.001) to the 1.540 Cargille® oil used in his method.

TABLE 2-7 The generic classes of synthetic fibers commonly found by the authors in forensic dust samples.

Generic	RRI[a]: $n\|/n\perp$	SE[b]	EB[c] (Range)	Relief	Usual Cross-section
Acetate	Both < 1.539	(+)	0.002–5	Med–Hi	Serrated
Triacetate	Both < 1.539	(+/−)	almost 0.0 (slight)	Med–Hi	Serrated
Acrylic	Both < 1.539	(−)	0.001–6	Low–Med	Bean, dog bone, mushroom, round, ovoid
Modacrylic					
(Verel®)	Both close to 1.539	(−)	0.001–3	Very Low	Dog bone, multilobed
(SEF®)	Both < 1.539	(−)	0.001–3	Low	Irregular, ribbon
(Dynel®)	Both < 1.539	(+)	0.002–5	Low–Med	Irregular
Aramid	Both > 1.539	(+)	0.22–71	Very Hi	Round, bean, peanut
Polyamide					
(Nylon 6, 6.6)	$n\| > 1.539$ / $n\perp < 1.539$	(+)	0.049–63	Low–Hi	Round, trilobal, tetralobal
(Qiana)	$n| > $ close to 1.539 / $n\perp < 1.539$	(+)	0.036	Low–Med	Trilobal
Glass, Mineral/Rock, Wool	Isotropic (Range 1.510–620)	...	......	Low–Hi	Round, off round, irregular
Olefin (Propylene)	Both < 1.539	(+)	0.028–34	Low–Med	Round, trilobal, delta, flat
Polyester	$n\| > 1.539$ / $n\perp$ close to 1.539/ ($n\perp > $ or $ < 1.539$)	(+)	0.098–0.180	Low–Hi	Round, ovoid polygonal donut, trilobal, swollen ribbon
Rayon (Viscose & Modified)	$n\| > 1.539$ / $n\perp < 1.539$	(+)	0.020–0.039	Low–Med	Serrated, multilobal bean, round

[a]RRI = Relative refractive indices

[b]SE = Sign of elongation

[c]EB = Estimated birefringence ($n\| - n\perp$).

(*Sources* of data for Table 2-7: references 23, 34, 84–90.)

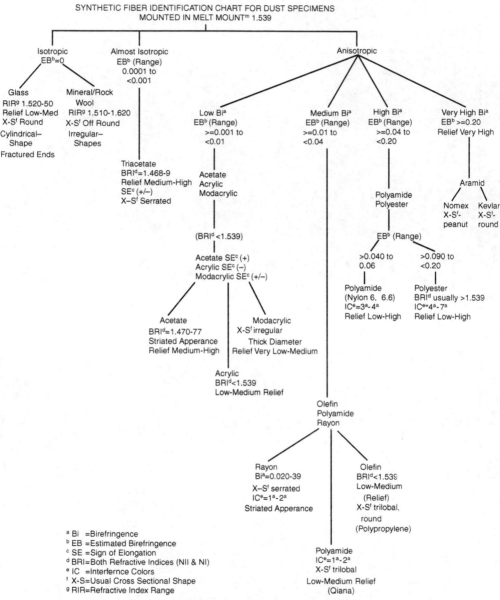

FIGURE 2-22 A flowchart for the preliminary identification of synthetic fibers commonly found in forensic dust specimens. (Sources of data: references 23, 34, 84–90.)

The minerals, glass, and related substances encountered in dust specimens usually originate from the soil located in the surrounding region, or from some other sources in the environment such as vegetation, animal activity, glass containers, building materials, vehicles, and safes. When a forensic dust specimen is mounted in Melt Mount® 1.539 and studied with PLM as described on pp. 30–31, tiny fragments of these types of materials are often observed. Just as hairs and fibers can be characterized and identified on the basis of their morphological appearance and optical properties, these materials also can be identified in the same manner.

It is the authors' combined experience that the two most commonly occurring minerals and mineral-like materials seen in dust specimens are grains of quartz and glass fragments. These two substances have similar morphological features, for example, conchoidal fractures and sharp edges, and thus appear quite similar when viewed under plane polarized light. However, as Miller points out and as most microscopists know, these two materials can be distinguished easily by the appearance of interference colors in quartz grains when viewed between crossed polars.[99] The authors often use parallel polars for this purpose because the morphology of each particle is visible, along with their apparent differences in optical properties (refer to Figure 2-23). Quartz has also been observed to exhibit orange/yellow dispersion colors at 25°C when mounted in Melt Mount® 1.539 and viewed with the central stop of a 10× dispersion staining objective apparatus.

Other commonly occurring minerals and related materials are depicted in Figures 2-24 through 2-27. Most of these substances are easily identified on the basis of their morphological appearances, and by a quick determination of some of their optical properties (degree of relief, birefringence, interference color, etc.). It is important to note that when a mineral is found in a dust specimen, its thickness is not known. Nevertheless, it is necessary to know the thickness of a mineral in order to obtain accurate birefringence measurements that can be used to help identify the mineral. The thickness of a mineral along the microscope's axis can be measured quite accurately using the micrometer located on the fine-adjustment focusing knob found on most high-quality microscopes. Once the mineral's thickness is known, its retardation can be estimated from the interference color(s) exhibited by the mineral grain. These two important pieces of data can be used, with the aid of an interference color chart or a simple formula, to estimate the mineral's birefringence. This information can be used

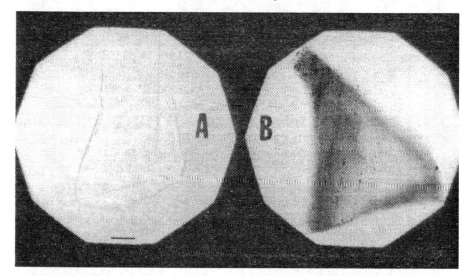

FIGURE 2-23 Differentiation of glass (A) and quartz (B) viewed with parallel polars. The specimens are mounted in Melt Mount® 1.539. The black bar is equal to 50 μm.

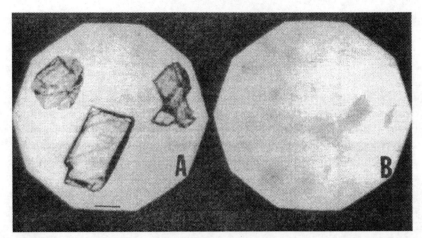

FIGURE 2-24   The appearance of calcite (A) and gypsum (B) in Melt Mount® 1.539 with plane polarized light. Note the various degrees of relief (shadowing). The black bar is equal to 50 μm.

to help identify the mineral. An illuminating discussion of the methods of optical crystallography, as well as an interference chart for the identification of common minerals, can be found in Bloss.[100] An excellent review of the essentials of polarized light microscopy can be found in a text written by McCrone, McCrone, and Delly.[101]

Another advantage of Melt Mount® 1.539 is that the orientation of a mineral grain can be changed by rolling the crystal as described by McCrone.[102] However, unlike Aroclor® 1260, the Melt Mount® preparation must be slightly heated on a

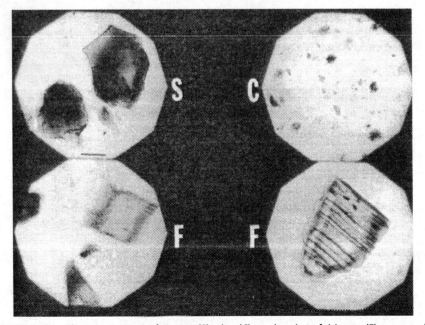

FIGURE 2-25   The appearance of quartz (S), clay (C), and various feldspars (F) mounted in Melt Mount® 1.539 and viewed with parallel polars. The black bar is equal to 50 μm.

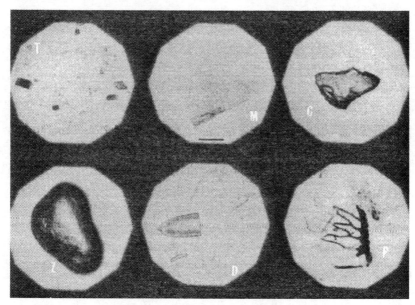

FIGURE 2-26   The appearance of tourmaline (T), biotite mica (M), garnet (G), zircon (Z), diatomaceous earth (D), and peat (P) mounted in Melt Mount® 1.539. Note the various degrees of relief exhibited by the mineral specimens. The observations were made with plane polarized light. The black bar is equal to 50 μm.

warm hotplate before rolling the crystal. Crystal rolling can be used to obtain vital crystallographic data concerning the specimen, which can be used to identify the questioned mineral. Crystal rolling can also be used to help measure a crystal fragment's thickness. After gently heating, one simple rolls the crystal fragment into the desired orientation and measures its width with a calibrated ocular micrometer. See Table 2-8 for a list of the various minerals and related materials encountered by the

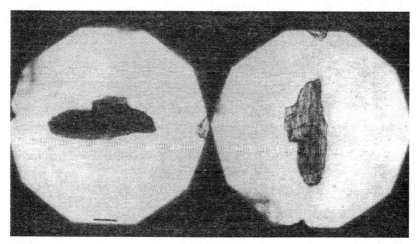

FIGURE 2-27   Hornblende (amphibole) mounted in Melt Mount® 1.539 shows pleochroism when rotated in plane polarized light. The black bar is equal to 50 μm.

TABLE 2-8 The minerals and associated materials encountered by the authors in forensic dust specimens. The specimens are described as they appear in Melt Mount® (MM) RI = 1.539.

Specimen	Color(s) (transparency)	Cleavage or Form	Relief[a]	Bi[b]	Remarks
Glass	Colorless, brown, amber, green (transparent)	Conchoidal fracture	Very low to high	None	Sharp edges RI range: 1.510–1.580 Strained Bi[b]
Quartz SiO_2	Colorless (transparent)	Conchoidal fracture, rounded	Low	Low	RIs > MM, edges sharp or round Inclusions common Exh.(+) Uniax. IF[c]
Calcite $CaCO_3$ (limestone)	Colorless (transparent)	Rhombic	Hi	Very high	High IC[d] Twinning common Like dolomite
Gypsum (plaster)	Colorless (transparent)	Rhombic & irregular	Low	Med	RIs <MM Surface rough
Halite NaCl	Colorless (transparent)	Cubic	Low	None	Isotropic RI > MM (1.544)
Feldspars	Colorless (transparent)	Rhombic, equant, & prismatic	Low–med	Low–Med	Twin lamellae Albite RIs ≤ MM Labradorite RIs > MM Microcline RIs < MM Orthoclase RIs < MM

	Color (transparency)	Form	Relief[a]	Birefringence[b]	Remarks
Micas	Colorless, grayish green, yellowish brown (transparent)	Irregular flakes	Low–med	Med–high	Pleochroic; cleavage perfect multilayered; Exh. (+−)Biax. IF[c]
Garnet	Colorless to pink (transparent)	Conchoidal fracture, rounded	High	None	Isotropic; Rls > MM; Wea< Bi[b]
Zircon	Colorless to amber (transparent)	Rounded	Very high	Med–high	Can appear opaque/relief; Rls > MM
Tourmaline	Colorless to yellow brown (transparent)	Irregular fragments, prismatic	Med–high	Med	Pleochroic; Color varies: blue, green, pink, black
Hornblende	Green (transparent)	Plates & irr. blades	Med–high	Med	Pleochroic; Rls > MM
Vegetable matter	Green, brown (transparent to opaque)	—	Med	Low	Color varies; Cellular form; Bi[b] varies
Diatoms	Colorless (transparent)	—	High	None	Fine structure; Form varies

[a]Relief: Very low—Invisible; Low—Edges visible; Med—Edges distinct; High—Heavy edges shadowing; Very high—Particle almost opaque.

[b]Birefringence: Low 0.001–.01; Med > 0.01–.05; High > 0.05–.10; Very high > 0.1.

[c]IF: Interference figure.

[d]IC: Interference colors

(Source of data: references 23, 96, 98, 100, 101, 104, 105.)

TABLE 2-9 A data sheet for the identification of minerals and related materials. Enter the required data.

Mineral & Related Materials Data Sheet

Morphology

Crystalline form or shape:_____

Cleavage/fracture:_____

Twinning/type:_____

Thickness in μm along microscope's optic axis:_____

Optical Data (plane polarized light)

Color:_____   Transparency:_____

Relief relative to Melt Mount® 1.539—plane polarized light

Very low_____   Low_____   Medium_____   High_____   Very high_____

Pleochroic: Yes_____   No_____   Colors:_____

Optical Data (crossed polars)

Isotropic_____   Anisotropic_____

Estimated retardation in nanometers (nm):_____

(interference colors)

Estimated birefringence:_____

Sign of elongation: Positive_____   Negative_____

Extinction:_____

Other Information

Magnetic: Yes_____   No_____

Other:_____

authors in their casework. The physical and optical appearance of each substance in Melt Mount® 1.539 is noted in this table. To determine the identity of an unknown mineral or related substance the data in Table 2-9 are compared with the information in Table 2-8, with a Michel Levy interference color chart, with known published data, and with known standards mounted in Melt Mount® 1.539. If a comparison of questioned and known specimens is desired, it can be carried out in the manner previously described for synthetic fibers. When necessary, a mineral grain can be isolated as previously described, and identified by the use of spindle stage methods.[103]

Finally, microscopists who wish to identify the minerals or associated materials that commonly occur in dust specimens should first have a working knowledge of the minerals composing the geographic region served by their laboratories, as well as common building materials, common inorganic salts, and various types of glass. A set of standards containing these materials mounted in Melt Mount® 1.539 should also be available. These materials should be studied thoroughly so that they are easily recognized. This should be done before any attempts at identifications are made in casework.

Miscellaneous Substances

McCrone and Delly[106] advocate that a variety of microscopic particles be identified by sight, *in situ,* on the basis of their characteristic morphologies and simple optical properties with the aid of PLM. Vegetable fibers, paper fibers, cordage fibers, paint chips, starch grains, feathers, insect parts, and so forth are just a few of the substances that can be identified in this manner. It has been the authors' combined experience that these materials frequently occur in forensic dust specimens. A few of these substances are shown as they appear in Melt Mount® 1.539 in Figures 2-28 through 2-33.

Wood fibers, which usually originate from paper products and sawdust, are ubiquitous in our environment and are consequently found in dust specimens (see Figure 2-28). Wood (paper) fibers can be identified on the basis of their microscopic morphology. Atlases such as the ones prepared by Parham and Gray[107] and Côté[108] are quite useful when attempting to identify wood fibers as to their species of origin. Cotton fibers are also abundant in our surroundings and are thus often seen in forensic dust specimens (see Figure 2-29). Cotton fibers are easily recognized on the basis of their characteristic morphology and their lack of extinction when viewed between crossed polars.[109] Other vegetable fibers that are commonly observed in forensic dust specimens are sisal, manila, flax, and ramie (see Figures 2-30 and 2-31). An excellent text by Catling and Grayson[110] concerning the identification of vegetable fibers in the forensic laboratory has been found invaluable when identifying these vegetable fibers. This text also contains a wealth of information on the identifying features of several other commonly used vegetable fibers.

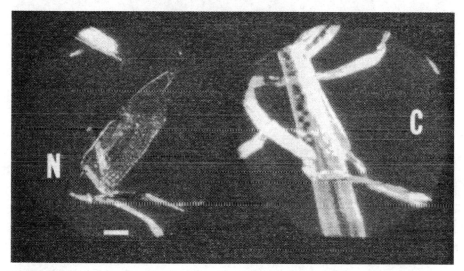

FIGURE 2-28   Nonconiferous (N) and coniferous (C) wood fibers mounted in Melt Mount® 1.539 and viewed between crossed polars. Note the vessel element on the left, and the tracheid fiber on the right. The white bar is equal to 40 μm.

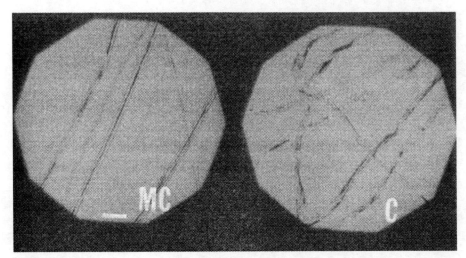

FIGURE 2-29 Mercerized cotton fibers (MC) and cotton fibers (C) are shown as they appear mounted in Melt Mount® 1.539 when viewed with plane polarized light. Note the many convolutions in the untreated cotton fibers as compared to the mercerized fibers. The white bar is equal to 40 μm.

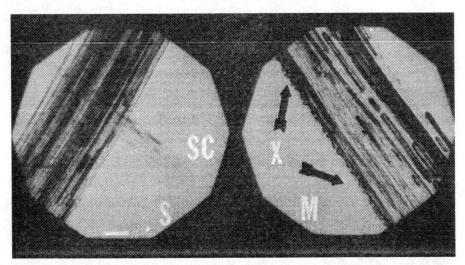

FIGURE 2-30 Sisal fibers (S) are shown on the left. Note the spiral cell (SC), which exhibits a negative sign of elongation. Manila fibers (M) are shown on the right, note the row of stegmata crystals (X). Both specimens are mounted in Melt Mount® 1.539 and observed with plane polarized light. The white bar is equal to 40 μm.

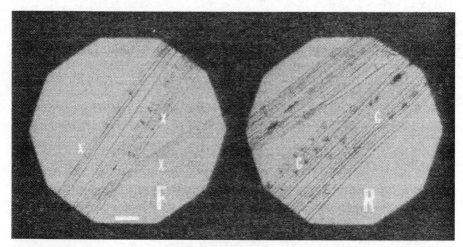

FIGURE 2.31   The appearance of flax fibers (F), and ramie fibers (R) in Melt Mount® 1.539 when viewed with plane polarized light. Note the cross markings (X) on the flax fibers and the row of star-shaped crystals (C) along the ramie fibers. The white bar is equal to 40 μm.

Grains of starch are seen on a routine basis in casework. Their source is usually food products, surgical gloves, baby powder, and so forth. Most grains of starch can be identified on the basis of their morphology. Figure 2-32 depicts a typical potato starch grain as it appears when observed between crossed polars.

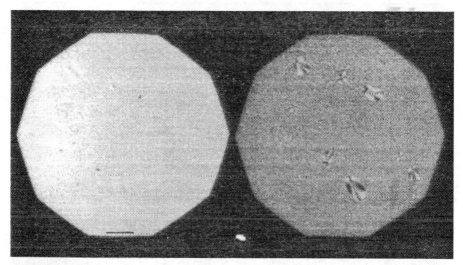

FIGURE 2-32   Potato starch mounted in Melt Mount® 1.539. On the left, the specimen is viewed with plane polarized light; on the right, the specimen is viewed between crossed polars 10° off extinction. The black bar is equal to 50 μm.

The black cross that is exhibited indicates that the particle is a starch grain, and its shape identifies it as potato starch. Most types of starch can be identified by the shape and size of their grains. Several types of starch are shown and described in the literature.[111]

Feathers found in dust specimens usually originate from domesticated birds raised for use as food, such as ducks, chickens, and turkeys, or those that are commonly found in our environment, such as pigeons. Feathers removed from birds used as food are frequently used as fillers in items such as jackets, coats, and pillows, to name just a few; consequently, they find their way into the dust found in many places. Feathers can be identified morphologically. One can usually determine the bird family from which a feather originated on the basis of the structure of its down.[112] Figure 2-33 shows the downy structure of feathers of three common birds of commercial importance.

Dust Comparison

Once the trace evidential contents of the questioned or known dust specimens have been identified, the information can be compiled on a tabulation sheet such as the one shown in Table 2-10. The data recorded on this sheet make the final comparison and interpretation of the information much easier. The data compiled with the tabulation sheet can easily be adapted to form a computer database that could be interpreted by the use of artificial intelligence. Therefore, a tabulation sheet should be prepared for each dust specimen. Finally, the tabulation sheet can be useful when preparing or presenting court exhibits or testimony.

Conclusion

This chapter is presented to illustrate how powerful the method of PLM is in the identification and characterization of forensic dust specimens. It is not meant to be a

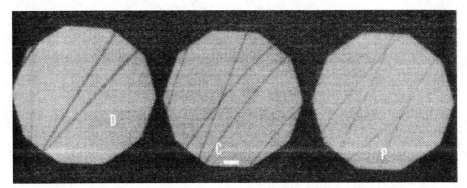

FIGURE 2-33 Feathers commonly found in dust as they appear in Melt Mount® 1.53. From left to right, duck (D), chicken (C), and pigeon (P). The white bar is equal 30 μm.

TABLE 2-10 A tabulation sheet for the characterization and comparison of questioned and known forensic dust specimens. Circle or write in the response.

Dust Tabulation Sheet   Specimen No._____

Dust specimen source: Questioned_____ Known_____
Human Hair: Yes_____   No_____
   Racial origin: Caucasoid_____   Mongoloid_____   Negroid_____   Mixed_____
   Somatic origin: Head_____   Pubic_____   Other_____
   No. of hair types:_____   Race(s):_____   Body area(s):_____
Animal Hair: Yes_____   No_____
   Guard hair_____   Tactile hair_____   Fur_____   Other_____
   Species of origin: Dog_____   Cat_____   Other_____
   No. of different species:_____
Synthetic Fibers: Yes_____   No_____
   Generic classes: Acetate   Triacetate   Acrylic   Aramid
    Modacrylic   Polyamide   Polyester   Rayon   Olefin
    Glass   Mineral   Other_____
No. of different types of each generic class: Acetate_____
   Triacetate_____   Acrylic_____   Aramid_____   Modacrylic_____
   Polyamide_____   Polyester_____   Olefin_____   Rayon_____
   Glass_____   Mineral_____   Other_____
Vegetable Fibers: Yes_____   No_____
   Type present: Cotton_____   Ramie_____   Sisal_____   Flax_____
       Other_____
Minerals, Glass, and Related Materials: Yes_____   No_____
   Type present: Quartz_____   Glass_____   Other_____
Miscellaneous Substances: Yes_____   No_____
   Type present_____
No. of similar materials in questioned and known dust_____
No. of dissimilar materials in questioned and known dust_____
Known and questioned: Similar_____   Dissimilar_____   Both_____

complete discussion of the topic, but rather to serve as an introduction and preliminary guide to the analysis of forensic dust specimens. It is designed to show just how much investigative information and data a forensic microscopist can obtain from a dust specimen, armed only with a polarized light microscope, a knowledge of parti cle morphology; a set of standards mounted in an appropriate medium; a few good atlases, whether published or self-prepared; a handbook; and the desire to identify and characterize forensic dust specimens. It is hoped that this chapter will serve to inspire more forensic scientists to use PLM in their everyday casework to help reconstruct and solve crimes.

References

1. W.C. McCrone, "Particle Analysis in the Crime Laboratory," in *The Particle Atlas*, vol. 5, W. C. McCrone, J. G. Delly, and S. J. Palenik, eds. Ann Arbor, MI: Ann Arbor Science Publishers (1979), pp. 1379–1401.

2. N. Petraco, "The Occurrence of Trace Evidence in One Examiner's Casework," *J. Forensic Sci.*, 30 (1985), 485–93.

3. McCrone [op cit., p. 1379].

4. H. Gross, *Criminal Investigation*, adapted from *System Der Kriminalistik*, by J. C. Adams. London, England: Sweet and Maxwell Limited (1924), pp. 144–47.

5. A. Schneider, "Police Microscopy," *J. Criminal Law Criminol. Pol. Sci.*, 11 (1920), 217–21.

6. E. Locard, "The Analysis of Dust Traces," *Am. J. Police Sci.*, 1 (1930), Part I, 276–98; Part II, 401–18; Part III, 496–514.

7. H. T. F. Rhodes, *Clues and Crime.* London: John Murray (1933), pp. 33–35.

8. H. Söderman and J. J. O'Connell, *Modern Criminal Investigation.* New York and London: Funk and Wagnalls (1935), pp. 243–50.

9. A. Lucas, *Forensic Chemistry and Scientific Criminal Investigation.* New York: Longmans, Green & Co.; London, Edward Arnold & Co. Publishers Limited (1935), pp. 64, 152–60.

10. C. H. O'Hara and J. W. Osterburg, *An Introduction to Criminalistics.* New York: The MacMillan Co. (1949), pp. 30–36.

11. P. L. Kirk, *Crime Investigation.* New York: Interscience Publishers (1953), pp. 3–11.

12. L. C. Nickolls, "The Identification of Stains of Nonbiological Origin," in *Methods of Forensic Science*, vol. 1, F. Lundquist, ed. New York: Interscience Publishers (1962), pp. 335–71.

13. M. Frei-Sulzer, "Coloured Fibres in Criminal Investigations with Special Reference to Natural Fibers," in *Methods of Forensic Science*, vol. 4, A. S. Curry, ed. New York: Interscience Publishers (1965), pp. 141–75.

14. S. J. Palenik, "The Determination of Geographical Origin of Dust Samples," in *The Particle Atlas*, vol. 5, W. C. McCrone, J. G. Delly, and S. J. Palenik, eds. Ann Arbor, MI: Ann Arbor Science Publishers (1979), pp. 1347–61.

15. M. C. Grieve, "The Role of Fibers in Forensic Science Examinations," *J. Forensic Sci.*, 28 (1983), 877–87.

16. W. Fong, "Fiber Evidence: Laboratory Methods and Observations from Casework," *J. Forensic Sci.*, 29 (1984), 55–63.

17. H. A. Deadman, "Fiber Evidence and the Wayne Williams Trial," *FBI Law Enforce. Bull.*, March (1984), 13–20, and May (1984), 10–19.

18. R. Saferstein, *Criminalistics*, 9th edition. Englewood Cliffs, NJ: Prentice-Hall, Inc. (2007), pp. 208–245.

19. P. R. DeForest, R. E. Gaensslen, and H. C. Lee, *Forensic Science: An Introduction to Criminalistics.* New York: McGraw-Hill (1983), pp. 146–67.

20. B. D. Gaudette, "Fibre Evidence," *RCMP Gazette*, 47:12 (1985), 18–20.

21. R. Saferstein, ed. *Forensic Science Handbook*, vol. I, 2nd ed., (2002); vol. II (2005). Englewood Cliffs, NJ: Prentice-Hall, Inc.

22. N. Petraco, "Trace Evidence—The Invisible Witness," *J. Forensic Sci.*, 31 (1986), 321–28.

23. W. C. McCrone and J. G. Delly, eds., *The Particle Atlas*, 2nd ed. Ann Arbor, MI: Ann Arbor Science Publishers: vol. 1 (1973), vol. 2 (1973), vol. 4 (1973), and W. C. McCrone, J. G.

Delly, and S. J. Palenik, eds., vol. 5 (1979).

24. W. J. Graves, "A Mineralogical Soil Classification Technique for the Forensic Scientist," *J. Forensic Sci.*, 24 (1979), 323–38.

25. W. Fong, "Rapid Microscopic Identification of Synthetic Fibers in a Single Liquid Mount," *J. Forensic Sci.*, 27 (1982), 257–63.

26. N. Petraco, "A Microscopical Method to Aid in the Identification of Animal Hair," *The Microscope*, 35 (1987), 83–92.

27. N. Petraco, and T. A. Kubic, *Color Atlas and Manual of Microscopy for Criminalists, Chemists, and Conservators*. Boca Raton, FL: CRC Press (2004).

28. P. R. DeForest, "Foundations of Forensic Microscopy," in *Forensic Science Handbook*, vol. I, 2nd ed., R. Saferstein, ed. Englewood Cliffs, NJ: Prentice-Hall, Inc. (2002), pp. 216–319.

29. R. E. Bisbing, "The Forensic Identification and Association of Human Hair," in *Forensic Science Handbook*, vol. I, 2nd ed., R. Saferstein, ed. Englewood Cliffs, NJ: Prentice-Hall, Inc. (2002), pp. 390–428.

30. R. D. Koons, et. al., "Forensic Glass Comparisons," in *Forensic Science Handbook*, vol. I, 2nd ed., R. Saferstein, ed. Englewood Cliffs, NJ: Prentice-Hall, Inc. (2002), pp. 162–213.

31. J. I. Thornton, "Forensic Paint Examination," in *Forensic Science Handbook*, vol. I, 2nd ed., R. Saferstein, ed. Englewood Cliffs, NJ: Prentice-Hall, Inc. (2002), pp. 429–478.

32. R. C. Murray and L. P. Solebello, "Forensic Examination of Soil," in *Forensic Science Handbook*, vol. I, 2nd ed., R. Saferstein, ed. Englewood Cliffs, NJ: Prentice-Hall, Inc. (2002), pp. 616–633.

33. S. Palenik and C. Palenik, "Microscopy and Microchemistry of Physical Evidence," in *Forensic Science Handbook*, vol. II, 2nd ed., R. Saferstein, ed. Englewood Cliffs, NJ: Prentice-Hall, Inc. (2005), pp. 176–230.

34. M. B. Eyring and B. D. Gaudette, "The Forensic Aspects of Textile Fiber Examination," in *Forensic Science Handbook*, vol. II, 2nd ed.; R. Saferstein, ed. Englewood Cliffs, NJ: Prentice-Hall, Inc. (2005), pp. 232–295.

35. Eyring [op. cit., pp. 233–238].

36. L. C. Nickolls, "The Identification of Stains of Nonbiological Origin," in *Methods of Forensic Science*, vol. 1; F. Lundquist, ed. New York: Interscience Publishers (1962), pp. 335–37.

37. E. Locard, "L'analyse des poussieres en criminalistique," in *Revue Internationale de Criminalistique*, 1 Juillet (1929), pp. 176–249.

38. Palenik [op cit., *Forensic Science Handbook*, vol. II, 2nd ed., pp. 178–183].

39. M. Frei-Sulzer, "Preserving Micro-Traces Under Adhesive Bands," *Kriminalistik*, No. 19/20 (1951), pp. 190–94.

40. E. Martin, "The Behavior of Textile Fibres in Contact with the Glue of Adhesive Transparent Strips Used for Collecting Specimens," *Internat. Crim. Pol. Rev.*, 188 (1965), 135–41.

41. Grieve, M. C., and Garger, E. F., An Improved Method for Rapid and Accurate Scanning of Fibers on Tape," *J. Forensic Sci.*, 26 (1981), 560–63.

42. M. Y. Choudhry, "A Novel Technique for the Collection and Recovery of Foreign Fibers in Forensic Science Casework," *J. Forensic Sci.*, 33 (1988), 249–53.

43. P. L. Kirk, "Microscopic Evidence—Its Use in the Investigation of Crime," *J. Crim. Law Criminol. Pol. Sci.*, 40 (1949–1950), 362–69.

44. N. Petraco, "A Simple Trace Evidence Trap for the Collection of Vacuum

Sweepings," *J. Forensic Sci.,* 32 (1987), 1422–25.

45. N. Petraco, "The Occurrence of Trace Evidence in One Examiner's Casework," *J. Forensic Sci.,* 30 (1985), 486.

46. Palenik [op cit., *Forensic Science Handbook,* vol. II, 2nd ed., pp. 179–180].

47. P. R. DeForest, S. Ryan, and N. Petraco, "Melt Mount® Stick Mounting Medium," *The Microscope,* 35 (1987), 261–66.

48. P. R. DeForest, B. Shankles, R. L. Sacher, and N. Petraco, "Melt Mount® 1.539 as a Mounting Medium for Hair," *The Microscope,* 35 (1987), 249–59.

49. E. A. Chille, R. E. Gorgon, R. A. Adamo, and P. R. DeForest, "Studies of Hair Deterioration—Interior Environments," presented at the 11th Meeting of the International Association of Forensic Sciences, Vancouver, B.C., Canada, August 2–11, 1987.

50. P. R. DeForest, N. Petraco, and R. A. Adamo, "Significance of Environmental Exposure in the Interpretation of Hair Evidence," presented at the 11th meeting of the International Association of Forensic Sciences, Vancouver, B.C., Canada, August 2–11, 1987.

51. J. W. Hicks, *Microscopy of Hair,* Issue 2. Washington, DC: U.S. Government Printing Office (1977), p. 6.

52. N. Petraco, "The Replication of Hair Cuticle Scale Patterns in Melt Mount®," *The Microscope,* 34 (1986), 341–45.

53. Bisbing [op cit., pp. 201–2].

54. Hicks [op cit.,pp. 7–10].

55. N. Petraco, C. Frass, F. X. Callery, and P. R. DeForest, "The Morphological and Evidential Significance of Human Hair Roots," *J. Forensic Sci.,* 33 (1988), 68–76.

56. Bisbing [op cit., p. 407–408].

57. J. Glaister, *A Study of Hairs and Wools Belonging to the Mammalian Group of Animals, Including a Special Study of Human Hair, Considered from Medico-Legal Aspects.* Cairo, Egypt: MISR Press, (1931), p. 155.

58. S. Smith and J. Glaister. *Recent Advances in Forensic Medicine,* 2nd edition, Philadelphia, PA: Blakiston's Son & Co., Inc. (1939), pp. 118–24.

59. B. D. Gaudette and E. S. Keeping, "An Attempt at Determining Probabilities in Human Scalp Hair Comparison," *J. Forensic Sci.,* 19 (1974), 601–02.

60. B. D. Gaudette, "Probabilities and Human Public Hair Comparison," *J. Forensic Sci.,* 21 (1976), 515–16.

61. Hicks [op cit.,pp. 6–27].

62. Bisbing [op cit.,pp. 406–413].

63. McCrone [op cit., p. 1383].

64. S. A. Shaffer, "A Protocol for the Examination of Hair Evidence," *The Microsocpe,* 30 (1982), 151–61.

65. M. A. T. Strauss, "Forensic Characterization of Human Hair I," *The Microscope,* 31 (1983), 15–29.

66. B. D. Gaudette, "Forensic Hair Comparisons," *Crime Lab. Dig.,* 12(1985), 44–59.

67. H. C. Lee and P. R. DeForest, "Forensic Hair Comparison," in *Forensic Science,* vol. 3; C. H. Wecht ed. New York: Matthew Bender (1987), pp. 37A-8, 9.

68. Gross [op cit., pp. 131–38].

69. Locard [op cit.,Part I, pp. 276–98].

70. H. Söderman and E. Fontell, *Handbok I. Kriminalteknik.* Stockholm (1930), pp. 534–52.

71. Glaister [op cit.]

72. Smith and Glaister [op cit., pp. 86–124].

73. P. L. Kirk, *Crime Investigation.* New York: Interscience Publishers (1953), pp. 152–75.

74. Hicks [op cit., pp. 28–40].

75. H. Sato, M. Yoshino, and S. Seta, "Macroscopical and Microscopical Studies of Mammalian Hairs with Special Reference to the Morphological Differences," *Rep. Natl. Res. Inst. Pol. Sci.,* 33:1 (1980), 1–16.

76. N. Petraco, "A Modified Technique for the Cross Sectioning of Hairs and Fibers," *J. Pol. Sci. Admin.,* 9 (1981), pp. 448–50.

77. A. B. Wildman, *Microscopy of Animal Textile Fibres.* Leeds: WIRA (1954).

78. A. S. Adorjan and G. B. Kolenosky, *A Manual for the Identification of Hairs of Selected Ontario Mammals,* Research Report (Wildlife), No. 90, Dept. of Lands and Forests, Ontario (1969).

79. T. D. Moore, L. E. Spence, and C. E. Dugnolle, *Identification of the Dorsal Guard Hairs of Some Mammals of Wyoming,* W. G. Hepworth, ed. Cheyenne, WY: Dept. of Fish and Game (1974).

80. H. Brunner, and B. J. Coman, *The Identification of Mammalian Hair.* Melbourne: Inkata Press (1974).

81. H. M. Appleyard, *Guide to the Identification of Animal Fibres,* 2nd edition. Leeds: WIRA (1978).

82. McCrone [op cit., pp. 1383–84].

83. W. Hanley, personal communication.

84. M. E. O'Neill, "Police Microanalysis— II. Textile Fibers," *J. Am. Inst. Crim. Law Criminol.,* 25 (1934), 835–42.

85. A. Longhetti and G. W. Roche, "Microscopic Identification of Man-Made Fibers from the Criminalistics Point of View," *J. Forensic Sci.,* 3 (1958), 303–29.

86. R. A. Rouen and V. C. Reeve, "A Comparison and Evaluation of Techniques for Identification of Synthetic Fibers," *J. Forensic Sci.,* 15 (1970), 410–32.

87. L. Forlini and W. C. McCrone, "Dispersion Staining of Fibers," *The Microscope,* 19 (1971), 243–54.

88. The Textile Institute, *Identification of Textile Materials,* 7th edition. Manchester, England: The Textile Institute (1975).

89. National Bureau of Standards, *Reference Collection of Synthetic Fibers.* McLean, VA: U.S. Dept. of Commerce (1984).

90. N. Petraco, P. R. DeForest, and H. Harris, "A New Approach to the Microscopical Examination and Comparison of Synthetic Fibers Encountered in Forensic Science Cases," *J. Forensic Sci.,* 25 (1980), 571–82.

91. L. J. Goin and P. L. Kirk, "Application of Microchemical Techniques: Identity of Soil Samples," *J. Crim. Law Criminol. Pol. Sci.,* 38 (1947–48), 267–81.

92. Kirk [op cit., pp. 249–56, 680–84].

93. D. Smale and N. A. Trueman, "Heavy Mineral Studies as Evidence in a Murder Case in Outback Australia," *J. Forensic Sci. Soc.,* 9 (1969), 123–28.

94. F. Fitzpatrick and J. I. Thornton, "Forensic Science Characterization of Sand," *J. Forensic Sci.,* 20 (1975), 460–75.

95. R. J. Dudley, "The Particle Size Analysis of Soils and Its Use in Forensic Science—The Determination of Particle Size Distributions within the Silt and Sand Fractions," *J. Forensic Sci. Soc.,* 16 (1976), 219–29.

96. R. C. Murray and J. C. F. Tedrow, *Forensic Geology,* 2nd ed., Engflewood Cliffs, JN: Prentice-Hall (1992).

97. S. J. Palenik, "Microscopy and the Law," *Indust. Res. Devel.,* March (1979), 85–88.

98. W. C. McCrone, "Soil Comparison and Identification of Constituents," *The Microscope,* 30 (1982), 17–25.

99. R. D. Koons, et. at, "Forensic Glass Comparisons," in *Forensic Science Handbook,* vol. I, 2nd ed., R. Saferstein, ed. Englewood Cliffs, NJ: Prentice-Hall, Inc. (2002), p. 181.

100. F. D. Bloss, *An Introduction to the Methods of Optical Crystallography.* New York: Holt, Rinehart and Winston, Inc. (1961).

101. W. C. McCrone, L. B. McCrone, and J. G. Delly, *Polarized Light Microscopy,* Ann Arbor, MI: Ann Arbor Science Publishers, Inc. (1978).

102. W. C. McCrone, "Particle Characterization by PLM—Part III: Crossed Polars," *The Microscope,* 31 (1983), 195–96.

103. F. D. Bloss, *The Spindle Stage: Principles and Practice.* Cambridge, England: Cambridge University Press (1981).

104. W. J. Graves, "A Mineralogical Soil Classification Technique for the Forensic Scientist," *J. Forensic Sci.,* 24 (1979), 331–37.

105. M. Fleischer, R. E. Wilcox, and J. J. Matzko, *Microscopic Determination of the Non-opaque Minerals,* U.S. Geological Survey Bulletin 1627. Washington, DC: U.S. Government Printing Office (1984).

106. W. C. McCrone and J. G. Delly, eds., *The Particle Atlas,* 2nd edition. Ann Arbor, MI: Ann Arbor Science Publishers: vol. 1 (1973), Introduction.

107. R. A. Parham and R. L. Gray, *The Practical Identification of Wood Pulp Fibers.* Atlanta, GA: Tappi Press (1982).

108. W. A. Côté, ed. *Papermaking Fibers: A Photomicrographic Atlas.* Syracuse, NY: Syracuse University Press (1980).

109. McCrone and Delly, eds. [op cit., pp. 352–3].

110. D. M. Catling and J. E. Grayson, *Identification of Vegetable Fibres.* London, England: Chapman Hall, Ltd. (1982).

111. McCrone and Delly, eds. [op cit., pp. 457–62].

112. Metropolitan Police Forensic Science Laboratory, *Biology Methods Manual.* London, England: Commissioner of Police of the Metropolis (1978), pp. 6–9 to 6–11.

3

Forensic Applications of Infrared Spectroscopy

Edward M. Suzuki, Ph.D.
Washington State Crime Laboratory
Washington State Patrol

The first measurements of the infrared absorptions of molecules occurred in the 1880s,[1] and the early spectroscopists performing these analyses recognized the potential of using this method to identify organic compounds.[1-3] These measurements were made using primitive devices, however, with the analyst manually recording the absorption of each wavelength; this tedious process required several hours for each sample. In computer-age parlance, it was not what one would consider a particularly *user-friendly* technique. Consequently, for many decades infrared spectroscopy remained an esoteric research tool used to study the structures of small molecules.

During World War II, interest in several defense projects—particularly the large-scale production of synthetic rubber—prompted the development of improved infrared instruments and the first practical commercial spectrometers appeared after the war. Following this, infrared spectroscopy grew rapidly from obscurity to become an important analytical tool encompassing a wide variety of applications in virtually every field of chemistry as well as many other fields, including physics, astronomy, environmental sciences, atmospheric sciences, geology, the biological sciences, and some engineering disciplines.

From an analytical chemistry perspective, infrared spectroscopy has few peers in terms of its wide applicability and versatility. The only compounds that do not absorb in the mid-infrared region are homonuclear diatomic molecules (e.g., H_2, N_2, I_2) and some simple inorganic salts (which do absorb in the far-infrared region). Solids, liquids, and vapors may all be readily analyzed. The method is an excellent means of determining the presence of functional groups in organic compounds, of obtaining information about the presence of many common inorganic cations or anions (e.g., NH_4^+, CO_3^{-2}, SO_4^{-2}), and of determining the generic type of a polymeric substance. Certainly one of its greater attributes is its specificity, and an infrared analysis constitutes an unequivocal identification for many compounds, particularly low- to moderate-molecular-weight organic compounds, low-molecular-weight inorganic compounds analyzed in the vapor phase under high resolutions, and some other inorganic compounds.

Considering these features and the overall dependability, ease of operation, and modest cost of an infrared spectrometer, it is not surprising that this instrument plays a prominent role in the forensic science laboratory. Few such laboratories may be found that are not so equipped, and the infrared spectrometer may be the workhorse for the analysis of certain types of evidence. In view of the limitless variety of materials that may be subject to a forensic examination, it could be argued that the only other instrument having a wider applicability in terms of providing meaningful information for the forensic scientist is the microscope.

Until the 1980s, this may have been largely an academic argument, because many of the materials normally encountered in forensic casework were too small for infrared analyses using dispersive spectrometers. This situation changed dramatically in the early 1980s when low-cost dependable Fourier transform infrared (FT-IR) spectrometers were first introduced commercially, and this soon led to a veritable revolution regarding the use of infrared spectroscopy in the forensic science laboratory.

Although FT-IR instruments have been available commercially since the late 1960s, these earlier models were quite expensive (costing more than $100,000) and plagued with mechanical difficulties; consequently, they were not widely used. Following the introduction of the new generation of low-cost dependable FT-IR instruments, however, dispersive spectrometers soon became obsolete. Accompanying this transition—and primarily in response to it—a number of sampling accessories using dispersive spectrometers, which previously were considered marginal or impractical, reemerged. The full potentials of these accessories, including the diamond anvil cell, diffuse reflectance, attenuated total reflectance, and the infrared microscope (which actually has been in existence since the late 1940s), were now realized, and today they are used routinely in forensic science laboratories throughout the world. At the same time, new accessories were introduced—and continue to be introduced—including devices that perform "on-the-fly" gas chromatographic effluent analysis, gas chromatographic cryogenic effluent trapping, photoacoustic spectroscopy, and the development of an attenuated total reflectance objective for the infrared microscope. Portable FT-IR units suitable for field operations, such as crime scene investigations, have also recently become available.

Because there are now a host of FT-IR sampling accessories, each with its merits and limitations, forensic scientists must decide which accessories—or more likely, which combination of accessories—are most appropriate to meet their needs. One of the goals of this chapter is to assist in this task by providing information about the suitability of the various methods for different types of evidence. The basic operation of each accessory is reviewed, with a heavy emphasis on explaining how the mechanism of the analysis process may affect the spectral data that result. In particular, the differences that can occur between spectra of the same compound analyzed by various accessories or methods are discussed. For some methods, sample preparation has little bearing on the quality of the spectral data obtained, whereas for others, it has very pronounced effects, and the factors that cause this are described.

Forensic scientists should understand how an FT-IR spectrometer itself operates, as it is based on an entirely different principle from that used on a dispersive instrument. Along with discussions of instrumentation, sampling methods/accessories, and data evaluation and interpretation, this chapter describes features of infrared spectroscopy that have made it the method of choice for the examination of some types of evidence, the advantages of using the technique in some cases to complement the information provided by other methods, and the limitations of infrared analysis for forensic examinations. Some basic theory of infrared spectroscopy is also included so that the forensic scientist may gain a better understanding of *why* this is so.

THEORY

An infrared spectrum is produced by the absorption of certain frequencies of radiation by a collection of molecules. This absorption produces an increase in the *vibrational* energies of these molecules. The full theoretical treatment of this process involves a considerable amount of mathematics and quantum mechanics and is beyond the scope of this chapter; however, some of the underlying principles involved and the consequences of the quantum mechanical solutions are presented so the reader may better understand the reason that an infrared spectrum provides the type of information it does.

The Electromagnetic Spectrum

Visible light makes up only a small part of the total electromagnetic spectrum. All radiation of this spectrum may be characterized by either its wavelength, λ, or its frequency, v. In a vacuum, electromagnetic radiation travels at the speed of light, c, and $\lambda v = c$. The wave nature of radiation may be viewed as an oscillating electric field, together with an oscillating magnetic field that is perpendicular to the electric field; both fields are perpendicular to the direction of travel of the wave (Figure 3-1). It is impossible to have an oscillating electric field without a corresponding oscillating magnetic field, as a changing electric field generates a magnetic field and a changing magnetic field generates an electric field. This is, in fact, one way to visualize the propagation of electromagnetic radiation.

Although many common phenomena can be explained in terms of the wave nature of radiation, in many instances radiation behaves as if it were made up of particles. Such a particle is referred to as a *photon*, and the energy of a single photon is given by $E = hv$, where h is Planck's constant and v is the frequency of the radiation. (This equation thus recognizes both the particle and the wave nature of radiation.) The energy of a particular photon is thus proportional to its frequency. One can view a single photon as that unit of radiation emitted or absorbed by a single atom or molecule during a radiative transition.

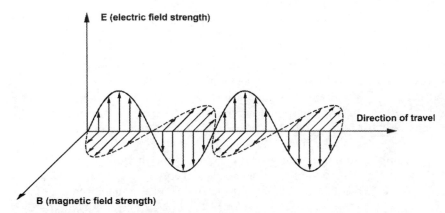

FIGURE 3-1   Depiction of the spatial variation of the electric and magnetic fields of electromagnetic radiation at a given instant of time. This wave travels to the right with a velocity of c in vacuum.

Figure 3-2 depicts the various regions of the electromagnetic spectrum. Because the spectrum consists of a continuum of wavelengths, there are no sharp demarcations between these regions. The absorption or emission of radiation by matter produces or results from different types of transitions, depending on the energy of the radiation. These are indicated on Figure 3-2 for the various regions along with some of the spectroscopic methods using these transitions. It is interesting to note that every one of the spectroscopic methods listed, except for microwave spectroscopy, has been used for forensic examinations. Neutron activation analysis is a type of gamma ray emission spectroscopy. Raman spectroscopy involves an *inelastic scattering process* (meaning that the scattered light has more or less energy than the incident light) and the monochromatic wavelength that is used can vary from near-ultraviolet to near-infrared radiation. In a conventional Raman analysis, this results in molecules having greater vibrational energies, with the Raman-scattered radiation having correspondingly less energy.

The frequencies occurring in the infrared region, 10^{11} to 10^{14} Hz [Hz (hertz) = cycles per second], are quite high. It is much more convenient to use the wavenumber to describe a particular frequency in this region. A *wavenumber* is the reciprocal of the wavelength expressed in centimeters, and is designated as cm^{-1}. The wavenumber is thus proportional to frequency and energy. The infrared region extends from approximately 13000 cm^{-1} (770 nm) to 10 cm^{-1} (300 GHz) and is divided into three subregions known as *near-infrared* (13000 to 4000 cm^{-1}), *mid-infrared* (4000 to 400 cm^{-1}), and *far-infrared* (400 to 10 cm^{-1}).

Vibration of Diatomic Molecules

The vibrational properties of diatomic molecules are examined first, because there is only a single vibrational mode to consider and many of the principles developed for this system also apply to polyatomic molecules. For both diatomic and polyatomic

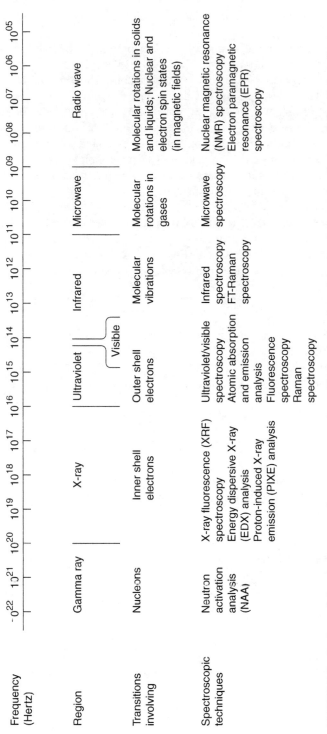

FIGURE 3-2 Regions of the electromagnetic spectrum, together with the nuclear/atomic/molecular processes that result from interactions with the radiation in each region, and some of the spectroscopic techniques based on these processes.

Frequency (Hertz)	10^{22} 10^{21}	10^{20} 10^{19} 10^{18} 10^{17}	10^{16}	10^{15} 10^{14}	10^{13} 10^{12}	10^{11} 10^{10} 10^{09}	10^{08} 10^{07} 10^{06} 10^{05}
Region	Gamma ray	X-ray	Ultraviolet		Infrared	Microwave	Radio wave
				Visible			
Transitions involving	Nucleons	Inner shell electrons	Outer shell electrons		Molecular vibrations	Molecular rotations in gases	Molecular rotations in solids and liquids; Nuclear and electron spin states (in magnetic fields)
Spectroscopic techniques	Neutron activation analysis (NAA)	X-ray fluorescence (XRF) spectroscopy Energy dispersive X-ray (EDX) analysis Proton-induced X-ray emission (PIXE) analysis	Ultraviolet/visible spectroscopy Atomic absorption and emission analysis Fluorescence spectroscopy Raman spectroscopy		Infrared spectroscopy FT-Raman spectroscopy	Microwave spectroscopy	Nuclear magnetic resonance (NMR) spectroscopy Electron paramagnetic resonance (EPR) spectroscopy

systems, the classical physics view is discussed, followed by the modification to these models imposed by quantum mechanics.

The vibrational motion of a molecule can be approximated by a simple model consisting of various masses (representing nuclei) held together by assorted springs (representing chemical bonds). Although somewhat simplistic, this model does provide a good qualitative description, considering that the actual process is one governed by the laws of quantum mechanics, not by classical physics. In the realm of quantum mechanics, one cannot specify the exact motion of, for example, an electron in an atom; however, macroscopic particles obey the laws of classical mechanics (which is really a limiting case of quantum mechanics applied to macroscopic objects). Because nuclei are considerably heavier than electrons, it is not entirely invalid to speak of their motions in this manner.

CLASSICAL DESCRIPTION OF THE VIBRATIONAL MOTIONS OF ONE- AND TWO-PARTICLE SYSTEMS   The model for the vibrational motion of a single particle consists of a mass attached to an ideal spring (Figure 3-3A). The equilibrium position of the spring is denoted by x_0 and the spring restoring force (F) is proportional to its displacement, $(x - x_0)$. Thus

$$F = -k(x - x_0) \qquad \textbf{3-1}$$

where x is the position of the mass m, and k is the force constant of the spring (that is, a measure of how stiff the spring is). The negative sign occurs because the force opposes any displacement; that is, for a value of x greater than x_0, the force vector is opposite in direction to a positive displacement. The potential energy for this system is given by

$$V(x) = \tfrac{1}{2}k(x - x_0)^2 \qquad \textbf{3-2}$$

which is a parabola (Figure 3-3B) and is known as a *harmonic potential function.*

Applying Newton's equation $(F = ma)$ to this system, one obtains an oscillatory motion with the position of the mass described by a sine wave (Figure 3-3C). The frequency of this system, known as the harmonic oscillator, is given by

$$v = \frac{1}{2\pi}\sqrt{\frac{k}{m}} \qquad \textbf{3-3}$$

As expected, the vibrational frequency of the particle increases as the spring becomes stiffer (i.e., k becomes larger) or the particle becomes lighter (i.e., m decreases). Also, according to this classical model, there are no restrictions on the amount of energy that the particle can possess. The two vertical dashed lines of Figure 3-3 indicate the bounds (turning points) of oscillation for the mass having a particular energy (depicted by the height of the horizontal dashed line of Figure 3-3B). At the turning points, all the energy of the particle is in the form of potential energy and the particle is momentarily not moving; at the equilibrium position, the particle has no potential energy and its kinetic energy is at a maximum. As the energy of the particle is increased, its amplitude of vibration increases, but its frequency remains the same.

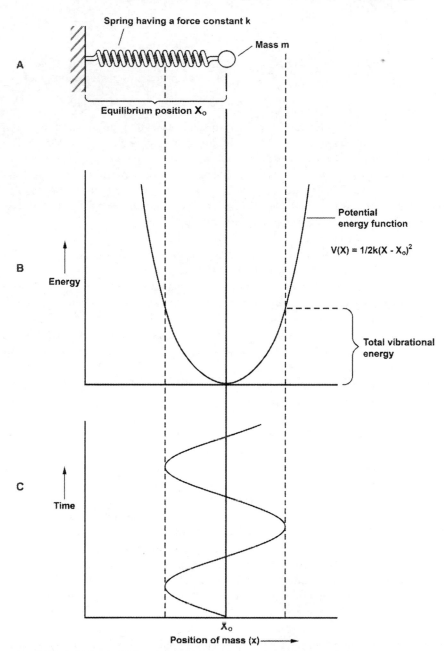

FIGURE 3-3   **(A)** Model for the vibration of a single particle consisting of a mass *m* attached to the end of an ideal spring having a force constant *k*. **(B)** The potential energy function for this system. **(C)** Displacement of the mass as a function of time. Note that the abscissa scale is the same for all three figures.

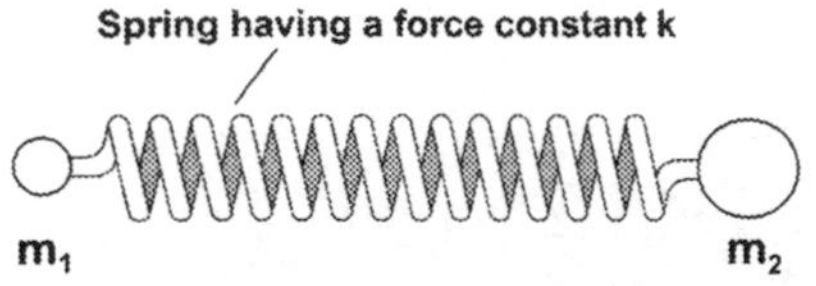

Spring having a force constant k

FIGURE 3-4   Two masses, m_1 and m_2, joined by an ideal spring having a force constant k.

m_1 m_2

Next, let us consider the two-particle system shown in Figure 3-4. In this case, there are two masses, m_1 and m_2, joined by a spring having a force constant k. The motions of both particles are restricted to a line. Since there are no external forces acting on this system, the center of mass must remain constant. From this, it follows that m_1 and m_2 must undergo a concerted motion; that is, they vibrate not only in phase, but with the same frequency. When Newton's equation is applied to this system, one obtains for the frequency of vibration

$$v = \frac{1}{2\pi}\sqrt{\frac{k}{\mu}} \qquad \text{where} \qquad \mu = \frac{m_1 m_2}{m_1 + m_2} \qquad \textbf{3-4}$$

and μ is known as the reduced mass. If one of the masses is considerably larger than the other (i.e., $m_2 \gg m_1$), the denominator in the expression for v can be approximated as m_2 and μ becomes m_1; the two-particle system then approximates the single-particle system m_1, where m_1 is the lighter mass. Figures 3-3b and 3-3c represent the potential function and motion for this two-particle system, where the abscissa is now the distance between the two masses.

QUANTUM MECHANICAL MODEL   The reader is probably most familiar with the manifestations of quantum mechanics for atomic systems, that is, the existence of discreet (quantized) energy levels (orbitals) for the various electrons of an atom. Quantization of energies is by no means limited to electronic systems, however, and also applies to other types of motions at the atomic (and subatomic) level, including vibration and rotation of molecules.

For a particle of mass m governed by a harmonic potential function with a force constant k (see Figure 3-3A), the quantum mechanical solutions permit a series of energies in which the differences between successive levels is constant. These results also apply to a two-particle system, such as a diatomic molecule, having a harmonic potential function. The quantum mechanical vibrational energy level diagram for a diatomic molecule with a harmonic potential function is shown in Figure 3-5, with the levels indicated within the potential function. The lowest level (the ground state) has a vibrational energy of $\frac{1}{2}hv$, where v is again given by Equation 3-4. The spacing between adjacent levels is hv, and is thus directly proportional to the frequency of vibration of the molecule. Each vibrational level is labeled by a number (the quantum number) beginning with zero.

In contrast to the classical description, where any vibrational energy is permitted, a diatomic molecule can thus have only certain discreet vibrational energies. For all of these energies, the frequency of vibration (Equation 3-4) remains constant, as in the classical case.

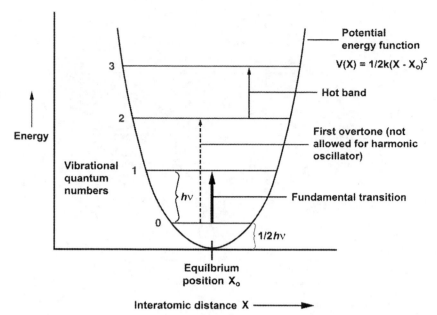

FIGURE 3-5 Vibrational energy level diagram for a diatomic molecule having a harmonic potential function. The energy levels are depicted within a harmonic potential function and the distance between adjacent levels is a constant given by $h\nu$.

Vibrational Transitions of Diatomic Molecules

Both the electric and magnetic fields of electromagnetic radiation (Figure 3-1) exert forces on molecules. The effects of the electric field, however, are considerably greater and are primarily responsible for the vibrational transitions that occur. Although the quantum mechanical model provides the best description of this process, the classical view provides a useful conceptualization of the absorption of infrared radiation.

CLASSICAL DESCRIPTION OF ABSORPTION OF INFRARED RADIATION   Before proceeding, it is necessary to review the concept of *dipole moment*. For a heteronuclear diatomic molecule (e.g., HCl, CO), the differing electronegativities of the two atoms result in an unequal sharing of the valence electrons that make up the chemical bond. A partial positive charge (designated as δ^+) thus resides at one end of the molecule, whereas the other end has a partial negative charge (designated as δ^-). The dipole moment, which is a vector quantity, is a measure of the net separation of charges throughout the molecule (and is not restricted to only diatomic molecules).

Imagine a diatomic molecule having a dipole moment; this molecule is vibrating at a frequency ν (given by Equation 3-4). Consider the effects of an electric field oriented parallel to the axis of this molecule. For the configuration depicted in Figure 3-6B, the effect of the electric field on the two ends of the molecule tends to stretch the two atoms apart, compared to when there is no electric field present (Figure 3-6A).

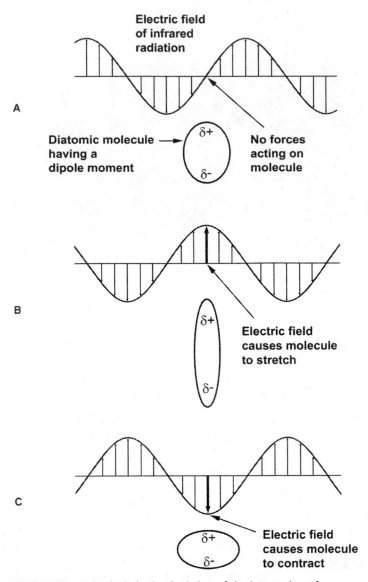

FIGURE 3-6 A classical physics depiction of the interaction of infrared radiation (illustrated by the oscillating electric field) with a diatomic molecule having a dipole moment. **(A)** When the electric field strength is zero, there are no forces acting on the molecule. **(B)** When the electric field is oriented parallel to the dipole moment of the molecule, this causes the molecule to stretch. **(C)** When the electric field is oriented antiparallel to the dipole moment of the molecule, this causes the molecule to contract. The alternating electric field vector of the radiation thus causes the molecule to vibrate at the same frequency as the radiation.

If the electric field is reversed (Figure 3-6C), the two atoms tend to be compressed. Because radiation is made up in part of an alternating electric field (Figure 3-1), it will successively stretch and compress a diatomic molecule that is oriented correctly.

For most radiation frequencies this induced motion has little effect, because the molecule is vibrating at its own natural frequency, and the intensity of the inducing electric field is relatively weak. When the frequency of the radiation matches that of the molecule, however, this radiant energy may be absorbed effectively, and this produces greater amplitudes of vibration for the diatomic molecules.

SELECTION RULES   For a vibrational transition to occur according to quantum mechanics, the energy of the photon of the exciting radiation must be the same as the energy difference between two discreet vibrational levels. Not every possible transition is permitted, however. The additional criteria that must be met for a radiative transition to occur are known as *selection rules*. Assuming a harmonic oscillator, the two selection rules for a diatomic molecule are: (1) the vibration of the molecule must produce a change in dipole moment; and (2) the vibrational quantum number can change only by ± 1 (the minus sign indicates emission of radiation—the selection rules apply for both excitation and emission).

Heteronuclear diatomic molecules generally have a permanent dipole moment. Because the dipole moment is a measure of the separation of charges, these dipole moments are expected to change during a vibration, and infrared absorptions occur for such molecules. Homonuclear diatomic molecules (such as H_2, O_2, and N_2) do not possess a permanent dipole moment. More important, because this lack of a dipole moment is not dependent on internuclear distance, there is no *change* in dipole moment for homonuclear diatomic molecules as they vibrate, and they do not absorb in the infrared region.

For most diatomic molecules, the ground vibrational state is the only level significantly populated at room temperature. Thus, for heteronuclear diatomics, the primary transition that occurs is from this ground state to the first excited state (the 0-to-1 transition of Figure 3-5). This absorption is known as the *fundamental transition*, or just the *fundamental*. Because the difference in energy between the 0 and 1 vibrational states is hv, **the frequency of radiation necessary to produce a fundamental transition is the same as the frequency of vibration of the molecule** (assuming a harmonic potential).

Although the 0-to-2 transition, known as the first *overtone* (see Figure 3-5), is not allowed, a very weak absorption is sometimes observed for this. As expected, this overtone occurs at a frequency very close to twice that of the fundamental.

For a few diatomic molecules having quite low vibrational frequencies, an appreciable fraction of the molecules may be in excited vibrational states at room temperature. For these molecules, vibrational transitions such as the 1-to-2 or 2-to-3 (Figure 3-5) may contribute to the spectrum. However, in most cases these transitions, known as *hot bands* or *difference bands,* are not readily apparent because they occur at nearly the same frequency as the fundamental transition.

ROTATIONAL ENERGY LEVELS   Along with the vibrational motion, a diatomic molecule can also rotate. Transitions between the quantized rotational energy levels of most molecules occur in the microwave region and are not of concern here. Rotations do affect the appearance of vapor infrared absorptions of relatively small molecules, however, and some discussion of molecular rotation is necessary.

The simplest model describing the rotation of a diatomic molecule assumes that the interatomic distance is constant (and hence is known as the *rigid rotor model*). Molecular vibrational frequencies are typically thousands of times greater than rotational frequencies; hence, numerous vibrations occur during the course of a single rotation. One may thus assume an average interatomic distance for a rotating diatomic molecule. For a diatomic molecule treated as a rigid rotor, the quantum mechanical rotational energy levels are given by

$$E_{rot} = J(J + 1) \, h \, B \qquad J = 0, 1, 2, 3, \ldots \qquad \text{3-5}$$

where J is the rotational quantum number and B is a rotational constant inversely related to the approximate size of the molecule (or more specifically, to the *moment of inertia* of the molecule).

SPECTRA OF CARBON MONOXIDE AND HYDROGEN CHLORIDE VAPORS   The infrared spectrum of carbon monoxide vapor, acquired at a resolution of 0.5 cm^{-1}, is shown in Figure 3-7A. Instead of a single absorption, a series of peaks is observed, each of which represents a specific rotational transition that occurs together with the fundamental vibrational change; this series of absorptions is thus referred to as a *vibrational–rotational spectrum*.

The rotational energy levels of a diatomic molecule, treated as a rigid rotor, were given by Equation 3-5. Because the spacings between these rotational levels are considerably smaller than those between the vibrational states, a vibrational–rotational energy diagram similar to that depicted in Figure 3-8 results.

Just as in the case of vibration, there are selection rules governing rotational transitions, including those that accompany a vibrational change. For a heteronuclear diatomic molecule, the selection rule for a rotational transition that occurs with a fundamental is $\Delta J = \pm 1$. The allowed vibrational–rotational transitions for a heteronuclear diatomic molecule are depicted in Figure 3-8 for the first few rotational energy levels. The relative position that each designated absorption occupies in the infrared spectrum is indicated beneath each transition.

Note that the fundamental transition between $J = 0$ states (indicated by the dashed line in Figure 3-8) is not allowed because it corresponds to $\Delta J = 0$ [this is also true for the other J states as well; for example, a diatomic molecule in the ground vibrational state and in the second excited rotational state ($J = 2$) cannot absorb infrared radiation to go to the first excited vibrational state in the second excited rotational state]. This "missing" absorption results in a gap in the middle of the series of peaks (Figure 3-7A) that otherwise appear to be spaced approximately equally. For the harmonic oscillator rigid rotor model of a diatomic molecule, the energy difference between adjacent peaks (excluding the gap) is a constant value given by $2B$, where B is the rotational constant (Equation 3-5). In reality, the difference between

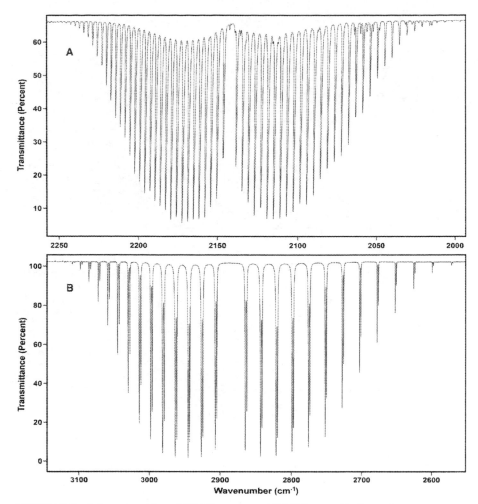

FIGURE 3-7 Infrared spectra of **(A)** CO vapor and **(B)** HCl vapor. Both spectra were acquired at a resolution of 0.5 cm^{-1}.   (*Source:* HCl spectrum courtesy of Mark Strongman, Washington State Crime Laboratory.)

two adjacent peaks decreases with increasing frequency (Figure 3-7A). This results from a deviation of the true potential function of a diatomic molecule from a parabola (Figure 3-3B) and the fact that a real molecule is not a rigid rotor. For example, molecules in higher rotational states rotate faster, which causes the interatomic distance to increase as a result of the centrifugal force (which is not really a force but arises from inertia). The rotational "constants" thus decrease as J increases because the molecules are getting larger.

Several very weak peaks that do not appear to be part of the regular pattern of Figure 3-7A are interspersed with the main absorptions. These are the result of vibrational–rotational transitions of ^{13}CO.

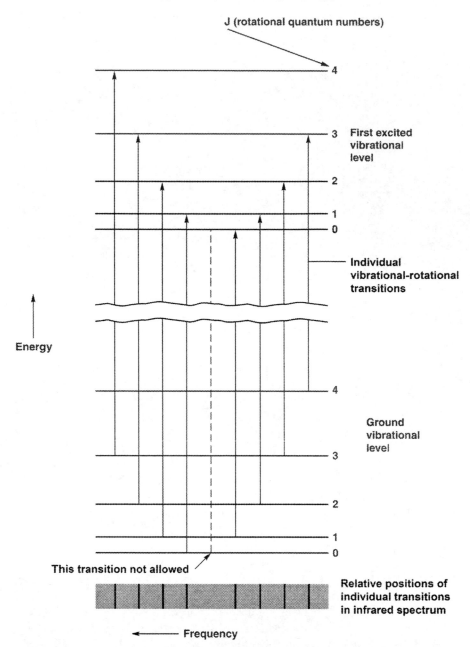

FIGURE 3-8   An energy diagram showing the first five rotational states for both the ground vibrational level and the first excited vibrational level of a diatomic molecule. The allowed vibrational–rotational transitions are indicated by arrows, and the relative positions that these transitions occupy in an infrared spectrum are indicated at the bottom.   (*Source:* Adapted from G. M. Barrow, *Introduction to Molecular Spectroscopy*, New York: McGraw-Hill, Inc., 1962, p. 140.)

The vibrational–rotational spectrum of hydrogen chloride vapor, acquired at a resolution of 0.5 cm^{-1}, is shown in Figure 3-7B. The doublet observed for each transition arises from chlorine isotopic splitting; the higher-frequency absorption is the result of H^{35}Cl, whereas the lower one is the result of H^{37}Cl (the isotopic ratio of ^{35}Cl to ^{37}Cl is close to 3:1, but the relative intensities of the doublets do not appear to exhibit this ratio because a logarithmic scale is involved).

The relative intensities of the series of peaks observed in the CO and HCl spectra (excluding the doublet nature for the latter) are determined by two factors: the population of molecules in each of the rotational states (of the ground vibrational state) and a degeneracy factor. Degeneracy occurs when several distinct quantum mechanical states have the same energy (a more familiar example of degeneracy occurs for atomic orbitals; the reader may remember that the three p orbitals have the same electronic energies, as do the five d orbitals).

Other heteronuclear diatomic molecules give spectra qualitatively similar to those of Figure 3-7, but for the majority of these in which neither atom is hydrogen, the spacings between adjacent lines are smaller because the rotation constants B are smaller.

Vibration of Polyatomic Molecules

A single particle has three degrees of freedom corresponding to its ability to move independently along any of three mutually perpendicular directions. For a system of N particles, there are a total of $3N$ degrees of freedom. For a bound system of N particles (such as a molecule), three of these correspond to the translational motion of the center of mass of the entire system and three more to the rotational motion (corresponding to components of the rotation of the molecule about any of three mutually perpendicular axes). For linear molecules however, there are only two rotational degrees of freedom, because rotation about the axis of such a molecule is not possible. For a system of N bound particles, there are thus $3N - 6$ or $3N - 5$ remaining degrees of freedom. These all correspond to internal (vibrational) motions of the system.

CLASSICAL DESCRIPTION OF THE VIBRATIONAL MOTIONS OF MULTIPARTICLE SYSTEMS   As a classical model for the vibration of a polyatomic molecule, consider again a macroscopic system consisting of various masses held together by assorted springs, such as the system depicted in Figure 3-9. To a good approximation, the translational and rotational motions of such a system may be treated independently of the vibrational motion. For a discussion of the vibrational motion, we thus assume a stationary frame of reference (the whole of which may be rotating and moving through space).

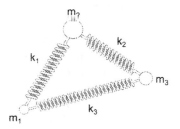

FIGURE 3-9   Three masses, m_1, m_2, and m_3, joined by three springs having force constants k_1, k_2, and k_3.

In general, the masses and spring force constants of a multiparticle system may all be different (Figure 3-9). The overall vibrational motion of such a system may appear to be quite complex and may vary depending on how the system is set into motion (e.g., by striking one of the masses). Outwardly, there might not appear to be any order to this system or any manner in which to describe its motion. **All of the vibrational motions that occur, however, are actually superpositions of a fixed number of fundamental types of vibrations, each of which has definite properties.** There are $3N - 6$ ($3N - 5$ for linear systems) of these fundamental vibrations and they are known as *normal modes,* which have the following properties: (1) For a given normal mode, all of the N masses vibrate in phase and at the same frequency, although each may have its own amplitude (which, again, is a consequence of the center of mass remaining constant); (2) each normal mode vibrates independently of the others; and (3) in general, each normal mode has a different frequency of vibration.

Because the N masses all move in phase, each reaches its maximum *amplitude* (turning point) and equilibrium position at the same time. Each normal mode can thus be described by a single parameter (which thus accounts for the $3N - 6$ or $3N - 5$ vibrational degrees of freedom). Assuming again that the springs are ideal, each normal mode has its own harmonic potential function similar to Figure 3-3B. There is, however, no single expression (similar to Equation 3-4) for the frequency of all normal modes. In principle, it is possible to derive a frequency expression for a given normal mode, and this expression depends on the equilibrium geometry of the system, the masses of the particles, the values of the various force constants, and the nature of the particular normal mode (i.e., the type of motion involved).

For a macroscopic system, each of the $3N - 6$ (or $3N - 5$) normal modes can have any energy, which is manifested as differences in the vibrational amplitudes. These different amplitudes, together with the various phase relationships that are possible, lead to the variety and complexity of the overall motions that can occur.

VIBRATIONAL ENERGY LEVELS AND TRANSITIONS OF POLYATOMIC MOLECULES   To correctly describe the vibrational behavior of a polyatomic molecule, quantum mechanics must again be used. Assuming that the potential energy function for each normal mode of the molecule is harmonic, the quantum mechanical solutions consist of discrete and equally spaced vibrational energy levels (similar to Figure 3-5 for a diatomic molecule) for each normal mode. The ground vibrational state of each mode has an energy of $\frac{1}{2}hv_i$, where i represents one of the $3N - 6$ or $3N - 5$ normal modes, and the spacing between adjacent levels is hv_i, where v_i is the vibrational frequency of that particular mode.

The selection rules for radiative transitions involving each normal mode are the same as for the diatomic case: (1) The photon must have the same energy as the difference between two states; (2) the vibrational quantum number must change by ± 1; and (3) the vibration of the normal mode must involve a dipole moment change. For some polyatomic molecules (especially highly symmetrical ones), some of the normal modes do not involve a dipole moment change, whereas others do. The former modes are known as *infrared inactive,* whereas the latter are *infrared active.* **The infrared spectrum of a polyatomic molecule consists primarily of the fundamentals of the infrared active normal modes.**

As in the case of a diatomic molecule, overtones can also occur, although they are generally much weaker than fundamentals. In addition, for a polyatomic molecule, another type of absorption is possible. A *combination band* results when a single photon simultaneously causes transitions involving two or more normal modes. As with overtones, these bands are very weak, and normally only combination bands involving two fundamentals are observed; as expected, the frequency of such a band is very close to the sum of the frequencies of the two individual fundamentals. Hot bands are also possible, including transitions to combination levels.

NATURE OF NORMAL MODES   As every organic chemist knows, an infrared spectrum provides functional group information based on certain characteristic absorptions that occur within a relatively narrow range of frequencies. The forensic drug chemist, however, uses infrared spectroscopy because it can be used to distinguish among closely related compounds such as positional isomers, geometric isomers, diastereomers, and so forth. Both of these seemingly contradictory features of an infrared spectrum arise from some properties of normal modes.

In general, each atom of a molecule participates in each normal mode. In many cases, however, the vibrational amplitudes of one, two, or three of the atoms may be considerably greater than those of the remaining atoms, and a vibration that is essentially localized results. Such cases occur when: (1) the mass of a particular atom or group of atoms is significantly greater or less than those of the rest of the molecule; or (2) the force constant (bond strength) between two atoms differs significantly from the other force constants in the molecule.

For organic compounds, the hydrogen atoms have much lower mass than any of the other atoms. Many of the normal modes for such compounds may thus be viewed as essentially hydrogen motions (recall that for a diatomic molecule, the reduced mass approached the mass of the lighter atom as the mass of the other atom was increased—the two-particle system thus reduced to a one-particle system). The frequencies of these hydrogen modes thus tend to be largely independent of the rest of the molecule, and the small differences that occur between them usually depend primarily on the force constants involved. As such, these fundamentals normally occur in well-defined characteristic regions, especially for the hydrogen stretching fundamentals, which are far removed in frequency from fundamentals involving other normal modes of organic compounds. For atoms that are considerably heavier than the carbon atoms that comprise the skeletal frame of an organic compound, a somewhat similar situation occurs. The C—Cl and C—Br stretching modes, for example, have characteristic frequencies.

When the bond between two particular atoms in a molecule is significantly stronger than other nearby bonds, one of the normal modes of the molecule is found to consist primarily of a stretching motion between these two atoms, with little participation from neighboring atoms. This occurs even if the masses of the two atoms are the same or similar to those of its neighbors. This particular normal mode is thus largely independent of the rest of the molecule and is similar to the vibration of a diatomic molecule. Like the modes involving hydrogen, these stretching modes have fundamentals that occur in characteristic regions. Examples of such bonds include C=O, C=C, C≡C, and C≡N. The stretching fundamentals of these groups occur, for the most part, in the region between the hydrogen stretching absorptions and the absorptions of the rest of the molecule (the diagnostic value of these fundamentals also depends on their intensities, discussed later in the chapter).

In general, the functional groups of organic compounds involve heteroatoms having different masses and bond strengths from those of carbon, or they involve carbon atoms having different bond strengths. These differences, and the localized normal modes that result from them, give rise to the characteristic functional group absorptions.

When the masses or bond strengths of a molecule (or portions of a molecule) do not differ significantly, many of the normal modes involve considerable participation by each of the atoms. For such cases, characteristic fundamentals do not occur and the particular absorption pattern is quite dependent on the configuration of the masses and the bonds involved. Any change of this configuration, such as in its geometry, addition of another mass, and so on, in general changes the normal mode characteristics and the resulting absorption pattern. An example of such a case is the carbon skeletal modes of a typical organic compound. Because the carbon atoms all have the same mass and the bond strengths between (singly bonded) carbon atoms are similar, *coupling* occurs between the various carbon stretching motions (and bending motions, as well). Instead of each individual C—C bond stretching independently, concerted motions involving the entire carbon framework, or large portions of the framework, occur. The various normal modes involving the carbon skeleton are thus quite complex and C—C stretching fundamentals tend to occur over a wide ($1200–800$ cm^{-1}) frequency region. Because the frequencies and intensities of these carbon skeletal absorptions (plus some others) tend to be peculiar to each individual compound, the portion of the spectrum from 1400 to 800 cm^{-1} is often referred to as the *fingerprint region.*

Coupling also occurs for more localized vibrations when equivalent atoms or groups of atoms are in fairly close proximity. The methylene (CH_2) group, for example, consists of two equivalent hydrogen atoms. Instead of two independent C—H stretching modes, the two vibrations couple, and two modes consisting of a symmetric stretch (where the two bonds stretch in phase) and an antisymmetric stretch (in which one bond is stretching while the other is compressing) result. The bending modes likewise couple. The two in-plane bending vibrations are referred to as *scissoring and rocking modes,* while the out-of-plane vibrations are called *wagging and twisting modes.* When the equivalent atoms of a molecule are relatively far apart, coupling no longer occurs and two independent vibrations result.

VIBRATIONAL–ROTATIONAL TRANSITIONS OF POLYATOMIC MOLECULES   The rotational energy levels given by Equation 3-5 apply not only to diatomic molecules but to all linear molecules and a few other very symmetric polyatomic molecules (such as methane) that have only a single rotational constant. In general, two types of vibrational–rotational patterns may be observed for such molecules. Some of the absorptions are similar to those of Figure 3-7 with a "missing" transition in the middle, whereas others have a prominent spike in this position. These two types may be seen in Figures 3-10D and 3-10E, respectively, which are absorptions of carbon dioxide.

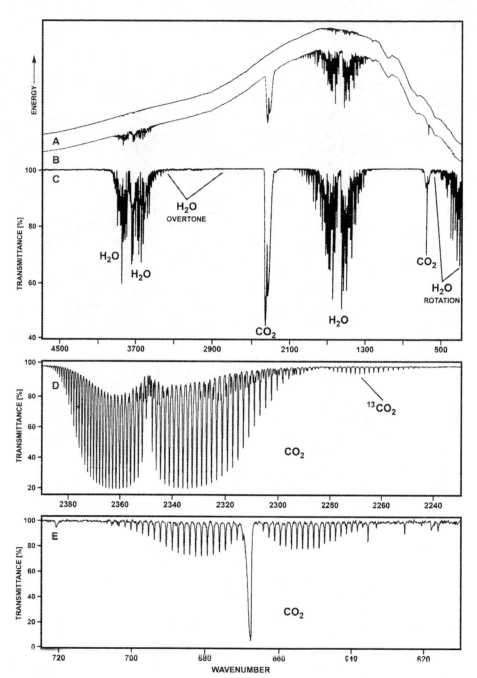

FIGURE 3-10 **(A)** An open beam reference spectrum collected at a resolution of 4 cm^{-1} with the instrument housing purged with dry nitrogen. **(B)** An open-beam sample spectrum collected at a resolution of 4 cm^{-1} resolution with the instrument housing unpurged. **(C)** A ratioed spectrum [obtained by dividing spectrum **(B)** by spectrum **(A)**] depicting the atmospheric absorptions of water and carbon dioxide vapors. **(D)** An expanded view of the carbon dioxide antisymmetric stretching absorption acquired at a resolution of 0.125 cm^{-1}. **(E)** An expanded view of the carbon dioxide bending absorption acquired at a resolution of 0.125 cm^{-1}.

The spike arises from rotational transitions where $\Delta J = 0$, which are allowed in certain cases.

The vast majority of polyatomic molecules have two or three rotational constants. Rotational constants of molecules are very much like indices of refraction[a] for crystalline materials, as the number of values that they may assume are determined by the symmetry properties of the system. Also, there are principal values for both rotational constants and indices of refraction relative to certain orientations of the molecule or the crystal lattice; for other orientations, there are intermediate values for these constants that assume a continuum of values between these principal values.

For polyatomic molecules with two or three rotational constants, the high resolution vapor spectra consist of absorptions with vibrational–rotational lines that exhibit irregular patterns, as observed for ammonia (Figure 3-11) and water (Figure 3-10C) vapors. The shape of the band, however, is often more or less symmetric about the center of the band. For larger molecules for which the individual vibrational–rotational transitions cannot be resolved, only the overall contour of the absorption pattern is observed. This is illustrated by the absorptions of carbon dioxide collected using two different spectral resolutions. At a resolution of 0.125 cm^{-1}, the individual transitions are readily seen (Figures 3-10D and 3-10E), but at a 4 cm^{-1} resolution (Figure 3-10C), only the overall contours are discernable.

SPECTRA OF WATER AND CARBON DIOXIDE VAPORS   Water is composed of three atoms in a nonlinear configuration and thus has three ($3N - 6 = 3$) normal modes. These normal modes are shown schematically in Figure 3-12A. The direction of vibration of each atom is depicted by an arrow; the relative lengths of the arrows are intended to show the relative amplitudes involved (not the actual to-scale amplitudes, which are smaller). As expected, the modes consist primarily of hydrogen motions and may be described as an antisymmetric O—H stretch, a symmetric O—H stretch, and a scissoring vibration. The fundamentals for these three modes (for H_2O vapor) occur at 3756, 3652, and 1595 cm^{-1}, respectively. The scissoring mode has a lower frequency because the "bond" between the two hydrogen atoms is considerably weaker than the O—H bonds.

The three fundamentals of H_2O vapor may be seen in Figure 3-10C, which depicts atmospheric absorptions. Note also the presence of a weak system centered near 3200 cm^{-1} resulting from the overtone of the scissor mode, and the pure rotational transitions of water vapor seen below 600 cm^{-1}.

For carbon dioxide, which is linear, there are four ($3N - 5 = 4$) normal modes. These are shown schematically in Figure 3-12B. They may be described as an antisymmetric C=O stretch, a symmetric C=O stretch, and a bending mode. The latter vibration can occur independently in two perpendicular planes, with each mode having

---

[a]Linear molecules and molecules with very high symmetries having a single rotational constant are analagous to an isotropic substance, which has a single index of refraction. Less-symmetric molecules have either two or three principal rotational constants, similar to birefringent materials that have two or three principal indices of refraction. The values of the rotational constants for such materials are depicted in a three-dimensional figure entirely analogous to the indicatrix.[4]

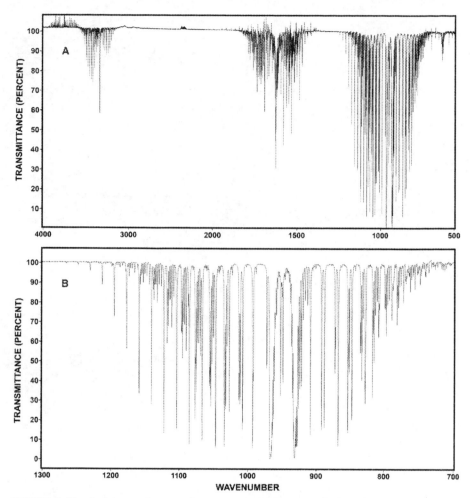

FIGURE 3-11 Spectrum of ammonia vapor acquired at a resolution of 0.5 cm^{-1} depicted between **(A)** 4000 and 500 cm^{-1} and **(B)** 1300 and 700 cm^{-1}. The weak inverse peaks (above 3500 cm^{-1}, near 2350 cm^{-1}, and between 1800 and 1400 cm^{-1}) are the result of water vapor and carbon dioxide.   (*Source:* Courtesy of Martin McDermot, Washington State Crime Laboratory.)

the same frequency; this is thus a doubly degenerate vibrational mode. The symmetric stretch does not involve a dipole moment change and is infrared inactive. Only two main absorptions are therefore observed for CO_2 (Figure 3-10C): the fundamentals of the antisymmetric stretch (centered at 2349 cm^{-1}; Figure 3-10D) and the degenerate bend (centered at 667 cm^{-1}; Figure 3-10E). Absorptions of $^{13}CO_2$ are also observed in Figure 3-10D, with the higher-frequency members interspersed with those of $^{12}CO_2$. Although carbon 13 has an isotopic abundance of only 1% of that of carbon 12, the $^{13}CO_2$ absorptions are readily observed because a logarithmic

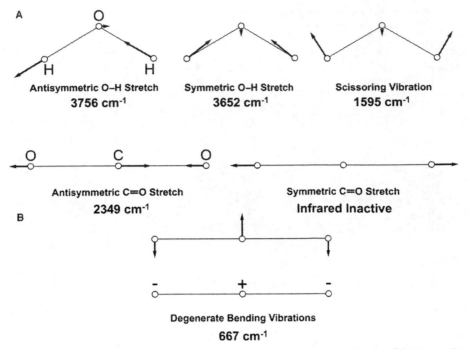

FIGURE 3-12 (A) Schematic depiction of the three normal modes of water. (B) Schematic depiction of the four normal modes of carbon dioxide.

scale is involved. The spike of the $^{13}CO_2$ bending vibration is not apparent in Figure 3-10E as it overlaps one of the transitions of $^{12}CO_2$. Several weak peaks that are not associated with the vibrational–rotational series of the bending fundamental are also observed in Figure 3-10E. The weak peaks at 721 (above the "E") and 619 cm^{-1} are hot bands of carbon dioxide, whereas the others are pure rotational transitions of water vapor.

When sufficient sample is analyzed, two other weaker absorptions of carbon dioxide may also be observed between 3800 and 3500 cm^{-1} (Figure 3-13). These are overtone/combination bands, including a transition to a combination level that includes the infrared inactive symmetric stretch.

Factors Affecting Infrared Spectra

MOLECULAR SYMMETRY   There are several reasons why exactly $3N - 6$ (or $3N - 5$) strong absorptions do not usually occur in the infrared spectrum of a particular compound. We have already discussed some of these, including normal modes that do not involve a dipole moment change and degeneracy. Both factors occur for molecules (or portions of molecules) having high degrees of symmetry. Using a method involving group theory, it is possible to predict for a particular molecule exactly how many degenerate normal modes occur and also the number of infrared active modes;

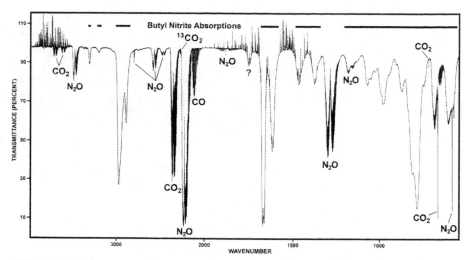

FIGURE 3-13 Spectrum of the vapors above a bottle of a decades-old sample of butyl nitrite collected at a spectral resolution of 0.5 cm^{-1}. The butyl nitrite absorptions are indicated by horizontal lines above the peaks. The inverse peaks above 3500 cm^{-1} and centered near 1600 cm^{-1} are the result of water vapor. (*Source:* Courtesy of Steve Reid, Washington State Crime Laboratory.)

one need know only the structure of the molecule. What is most important for our purposes, however, is a practical consequence of symmetry: A small structural change may destroy symmetry and thereby have a major effect on the infrared spectrum. This occurs as a result of several factors, including loss of the degeneracy, inactive modes becoming active, new fundamentals involving any added group, and peak shifts of the existing fundamentals. Symmetry thus plays a role—albeit one that is not normally recognized or fully appreciated—in the discriminating feature of an infrared spectrum.

As an example of this, consider the differences between the spectra of benzene (Figure 3-14B) and fluorobenzene (Figure 3-14C); that is, changes that result from substitution of a fluorine atom for a hydrogen atom. It is clear that these differences involve more than simply "addition" of C—F stretching and bending fundamentals to the spectrum of benzene. Because of its very high symmetry, only 4 of the 30 normal modes of benzene are infrared active (10 of the modes are doubly degenerate). Fluorobenzene, in contrast, has no degenerate modes and 27 of the 30 are infrared active. Although most compounds are not as symmetrical as benzene, many do contain symmetrical moieties and these same principles still apply, albeit with results that are usually not as pronounced.

OTHER FACTORS Apart from symmetry, there are several other reasons why all of the fundamentals of the infrared active modes of a particular compound may not be observed. The intensity of a particular infrared absorption depends on the amount of dipole moment change that occurs for a given normal mode. This change varies

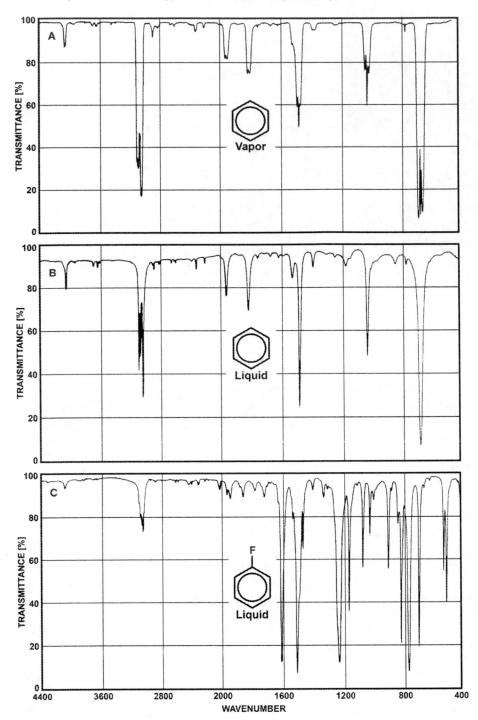

FIGURE 3-14   Spectra acquired at a resolution of 4 cm^{-1} of (A) benzene vapor, (B) benzene liquid, and (C) fluorobenzene liquid.

considerably depending on the type of vibration involved and, even though a particular mode is active, its fundamental may be too weak to be observed under normal conditions.

Like the frequencies of normal modes, the dipole moment changes can be both characteristic for certain vibrations and variable for others. The C=O stretch, for example, is usually one of the strongest absorptions in the spectrum, whereas C=C and C≡C stretching fundamentals are usually weak. The intensities of the carbon skeletal absorptions, like their frequencies, tend to vary and this, too, adds an element of individuality to an infrared spectrum.

Even if not especially weak, a fundamental still may not be readily observed if it happens to occur in the same region as another stronger absorption. As noted, if two or more similar vibrations share a common atom or are otherwise in close proximity, coupling can occur and this tends to split apart the resulting normal mode frequencies rather than to cause them to coalesce. Two absorptions that overlap, in contrast, are unrelated either because they have different symmetry properties or else the vibrational motions are physically isolated from one another in the molecule.

For large molecules, the vibrations of equivalent atoms that are relatively far apart in the molecule are also decoupled, and their fundamentals occur at the same, or nearly the same, frequencies. This is particularly evident in the spectra of large molecules composed of repeating units, that is, polymeric materials. Because of this, the spectra of some polymers can closely resemble those of their constituent monomers.

In addition to fundamentals, weaker absorptions of various overtone and combination bands may also be observed, especially in those regions (such as 2800 to 1800 cm^{-1}) normally devoid of fundamentals. In certain cases where an overtone or combination band occurs very close to a fundamental, *Fermi resonance* may occur. Assuming certain conditions are met, the two vibrational states (i.e., the first excited vibrational level of one normal mode and the overtone or combination level involving one or more other different normal modes) become mixed and two (or more) strong absorptions may result. As discussed earlier, four modes of benzene are infrared active, yet six relatively strong absorptions occur (Figure 3-14B). The two extra absorptions in the C—H stretching region result from Fermi resonance involving two combination levels and a C—H stretching mode. Hot bands, although normally weak, may also contribute to a spectrum.

In the foregoing discussions, it has been assumed that a particular compound exists as a single structure. The existence of different conformations for some molecules, or the formation of tautomers, may result in additional absorptions.

PHYSICAL STATE   The physical state of a particular compound, that is, whether it is analyzed as a vapor, liquid, crystalline solid, or noncrystalline solid, has a strong bearing on the appearance of its infrared spectrum. In the vapor phase at sufficiently low pressures, each molecule is essentially isolated and unaffected by its neighbors. Because of molecular rotation, each absorption band consists of a series of very narrow vibrational–rotational lines. As mentioned, for most molecules the spacings between adjacent lines are usually too small (0.01 cm^{-1} or less) to be resolved, and instead, the band contour of the vibrational–rotational structure is observed. In general, there may be some differences in the shapes of the band contours between different absorptions of a particular compound because of differences in rotational selection rules (which are determined by the types of normal modes involved). These differences may be seen in the spectrum of benzene vapor (Figure 3-14A).

The differences between the spectra of vapors and condensed phases arise from various types of intermolecular interactions. For liquids, these interactions tend to hinder the molecular rotations and effectively broaden the individual vibrational–rotational lines so that they merge into a single band. Molecular associations, such as hydrogen bonding, dipole interactions, formation of dimers, and so on, may result in peak shifts, band broadening, or the appearance of new absorptions.

The most familiar example of this occurs as the result of hydrogen bonding. When alcohols are analyzed as vapors, little or no hydrogen bonding can take place and the O—H stretching fundamental is seen as a relatively sharp absorption that occurs between 3700 and 3600 cm^{-1}. In a crystalline solid where hydrogen bonding usually occurs, this weakens the O—H bond because the hydrogen atom now forms associations with other atoms. Consequently, the frequency of the alcohol O—H stretch is lowered and is seen in the 3400 to 3300 cm^{-1} region. In certain cases where strong intramolecular hydrogen bonds may form, this frequency may occur as low as 3100 cm^{-1}. The alcohol molecules occupy well-defined sites in the crystal lattice and the configuration of two (or more) molecules involved in hydrogen bonding is repeated throughout the lattice structure. The O—H stretching absorption is thus relatively sharp in spectra of many crystalline solids.

In contrast, for liquids there are a wide variety of different configurations that two (or more) hydrogen bonded molecules may assume relative to one another (and this is constantly changing). This results in different bond strengths and reduced masses for these various configurations. The O—H stretching absorption is thus quite broad in the spectrum of an alcohol analyzed as a liquid because it represents, in effect, an overlap of a continuum of peaks of different frequencies reflective of the various configurations. As observed for solids, the frequency of the alcohol O—H stretching absorption in liquids is usually centered in the 3400 to 3300 cm^{-1} region.

The spectrum of a solid composed of a noncrystalline glass is often very similar in appearance to that of the same material analyzed as a liquid. In contrast, the spectrum of a crystalline solid usually consists of a number of relatively sharp absorptions, often with peak splittings and other extra absorptions not observed for the vapor and liquid phase spectra. The relative sharpness of these absorptions results from the fact that molecular rotations do not occur, and within the unit cell of the crystal, each of the molecules occupies a definite, well-defined position. Because of the close proximity of neighboring molecules in the crystalline state, strong interactions may occur. These interactions often result in splittings for some absorptions arising from the differing environments that each of the molecules that make up the unit cell may experience. In some cases, this may result in loss of degeneracy for some normal modes (i.e., the environment around a symmetrical molecule in a lattice may not be entirely symmetrical), which may also produce extra absorptions.

The spectrum of a crystalline solid is thus dependent to some extent on the particular arrangement of molecules in the crystal unit cell—that is, the nature of the lattice. As such, different crystal forms of the same substance (polymorphism) usually exhibit distinguishable infrared spectra. Similarly, certain racemic mixtures in which the *d* and *l* enantiomers combine into a single mixed crystal (known as a *racemate,* as opposed to the *eutectic mixture,* in which distinct crystals of *d* and distinct crystals of *l* occur) generally have distinguishable spectra from the pure *d* or pure *l* (or eutectic mixture) spectra.

SPECIFICITY AND LIMITATIONS OF INFRARED SPECTROSCOPY

The individualizing feature of an infrared spectrum has sometimes been compared with that of a fingerprint. Uncritical acceptance of this analogy, however, may be misleading for two reasons. First, the forensic scientist may feel that because an infrared analysis was performed on a sample, an unequivocal conclusion can be drawn *per se*, regardless of the quality of the spectral data. Spectra obtained from poorly prepared samples may be given unwarranted weight because "the method is so specific." In fact, the nature of a spectrum—and hence its value as an identification tool—can be quite dependent on sample preparation. **Proper sampling and interpretation of spectral data should not be relegated to a back seat because of any perceived notions about the specificity of the technique.**

Second, on a more fundamental level, there are some classes of compounds for which an infrared spectrum provides only limited information and cannot be used by itself to identify a specific member of such a class. Although infrared spectroscopy is indeed an excellent identification tool for many compounds (and for these, a fingerprint analogy is not unjustified if the technique is properly employed), this is not true for *all* infrared-absorbing compounds. Because any substance can potentially be analyzed as evidence, it is important that the forensic scientist be aware of the limitations—as well as the merits—of infrared spectroscopy as applied to a wide variety of compounds and materials.

Vapor Spectra of Small Molecules

As observed for carbon monoxide (Figure 3-7A), hydrogen chloride (Figure 3-7B), water (Figure 3-10C), carbon dioxide (Figures 3-10D, 3-10E, and 3-13), and ammonia (Figures 3-11A and 3-11B), the high-resolution vapor-phase spectra of low-molecular-weight compounds, whether organic or inorganic, are *extremely* distinct. Because the rotational constants for such molecules are relatively large, the individual vibrational–rotational transitions of each absorption can be resolved clearly, resulting in a plethora of data that can be used to characterize these substances. For the simplest infrared-absorbing system, namely a heteronuclear diatomic molecule, there is a single fundamental. Even in this case, however, a wealth of individualizing features is observed, as seen for carbon monoxide and hydrogen chloride (Figure 3-7). The distinguishing features include the position of the band, the spacings between adjacent lines (which are very narrow), the degree to which the spacings decrease with increasing frequency, the number of observed lines and their relative intensities, and the presence or absence of isotope absorptions. The number of stable heteronuclear diatomic molecules is very limited, and all of the high-resolution vapor data for these compounds fully confirm these arguments.

Molecules composed of three or more atoms have at least two[b] infrared active fundamentals, each of which consists of a series of vibrational–rotational transitions. For linear molecules and others having a single rotational constant, the spacings between adjacent vibrational–rotational lines are regular, as observed for carbon dioxide (Figures 3-10D and 3-10E). For less symmetrical molecules, irregular patterns occur, as observed for water (Figure 3-10C) and ammonia (Figure 3-11). Isotopic absorptions, overtone/combination bands, and hot bands may also be observed for some molecules.

Vapor state considerations aside, there are other reasons why the spectra of relatively small molecules are so distinct. Small molecules are often quite symmetrical or they have prominent symmetrical moieties. Small structural changes are thus likely to produce major spectral differences. Even when symmetry is not involved, however, the effects of even minor structural modifications on the molecule tend to be much more pronounced when its framework is small. The addition of a single methylene (CH_2) unit to a polyethylene molecule, for example, produces no discernable changes in its infrared spectrum. The addition of a methylene unit to methane, in contrast, results in very pronounced spectral changes, as this "doubles" the molecule (in addition to decreasing symmetry).

Owing to all of these factors, such small molecules can be readily identified, even when several other strong absorptions are present. This is illustrated by the spectrum of the vapors above an old sample of butyl nitrite (Figure 3-13) obtained at a resolution of 0.5 cm^{-1}. Along with absorptions of butyl nitrite vapor (indicated by the horizontal lines above the spectrum in Figure 3-13), carbon dioxide, and inverse peaks of water vapor, absorptions of nitrous oxide and carbon monoxide are clearly visible. Nitrous oxide (N_2O) is a linear molecule and an expansion of the nine N_2O absorptions seen in this figure would result in data similar to those seen in Figures 3-10D or 3-10E (the data for N_2O, however, would be more distinct using a resolution of 0.125 cm^{-1} rather than 0.5 cm^{-1}). Although only a single series is observed for CO (and not even a complete series at that, because the members of the higher frequency branch overlap the absorptions of N_2O), there can be no question about the presence of CO in this sample, because even these limited absorptions result in a *unique pattern* that no other compound or even combinations of compounds can duplicate.

---

[b]The only exception to this is a homonuclear triatomic molecule, where each atom occupies the corners of an equilateral triangle, with the three atoms being chemically equivalent. For this case (for which there are no common examples), there are three ($3N - 6 = 3$) normal modes. In one mode involving a symmetric stretching motion known as *ring breathing*, all the atoms are moving away from (or toward) the center of the triangle, and this mode is infrared inactive. The second mode, called a *ring deformation vibration*, involves both stretching and bending motions and although infrared active, is doubly degenerate. There is therefore only one main infrared absorption for such molecules. Ozone is a homonuclear triatomic molecule, but its three oxygen atoms (which are in a bent configuration) are not equivalent, and ozone has three infrared active fundamentals.

Organic Compounds

It is for organic compounds that the attributes normally associated with infrared spectroscopy, namely its ability to provide functional group information and to permit differentiation between closely related structures, are most evident. (The reasons for this were described in the previous section.) For most forensic analyses, it is the individualizing features of infrared spectroscopy that make it such a valuable tool for identification or comparison purposes. For the analysis of unknown materials, the functional group information can also be valuable.

HOMOLOGOUS SERIES   For the vast majority of low- to moderate-weight organic compounds, any alteration of structure produces changes in normal modes, and this results in distinct spectral changes. In certain cases, however, the resulting spectral differences may not be observable. This may happen if the differences (1) affect only those absorptions that are very weak, infrared inactive, or occur outside of the spectral region examined; or (2) produce new absorptions that overlap existing ones or cause frequency and intensity changes that are too small to be detected.

This situation occurs for organic compounds composed of, or incorporating a moderate to large number of, repeating structural units. The best examples of such compounds are members of various homologous series. Although infrared spectroscopy can be used to differentiate between the lowest members of such series, doing so becomes increasingly difficult as the number of repeating units increases.

Consider, for example, the series consisting of straight chain hydrocarbons (normal alkanes). The infrared spectra of methane, ethane, propane, and *n*-butane (as vapors) are easily distinguished (this is also true for these substances analyzed as liquids). The differences in the spectra of *n*-pentane and the higher members, however, become less distinct as the major absorptions for these are all similar (Figure 3-15). The weaker absorptions can be used to distinguish among the lower members, up to a carbon number of 20 or so,[5] but the differences become quite minor.

The same situation occurs for other homologous series, and it is clear that an infrared analysis cannot normally be used to identify an individual member of such a series, except for the lowest members. Infrared spectroscopy, however, is an excellent means of determining *which* particular series is involved. Fats and oils, for example, are composed of mixtures of glycerol triesters of various fatty acids (both saturated and unsaturated). Although infrared spectroscopy cannot usually distinguish between different saturated fats or between different unsaturated fats, it can be used to distinguish between saturated and unsaturated fats (and also provide some measure of the degree of unsaturation).

In a similar vein, infrared spectroscopy cannot be used to determine the molecular weights of polymers, nor is it sensitive to sequence differences in polymers composed of several different units. As such, it is not useful for protein or DNA sequence analyses.

COMPARISON OF INFRARED AND GAS CHROMATOGRAPHY/MASS SPECTRAL DATA   Because gas chromatography/mass spectrometry (GC/MS) is also one of the methods that the forensic scientist may use for the analysis of organic compounds, it

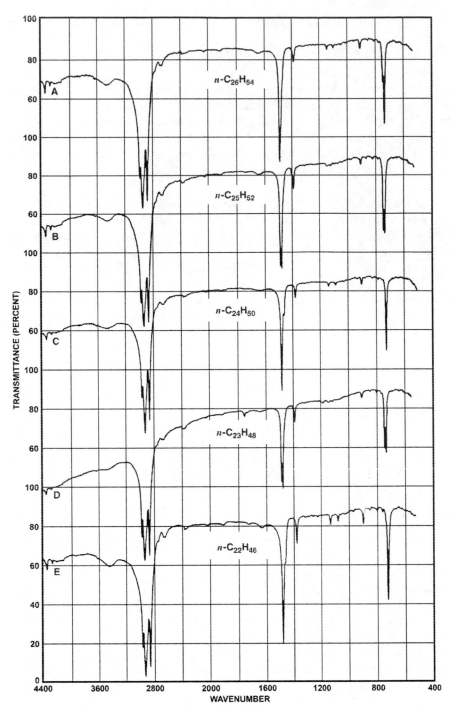

FIGURE 3-15 Spectra of five normal hydrocarbons in KBr pellets: **(A)** hexacosane, **(B)** pentacosane, **(C)** tetracosane, **(D)** tricosane, and **(E)** docosane. Note, in particular, the similarities between spectra within the even-numbered subseries and within the odd-numbered subseries. (*Source:* From Reference 5, copyright ASTM, reprinted with permission.)

is worthwhile to compare, in very general terms, the discriminating abilities of infrared spectroscopy and GC/MS (using electron impact ionization). In many respects, these two methods are highly complementary, because the weaknesses of one are often the strengths of the other. The differentiation of many volatile homologous series members, for example, is usually easily accomplished with GC/MS owing to differences in molecular weights. This normally results in differences in both GC retention times and MS molecular ions.

The converse involves the differentiation of isomers. Mass spectral data often are quite similar for some isomers, especially diastereomers and positional isomers. In some cases, such isomers may also exhibit very similar GC retention times because they have identical molecular weights. In contrast, the infrared spectra of most isomers are quite distinct, and normally there are several conspicuous spectral features that serve to differentiate among them (as opposed to minor differences in the intensity ratios of certain fragments, as may occur for the corresponding mass spectral data). An exception to this involves the differentiation of positional isomers where a double bond occurs near the middle of a moderate to long unbranched chain. This situation is not unlike that of a homologous series, and the infrared data for such isomers may be quite similar. Although GC retention times may also be similar for these isomers, their mass spectra are often distinct because the unsaturation produces a "weak spot" in the molecule about which fragmentation occurs.

Inorganic Compounds

IONIC SALTS In addition to homonuclear diatomic molecules (which are mostly gases), some inorganic salts also do not absorb in the mid-infrared region. These are *ionic salts,* that is, salts composed of monoatomic cations and anions such as NaCl, KBr, and CaF_2. Each ion in the crystal lattice has an equilibrium position and experiences a restoring force if it is displaced from this position. The ions are vibrating about their equilibrium positions and the lattice vibrational energies are quantized similar to molecular vibrations. The ionic forces that hold the lattice together may provide a strong overall binding energy, but these electrostatic forces are not directional like covalent bonds. Consequently, they provide relatively weak restoring forces for the vibrations of ions against one another and the infrared active transitions between vibrational modes of a crystal lattice (known as *phonons* because they include vibrational modes that transmit sound through a crystal) occur in the far-infrared region. Such salts are thus used as windows for the mid-infrared region.

Consistent with the principles of vibrating systems discussed previously (Equation 3-3), salts involving heavier ions generally tend to absorb at lower frequencies than those composed of lighter ones. This trend may be seen in the following series, which lists three alkali halide salts used as infrared windows, their molecular weights (MW), and the far-infrared regions where they begin to absorb: NaCl, MW 58, 625 cm^{-1}; KBr, MW 119, 400 cm^{-1}; and CsI, MW 260, 200 cm^{-1} (decreasing force constants might also be involved here, because the ions are getting larger). Because CsI is transparent over the widest range, it is used in extended-range FT-IR spectrometers.

For the analysis of unknown materials, it might be assumed that if no infrared absorptions occur, no useful analytical data are obtained. In view of the paucity of nonabsorbing compounds, however, this information has actually eliminated millions of compounds from consideration, including all organic compounds and the vast majority of inorganic ones.

COVALENT SALTS   The term *covalent salts* is used to denote those salts composed of one or more complex ions, that is, ions consisting of two or more atoms between which covalent bonds occur. Examples of such compounds include K_2CO_3, NH_4Cl, and $FeNH_4SO_4 \cdot 12H_2O$. For such salts, mid-infrared absorptions arising from transitions involving the normal modes of the complex ion(s) occur (a possible exception to this involves homonuclear diatomic ions such as the acetylide anion, C_2^{-2}). Covalent salts generally exhibit far fewer absorptions than typical organic compounds. This arises from both the relative simplicity of most covalent ions and their high symmetries. Group theory predicts, for example, that five-atom tetrahedral molecules or ions (including CH_4, NH_4^+, SO_4^{-2}, PO_4^{-3}, ClO_4^-, etc.) will have only two infrared active fundamental absorptions. This may be seen from spectra of potassium sulfate (Figure 3-16C) and potassium perchlorate (Figure 3-16D). Strictly speaking, this prediction applies to molecules in the vapor state where intermolecular interactions are minimal, but only two strong absorptions are observed for many tetrahedral ion salts. The effects of neighboring ions or molecules may have a strong influence on spectra of crystalline materials, as discussed previously, and loss of symmetry resulting from local environments in the crystal lattice is a major factor in the appearance of "extra" absorptions or peak splittings, as observed for sodium sulfate (Figure 3-16B).

Compounds that include one or more molecules of hydration also have absorptions arsing from modes of water, as seen in spectra of calcium sulfate dihydrate (Figure 3-16A) and magnesium nitrate hexahydrate (Figure 3-17C). For ionic salts that are hydrated, the spectra consist primarily of hydrated water absorptions, as observed for nickel (II) chloride hexahydrate ($NiCl_2 \cdot 6H_2O$, Figure 3-18B), strontium chloride hexahydrate ($SrCl_2 \cdot 6H_2O$, Figure 3-18C), cobalt chloride hexahydrate ($CoCl_2 \cdot 6H_2O$, Figure 3-18D), and copper (II) chloride dihydrate ($CuCl_2 \cdot 2H_2O$, Figure 3-18E). In general, the absorptions of water of hydration are sharper than those of water itself (Figure 3-18A) or water adsorbed onto the surfaces of samples, because the hydrated water molecules occupy well-defined positions in the crystal lattice. The hydrated water absorptions often exhibit structures and may differ between various salts, particularly in the far-infrared region. The spectrum of water vapor consists of vibrational–rotational transitions of the two O—H stretches and a scissoring mode, along with pure rotational transitions below 600 cm^{-1} (Figures 3-10C and 3-12). For liquid water (Figure 3-18A), the two O—H stretches coalesce into a single broad feature and the low-frequency broad absorption arises from hindered rotations of water. For water of hydration, the low-frequency absorptions may include torsional modes with hydrogen atom motions similar to those of CH_2 twisting and wagging vibrations, lattice vibrations of water, lattice vibrations of the cations and anions, or a combination of these.

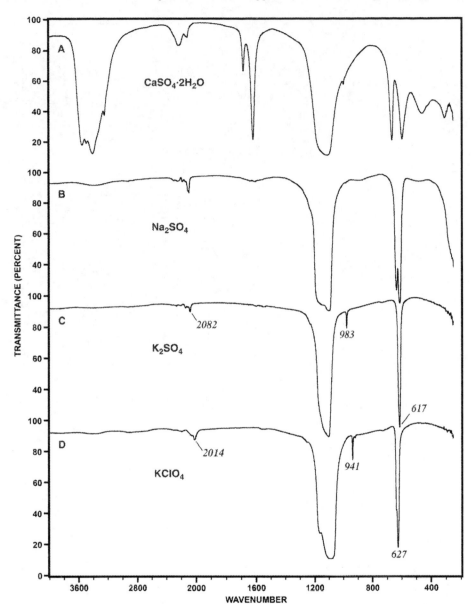

FIGURE 3-16 Spectra of three sulfate salts and potassium perchlorate obtained as thin films on a single anvil of a diamond anvil cell. **(A)** Calcium sulfate dihydrate (gypsum $CaSO_4 \cdot 2H_2O$); **(B)** sodium sulfate (Na_2SO_4); **(C)** potassium sulfate (K_2SO_4); and **(D)** potassium perchlorate ($KClO_4$).

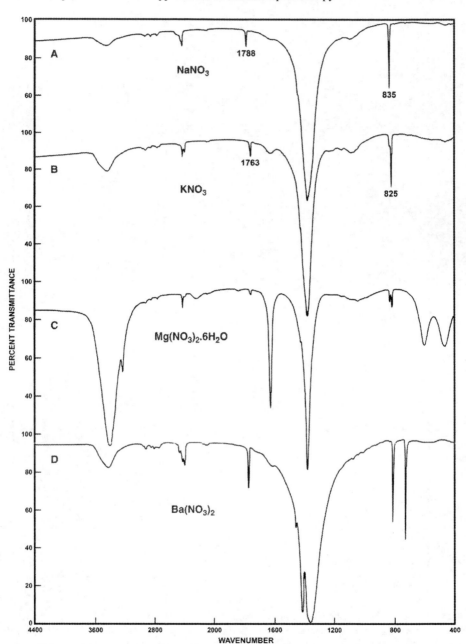

FIGURE 3-17 Spectra of four nitrate salts analyzed as KBr pellets: **(A)** sodium (NaNO$_3$); **(B)** potassium (KNO$_3$); **(C)** magnesium (Mg[NO$_3$]$_2$ · 6H$_2$O); and **(D)** barium (Ba[NO$_3$]$_2$).

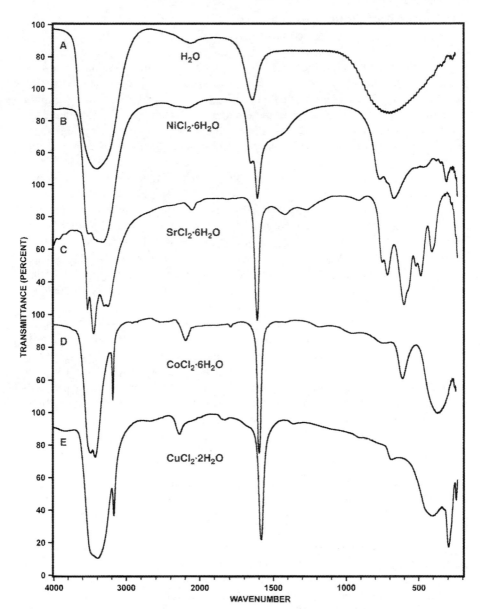

FIGURE 3-18   Spectra of water and four hydrated chloride salts: **(A)** Water in a diamond anvil cell. The weak oscillations observed for the lower-frequency portion of the spectrum are the result of interference fringes; **(B)** nickel chloride hexahydrate ($NiCl_2 \cdot 6H_2O$); **(C)** strontium chloride hexahydrate ($SrCl_2 \cdot 6H_2O$); **(D)** cobalt chloride hexahydrate ($CoCl_2 \cdot 6H_2O$); and **(E)** copper chloride dihydrate ($CuCl_2 \cdot 2H_2O$). All salts were analyzed as thin films on a single anvil of the diamond anvil cell.

For covalent salts that are not hydrated, only the vibrational transitions of the complex ion are observed in the mid-infrared regions and very similar spectra can sometimes occur for different salts of a given cation or anion. The spectra of $NaNO_3$ (Figure 3-17A) and KNO_3 (Figure 3-17B), for example, are quite similar. These similarities are sometimes greatest when the nonabsorbing ions involved are successive members within a particular chemical group (e.g., sodium and potassium, strontium and barium). For a few complex ions, in fact, there is a systematic variation in the absorption frequencies as one progresses through such a group for the nonabsorbing ion.[6] In general, however, no such relationship exists and there may be notable differences between the spectra of various salts of a particular cation or anion, even when hydration is not involved (for example, compare Figures 3-16B and 3-16C, and Figures 3-17B and 3-17D).

Usually, the differences between the spectra of various common complex ions are distinct enough so that one can usually determine the type of ion involved. There are, however, a few exceptions. K_2SO_4 (Figure 3-16C) and $KClO_4$ (3-16D), for example, give quite similar spectra. Such cases invariably involve very similar ions: ClO_4^- and SO_4^{-2} are both tetrahedral oxide anions having similar bond strengths and central atom atomic weights; their vibrational modes and frequencies are thus similar.

In view of the foregoing discussion, it should be clear that mid-infrared spectroscopy alone is not always sufficient to characterize completely some inorganic salts, and especially those that consist of or include nonabsorbing cations or anions. For these, further analysis using microscopy, elemental methods, capillary electrophoresis, ion chromatography, X-ray diffraction, "wet" chemical or physical methods, or others should be conducted to provide additional data that confirm, complement and extend the information provided by infrared spectroscopy.

INSTRUMENTATION

In a dispersive infrared spectrometer a dispersing element, such as a grating or a prism, produces a narrow band of infrared wavelengths. The sample absorption occurring for each of these bands is compared with that occurring for a reference beam; by continuously varying the wavelength of the chosen band (by selectively changing the orientation of the grating or prism), one obtains a spectrum. With an FT-IR spectrometer, all of the radiation from the polychromatic source is analyzed at the same time and based on an interferogram that is produced, a *mathematical dispersion* is computed, which produces a spectrum. This method of analysis has several advantages over dispersive sampling. Because all the wavelengths are analyzed simultaneously (a process known as *multiplexing*), an FT–IR instrument requires considerably less time to acquire a spectrum. In a dispersive instrument, various slits are used to isolate a band of wavelengths, and this reduces the amount of available energy. In an FT-IR instrument, there are no slits and the throughput energy is higher. There are other advantages as well, including a higher wavelength precision and a greater photometric accuracy. The multiplexing and increased throughput advantages, however, are the ones primarily responsible for most of the observed benefits. An interferogram can be generated in a fraction of a second and numerous interferograms can be averaged to increase the signal-to-noise ratio. This feature, together with the increased energy throughput, permits quite small areas to be effectively analyzed. In short, two factors of particular concern to the forensic scientist are addressed by this instrument: speed and sensitivity (the latter also makes possible another important consideration, namely, *convenience*, by permitting various labor-saving accessories to be used).

The Michelson Interferometer

The basic components of a Michelson interferometer, the most common type used for an FT-IR instrument, are shown in Figure 3-19. They consist of a source, which emits a continuum of infrared wavelengths; a beam splitter (typically oriented 45° relative to the light path) that, for simplicity, we assume transmits exactly half of the incident radiation and reflects the other half; two plane mirrors, one of which is free to move in the direction of the light path and the other stationary; and a detector. The stationary mirror is located at a distance D_s (based on the center of the beam splitter) from the beam splitter. The distance of the movable mirror from the beam splitter at any instant is denoted by D_m.

A collimated (parallel) beam from the source is incident on the beam splitter, and half of this radiation is reflected and travels to the stationary mirror, then back to the beam splitter. The other half is transmitted and travels to the movable mirror, then back to the beam splitter. At the beam splitter, the portion of the radiation from

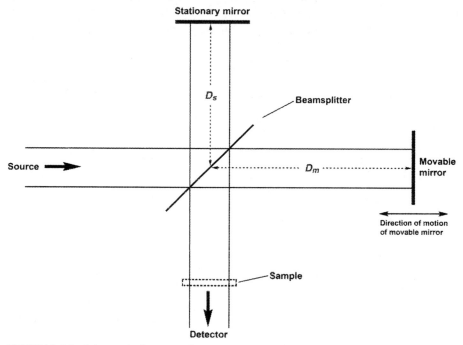

FIGURE 3-19 Schematic diagram of a Michelson interferometer.

the movable mirror that is reflected from the beam splitter recombines with the portion of the radiation from the stationary mirror that is transmitted through the beam splitter, and this recombined beam then travels to the detector.

Consider first the case of a single wavelength of radiation emitted by the source. This monochromatic radiation has a wavelength λ and a frequency v. When the movable mirror is at the same distance from the beam splitter as the stationary mirror ($D_m = D_s$), there is no difference in the path lengths experienced by the components traveling to the two mirrors. Note that this is true for every ray of the parallel beam, even though the actual path lengths may differ between different rays. The beams from the two mirrors, on recombining, are in phase and interfere constructively; the intensity of the radiation reaching the detector is at a maximum. When the movable mirror is moved a distance $\lambda/4$ away from the beamsplitter ($D_m = D_s + \lambda/4$), the component that goes to the movable mirror must travel a distance $\lambda/2$ greater than its counterpart. On recombining, the two components are exactly 180° out of phase, and therefore they interfere destructively; no radiation travels to the detector. When $D_m = D_s + \lambda/2$, the two components are again in phase, and so forth.

The difference in pathlength between the two components is known as the *retardation*, δ, where $\delta = 2(D_m - D_s)$. For a monochromatic source, the intensity of radiation reaching the detector varies sinusoidally as a function of the retardation and is proportional to $(1 + \cos 2\pi\delta/\lambda)$. Because $v = 1/\lambda$, this becomes $(1 + \cos 2\pi\delta v)$, where v is expressed in wavenumbers.

Consider now the usual case of a polychromatic source emitting a continuum of wavelengths. Each individual wavelength that composes the polychromatic source produces its own intensity pattern proportional to $(1 + \cos 2\pi\delta v)$, independently of all others. The intensities of each of these differ, however, as a result of differences in the source output, beam splitter efficiency, detector response, and other factors, all of which depend on v. Let $B(v)$ be the function that describes the net effect of all of these factors, that is, $B(v)$ is an effective source spectrum. For a particular frequency v, the intensity (I_v) recorded by the detector, as a function of the retardation δ, is therefore

$$I_v(\delta) = B(v)[1 + \cos 2\pi\delta v] \qquad \textbf{3-6}$$

The actual intensity measured for a polychromatic source is the sum of all of these or, because a continuum is involved, the integral

$$I_T(\delta) = \int_0^\infty B(v)[1 + \cos 2\pi\delta v]\, dv \qquad \textbf{3-7}$$

where the summation occurs for all possible frequency values. $I_T(\delta)$, the detector output as a function of retardation, is known as an *interferogram*.

By continuously recording the output of the detector as the movable mirror traverses its course, an interferogram is generated. When $D_m = D_s$ ($\delta = 0$), all the frequencies of the source recombine in phase and the interferogram has its maximum intensity; for no other values of δ are all of the frequencies again in phase, and the $\delta = 0$ peak leads to a conspicuous spike in an interferogram, known as the *centerburst*. The interferogram should be symmetrical about this point, although, in practice, this is not usually the case. This asymmetry results primarily from artifacts produced electronically and is corrected for.

For purposes of obtaining a spectrum, only the second term of Equation 3-7 is required. This is the oscillating portion of the interferogram given by

$$I(\delta) = \int_0^\infty B(v) \cos 2\pi \delta v \cdot dv \qquad \textbf{3-8}$$

Equation 3-8 is one part of a mathematical relationship known as a cosine Fourier transform pair, the other part being

$$B(v) = \int_{-\infty}^\infty I(\delta) \cos 2\pi v \delta \cdot d\delta \qquad \textbf{3-9}$$

In this equation, the distribution of frequencies recorded by the detector, $B(v)$, is given as a cosine *Fourier transform* of the interferogram, $I(\delta)$. **Mathematically, a cosine Fourier transform may be viewed as a process that picks out from a particular function (in this case, the interferogram) the relative contributions of each of the cosine curves comprising this function.** By measuring an interferogram and computing its Fourier transform (Equation 3-9), one thereby obtains an instrument-detected spectrum of the source.

SPECTRAL RESOLUTION   On paper, Equation 3-9 produces a spectrum having an infinite resolution; this requires, however, that the movable mirror be scanned over an infinite distance. Because $I(\delta)$ and the cosine function are both symmetrical about $\delta = 0$, the integration of Equation 3-9 can be performed from $\delta = 0$ to $\delta = \infty$ (and multiplied by 2), but this still requires an infinite distance for the mirror to travel. Obviously, this cannot be done, and in practice the movable mirrors of most FT-IR interferometers travel a span consisting of, at most, a few centimeters from one or both sides of the zero retardation point. This amounts to a truncation of the interferogram or integration of Equation 3-9 over a finite range of retardations. This truncation has two effects on the spectral data obtained from such interferograms.

The primary consequence of limiting the retardation range is that spectral resolution decreases. **The resolution, in fact, is directly proportional to the maximum retardation** (and thus to the maximum distance that the movable mirror travels to one side of the zero retardation point). In order to produce two well-resolved peaks for two closely spaced absorptions having frequencies v_1 and v_2 (where $v_1 - v_2 = \Delta v$), the maximum retardation must be $1/\Delta v$ or greater. To resolve two peaks separated by $0.5\ \text{cm}^{-1}$, for example, the maximum retardation must be 2 cm or greater (i.e., the movable mirror must travel at least 1 cm from the zero retardation point).

Some insight into the reason why resolution increases with maximum retardation may be gained by considering the nature of the interferogram produced by a dichromatic source. Assume that this source produces two equally intense monochromatic wavelengths having very similar frequencies, denoted by v_1 and v_2 ($v_1 - v_2 = \Delta v$). Each of these frequencies produces its own interferogram, the oscillating portions of which are described by $\cos 2\pi v_1 \delta$ and $\cos 2\pi v_2 \delta$. The total interferogram is the sum of these two, and when two cosine functions having similar frequencies are added, a pattern of beats is produced, as depicted in Figure 3-20. The zero retardation of the total interferogram corresponds to a maximum in those beats, whereas the next maximum occurs at a retardation of $1/\Delta v$. For higher retardation values, the pattern is repeated; hence, one complete cycle of the interferogram occurs between $\delta = 0$ and $\delta = 1/\Delta v$. Thus, the essential information required to identify two closely spaced frequencies separated by Δv is present in an interferogram having a maximum retardation of $1/\Delta v$. The smaller the value of Δv (i.e., the closer together the two frequencies are), the greater the maximum retardation must be in order to obtain a complete cycle of the beat pattern. Although this example involved an emission spectrum, the same arguments apply in the case of absorption.

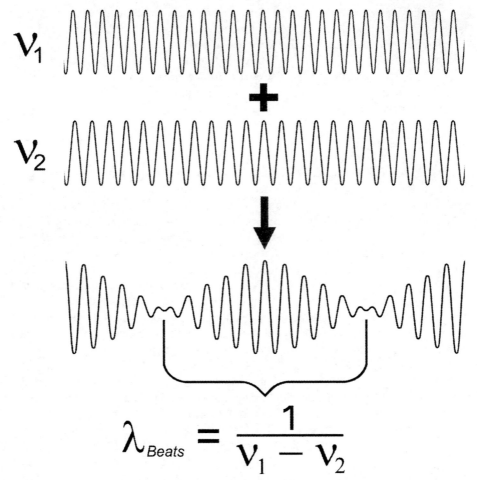

FIGURE 3-20   Depiction of the addition of two waves having similar frequencies to produce a beat pattern in the resulting wave. The frequencies of the two waves are v_1 and v_2, and the wavelength of the beat pattern increases as the difference between v_1 and v_2 decreases.

For a dispersive instrument, spectral resolution is dependent on the width of the slit used to isolate a band of wavelengths dispersed by a prism or grating; this width varies depending on the amount of energy in the band and the spectral resolution varies. **An FT-IR spectrometer, in contrast, has a constant resolution.** If a comparison is made between a spectrum acquired using an FT-IR spectrometer and one produced on a dispersive instrument, differences in the resolutions of some closely spaced peaks might be noted, even if the dispersive-instrument data were collected at the same nominal resolution as the FT-IR instrument. Specifically, the absorptions occurring at both ends of the dispersive-generated spectrum may not be as well resolved as those observed for the FT-IR spectrum, because there is less energy at the ends of the spectrum and wider slits are used (for the same reason, the FT-IR spectrum exhibits more noise at both ends of the spectrum).

APODIZATION   A second consequence of the truncation of the interferogram is that a distorted band shape occurs for very sharp absorptions. Consider again a monochromatic source of radiation having a frequency v_1; the "spectrum" of this source should consist of a single line at a frequency of v_1. The oscillating portion of this monochromatic source interferogram is proportional to $\cos 2\pi v_1 \delta$, and integration of this function over *all* values of δ (Equation 3-9) gives $B(v) = 0$, except for $v = v_1$ as expected. When this same integration is performed for a truncated interferogram (i.e., for a finite range of retardations from $-d$ to d), however, the shape of the resulting peak is not a line, but instead has a form related to the function $(\sin 2\pi v d)/(2\pi v d)$ centered around v_1. This function has prominent oscillatory "ringing" patterns flanking the central peak. The width of this central peak is equal to $1/d$ (therefore, the larger the maximum retardation d, the narrower is the peak—this too reflects the relationship between maximum retardation and resolution). To minimize these artifactual sidebands, the truncated interferogram is multiplied by a function that results in more weight being given to the center ($\delta = 0$) and the lower values of δ. This process is known as *apodization*. Apodization not only reduces the band shape distortions, but also decreases the noise in the transformed spectrum. Some decrease in resolution also occurs, however. A number of different apodization functions have been used, including triangular (for which the weighting factor decreases linearly with increasing $|\delta|$ to a value of zero for the maximum retardation), trapezoidal (which may be viewed as triangular with its top cut off), a cosine or cosine-squared function, and so forth. An unapodized interferogram is sometimes referred to as having a *boxcar apodization,* because it may be viewed as a product of a rectangular function [$F(x) = 1$ for $|\delta| < d$; $F(x) = 0$ for $|\delta| > d$, where d is the maximum retardation] and the "true" infinite interferogram.

DATA ACQUISITION   Although the interferogram output from the detector is an analog signal, only a discrete number of data points are actually recorded, because the data must be processed by a digital computer. For signal averaging to be effective, an interferogram reading must be collected at the same mirror position for each scan. This is accomplished by the use of a reference interferogram produced by a helium–neon laser, which emits a monochromatic red line at 632.8 nm. The sinusoidally varying interferogram of the laser (which has its own detector separate from that used for the infrared beam) is used as a "ruler" to indicate the precise position of the movable mirror; from the centerburst signal of the regular interferogram, one need count only the number of fringes of this laser interferogram that have occurred to know the exact position of the movable mirror. These fringes are thus used to signal when a data point is to be collected and because the frequency of laser is invariant, it also serves as the internal calibration device for the spectrometer. A schematic diagram of a typical FT-IR instrument, based on the Michelson interferometer, is shown in Figure 3-21.

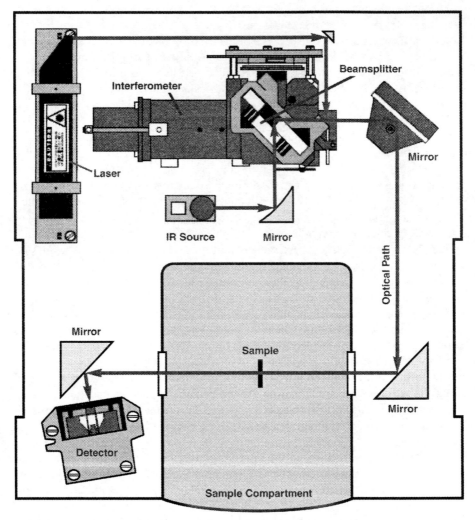

FIGURE 3-21 Schematic diagram of the Nicolet Series 4700 FT-IR spectrometer. (*Source:* Reprinted with permission from the Thermo Fisher Scientific Company.)

GENERATION OF A SPECTRUM   As indicated previously, the Fourier transform of an interferogram produces an instrument-detected spectrum of the source (or the source minus the wavelengths absorbed by the sample) and not a conventional ra-tioed spectrum. Even when a sample is not present, this detected source spectrum is different from the actual distribution of infrared frequencies emitted by the source, because the beam splitter efficiency, detector response, mirror reflectivities, and so forth, are nonlinear through the mid-infrared region. Further, the interferogram is amplified electronically, and this process also is not entirely linear with respect to in-terferogram frequency. All of these effects are essentially constant from scan to scan, however, and by ratioing the spectrum obtained with a sample in the beam to that ob-tained without a sample, the transmittance spectrum of the sample is obtained.

Figure 3-10A depicts what a typical instrument-detected FT-IR source spec-trum looks like, that is, a background scan obtained without a sample in the beam. The instrument housing was purged with dry nitrogen for this, and a deuterated triglycine sulfate detector was used. As a "sample," a scan of a normal atmosphere was made (the instrument housing was not purged), giving the spectrum depicted in Figure 3-10B. This is the spectrum that was actually generated from the interfero-gram collected for this sample, but the instrument automatically ratios this scan to that of the stored background (Figure 3-10A) to give a normal transmittance spec-trum as shown in Figure 3-10C.

Because of the absorptions of water and carbon dioxide vapors, purging of the instrument housing with dry and carbon dioxide–free nitrogen is highly recommended. This not only makes interpretation of spectral data easier (especially if the spectrum of a sample with weak absorptions is obtained), but also protects the optics of the instrument. In the case of an extended-range FT-IR instrument equipped with CsI optics, this should be considered mandatory to protect the hygroscopic CsI optical elements.

SPECTRAL NOISE   The noise in a spectrum generated from an interferogram is de-termined by a number of factors, including the spectral resolution, the number of scans that are averaged, and the type of detector that is used. For a ratioed spectrum (i.e., a normal transmittance spectrum), the variation in the noise level with frequency results mostly from the nonlinear shape of two ratioed spectra. Assume, for example, that the noise level of the reference scan of Figure 3-10A is 1% of its maximum height (which occurs near 2000 cm^{-1}) and is constant for all frequencies. At both ends of this spectrum, where the curve drops off, this 1% noise becomes a significant fraction of the height of the spectrum. When ratioed, both ends of the resulting trans-mittance spectrum therefore exhibit greater relative noise (this is usually explained as resulting from the low energy at the ends, which is simply another means of ex-pressing this limitation).

The signal-to-noise ratio (SNR) for an FT-IR instrument is inversely related to the spectral resolution, all other things being equal. Doubling the resolution (e.g., in-creasing the resolution from 4 cm^{-1} to 2 cm^{-1}) decreases the SNR by a factor of 2. This formula applies for equal collection time intervals and *not* the total number of scans averaged. The reason for this is that the interferometer is scanning for a longer time period when resolution is increased because the movable mirror has to travel a greater distance. In addition, the diameter of the infrared beam (controlled by an aperture) is also decreased when resolution is increased. This is done to minimize the contribution of nonparallel beams that reach the detector, because such beams limit the resolution that can be achieved. Decreasing the aperture diameter also causes the SNR to decrease.

The SNR is proportional to the square root of the measurement time. When the spectral resolution remains the same, this is tantamount to the SNR being proportional to the square root of the total number of scans that are averaged. To double the SNR, four times as many scans are required.

Considering all of these factors, doubling the spectral resolution requires increasing the collection time by a factor *greater* than 4 to maintain the same SNR. Therefore, a resolution higher than necessary should not be used. For the vast majority of evidence analyzed in the forensic science laboratory, spectral resolutions greater than 4 cm^{-1} do not result in spectra having significantly increased detail, except for those few samples involving relatively small molecules analyzed as vapors. An optimal resolution for almost all such samples is thus 4 cm^{-1}.

It should be remembered that the SNR is also determined by the SNRs of both the reference and the sample spectra. If one of these was collected with significantly fewer scans than the other, its SNR will be the one that primarily determines the SNR of the ratioed data. If the limiting factor is the reference spectrum, there is little to be gained by increasing the number of sample scans much beyond that used for the reference, because the SNR of the ratioed spectrum will not improve by much. If a reference spectrum is to be stored and used for a number of samples, there is merit in using a relatively large number of scans for the reference because the SNR of the sample will then determine the overall SNR; if there is a lot of noise in the ratioed spectrum, it can be reduced by collecting more sample scans rather than having to rerun both the reference and the sample.

For more information on FT-IR instrumentation, the reader is referred to the definitive work on this subject (the FT-IR "bible") by Griffiths and de Haseth.[7]

Detectors

There are two types of detectors used on FT-IR spectrometers: deuterated triglycine sulfate (DTGS) pyroelectric detectors and mercury cadmium telluride (MCT) photoconductivity detectors. In some cases, a particular accessory dictates which detector *must* be used, whereas for others, analysts may be able to choose which is most appropriate to meet their particular needs (which should be determined by the types of evidence analyzed routinely on that instrument).

DEUTERATED TRIGLYCINE SULFATE PYROELECTRIC DETECTORS   Single crystals of pyroelectric materials, such as DTGS, develop opposite charges on two crystal faces, which originate from the dipole moments of the individual molecules and their orientations in the crystal lattice. The amount of charge produced depends on the temperature of the crystal and when the temperature changes, a current flows in the crystal in response to the changing polarity. When used as an infrared detector, a single crystal of DTGS has a blackened coating on one surface to absorb radiation, and the device responds to changes in the intensity of radiation focused onto the coating.

The advantages of the DTGS detector include a very wide spectral range, a high linearity, and the ability to operate at room temperature. The detector is sensitive down to 50 cm^{-1}, so the low frequency limit of an FT-IR spectrometer equipped with this detector is determined by the optics of the instrument (i.e., whether the beam splitter and the windows use KBr or CsI) and not by the detector.

As a thermal sensing device that responds to temperature changes, this detector must be able to dissipate the heat it receives rapidly. Because it is not able to do so instantaneously, it does not respond well to high-frequency changes in temperature. Consequently, there is a limit to how fast the movable mirror of an FT-IR instrument can be scanned when using a DTGS detector, as too high a velocity results in loss of sensitivity for the higher frequencies of the interferogram (and hence in the spectrum itself, because the frequencies in an interferogram are proportional to the frequencies of the source). For most FT-IR systems, the software operating the spectrometer has been designed so that when the user indicates that a DTGS detector is to be used (if there is a choice), it automatically sets the scanning velocity of the movable mirror to accommodate this detector.

MERCURY CADMIUM TELLURIDE PHOTOCONDUCTIVITY DETECTORS   The MCT detector consists of a thin layer (10 to 20 μm) of mercury cadmium telluride with a voltage applied across two faces. When there is no infrared light striking the detector, little current is generated, because the material is a semiconductor. An infrared photon having sufficient energy can cause an electron of the detector to be promoted from the valence band to the conduction band, and when such photons are absorbed by the detector, this increases its conductivity. Such devices are therefore referred to as *photoconductivity detectors*.

Compared to the DTGS detector, MCT detectors are more sensitive, can be scanned at higher rates, and have excellent low-light capabilities (the sensitivity of the broadband MCT detector is roughly four times that of the DTGS detector). They are more expensive, however, and must be kept cold with liquid nitrogen during operation. To keep atmospheric constituents from condensing onto the cooled detector surface, the detector housing is evacuated. After five years or so, this housing may require re-evacuation; the need for this is apparent when the liquid nitrogen Dewar has to be filled frequently.

The increased sensitivity of MCT detectors comes at a price, because they have more limited spectral ranges. There is, in fact, an inverse relationship between sensitivity and spectral range. The sensitivity of the MCT detector is determined by the ratio of the three constituents (mercury, cadmium, and tellurium) that make up the detector, and the more sensitive the detector, the higher is its low-frequency cut-off point. Although these values form a continuum, MCT detectors are classified as broadband and narrowband (and sometimes as mediumband) according to their low-frequency cut-off points, which can vary from 800 to 400 cm^{-1}. Narrowband detectors have cutoff points near 700 cm^{-1} or higher, whereas broadband detectors have cutoff points near 450 cm^{-1} or lower. Because of its high sensitivity, MCT detectors are required with low-throughput accessories, such as the infrared microscope and GC/FT-IR attachments, and these normally use dedicated detectors separate from that used on the interferometer bench.

MCT detectors are excellent at detecting low levels of infrared light, but at the same time, they can also be easily saturated if the intensity of light reaching the detector is too high. This is not normally a problem with most FT-IR accessories because they involve a considerable loss of energy. However, if a sample is analyzed with an open beam (such as might occur with a KBr pellet or a vapor cell) on an instrument with a MCT detector, the detector will likely saturate and an attenuation screen should be placed in the beam.

ANALYSIS TECHNIQUES AND ACCESSORIES

The specialized sampling techniques and accessories are what make the FT-IR spectrometer such an indispensable tool for analyzing the wide variety of materials submitted to the forensic science laboratory. Although traditional sampling methods—which were designed for use on dispersive instruments—can be used with an FT-IR spectrometer, they are not exploiting the full capabilities of this device. The KBr pellet method, for example, has long been used for the analysis of powdered solid samples. This technique requires a fair amount of sample preparation and the main advantage that an FT-IR spectrometer provides over a computerized dispersive instrument for analyzing a pellet is a shorter collection time. As noted, if a MCT detector is used on an FT-IR instrument for such an analysis, an attenuation screen must be placed in the beam to avoid detector saturation. Clearly, there is energy being wasted here and the use of a more suitable FT-IR accessory requires less sample preparation, permits significantly smaller sample sizes, or allows the user to obtain spectra of intractable materials that are not amenable for analysis using KBr pellets. An analyst using an FT-IR spectrometer for the routine analysis of pellets is thus utilizing only a portion of the available technology. This is unfortunate as those accessories most likely to be used in lieu of this method cost only a fraction of the price of the FT-IR spectrometer itself.

Diamond Anvil Cell

The diamond anvil cell (DAC) was originally intended as a device to study spectroscopically the behavior of substances under high pressures, but later it was found to be a convenient means to analyze small amounts (1 to 10 μg) of materials without regard to pressure.[8–11] It has been used since 1959,[12] and the first forensic applications of this device were reported in 1965.[13,14] Until the 1980s, the high-pressure version of the DAC was used with spectra collected on dispersive spectrometers. Although this configuration allowed the acquisition of data for materials that were otherwise difficult to handle, the resulting spectra were far from optimal. Because of the low throughputs of this accessory, both the SNR and spectral resolution usually suffered and alignment problems were not uncommon. In addition, the spectra consisted of sample absorptions together with those of diamond, as there was no means to compensate for the broad diamond features and only the region below 1800 cm^{-1} was normally examined.

With an FT-IR instrument, a "normal" spectrum can be readily obtained by ratioing the sample scan to that of the DAC without a sample, and numerous scans can be averaged to give excellent SNRs. In 1984, the low-pressure DAC was introduced and this modification had several advantages over its high-pressure predecessor. Because the diamond anvils are not as thick as those of the high-pressure DAC, spectral data could be obtained for the 2400 to 1800 cm^{-1} region where the diamonds absorb. The low-pressure DAC is also more compact and less expensive than the high-pressure version, and it can be used with both a beam condenser and an infrared microscope (the thicker anvils of the high pressure DAC prevented its use on an infrared microscope because the refractive diamonds produced a pronounced defocusing of the infrared beam). The low-pressure DAC is now the one predominantly used in forensic science laboratories in the United States.

This device, also known as the miniature DAC, consists of two diamond windows (anvils), each embedded in the center of a triangular-shaped metal holder. The windows are each 1 mm thick and the aperture of the holder is 0.8 mm in diameter. Three screws are used to keep the two holders together but are not intended to exert much pressure on the sample. The diamonds used for infrared spectroscopy are Type IIa diamonds. *Type II* refers to diamonds that contain little or no nitrogen, the most common impurity in diamonds; the *a* designation refers to diamonds that lack other impurities, such as boron, which produce color. Both properties are required for infrared spectroscopy because nitrogen and other impurities produce infrared absorptions. Because Type IIa diamonds are quite rare and are highly desired in the gem industry because of their clarity and lack of color, they are more expensive than most other diamonds. In 2007, the manufacturer of the DAC, High Pressure Diamond Optics, began using synthetic diamonds because of their increased availability and the fact that they have identical performance characteristics to those of natural diamonds.

The transmittances of a single anvil and both anvils of the low-pressure DAC are depicted in Figures 3-22A and 3-22B, respectively.[15] Although the broad features between 2400 and 1800 cm^{-1} may appear to be strong absorptions, they are actually quite weak because they represent the absorptions of a specimen 1-mm thick (for a single anvil, Figure 3-22A). A typical sample used for infrared analysis is between 1- and 10-μm thick (undiluted), so these absorptions are for a material 100 to 1000 times as thick as a conventional sample. These unusual features, which occur in the region normally associated with stretching absorptions of triple-bonded organic compounds or those having two adjacent double bonds (such as carbon dioxide—see Figure 3-10C), are overtone/combination transitions of the lattice vibrations of diamond.[16] The carbon stretching absorptions, which one might expect to occur near 1000 cm^{-1}, are infrared inactive so only these very weak features are observed. There are no other diamond absorptions down to at least 10 cm^{-1} (which is where the microwave region begins), so diamond windows are transparent throughout the far-infrared region, unlike salt windows.

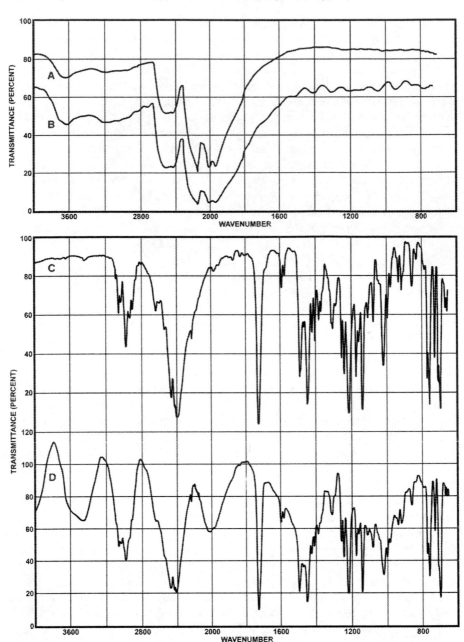

FIGURE 3-22   Infrared microscope spectra of **(A)** a single anvil of the low-pressure DAC; **(B)** both anvils of the low-pressure DAC; **(C)** diphenoxylate hydrochloride pressed onto a single anvil of the low-pressure DAC; and **(D)** diphenoxylate hydrochloride pressed between both anvils of the low-pressure DAC using a reference spectrum of the empty DAC without KBr.   (*Source:* From Reference 15, copyright ASTM, reprinted with permission.)

The diameter of the infrared beam passing through the center of the sample compartment of a typical FT-IR instrument is 1 cm (10 mm) or so. Because the aperture of the DAC is 0.8 mm, only 0.6% of this beam passes through the DAC were it placed in the beam directly. A 4X or 5X beam condenser is thus used with the DAC and a 5X beam condenser condenses a 10mm diameter beam to 2mm, so that roughly 16% of the beam energy now passes through the DAC.

In addition to its transparency in most of the infrared region, the other properties of diamond that make it such a valuable window material include its hardness, inertness and virtual indestructibility. Unlike other infrared window materials, it cannot be scratched (except by another diamond) or easily broken, and it thus provides an ideal substrate for pressing samples to flatten them. Overall, the DAC technique is the most versatile and useful method for preparing and securing the extremely wide variety of samples (including powders, fibers, paints, plastics, rubbers, adhesives, foams, geological specimens, building materials, etc.) submitted as evidence. Because of its inertness, the DAC has also been used to analyze liquids, including corrosive liquids such as sulfuric acid,[9] although a diamond-coated ATR accessory now provides a more convenient alternative for these.

Sample preparation is minimal with the DAC. For powders and pliable objects, one simply squeezes a small amount of material between the two anvil faces to form a uniform film. Thin slices of harder objects such as plastics may be obtained using a scalpel, whereas the hardest objects may be scored with a diamond-tipped scribe to produce a small amount of powder. For a reference spectrum, KBr or CsI should *always* be used in the DAC. This not only protects the anvils from coming into direct contact with one another, but also minimizes interference fringes.

INTERFERENCE FRINGES Interference fringes can occur whenever a sample (or window) has very parallel faces and is situated perpendicular to the infrared beam. Most analysts have probably seen interference fringes in spectra of polystyrene calibration films, and weak fringes can be seen below $1500 \ cm^{-1}$ in the DAC spectrum of water in Figure 3-18A and below $1600 \ cm^{-1}$ in the spectrum of both anvils of the DAC (Figure 3-22B). There are very pronounced interference fringes in the DAC/infrared microscope spectrum of Figure 3-22D.

Figure 3-23A depicts six possible paths for light incident on a sample sandwiched between two windows; the reflected beams are shown returning on different paths than the incident beams for clarity, although for perpendicular incidence they overlap. Rays 1 through 4 represent reflection from each of the four interfaces. These four do not contribute to the spectrum, other than causing some loss of the intensity of the incident beam, because they do not reach the detector. Ray 5 reflects from the two window-sample interfaces, whereas Ray 6 travels through the two windows and the sample. If the thickness of the sample is D, Ray 5 travels an extra distance of $2D$ compared to Ray 6. If this extra distance is a multiple of the wavelength (which is λ/n in the sample, where λ is the wavelength in vacuum and n the index of refraction of the sample), constructive interference results if Rays 5 and 6 are coincident. As the wavelength becomes larger or smaller and the extra distance becomes a multiple of half a wavelength, destructive interference occurs. As the wavelength changes,

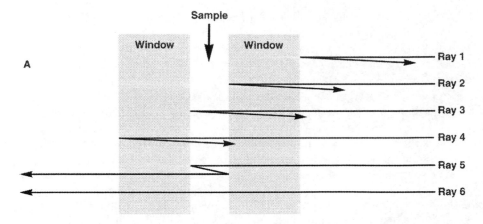

Reference of Empty DAC

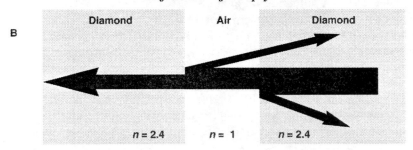

Sample in DAC

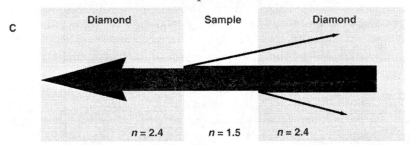

FIGURE 3-23 **(A)** Six of the possible paths that light rays may take when encountering a sample sandwiched between two windows. **(B)** Transmitted and reflected rays for light traveling through an empty DAC. **(C)** Transmitted and reflected rays for light traveling through a DAC containing a sample. Because the reflection losses are greater for **(B)**, a greater fraction of the incident light reaches the detector for **(C)** (for wavelengths where the sample does not absorb), resulting in spectral baselines that are higher than 100% transmittance. The reflected rays are all depicted as returning at an angle for clarity.

constructive and destructive interference alternate and an oscillating pattern occurs in the spectrum. The number of fringes increases as the thickness of the sample increases and there is a simple formula[17] to calculate the thickness of the sample if its refractive index is known.

Note that fringes do not occur if the sample happens to have the same index of refraction as the window. Conversely, fringes tend to be more prominent when there is a large difference in index of refraction between the window material and the sample, because the reflection at the sample-window interface is greater. Interference fringes are more prevalent using diamond windows because of its high index of refraction. The indices of refraction at 2000 cm^{-1} for some relevant materials are diamond 2.4, KBr 1.54, CsI 1.75, and organic compounds ~1.5.

When an empty DAC is used as a reference spectrum, there is more reflection occurring at the two air-diamond interfaces than would be the case if KBr or CsI were used, because there is more of a difference in the index of refraction between the air and diamond compared to salt and diamond. The relative intensity of Ray 5 compared to Ray 6 is thus greater when an empty DAC is run and noticeable interference fringes can usually be seen in such reference scans. Fringes are less pronounced for the sample compared to an empty DAC because the index of refraction of the sample is always higher than that of air. Note that even if there are no fringes in the sample scan, they appear in the ratioed spectrum if there are fringes in the reference scan.

Although not depicted in Figure 3-23A, interference between Rays 5 and 6 is not the only possible source of fringes in a spectrum, as six different plates sandwiched between two interfaces are actually present (and these all have different thicknesses if the two anvils have different thicknesses). In practice, however, only one or two sets of fringes are usually apparent.

Although it may not be possible to completely eliminate fringes when using the DAC, there are some ways to minimize them, in addition to using KBr or CsI in the reference scan. One method is to apply uneven pressure to the sample and to the KBr or CsI so that one corner of the DAC is pressed down more than the other two. This forms a wedge-shaped cross-section for the sample and the KBr or CsI, and if pronounced enough, interference fringes will not be observed because constructive (and destructive) interference do not occur at the same time for every ray passing through the sample. In addition, because one or more of the faces is no longer exactly perpendicular to the beam, Rays 5 and 6 may no longer be coincident after exiting from the second window, which may also decrease fringes. For the same reason, if the DAC can be tilted slightly so that its faces are no longer exactly perpendicular to the beam (this is more easily done when using an infrared microscope than a beam condenser), this might likewise reduce interference fringes.

A third method to avoid fringes is to use single anvil analysis.[15,18] For this, the sample is pressed together as usual, then the two anvils are separated and if the entire sample is found to be attached to one anvil, that anvil alone is used for analysis. This requires that the particular anvil chosen be run as a reference because the two anvils are not exactly alike, and this can be done by using prestored reference spectra of each anvil or running the reference after the sample. For single anvil analysis, there is no need to use KBr or CsI for the reference spectrum. This method of analysis is more easily performed for some types of samples (such as a single slice of a paint or plastic) than others, and is not applicable for elastic materials that must be kept compressed. It can be used for some powders, although this may require some patience on the part of the analyst to ensure that all of the sample adhers to one side only (the spectra of the powders of Figures 3-16A–D and 3-18B–E were all obtained using a single anvil).

As noted, the DAC may be used with the infrared microscope. For these analyses, the single anvil method is preferred, as interference fringes are often more pronounced because very small analysis areas are involved and the differences in thickness across a sample tend to be less. The strong interference fringes in the infrared microscope spectrum of Figure 3-22D resulted from use of a reference scan with an empty DAC without KBr; as a comparison, the same sample (diphenoxylate hydrochloride) was analyzed on a single anvil giving the fringe-free spectrum depicted in Figure 3-22C.

SPECTRAL VARIABILITIES AND ARTIFACTS   One seemingly puzzling occurrence might also be observed when using an empty DAC as a reference, namely, spectral baselines that are higher than 100% (Figure 3-22D). This occurs because more of the infrared beam is reflected back to the source from an empty DAC compared to when a sample is present, as illustrated in Figures 3-23B and 3-23C. More light therefore reaches the detector (for spectral regions where there is no absorption) for the sample than for the reference. This effect is also minimized by using KBr or CsI in the DAC.

In general, inorganic compounds have higher absorption coefficients and indices of refraction than organic compounds. Some inorganic compounds are such strong infrared absorbers that it is difficult to form a film thin enough—even when pressed between two diamonds—such that its strongest peaks have not "bottomed-out." These compounds are best analyzed diluted with KBr or CsI.

In some cases, dilution with CsI may also help reduce absorption band distortions. These distortions originate from the large change in index of refraction across an absorption band. Figures 3-24A and 3-24B depict, respectively, the absorption coefficient and index of refraction of a compound as a function of frequency. The index of refraction has a derivative shape that reaches its maximum value on the low frequency side of the absorption band. The behavior in the region where the index of refraction is increasing rapidly as the frequency decreases is known as *anomalous dispersion*, because the index of refraction generally decreases with decreasing frequency. Although one might not expect the index of refraction to influence the absorption spectrum of a compound, it can, in fact, have a very pronounced effect, depending on the analysis technique and in some cases, the method of sample preparation. The manifestations of this effect on spectral data, if significant, are discussed for each analysis technique.

The change in index of refraction across an absorption band is generally greater for inorganic compounds and they tend to be more prone to absorption band distortions. Although such distortions may be less of a concern for comparative analyses when using the same method for both known and questioned samples,

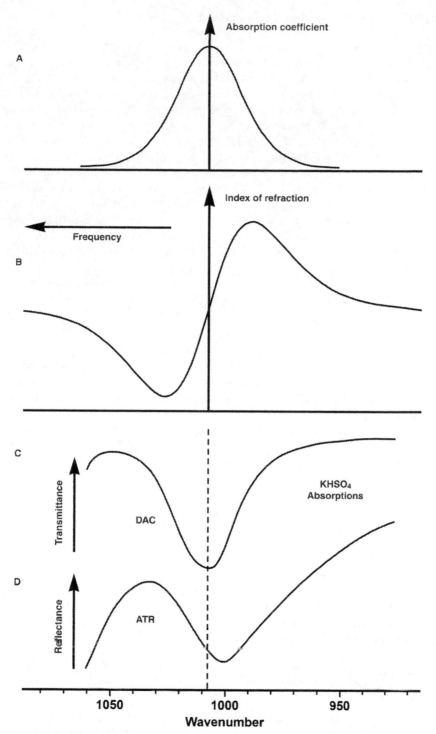

FIGURE 3-24 **(A)** The absorption coefficient of a compound as a function of frequency. **(B)** The index of refraction as a function of frequency. **(C)** The 1007 cm^{-1} absorption of KHSO$_4$ analyzed using the DAC. **(D)** This same absorption as observed in the ATR spectrum of KHSO$_4$ obtained using a single-pass diamond ATR accessory.

comparison to data obtained by other techniques or to library spectra may pose questions. Further, in the case of a few inorganic compounds analyzed using the DAC, differences can occur for the same compound in different matrices. An example of this is a minor but noticeable distortion[19] of the absorption band of rutile (titanium dioxide). The spectrum of rutile consists of a very broad absorption between 800 and 250 cm^{-1} with two low-frequency spikes below 450 cm^{-1} and two minor lobes above and below 600 cm^{-1} (Figures 3-25A and 3-25B). In spectra of rutile taken using CsI pellets or DRIFTS, the higher-frequency lobe has a greater intensity, and this is also observed for the absorptions of rutile in spectra of paints analyzed as thin slices (Figure 3-25B) or in the DAC. In contrast, the DAC spectrum of neat rutile has a greater intensity for the lower-frequency lobe; and although this intensity decreases somewhat when rutile is diluted with excess CsI, the enhanced intensity of the lower-frequency lobe is still noticeable (compare Figures 3-25A and 3-25B). This effect arises from differences in the amount of light reflected from the diamond–rutile interfaces for the high- and low-frequency lobes. Because the index of refraction of rutile is much higher in the vicinity of the low-frequency lobe (see Figures 3-24A and 3-24B), there is more reflection for these frequencies compared to those of the high-frequency lobe. This reflection loss is manifested in the spectrum as what appears to be a greater absorption for the lower frequency lobe. In DAC spectra of paints containing rutile, this effect is not evident because the small particles of rutile are dispersed in the binder matrix and there is minimal contact between the rutile particles and the diamond windows. This effect is also observed for anatase (a second polymorph of titanium dioxide), for Nickel Titanate (compare the low frequency lobes of Figures 3-25C and 3-25D), and for other titanates.[19]

Although not common, pressure effects might also occur when using the DAC. Excess pressure may cause a compound to lose its crystallinity, that is, to form an amorphous or glass-like structure, and this usually results in absorption bands becoming broader or coalescing. Other pressure-induced changes that might occur include a transition to a different crystal form (if the material is polymorphic), a tautomeric shift (i.e., a shift in the equilibrium that produces an increase in the concentration of one tautomer at the expense of the other), or possibly even sample decomposition. With the low-pressure DAC, the main source of pressure occurs when a powder or other solid material is pressed to form a thin film. Some of the transitions noted previously are irreversible, and even when pressure is removed, spectra different from those of the original substance result. In other cases, the changes are reversible but still might occur if the pressure exerted to keep the two anvils together is sufficient to cause effects. If a pressure-induced transition is suspected, an alternative method that avoids exerting pressure on the sample should be used.

Infrared Microscope

The infrared microscope permits an analyst to view a sample optically, then to select that portion of the specimen that is to be analyzed by the FT-IR spectrometer. The latter is usually done by transmittance sampling with the microscope acting as a

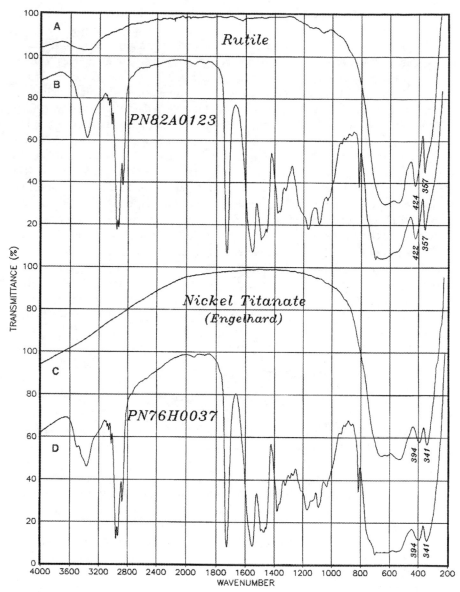

FIGURE 3-25   Spectra of rutile, Nickel Titanate, as well as two automotive paints that contain these two pigments. The pigments were diluted with CsI and pressed onto a single anvil of a DAC. The paints, from the *Reference Collection of Automotive Paints*, were analyzed as thin slices held over a 1-mm diameter aperture. **(A)** Rutile. **(B)** A white nonmetallic acrylic melamine enamel, PN82A0123, that contains a large amount of rutile. **(C)** Nickel Titanate. **(D)** A yellow nonmetallic acrylic melamine enamel, PN76H0037, that contains a large amount of Nickel Titanate.   (*Source:* From Reference 19, copyright American Academy of Forensic Sciences, reprinted with permission.)

beam condenser and the aperture defining the area of analysis. Reflectance measurements or use of an ATR objective are also options available on some systems.

The main limitation of infrared spectroscopy for the examination of many types of evidence has traditionally been the inability to examine very small samples. The infrared microscope addresses this problem; in essence, this accessory extends the applications of the DAC to much smaller particles, the dimensions of which are limited only by diffraction. With the DAC, a sample should have a diameter of approximately 0.8 mm (800 μm) when flattened (particles smaller than this can be analyzed because flattening spreads the particle out). With the infrared microscope, samples having dimensions down to around 10 μm (which is the wavelength corresponding to 1000 cm^{-1}) may be examined. This represents a factor of 6,400 decrease in particle size, and nanogram quantities of materials can routinely be analyzed. In addition, because this accessory allows the user to delineate (within the constraints of the aperturing device) the area to be examined, analyses of specified regions of inhomogeneous materials can be made *in situ* and a compositional topography determined.

Because of the very small sample sizes that may be subjected to analysis, almost all infrared microscopes come equipped with narrowband MCT detectors. This results in the main limitation of this accessory, namely, its more limited spectral range. The types of compounds and evidence affected are described later. For more information about various aspects of the infrared microscope, the reader is referred to Chapter 4 of this *Handbook*.

Attenuated Total Reflectance

Attenuated total reflectance (ATR) was introduced in 1959,[20] but this analysis method was not widely used in forensic science laboratories until quite recently. This occurred only after the introduction of single-pass accessories[21] and ATR objectives for infrared microscopes. Portable FT-IR systems with dedicated ATR units have also recently been introduced. The ATR method of analysis, however, may produce spectra with notable differences compared to those acquired using transmittance methods. In addition, the differential nature of the sampling process may raise interpretation questions when some inhomogeneous materials are examined if analysts are not familiar with the mechanism of ATR absorption. This section thus examines in some detail the nature of the ATR analysis process. Although "ATR" is now the dominant acronym used for this technique, it is also referred to as *IRS (internal reflection spectroscopy)*.

ATR ANALYSIS PROCESS   Figure 3-26 depicts reflection and refraction when a light ray travels from a medium having a high index of refraction into one having a lower index of refraction for various angles of incidence. The refracted rays bend away from the normal, and as the angle of incidence becomes larger, a point is reached where the refracted ray travels parallel to the interface surface. For all angles greater than this value, known as the *critical angle*, there is no refracted ray and total internal reflection occurs. The incident ray and the totally reflected ray have the same intensity and in the vicinity of the reflection point, there is interference between

Medium having a lower index of refraction

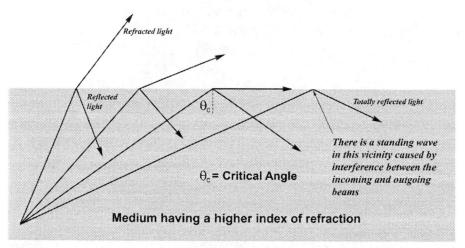

FIGURE 3-26   Reflection, refraction, and total internal reflection of light rays passing from one medium (shaded) to another medium with a lower index of refraction, shown for various angles of incidence. As the angle of incidence increases beyond the critical angle, θ_c, there is no longer a refracted ray and total internal reflection occurs. In the vicinity of the region where total internal reflection occurs, there is interference between the incident and reflected rays, which produces a standing wave composed of oscillating electric and magnetic fields.

the incoming and outgoing waves. This produces a standing wave, that is, one that is not propagating. The standing wave is composed of oscillating electric and magnetic fields that are perpendicular to one another; the one of interest here is the oscillating electric field because it is primarily responsible for most absorption of electromagnetic radiation (excluding magnetic resonance techniques). The standing wave extends into the medium having a lower index of refraction, where it is called the *evanescent wave*. The intensity of the evanescent wave decreases exponentially away from its source (Figure 3-27), which is near the point where reflection occurs in the higher index of refraction medium. As an oscillating electric field, the evanescent wave can cause vibrational transitions just as light of the same wavelength that is traveling through the sample can be absorbed (see Figure 3-6). Hence, if there is a sample located at the surface, some of the energy of the evanescent wave can be absorbed and the intensity of the totally reflected light is attenuated.

A formula[22] for the penetration depth of the evanescent wave, d_p, is given by

$$d_p = \frac{\lambda}{2\pi n_0 \sqrt{\sin^2\theta - n^2/n_0^2}}$$ **3-10**

where λ is the wavelength of light, n_0 is the index of refraction of the ATR element, n is the index of refraction of the sample, and θ is the angle of incidence. This formula represents the distance from the surface where the intensity of the electric field of the evanescent wave drops to $1/e$ of its value at the surface, where e (2.718 ...) is the base

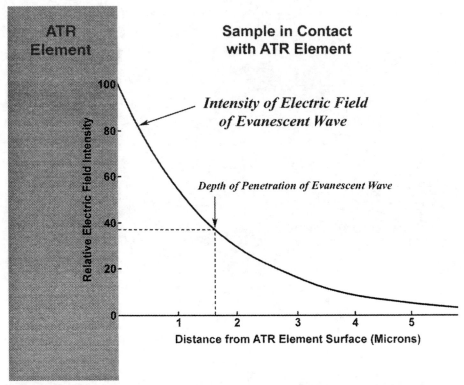

FIGURE 3-27 The relative intensity of the electric field of the evanescent wave as a function of distance from the surface of the ATR element (shaded). The intensity decreases exponentially from the surface, but the exact function depends on the indices of refraction of the element and the sample, the angle of incidence, and the wavelength of light. The *penetration depth of the evanescent wave* is defined as the distance from the surface where electric field drops to 37% of its value at the surface. The values depicted in this figure are roughly those for a diamond ATR element, an angle of incidence of 45°, a sample consisting of an organic compound, and a wavelength near 8.5 microns (1200 cm^{-1}).

of the natural logarithm system. This fraction is 37% and D_p represents the depth within which most of the absorption occurs, but because the intensity never really drops to zero, there can still be minor contributions from beyond this depth. Strictly speaking, this equation only applies in the absence of absorption, but it has been found to be a good approximation for absorbing samples as long as θ is not close to the critical angle. Note that the wavelength of the analysis, λ, is in the numerator of this expression with all of the other terms in the denominator. For a typical organic compound analyzed on an ATR accessory with a diamond element and an incident angle of 45°, the value of the denominator is approximately 5.0, so the penetration depth is roughly two-tenths of a wavelength.

ATR SAMPLE AND ANALYSIS REQUIREMENTS   In view of the ATR mechanism of absorption, one can see that there are two requirements for an ATR analysis. First, the sample must have an index of refraction lower than that of the ATR element, otherwise refraction will occur and there will no longer be total reflection at the surface. In fact, the index of refraction of the sample should be substantially lower, and this is determined by the angle of incidence. This requirement is expressed quantitatively in the denominator of Equation 3-10, where the term n^2/n_0^2 must not exceed $\sin^2\theta$, lest the square-root term become negative. The maxiumum value that $\sin^2\theta$ can assume is one, when the incident beam is parallel to the surface, and this is the only time when the index of refraction of the sample can be close to the index of refraction of the element; for less oblique angles, it must become progressively less, because $\sin^2\theta$ decreases as θ decreases.

The ATR element of an accessory should thus have a high index of refraction so that a wide variety of compounds can be analyzed. Typical element materials used in commercial devices include silver chloride ($n = 2.0$), zinc selenide ($n = 2.4$), thallous bromideiodide (KRS-5, $n = 2.4$), diamond ($n = 2.4$), silicon ($n = 3.4$), and germanium ($n = 4.0$), where the cited indices of refraction are for 2000 cm^{-1}; as a comparison, a typical organic compound has an index of refraction of 1.4 to 1.5. Diamond elements are actually diamond coated, with the bulk of the element composed of one of the other listed materials. The ATR properties are determined by diamond because it makes up the interface, but the other material (known as the *focusing device* and not the element) determines the low-frequency limit of the accessory, because all such materials begin to absorb in the far-infrared region at higher frequencies than diamond. A schematic diagram of a typical diamond-coated single pass ATR accessory is depicted in Figure 3-28.

Although it might appear that having an element with the highest possible index of refraction is desirable for all analyses, this is not necessarily the case. Equation 3-10 indicates that as the index of refraction of the element (n_0) increases, the penetration depth of the evanescent wave decreases. In the case of a very thin

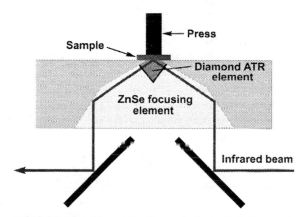

FIGURE 3-28   Schematic diagram of a typical diamond-coated single-pass ATR accessory with a zinc–selenide focusing element.

deposit or film on a substrate (such as a paint smear), this can be an advantage, but it also means that the absorption intensities are weaker (that is, the SNR will be less). There is a tradeoff here, so there is no one element material that is optimal for all types of evidence.

The very shallow penetration depth of the evanescent wave (Figure 3-27) gives rise to the second requirement for a successful ATR analysis: the sample must be in intimate contact with the element and there should be no air gaps between the sample and the element. Commercial ATR accessories are thus designed with a mechanism to press the sample against the element, usually consisting of a cylindrical piston that exerts a preset pressure on the sample.

As noted, the typical thickness of a transmittance sample (undiluted) for infrared analysis is between 1 and 10 microns, whereas the maximum penetration depth of an ATR analysis is normally of the order of a few microns. ATR peaks thus rarely bottom out, and most materials can be analyzed intact; there is no need to thin a solid sample or dilute it with KBr or CsI. For liquids, a drop or two is simply placed over the element and even strong infrared absorbers do not present a problem, as illustrated by the ATR spectrum of water (obtained using a single-pass accessory with a diamond-coated element; Figure 3-29A). With the use of a diamond-coated element, spectra of corrosive liquids, such as concentrated acids or bases, can also be readily obtained (Figures 3-29B–I). Although these corrosive liquids do not damage the diamond, their analysis time should be kept to a minimum to protect the stainless-steel surface surrounding the diamond window, and this area should be washed liberally with water following such an analysis. Note that, as in the case of salts having non-absorbing ions, the spectra of concentrated HCl (Figure 3-29G), HBr (Figure 3-29H), and HI (Figure 3-29I) are quite similar. Such infrared data should thus be viewed as providing class characteristics or screening information, and additional methods are required for identification. For HCl (Figure 3-7B) and HBr, high-resolution vapor infrared spectra can be used.

Because of their durability and inertness, diamond-coated elements are strongly recommended for use on single-pass ATR accessories. Unlike other element materials, diamond does not scratch, and as illustrated, there are few limitations to the types of samples that can be analyzed, other than that involving the index of refraction.

In addition to powders and liquids, ATR provides a convenient means to analyze gels, pastes, and other materials having semisolid consistencies; the outer layers of a multilayered paint chip or plastic laminate; both surfaces of tape; and other inhomogeneous materials where a spectrum of the outer surface portion is sought. When an outer layer or other inhomogeneous material is examined, it is important to obtain a spectrum of the substrate or adjacent material to determine if there are contributions to the spectrum from this material.

CHARACTERISTICS OF ATR SPECTRA   One significant difference that is observed between ATR and transmittance spectra of the same compound is the occurrence of enhanced relative intensities for the lower-frequency ATR absorptions. This results from the effective sampling depth of an ATR analysis being proportional to the wavelength. This difference may be seen by comparing the relative intensities of the

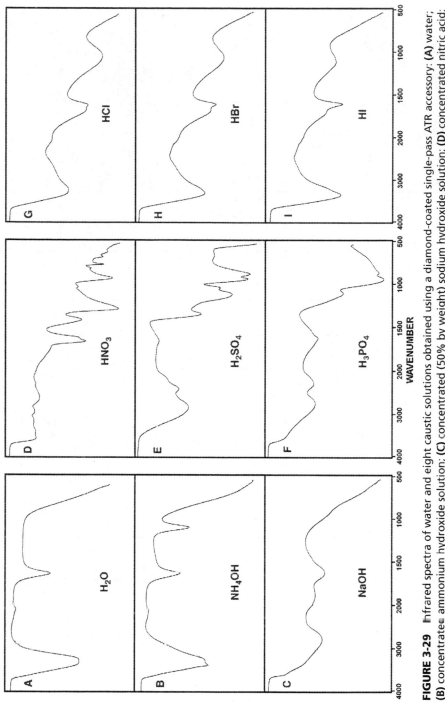

FIGURE 3-29 Infrared spectra of water and eight caustic solutions obtained using a diamond-coated single-pass ATR accessory: **(A)** water; **(B)** concentrated ammonium hydroxide solution; **(C)** concentrated (50% by weight) sodium hydroxide solution; **(D)** concentrated nitric acid; **(E)** concentrated sulfuric acid; **(F)** concentrated phosphoric acid; **(G)** concentrated hydrochloric acid; **(H)** concentrated hydrobromic acid; and **(I)** concentrated hydriodic acid. The ordinate scales for all spectra are shown between 100 and 0% reflectance.

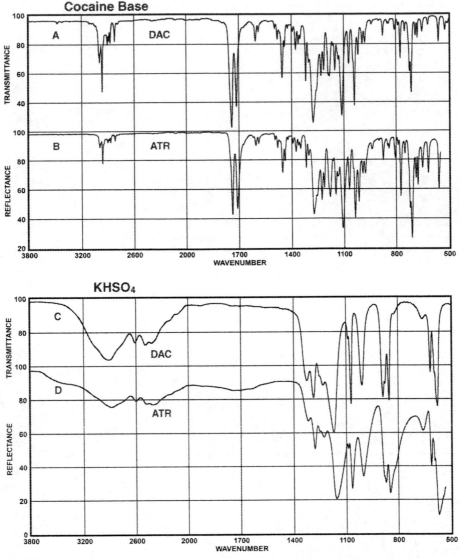

FIGURE 3-30 **(A)** DAC spectrum of cocaine base. **(B)** ATR spectrum of cocaine base obtained using a diamond-coated single-pass ATR accessory. **(C)** DAC spectrum of KHSO$_4$. **(D)** ATR spectrum of KHSO$_4$ obtained using a diamond-coated single-pass ATR accessory.

cocaine base absorptions acquired using a DAC (Figure 3-30A) and a single-pass ATR accessory (Figure 3-30B).

ATR spectra may exhibit one other significant difference compared to transmittance data, although the extent to which this occurs varies between compounds. Because of anomalous dispersion, the index of refraction of a compound is higher on the low-frequency side of an absorption band (Figures 3-24A and 3-24B). From Equation 3-10, it can be seen that as the index of refraction of a sample increases, the penetration depth also increases. The lower frequencies of an absorption band thus penetrate deeper into the sample, and this causes a skewing of the band shape. This may be manifested as both a peak shift (to lower frequencies) and a low-frequency shoulder. This skewing can be seen clearly for most of the ATR absorptions of $KHSO_4$ (Figure 3-30D) compared to its DAC absorptions (Figure 3-30C). A peak shift for the 1007 cm^{-1} $KHSO_4$ DAC absorption is seen clearly in expanded views of the ATR (Figure 3-24D) and DAC (Figure 3-24C) bands, and an extended low-frequency tail for the ATR absorption is evident. The increase in the index of refraction across an absorption band is generally greater for inorganic compounds, so these effects tend to be more pronounced for such compounds.

ATR correction programs that adjust the relative intensities of an ATR spectrum to make them similar to those of transmittance spectra are included in the software of most FT-IR systems. Such programs, however, simply multiply the spectrum (in absorbance) by a factor proportional to $1/\lambda$; **they do not correct for peak shifts and skewed bands,** as these are peculiar to each compound. ATR users should thus generate their own in-house libraries acquired on the same accessory used for analysis.

ANALYSIS OF INHOMOGENEOUS SAMPLES   Before the advent of an ATR objective for the infrared microscope, thin paint smears were among the most intractable evidence items to examine using infrared spectroscopy, as they were difficult or impossible to remove intact. With an ATR objective, paint smears can be analyzed *in situ*. Because the smears may be quite thin, it is important to always examine the spectrum of the substrate for comparison. Figure 3-31B is the spectrum of a green paint smear on a white automotive paint, obtained *in situ* using an ATR objective of an infrared microscope with a zinc selenide element. The ATR spectrum of the white automotive paint substrate is shown in Figure 3-31A, and the ATR spectrum of the green paint itself is depicted in Figure 3-31C. All of the absorptions of the green paint (Figure 3-31C) are present in the spectrum of the smear (Figure 3-31B), but the latter also has absorptions of the white substrate paint (Figure 3-31A). These include barely discernable absorptions of styrene above 3000 cm^{-1}, a very weak absorption of acrylonitrile near 2240 cm^{-1}, and a strong tail at the low-frequency end of the spectrum arising from titanium dioxide (Figure 3-25A). Although the baseline of the green paint spectrum (Figure 3-31C) drops in the low-frequency region, its slope is more gentle than that of the tail of the smear spectrum and white paint. Similar gentle slopes are also observed for many ATR spectra where titanium dioxide is not present, and a large amount of this pigment is not indicated for the green paint.

The *in situ* analysis resulted in observation of both smear and substrate absorptions, but because of differences in ATR penetration depths, the lower-frequency absorptions of the substrate paint appear much more prominently in the smear spectrum. Germanium elements are useful for cases such as this because of its shallow penetration depths. However, even if this sample were analyzed using a germanium element, it is possible that titanium dioxide absorptions might still be observed (although they would be expected to be diminished in comparison to Figure 3-31B).

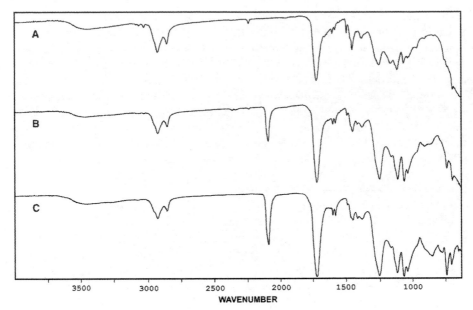

FIGURE 3-31 Spectra obtained using a zinc–selenide ATR objective of an infrared microscope of **(A)** a white automotive paint; **(B)** a green smear on the white automotive paint, analyzed *in situ*; and **(C)** the green automotive paint that is the source of the smear. (*Source:* Courtesy of John Reffner, Spectra-Tech.)

Analysts examining paint smears and other thin layers or deposits using ATR accessories should thus always be cognizant of the possible effects of penetration depth differences. This example also illustrates the desirability of having more than one type of ATR element available for use—particularly when a very wide variety of different objects may be subject to infrared examination—although this might not be practical for every laboratory.

FAR-INFRARED ANALYSES With the use of a thallous bromideiodide (KRS-5) element run on an extended range FT-IR spectrometer, it is possible to obtain ATR data down to 300 cm^{-1} (a diamond-coated KRS-5 element is much preferred, however, because KRS-5 is quite soft and thallium is very toxic). For the routine collection of far-infrared data, however, a beam condenser/DAC configuration is generally a more useful option for several reasons: (1) Somewhat smaller sample sizes can be analyzed using the DAC, which has an aperture of 0.8 mm versus 1 mm for a single-pass ATR accessory, and with the DAC, there is a convenient means to produce thinner and wider films; (2) the inorganic compound absorptions that may be sought in the far-infrared region are much less prone to anomalous dispersion distortions using transmittance analysis; (3) the vast majority of far-infrared data of inorganic compounds in spectral libraries was acquired using transmittance methods; (4) there are no restrictions on the index of refraction of the sample and even quite refractory inorganic compounds can be readily analyzed; and (5) ATR spectra typically exhibit a drop in their baselines for the lower frequencies (see, e.g., Figures 3-29D, 3-30A–I, and 3-31A–C), which is even more pronounced in the far-infrared region; this may make interpretation more difficult, as encountered with the green paint (Figure 3-31C) when trying to determine how much titanium dioxide might be present. If an ATR accessory is used for far-infrared analyses, it might help to use an ATR correction because this should help flatten the baseline.

For more information regarding ATR spectroscopy, the reader is referred to comprehensive treatments by Harrick[23] and Mirabella.[24–26]

Diffuse Reflectance (DRIFTS)

Diffuse reflectance measurements have been made in the mid-infrared region with dispersive instruments since the early 1960s,[27,28] but it was only with the use of an FT-IR spectrometer that it became practical to use such an accessory for routine analysis. Willey[29] was the first to demonstrate diffuse reflectance sampling on an FT–IR instrument, and Griffiths and coworkers performed most of the early studies on this technique.[30–48] The latter workers coined the acronym *DRIFT* (diffuse reflectance infrared Fourier transform) spectroscopy (DRIFTS) to describe this technique.

For the DRIFTS analysis of powdered samples, the powder is normally mixed with excess KBr similar to what is done for the preparation of a KBr pellet. There is no need to press a pellet, however, as one simply places this mixture into a sample cup. A reference spectrum of KBr is run and when ratioed and appropriately formatted, a spectrum very similar to that obtained with a KBr pellet results. DRIFTS sample cups are normally a few millimeters deep so that the powder can meet the requirement of "infinite" thickness. A DRIFTS sample meets this criterion if, by making it thicker, there is no longer any increase in the intensities of the absorption bands that are produced. This criterion is required by the mathematical model that was developed to describe diffuse reflectance sampling quantitatively, known as the *Kubelka–Munk model*.[49] Infinite thickness is realized for most infrared samples diluted with KBr when they are approximately 3 mm deep.[34]

THE KUBELKA–MUNK MODEL OF DIFFUSE REFLECTANCE   In the Kubelka–Munk model, the sample is a homogeneous medium that can both absorb and scatter light. Because scattering in the medium (caused by reflection, refraction, or diffraction) is a random process, radiation penetrating the sample surface quickly becomes isotropic, that is, the radiation is now traveling in all directions. Consider a very thin plate that is parallel to the surface of the sample, of thickness dx, located a distance x below the sample surface. The extension of the sample in the yz plane is assumed to be large enough so that edge effects are negligible. The intensity of the radiation incident on the plate from above is $I(x)$, whereas the intensity incident from below is $J(x)$. Because the radiation is isotropic, the distance, on average, that a light ray travels when passing through the plate is not dx but $2dx$ (which arises from integrating $dx/\cos\theta$ for all values of the incident angle θ).

Absorption and scattering in the medium are governed by an absorption coefficient, k, and a scattering coefficient, s. These constants represent the fractions of the light that are absorbed and scattered, respectively, in a unit distance; for this model, scattering refers specifically to the deflection of a light beam that causes it to go from an upward direction to a downward one, or vice versa, and not to any random deflection. The change in the intensity of $I(x)$ as it passes through the plate is

$$dI(x) = -kI(x)2dx - sI(x)2dx + sJ(x)2dx \qquad \textbf{3-11}$$

where the first two terms represent the fractions of the incident ray that are absorbed and scattered backward, respectively, and the third term represents the contribution to $I(x)$ from light scattered (downward in this case) from the light incident on the plate from below. Likewise, the change in the intensity of $J(x)$ as it passes through the plate from below is

$$-dJ(x) = -kJ(x)2dx - sJ(x)2dx + sI(x)2dx \qquad \textbf{3-12}$$

Equations 3-11 and 3-12 have opposite signs because they represent light traveling in opposite directions. The values of $J(x)$ and $I(x)$ at the surface are designated J_0 and I_0 and the two differential equations 3-11 and 3-12 can be solved to give an equation relating the diffuse reflectance from the sample, $R_\infty = J_0/I_0$, in terms of k and s:

$$\frac{(1 - R_\infty)^2}{2\,R_\infty} = \frac{k}{s} \qquad \textbf{3-13}$$

The absorption coefficient, k, is proportional to the product of the sample absorptivity, a, and concentration, c, and the equation can be rewritten as

$$F(R_\infty) = \frac{(1 - R_\infty)^2}{2\,R_\infty} = \frac{k}{s} = k'ac \qquad \textbf{3-14}$$

where k' is a constant and the expression $F(R_\infty)$ is known as the Kubelka–Munk function.

Transmittance sampling is governed by the more familiar Beer–Lambert equation, $A = abc$, where A is the absorbance [which is equal to the $\log_{10}(100/\%T)$, where $\%T$ is the percent transmittance], a is the sample absorptivity, b is the path length, and c is the sample concentration. The Kubelka–Munk function $F(R_\infty)$ is thus entirely analogous to the absorbance, $A = abc$, in transmittance analysis, because both equations express a quantity related to the amount of the incident light absorbed by a sample to its absorptivity and concentration. Note, however, that there is no term in the Kubelka–Munk function for the path length b, because there is no definite pathlength.

For further details of the Kubelka–Munk model, the reader is referred elsewhere.[49–52]

ANALYSIS METHODS In Equations 3-13 and 3-14, R_∞ varies between 0 and 1. An absolute measurement is not being made, however, and the reflectance of a sample relative to a nonabsorbing material (usually the KBr used to dilute the sample) is measured, giving the relative percentage of reflectance. For some commercial

DRIFTS accessories, both macro- and micro-sample cups are available, but the latter are preferred because they require less sample. Regardless of size, sample cups should be filled to the top with powder and leveled. For most accessories, the collection optics were designed to gather light from a small area and a very specific height (i.e., from a focal plane that is situated at the top of the sample cup). If the level of the sample is much above or below this plane, less light is collected. This not only decreases the collection efficiency, but if different powder levels are used for reference and sample, baselines significantly above or below 100% may result for the ratioed spectrum. With most commercial DRIFTS micro-sample cups, it is easy to produce flat sample surfaces at just the right height because the cups have a volcano shape with beveled outside edges, and one simply uses a spatula to scrape across the top of the cup to remove excess powder. Sample powders must also be ground to small particle sizes to minimize spectral distortions.

Presentation of spectral data in either reflectance or in the Kubelka–Munk format (Equation 3-14), which is linear in sample concentration similar to the absorbance format, are standard options with most FT-IR software; one reason why it is not desirable to have a reflectance spectrum with a baseline above 100% is that Equation 3-14 produces meaningless values when R_∞ is greater than 1. By convention, the Kubelka–Munk data are shown with absorptions increasing in the upward direction similar to a spectrum presented in the absorbance format. With some software, the Kubelka–Munk data can then be converted to a transmittance-like logarithmic scale (using an absorbance to transmittance conversion), and such presentations can be quite useful[5] for facilitating comparisons to spectra obtained in transmittance, because they are often nearly identical in appearance to KBr pellet spectra.

In comparison to KBr pellet sampling, DRIFTS offers several advantages. Already mentioned was the lack of a need to press a pellet, but, equally important, DRIFTS is a much more sensitive technique and has a considerably greater concentration range. In practical terms, these two factors mean that samples rarely have to be rerun, either because there is too little or too much analyte present. The sensitivity and very wide concentration range of DRIFTS are illustrated in Figure 3-32, which depicts DRIFTS spectra of codeine base obtained over a 100-fold concentration range. Figure 3-32A is the reflectance spectrum of a 500:1 dilution with KBr, and the transmittance format of this spectrum is depicted in Figure 3-32C. Figures 3-32D and 3-32E are transmittance format data for two other dilutions, 50:1 and 5:1, respectively. As a comparison, the KBr pellet spectrum of codeine base is shown in Figure 3-32F and the gross similarities between the DRIFTS data and the transmittance spectrum can be seen. Note that the DRIFTS data have very flat baselines and lack the broad O—H stretching band of adsorbed water often observed for KBr pellet spectra. The flat baselines may be beneficial when performing spectral searches of DRIFTS data, because strongly sloping baselines may present a problem, depending on the type of search algorithm used.

Because of the wide concentration range of DRIFTS, neat powders may be analyzed in some cases. Compounds analyzed in this manner should be relatively weak infrared absorbers and must be ground to very small particle sizes to minimize

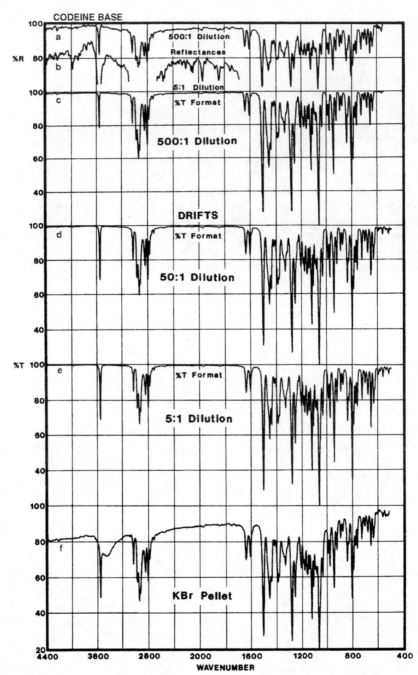

FIGURE 3-32 Spectra of codeine base. **(A)** DRIFTS spectrum of a 1:500 dilution with KBr depicted in the reflectance format. **(B)** Portions of the reflectance spectrum of a 1:5 dilution with KBr depicting the weak overtone/combination bands. **(C)** Spectrum A shown in the transmittance format. **(D)** DRIFTS spectrum of a 50:1 dilution with KBr shown in the transmittance format. **(E)** DRIFTS spectrum of a 5:1 dilution with KBr shown in the transmittance format. **(F)** KBr pellet spectrum.

specular reflectance distortions (discussed later). Figure 3-33A depicts the reflectance spectrum of PCP base ground to a fine powder and analyzed neat,[53] while the transmittance format of this data is shown in Figure 3-33C. Analogous spectra of suspected PCP from a case are presented in Figures 3-33B and 3-33D, respectively, whereas the spectrum of PCP base in a KBr pellet is shown in Figure 3-33E for comparison. Even for neat samples, spectra virtually identical to transmittance data are obtained with DRIFTS. Note that in the reflectance spectra (Figures 3-33A and 3-33B), the intensities of the very weak overtone/combination bands (above 3200 cm^{-1} and between 2600 and 1600 cm^{-1}) are enhanced significantly compared to their values in the pellet spectrum. These usually very weak features can be useful for providing additional characterizing and individualizing data for distinguishing between similar compounds.[5,53] Although the intensities of the very weak peaks are enhanced, the stronger absorptions are compressed (compare the strong peaks below 1600 cm^{-1} in Figures 3-33A and 3-33C). Consequently, for such concentrated samples, it is useful to present the data in both reflectance and transmittance formats to be able to observe the spectral details for the entire range of absorption intensities.

A second mode of DRIFTS analysis involves deposition of a solution containing an analyte (using a fairly volatile solvent) onto KBr prepacked in a cup. This method is more sensitive than mixing the same amount of analyte with KBr, with sensitivities of approximately 100 ng or less (depending on the analyte). Figures 3-34A and 3-34B depict reflectance and transmittance format spectra, respectively, of 0.02 microliter of phenyl-2-propanone (P2P) liquid that was deposited from a diethylether solution onto KBr. As a comparison, the spectrum of P2P liquid held between two KBr plates is shown in Figure 3-34C, and the excellent agreement between the data obtained by the two methods can be seen. The liquid film spectrum, however, required several drops of liquid for analysis.

A few materials, including some tablets,[31,53] polymeric foams,[54,55] or metallic paints,[56–58] can be analyzed directly using DRIFTS, but significant specular reflectance distortions occur in the spectra of most other materials analyzed directly. Some materials can also be rubbed on an abrasive silicon carbide disk, which produces a powder of the material that is then directly analyzed by DRIFTS.[59]

DRIFTS SAMPLING PROCESS When the scattering coefficient of Equation 3-11 is zero and the transmittance through a finite layer is calculated, the Kubelka–Munk equation reduces to the Beer–Lambert equation. The absorption process is the same for both modes of analysis and the primary difference between them lies in the nature of the pathlengths that the infrared radiation experiences.

In transmittance analysis, all of the light reaching the detector has traveled through the same thickness of sample and each photon has the same probability of being absorbed. A thicker sample results in greater absorption intensities. In DRIFTS analysis, there is no definite pathlength and a large number of different random routes, including multipass (zigzag) and serpentine routes, occur. In the absence of absorption, there is, however, an average or effective pathlength and this is determined solely by the scattering coefficient, s, in Equation 3-14. As s decreases (i.e., as the matrix becomes less opaque and more transparent), the penetration depths and average pathlengths increase. When the absorption coefficient, k, is nonzero, the

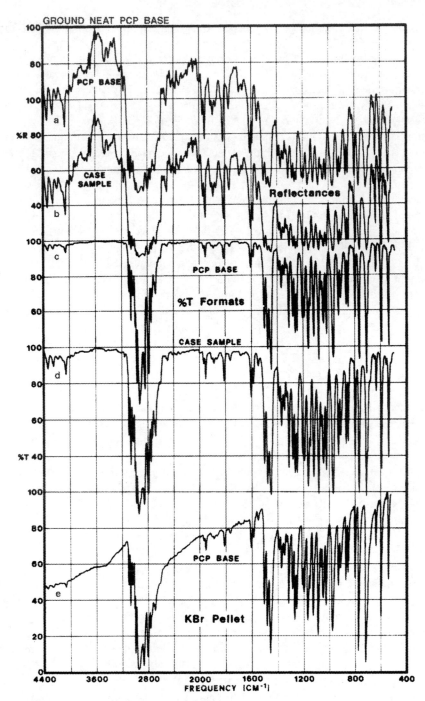

FIGURE 3-33 **(A)** DRIFTS reflectance spectrum of PCP base ground to a fine powder and analyzed neat. **(B)** DRIFTS reflectance spectrum of a case sample ground to a fine powder and analyzed neat. **(C)** Spectrum **(A)** depicted in the transmittance format. **(D)** Spectrum **(B)** depicted in the transmittance format. **(E)** KBr pellet spectrum of PCP base. (*Source:* From Reference 53, copyright ASTM, reprinted with permission.)

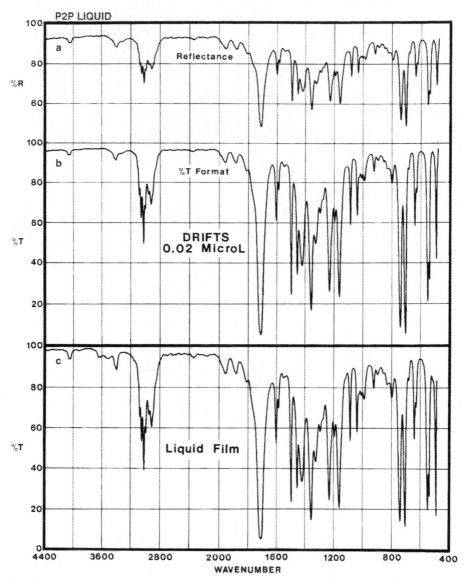

FIGURE 3-34   (A) DRIFTS reflectance spectrum of 0.02 microliter of P2P liquid deposited onto KBr from a diethylether solution. **(B)** Spectrum **(A)** depicted in the transmittance format. **(C)** Spectrum of P2P liquid pressed between two KBr plates.

absorption process itself contributes to shorter average pathlengths. Rays of a strongly absorbing wavelength, for example, do not travel far before an absorption occurs or the ray is scattered back to the surface. Even for very strongly absorbing wavelengths of neat powders, however, not all of the light is absorbed because some rays have been scattered back to the surface after traveling only a short distance. DRIFTS peaks therefore rarely bottom out (for R_∞ in Equation 3-14 to reach zero requires that either the absorption coefficient k be infinite or that the scattering coefficient s be zero, neither of which can occur). For weakly absorbing wavelengths, the opposite situation occurs and these rays are free to travel large distances before they are absorbed or scattered back to the surface. Such weakly absorbing wavelengths thus experience greater average pathlengths than those that absorb strongly. This differential analysis process is reflected in the gross appearance of a reflectance spectrum, and explains the enhanced intensities of the very weak peaks and the compression or "crunching" of the strong absorptions. DRIFTS differential pathlenghs are thus the reason for the increased sensitivity and very wide concentration range of this technique.

DIFFUSE VERSUS SPECULAR REFLECTANCE   When a collimated beam is incident on a flat mirror, all of the specularly reflected light travels in the same direction because the angle of incidence is equal to the angle of reflection. If this same beam is incident on a matte surface, such as the collection of nonabsorbing particles, individual rays may still be reflected from the particle surfaces such that the angle of incidence is equal to the angle of reflection. However, because the surface is irregular, many of the reflected rays are now traveling in different directions. Although this collection of reflected rays appears "diffuse," this type of reflection is still considered "specular." At the same time, there are contributions from reflected rays that have penetrated the sample surface, traveled various routes, then returned to the surface. The latter constitutes *diffuse reflectance*, and the distinguishing feature here is the fact that diffuse reflectance rays have traveled through the sample; that is, such rays penetrated the sample surface rather than being reflected from it. This distinction is mostly a moot point when the sample is not absorbing. **However, with an absorbing sample, this distinction is a critical one that determines the information content of the reflected light and also explains several artifacts that may occur in absorption spectroscopy.**

The reflection at an interface between two media having different indices of refraction has been discussed on several occasions. For light perpendicularly incident on such an interface where the two media have indices of refraction of n_1 and n_2, the reflection, R_p, is given by one of the Fresnel equations:

$$R_p = \frac{(n_1 - n_2)^2}{(n_1 + n_2)^2} \qquad \textbf{3-15}$$

When one medium is air and the index of refraction of the substance is n, this becomes

$$R_p = \frac{(n - 1)^2}{(n + 1)^2} \qquad \textbf{3-16}$$

When light from air is incident on a surface that can absorb all or part of the radiation, another modification of this equation is required. For light that is perpendicularly incident on an absorbing medium having an absorption coefficient, a, and an index of refraction, n, the specular reflection, R_p, is given by

$$R_p = \frac{(n - 1)^2 + a^2\lambda^2/16\pi^2}{(n + 1)^2 + a^2\lambda^2/16\pi^2} \qquad \textbf{3-17}$$

where λ is the wavelength of light.

As n increases in Equation 3-16, the 1 terms in both the numerator and denominator become less of a factor and the ratio slowly approaches 1 asymptotically. This is consistent with the observation that materials with high indices of refraction tend to be more reflective. For a material that can absorb certain wavelengths of the incident light, this same formula (Equation 3-16) applies for the nonabsorbing regions as well (because a in Equation 3-17 is zero), but how is the reflectance affected in a region where there is a strong absorption? According to Equation 3-17, when a is very large, the second terms in the numerator and denominator (which are identical) also cause the reflectance to approach one, but at a faster rate than that caused by an index of refraction increase. Although this premise may seem completely contrary to "common sense," **under certain conditions a material that absorbs strongly also reflects more light in the spectral region where the absorption occurs**. Equation 3-17 assumes a plane surface and perpendicular incidence, but it also describes qualitatively the reflection behavior for other angles, and for reflection from particles that are large compared to the wavelength of light. As the particle size decreases, however, the ratio of diffuse reflectance (as defined previously) to specular reflection increases.

Although this specular reflectance behavior may appear quite perplexing, it explains the workings of a very simple and common device that the reader likely uses on a daily basis (or more frequently for some): a mirror. The reason a mirror is a better reflector than a glass plate (which with $n = 1.5$ gives 0.04 for Equation 3-16, meaning only 4% of perpendicularly incident light reflects back from glass) is the metal coating (usually aluminum) of the mirror. Metals have very high indices of refraction and absorption coefficients, and Equation 3-17 may be close to 1 for some polished metal surfaces. However, if a shiny metal is ground to a very fine powder, it appears black because the increased diffuse reflectance now causes most of the incident light to be absorbed.

Another example of this effect is the *bronzing* of some dried inks. Such inks exhibit areas of luster that appear to be the complementary color of the ink itself. A dark blue ink may, for example, exhibit areas with a metallic appearance and a bronze hue. This is caused by a high concentration of strongly absorbing pigment particles forming a smooth film over the paper fibers, and this portion of the ink reflects more of the wavelengths that are normally absorbed by the pigment.

SPECULAR REFLECTANCE ANALYSIS   According to Equation 3-17, light incident on the surface of a material that has high indices of refraction and absorption coefficients reflects more of the wavelengths that absorb strongly. The reflectance spectrum of such a material should thus resemble an absorbance spectrum or an "upside down" transmittance spectrum. In general, inorganic compounds have higher absorption coefficients and indices of refraction than organic compounds, so they likely produce more specular reflectance when analyzed directly. Figures 3-35A and 3-35C are DAC spectra of two off-white materials that were suspected to be "rock" cocaine samples. Because they were both quite hard, a diamond scribe was used to form small amounts of powder for the DAC analyses. Both of the materials were also analyzed intact, with their surfaces situated at the focal plane of a DRIFTS accessory, giving the reflectance spectra shown in Figures 3-35B and 3-35D (reference spectra for these were obtained from the reflection of a mirror located at the focal plane of

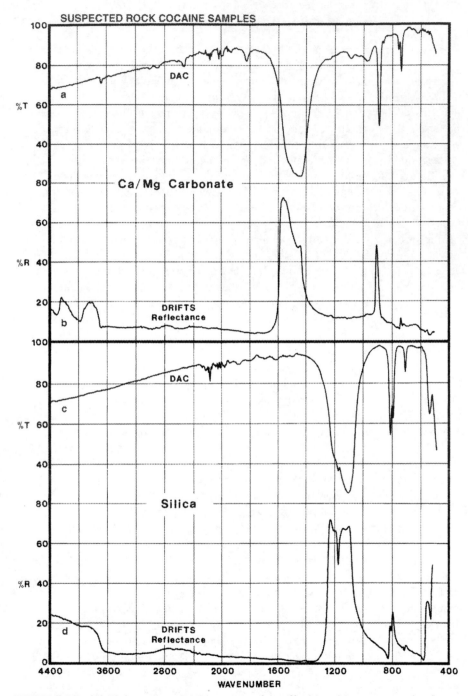

FIGURE 3-35 **(A)** High-pressure DAC spectrum of an off-white object suspected to be cocaine base (dolomite). **(B)** DRIFTS reflectance spectrum of this object analyzed intact using a mirror to collect the reference spectrum. **(C)** High-pressure DAC spectrum of an off-white object suspected to be cocaine base (quartz). **(D)** DRIFTS reflectance spectrum of this object analyzed intact using a mirror to collect the reference spectrum.

the accessory). The first sample (Figures 3-35A and 3-35B) was identified as dolomite (with the infrared spectrum indicating a carbonate similar to calcium carbonate and XRF data indicating the presence of calcium and magnesium), whereas the second sample is quartz. It should be emphasized that Figures 3-35B and 3-35D are *not* presented in absorbance and are raw reflectance data; the samples are not reflecting much of the incident light except where they normally absorb.

Even for materials with very high indices of refraction and absorption coefficients and very smooth surfaces, specular reflectance spectra are never an exact mirror image of the corresponding transmittance data (Figure 3-35). Some diffuse reflectance always occurs (Equation 3-17 is always less than 1), and this is more likely to be the case for the weaker absorptions. The maxima for the absorption coefficient and the index of refraction do not coincide (Figures 3-24A and 3-24B), and this situation is further complicated for birefringent materials. Because of this, the peak of an absorption maximum in diffuse reflectance and the corresponding peak of the reflectance maximum in specular reflectance usually occur at different frequencies, and derivative-shaped peaks are common in reflectance spectra of most objects analyzed intact. The ratio of specular to diffuse reflectance is also dependent on the surface characteristics of the sample, or the sample particle sizes. Specular reflectance analyses, however, can still be useful for screening, differentiation, and in a few cases, comparative analyses because no sample preparation is required, and even very hard materials are readily subject to examination. Specular reflectance analyses can be performed using either a DRIFTS accessory or the reflectance mode of an infrared microscope, with the sample surface located at the focal plane of the accessory.

As noted, a few organic polymeric foams[54,55] produce primarily diffuse reflectance when analyzed directly. This is possible for these materials because of their matte surfaces and, especially, their very low densities. The latter results in very low absorption coefficients (per unit distance), although minor distortions of some absorptions may still occur because of specular reflectance. To obtain distortion-free spectra of neat powders, samples with relatively low absorption coefficients and indices of refraction are required (which limits this technique to some organic compounds), and the powder particle sizes should be very small to ensure that almost all of the light incident on the powder undergoes diffuse and not specular reflectance.

Readers may encounter the term *specular reflectance analysis* as used in a somewhat different context than described here. *Specular reflectance accessories* were originally designed for use on dispersive spectrometers and were similar to DRIFTS accessories except that a mirror was located at the focal plane of the optics. A solution of a soluble analyte was deposited onto the mirror and the solvent allowed to evaporate, leaving a thin cast film of the sample. The incident infrared beam passed through the cast film, reflected off the mirror, then passed through the film again, producing a double-pass transmittance analysis. This type of analysis is now more commonly referred to as *reflection–absorption* to distinguish it from the specular reflectance analysis described earlier. Cast films are now more readily analyzed using a single-pass ATR accessory because the thickness of the sample is much less of a concern. The reflection–absorption method is most useful for the *in situ* analysis of thin films on reflective substrates, such as coatings on metal containers, and an infrared microscope is usually the preferred accessory, because it allows small select areas of the sample to be analyzed.

DRIFTS SPECTRAL VARIABILITIES AND ARTIFACTS   In the preparation of a KBr pellet, failure to grind the sample thoroughly results in opaque pellets and strongly sloping spectral baselines. Because sloping baselines are rare with DRIFTS, users of this technique may fail to grind their powders sufficiently. This results in variations in relative peak intensities and peak shapes caused by specular reflectance from the analyte particle surfaces. Because specular reflection increases as the absorption coefficients of the compound increase, there is more reflection for the stronger absorbing wavelengths. Wavelengths of weak absorptions, in contrast, are more likely to penetrate the particle surfaces and be absorbed. Compared to the DRIFTS spectrum of a sample that was ground thoroughly, the relative intensities of the weaker peaks are enhanced. Specular reflectance from the analyte particle surfaces also depends on indicies of refraction, and because of anomalous dispersion (Figure 3-24B), distortions of the absorption band shapes may occur. This is particularly true for inorganic compounds, which should be ground very thoroughly and diluted with a large amount of KBr to avoid or minimize such distortions.

As with the KBr pellet method, grinding the analyte with KBr may result in interactions between the sample and the matrix. The most common of these occurs when a salt, either organic or inorganic, undergoes ion exchange with KBr. This is illustrated by data collected for ephedrine sulfate.[15] The DAC spectrum of neat ephedrine sulfate is depicted in Figure 3-36A. When ephedrine sulfate and excess KBr are ground together for only a short period of time and pressed into a KBr pellet, spectra such as that shown in Figure 3-36B result. This spectrum is similar to that of the neat sample with a few minor differences. This same ephedrine sulfate/KBr mixture was then ground further—to the same extent as would be usually used—and the KBr pellet spectrum shown in Figure 3-36C was obtained. This spectrum differs considerably from that of ephedrine sulfate (Figure 3-36A), but is nearly identical to the KBr pellet spectrum of ephedrine HCl (Figure 3-36D), with the exception of two strong absorptions (near 1100 and 620 cm^{-1}) consistent with those of K_2SO_4 (Figure 3-16C). It is thus evident that an ion exchange occurred when ephedrine sulfate and KBr were ground together, producing ephedrine hydrobromide and potassium sulfate. Identical spectra are obtained using DRIFTS, so it is clear that the grinding process causes the ion exchange and not the pressure applied to create a pellet. The strong similarities between Figures 3-36C and 3-36D also suggest that the latter is probably the spectrum of ephedrine HBr and not ephedrine HCl, so an ion exchange likely also occurred when ephedrine HCl was ground with excess KBr. Ion exchange with the salt matrix has also been observed for methamphetamine salts,[60] and likely occurs for many other salts as well.

Although less common than ion exchange, oxidation–reduction reactions involving analyte and KBr may also occur during the grinding process. An oxidizing agent may, for example, oxidize bromide anion to free bromine (Br_2), which is brown; production of a brown color during the grinding process (along with possibly a faint pungent odor of Br_2) should alert the analyst that such a reaction might be

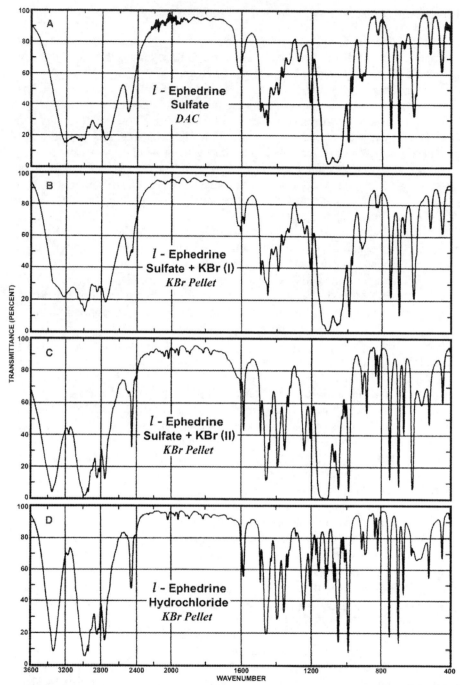

FIGURE 3-36 (A) High-pressure DAC spectrum of *l*-ephedrine sulfate. (B) KBr pellet spectrum of *l*-ephedrine sulfate ground together with excess KBr for a short period. (C) KBr pellet spectrum of *l*-ephedrine sulfate ground together thoroughly with excess KBr. (D) KBr pellet spectrum of *l*-ephedrine hydrochloride. (*Source:* From Reference 15, copyright ASTM, reprinted with permission.)

occurring. For cases where ion exchange or a reaction with KBr may be a problem, alternative methods that do not require mixing with KBr, such as the use of the DAC or a single-pass ATR accessory, should be considered.

As discussed for the DAC, in a few cases the analyte may be pressure sensitive, and the pressure induced when grinding the powder for a DRIFTS analysis may be sufficient to cause a transformation. Because the use of the DAC is not usually a viable alternative in such a case, a possible solution might be to press the powder gently onto the element of a single-pass ATR accessory without using the accessory press, or possibly to deposit a solution of the analyte onto the element to form a film (although this process itself might also cause a transformation—see later). Alternatively, if the particle sizes of the sample are already quite small, simply diluting the powder with excess KBr without grinding and using DRIFTS may be a solution. This method was found to be a useful means to obtain spectra of a group of pressure-sensitive organic pigments, the benzimidazolones,[61] which were found to undergo transformations readily when analyzed using a DAC or when subjected to grinding.

The method of depositing a solution of analyte onto KBr is a more sensitive mode of DRIFTS analysis, but also one that may result in more spectral variabilities. The deposition process itself is not unlike that of performing column chromatography, as the analyte absorbs onto the KBr particle surfaces. This results in a particularly efficient matrix for DRIFTS analysis if each of the KBr particles is coated with analyte. Further, the analyte tends to be concentrated near the surface of the KBr where most of the DRIFTS analysis takes place. However, if there is only a small amount of analyte and it is located in a thin zone near the surface, the Kubelka–Munk criteria of uniform sample and infinite thickness are not met, which affects the relative peak intensities of the spectrum. In the extreme case of a very small amount of analyte, the analyte absorbed onto the KBr particles may consist primarily of a monolayer. Because of strong interactions between the analyte and the KBr surface, this may produce spectra with notable differences compared to those normally obtained. This only occurs, however, when very small amounts of sample are analyzed, so it is not likely to be encountered often.

Two other effects may also be observed with analyte depositions, but these are not limited to DRIFTS and may be observed with other infrared analysis methods as well. When an analyte is dissolved in a solvent and the solvent is allowed to evaporate, the analyte may recrystallize immediately or it may first form a noncrystalline glass. In some cases, the glass spontaneously crystallizes with time, but this is not always the case. When grinding such a noncrystalline material with KBr, the trituration (scratching) process itself often causes the material to crystallize. When an analyte is deposited from solution onto KBr, however, this may not occur, and spectra of the noncrystalline glass may result. Regardless of which analysis method is used, for compounds that are very difficult to crystallize, spectra of the material in the noncrystalline form should be acquired and used as a reference (the noncrystalline form can usually be readily produced by simply evaporating a solution of the standard). For polymorphic compounds that are dissolved in a solvent, an additional complication arises because it is not always known which polymorph will crystallize, and a mix of polymorphs might even result. It may be necessary to acquire reference spectra of each polymorph (or even mixed polymorphs), but the first preference is to use a method that avoids dissolution in a solvent.

Vapor Cells

Vapor cells are one of the few infrared accessories that have not changed since the era of dispersive spectrometers, but with FT-IR instruments, high-resolution vapor spectra (0.125 cm^{-1} or higher) with excellent SNRs can be readily obtained with such devices. As noted, high-resolution data are required to observe the individual vibrational–rotational transitions of small molecules.

The typical length of an infrared vapor cell is 10 cm and sample vapor pressures significantly less than 1 atmosphere are normally sufficient to produce strong absorptions. Cells with demountable windows, which are pressed against rubber O-rings with screw-on caps, are preferred because they allow the windows (usually KBr) and the inside of the cell to be polished or cleaned periodically.

A large-volume syringe is a useful device to draw a sample of vapor and inject it into the cell, which typically has two ports with valves for filling or emptying the cell. Usually, the vapors above a liquid are analyzed and the syringe tip can be positioned in the mouth of the container to draw a headspace sample and then inject it into the cell; it may be necessary to do this several times, depending on the volume of the syringe and the vapor pressure of the analyte above the liquid. As a reference spectrum, a similar volume of air drawn from the same area in the room where the sample was collected can be used (this is much more important when low concentrations of sample are involved). Alternatively, for vapors collected from aqueous solutions (such as hydrochloric acid or ammonium hydroxide), it might be helpful to collect the vapors above water as a reference.

In any case, it is likely that there will be differences in the concentrations of water vapor and carbon dioxide in the cell for the reference versus the sample. Inverse peaks of these atmospheric constituents (indicative of more water or carbon dioxide in the reference than in the sample—see Figure 3-13) as well as "normal" peaks may occur, and it is important to remember that absorptions of these may arise from vapors in the cell, the instrument compartment, or both. For FT-IR instruments equipped with a purge system where the flow of purge gas can be controlled, some compensation for water vapor and carbon dioxide can be made by controlling the amount of atmospheric gases in the instrument. Spectral subtractions using stored spectra of water vapor and carbon dioxide vapors (obtained at the same resolution as sample) can also be performed, and these should produce "clean" results because the interactions between the vapors are minimal. However, for the vapor samples that are likely to be analyzed in forensic laboratories (such as CO, Figure 3-7A, HCl, Figure 3-7B; NH$_3$, Figure 3-11; and N$_2$O, Figure 3-13), weak or even moderate absorptions of water vapor and carbon dioxide are not usually a problem.

When high spectral resolutions are used, longer collection times are normally required. The total collection time should be dictated by the intensities of the vapor absorptions (i.e., the amount of sample) and the analyst's ability to distinguish the analyte peaks of interest clearly from noise.

Gas Chromatography/Fourier Transform Infrared (GC/FT-IR) Spectroscopy

The characterization, identification, and comparison of materials comprised of various mixtures are prominent problems faced by the forensic scientist. For complex mixtures, and especially for limited sample sizes, the various chromatographic methods have been the clear choice for achieving separations. As a means of identifying one or more of the components of the mixture, however, chromatography alone is usually not sufficient. Individually, these components may be identified using spectrometric methods, but these methods are almost never useful in identifying constituents of an unresolved complex mixture. The coupling of chromatography and one or more spectrometric analyses, however, produces an extremely powerful tool, and these methods (variously referred to as hyphenated,[62-65] hybrid, slashed, combined, or coupled techniques) have revolutionized the analyses of complex mixtures.

The forensic scientist is probably most familiar with one of the earliest such pairings, gas chromatography/mass spectrometry (GC/MS), which is undoubtedly the most widely used coupled technique in the forensic science laboratory. Hyphenated techniques involving infrared spectroscopy, in contrast, were never practical using dispersive instruments because of their low sensitivities and slow scanning speeds. Such techniques are possible with an FT-IR spectrometer, however, and since the 1980s, at least four different configurations coupling chromatography with infrared spectroscopy have been manufactured commercially. In one of these, known as the Cryolect™, the effluent from a GC was trapped in a cryogenically cooled (10–15° K) argon matrix,[66] and a thin-layer chromatography/FT-IR system, known as the Chromalect™, was also marketed.[67] Although both the Cryolect and the Chromalect had considerable potential for forensic applications, neither was a commercial success and they are no longer sold. Two coupled FT-IR accessories that are available include GC/FT-IR and another GC/FT-IR cryogenic trapping system. The former is discussed in this section.

Analogous to a GC/MS analysis, a GC/FT-IR system continuously collects spectral data as the eluants emerge from a GC column and stores these data "on-the-fly." A heated transfer line from the column directs the eluant through a light pipe, which consists of a heated narrow tube. The light pipe, which is coated on its inner surface with an inert reflective material such as gold, is usually around 10 or 15 cm long, with an inner diameter of 1 mm. A GC/FT-IR system usually requires an MCT detector because of its greater sensitivity and faster scan rate. Analogous to the total ion chromatogram of GC/MS, GC/FT-IR employs a total response chromatogram reflecting the infrared absorption intensities of the eluants. This response chromatogram is usually based on a Gram–Schmidt reconstruction,[68] which, by processing interferograms, gives a measure of the total infrared absorbance for the entire spectral range. Chromatograms can also be reconstructed based on absorptions that occur in selected regions of the spectrum.

Because the absorptions of a heated vapor are being measured, the appearance of a GC/FT-IR spectrum differs somewhat from that of the same material analyzed in a condensed phase—particularly solids. The infrared absorptions of crystalline organic compounds, for example, are typically fairly sharp and may occur as multiplets because of crystal lattice effects. GC/FT-IR spectral bands, in contrast, tend to be broader with less structure present. A spectral resolution of 8 cm^{-1} is typically used with GC/FT-IR systems, because this permits a faster collection time and there is usually no significant loss in spectral detail.

As a result of these spectral differences, the reference library for a GC/FT-IR analysis should consist of vapor spectra. Because GC/FT-IR spectra do not, in general, exhibit as much detail as crystalline solid spectra, there may be fewer spectral features present for differentiating between some closely related compounds. In addition, many GC/FT-IR systems use a narrow-band MCT detector, which limits the spectral range. However, GC/FT-IR spectra tend to be highly reproducible, and problems with formation of noncrystalline glasses, polymorphism, hydration, impurity bands, and so on, do not occur (assuming a complete chromatographic separation has occurred). Relatively minor spectral differences, together with chromatographic retention times, may thus be used for differentiating between similar compounds.

Further discriminating information may be obtained with the use of a gas chromatography/Fourier transform infrared spectroscopy/mass spectrometry (GC/FT-IR/MS) system. This double-hyphenated technique is particularly appropriate because of the complementary nature of infrared and mass spectral data, and this instrument has been widely touted for its ability to readily distinguish between closely related isomers and individual members of a homologous series. An example of this is shown in Figure 3-37, which depicts[69] infrared and mass spectral data for two isomers, amphetamine and N-methylphenethylamine, obtained using a GC/FT-IR/MS instrument.

A GC/FT-IR/MS system may be configured either in series (with the FT-IR analysis occurring first, because it is nondestructive) or in parallel. For the latter, the majority of the GC eluant is directed to the light pipe, as the infrared analysis requires more sample than the mass spectral analysis. An additional option is to have a completely parallel system involving two separate GC columns, which may further utilize the selectivity of two different GC liquid phases.

For more information about GC/FT-IR[70–73] and GC/FT-IR/MS,[74–79] the reader is referred elsewhere.

Gas Chromatography/Cryogenic Trapping Infrared Analysis

A GC/FT-IR analysis provides an excellent means to obtain spectra of individual volatile components in a mixture, but the infrared end of this combined technique is not optimal regarding sensitivity. The primary limiting factor here is the short residence time of the analyte in the light pipe, and the normal method of increasing the SNR by averaging more scans is thus not applicable. One solution to this problem is to condense the GC analytes as they elute. In the Cryolect, analytes were trapped in an argon matrix, but this required an expensive cryogenic refrigeration system to freeze argon. As an alternative, the FT-IR analysis of GC components condensed as solid films at liquid nitrogen temperatures or higher has been performed.[80–82] This method allows a more commercially viable cryo-trapping accessory to be manufactured, because an elaborate refrigeration system is not required.

The condensing surface for a cryo-trapping system may consist of either a window for transmittance analysis or a reflective substrate for reflection-absorption

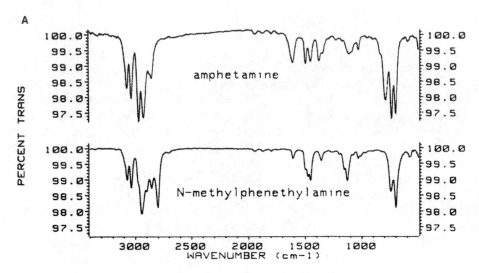

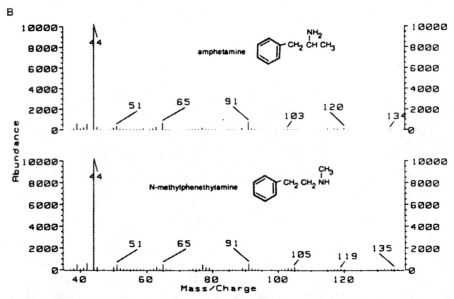

FIGURE 3-37   Infrared and mass spectra of two isomers, amphetamine and N-methylphenethylamine, obtained using a GC/FT-IR/MS instrument. **(A)** Infrared spectra. **(B)** Mass spectra.   (*Source:* From Reference 69, reproduced from the *Journal of Chromatographic Science* by permission of Preston Publications, a division of Preston Industries, Inc.)

analysis. Because the surface is moving, the GC components are separated spatially along a segment of the window or substrate. The temperature of the surface is below the freezing points of the analytes so they all condense to form solid films, but also well above the boiling point of the helium carrier gas. The system is under a high vacuum to prevent condensation of water and carbon dioxide onto the surface and to remove helium and sublime any ice that may form.

The incident beam of the FT-IR spectrometer is focused on the very small area where an analyte film has just been deposited, so spectra are collected and stored in real time (except for a slight delay between condensation and analysis because the surface is moving slowly). Unlike a conventional or lightpipe GC/FT-IR analysis, the separated components may later be reexamined on the cooled disk, resulting in much lower detection limits.

Various methods may be used to construct an FT-IR chromatogram "on-the-fly," such as recording the absorbance value of the strongest peak of each spectrum, or the sums of the absorbance values of several of the strongest peaks. Reconstructed chromatograms based on the absorption or absorptions in a specific spectral window or windows can also be produced.

An example of a commercial GC/cryo-trapping FT-IR system is the DiscovIR-GC™, which was introduced in 2006. In this system, the GC effluent is condensed onto a revolving zinc selenide disk held between $-100°C$ and $-30°C$. The temperature is controlled by liquid nitrogen cooling and use of a heater. The width of the track that is subject to infrared analysis is 100 μm and a narrowband MCT detector is used with a spectral range of 4000 to 700 cm^{-1}. During the analysis, interferograms are collected at the rate of up to two scans per second (achieved when using a spectral resolution of 8 cm^{-1}). Approximately 50 hours of chromatographic samples can be stored on the disk at one time. The sensitivity of this system is in the range of a few hundred picograms. Spectra of amphetamine, methamphetamine, and phentermine obtained using the DiscovIR-GC are depicted in Figures 3-38A, 3-38B, and 3-38C, respectively. Note the differences between the spectra of amphetamine obtained as a solid film (Figure 3-38A) and as a vapor using GC/FT-IR (Figure 3-37A).

Photoacoustic Spectroscopy

The *photoacoustic effect*, a process by which radiant energy is converted into acoustic energy, was discovered by Alexander Graham Bell in 1880 (at about the same time, Bell arranged a research grant for Albert Michelson that funded the development of the interferometer). When light is absorbed by a confined gas, the heating effects cause the pressure of the gas to increase. If this light is modulated (i.e., turned on and off repeatedly), the pressure of the gas also increases and decreases. The propagation of this oscillating pressure is sound (for those frequencies to which our ears respond), and a microphone can be used to detect these pressure differences. For a solid or liquid sample surrounded by a confined gas, a similar effect occurs as thermal transfer from the heated sample to an envelope of surrounding gas causes this gas to expand.

As described previously, the intensity of each wavelength of infrared radiation passing through an FT-IR spectrometer is modulated as a result of the interference

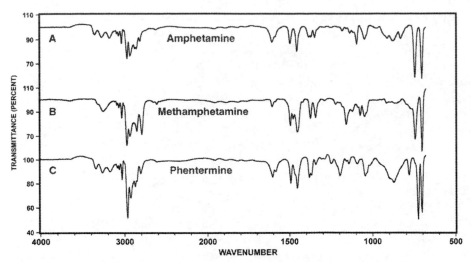

FIGURE 3-38 Spectra of three phenylethylamines obtained using a GC/Cryo-Trapping/FT-IR system, the DiscovIR-GC. The three were separated by gas chromatography and deposited onto a cooled zinc–selenide disk. **(A)** Amphetamine. **(B)** Methamphetamine. **(C)** Phentermine. (*Source:* Data courtesy of Spectra Analysis, Inc.)

caused by the pathlength differences. The rate of this modulation is directly proportional to both the wavenumber and the mirror velocity. Light from an FT-IR instrument can therefore be used to produce a photoacoustic effect, which may be detected if the mirror velocity is such that the modulation frequencies fall within the response range of the microphone.

The use of an FT-IR instrument to obtain a photoacoustic infrared spectrum of a solid was first reported in 1979.[83,84] Shortly thereafter, FT-IR photoacoustic accessories became available commercially. A photoacoustic accessory for condensed phase samples consists of a small chamber housing a sample cup, a salt window through which the infrared beam passes, and a microphone detector. The amplified acoustic interferogram from the microphone is processed by the FT-IR in a manner similar to what is done for a conventional interferogram. An acoustic interferogram normally exhibits a relatively large frequency-dependent phase shift, caused by the lag time involved in the thermal transfer process.

Because a photoacoustic signal is generated only for absorbing wavelengths, no detector response occurs for nonabsorbing spectral regions. An unratioed photoacoustic spectrum thus has the appearance of an absorbance format plot, with upward-tending peaks indicative of absorptions. To compensate for the wavelength intensity differences of the source, the photoacoustic spectrum of an essentially totally absorbing substance, such as carbon black, is often used as a reference. This reference spectrum is similar in appearance to a normal reference spectrum obtained using a DTGS detector, and such spectra are sometimes used in lieu of a carbon black photoacoustic reference.

In photoacoustic spectroscopy, only those portions of the sample that can transfer their acquired heat rapidly to the surrounding gas contribute to the analysis process. The effective sampling depth of this method is thus relatively shallow (typically of the order of tens of micrometers) and depends on a number of factors, including the modulation rate, wavelength, and thermal transfer properties of the material. Because the bulk of most objects is not being analyzed, this technique permits many materials to be analyzed intact without any sample preparation. Specular reflectance distortions are minimal and photoacoustic spectra are much less dependent on sample morphology or particle size[85,86] than most other techniques.

One interesting feature of photoacoustic spectroscopy is the ability to vary the sampling depth. This capability results from the signal generation process, which involves heat transport from within the sample to the surface where the photoacoustic signal is then generated in the gas. If the modulation frequency of the light generating the photoacoustic signal is increased, there is less time for heat transport to occur within the sample because of the finite velocities of the thermal waves. This results in a shallower sampling depth. The modulation frequency of a photoacoustic measurement can easily be varied by changing the interferometer mirror velocity.

This feature can be quite useful when analyzing some inhomogeneous materials. As an example, Figure 3-39 depicts how this process may be used to help deduce the compositions of a bicomponent fiber. Figures 3-39B and 3-39C depict photoacoustic spectra of a single 20-μm diameter bicomponent fiber composed of a nylon sheath and a polyester (PET) core obtained using two different mirror velocities. Figure 3-39B was obtained with a mirror velocity of 20 kHz (which denotes the frequency of the

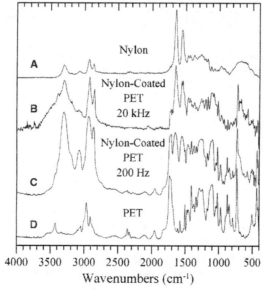

FIGURE 3-39 Spectra of a single 20-μm diameter bicomponent fiber consisting of a polyester (PET) core and a nylon sheath compared to spectra of nylon and polyester. All data were obtained using a photoacoustic accessory. **(A)** Nylon. **(B)** A shallow (20 kHz) sampling of the bicomponent fiber. **(C)** A deep (200 kHz) sampling of the bicomponent fiber. **(D)** Polyester. (*Source:* Figure courtesy of Dr. John F. McClelland, Iowa State University, reprinted with permission.)

helium–neon laser interferogram) and Figure 3-39C shows data for the same sample obtained using a 200-Hz mirror velocity (representing a 100-fold reduction in mirror velocity). As a comparison, photoacoustic spectra of nylon and polyester fibers are shown in Figures 3-39A and 3-39D, respectively. For the shallower sampling, the spectrum (Figure 3-39B) is primarily that of nylon (Figure 3-39A), whereas prominent absorptions of both nylon and polyester (Figure 3-39D) are seen for the deeper sampling (Figure 3-39C).

As an alternative to the use of a microphone, the deflection of a laser beam that passes above the surface of the sample may be used to detect a heating effect. This deflection arises from variations in the refractive index of the gas caused by the modulated incident radiation. A technique based on this detection scheme, known as *FT-IR photothermal beam deflection spectrometry*, has been developed[87] and produces spectral data similar to those obtained by the photoacoustic method. One of the advantages of this system is that relatively large objects that may not fit into the photoacoustic chamber can be analyzed. For more information about photoacoustic and photothermal beam deflection spectroscopies, the reader is referred elsewhere.[88–94]

SPECTRAL DATA EVALUATION AND INTERPRETATION

Spectral data interpretation specific to each of the FT-IR sampling accessories and analysis methods is emphasized in the preceding section. Here, the discussion involves some aspects of data evaluation and interpretation that occur for all analysis methods or span several different methods.

Atmospheric Absorptions

Even for instruments purged with air from driers, weak absorptions of water vapor and carbon dioxide (Figure 3-10C) might still be observed in some spectra. The importance of recognizing these features as arising from atmospheric constituents cannot be overemphasized, as forensic scientists have been known to attribute them to samples or to absorptions of both questioned and control samples in cases involving comparisons. This may be more of a problem with the two carbon dioxide absorptions because they appear to be more like those of samples, whereas the O—H stretches and pure rotations of water vapor, if weak, are more likely to be attributed to noise. If there is a question as to the identity of such a peak or peaks, analysts should examine the rest of the spectrum for other absorptions of the atmospheric constituent that is suspected. If a sharp peak at 667 cm^{-1} is observed, for example, the 2350 cm^{-1} doublet of carbon dioxide should also be sought to confirm that extraneous features are present. If absorptions of atmospheric constituents cannot be avoided, they should be removed using correction software because their presence may otherwise mask the identity of some minor constituents in certain types of evidence, as discussed later.

Sample Effects

The nature of certain samples may cause what appear to be anomalous or "poor" spectra, although these result from the inherent properties of the materials and not from lack of sufficient sample preparation. Two examples are presented.

The spectrum of a heavily pigmented metallic automotive paint analyzed with a DAC is depicted in Figure 3-40B. The very low baseline of this spectrum might lead an analyst to conclude that the sample is too thick and to prepare a thinner slice. The simplest means to determine if the sample is too thick, however, is to see if the strongest peaks have bottomed out (as occurs for the strongest absorptions of Figure 3-40G). This is not the case here. The low baseline is caused by the presence of a very high concentration of opaque metal flakes. The baseline of 17% suggests that the metal flakes are blocking roughly 83% of the infrared light incident on this paint slice.

Because of properties of the logarithmic scale, the data obtained by presenting this spectrum full scale from 18% to 0% transmittance is *identical* to that obtained by converting the spectrum to absorbance, subtracting a constant, then converting it back to transmittance (i.e., to performing a baseline adjustment). For either type of expansion, the spectrum depicted in Figure 3-40A results. This holds true, however, only if data are presented between a specified value and 0%T (and the sample has also covered the entire area through which the beam passes).

The spectra of two automotive paints, obtained as thin slices placed over a 1-mm diameter aperture, are shown in Figures 3-40E and 3-41A. Analysts—particularly those who have used KBr pellets—may associate strongly sloping baselines with poor or inadequate sample preparation. The sloping baselines of these two spectra, however, are caused by the presence of large amounts of carbon black in these two black nonmetallic finishes. Carbon black absorbs the higher frequencies of infrared light more strongly, and other materials containing large amounts of this pigment, such as tire rubber, also produce spectra exhibiting this effect.

Sample Preparation Effects

Figure 3-40F is the spectrum of a white interior house paint analyzed as a slice placed over a 1-mm diameter aperture. This paint spectrum contains broad peaks of a silicate and titanium dioxide but they have not bottomed out as they have for the spectrum of a thicker slice of this same paint (Figure 3-40G). This thicker slice was rerun, giving the spectrum shown in Figure 3-40H; the question then is, what is causing this strange-looking result? For Figure 3-40G, the slice covered the entire area of the aperture; but for the second analysis, the slice was moved so that it covered only a portion of this area. In fact, Figure 3-40H indicates that for the second analysis, the slice covered nearly 40% of the area because 60% of the incident light beam is still reaching the detector for those frequencies completely absorbed by the sample (slightly more light can be seen to be reaching the detector for the longer wavelengths that are completely absorbed—this is caused by stray light arising from diffraction, which affects the longer wavelengths more).

For spectra where the strongest absorptions have very flat bottoms, as in Figure 3-40H, it is easier to recognize the effects of not having a sample that completely covers the area through which the infrared beam passes. This is not usually the case, however, and the point to remember is that by having "holes" in the sample, distorted spectra may result. When not severe, this is manifested as differences in relative peak intensities.

Although it is thus desirable to prepare samples such that the entire analysis area is occupied, this may not always be feasible. This is rarely a problem when

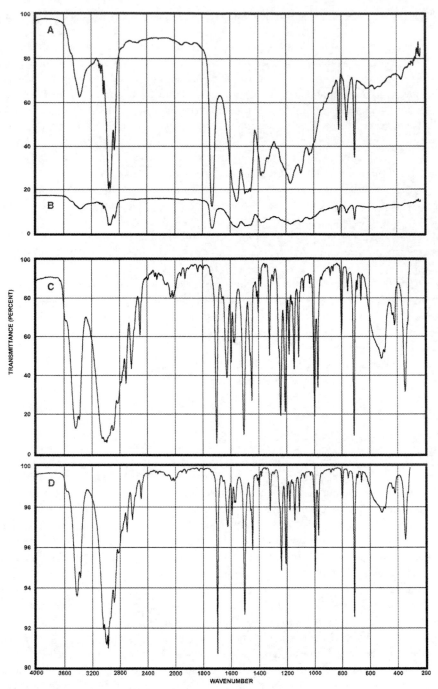

FIGURE 3-40 Spectra of **(A)** a silver metallic acrylic melamine enamel automotive paint pressed onto a single anvil of the DAC. The paint contains a very high concentration of metal flakes and the baseline of the spectrum was adjusted. **(B)** Same data as **(A)** before the baseline was adjusted. **(C)** Cathinone hydrochloride in a DAC. **(D)** Same data as **(C)** compressed and depicted between 100% and 90% transmittance.

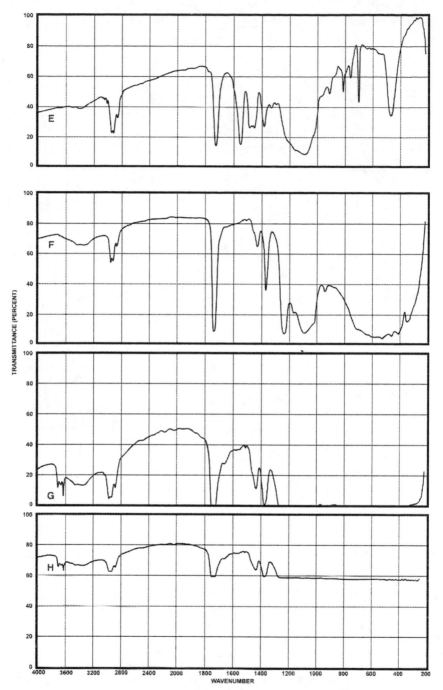

FIGURE 3-40 *Continued*   **(E)** A black nonmetallic acrylic melamine enamel automotive paint analyzed as a thin slice placed over a 1-mm aperture. The paint has a flat finish caused by the presence of a large amount of a silica extender pigment. **(F)** A white latex house paint analyzed as a thin slice placed over a 1-mm aperture. **(G)** A thicker slice of the house paint in **(F)**. **(H)** The same slice as **(G)**, repositioned so that it covers only a portion of the aperture.

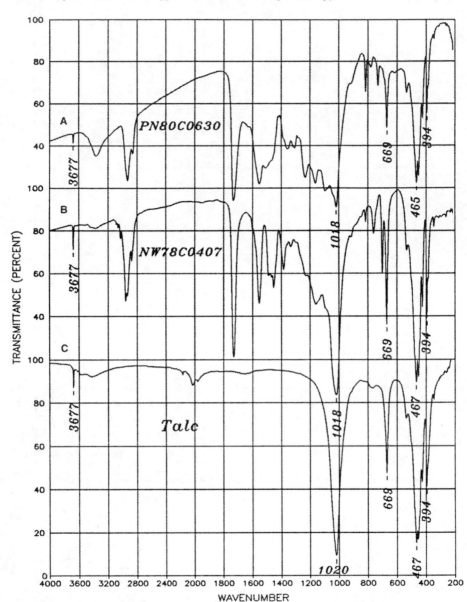

FIGURE 3-41 Spectra of talc and two black nonmetallic acrylic melamine enamel automotive paints from the *Reference Collection of Automotive Paints* analyzed as a thin slices placed over a 1-mm aperture. Both paints have flat finishes caused by the presence of large amounts of talc. **(A)** PN80C0630. **(B)** NW78C0407. **(C)** Talc and excess CsI in a DAC. (*Source:* From Reference 95, copyright ASTM, reprinted with permission.)

using the infrared microscope, where an aperture is chosen for a particular specimen, but it may occur when an analyst wishes to obtain far-infrared data for a sample and there is not enough material to completely cover the face of a DAC. In cases where a large analysis area is unoccupied, a better representation of the spectrum is obtained by presenting full scale the spectrum depicted between the baseline and the normal bottom, if this can be estimated (i.e., if the sample occupies roughly 60% of the analysis area, then data should be depicted from the baseline to 40%T or so).

Nonlinear Scale Effects

When transmission methods are used for analysis, spectral data may be presented in either percent transmittance or in absorbance. There are merits and limitations to both formats, but in general, the transmittance presentation is preferred for most forensic analyses because its logarithmic scale allows the weaker absorptions of the sample to be observed more readily. More peaks can thus be used for characterizing or comparing evidence, and this feature is especially helpful when analyzing materials comprised of several components. These include many synthetic polymeric substances (plastics, rubbers, foams, adhesives, tapes, etc.), building materials, paints, and other composites, all of which many contain varying quantities of inorganic constituents. The quantities of one or more of the constituents may be minor and they are more readily detected in transmission spectra.

Although the absorbance mode allows one to make a better comparison between the relative intensities of two absorptions, minor differences in intensities are generally not reliable indicators of differences between two spectra or two samples. To attach significance to such minor differences would require ideal samples and a considerable amount of background work, including demonstrating that the precision of the method is high enough to justify such an opinion, and also that the sample or samples are not inhomogeneous. For materials that are not isotropic, such as drawn fibers or sheets of plastic and single crystals, the orientation of the sample in the beam may also affect relative peak intensities, and as demonstrated, when the analysis area is not completely covered with sample, this can likewise occur.

One feature of the transmittance scale is the compression of absorptions as the baseline gets lower. In absorbance, there is no upper limit to the intensity of a peak, whereas in transmission, the scale ends at 0%T, so if the baseline is low, peaks *appear* to be less intense. The absorption intensities of the paint spectrum having a low baseline (Figure 3-40B) are not weak, as seen in the baseline-adjusted presentation of this same data (Figure 3-40A). This compression effect may be especially deceiving when a spectrum has a strongly sloping baseline and one is comparing relative intensities for peaks at high and low frequencies. The sharp hydroxyl stretch of talc at 3677 cm^{-1}, for example, may appear to be weaker than normal as a result of the pronounced baseline slope (compare Figures 3-41A and 3-41C). If such spectra are subject to baseline flattening (as opposed to a baseline adjustment, which only raises or lowers the entire spectrum), this should always be done in absorbance and not in percentage transmittance; otherwise, relative peak intensities are not reproduced faithfully.

There are two ways of producing an ordinate expansion for a spectrum presented in transmittance, and it is important to note that these two presentations may produce spectra that appear to have different relative intensities. This difference is most pronounced when a sample with very weak absorptions is compared to one with normal intensities, and two different transmission scales are used. Figure 3-40C is the DAC spectrum of cathinone HCl depicted between 100%T and 0%T, with the strongest peak having an intensity of 5%T. This same data was converted to absorbance, scaled by a factor of 0.035, then converted back to transmittance (to produce data that would be obtained if a much thinner sample were analyzed). The strongest absorption is now at 91%T and data are depicted full scale between 100%T and 90%T (Figure 3-40D). Note the differences in the relative intensities between Figures 3-40C and 3-40D when comparing the strong and weak absorptions. It should be reiterated that this does not occur if spectral data between a given%T value and 0%T are depicted full scale. Also, this example represents what is likely a worst-case scenario, because it represents a difference in sample thickness of a factor of 28, but differences in the amounts or sizes of material received for questioned and known specimens are likely the norm in forensic science, and analysts should be aware of this possibility when comparisons of spectra are made in this manner.

Low-Frequency Absorptions

The infrared microscope has assumed a very prominent role in the forensic science laboratory because it allows for the analysis of very small items of evidence. However, the limited spectral range of this accessory prevents the observation of low-frequency absorptions. With the use of an extended range FT-IR spectrometer equipped with CsI optics and a DTGS detector, spectral data to 225 cm^{-1} can be obtained. Forensic scientists should thus be aware of the types of compounds that have absorptions in the 700 to 200 cm^{-1} region that are important in characterizing or identifying them.

As noted previously, the 1400 to 800 cm^{-1} spectral region (the *fingerprint region*) is particularly useful for differentiating between closely related organic compounds, owing to the vibrations of compounds based on a carbon skeleton. Although a few organic compounds have characteristic absorptions below 700 cm^{-1}, such as the stretching modes of bromides and iodides, even these compounds can usually be identified based solely on the absorptions above this region.

The term *fingerprint region* does not apply to inorganic compounds, however, and these often have more characteristic absorptions *below* 800 cm^{-1}. There are several reasons for this. Because most inorganic compounds are composed of heavier atoms than those of organic compounds, they tend to have lower vibrational frequencies. Also, for some inorganic compounds, bonding that is intermediate between covalent and ionic occurs, and as noted for ionic salts, the coulombic forces are not directional and the weaker force constants between adjacent ions or atoms cause their vibrations to occur at lower frequencies.

For some inorganic compounds, all or most of their absorptions occur below 700 cm^{-1}. Many inorganic oxide salts, for example, fall into this category, as illustrated by the absorptions of the nine oxides depicted in Figure 3-42[95] (these spectra

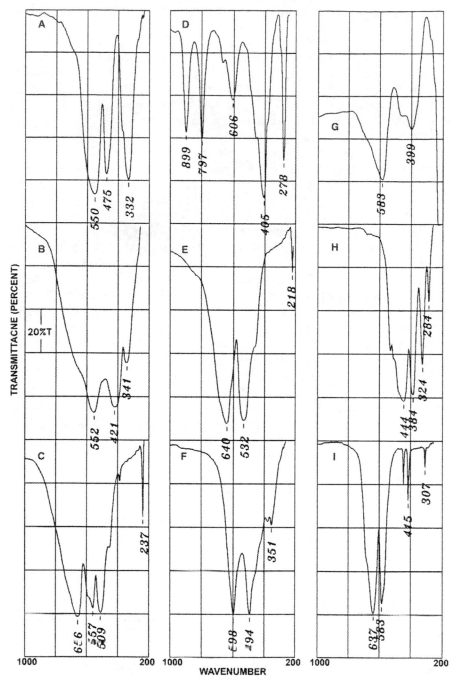

FIGURE 3-42 DAC spectra of nine inorganic oxide paint pigments (diluted with CsI) in the 1000 to 200 cm⁻¹ region. (**A**) Ferric oxide. (**B**) Zinc iron ferrite brown spinel. (**C**) Cobalt aluminate blue spinel. (**D**) Hydrous ferric oxide. (**E**) Cobalt chromite blue-green spinel. (**F**) Zinc iron chromite brown spinel. (**G**) Black iron oxide. (**H**) Lead (III) oxide. (**I**) Chromium (III) oxide. (*Source:* From Reference 95, copyright ASTM, reprinted with permission.)

also serve to illustrate the differences in absorption patterns that can occur for oxides). The nine, all of which have been used as paint pigments, have only weak or no significant absorptions above 1000 cm^{-1}. Of the nine, the two most common pigments are ferric oxide (Fe_2O_3) and hydrous ferric oxide ($FeO \cdot OH$), and ferric oxide has no absorptions above 700 cm^{-1} (Figure 3-43A). The spectrum of a maroon nonmetallic automotive finish that contains this pigment is shown in Figure 3-43B, and analysis of such of a paint using an infrared microscope (with a narrowband MCT detector) would not reveal the presence of this pigment.

Hydrous ferric oxide (Figure 3-43D) has an O—H stretching absorption near 3100 cm^{-1} and two other weak peaks above 700 cm^{-1}, but the two main absorptions occur below 450 cm^{-1}. In the spectrum of a yellow nonmetallic automotive finish (Figure 3-43E) that contains a large amount of this pigment, all of the peaks of hydrous ferric oxide are observed, although the two low-frequency absorptions are the most conspicuous. For the spectrum (Figure 3-43F) of a green metallic automotive finish that contains a lesser amount of hydrous ferric oxide, only the two far-infrared absorptions are observed. The spectrum of a brown nonmetallic automotive finish that contains both ferric oxide and hydrous ferric oxide is shown in Figure 3-43C. Hydrous ferric oxide is almost always used (for automotive paints[95]) in lower concentrations than that found in the paint chosen for Figure 3-43E, so in most cases, it too cannot be identified using an infrared microscope. Figure 3-44C and 3-44D depict spectra of two yellow nonmetallic automotive finishes that have the same color and similar infrared absorptions; the main distinguishing feature is the presence of a weak hydrous ferric oxide peak at 270 cm^{-1} for the latter spectrum.

The most common pigment used in paint is titanium dioxide. This compound can exist in three different polymorphic forms and two of them, rutile and anatase, are used in paints; the spectra of the two (Figures 3-44B and 3-44A, respectively) can be distinguished based on far-infrared absorptions. When paints containing large amounts of titanium dioxide are analyzed using the infrared microscope, only the high-frequency shoulder of the broad titanium dioxide absorption is normally observed (Figure 3-31A).

Most inorganic compounds have one or more strong absorptions above 700 cm^{-1}, as well as absorptions between 700 and 200 cm^{-1}; the latter assume more importance for characterization if there is only one absorption above 700 cm^{-1}. Sulfate salts, for example, have one strong absorption (the antisymmetric S—O stretch) near 1100 cm^{-1}, together with one or more weaker absorptions below 700 cm^{-1} (Figure 3-16). Some inorganic compounds have quite distinct absorptions above 700 cm^{-1}, but even for these, the observation of the low-frequency absorptions may be helpful for several reasons:

1. Inorganic compounds typically have far fewer absorptions than organic compounds.
2. In some cases, the far-infrared absorptions may provide more distinguishing characteristics (Figure 3-18) than those above 700 cm^{-1}.
3. Far-infrared absorptions of some inorganic compounds are quite strong (see, e.g., Figures 3-18, 3-41C, 3-45C, and 3-46C).

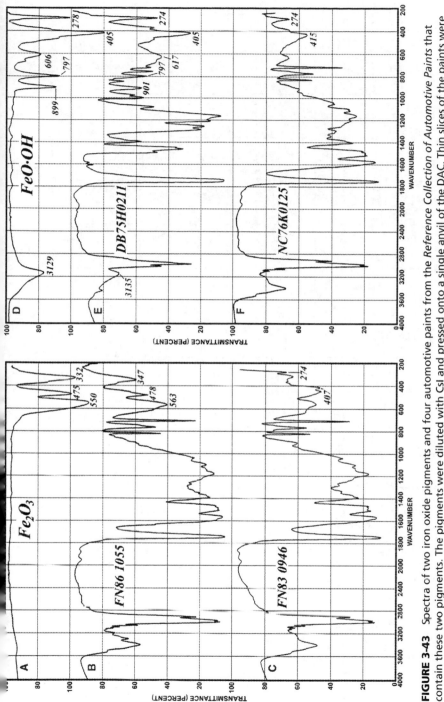

FIGURE 3-43 Spectra of two iron oxide pigments and four automotive paints from the *Reference Collection of Automotive Paints* that contain these two pigments. The pigments were diluted with CsI and pressed onto a single anvil of the DAC. Thin slices of the paints were placed over a 1-mm diameter aperture. **(A)** Ferric oxide, Fe_2O_3. **(B)** A red–maroon nonmetallic acrylic melamine enamel, FN86 1055, that contains ferric oxide. **(C)** A brown nonmetallic acrylic melamine enamel, FN83 0946, that contains ferric oxide. **(D)** Hydrous ferric oxide, FeO·OH. **(E)** A yellow nonmetallic acrylic lacquer, DB75H0211, that contains a large amount of hydrous ferric oxide. **(F)** A green metallic acrylic melamine enamel, NC76K0125, that contains a small amount of hydrous ferric oxide. (*Source:* From Reference 95, copyright ASTM, reprinted with permission.)

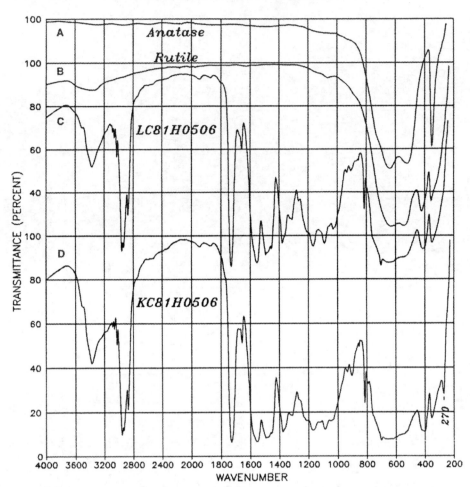

FIGURE 3-44   Spectra of anatase, rutile, and two yellow nonmetallic acrylic melamine enamel automotive paints from the *Reference Collection of Automotive Paints* that have the same color and similar infrared spectra. The two pigments were diluted with excess CsI and pressed onto a single anvil of a DAC. The two paints were analyzed as thin slices placed over a 1-mm aperture. **(A)** Anatase. **(B)** Rutile. **(C)** LC81H0506. **(D)** KC81H0506. The main difference between the spectra of the two paints is the presence of a weak peak of hydrous ferric oxide at 270 cm^{-1}.   (*Source:* From Reference 95, copyright American Academy of Forensic Sciences, reprinted with permission.)

4. For the analysis of some materials comprised of an organic binder and inorganic extender pigments, the inorganic pigment absorptions may be obscured in the mid-infrared region; however, because organic compound absorptions are usually weak in the far-infrared region, the low-frequency inorganic compound absorption may be observed more clearly.

This last point is illustrated by the spectrum of the black nonmetallic automotive finish of Figure 3-40E, which has a very broad absorption near 1100 cm^{-1}. This

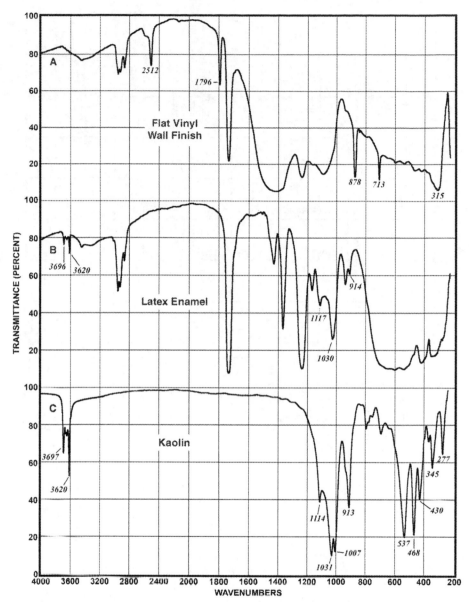

FIGURE 3-45   Spectra of **(A)** Ameritone flat vinyl interior house paint that contains a silicate, an oxide, and a large amount of calcite. **(B)** Parker Paint latex enamel interior house paint that contains kaolin and a large amount of rutile. **(C)** Kaolin diluted with excess CsI and pressed onto a single anvil of a DAC. Both paints were analyzed as thin films pressed onto a single anvil of a DAC.

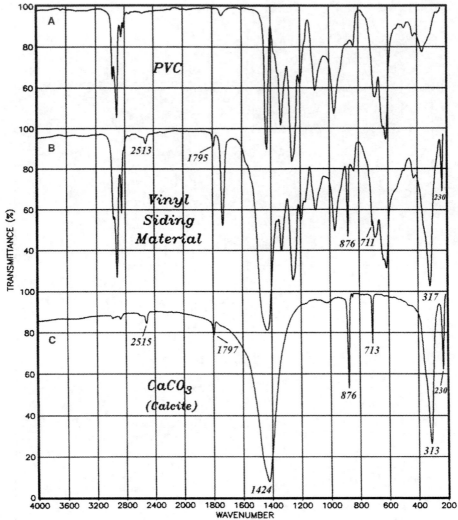

FIGURE 3-46 Spectra of **(A)** Poly(vinyl chloride) pressed onto a single anvil of a DAC. **(B)** A thin slice of a vinyl siding material placed over a 1-mm aperture. **(C)** Calcium carbonate (calcite) diluted with excess CsI and pressed onto a single anvil of a DAC.

may be the result, in part, of a silicate, but some acrylic binders also have a broad strong absorption in this region. The absorption near 470 cm^{-1}, however, confirms the presence of a form of silica.[95]

For laboratories having both extended range FT-IR and infrared microscope capabilities, the type of evidence under examination, its size, and the extent to which an infrared analysis will add to the information obtained by other methods should all be considered when determining which option to use. In general, however, if the evidence consists of or may contain a significant quantity of an inorganic constituent(s), an extended range analysis should be considered if there is sufficient sample.

Absorptions of Organic and Inorganic Compounds:
A Comparison

The forensic scientist may be asked on occasion to identify a totally unknown material, the nature of which must be determined in order to assess its relevance as evidence. Because the material can be any compound, mixture, manufactured product, or practically any other physical object, the analysis of unknown materials is one of the more challenging tasks faced by the forensic scientist. Infrared spectroscopy is an excellent tool for screening unknown materials because the list of compounds that do not absorb in the mid-infrared region is extremely limited, and as noted, for compounds that do not, the analyst has a clear direction in which to proceed.

Although many of the unknown materials are not single components, this discussion proceeds with the assumption that each individual component has been isolated, physically if not categorically, by successive identification of components. An important distinction for the analysis of an unknown is whether the material is an organic or inorganic compound, because this knowledge dictates the course of further analysis. In the vast majority of cases, this can be determined very rapidly by simply examining the infrared spectrum of the material.

Figures 3-47A through 3-47K are infrared spectra of some organic compounds, whereas Figures 3-47M through 3-47X are spectra of some inorganic compounds. Even a cursory examination of these spectra reveals some obvious differences. In general, organic compound absorptions are numerous, narrow in breadth, and span a relatively wide range of frequencies. Inorganic compound absorptions, in contrast, tend to be fewer in number, broader in breadth (for some, but not all absorptions), and in many cases, tend to be concentrated more in low frequency portion of the spectrum. The positions of many organic compound absorptions fall into well-defined regions, and simply knowing a few of these is usually more than adequate for making the distinction of interest here (the Bibliography contains many references devoted to functional group analysis of organic compounds using infrared and other methods). Almost all organic compounds, for example, have C—H stretching absorptions near 3000 cm^{-1}, whereas these do not occur in spectra of inorganic compounds (although broader O—H stretching absorptions might occur in that region in some cases).

Two spectra that are of borderline nature serve to illustrate the exceptions to these rules, and also how they may still be used to provide some insights. The spectrum of Figure 3-47K has sharp absorptions but they are not numerous. The C—H stretching absorptions of this spectrum, however, clearly indicate that the compound is organic (further analysis would also indicate the presence of characteristic C—H bending vibrations). The spectrum is that of polyethylene, which has one of the simplest infrared spectra for a large organic compound (see also Figure 3-15).

The spectrum of Figure 3-47L also has relatively few absorptions, including a broad band between 1100 and 1000 cm^{-1}. It has weak C—H stretching absorptions, however, indicating that the compound is organic, or contains an organic moiety. The spectrum is that of silicone rubber, poly(dimethylsiloxane); it contains absorptions of both types of compounds, because this polymer consists of a $(Si-O-)_n$ backbone with two methyl groups attached to each silicon atom. The broad absorption arises

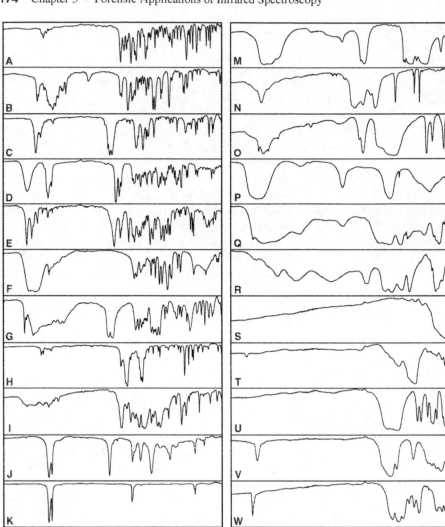

FIGURE 3-47   DAC spectra of eleven organic compounds and twelve inorganic compounds. **(A)** Alprazolam. **(B)** 2,4,5-Trimethoxyamphetamine HCl. **(C)** Allyl-phenyl barbituric acid. **(D)** Methandrostenolone. **(E)** Methocarbamol. **(F)** Myo-inositol. **(G)** Citric acid. **(H)** 3,4-Dinitrotoluene. **(I)** Methylene Blue. **(J)** Poly(ethylene/vinyl acetate). **(K)** High-density polyethylene. **(L)** Poly(dimethylsiloxane). **(M)** Ammonium molybdate. **(N)** Cerric ammonium nitrate. **(O)** Ferric ammonium sulfate. **(P)** Magnesium sulfate heptahydrate. **(Q)** Calcium phosphate monobasic monohydrate. **(R)** Sodium phosphate dibasic. **(S)** Zincite. **(T)** Scheelite. **(U)** Orthoclase. **(V)** Amblygonite. **(W)** Prehnite. **(X)** Bauxite.

from a Si—O stretch, which is observed in spectra of all silicates (Figures 3-41C, 3-45C, 3-47W, and 3-47X).

Broad absorptions do occur in spectra of organic compounds (Figures 3-47B, 3-47D, 3-47F, 3-47G, and 3-47I), often caused by hydrogen bonding, whereas relatively sharp O—H stretches are observed in spectra of many minerals (Figures 3-41C, 3-45C, 3-47V, 3-47W, and 3-47X). The cited differences are only general trends, but they can serve as a helpful guide when forensic scientists are faced with spectra of unknown substances.

Many materials encountered in trace analysis consist of polymeric organic binders and one or more inorganic extender pigments, and infrared spectra of these have absorptions characteristic of both types of compounds. The inorganic pigment absorptions are often easily identified in such spectra because they are broader than the other absorptions. Mostly, however, they are often readily recognized because the same ones tend to be used for a wide variety of different materials.

Absorptions of Talc, Kaolin, and Calcium Carbonate

Forensic scientists using infrared spectroscopy are likely to encounter three inorganic extender pigments—talc, kaolin, and calcium carbonate—more than any others. They may occur in certain exhibits submitted as suspected controlled substances, but trace analysts will almost certainly encounter them on a routine basis, as they are so prevalent in many of the types of evidence that they analyze: paints, explosives, cosmetics, building materials, plastics, rubbers, foams, adhesives, tapes, paper products, and others.

Spectra of talc, kaolin, and calcium carbonate are shown in Figures 3-41C, 3-45C, and 3-46C, respectively. Nature has provided infrared analysts with convenient "handles" in the case of talc and kaolin—two layer-type silicates, as each produces distinct, easy-to-recognize O—H stretching absorptions. For talc, this consists of a sharp spike at 3677 cm^{-1}; and for kaolin, a quadruplet of sharp peaks, with the two strongest occurring at 3697 and 3620 cm^{-1}. Although they are not strong absorptions, they occur in a region usually devoid of other absorptions of the materials in which these extender pigments are used. The talc 3677 cm^{-1} peak is seen in spectra of two automotive finishes (Figures 3-41A and 3-41B), along with most of the other absorptions of talc. The kaolin multiplet, although weak, can be seen in the spectrum of an interior house paint (Figure 3-45B). The house paint that was used to obtain the spectra depicted in Figures 3-40F and 3-40G also contains a small amount of kaolin, although the kaolin multiplet is only observed in the spectrum of the thick sample (Figure 3-40G).

The two common polymorphs of calcium carbonate are calcite and aragonite. The source of the latter polymorph is usually sea shells and its spectrum can be distinguished from that of calcite (Figure 3-46C) from the higher frequency of the C—O stretching absorption, which is centered at 1500 cm^{-1} rather than near 1420 cm^{-1} for calcite, weak sharp peaks at 1083 and 700 cm^{-1}, and a shift in the 876 cm^{-1} peak to 860 cm^{-1}. The calcite spectrum, however, is very similar to that of dolomite (Figure 3-35A). Although they are very weak absorptions, the spectrum of calcium carbonate also has features that can sometimes serve as handles. They consist of two overtone/combination bands at 2515 and 1797 cm^{-1} (Figure 3-46C; the latter occurs at 1787 cm^{-1} in aragonite), which likewise occur in regions where few other absorptions are observed. The 1797 cm^{-1} peak, for example, has a higher frequency than any carbonyl bands of the materials of interest, as such carbonyls are predominantly those of esters, which absorb near 1735 cm^{-1}. The two very weak calcite peaks can be seen in the spectrum of a vinyl siding material (Figure 3-46B). They are quite conspicuous in the spectrum of an interior house paint that contains a large amount of calcite (Figure 3-45A).

Because of the prevalence of the three extender pigments and the fact that they may serve as distinguishing features in the spectra of some materials containing them, their infrared handles, as well as the frequencies of a few of their other absorptions, are well worth committing to memory.

INFRARED ANALYSIS OF EVIDENCE

For each of the types of evidence discussed in this section, the review of the literature may cite older references where a dispersive spectrometer or KBr pellets, or both, were used for analysis. These are included because they may contain useful reference spectra, isolation or sample preparation techniques, or other pertinent information relating to the analysis of the evidence.

Controlled Substances

For the identification of a controlled substance, the forensic drug chemist must prove that a sample contains the reported compound to the exclusion of all others. To accomplish this, the analytical data collected for the compound must allow the analyst to distinguish it from all the millions of other possibilities. Obviously, direct comparison of such data to those of each of the other compounds is not practical, and the forensic chemist relies instead on an established body of knowledge. This knowledge consists of both empirical data and, as noted by Siegel[96] in Volume II of this *Handbook* series, theoretical considerations.

Empirically, the relevant analytical data for the millions of known compounds should be distinguishable from those of the compound of interest. Because these data may not always be readily available, there should also be a firm theoretical basis that indicates that such data will differ from those of the compound of interest. This should also be true for compounds not currently known to exist, because one can never exclude the possibility that such a substance might be illicitly manufactured and submitted to a forensic laboratory for examination. This has, in fact, occurred[97–105] on several occasions.

In both respects, theoretical and empirical, infrared spectroscopy fulfills these criteria. Because controlled substances are organic compounds having moderate molecular weights, they are among the substances for which the individualizing features of this method are most apparent. The only repeating structural unit of concern is a methylene (CH_2) group, but the number of units involved (e.g., in barbiturates or cannabinoids) is small enough that it does not present a problem.

The vast amount of existing empirical data also confirms and solidifies the theoretical foundation. As is true for most other analytical methods, the compounds most likely to produce infrared spectra similar to those of a given substance are those having similar structures, and statistical analyses of the infrared spectra of some illicit drugs also confirm this.[106] Studies of various forensic identification procedures have thus concentrated on isomers, homologs, and other compounds very similar to a specific controlled substance. In none of these studies, or any others, has there ever been a case in which such a compound was found to give an infrared spectrum identical to that of a controlled substance.

Some of the closely related structures, however, may have spectra very similar to that of a particular substance, especially for higher-molecular-weight compounds. It is thus imperative that the appropriate techniques regarding both compound isolation and spectroscopic sample preparation be used by the forensic chemist to ensure that optimal spectral data are obtained. Knowledge of the relevant properties of a particular compound that may affect its spectrum, such as polymorphism, hydration, formation of complexes with certain solvents, difficulties in crystallization, and so on, is also important so that the analyst is able to interpret properly any spectral variabilities that may occur. To gauge better the quality of spectral data necessary for unequivocal identification, analysts should (preferably early in their training) examine the spectra of a number of closely related compounds to get a feel for the discriminating features of an infrared spectrum.

SCREENING AND UNKNOWN ANALYSES Although not usually viewed as a screening technique, infrared spectroscopy can, in fact, be quite valuable for this purpose in some cases. It is useful for screening samples for which a complete compositional determination is sought, for example, because virtually all of the constituents of a typical drug mixture have infrared absorptions (a possible exception to this may be table salt, but it is not a common diluent). The infrared spectrum of a mixture thus provides an overall absorption profile, the peaks of which should be accounted for as the analyst proceeds to isolate and identify each of the major components.

Infrared screening is particularly useful for mixtures containing sugars, starch, cellulose, or inorganic diluents (such as talc or sodium bicarbonate) because these diluents are not normally detected by common screening methods, such as color tests, ultraviolet spectroscopy, or gas chromatography. Also, these substances usually do not have strong absorptions above 1600 cm^{-1}, leaving a "carbonyl window" region open. This is significant because many, if not a majority, of controlled substances contain a carbonyl group, which produces a strong characteristic absorption in the 1650 to 1750 cm^{-1} region.

The identification of an unknown substance based on its infrared spectrum is facilitated by use of computerized search systems, which are part of the standard software of most FT-IR instruments (although large libraries are not usually included and must be purchased separately). For mixtures containing a significant quantity of a diluent or diluents, however, search systems are of more limited use (although the main absorbing component may appear in the hit list), unless various mixtures are included in the search library.

A program for searching spectral data of some drugs of abuse has been described,[107] as have combined search methods that use infrared data together with other spectroscopic data.[108,109] Although computerized infrared search systems are a very useful tool for the forensic chemist, it should be remembered that they are, in fact, nothing more than efficient screening devices, and **an identification is made by the forensic chemist—not the computer.**

DETERMINATION OF DRUG FORM   Many controlled substances occur in different forms (i.e., free base or free acid versus various salts), and this information is relevant for quantitative analysis and in comparing exhibits for intelligence purposes. In a few cases, the form of the drug must also be determined and specified explicitly because the statutes governing the particular substance distinguish among these forms.

The general form of a drug can be determined from its infrared spectrum. Data for *l*-ephedrine base and three of its salts are depicted in Figure 3-48. The spectra of the base (Figure 3-48C), hydrochloride salt (Figure 3-48B), sulfate salt (Figure 3-48E) and nitrate salt (Figure 3-48F) are all readily distinguished. Spectra of the latter two were obtained as smears on a salt plate to avoid ion exchange problems, as discussed previously, and if a distinction between hydrochloride and hydrobromide salts is desired, use of a method that does not involve grinding with KBr should be considered. Salts of more complex anions, such as tartrate, succinate, mandelate, or citrate, also give distinct spectra.

Salts of acidic drugs likewise can be distinguished. Dissociated forms of imides (e.g., barbiturates), carboxylic acids, and phenols, for example, all give spectra quite distinct from those of their free-acid forms. It may not be possible, however, to determine the specific cation involved in these salts based solely on their mid-infrared spectra.

Some drugs are polymorphic, and as described previously, the differences in the lattice structures of these crystal forms usually result in noticeable spectral differences. Heroin base, for example, can exist in one of two crystal forms,[110,111] and their spectra can be distinguished[15] (Figure 3-49A and 3-49B). Many barbiturates are polymorphic, and differences in their spectra have also been noted.[112,113] In addition to polymorphism, some drugs can occur in either anhydrous or hydrated forms. The spectral differences between these are usually more pronounced than those between polymorphs as a result of the presence of additional absorptions of water of hydration (see Figure 3-18). Compare, for example, Figures 3-48C and 3-48D, which are spectra of anhydrous and hydrated ephedrine, respectively; note the additional absorptions of hydrated water above 3200 cm^{-1} and at 1640 cm^{-1} and 540 cm^{-1} in Figure 3-48D, as well as other spectral differences. Codeine base may crystallize as either the anhydrous form or as a monohydrate, and because of this, the need to interpret infrared data properly has been described.[114,115] Water is not the only substance that can be associated with a drug in a crystal lattice, and, although not common, other solvents have been known to do so. Infrared spectra of O^6-acetylmorphine recrystallized from solvent mixtures of ethyl acetate, for example, differ from that of O^6-acetylmorphine because of the presence of ethyl acetate solvent of crystallization.[116,117]

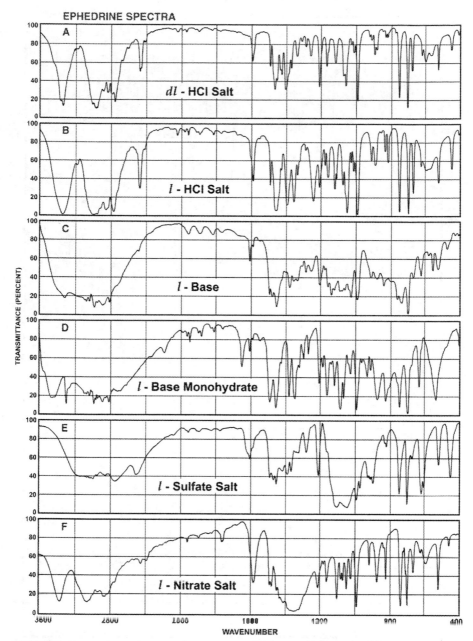

FIGURE 3-48 Spectra of various forms of ephedrine: **(A)** *dl*-HCl salt in a KBr pellet. **(B)** *l*-HCl salt in a KBr pellet. **(C)** *l*-Base (anhydrous) oil pressed between two KBr windows. **(D)** *l*-Base monohydrate smeared onto a KBr window. **(E)** *l*-Sulfate salt smeared onto a KBr window, baseline flattened. **(F)** *l*-Nitrate salt smeared onto a KBr window.

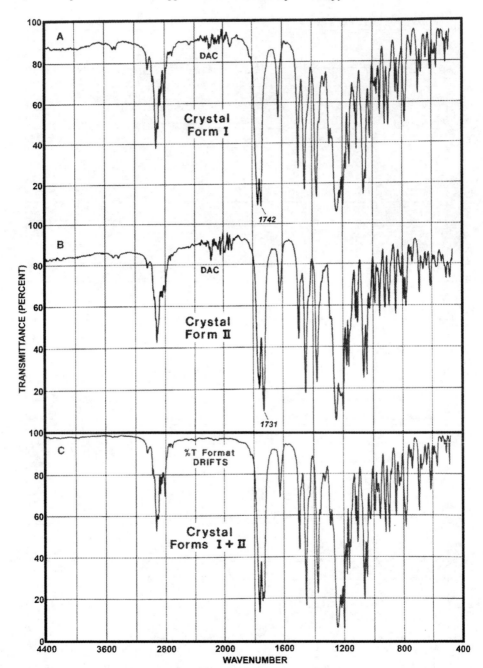

FIGURE 3-49 **(A)** High-pressure DAC spectrum of heroin base, Form I. **(B)** High-pressure DAC spectrum of heroin base, Form II. **(C)** DRIFTS spectrum in the transmittance format of a mixture of heroin base, Forms I and II. (*Source:* From Reference 15, copyright ASTM, reprinted with permission.)

Although infrared spectroscopy (excluding infrared circular dichroism techniques) cannot be used to identify optical isomers directly, it sometimes can serve to distinguish between an optical isomer and its racemic mixture. As noted, this may be possible if the racemic mixture consists of a mixed crystal. An example of this is *dl*-ephedrine hydrochloride, which may be seen (Figure 3-48A) to have a spectrum distinguishable from that of the *l* (or *d*) isomer (Figure 3-48B). By means of derivatization with an optically active reagent, it is possible to identify enantiomers indirectly by infrared analysis because this amounts to a differentiation of diastereomers. This derivative can include a salt where both the cation and anion are optically active, as shown by a procedure to identify the optical isomer of amphetamine using *d*-mandelic acid.[118]

IDENTIFICATION METHODS   A single-pass ATR accessory is likely the most useful technique for the routine analysis of suspected controlled substances and related compounds, because it requires the least amount of sample preparation of any of the common methods and it has a high sensitivity. As discussed previously, a diamond-coated ATR element is preferred because of its durability and the wide range of materials that may be subjected to analysis. Reference data for standards should consist of ATR spectra because of the differences between transmission and ATR absorptions, as emphasized for cocaine,[119] and a library of 455 controlled and noncontrolled solid drug standards using a diamond ATR accessory has been produced.[120]

Some drug samples may be analyzed directly without preparation using DRIFTS or one of the photothermal methods. The direct analyses of certain pharmaceutical tablets, including Empirin™ [31,32] and Doriden™ (glutethemide)[53] using DRIFTS, and Empirin[88] and an aspirin tablet[84] using photoacoustic spectroscopy, have been reported. The direct analyses of neat powders using DRIFTS[30,34,40,53] and photothermal methods[85–88] have also been described. The spectra obtained by direct DRIFTS analysis and the photothermal methods differ from each other and from transmittance spectra because of specular reflectance, thermal transfer and saturation effects, as well as other factors. In general, the photothermal methods produce spectra that are less dependent on particle size, sample morphology, and surface characteristics than DRIFTS. In either case, reference data generated by the same method should be used.

For some powder mixtures, the analyst may be able isolate a drug particle of interest by simply removing it from the mixture, followed by an analysis using the DAC,[15] infrared microscope,[15,121] or ATR. The powder is viewed with a stereomicroscope, and a particle of interest (which often has a distinct morphology) is removed with a probe or a pair of microforceps. Low microgram to nanogram quantities of material can be analyzed in this manner, and because the sample is not dissolved in solution, problems with recrystallization, polymorphism, hydration, or ion exchange do not occur. This method is especially useful for isolating and identifying individual crystals of drugs that exhibit polymorphism, including heroin base (Figures 3-49A and 3-49B), barbiturates,[121] and other drugs.[122,123]

For other complex mixtures, one of the hyphenated techniques may be helpful. The use of GC/FT-IR for forensic drug analysis has been described, and this work[124]

illustrated the differentiation of some isomer pairs, including cocaine/pseudoco-
caine, phentermine/methamphetamine, and lysergic acid diethylamide (LSD)/lyser-
gic acid methylpropylamide (LAMPA) using this method. GC/FT-IR has also been
used for the differentiation of five monomethlyfentanyl isomers[125] and for the analysis of various alkyl nitrites.[126] GC/FT-IR was compared to GC/cryo-trapping FT-IR
for the analysis of barbiturates,[127] and the latter was found to have detection limits
nearly two orders of magnitude lower. The benefits of using GC/FT-IR/MS have
been described in a study of the identification of amphetamine and eleven of its side-
chain isomers[69] (see Figure 3-37) and other controlled substances.[128] Some of the
advantages of a hyphenated technique may be obtained by using gas, liquid, or thin-
layer chromatography manually in a preparative mode, followed by an infrared identification. The analysis of drugs of abuse using a system that collects GC eluants in a
vapor cell has been reported,[129] as has a method for identifying cannabinoids collected from a GC outlet and condensed onto KBr packed into a pipette.[130] A method
similar to the latter has also been used for the identification of heroin.[131] A comparative study of microinfrared techniques used to identify drugs isolated by preparative
GC or TLC has been performed.[132] High-performance liquid chromatography
(HPLC) may be used instead of GC for preparative infrared analysis, and this
method has been used for the identification of cocaine[133] and heroin.[134]

The quantitative analysis of cocaine and heroin using infrared spectroscopy
has been described,[135] and this method was also used for a survey and comparison of
heroin seizures.[136] Several studies have examined the specificity of various procedures used for the forensic identification of heroin by collecting and comparing data,
including infrared spectra, for a variety of compounds similar to heroin.[137–140] A
similar study was conducted for some mono-methoxy positional isomers of amphetamine, methamphetamine and P2P.[141] In anticipation of the future abuse of a
new group of "designer drugs," the methoxycathinones, infrared and other data for
several homologs of 3,4-methylenedioxycathinone (MDCATH) were obtained.[103]
Infrared spectra of cocaine[142] and its disastereomers,[143–145] and synthetic impurities
of cocaine[146–150] have been published, as have data for other analgesics,[151–153]
stimulants,[154–159] sedatives,[160–165] steroids,[166–168] GHB,[169–171] adulterants and diluents
in cocaine samples,[172] and excipients of illicit tablets.[173] Microcrystal tests have been
combined with an infrared microscope analysis of the microcrystals for the identification of cocaine, heroin, phencyclidine, and other controlled substances.[174,175]

Hallucinogenic compounds of interest to the forensic chemist often have low
dosages (less than 1 mg), and they may occur in matrices (e.g., blotter paper, sugar
cubes, gelatin, mushrooms, cacti) from which isolation of a particular compound is
difficult. These features make them ideal for analysis using one of the hyphenated
techniques, and the identification of LSD using GC/FT-IR[124] has been reported, as
has a GC/FT-IR analysis of cannabinoids.[176] The low dosages of LSD also suggest
the use of an infrared microscope, and a method employing a TLC/wick-evaporation
isolation technique has been found to give high-quality spectra of LSD.[177]

The infrared analysis of LSD and other hallucinogens using conventional isolation
and analysis techniques has also been described,[178–182] along with methods for the identification of psilocin[183,184] and mescaline/peyote alkaloids[185] extracted from mushrooms

and cacti, respectively. Infrared data have been published for a number of phencyclidine analogs,[100,186–190] methoxysubstituted amphetamine compounds,[103,191–206] and tryptamine-related compounds.[207,208] Photoacoustic spectroscopy has been used for the quantitative analysis of phencyclidine and phenobarbital in complex mixtures,[209] including samples diluted with lactose and parsley.

In addition to the aforementioned references, infrared spectra and isolation procedures for a number of controlled substances have been published in *Microgram*, a DEA publication with a restricted circulation. Several books or compilations of infrared and other spectral data that should be of interest to the forensic drug chemist include the comprehensive compilation by Mills et al.,[210] *Clarke's Analysis of Drugs and Poisons,*[211] and the *Analytical Profiles* series produced by CND Analytical, Inc. Other books containing reference infrared spectra of drugs and related materials are cited in the Bibliography.

CHEMICALS FROM CLANDESTINE LABORATORIES   In order to provide evidence regarding manufacture of a controlled substance, the forensic chemist may be asked to analyze various solvents, reagents, precursors, intermediates, by-products, and products confiscated from a clandestine laboratory. For many of these materials, infrared spectroscopy may be used for identification. Volatile reagents and solvents (e.g., acetone, diethyl ether, chloroform, methanol, ethyl acetate, methylamine) may be analyzed using ATR, GC/FTIR, or a vapor cell, whereas unknown liquids, including corrosives (Figure 3-29), may be readily screened using ATR with a diamond element. Hydrochloric acid (Figure 3-7B) and ammonia (ammonium hydroxide solution, Figure 3-11) can be identified using a vapor cell. For complex mixtures that potentially may contain solvents, starting materials, catalysts, intermediates, and by-products along with final product, one of the hyphenated techniques, particularly GC/FT-IR/MS, may be useful. The possibility that such a mixture may be altered by the temperature of the GC injection port, however, should be considered when using a GC technique.

Infrared data have been published for some contaminants in the clandestine preparation of amphetamine,[212] methamphetamine,[212–214] 4-methoxyamphetamine[215] and *N*-ethyl-1-phenylcyclohexylamine.[216] Similar data have also been presented for compounds associated with the synthesis of phenyl-2-propane (P2P) from phenyl-propenes,[217] precursors, intermediates, and impurities of the synthesis of 3,4-methylenedioxyamphetamine,[218] precursors of monoethoxyamphetamines,[219] precursors and products of the synthesis of methaqualone and mecloqualone,[220] and ephedrone,[221] a ketone product of methamphetamine. Infrared and other data were used to determine the structure of the main byproduct (1-(1′,4′-cyclohexadienyl)-2-methylamino propane—usually referred to as the *150 compound*) of the synthesis of methamphetamine using the lithium-ammonia (Birch) reduction reaction.[222] GC/FT IR data have been used to identify various by-products in the synthesis of P2P, which allowed a determination of the specific route used to produce this precursor.[223]

A comprehensive set of references from *Microgram* and other sources relating to the clandestine synthesis of a number of controlled substances has been compiled by the Clandestine Laboratory Investigating Chemists organization, and they include a large number of infrared spectral and other data.

Toxicology

Infrared spectroscopy has been used for the identification of a variety of materials extracted or removed from various tissues and blood. It is especially useful for the identification of nonvolatile samples because these are not amenable to analysis using GC/MS. As an example, an infrared analysis was used for the determination of polydimethylsiloxane (silicone oil) recovered from blood and internal organs in a fatality related to tissue augmentation with this polymer.[224] Cases have also been reported where infrared analyses were used in death investigations following suspected ingestions of monochloronapthalene,[225] a wood preservative, and endosulfan,[226] an insecticide. A method has been described for the extraction of unmetabolized ibogaine from blood, urine, or tissue, followed by an infrared identification.[227]

As discussed, high-resolution vapor spectra can be used for the unequivocal identification of some low-molecular-weight compounds, even when other strong absorptions are present. This method has been used to identify toxic or medicinal gases and mixtures, including carbon monoxide[228] and other gases (nitrous oxide, ethylene, methane, ether, etc.) extracted from blood[229] or from tissue samples.[230] The analysis of medicinal gases for trace vapor impurities using a 10-m gas cell has also been reported.[231]

For some field instruments, breath alcohol is measured by having a subject blow into a vapor cell, then measuring the absorptions of two wavelengths in the C—H stretching region. The ratio of the two absorptions are compared to ensure that no interfering substances are present. Two studies examined the feasibility of using an FT-IR instrument for measuring breath alcohol, with the intent of also determining the identities of other vapors that might be released from the lungs of subjects.[232, 233]

The aforementioned applications notwithstanding, infrared spectroscopy has not been a tool historically associated with forensic toxicology. The reasons for this are clear: toxicological samples are often characterized by their low concentrations, complex matrices, and the presence of various metabolites. Chromatographic methods and GC/MS have thus been the standard tools of the trade, but hyphenated techniques involved infrared spectroscopy, especially GC/FT-IR and GC/FT-IR/MS, are increasingly being applied to toxicological problems. GC/FT-IR has been used, for example, for the analysis of postmortem blood in a paraquat poisoning,[234] the determination of acetone in lung extracts and trichloroethylene in blood extracts,[234] the detection of amphetamine and methamphetamine in urine,[235] and for other forensic toxicological applications.[236] A number of volatile organic compounds were identified in extracts of blood that were first concentrated using a purge and trap method followed by a GC/FT-IR analysis.[237] A comparison of GC/MS using an ion-trap instrument and GC/FT-IR was conducted for the analysis of stimulants in drug testing.[238] GC/FT-IR/MS has been used for the qualitative and quantitative analysis of amphetamine, methamphetamine, and related analogs extracted from urine.[239]

The infrared microscope has been used to analyze hair samples for drugs of abuse[240] and to determine the distribution of these drugs in hair.[241] It has also been used for the analysis of very small quantities of nonvolatile biological materials, such as tissue deposits,[242,243] and cells and tissue itself.[244,245]

Paint

Paint evidence is normally subjected to a comparative analysis by the forensic scientist to determine if two samples could have originated from a common source. In some cases, an identification of an automotive paint may be required to determine the type of vehicle involved in a hit-and-run incident. Although not common, the forensic scientist may even be asked to determine if a particular material *is* paint, and if so, what type and how this might relate to the circumstances of an investigation. For any paint examination, characteristics that allow the forensic scientist to distinguish between different finishes are a primary consideration in selecting analytical methods.

Dried paint consists of a polymeric organic binder and inorganic and organic pigments and additives. The properties of a paint that may serve as discriminating features include its color, luster (high gloss to flat), type (metallic, nonmetallic, pearlescent, and special effects, as applicable), layer structure, chemical composition, and surface characteristics (weathering, defects, presence of texture particles, etc.). Determination of chemical composition not only serves to distinguish paints, but also provides indispensable information for establishing whether a material is paint, the type of paint, how common it might be, and in the case of an automotive finish, the type of vehicle that could have been its source (using an appropriate database based on compositions and other characteristics).

Infrared spectroscopy is an excellent means to determine paint composition and is the main tool used both in the paint industry and by forensic scientists to identify paint binders. It is also used for the *in situ* identification of other major paint components. In a few cases, minor components may be identified if they produce absorptions that occur in isolated spectral regions.

Although all paints are composed of a binder, the amounts and types of pigments vary considerably, depending on the intended purpose of the finish. The infrared spectra of various types of paint reflect this gradation, and in general, they are very different for each type of paint. The different types are thus discussed separately.

Before proceeding, it is worth reviewing briefly what a *pigment* is. According to paint industry terminology, a pigment is used to impart color, opacity, or modify physical properties of the paint. Pigments are also insoluble unlike dyes. Rutile and anatase are pigments because they have high[c] indices of refraction (2.7 and 2.5, respectively) and are used primarily to produce opacity (the mechanism of production of opacity was described earlier by the Kubelka–Munk equations). Extender pigments, such as talc (1.6), kaolin (1.6), or calcium carbonate (1.6), have indices of refraction that are close to those of binders, which are typically around 1.5. If they were exactly the same, they would not produce any opacity and would serve mostly to extend the binder, that is, to produce bulk at a lower cost. Because they are not quite the same, extender pigments may contribute to opacity and are used to modify luster or texture, to increase viscosity of a (wet) paint, to lower costs, or for other purposes.

---

[c]In general, there is a positive correlation between index of refraction and atomic number, but titanium has a relatively low atomic number. The high indices of refraction of rutile and anatase can be explained by Figures 3-24A and 3-24B. Both polymorphs have intense absorptions in the ultraviolet region and the low frequency "tail" of Figure 3-24B for rutile and anatase occurs in the visible region.

AUTOMOTIVE FINISH LAYERS During the 1970s and 1980s, the two predominant types of binders that were used for original finishes of North American automobiles were the acrylic lacquer and the acrylic melamine enamel. Earlier, in the 1960s, alkyd enamels or alkyd melamine enamels were also used, especially on trucks. The period from roughly the mid-1980s to the mid-1990s saw very significant changes in the compositions of automotive finishes. For binders, this included discontinuation of the use of acrylic lacquers (which had been used from the 1960s to the early 1990s[246] on many General Motors vehicles) and the introduction of several new types, including the polyester melamine, acrylic urethane, acrylic silane, and acrylic epoxy. Some pigments, including Prussian Blue[247] and the widely used lead chromates,[95] were phased out, and at the same time, new pigments were introduced.[248] The transition from monocoats to predominantly basecoat/clearcoat finishes also occurred during this period, and this, in turn, made possible other significant changes in pigmentation. A clearcoat provides both protection (especially from ultraviolet light) and gloss, and its introduction allowed the use of some pigments that previously were not light-fast enough to meet the stringent requirements of an automotive finish. In other cases, pigments that could not be used in high pigment loads because they adversely affected gloss in a monocoat became more common. Still others that could not be used at all for this same reason, including pearlescent and other special effects pigments, were added to the palette of automobile color stylists. It should be stressed that these changes were for North American vehicles, and although many of them also occurred for paints on imports, this was not always the case. Use of lead chromate pigments, for example, continued[249] for European vehicle finishes after they had been discontinued in North America. Also, all these changes did not necessarily occur for North American refinishes; Prussian Blue, for example, continued to be used in such paints.[250] Overall, automotive finishes became more diverse in terms of color, layer sequence (there are now tinted clearcoats, tricoat systems, and color-coordinated undercoats), microscopic characteristics, and composition. Paints used on individual vehicle parts have also become more diverse as a result of increased use of plastic parts, particularly for bumpers, as these typically have a totally different coating system from that used for metal substrates.

Binder Absorptions The identification of paint binders based on their infrared absorptions has been emphasized in much of the literature pertaining to the forensic analysis of paints. An excellent in-depth review of this subject is presented by Ryland,[246] and it includes reference spectra of the major types of paint binders together with a classification flow chart for identifying them. Paint analysts are cautioned against blindly following flow charts for binder identification, however, as the presence of major absorptions of pigments can easily lead to misidentification. Such charts are intended for paint spectra lacking such absorptions or for use by analysts who already possess some recognition skills regarding binder and pigment absorption patterns.

The spectrum of a yellow nonmetallic acrylic lacquer is shown in Figure 3-43E. The acrylic lacquer binder is comprised primarily of poly(methyl methacrylate) and its spectrum is nearly identical to that of this plastic. As discussed, Figure 3-43E also contains absorptions of hydrous ferric oxide (Figure 3-43D).

Although acrylic lacquer binders are no longer used for original finishes on North American automobiles, acrylic melamine enamels continue to be very common binders for both basecoats and clearcoats. The spectrum of a silver metallic acrylic melamine enamel is depicted in Figure 3-40A, and as this paint contains very little pigmentation, the absorptions are those of the binder alone. This binder consists of an acrylic backbone cross-linked with melamine, which produces two very characteristic triazine ring vibrations at 1550 cm^{-1} (broad and usually quite strong) and 815 cm^{-1} (sharp and weaker than the 1550 cm^{-1} absorption). These two absorptions are observed in spectra of other melamine-containing binders, including alkyd melamines and polyester melamines. Acrylic melamine enamel binders also frequently contain styrene (which is incorporated into the backbone). Styrene produces three groups of absorptions, consisting of the aromatic C—H stretches above 3000 cm^{-1} (weak to very weak), two very weak "blips" between 2000 and 1800 cm^{-1} arising from overtone/combination bands of monosubstituted benzene rings, and two aromatic C—H out of plane bends at 760 and 700 cm^{-1} (medium to very weak). These absorptions are also observed in spectra of other paint binders that contain styrene. The characteristic absorptions of both melamine and styrene can be seen in Figures 3-40A, 3-40E, 3-43B, 3-43C, 3-43F, 3-44C, and 3-44D. The two melamine absorptions and the C—H stretches and two overtone/combination bands of styrene can also be seen in Figures 3-25B and 3-25D, although the styrene 760 and 700 cm^{-1} peaks are mostly obscured. Less often, spectra of acrylic melamine enamels contain very little if any absorptions of styrene, and this can serve as one means to differentiate between different formulations of this binder. In some cases, there may be minor differences in the 1400 to 900 cm^{-1} spectral region (compare Figures 3-43C and 3-43F), reflecting differences in the types of acrylic monomers used.[251]

One acrylic monomer, acrylonitrile, produces a characteristic nitrile (—C≡N) stretching absorption at 2239 cm^{-1}. Although this monomer is a quite minor component of the paint, its presence is readily detected[247] because this absorption occurs in the overtone/combination region normally devoid of significant features. Two other components[247] of certain paints also produce absorptions in this region. A blue inorganic pigment, Prussian Blue (which is composed of iron and other cations with the $[Fe(CN)_6]^{-4}$ anion) produces a cyano (C≡N$^-$) stretching absorption at 2090 cm^{-1}, and an isocyanate (—N=C=O) residue, resulting from the presence of unreacted starting material in a two-component urethane, produces an absorption in the 2260 to 2270 cm^{-1} region.

Characteristic absorptions of other binders used in automotive finish layers are discussed by Ryland[246] and Thornton.[252] Infrared spectra of some black nonmetallic basecoat/clearcoat finishes were the subject of a collaborative study[253] that demonstrated the discriminating characteristics of this method for some newer original finishes. This study also found that even with analysts in eight laboratories using a variety of FT-IR instruments, similar spectra were obtained, with the exception of data collected using ATR accessories. The significance of minor differences in the infrared spectra of some automotive topcoats was evaluated,[254] and a study of the infrared spectra of automobile refinish paints found considerable variations in their compositions as well as typical differences in the types of binders used in refinishes versus original finishes.[255]

Pigment Absorptions   Spectra of automotive finish layers exhibit a very wide range of pigment absorption intensities. When examining infrared spectra of colored layers, paint analysts may find it puzzling that the spectrum of a finish having a dark shade in one hue has no observable pigment absorptions, whereas that of a lighter shade of a different hue has an abundance of such peaks. A brief discussion of why this occurs and what colors of paint can be expected to produce prominent pigment absorptions is thus presented. These are only trends, however, and there are exceptions. They are based on a study[19,61,95,247,248,256,257] of U.S. automobile original finishes (1974–1989) from the *Reference Collection of Automotive Paints*, spectra of more recent finishes, and information provided by paint manufacturers and automobile color stylists.

As expected, spectra of clearcoats consist predominantly of binder absorptions. Some clearcoat spectra, however, may also have weak to moderate absorptions of synthetic silica. Synthetic silica is used in some clearcoats and certain metallic paints to increase the viscosity of a wet paint to aid in its application (i.e., to keep the paint from dripping when sprayed onto a vertical surface). The far-infrared absorption of synthetic silica (at 470 cm^{-1} in Figure 3-40E) may be the most clearly observed feature in such spectra, as the Si—O stretch near 1100 cm^{-1} may be partially obscured by C—O stretches of the binder.

Metallic paints of a given color normally contain a lower concentration of pigments than nonmetallic paints, as the metallic finishes must be transparent enough for the metal flakes to be observed (which is why there is no such thing as a white metallic finish, although off-white pearlescent paints may be encountered). In most cases, organic pigments have greater tinctorial strengths, smaller particle sizes, and lower indices of refraction than inorganic pigments, and the latter two properties make them more transparent. For these reasons, organic pigments tend to be more prevalent in metallic finishes. Although some inorganic pigments are used in metallic finishes (such as ferric oxide and hydrous ferric oxide; see Figure 3-43F), they are never used in high pigment loads. Small amounts of rutile, for example, may be used in metallic paints, but its absorptions are usually too weak to be identified clearly. Some other inorganic pigments are never used in metallic finishes. Silver and gray shades of metallic finishes often contain little pigmentation or only carbon black, as their hues or visual effects arise primarily from the metal flakes; spectra of these thus consist predominantly of binder absorptions. As noted, spectra of metallic finishes containing a high concentration of flakes exhibit low baselines (Figure 3-40B). Generally speaking, spectra of metallic finishes thus contain weaker pigment absorptions than those of nonmetallic finishes of similar colors.

Spectra of white paints always contain very strong absorptions of rutile, as do those of all other nonmetallic colors in the very light shades, including sky blue, pink, gray, tan, and others that might be described as having pastel or "creamy" hues. Spectra of these lighter shades typically do not contain absorptions of color-imparting pigments. Spectra of black finishes (nonmetallic and metallic) almost never contain pigment absorptions, as they normally contain carbon black, which does not produce a specific infrared absorption. As noted, such spectra often exhibit strongly sloping baselines (Figures 3-40E and 3-41A).

Spectra of red paints usually contain the most and strongest pigment absorptions, followed by oranges and yellows. Spectra of blue paints rarely contain pigment absorptions, and this is true to a lesser extent for greens. This effect can be explained by Figures 3-24A and 3-24B and the Kubelka–Munk model (Equation 3-14). Blue and green pigments absorb orange and red colors, and the low-frequency tails of Figure 3-24B arising from these absorption bands occur in the near-infrared region (it might help here to recall that color sequence of violet, blue, green, yellow, orange, and red represents decreasing frequencies). This has no effect on the blue and green wavelengths that are used for viewing such paints. In contrast, red, orange, and yellow paints absorb blue, green, and violet colors, and the tails of Figure 3-24B occur for those wavelengths that are used for viewing paints containing these pigments. These pigments thus have high indices of refraction for their viewing wavelengths and this causes their scattering coefficients (k in Equation 3-14) to be higher than those of blue and green pigments. Consequently, the average penetration depths of light of the viewing wavelengths for red, orange, and yellow paints are less than those for blue and green paints. Were the same concentration of a blue pigment and red pigment that have exactly the same tinctorial strengths used for two paints, the red paint would appear to have a much paler shade. Conversely, because the viewing wavelengths of blue and green paints penetrate deeper into the finish, less pigment is required to impart color.

Another reason that spectra of blue paints rarely have noticeable pigment absorptions is that the most common blue pigment used in an automotive paint, Copper Phthalocyanine Blue, is both a very intense absorber of visible light and a relatively weak absorber of infrared light (because of its high symmetry). The concentrations used for most blue paints are thus too low to produce significant infrared absorptions. This is not the case, however, for Prussian Blue. Like most inorganic pigments, Prussian Blue is a weak absorber of visible light and a strong absorber of infrared light, so heavier pigment loads are required to produce color. Its main absorption at 2090 cm^{-1} is thus readily seen in paint spectra (as noted), even when small amounts of Prussian Blue are used.[247]

The most common pigment absorption observed in spectra of green paints, both metallic and nonmetallic, is—ironically—a yellow pigment, hydrous ferric oxide (Figure 3-43F). There are two green phthalocyanine pigments that may be used in automotive paints. Like Copper Phthalocyanine Blue, however, their absorptions are normally too weak to be observed. The two green pigments are also more expensive than Copper Phthalocyanine Blue, and a combination of Copper Phthalocyanine Blue and hydrous ferric oxide is often used as an alternative means to formulate a green shade. Only the absorptions of the latter are observed in paint infrared spectra.

The color-imparting inorganic pigments that have been identified *in situ* in automotive finishes using infrared spectroscopy include ferric oxide[95] (Figures 3-43A, 3-43B and 3-43C), hydrous ferric oxide[95] (Figures 3-43D, 3-43E and 3-43F), Chrome Yellow,[95] Molybdate Orange[95], silica-encapsulated versions[95] of Chrome Yellow and Molybdate Orange, Nickel Titanate[19] (Figures 3-25C and 3-25D), Chrome Titanate,[19] and Prussian Blue.[247] Hydrous ferric oxide was found in the widest range of paint colors, including yellow, orange, red, brown, and green nonmetallic and yellow, orange, brown, olive, and green metallic paints.[95] It is particularly prevalent in finishes having pale yellow and beige nonmetallic shades, and usually only a weak peak near 270 cm^{-1} on the low-frequency shoulder of the rutile structure is seen in spectra of such paints (see, e.g., Figure 3-44D). As noted, Prussian Blue and the lead chromate pigments (Chrome Yellow and Molybdate Orange) are no longer used in North American automobile original finishes.

Some organic pigments or classes of organic pigments that have been identified in automotive finishes using infrared spectroscopy include benzimidazolones,[61] quinacidones,[256] DPP Red BO,[248] Thioindigo Bordeaux,[248] Isoindolinone 3R,[257] Isoindoline Yellow,[257] Anthrapyrimidine Yellow,[257] perylenes,[258] and others.[258] In general, the absorptions of organic pigments can be recognized in spectra of colored finish layers by their narrow breadths and in many cases, the number of absorptions (i.e., the same criteria already discussed for distinguishing between the absorptions of organic and inorganic compounds in general). However, there are no simple criteria for determining *how many* different organic pigments are present other than comparing the absorptions to those of known pigments, although certain combinations are much more common than others[19,61,95,248,256,257] (including combinations with inorganic pigments).

The use of significant amounts of extender pigments in a monocoat, excluding synthetic silica (as noted), is very rare. High concentrations of extender pigments adversely affect gloss, and the only paints from the *Reference Collection of Automotive Paints* that contained noticeable infrared absorptions of extender pigments were a few black nonmetallic monocoats having flat or satin finishes. The extender pigments that were identified[95] in these paints include talc (Figures 3-41A, 3-41B, and 3-41C), synthetic silica (Figure 3-40E), and diatomaceous silica, and it is clear that the three are serving as flatting agents. Because gloss is produced by the clearcoat in a basecoat/clearcoat finish system, it is possible that the basecoats of such systems might contain higher concentrations of extender pigments, and the most common extender pigment found in a basecoat is barium sulfate, which is used as an anti-settling agent for the pigments.

AUTOMOTIVE UNDERCOATS   Automotive undercoats generally have very different compositions from finish layers. This is reflected in their colors, textures, infrared spectra, and other properties. Adhesion to both the substrate and the overlaying coat is a primary consideration of an undercoat, and this is achieved, in part, by having matte surfaces. Consequently, undercoats almost always contain significant quantities of titanium dioxide or, more often, extender pigments. In addition, the binders used in undercoats are usually (but not always) different from those used in finish layers, and include epoxy, acrylic, alkyd, nitrocellulose, polyester, meleinised oils, and meleinised polybutadiene. The pigments and extender pigments that are used in undercoats include titanium dioxide, barium sulfate, calcium carbonate, silica, talc, kaolin, ferric oxide, chromates, phosphates, and others. Often, these are used in various combinations and it is this possibility, together with the different binders and their combinations and modifications, that produces the diversity in undercoat compositions.

One very common binder that is used in an undercoat is epoxy. These are aromatic epoxies that produce a characteristic sharp ring expansion absorption at $1510\,\mathrm{cm}^{-1}$ (see Figure 3-50G); other absorptions of epoxies that might be observed are given elsewhere.[246,252] Epoxies used in undercoats almost always use a copolymer of an acrylic or polyester, so a carbonyl ester absorption is normally also observed. Spectra of acrylic epoxy binders that are used in some finish layers do not contain the $1510\,\mathrm{cm}^{-1}$ absorption because they are aliphatic epoxies (which are more durable to light exposure).

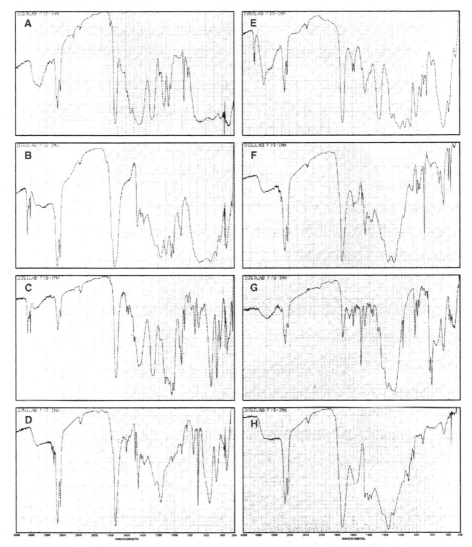

FIGURE 3-50 Spectra of eight automotive undercoats used in a collaborative study to determine if the binders and pigments used in undercoats could be readily identified using infrared spectroscopy. (*Source:* From Reference 259, copyright Canadian Society of Forensic Sciences, reprinted with permission.)

A collaborative study[259] involving the infrared analysis of undercoats has demonstrated that even when two or more pigments are present, it is usually possible to identify the pigments and the major binder components based on their absorptions.[260] Spectra of the eight undercoats used in this study are shown in Figures 3-50A–H, and the binders, pigments, and extender pigments that were identified include the following: Figure 3-50A: Alkyd, titanium dioxide, calcite; Figure 3-50B: Acrylic, titanium dioxide, kaolin; Figure 3-50C: Alkyd, epoxy, calcite, kaolin; Figure 3-50D: Acrylic, styrene, ferric oxide; Figure 3-50E: Alkyd, talc; Figure 3-50F: Acrylic, styrene, quartz; Figure 3-50G: Acrylic, epoxy, barium sulfate, quartz, ferric oxide; Figure 3-50H: Acrylic, strontium chromate. A hierarchical classification system was used that allows for the ambiguities that invariably arise when absorptions of several components are present and some characteristic features are obscured. The far-infrared absorptions of Figure 3-50A, for example, do not provide a definitive differentiation between rutile (Figure 3-44B) and anatase (Figure 3-44A), although they appear to be those of rutile. In cases such as this, analysts may choose to identify the pigment under the more generic classification as titanium dioxide or oxide (or calcium carbonate or carbonate rather than calcite or aragonite).

Rodgers et al.[251,261–262] performed most of the early work on the forensic identification of automotive paint constituents using infrared spectroscopy. Although data for this work were obtained using a DAC on a dispersive instrument, this series of papers still provides an excellent primer on this subject and is highly recommended.

VEHICLE IDENTIFICATION   Until 1989, a collection of original finishes used on U.S. automobiles (1974–1989), the *Reference Collection of Automotive Paints,* was available commercially to assist forensic paint examiners to identify paint evidence in hit-and-run cases. The limitations of this collection, however, were that it did not include paints from import vehicles, nor did it include the complete paint system (including primers and other undercoats). Forensic laboratories of the Royal Canadian Mounted Police (RCMP), in contrast, maintained reference panels of complete automotive finish systems, and RCMP scientists devised various automotive paint classification schemes, based on infrared and other data for each layer, to assist in vehicle identification.[251,259, 261–268]

In 1994, a committee of international forensic paint examiners, then known as TWGPAINT (now part of SWGMAT, the Scientific Working Group for Materials Analysis), was formed. One of the first priorities of this committee was to address the issue of lack of sufficient databases for paints, particularly in regard to identification of vehicles following the termination of the *Reference Collection of Automotive Paints.* TWGPAINT obtained funding from both the U.S. National Institute of Justice (NIJ) and the National Institute of Standards and Technology (NIST) to expand the existing database of the RCMP Laboratories, known as the Paint Data Query (PDQ) system. In this collaborative program involving the FBI and RCMP Laboratories, participating American forensic laboratories collect samples for PDQ that consist of the complete automotive finish systems removed from vehicles from salvage yards, repair shops, or other sources. The VIN (vehicle identification number) is also included with each sample to establish the make, model, year, and manufacturing plant of the paint. The RCMP Laboratories then obtain extended-range infrared spectra of each layer, together with other information, for entry into the PDQ database. Participating laboratories are provided with the database, which includes both text and infrared spectral search capabilities. Compositional data for each layer of an unknown paint system can be entered using a hierarchical classification system similar to that used for the undercoat collaborative study cited previously. More information about PDQ is given elsewhere.[269]

ARCHITECTURAL COATINGS   In most respects, architectural coatings (house paints) are quite different from automotive finishes, especially when considering interior latex paints. Probably the most obvious difference is the extremely wide range of colors exhibited by automotive paints (in North America, at least), as well as the fact that they include metallic and pearlescent finishes and they almost always have very high sheens. Automotive colors are often very vivid and bright. House paints tend to occur in more pastel and subdued hues, particularly for interior paints for which off-white shades are common, and they usually have semi-gloss to flat lusters. Original automotive finish systems also have a well-defined layer sequence with a primer, undercoat(s), and finish system that usually has a clearcoat. House paints, in contrast, normally have at most a primer/sealer layer with a finish layer(s) (or many layers if repainted).

Because of the extremely wide range of colors and styles exhibited by automotive finishes, a color and microscopic examination by itself serves to distinguish a very large percentage of them, as demonstrated by many studies.[270–275] This is likely not the case with interior housepaints, and although many off-white shades and lusters can be distinguished by color and microscopic characteristics, paint composition may assume a more important role in characterizing and distinguishing them.

The binders that have been used for water-borne (latex) house paints include polyvinyl acetate (PVA)–acrylic, acrylic, styrene–acrylic, styrene–butadiene, and PVA–polyethylene, but PVA–acrylics and acrylics are now the most common types used in interior finishes. Alkyd-modified latex paints have also been recently introduced. Acrylics are high-performance latex binders that are more common for higher-gloss interior finishes and exterior finishes. Alkyds, polyurethanes, acrylics, and nitrocellulose are used in oil-base house paints, although alkyds are the most common. Many of the same pigments and extender pigments used for automotive undercoats, especially titanium dioxide, calcium carbonate (calcite and aragonite), silica, talc, kaolin, and barium sulfate, are also used in house paints. In addition, house paints may contain mica, zinc oxide, gypsum, dolomite, wollastonite, magnesite, and bentonite, and like automotive undercoats, various combinations of pigments and extender pigments may be used.

Although they tend to be more prevalent in low lusters, house paints run the gamut in gloss levels and are sometimes classified by their sheen gradations as flat, eggshell, pearl, satin, semi-gloss, and gloss. In general, the lower the luster of the finish, the larger the quantities of extender pigments that are used, because these serve, in part, as flatting agents. This difference is reflected in infrared spectra of house paints and is illustrated by the absorptions of three off-white interior latex paints depicted in Figures 3-40F, 3-45A, and 3-45B. Figures 3-40F and 3-45A are spectra of flat finishes. The spectrum of Figure 3-40F has strong absorptions of rutile (Figure 3-44B) and likely silica (based on absorptions near 1100 and 470 cm^{-1}), and a very weak absorption of kaolin (Figures 3-40G and 3-45C), whereas Figure 3-45A has strong absorptions of calcite (Figure 3-46C), likely silica, and an oxide (the very broad low-frequency absorption beginning near 950 cm^{-1}). The spectrum of the semi-gloss paint of Figure 3-45B contains a strong absorption of rutile, a weak absorption of kaolin, and several absorptions of the PVA–acrylic binder.[246] Spectra of most flat finishes are dominated by the presence of strong broad absorptions of titanium dioxide and extender pigments, and in many cases, only a few binder absorptions are observed (compare Figures 3-45A and 3-45B). Differences in the absorptions of pigments—and especially extender pigments—thus serve as the main means to distinguish between infrared spectra of many interior house paints. Because they tend to occur in pastel shades, large amounts of color-imparting pigments are not required for most interior house paints, and absorptions of these pigments are not normally observed in infrared spectra.

Composition-wise, oil-base house paints and transparent finishes (such as varnish, shellac, or clear lacquer) are sometimes more like automotive finishes because similar binders can be used, although when the entire coating system is present, they are not likely to be confused. Spectra of high-gloss transparent finishes consist predominantly of the binder, whereas spectra of semi-gloss transparent finishes may contain absorptions of the extender pigment used as the flatting agent.

A combination of FT-IR and Raman spectroscopy was used to study the discrimination between some lilac[276] and white[277] house paints and their resins,[278] and the two methods were found to be complementary in their discriminating abilities. In lilac paints, the two strongest scattering constituents were often found to be Violet 23 and Copper Phthalocyanine Blue, the absorptions of which are not observed in infrared spectra. However, a study[250] of automotive paints using Raman spectroscopy found that silicates (talc, kaolin, silica, mica, etc.), which are very common extender pigments in house paints, are very weak Raman scatterers, and even when present in high concentrations in a paint (regardless of type of paint), their peaks are not observed.

OTHER COATINGS The binders that have been cited for automotive finish layers, undercoats, and house paints are also used for many other types of coatings. The specific type, however, depends strongly on the intended applications of the coating and especially, the degree to which they may be subjected to light and moisture exposure. Bicycle paints, for example, are usually similar to those used for automobiles, whereas binders containing aromatic epoxies, which are not light-fast, are usually limited to undercoats and interior applications. The color-imparting pigments may or may not be the same as those cited for automotive finishes. In general, paints that are intended for long-term outdoor use or that otherwise require high-performance pigments often contain the same pigments used for automotive paints. The less-expensive pigments (mostly inorganic, but also Copper Phthalocyanine Blue) are also likely to be found in a variety of coatings. For organic pigments, which generally cost more than inorganic pigments, less-expensive ones than those used for automobiles are likely to be encountered for these other paints.

The extent to which pigment and extender pigment absorptions occur in the spectra of various coatings follows the same guidelines discussed for automotive and house paints. Spectra of transparent coatings contain few if any such absorptions, and these absorptions become progressively more prominent as coatings become more translucent. Spectra of paints with pastel shades likely contain only absorptions of titanium dioxide and extender pigments, whereas those with vivid nonmetallic hues, especially in reds, oranges, and yellows, likely contain absorptions of inorganic pigments, organic pigments, or both.

The ability to discriminate between 40 green spraypaints was examined using a combination of FT-IR and Raman spectroscopy.[279] As in the study of house paints using these two methods, the two techniques were found to be complementary. No information about binders was obtained with Raman spectroscopy, for example, but both of the green phthalocyanine pigments mentioned earlier were readily identified in Raman spectra of some of the spray paints. Discrimination studies involving black[280] and red[281] spraypaints were also conducted, using a combination of optical microscopy, infrared spectroscopy and X-ray fluorescence spectrometry,

The Federation of Societies for Coatings Technology has compiled what is undoubtedly the most useful collection of reference infrared spectra of binders, pigments, and additives for various types of paints. It should be noted that newer editions of this collection are not simply updates and duplicates of older editions. The first edition[282] consists of far-infrared data collected to 200 cm^{-1}, whereas the fourth edition[283] has data to 400 cm^{-1}, so the first edition is the most useful one for identifying many inorganic paint constituents.

ANALYSIS METHODS   KBr pellets or micropellets,[255,284–289] DACs,[10,14,251,259,261,262,271] and multipass ATR accessories[289,291,292] have all been used for the analysis of paints using dispersive spectrometers. Cast films[285,289] of lacquers and condensates of paint pyrolysis products[285,289,293,294] have also been analyzed on such instruments. DAC spectra obtained using a dispersive instrument contain strong absorptions of diamond (Figure 3-22B), whereas ratioed spectra free of diamond absorptions are obtained with FT-IR spectrometers, and both high[11,57,58,295] and low[296,297] pressure DACs have been used for the FT-IR analysis of paints. With the high-pressure DAC, weak absorptions of acrylonitrile, Prussian Blue, or isocyanate residues of urethanes are not normally observed because of the high noise levels that occur in the region where the diamonds absorb (see, e.g., Figures 3-49A and 3-49B). The outer layers of a multi-layered paint can be analyzed with a single-pass ATR accessory, but analysts should remember that such spectra differ in intensity ratios if compared to transmission data, and pronounced band shape and frequency differences may occur if the paint contains inorganic components (compare Figures 3-30C and 3-30D).

For DAC or infrared microscope[123,298] analyses, samples of individual layers of a multilayered paint can be obtained using manual sectioning with a sharp scalpel or other device, or by using a microtome.[299] With the infrared microscope, each layer of a thin cross-section of a multilayered paint can be sequentially analyzed. Such cross-sections should be pressed flat before analysis, either with a roller device, a DAC, or some other means. This not only produces a sample with a more uniform thickness, but more importantly, increases the width of each layer. The latter makes it easier to avoid diffraction-induced stray light effects, which may occur if the edge of the aperture is set too close to the adjacent layer. Every effort should thus be made to set aperture edges as far away from adjacent layers as practical. Analysts should also compare their spectrum to those of the two adjacent layers (or layer) for evidence of spurious absorptions. The applications of chemical infrared imaging for the analysis of multilayered paint has recently been demonstrated, using an infrared microscope and a focal plane array detector system.[300,301] The infrared microscope can also be used for the analysis of very small cast films of paint pyrolyzates evaporated onto a salt window.[302] A summary of paint sample preparation methods for the infrared microscope is provided by Allen.[303]

The infrared microscope is particularly useful for the analysis of paint smears.[304] If the smear cannot be physically separated from the substrate, an ATR objective for the microscope is the best means to conduct an *in situ* analysis,[305] and a germanium element should be used if available. The effects of penetration depth differences should always be considered when performing such examinations (Figure 3-31). A combination of microscopy, solubility tests, and infrared spectroscopy using an ATR objective has been used for the analysis of thin paint smears involving two automobiles and a motor bike.[306]

Thin coatings on metal or other reflective substrates can be sampled directly using reflection-absorption analysis with an infrared microscope in the reflectance mode.[307] This method is applicable to coatings on an aluminum beverage can, for example, and has been used for the nondestructive analysis of a latex coating on a lottery ticket in a possible fraud case.[308] A variation of a reflection–absorption analysis has been used for the direct analysis of reference panels of metallic monocoats using a DRIFTS accessory.[57,58]

The role that infrared spectroscopy and other methods play in a comprehensive analysis of paint evidence has been recently reviewed by Ryland et al.,[309] whereas Hartshorn reviews the FT-IR analysis of paints from the perspective of the coatings industry.[310]

COMPARISON OF INFRARED AND PYROLYSIS GAS CHROMATOGRAPHY DATA   Pyrolysis gas chromatography (PGC) and pyrolysis gas chromatography/mass spectrometry (PGC/MS) are also used by forensic scientists to examine paint evidence, and a brief comparison of these methods to infrared spectroscopy is worth discussing. Generally, the data obtained by these two techniques are highly complementary. Infrared spectroscopy is an excellent means of identifying various types of polymers, for example, but is limited in its ability to detect most minor components that might be present along with the primary constituent. It also is of very limited value in characterizing binders when large amounts of extender pigments are present, as is the case for many flat interior house paints. Pyrolysis methods provide indirect information about polymers, through inferences made from the thermal degradation products identified, and give valuable information about the minor organic constituents present. For coatings where the differences in formulations are based primarily on minor components (such as differences in the types or amounts of various modifiers, drying oils, plasticizers, driers, and other organic additives), pyrolysis methods usually provide superior discrimination. They are, for example, the best techniques to determine the composition of various acrylic monomers used in an acrylic melamine enamel or an acrylic lacquer. Structural features that could be important in distinguishing between different paints may be destroyed by the pyrolysis process, however. For the differentiation of alkyd resins, it was found[311] that, although overall, PGC was more discriminating than infrared spectroscopy, the latter permitted a clear distinction between ortho- and isophthalic acid alkyds, whereas the former did not. The primary limitation of PGC and PGC/MS is that information about inorganic constituents cannot be obtained. As noted, inorganic pigments and extender pigments are strong absorbers of infrared light, so their absorptions are usually readily observed in paint spectra.

Because of the complementary nature of the two techniques and their respective inherent limitations, there is considerable merit in performing both examinations.[246,311,312] In situations where only a single technique is to be used, the type of paint involved should be a consideration. Paints that may contain a variety of inorganic constituents, for example, might be better characterized and differentiated using infrared spectroscopy, as demonstrated in a study of 31 house paints.[313] In line with this, the use of an infrared analysis for automotive undercoats and a PGC analysis for topcoats has been reported.[314] In cases where the amount of sample is limited and both techniques are to be used, the infrared analysis should be conducted first, because it is nondestructive, and the same sample can then be used for a PGC or PGC/MS analysis.

Fibers

Infrared spectroscopy plays an important role in any systematic scheme[315–319] involving the forensic analysis of fibers. This method is particularly helpful for some fibers (such as modified acrylics) for which a microscopic examination may not permit variations within a class to be distinguished, or for identifying fibers that are not commonly encountered. In addition, in a few cases it may provide information about fiber dyes or pigments and inorganic constituents, such as delustering agents, fire retardants, and so forth.

Fibers have traditionally been one of the more intractable materials routinely encountered by the forensic trace analyst as far as infrared analysis is concerned. A conventional dispersion in a KBr pellet is nearly impossible to achieve and tiny snippings of fibers, with or without further grinding, have been pressed with KBr instead.[320–322] A modification of this technique involves using a lead foil with an aperture of approximately 0.25 mm.[323] In either case, specimens having a nonuniform distribution of sample may result and as discussed, this can affect relative peak intensities. To avoid this, cast films[321,323–326] or evaporated residues of solutions mixed with KBr[327,328] have been used. These are not universally applicable, however, because not all fibers are amenable to such sampling. Also, dimethyl formamide, one of the solvents used to form cast films, binds very strongly with some fibers,[322,329] and this may produce residual amide absorptions in the resulting spectra. Strands of some fibers have been stretched across a window and sampled directly.[330–332]

The aforementioned methods have been used primarily on dispersive instruments. Two accessories that have been used with both dispersive and FTIR spectrometers for fiber analyses include ATR and the DAC. Multipass ATR accessories require a considerable amount of sample,[333–335] so single-pass accessories[21,336–339] are preferred. DAC spectra of fibers have been obtained using dispersive[14,340,341] and FT-IR[342–344] spectrometers. Several segments of fibers must normally be used with the DAC, however, because the diameters of most fibers are considerably less than the 0.8 mm (800 μm) aperture of this device. Single strands of flattened fibers have been analyzed with an FT-IR instrument using a beam condenser together with a 1.5×35 μm aperture.[345]

In view of the morphology, size, and consistency of fibers, the infrared microscope is the method of choice for an infrared analysis, using either transmittance[315,316,346–361] or an ATR objective.[305,362] Reflection–absorption using an infrared microscope may be used in cases where a smear of a fiber has transferred onto a reflective surface. Smears of Kevlar fibers on bullets were identified in this manner, for example, when bullets from several firearms of various calibers were analyzed after they struck a Kevlar bulletproof vest.[363]

Most synthetic fibers exhibit some degree of ordered molecular orientation that results from the drawing process used in their manufacture. The analysis beam of an FT-IR instrument is partially polarized, so the orientation of a sample that is not isotropic, such as a fiber, can affect its spectrum (some insight into why this occurs may be obtained from Figure 3-6). This may affect the relative peak intensities of a spectrum and although likely to be a minor effect, it is a good practice to use the same analysis orientation for fibers when conducting comparisons. Pressing a fiber to flatten it may also affect the molecular orientation,[349,350,357] so fibers that are being compared should be treated in the same manner in this regard also. With the use of a completely polarized incident beam on an infrared microscope, the orientation effects have been used to obtain dichroic ratio measurements for fibers to provide information regarding manufacturing differences[364,365] and to study the microstructure of cellulosic fibers.[361]

Because selected small areas can be analyzed with the microscope, it is possible to obtain spectra of individual lobes of a bicomponent fiber,[121,326] or their sheath and cores if they are made up of these components.[350] Bicomponent fibers have also been analyzed using infrared chemical imaging,[366] and as described previously, depth profiling using photoacoustic spectroscopy can be used (Figure 3-39) to deduce the compositions of the sheath and core.[92] For some nonwoven fabrics, it is possible to obtain spectra of both the fibers and the adhesive used as a binder.[121] The infrared microscope has also been used to determine the methyl acrylate content of some acrylic fibers[348] and to distinguish between 48 colorless acrylic fibers based on carbonyl, acrylic, and methylene absorption intensity ratios.[360]

Some of the within-genera compositional distinctions that have been made based on infrared data include differences in some acrylics,[326,329,348,349,351,353,355,360,367] modified acrylics,[325,356] polyesters,[328,334,349,359,365,368] nylons,[349,369] polyvinyl chlorides,[370] polyolefins,[341,352] polyurethanes,[371] and other nitrogen-containing fibers.[372] Cellulose acetate has been distinguished from cellulose triacetate based on significant differences in the relative intensities of O—H and C—H stretching absorptions.[343,349] Changes in the infrared spectrum of Orlon (acrylic) arising from different dyeing processes have been reported,[343] and the characteristic absorptions of a number of dyes used in colored acrylic fibers were identified.[355] Likewise, changes in the spectra of polypropylene fibers arising from dye-receptive additives have been noted.[341] A combination of infrared, Raman, and visible microspectroscopy were used to characterize various pigments used in polypropylene fibers.[352] Three new classes or types of fiber—Lyocell,[354] Nylon 6 block co-polymers,[354] and polylactic acid (PLA)[358]—were characterized using infrared and other methods.

The thermal degradation of fibers that had been melted, decomposed, burned, or incinerated has been studied using the infrared microscope,[373] and the infrared microscope, differential scanning calorimetry and optical microscopy were used to study the effects of exposure to the elements on polyester fibers.[374] ATR and polarized ATR were used for the characterization of historic silk,[375] and the location of a finishing agent in a polyester fiber was studied by a combination of FT-IR photoacoustic spectroscopy and X-ray photoelectron spectroscopy.[376] The discrimination of trace quantities of acrylic and polyamide fibers were compared in a study using both infrared spectroscopy and PGC.[377]

Explosives

The ingredients and residues associated with various explosive devices are composed of a wide variety of different substances, including organic compounds, inorganic salts, and polymers. This wide variety makes infrared spectroscopy an ideal tool, not only for screening such substances, but also for identification. Most systematic approaches[378–388] to examining explosives or their residues include an infrared analysis, and this method figures particularly prominently in many of the more comprehensive schemes.[378–380] Some of the specific types of explosives that have been analyzed using infrared spectroscopy include dynamite,[389] black powder,[390] smokeless powder,[391,392] C-4[393,394] and other military explosives,[395] flash powder,[396] monomethylamine nitrate,[397] nitrotoluenes,[398,399] triacetonetriperoxide,[400–402] silver fulminate,[403] and others.[404–408] Materials associated with explosive devices, such as pipe-bomb fillers,[409] adulterants used in improvised devices,[410] or blasting-cap leg wire insulation,[411–413] have likewise been identified using this technique.

Infrared spectroscopy is particularly helpful for the analysis of unusual or unexpected substances associated with explosive devices.[400,409,410,414–417] One of the advantages of this technique for this type of analysis is that, as discussed earlier, analysts can often recognize immediately from the spectrum of an unknown compound whether it is organic or inorganic, and this distinction provides important clues as to the nature of the explosive material, residue, or device used.

Some of the more common inorganic salts encountered in the analysis of explosives and their residues include nitrates, sulfates, chlorates, perchlorates, carbonates, oxides, and ammonium cations. Nitrates (Figure 3-17), sulfates (Figure 3-16), perchlorates (Figure 3-16D), chlorates, and carbonates (Figure 3-35A and 3-46C) all produce strong, broad antisymmetric oxygen-stretching fundamentals that occur between 1500 and 1000 cm^{-1}; depending on the particular salt involved, one or two sharp absorptions due to oxygen bending fundamentals occur at lower frequencies.[6,418] As noted, potassium sulfate (Figure 3-16C) and potassium perchlorate (Figure 3-16D) have very similar infrared spectra, but they can be easily distinguished using "wet" chemical methods (such as a sulfate test using barium chloride, or a test for oxidants using diphenylamine reagent), ion chromatography, capillary electrophoresis, or other methods. Even when mixtures involving these salts are involved, the individual components can usually be recognized from their characteristic absorptions.[378]

For organic compounds, two functional groups of particular importance in explosives analyses include nitro (—NO$_2$) and nitrate (—ONO$_2$), both of which produce strong characteristic absorptions.[419,420] The specific frequencies observed for these groups can also yield considerable information about the type of nitro or nitrate compound involved.[386,420] For some organic unknowns, an integrated approach involving consideration of data from a variety of spectroscopic methods, including infrared, ultraviolet, NMR (proton and carbon-13), and mass spectrometry may be required.[400,414–416]

In line with the diversity of materials encountered in explosives analyses, a variety of infrared analysis methods, including KBr pellets or micropellets,[378,385,389,390,393,395–398,400,402,403,406–408,416,417] nujol mulls,[406] solutions in various solvents,[385,389,393,395,399,404–406,410] capillary films,[398,406,414] and the DAC[378,390,391,395,411–413] have been used with dispersive instruments. These methods can also be used on an FT-IR,[391,409,421] although accessories that provide better sensitivity and require less sample preparation are now available. Solutions can be analyzed with a single-pass diamond ATR accessory, for example, providing better solvent compensation than possible with transmittance methods. Heat- and shock-sensitive compounds, such as nitroglycerin, are conveniently analyzed as residues deposited from solution using either ATR[394] or DRIFTS; this is preferred to methods such as the DAC that require application of pressure. ATR can also be useful for the direct analysis of some gels or water slurries. For greater sensitivity, the infrared microscope may be helpful, and this accessory has been used for the analysis of individual propellant particles of smokeless powder.[392] When inorganic salts are involved, however, a DAC/extended-range analysis is usually preferred.

For the analysis of complex mixtures, one of the hyphenated techniques may be ideal. GC/FT-IR is a useful complement to GC/MS for the analysis of nitro or nitrate compounds, for example, because such compounds may produce similar mass spectra. The feasibility of using a FT-IR spectrometer as an on-the-fly detector for explosives eluting from a HPLC has been examined.[421,422] Supercritical fluid chromatography (SFC) has been performed on both methylene chloride and supercritical carbon dioxide extracts of double-base smokeless powders, using on-line FT-IR detection,[423] whereas on-line gel permeation chromatography/Fourier transform infrared (GPC/FT-IR) spectroscopy has been used to determine the nitrogen content of cellulose nitrates.[424] Nitrocellulose and pulp in smokeless powder have also been measured using a thermogravimetric analysis/Fourier transform infrared (TGA/FT-IR) procedure.[425]

The mechanism involved in the explosive reaction between swimming pool chlorine (calcium hypochlorite) and brake fluid (polyethylene glycol), a possible improvised explosive mixture, has been studied by means of vapor infrared spectra of the gaseous products produced.[426] Differences in the surface characteristics of solid propellants containing cyclotrimethylene-trinitramine (RDX), nitrocellulose, and other compounds were studied using FT-IR photoacoustic spectroscopy.[427]

Synthetic Polymers

In addition to paints and fibers, the forensic scientist is likely to encounter a variety of evidence composed of or incorporating synthetic polymers. This is inevitable in view of the prevalence of such materials, including plastics, rubbers, foams, tapes, adhesives, laminates, composites, and building materials in our society. Infrared spectroscopy is one of the primary analytical tools of the polymer chemist, and numerous papers dealing with polymer spectroscopy—many of which may be of peripheral interest to the forensic scientist—have been published. Clearly, this is a broad and expanding subject, and the scope of the present section is limited to a discussion of the forensic aspects of polymer analysis using infrared spectroscopy.

One of the main concerns of the forensic scientist is to be able to distinguish between various materials composed of synthetic polymers. The situation for this type of evidence is not unlike that of paint evidence, because items composed of synthetic polymers sometimes contain appreciable amounts of inorganic extender pigments and other additives. Their absorptions, together with those of the polymer and associated compounds (such as plasticizers), can be used to characterize and differentiate such materials. The spectrum of the vinyl siding of Figure 3-46B, for example, contains strong absorptions of calcite (Figure 3-46C). Compared to the spectrum of PVC (Figure 3-46A), it also has enhanced C—H and carbonyl-stretching absorptions, both consistent with the presence of a phthalate plasticizer.

As in the case of paints, fibers and many other products, infrared spectroscopy is usually one of several tests that are used to characterize evidence, and this vinyl-siding example also serves as a reminder that infrared spectroscopy is only providing part of the picture (albeit a large part) regarding composition. The identity of the plasticizer, for example, is far from clear, and for many other polymers that do not contain a carbonyl group, the presence of carbonyl-stretching absorptions in their spectra may be more indicative of an ester copolymer than a plasticizer. The siding material used in this example also contains both rutile and Nickel Titanate, but the infrared data provide little evidence of their presence (other than a broad low-frequency shoulder in the 500 to 600 cm^{-1} region for Figure 3-46B compared to Figure 3-46A). Even if this sample happened to contain a large quantity of Nickel Titanate without rutile, other methods would still be required to identify this pigment because its infrared absorptions are very similar to those of rutile (Figure 3-25) and to those of other titanate pigments (which are all readily distinguished[19] based on elemental analysis data). In interpreting infrared spectra, forensic scientists should thus always be aware of both the information that this technique provides **and the information that it does not** (as emphasized previously for inorganic salts that include nonabsorbing cations or anions).

Materials composed of synthetic polymers span a range of physical character-istics and include hard plastics, rubbers, elastic foams, rigid forms, and films. Various infrared methods have thus been used for their analysis, including KBr pel-lets,[284,285] the DAC,[14] the infrared microscope,[121,428–432] DRIFTS,[54,55] ATR,[291] photoacoustic spectroscopy,[83] and pyrolysis GC/IR/MS.[77,78] The infrared method best suited for the analysis of a particular type of material is dictated by the nature of the material and its size. Although there is thus no universal method, the DAC/extended-range accessory is a useful option for many such materials, because it allows potentially important far-infrared data to be collected for inorganic constituents and it provides a convenient means to flatten and retain pliable materials such as foams or rubbers; hard plastics may be powdered with a diamond scribe or sliced with a scalpel. For materials having inhomogeneous compositions, such as laminates or composites, the infrared microscope or an ATR objective can be useful for analyzing individual components.[121,428–430] A comparison of some techniques used in the forensic science laboratory to characterize synthetic polymers was conducted,[433] and brief reviews of the analysis of polymers using FT-IR spectroscopy[434] and infrared and other techniques have been presented.[435]

ADHESIVE TAPES   Adhesive tapes have been used for a variety of purposes associ-ated with criminal activities, including restraining victims, wrapping packages con-taining bombs, drugs, or other illegal items, as reinforcement for pipebombs and other improvised explosive devices, as used on documents, and so forth. Forensic scientists may be asked to compare tapes, to determine the type of tape that is sub-mitted as evidence, to determine the manufacturer of a tape, or to determine if a ma-terial is tape. Tapes are composed of a backing and adhesive. Tapes requiring more strength may be further reinforced with a fabric or fibers. All three components have been analyzed using infrared spectroscopy.

The value of adhesive tape as evidence was examined in a study that compared 58 different tapes using a combination of microscopy, infrared spectroscopy, visi-ble–ultraviolet microspectrophotometry, and PGC/MS.[436] The backing and adhesive for each tape were analyzed using an infrared microscope, and the combined dis-criminating ability of the four methods was found to be very high. Merrill and Bartick[437] examined six different ATR methods for their ability to discriminate be-tween various types of duct tape, electrical tape, packaging tape, and office tape, with both sides of the tapes analyzed intact. An extended-range analysis using a sin-gle-pass ATR accessory with a diamond-coated KRS-5 element was found to be the technique of choice. Duct-tape backing was the focus of a study that examined 82 tapes using a single-pass ATR accessory, a macroscopic examination, and a micro-scopic examination of the backing cross sections.[438] For a few tapes, the infrared data revealed the presence of a multilayered backing that was not evident from the microscopic examination, because a second polymer coat was coextruded during the tape manufacturing process. PVC adhesive tapes[439] and PVC black electrical tapes[440] were characterized using infrared and other methods. The infrared data for these were differentiated by the absorptions of adhesives, copolymers, plasticizers, and inorganic constituents.

AUTOMOTIVE PARTS   Because they provide a number of benefits such as corrosion resistance, reduced weight, and lower cost, plastics and rubbers have assumed an increasingly important role in automobile manufacturing. Automobile side light plastics have been analyzed and differentiated using infrared and other methods.[441] A DAC on a dispersive instrument was used for this, whereas an ATR FT-IR analysis[442] and use of an ATR objective of an infrared microscope[443] were used for the examination of automobile rubber bumper guards. Bumper guards were also analyzed[444] using a combination of infrared microscopy, PGC, and X-ray analysis using a scanning electron microscope (SEM/EDX). Like paint, automotive repair body fillers may be encountered in transfers or as fragments left at the scene of a hit-and-run incident. Repair body fillers typically contain large amounts of inorganic extender pigments and infrared spectroscopy has been found to be useful for their differentiation.[445] Another study of body fillers using a combination of infrared spectroscopy, visible microspectrophotometry, density measurements, and SEM-EDX also confirmed this.[446] The ability to discriminate between automotive tire rubbers using an ATR objective of an infrared microscope, DRIFTS and PGC/MS was examined,[447] and PGC/MS was found to provide the best discrimination.

PLASTIC BAGS AND FILMS   Cleverley[448] studied the differentiation of low-density polyethylene plastic bags using infrared spectroscopy. Based primarily on the weaker absorptions observed for thick-film samples, he was able to distinguish two ethylene/vinyl acetate copolymer types and ten homopolymer types; seven other types produced small but reproducible differences in relative band intensities. The discriminating abilities of microscopy, infrared spectroscopy using a single-pass ATR accessory, and X-ray diffraction (XRD) were also examined for polyethylene plastic bags.[449] Microscopy was found to discriminate plastic bags by their morphological differences; XRD provided a discrimination based on crystallinity and the polyethylene films could be grouped into three classes: low-density, linear low-density, and high-density; and infrared spectroscopy provided a distinction based on molecular components. The suitability of various types of plastic bags as storage containers for fire debris evidence was examined in a study that used infrared spectroscopy as one of the methods used for this assessment.[450]

Plastic-wrap films have been analyzed using infrared spectroscopy[451] and a combination of infrared spectroscopy and thermal desorption gas chromatography.[452] Multilayer plastic packaging foils were analyzed using an ATR system on an infrared microscope.[453] This system was also used to obtain infrared images of the layers, and the data obtained were compared to those from PLM, SEM, and differential scanning calorimetry. The infrared method was found to provide superior discrimination to the combination of these three techniques, because it provided both spatial and chemical information.

OTHER   Infrared methods have been used to differentiate rubber shoe soles,[454] polymeric foams,[55,455] and plastic electrical wire insulation used for blasting caps.[411–413] Different brands of plastic reflective glitter particles, used in hair gels, cosmetics, and clothing, have been distinguished based on infrared and other data.[456] Infrared and other data have also been used for the identification and differentiation of various types of adhesives.[457–460] A single-pass ATR analysis and multivariate statistical methods were used for the discrimination of some nylon polymers.[461] In a study of plastic films used for passports, authentic and counterfeit passports could be distinguished based on differences in reflectance spectra obtained with an infrared microscope using polarized light.[462]

Two studies examined the discrimination of polydimethylsiloxane condom lubricants using infrared spectroscopy and other methods. In the first, the viscosities of ten different lubricant brands were compared by determining the average polymer chain lengths obtained by measuring the ratios of the dimethyl to trimethyl infrared absorptions.[463] The second study examined extracts of lubricants using infrared spectroscopy for the presence of polydimethylsiloxane and the spermicide nonoxynol-9, and also examined the use of desorption chemical ionization/mass spectrometry in conjunction with an infrared analysis.[464]

Document Examinations

The examination of questioned documents may occasionally entail the analysis of paper, ink, toner, or other document-associated items. This analysis may involve either a comparison or an attempt to determine the time frame in which a document was produced.[465,466] In either case, the compositions of the paper, ink or toner, or associated items may be sought, and infrared spectroscopy has been used for many such examinations.

PAPER COMPOSITIONS   Many types of paper contain various fillers and coatings, both organic and inorganic, and these may serve to distinguish documents. An ATR analysis was used to examine paper coatings and various types, including polyvinylchloride-acetate, acrylic, silicone, polyethylene, polystyrene, paraffin-impregnated, baryte, and assorted dyed papers, were identified and differentiated.[467] Probably the most common inorganic filler used in paper is kaolin, although the trend in recent years has been to produce longer-lasting acid-free paper using calcium carbonate and other alkaline fillers. Differences in kaolin and carbonate absorptions were among the features used to differentiate white papers in a study using DRIFTS, ATR, and multivariate statistical techniques.[468] A combination of infrared analysis using an ATR accessory and electron spectroscopy were used to determine whether aging effects could be detected for some historical documents.[469] The infrared microscope was used in a study of paper and differences in spectra arising from differences in the amounts of lignin present were noted.[470] This study also identified nylon fibers in currency notes that are woven into the cellulose matrix at random locations to help detect counterfeit currency. Ten samples of white paper from different manufacturers were analyzed in a study using DRIFTS and statistical methods, and all were distinguished.[471] Zinc oxide photocopy papers have also been characterized and distinguished using infrared and other methods.[472]

INKS Three FT-IR accessories, the DAC, infrared microscope, and DRIFTS, were evaluated for their applicability in analyzing ballpoint-pen inks.[473] For the nondestructive *in situ* analysis of ink on paper, DRIFTS appeared to be the best suited of the three methods. Analyses of ballpoint pen inks extracted from paper and analyzed using DRIFTS deposition[474] and deposition onto a KBr pellet[475] have been reported. Fifteen black inks were distinguished using *in situ* DRIFTS analyses and statistical methods.[471] Black inks have also been analyzed *in situ* using FT-IR photothermal beam deflection spectroscopy, and the spectra obtained permitted some differentiation and the determination of whether the inks contained carbon.[476] Blue ballpoint pen inks were analyzed using an infrared microscope and this permitted 108 inks to be classified into 35 subgroups.[477] Seventy samples of blue and black ballpoint pen and gel inks were analyzed using a combination of infrared and Raman spectroscopy and X-ray fluorescence (XRF) spectrometry.[478] The ink samples were analyzed in transmittance using an infrared microscope, and based on the combination of the three techniques, approximately 90% of the samples of the same type and color could be distinguished. Blue and black ballpoint-pen inks and liquid inks were also analyzed using a combination of microscopy, infrared spectroscopy using an infrared microscope, Raman spectroscopy, and thin-layer chromatography.[479] The feasibility of using an ATR objective of an infrared microscope to analyze inks *in situ* was demonstrated in a case where a carbon copy had been suspected of being altered.[443] Spectra of the ink of the carbon paper and that of a known carbon copy were similar and had strong peaks of Prussian Blue,[247] but the spectrum of the ink on the document in question lacked these peaks, indicating it was not from the carbon paper. Synchrotron radiation was used with an infrared microscope to obtain *in situ* reflectance spectra of inks on paper,[480] and ink removed from U.S. currency was analyzed using an infrared microscope.[470]

Current methods of ink dating consist, for the most part, of identification of the specific brand of ink involved together with knowledge of the time frames in which specific brands were manufactured. Some work has been performed, however, on correlating the age of ink with compositional changes that occur with time after the ink has been deposited. The possibility that the infrared spectrum of an ink might be reflective of such a change has been investigated, and, for one type of ink at least, the ratio of hydroxyl to methyl absorptions was found to vary with time,[481,482] thereby permitting some dating information.

An ink analysis that has generated considerable interest and controversy is the high-profile examination conducted by McCrone on the Vinland map. This map, purported to be from the fifteenth century, was analyzed by a number of laboratories, and carbon dating of the paper used for the map indicated it to be from the fifteenth century. McCrone[483,484] analyzed the map on two occasions. An infrared microscope analysis[483] of the ink medium indicated it to be composed of gelatin, a common medieval material used for inks. Using microscopy and other methods, McCrone also identified anatase in the ink, with the anatase having morphologies, particle sizes, and particle size distributions consistent with those of modern formulations.[484] Anatase was first manufactured as a paint pigment in the 1920s, and McCrone (and many others) concluded that the map is a forgery.

TONERS   Documents produced from photocopiers, laser printers, and fax machines have become very common in our society, and they are increasingly being submitted as evidence. These devices use toners rather than inks. The latter are applied as liquids, whereas toners are usually applied as powders that are heated to form a film that binds to paper. Common toner polymers include styrene/acrylics, polyesters, and epoxies, although many others have been used,[485] and carbon black and magnetite (Fe_3O_4) are common pigments. Prussian Blue and other pigments have also been used.

Kemp and Totty[486] were the first to examine toners using infrared spectroscopy. They prepared KBr micropellets of toners removed from documents, then classified toners into ten groups based on their infrared absorptions. Using Kemp and Totty's data, Williams[487] further subdivided the classes based on detailed interpretations of the absorptions, including identifying cyano peaks at 2090 cm^{-1} as those of Prussian Blue and demonstrating that the *ortho*, *meta*, and *para* isomers of polyesters (alkyds) could be distinguished.

Twenty-nine photocopy toners were extracted from documents using carbon tetrachloride and analyzed in transmittance using an FT-IR instrument, and the toners were classified into six groups based on their absorptions.[488] Using a DRIFTS analysis of toners removed from documents, 152 different black and colored toners were classified into 36 groups.[489,490] A combination of infrared spectroscopy and PGC was used to distinguish toners[491] and toners and adhesives[492] removed from documents. Black toners were also analyzed using a combination of infrared spectroscopy and PGC/MS,[493] or infrared spectroscopy and XRF spectrometry.[494] Seventy-five photocopy toners were analyzed by DRIFTS, SEM/EDX, and PGC, and the combination of DRIFTS and SEM/EDX was found to be the best approach, as it allowed 30 classes to be established.[495]

A heated iron was used to remove a small portion of toner from a document, and the portion then placed on a reflective surface in order to perform a reflection–absorption analysis using an infrared microscope.[496] Three techniques, DRIFTS, reflection–absorption, and use of a germanium or diamond ATR objective of an infrared microscope, were evaluated for their ability to obtain spectra of toners.[497] For *in situ* analyses, the germanium ATR element was preferred over diamond, because absorptions of the cellulose substrate were observed in spectra using the diamond element, which also exhibited more dispersion distortions owing to its lower index of refraction compared to germanium. Overall, reflection–absorption was deemed the optimum method considering quality of data, speed, and accessory cost, and these same authors then produced a searchable spectral library of 807 toners using reflection–absorption analysis.[498,499]

A study was conducted to determine if it is possible to distinguish between documents produced on a laser printer and a photocopier.[500] An extended range FT-IR analysis of toners using a DAC was one of the methods used in this study, and absorptions of magnetite (Black Iron Oxide, see Figure 3-42G) were observed in many of the toner spectra. Like carbon black, spectra of magnetite have pronounced sloping baselines; unlike carbon black, however, magnetite can be readily identified based on its absorptions using an extended range instrument. This study concluded that it is difficult to distinguish documents produced by these two devices because similar toners are often used.

OTHER DOCUMENT-RELATED ANALYSES   Correction fluids, which may appear on some questioned documents, have been characterized using DAC FT-IR data.[501] Both the binders and pigments of these fluids were found to be useful for this, and, as a result of manufacturers changing their formulations with time, it was found that some dating of fluids was possible. As cited earlier, the latex coating on a Connecticut state winning lottery ticket was analyzed intact using reflection–absorption with an infrared microscope, and this helped to authenticate the ticket, which originally was believed to be a counterfeit.[308] Adhesives associated with documents have been analyzed using infrared and other methods,[291,457,458] including adhesives used on postage stamps.[502,503]

Miscellaneous Evidence

Some types of evidence not routinely submitted to forensic science laboratories or that may be common but not normally subjected to infrared analysis are discussed in this section.

PETROLEUM PRODUCTS   Several types of petroleum products of interest to the forensic scientist have been analyzed using infrared spectroscopy. Cleverley found that each of the twenty different formulations of lubricating greases that he examined gave a different spectrum.[504] One of the main distinguishing features used for this was whether a soap (salt of a fatty acid) or a clay thickener was present. Bar soaps themselves were the subject of a study examining the discriminating ability of FT-IR spectroscopy (using a DAC) and an SEM/EDX analysis.[505] Some automobile lubricating oils have been differentiated using infrared methods,[506–509] including differentiation of used oils having different extents of decomposition.[510–512] The rate of oil degradation in a vehicle has also been studied using infrared spectroscopy.[513] Crude oil and various fuel oils have been examined to determine whether infrared data can be used to help identify the source of oil spills.[514–517] Because the primary constituents of most petroleum products consist of various straight-chain alkanes, the differences in the spectra of these products may be minor and usually arise from the presence of additives, aromatic compounds, and other components.

SOIL   The forensic characterization of clay minerals using infrared and other methods has been reported.[518,519] A novel technique to study the organic fraction of soils using infrared spectroscopy has been proposed.[520] The spectrum of a soil sample is obtained before and after an oxidative pyrolysis is conducted to remove all of the organic components. A spectral subtraction is then performed to obtain a spectrum of the organic components, and this method was found to increase the discrimination between soils that are otherwise similar. Bulk samples of air-dried soils have been analyzed directly using photoacoustic spectroscopy, and the information from such spectra was found to be similar to that obtained using transmittance methods, although the latter required considerably more sample preparation.[521]

HAIR AND COSMETICS   An FT-IR study was conducted to determine if there were differences among individuals in the ratios of the amide I and amide II infrared absorption bands of human hair.[522] Only minor differences were found, however. A high-resolution infrared image of the cross section of a human hair has been obtained using a germanium ATR objective of an infrared microscope and a focal plane array detector system.[523] The oxidation of human head hair produced by bleaching has been monitored using infrared spectroscopy, and, based on sulfonic acid group absorptions, some discrimination between treated and untreated hairs was possible.[524,525] Using a zinc selenide ATR objective of an infrared microscope, spectra of a hair before and after application of hairspray were taken.[443] A spectral subtraction then yielded a spectrum similar to that of the hairspray, except for weak residual amide absorptions of the hair.

Fifty-three cosmetic foundation products were the subject of a study to examine the discriminating abilities of DAC/FT-IR spectroscopy, SEM/EDX, and GC-FID.[526] It was found that each of the three methods alone had discriminating powers of 98.3%, 93.8%, and 82.0%, respectively, but in combination, it was 99.7%, indicating nearly total discrimination. Cosmetics also served as the basis for determining the driver of a vehicle in which four of the six occupants (four males and two females, including the suspected driver) were killed.[527] Cosmetic smears on the airbag were analyzed using the infrared microscope, PCG, SEM/EDX, and XRD. Although there was also DNA evidence found on the airbag, the judge in the case believed that its origin might possibly have arisen from an individual other than the driver, but he found the pattern and composition of the cosmetics smears on the airbag to be convincing evidence.

FINGERPRINTS   Long before DNA technology assumed a central role in the public's perception of an unequivocal means to identify an individual, there were fingerprints. Indeed, the association between a fingerprint and a specific individual has become so ingrained that it is often used as an analogy, such as when the term *fingerprint region* is used to describe a specific portion of the infrared spectrum (of an organic compound). Fittingly, fingerprints and infrared spectroscopy have now crossed paths.

In 2001, Wilkinson et al.[528] first demonstrated the feasibility of obtaining infrared spectra of individual particles of fingerprints using an infrared microscope with synchrotron radiation. In 2004, Williams et al.[529] demonstrated this capability using a conventional infrared microscope to obtain reflection-absorption spectra of components of fingerprints on a reflective surface. Using both a conventional infrared microscope and one with a synchrotron source, Grant et al.[530] then examined the feasibility of identifying various materials that volunteers had handled, including ibuprofen, vitamin C, non-dairy creamer, and Sweet'N Low®, before making prints on a reflective surface. The volunteers were asked to wipe their fingers prior to making prints so that no visible residues remained. The data collected allowed each of these substances to be identified from the spectra of the fingerprints.

Two methods to obtain infrared images of fingerprints have been reported more recently. In the first, reflectance spectra of fingerprints were collected using an infrared microscope, with the area of the fingerprint scanned sequentially.[531] The spectral data were then processed to form an image. A second method used an ATR accessory and a focal plane array detection system.[532]

ART AND ARTIFACT FORGERIES   Along with the Vinland map, McCrone[533] was also involved in another extremely controversial analysis involving the Shroud of Turin. Using microscopy and other tests, he concluded that the stains on the Shroud could not have originated from the time period in which they were thought to have been produced (a fact later confirmed by carbon dating of the Shroud and by other examinations).

Although historical artifacts and art are not usually analyzed in public forensic science laboratories, there is certainly a potential for this because it has been estimated that 15% of all artwork sold worldwide are forgeries.[534] Much of this may be unintentional, but certainly some of it also involves fraud. Like dating methods used in document analyses, the strongest indications of an art forgery (style considerations aside) are usually based on paint pigment and resin formulations that were used during certain time periods.[535–537] This was the basis for McCrone's conclusions regarding the Vinland map and other forgeries.[536] Because infrared spectroscopy has proved to be a valuable tool of the forensic paint examiner, it is not surprising that it is often used for detecting art forgeries and restorations.[538–546] Noninvasive procedures are preferred for the analysis of art and artifacts, and a fiber optics reflectance analysis using a portable FT-IR instrument has been proposed as one means to accomplish this.[547] Optimal infrared spectra are usually obtained using transmittance methods, however, and the infrared microscope is usually the method of choice.[539,542,544] Derrick, Stulik, and Landry[548] present a summary of the use of infrared spectroscopy for the analysis of materials found in cultural artifacts, including paintings, sculptures, and archaeological items.

In a case where a synthetic organic pigment is identified in a painting said to be from the nineteenth century or earlier, it is clear that this component was not used in the original work because organic pigments are of modern origin. A recent example illustrates, however, that synthetic organic pigments can also be useful in determining more modern forgeries.

In 2002, thirty-two previously unknown works by the American abstract expressionist artist Jackson Pollock were found in a storage locker of a friend of Pollock's. Some of the paintings began to be displayed at various art museums, but some were also sent to the Boston Museum of Fine Arts Laboratory, the Harvard Art Museum Laboratory, and Orion Analytical LLC.[549] All three laboratories examined deep layers of these paintings and identified several organic pigments and other paint ingredients that were first introduced decades after Pollock died in 1956. None of these constituents were found in any of the Pollock works known to be genuine. All three laboratories used infrared spectroscopy and other methods for their pigment identifications (Orion Analytical LLC, 2007, personal communication), and one of the organic pigments identified was DPP Red BO, a very common automotive paint pigment that was first introduced in 1985.[248]

OTHER APPLICATIONS   An infrared method has been developed to detect the nerve agent Sarin (isopropyl methylphosphonofluoridate, or GB) using DRIFTS and magnesium oxide as an a preconcentrating agent.[550] Infrared spectroscopy has been used to identify the active ingredients of various personal protection lachrymator devices that contain chloroacetophenone (CN),[551–553] *ortho*-chlorobenzal-malononitrile (CS),[551–554] and capsaicinoids.[552,555] In a case in which Roundup® (isopropylammonium glyphosate) was suspected of being placed in the tank of a lawn tractor, an analysis of the products of gasoline and Roundup using infrared spectroscopy was found to be consistent with the use of this herbicide.[556] For analyses involving game poaching, the FT-IR has also been used to screen suspected ivory for the presence of dahlite, a component of dentine.[557] Several small, yellow, plastic-like flakes were recovered from the body of a rape victim, and these were compared to the screen-printing ink from the jersey of the suspect. Using infrared spectroscopy, microscopy, and PGC, the flakes were found to be consistent with those from the jersey.[558] The difficulties in comparing cement-based safe insulations because of compositional changes arising from moisture effects have been described when using infrared spectroscopy.[559] The application of infrared imaging for the analysis of particles that have been lifted onto tape has been discussed, where an ATR objective of an infrared microscope was used with a focal plane array detector system.[560]

Contaminants

As evidenced throughout this chapter, the FT-IR and its accessories have been responsible for a quantum leap in the forensic scientist's ability to analyze ever smaller samples using infrared spectroscopy. As the size of evidence analyzed becomes smaller, the problems associated with contaminants may become more acute. For this brief discussion, contaminants are divided into two classes: those that are associated with pure substrates (substrates being materials such as fibers, paints, and fragments of an explosive device), which are referred to as *inherent contaminants*; and those that may be introduced during an analysis (*external contaminants*). The former, which are beyond the control of the analyst, are really an integral part of the evidence and may have considerable significance (indeed, a contaminant may be the evidence itself); the latter can be (mostly) controlled, and these contaminants are to be avoided, especially when dealing with microtrace evidence.[561]

Inherent contaminants may present difficulties when the substrate itself is the object of interest. Assuming that the contaminant and the substrate occur as discrete (nonuniform) units, it may be possible to separate them physically. The DAC or infrared microscope may then be useful for analysis. In many cases it may be possible to simply to press an appropriate area of the sample to form a film and sample a region of the substrate free of contaminants. Alternatively, an *in situ* analysis using an ATR objective of an infrared microscope may be used. If available, a germanium element is preferred because substrate absorptions are less likely to be observed, and the high index of refraction of germanium allows a greater variety of materials to be analyzed without producing spectral distortions.

Tungol et al.[350] discuss several examples of dealing with contaminants on fibers analyzed using an infrared microscope. Petraco and DeForest[562] discuss the infrared microscope analysis of contaminants transferred to bullets during flight to aid in establishing trajectories. Several contaminants that were responsible for producing paint defects were identified using a combination of microscopy and FT-IR analysis.[563] Infrared spectroscopy has also recently been used for the analysis of pollen.[564]

The control of external contaminants that may be introduced during sample isolation and preparation for infrared microanalysis has been described.[565] Aside from such contaminants, including those from solvent and reagent impurities, the primary source of external contaminants is dust. Dust from several different environments has been identified using optical microscopy,[566] whereas the infrared microscope has been used to study the composition of dust in both office and laboratory environments.[567] For the laboratory environments, cellulose was the most common constituent identified—primarily in the form of paper fibers, wood particles, and textile cotton. Polyamides were the second most common constituents, with most of these consisting of proteinaceous material in the form of flat, flaky particles (human epithelial cells); lesser amounts of hair and nylon fibers were included in this category. Other textile fibers, synthetic polymers, and cosmetics were also identified. In addition to the aforementioned, forensic laboratories performing frequent drug analyses might expect to find constituents of commonly encountered powders—such as cocaine hydrochloride or other drugs received in high volume—in their dust. For more information about the analysis of dust, the reader is referred to Chapter 2 of this *Handbook*.

ACKNOWLEDGMENTS

First Edition

I would like to thank Mr. George Ishii, Mr. Kay Sweeney, Dr. William Gresham, and Ms. Chesterene Cwiklik for their encouragement, comments, and, especially, for their foresight in promoting the purchase of our laboratory's first FT-IR instrument in 1981. Without the experience gained from using this instrument and a first-hand appreciation of its capabilities, producing this manuscript would have been a much more difficult (and abstract) task. I would also like to thank Deputy Chief Edward Crawford, who was instrumental in the purchase of our second FT-IR and infrared microscope; Captain Bruce Bjork, who overcame obstacles during the selection of our third and fourth FT-IRs; Ms. Tammy Usher, Ms. Vema Ayers, Ms. Linda Gamer, Ms. Phyllis Blair, Ms. Tanya Harrison, Ms. Kitty Moury, and Ms. Janene Rau, for their dedicated secretarial and word-processing work on a project that never seemed to end; Ms. Michele Derrick (The Getty Conservation Institute), for providing me with an extensive list of references pertaining to infrared analysis in art and archaeology; and the following individuals who took time to review this manuscript: Dr. Ed Bartick (FBI Forensic Science Research Unit), Ms. Ingrid Dearmore (WSCL), Dr. Larry Ellis (Bomem), Ms. Kerstin Gleim (WSCL), Dr. Gresham, Mr. Mike Grubb (WSCL), Dr. Howard Harris (Monroe County Public Safety Laboratory), Mr. Steve Hill (Digilab), Dr. Farida Holler (Digilab), Mr. Jerry Kacsir (Laser Precision Analytical), Mr. Alfred Low-Beer (NJ State Police Laboratory), Mr. Bill Marshall (WSCL), Mr. Erik Neilson (WSCL), Ms. Judy Nickels

(WSCL), Dr. Kent Oakes (National Fish and Wildlife Forensics Laboratory), Dr. John Reffner (Spectra Tech), Ms. Mary Tungol (FBI Laboratory), and Mr. Will Wihlborg (Spectra Tech). Finally, I would like to thank my wife **Joanne** and my two daughters, **Stacie** and **Stephanie,** for their encouragement and patience during the two-and-one-half-year period in which this manuscript was prepared.

Second Edition

I would like to thank again the contributions of the above individuals, plus those who have assisted in the extensive revisions to the first edition: Professor Joseph W. Nibler (Oregon State University), Professor Darren L. Williams (Sam Houston State University), Dr. John Reffner (Smiths Detection), and Professor Mary Tungol Carrabba (Southern Oregon University and Rogue River Spectroscopy, LLC), for their helpful discussions, and Professor Nibler, for being such a wonderful graduate thesis advisor; Mr. George Ishii (WSCL, retired), who very early in my career instilled in me a sense of obligation to contribute to the field of forensic science; Mr. Jim Tarver (WSCL), for his support of this project; Mr. Jeff Teitelbaum (WSP Forensic Laboratory Services Bureau), for his assistance in procuring references; Mr. Brett Bishop (WSCL) and Mr. Ray Kusumi (WSCL), for their assistance with *Photoshop*; all the forensic scientists who have taken the FBI Laboratory course, "Forensic Infrared Spectrometry for Trace Analysis," for their probing questions, which have been the main impetus behind the additions to the first edition; Ms. Lee Brun-Conti (ATF), Dr. Eric Buel (Vermont Forensic Laboratory), Ms. Helen Griffiths (Ventura County Forensic Laboratory), Mr. James Martin (Orion Analytical LLD), Dr. John McClelland (Iowa State University), Dr. Chris Palenik (Microtrace), Mr. Scott Ryland (Florida Department of Law Enforcement), Mr. Bob Shipman (Vermont Forensic Laboratory), Ms. Marianne Stam (California DOJ Riverside Laboratory), Dr. Jason Stenzel (WSCL), and Dr. Diane Williams (FBI Counterterrorism & Forensic Science Research Unit and Virginia Commonwealth University), for taking the time to review this manuscript, or portions thereof; and editor Dr. Richard Saferstein, for his patience with this contributor, who proved to be the *rate-determining step* for the production of this second edition. The author would also like to thank again his family, **Joanne, Stacie,** and **Stephanie,** for their love, encouragement, patience, and—above all—their support (with the able assistance of Bailey, an exuberant one-year-old *Canis lupus familiaris* pug–beagle hybrid) in helping to keep an obsessive perfectionist insomniac as sane as can be expected for one who works in a forensic science laboratory.

References

1. W. Abney and E. R. Festing, *Phil. Trans.*, 172 (1882): 887.
2. W. H. Julius, *Verhandl. Koniki. Akad. Weterschappen Amsterdam*, 1 (1892): 1.
3. N. C. Thomas, "The Early History of Spectroscopy," *J. Chem. Educ.*, 68 (1991): 631.
4. P. R. De Forest, "Foundations of Forensic Microscopy," in *Forensic Science Handbook*, vol. I, 2nd ed. R. Saferstein (Englewood Cliffs, NJ: Prentice-Hall, Inc., 2002), pp, 215–319.
5. E. M. Suzuki and W. R. Gresham, "Forensic Science Applications of

Diffuse Reflectance Infrared Fourier Transform Spectroscopy (DRIFTS): I. Principles, Sampling Methods, and Advantages," *J. Forensic Sci.*, 31 (1986): 931–52.

6. L. J. Bellamy, *The Infra-Red Spectra of Complex Molecules* (London: Chapman and Hall, 1975).

7. P. R. Griffiths and J. A. de Haseth, *Fourier Transform Infrared Spectroscopy*, 2nd ed. (New York: Wiley InterScience, 2007).

8. E. R. Lippincott, F. E. Welsh, and C. E. Weir, "Microtechnique for the Infrared Study of Solids," *Anal. Chem.*, 33 (1961): 137.

9. E. R. Lippincott, L. S. Whatley, and H. C. Duecker, "Microtechniques Using Miniaturized Diamond Optics," in *Applied Infrared Spectroscopy*, ed. D. N. Kendall (New York: Reinhold Publishing Corp., 1966), pp. 435–61.

10. J. R. Ferraro and L. J. Basile, "The Diamond Anvil Cell as a Sampling Device in IR," *Am. Lab.*, 11 (March 1979): 31–6.

11. K. Krishnan, S. L. Hill, and R. H. Brown, "FTIR Spectroscopy Using Diffuse Reflectance and a Diamond Cell," *Am. Lab.*, 12 (March 1980): 104–14.

12. C. E. Weir, E. R. Lippincott, A. Van Vankenburg, and E. N. Bunting, "Infrared Studies in the 1- to 15-Micron Region to 30,000 Atmospheres," *J. Res. Natl. Bur. Std. (US.) Sect. A*, 63 (1959): 55–62.

13. A. R. Corrigan, 5th International Criminology Congress, Montreal, Canada, 1965.

14. F. T. Tweed, R. Cameron, J. S. Deak, and P. G. Rogers "The Forensic Microanalysis of Paints, Plastics, and Other Materials by an Infrared Diamond Cell Technique," *Forensic Sci.*, 4 (1974): 211–8.

15. E. M. Suzuki, "Fourier Transform Infrared Analyses of Some Particulate Drug Mixtures Using a Diamond Anvil Cell With a Beam Condenser and an Infrared Microscope," *J. Forensic Sci.*, 37 (1992): 467–87.

16. J. C. Decius and R. M. Hexter, *Molecular Vibrations in Crystals* (New York: McGraw-Hill, 1977), pp. 113–23.

17. T. Conley, *Infrared Spectroscopy*, 2nd ed. (Boston: Allyn and Bacon, Inc., 1972).

18. D. Lin-Vien, B. J. Bland, and V. J. Spence, "An Improved Method of Using the Diamond Anvil Cell for Infrared Microprobe Analysis," *Appl. Spectrosc.*, 44 (1990): 1227–28.

19. E. M. Suzuki and M. X. McDermot, "Infrared Spectra of U.S. Automobile Original Finishes. VII. Extended Range FT-IR and XRF Analyses of Inorganic Pigments *in situ*—Nickel Titanate and Chrome Titanate," *J. Forensic Sci.*, 51 (2006): 532–58.

20. J. Fahrenfort, "Attenuated Total Reflection—A New Principle for the Production of Useful Infrared Reflection Spectra of Organic Compounds," in *Molecular Spectroscopy (Proceedings IV Int. Meeting, Bologna, 1959)*, vol. 2, ed. A. Mangini (London: Pergamon, 1962), p. 437.

21. N. J. Harrick, M. Milosevic, and S. L. Berets, "New Developments in Internal Reflectance Spectroscopy, Part 1: The Splitpea," *Am. Lab.*, 24 (February 1992): 50MM-50PP.

22. F. M. Mirabella, Jr., "Principles, Theory, and Practice of Internal Reflection Spectroscopy," in *Internal Reflection Spectroscopy: Theory and Applications*, ed. F. M. Mirabella (New York: Marcel Dekker Inc., 1993), pp. 17–52.

23. N. J. Harrick, *Internal Reflection Spectroscopy* (Pleasantville, NY: Harrick Scientific Products, Inc., 1987).

24. F. M. Mirabella, Jr., "Internal Reflection Spectroscopy," *Appl. Spectrosc. Rev.*, 21 (1985): 45–178.

25. F. M. Mirabella, Jr., *Internal Reflection Spectroscopy: Theory and Applications* (New York: Marcel Dekker Inc., 1993).

26. F. M. Mirabella, Jr. and N. J. Harrick, *Internal Reflection Spectroscopy: Review and Supplement* (Pleasantville, NY: Harrick Scientific Products, Inc., 1985).

27. J. U. White, "New Method for Measuring Diffuse Reflectance in the Infrared," *J. Opt. Soc. Am.*, 54 (1964): 1332–7.

28. W. R. Blevin and W. J. Brown, "An Infra-Red Reflectometer with a Spheroidal Mirror," *J. Sci. Instrum.*, 42 (1965): 385–9.

29. R. R. Willey, "Fourier Transform Infrared Spectrophotometer for Transmittance and Diffuse Reflectance Measurements," *Appl. Spectrosc.*, 30 (1976): 593–601.

30. M. P. Fuller and P. R. Griffiths, "Diffuse Reflectance Measurements by Infrared Fourier Transform Spectroscopy," *Anal. Chem.*, 50 (1978): 1906–10.

31. M. P. Fuller and P. R. Griffiths, "Infrared Analysis by Diffuse Reflectance Spectrometry," *Am. Lab.*, 10 (October 1978): 69–80.

32. P. R. Griffiths, D. Kuehl, and M. P. Fuller, "Applications of Fourier Transform Infrared Spectrometry in Forensic Analysis," in *Proceedings of the International Symposium on Instrumental Applications in Forensic Drug Chemistry* (Washington, D.C.: U.S. Government Printing Office, 1978), pp. 60–9.

33. M. P. Fuller and P. R. Griffiths, "Infrared Microsampling by Diffuse Reflectance Fourier Transform Spectroscopy," *Appl. Spectrosc.*, 34 (1980): 533–9.

34. P. R. Griffiths and M. P. Fuller, "Mid-Infrared Spectrometry of Powdered Samples," in *Advances in Infrared and Raman Spectroscopy*, vol. 9, eds. R. J. H. Clark and R. E. Hester (Philadelphia: Heyden and Sons, 1982), pp. 63–129.

35. S. A. Yeboah, S. Wang, and P. R. Griffiths, "Effect of Pressure on Diffuse Reflectance Infrared Spectra of Compressed Powders," *Appl. Spectrosc.*, 38 (1984): 259–64.

36. I. M. Hamadeh, S. A. Yeboah, K. A. Trumbull, and P. R. Griffiths, "Preparation of Calibration Standards for Quantitative Diffuse Reflectance Infrared Spectrometry," *Appl. Spectrosc.*, 38 (1984): 486–91.

37. C. M. Conroy, P. R. Griffiths, and K. Jinno, "Interface of a Microbore High-Performance Liquid Chromatograph with a Diffuse Reflectance Fourier Transform Infrared Spectrometer," *Anal. Chem.*, 57 (1985): 822–5.

38. P. J. Brimmer and P. R. Griffiths, "Effect of Absorbing Matrices on Diffuse Reflectance Infrared Spectra," *Anal. Chem.*, 58 (1986): 2179–84.

39. P. J. Brimmer, P. R. Griffiths, and N. J. Harrick, "Angular Dependence of Diffuse Reflectance Infrared Spectra, Part I: FT-IR Spectrogoniophotometer," *Appl, Spectrosc.*, 40 (1986): 258–65.

40. P. J. Brimmer and P. R. Griffiths, "Angular Dependence of Diffuse Reflectance Infrared Spectra, Part II: Effect of Polarization," *Appl. Spectrosc.*, 41 (1987): 791–7.

41. P. J. Brimmer and P. R. Griffiths, "Angular Dependence of Diffuse Reflectance Infrared Spectra, Part III: Linearity of Kubelka–Munk Plots," *Appl, Spectrosc.*, 42 (1988): 242–7.

42. M. L. E. TeVrucht and P. R. Griffiths, "Mixed Alkali Halide Dilution Matrices for Diffuse Reflectance Infrared Spectrometry: Effect of Particle Size," *Appl. Spectrosc.*, 43 (1989): 1293–4.

43. M. L. E. TeVrucht and P. R. Griffiths, "A Simple Sample Packing Accessory for Diffuse Reflectance Infrared Spectrometry," *Appl. Spectrosc.*, 43 (1989): 1492–4.

44. D. J. J. Fraser and P. R. Griffiths, "Effect of Scattering Coefficient on Diffuse Reflectance Infrared Spectra," *Appl, Spectrosc.*, 44 (1990): 193–9.

45. J. M. Olinger and P. R. Griffiths, "Effects of Sample Dilution and Particle Size/Morphology on Diffuse Reflection Spectra of Carbohydrate

Systems in the Near- and Mid-Infrared. Part I. Single Analytes," *Appl. Spectrosc.*, 47 (1993): 687–94.

46. J. M. Olinger and P. R. Griffiths, "Effects of Sample Dilution and Particle Size/Morphology on Diffuse Reflection Spectra of Carbohydrate Systems in the Near- and Mid-Infrared. Part II. Durum Wheat," *Appl. Spectrosc.*, 47 (1993): 695–701.

47. J. Mattia, P. C. Painter, D. A. Heaps, and P. R. Griffiths, "Effect of Hydration on Band Intensities in Diffuse Infrared Spectra of Samples in Alkali Halide Matices," *Appl. Spectrosc.*, 59 (2005): 140–3.

48. L. A. Averett and P. R. Griffiths, "Method to Improve Linearity of Diffuse Reflectance Mid-Infrared Spectroscopy," *Anal. Chem.*, 78 (2006): 8165–7.

49. P. Kubelka and F. Munk, *Z. Tech. Phys.*, 12 (1931): 593.

50. G. Kortum, *Reflectance Spectroscopy* (New York: Springer-Verlag, 1969).

51. W. W. Wendlandt and H. G. Hecht, *Reflectance Spectroscopy* (New York: John Wiley & Sons, 1966).

52. R. K. Vincent and G. R. Hunt, "Infrared Reflectance from Mat Surfaces," *Appl. Opt.*, 7 (1968): 53–9.

53. E. M. Suzuki and W. R. Gresham, "Forensic Science Applications of Diffuse Reflectance Infrared Fourier Transform Spectroscopy (DRIFTS): II. Direct Analysis of Some Tablets, Capsule Powders, and Powders," *J. Forensic Sci.*, 31 (1986): 1292–1313.

54. J. M. Chalmers and M. W. Mackenzie, "Some Industrial Applications of FT-IR Diffuse Reflectance Spectroscopy," *Appl. Spectrosc.*, 39 (1985): 634–41.

55. E. M. Suzuki and W. R. Gresham, "Forensic Science Applications of Diffuse Reflectance Infrared Fourier Transform Spectroscopy (DRIFTS): III. Direct Analysis of Polymeric Foams." *J. Forensic Sci.*, 32 (1987): 377–95.

56. D. B. Chase, R. L. Arney, and W. G. Holtje, "Applications of Diffuse Reflectance FT-IR to Pigment Photodecomposition in Paint," *Appl. Spectrosc.*, 36 (1982): 155–7.

57. E. M. Suzuki, "Forensic Science Applications of Diffuse Reflectance Infrared Fourier Transform Spectroscopy (DRIFTS): IV. Direct Analysis of Metallic Paints—Sampling Considerations," *J. Forensic Sci.*, 34 (1989): 164–79.

58. E. M. Suzuki and J. A. Brown, "Forensic Science Applications of Diffuse Reflectance Infrared Fourier Transform Spectroscopy (DRIFTS): V. Direct Analysis of Metallic Paints— Screening of Panels," *J. Forensic Sci.*, 34 (1989): 180–96.

59. W. D. Mazella and C. L. Lennard, "Use of a Silicon Carbide Sampling Accessory for the Diffuse Reflectance Infrared Fourier Transform Analysis of Samples of Interest to Forensic Science," *J. Forensic Sci.*, 36 (1991): 556–64.

60. J. S. Chappell, "Matrix Effects in the Infrared Examination of Methamphetamine Salts," *Forensic Sci. Int.*, 75 (1995): 1–10.

61. E. M. Suzuki and W. P. Marshall, "Infrared Spectra of U.S. Automobile Original Topcoats (1974–1989): III. *In Situ* Identification of Some Organic Pigments used in Yellow, Orange, Red, and Brown Nonmetallic and Brown Metallic Finishes—Benzimidazolones," *J. Forensic Sci.*, 42 (1997): 619–48.

62. T. Hirschfeld, "The Hy-phen-ated Methods," *Anal. Chem.*, 52 (1980): 297A–312A.

63. P. R. Griffiths, S. L. Pentoney, Jr., A. Giorgetti, and K. H. Shafer, "The Hyphenation of Chromatography and FT-IR Spectrometry," *Anal. Chem.*, 58 (1986): 1349A–66A.

64. J. A. deHaseth, "Hybridized Techniques: Hyphenated and Slashed Instrumental Methods," *Spectrosc.*, 2, No. 10 (1987): 14–6.

65. R. White, *Chromatography/Fourier Transform Infrared Spectroscopy and*

Its Applications (New York: Marcel Dekker, Inc., 1990).

66. G. T. Reedy, S. Bourne, and P. T. Cunningham, "Gas Chromatography/ Infrared Matrix Isolation Spectrometry," *Anal. Chem.*, 51 (1979): 1535–40.

67. H. Bui, "A Practical System for Hyphenated Thin-Layer Chromatography/Fourier Transform Infrared Spectroscopy," *Spectrosc.*, 2, No. 10 (1987): 44–5.

68. J. A. de Haseth and T. L. Isenhour, "Reconstruction of Gas Chromatograms from Interferometric Gas Chromatography/Infrared Spectrometry Data," *Anal. Chem.*, 49 (1977): 1977–81.

69. W. Duncan and W. H. Soine, "Identification of Amphetamine Isomers by GC/IR/MS," *J. Chromatogr. Sci.*, 26 (1988): 521–6.

70. P. R. Griffiths, J. A. de Haseth, and L. V. Azarraga, "Capillary GC/FT-IR," *Anal. Chem.*, 55 (1983): 1361A–87A.

71. K. Krishnan, "Advances in Capillary Gas Chromatography-Fourier Transform Interferometry," in *Fourier Transform Infrared Spectroscopy*, vol. 4., eds. J. R. Ferraro and L. J. Basile (New York: Academic Press, 1985), pp. 97–145.

72. R. L. White, "Gas Chromatography-Fourier Transform Infrared Spectroscopy," *Appl. Spectrosc. Rev.*, 23 (1987): 165–245.

73. W. Herres, *HRGC-FTIR: Capillary Gas Chromatography-Fourier Transform Infrared Spectroscopy* (New York: Huthig, 1987).

74. C. L. Wilkins, G. N. Giss, R. L. White, G. M. Brissey, and E. C. Onyiriuka, "Mixture Analysis by Gas Chromatography/Fourier Transform Infrared Spectrometry/Mass Spectrometry," *Anal. Chem.*, 54 (1982): 2260–4.

75. C. L. Wilkins, "Linked Gas Chromatography Infrared Mass Spectrometry," *Anal. Chem.*, 59 (1987): 571A–81A.

76. J. C. Demirgian, "Gas Chromatography-Fourier Transform Infrared Spectroscopy-Mass Spectrometry," *Trends Anal. Chem.*, 6 (1987): 58–64.

77. W. P. Duncan, "Use of GC-IR-MS and Pyrolysis for Polybutadiene Characterization," *Am. Lab.*, 20 (August 1988): 40–6.

78. R. Oguchi, A. Shimizu, S. Yamashita, K. Yamaguchi, and P. Wylie, "Polymer Analysis Using Pyrolysis-GC-FTIR-MS and GC-AED," *J. High Resolu. Chromatogr.*, 146 (1991): 412–6.

79. C. L. Wilkins, "Directly-Linked Gas Chromatography–Infrared–Mass Spectrometry (GC/IR/MS)," in *Handbook of Vibrational Spectroscopy*, eds. J. M. Chalmers and P. R. Griffiths (New York: John Wiley & Sons, 2002).

80. A. M. Haefner, K. L. Norton, P. R. Griffiths, S. Bourne, and R. Curbelo, "Interfaced Gas Chromatography and Fourier Transform Infrared Transmission Spectrometry by Eluite Trapping at 77K," *Anal. Chem.*, 60 (1988): 2441–4.

81. S. Bourne, A. M. Haefner, K. L. Norton, and P. R. Griffiths, "Performance Characteristics of a Real-Time Direct Deposition Gas Chromatography/Fourier Transform Infrared Spectrometry System," *Anal. Chem.*, 62 (1990): 2448–52.

82. M. T. Söderström and R. A. Ketola, "Identification of Nerve Agents and Their Homologues and Dialkyl Methylphosphonates by Gas Chromatography/Fourier Transform Infrared Spectrometry (GC-FTIR)," *Presenius J. Anal. Chem.*, 350 (1994): 162–7.

83. M. G. Rockley, "Fourier-Transformed Infrared Photoacoustic Spectroscopy of Polystyrene Film," *Chem. Phys, Lett.*, 68 (1979): 455–6.

84. M. G. Rockley, "Fourier-Transformed Infrared Photoacoustic Spectroscopy of Solids," *Appl. Spectrosc.*, 34 (1980): 405–6.

85. N. L. Rockley, M. K. Woodward, and M. G. Rockley, "The Effect of Particle

Size on FT-IR-PAS Spectra," *Appl. Spectrosc.*, 38 (1984): 329–34.

86. C. Q. Yang and W. G. Fateley, "The Effect of Particle Size on Fourier Transform Infrared Photoacoustic Spectra," *J. Mol. Struct.*, 146 (1986): 25–39.

87. M. J. D. Low, M. Lacroix, and C. Morterra, "Infrared Photothermal Beam Deflection Fourier Transform Spectroscopy of Solids," *Appl. Spectrosc.*, 36 (1982): 582–4.

88. D. W. Vidrine, "Photoacoustic Fourier Transform Infrared Spectroscopy of Solids and Liquids," in *Fourier Transform Infrared Spectroscopy*, vol. 3, eds. J. R. Ferraro and L. J. Basile (New York: Academic Press, 1982), pp. 125–48.

89. M. J. D. Low and J. M. D. Tascon, "An Approach to the Study of Minerals Using Infrared Photothermal Beam Deflection Spectroscopy," *Phys. Chem. Minerals*, 12 (1985): 19–22.

90. M. J. D. Low and P. G. Varlashkin, "Application of Infrared Fourier Transform Spectroscopy to Problems in Conservation. II. Photothermal Beam Deflection," *Stud. Conserv.*, 31 (1986): 77–82.

91. S. E. Bialkowski, *Photothermal Spectroscopy Methods for Chemical Analysis* (New York: John Wiley & Sons, 1995).

92. J. F. McClelland, R. W. Jones, and S. J. Bajic, "FT-IR Photoacoustic Spectroscopy," in *Handbook of Vibrational Spectroscopy*, eds. J. M. Chalmers and P. R. Griffiths (New York: John Wiley & Sons, 2002).

93. J. F. Power, "Beam Deflection Photothermal Spectroscopy," in *Handbook of Vibrational Spectroscopy*, eds. J. M. Chalmers and P. R. Griffiths (New York: John Wiley & Sons, 2002).

94. K. H. Michaelian, *Photoacoustic Infrared Spectroscopy* (New York: Wiley Interscience, 2003).

95. E. M. Suzuki, "Infrared Spectra of U.S. Automobile Original Topcoats. II. Identification of Some Topcoat Inorganic Pigments Using an Extended Range (4000–220 cm^{-1}) Fourier Transform Spectrometer," *J. Forensic Sci.*, 41 (1996): 393–406.

96. J. A. Siegel, "Forensic Identification of Illicit Drugs," in *Forensic Science Handbook*, vol II, 2nd ed. R. Saferstein (Upper Saddle River, NJ: Pearson Prentice-Hall, 2005), pp. 111–74

97. T. C. Kram, D. A. Cooper, and A. C. Allen, "Behind the Identification of China White," *Anal. Chem.*, 53 (1981): 1379A–86A.

98. W. A. Ayres, M. J. Starsiak, and P. Sokolay, "The Bogus Drug: Three Methyl & Alpha Methyl Fentanyl Sold as 'China White,'" *J. Psychoactive Drugs*, 13 (1981): 91–3.

99. G. L. Henderson, "Designer Drugs: Past History and Future Prospects," *J. Forensic Sci.*, 33 (1988): 569–75.

100. B. A. Lodge, B. Duhaime, J. Zamecnik, P. MacMurray, and R. Brousseau, "New Street Analogs of Phencylidine," *Forensic Sci. Int.*, 55 (1992): 13–26.

101. J. Carpenter, J. Hugel, and K. Weaver, "The Identification of *N*-(2-hydroxy-ethyl)amphetamine," *Can. Soc. Forensic Sci. J.*, 26 (1993): 143–6.

102. L. A. King, A. J. Poortman-van der Meer, and H. Huizer, "1-Phenylethylamines: A New Series of Illicit Drugs?" *Forensic Sci. Int.*, 77 (1996): 141–9.

103. T. A. Dal Cason, "The Characterization of Some 3,4-Methylenedioxycathinone (MDCATH) Homologs," *Forensic Sci. Int.*, 87 (1997): 9–53.

104. A. J. Poortman and E. Lock, "Analytical Profile of 4-Methyl-thioamphetamine (4-MTA), a New Street Drug," *Forensic Sci. Int.*, 100 (1999): 221–33.

105. H. Ohta, Y. Suzuki, R. Sugita, S. Suzuki, and K. Ogasawara, "A Confiscation Case Involving a Novel Barbiturate

Designer Drug," *Can. Soc. Forensic Sci. J.*, 33 (2000): 103–10.

106. W. W. Moss, F. T. Posey, and P. C. Peterson, "A Multivariate Analysis of the Infrared Spectra of Drugs of Abuse," *J. Forensic Sci.*, 25 (1980): 304–13.

107. N. H. Choulis, J. M. Krall, and N. G. Oarke, "Computers in Drug Analysis. Part I: Identification of Drugs of Abuse via IR Spectroscopy," *Pharmacie*, 34 (1979): 647–8.

108. R. E. Ardrey and C. Brown, "The Identification of Organic Compounds Using Spectroscopic Interpretation and a Computer Bank of Molecular Structures Stored in the Form of Their Wiswesser Line Notations," *J. Forensic Sci. Soc.*, 17 (1977): 63–71.

109. C. F. Hammer, "A Brief Review of the Computerized Identification of Known Compounds and the Elucidation of Unknown Structures," in *Proceedings of the International Symposium on Instrumental Applications in Forensic Drug Chemistry* (Washington, D.C.: U.S. Government Printing Office, 1978), pp. 83–90.

110. M. L. Borka, "The Polymorphism of Heroin and Its Forensic Aspects," *Acta Pharm. Svecica*, 14 (1977): 210–2.

111. M. Ravreby and A. Gorski, "Variations in the Infrared Spectra of Heroin Base," *J. Forensic Sci.*, 34 (1989): 918–27.

112. R. J. Mesley and R. L. Oements, "Infrared Identification of Barbiturates with Particular Reference to the Occurrence of Polymorphism," *J. Pharm. Pharmacol.*, 20 (1968): 341–7.

113. R. J. Mesley, "Spectra-Structure Correlations in Polymorphic Solids—II. 5,5-Disubstituted Barbituric Acids," *Spectrochim. Acta*, 26A (1970): 1427–48.

114. H. Kanai, V. Inouye, and R. Goo, "Anomalous Infrared Spectra of Codeine Free Base in Potassium Bromide Pellet," *Anal. Chem. Acta.*, 173 (1985): 373–5.

115. R. O. Allen, "UV and IR Spectroscopy in Controlled Substance Analysis," in *Proceedings of the International Symposium on the Forensic Aspects of Controlled Substances*, (Washington, D.C.: U.S. Government Printing Office, 1988), pp. 55–65.

116. H. D. Beckstead and G. A. Neville, "A Novel Application of Headspace and GC-FT-IR Analysis to Identify the Ethyl Acetate Complex of O^6-Acetylmorphine," *Can. Soc. Forensic Sci. J.*, 20 (1987): 71–6.

117. H. D. Beckstead and G. A. Neville, "Fourier Transform Infrared (FT-IR) Characterization of the Ethyl Acetate Complex of O6-Acetylmorphine," *J. Forensic Sci.*, 33 (1988): 223–9.

118. J. A. Heagy, "Infrared Method for Distinguishing Optical Isomers of Amphetamine," *Anal. Chem.*, 42 (1970): 42.

119. C. V. Koulis, J. A. Reffner, and A. M. Bibby, "Comparison of Transmission and Internal Reflection Spectra of Cocaine," *J. Forensic Sci.*, 46 (2001): 822–9.

120. C. V. Koulis, K. J. Hymes, and J. L. Rawlins, "A New Infrared Spectral Library of Controlled and Non-controlled Drug Standards Using Internal Reflection Spectroscopy," *J. Forensic Sci.*, 45 (2000): 876–81.

121. J. A. Reffner, J. P. Coates, and R. G. Messerschmidt, "Chemical Microscopy with FTIR Microspectrometry," *Am. Lab.*, 19 (April 1987): 86–97.

122. J. A. Reffner, "FT-IR Microspectrometry: Applications in Pharmaceutical Research," in *Infrared Microspectroscopy*, eds. R. G. Messerschmidt and M. A. Harthcock (New York: Marcel Dekker, Inc., 1988), pp. 179–96.

123. J. P. Beauchaine, J. W. Peterman, and R. J. Rosenthal, "Applications of FT-IR/ Microscopy in Forensic Analysis," *Mikrochim. Acta 1988*, I, 133–8.

124. K. Kempfert, "Forensic Drug Analysis by GC/FT-IR," *Appl. Spectrosc.*, 42 (1988): 845–9.

125. S. Suzuki, "Studies on Fentanyl and Related Compounds: II. Spectrometric

Discrimination of Five Monomethylated Fentanyl Isomers by Gas Chromatography/Fourier Transform-Infrared Spectrometry," *Forensic Sci. Int.*, 43 (1989): 15–9.

126. M. E. Kurz, J. R. Witherspoon, S. Savage, and S. Johns, "Analysis of Alkyl Nitrites by Gas Chromatography-Infrared Spectroscopy," *J. Forensic Sci.*, 37 (1992): 1662–72.

127. K. L. Norton and P. R. Griffiths, "Comparison of Direction Deposition and Flow-Cell Gas Chromatography-Fourier Transform Infrared Spectrometry of Barbiturates," *J. Chromatogr. A*, 703 (1995): 383–92.

128. W. P. Duncan and D. G. Deutsch, "The Use of GC/IR/MS for High-Confidence Identification of Drugs," *Clin. Chem.*, 35 (1989): 1279–81.

129. R. Saferstein and J. J. Manura, "Routine Analysis of Drugs of Abuse by GC/IR," *Am. Lab.*, 10 (February 1978): 125–9.

130. R. C. Backer, W. N. Jensen, A. G. Beck, and R. J. Barnett, "A Simple Method for the Infrared Identification of Cannabinoids of Marihuana Resolved by Gas Chromatography," *J. Forensic Sci.*, 15 (1970): 287–91.

131. R. C. Shaler and J. H. Jerpe, "Identification and Determination of Heroin in Illicit Seizures by Combined Gas Chromatography-Infrared Spectrophotometry," *J. Forensic Sci.*, 17 (1972): 668–73.

132. W. L. Brannon, "Comparative Study of Micro Infrared Techniques," *J. Assoc. Off. Anal. Chem.*, 53 (1970): 599–608.

133. W. A. Trinler and D. J. Reuland, "Unequivocal Determination of Cocaine in Simulated Street Drugs by a Combination of High-Performance Liquid Chromatography and Infrared Spectrophotometry," *J. Forensic Sci.*, 23 (1978): 37–43.

134. D. J. Reuland and W. A. Trinler, "An Unequivocal Determination of Heroin in Simulated Street Drugs by a Combination of High-Performance Liquid Chromatography and Infrared Spectrophotometry Using Micro-Sampling Techniques," *Forensic Sci.*, 11 (1978): 195–200.

135. M. Ravreby, "Quantitative Determination of Cocaine and Heroin by Fourier Transform Infrared Spectrophotometry," *J. Forensic Sci.*, 32 (1987): 20–37.

136. R. Levy, M. Ravreby, L. Meirovich, and O. Shapira-Heiman, "A Survey and Comparison of Heroin Seizures in Israel During 1992 by Fourier Transform Infrared Spectrophotometry," *J. Forensic Sci.*, 41 (1996): 6–11.

137. W. D. Beazley, "Analytical Characterization of Isoheroin," *J. Forensic Sci.*, 30 (1985): 915–21.

138. F. Medina, III, "The Identification of Heroin and Three Structurally Related Isoheroins," *J. Forensic Sci.*, 34 (1989): 565–78.

139. C. C. Clark, "A Study of Procedures for the Identification of Heroin," *J. Forensic Sci.*, 22 (1977): 418–24.

140. J. J. Manura, J. M. Chao, and R. Saferstein, "The Forensic Identification of Heroin," *J. Forensic Sci.*, 23 (1978): 44–56.

141. T. A. Dal Cason, "A Re-examination of the Mono-methoxy Positional Ring Isomers of Amphetamine, Methamphetamine and Phenyl-2-propanone," *Forensic Sci. Int.*, 119 (2001): 168–94.

142. S. H. Elsherbini, "Cocaine Base Identification and Quantification," *Forensic Sci. Rev.*, 10 (1998): 1–12.

143. J. A. Siegel and R. A. Cormier, "The Preparation of *d*-Pseudococaine from *l*-Cocaine," *J. Forensic Sci.*, 25 (1980): 357–65.

144. A. C. Allen, D. A. Cooper, W. O. Kiser, and R. C. Cottrell, "The Cocaine Diastereomers," *J. Forensic Sci.*, 26 (1981): 12–26.

145. J. F. Casale, "A Practical Total Synthesis of Cocaine's Enantiomers," *Forensic Sci. Int.* 33 (1987): 275–98.

146. D. A. Cooper and A. C. Allen, "Synthetic Cocaine Impurities," *J. Forensic Sci.*, 29 (1984): 1045–55.

147. J. M. Moore, "Identification of *cis*- and *trans*-Cinnamoylcocaine in Illicit Cocaine Seizures," *J. Assoc. Off. Anal. Chem.*, 56 (1973): 1199–1205.

148. J. F. Casale, "Detection of Pseudoecgonine and Differentiation from Ecgonine in Illicit Cocaine," *Forensic Sci. Int.*, 47 (1990): 277–87.

149. L. M. Brewer and A. Allen, "*N*-Formyl Cocaine: A Study of Cocaine Comparison Parameters," *J. Forensic Sci.*, 36 (1991): 697–707.

150. J. G. Ensing and J. C. Hummelen, "Isolation, Identification, and Origin of Three Previously Unknown Congeners in Illicit Cocaine," *J. Forensic Sci.*, 36 (1991): 1666–87.

151. J. E. Wallace, J. D. Biggs, and E. V. Dahl, "A Rapid and Specific Spectrophotometric Method for Determining Propoxyphene," *J. Forensic Sci.*, 10 (1965): 179–91.

152. D. R. Wilkinson, F. Pavlikowski, and P. Jensen, "Identification of Drugs and Their Derivatives," *J. Forensic Sci.*, 21 (1976): 564–74.

153. D. Cooper, M. Jacob, and A. Allen, "Identification of Fentanyl Derivatives," *J. Forensic Sci.*, 31 (1986): 511–28.

154. E. G. C. Clarke and H. Leach, "The Identification of Phenatine," *J. Forensic Sci. Soc.*, 7 (1967): 182–3.

155. R. J. Warren, P. P. Begosh, and J. E. Zarembo, "The Identification of Amphetamines and Related Sympathomimetic Amines," *J. Assoc. Off. Anal. Chem.*, 54 (1971): 1179–91.

156. F. T. Davis and M. E. Brewster, "A Fatality Involving U4Euh, a Cyclic Derivative of Phenylpropanolamine," *J. Forensic Sci.*, 33 (1988): 549–53.

157. R. F. X. Klein, A. R. Sperling, D. A. Cooper, and T. C. Kram, "The Stereoisomers of 4-Methylaminorex," *J. Forensic Sci.*. 34 (1989): 962–79.

158. A. W. By, B. A. Dawson, B. A. Lodge, and W. W. Sy, "Spectral Distinction Between *cis*- and *trans*-4-Methylaminorex," *Forensic Sci. Int.*. 43 (1989): 83–91.

159. F. T. Noggle, Jr., C. R. Clark, and J. DeRuiter, "Liquid Chromatographic and Spectral Analysis of the Stereoisomers of Dimethylaminorex," *J. Assoc. Off. Anal. Chem.*, 75 (1992): 423–7.

160. J. L. Hamilton, "Collaborative Study of the Analysis of Pentaerythritol Tetranitrate and Meprobamate in Tablets," *J. Assoc. Off. Anal. Chem.*, 53 (1970): 594–8.

161. P. Daenens and M. Van Boven, "The Identification of Quinazolinones on the Illicit Market," *J. Forensic Sci.*, 21 (1976): 552–63.

162. T. A. Dal Cason, S. A. Angelos, and O. Washington, "Identification of Some Chemical Analogues and Positional Isomers of Methaqualone," *J. Forensic Sci.*, 26 (1981): 793–833.

163. C. C. Clark, "The Identification of Nitromethaqualone and Its Differentiation From Some Positional Isomers," *J. Forensic Sci.*, 33 (1988): 1035–44.

164. E. M. Suzuki and W. R. Gresham, "Identification of Some Interferences in the Analysis of Clorazepate," *J. Forensic Sci.*, 28 (1983): 655–82.

165. D. K. Kulia, B. Muhkopadhyay, and S. C. Lahiri. "Identification and Estimation of Methaqualone in Toffee Samples Using Gas Chromatography-Mass Spectrometry, Fourier Transform Infrared Spectrometry, and High-Performance Thin-Layer Chromatography," *Forensic Sci. Commun.*, 8 (2006): 1–7.

166. M. J. Walters, R. J. Ayers, and D. J. Brown, "Analysis of Illegally Distributed Anabolic Steroid Products by Liquid Chromatography with Identity Confirmation by Mass

Spectrometry and Infrared Spectrophotometry," *J. Assoc. Off. Anal. Chem.*, 73 (1990): 904–26.

167. P. D. Colman, E. A. Hearn, R. W. Taylor, and S. D. Le, "Anabolic Steroids—Analysis of Dosage Forms from Selected Case Studies from the Los Angeles County Sheriff's Scientific Services Bureau," *J. Forensic Sci.*, 36 (1991): 1079–88.

168. D. M. Chiong, E. Consuegra-Rodriguez, and J. R. Almirall, "The Analysis and Identification of Steroids," *J. Forensic Sci.*, 37 (1992): 488–502.

169. J. S. Chappell, A. W. Meyn, and K. K. Ngim, "The Extraction and Infrared Identification of *gamma*-Hydroxybutyric Acid (GHB) from Aqueous Solutions," *J. Forensic Sci.*, 49 (2004): 52–9.

170. J. V. DeFrancesco, M. R. Witkowski, and L. A. Ciolino, "GHB Free Acid: I. Solution Formation Studies and Spectroscopic Characterization by ¹HNMR and FT-IR," *J. Forensic Sci.*, 51 (2006): 321–9.

171. M. R. Witkowski, L. A. Ciolino, and J. V. DeFrancesco, "GHB Free Acid: II. Isolation and Spectroscopic Characterization for Forensic Analysis," *J. Forensic Sci.*, 51 (2006): 330–9.

172. M. Lopez-Artiguez, A. Camean, and M. Repetto, "Unequivocal Identification of Several Common Adulterants and Diluents in Street Samples of Cocaine by Infrared Spectroscopy," *J. Forensic Sci.*, 40 (1995): 602–10.

173. P. J. Gomm and I. J. Humphreys, "Identification of the Major Excipients of Illicit Tablets Using Infrared Spectroscopy," *J. Forensic Sci. Soc.*, 15 (1975): 293–9.

174. D. Wielbo and I. R. Tebbet, "The Use of Microcrystal Tests in Conjunction with Fourier Transform Infra-Red Spectroscopy for the Rapid Identification of Street Drugs," *J. Forensic Sci.*, 37 (1992): 1134–48.

175. D. Wielbo and I. R. Tebbet, "The Use of Microcrystal Tests in Conjunction with Fourier Transform Infra-Red Spectroscopy for the Rapid Identification of Street Drugs: Determination of Interference by Common Diluents," *J. Forensic Sci. Soc.*, 33 (1993): 25–32.

176. M. Deveaux and J. Huvenne, "Toxicological Applications of Gas Chromatography Using Fourier Transform Infrared Spectrometry Detection," *Trends Anal. Chem.*, 4 (1985): 149–55.

177. H. A. Harris and T. Kane, "A Method for Identification of Lysergic Acid Diethylamide (LSD) Using a Microscope Sampling Device with Fourier Transform Infrared (FT/IR) Spectroscopy," *J. Forensic Sci.*, 36 (1991): 1186–91.

178. C. C. Cromp and F. G. Tumey, "Infrared Identification of LSD and Related Compounds, *J. Forensic Sci.*, 12 (1967): 538–46.

179. R. J. Mesley and W. H. Evans, "Infrared Identification of Lysergide (LSD)," *J. Pharm. Pharmacol.*, 21 (1969): 713–20.

180. S. W. Bellman, J. W. Turczan, and T. C. Kram, "Spectrometric Forensic Chemistry of Hallucinogenic Drugs," *J. Forensic Sci.*, 15 (1970): 261–86.

181. M. D. Miller, "Isolation and Identification of Lysergic Acid Amide and Isolysergic Acid Amide as the Principal Ergoline Alkaloids in *Argyreia hervosa*, a Tropical Wood Rose," *J. Assoc. Off. Anal. Chem.*, 53 (1970): 123–6.

182. K. Bailey, D. Verner, and D. Legault, "Distinction of Some Dialkyl Amides of Lysergic and *iso*-Lysergic Acids From LSD," *J. Assoc. Off Anal. Chem.*, 59 (1973): 88–99.

183. J. F. Casale, "An Aqueous–Organic Extraction Method for the Isolation and Identification of Psilocin from Hallucinogenic Mushrooms," *J. Forensic Sci.*, 30 (1985): 247–50.

184. R. E. Lee, "A Technique for the Rapid Isolation and Identification of Psilocin

from Psilocin/Psilocybin Containing Mushrooms," *J. Forensic Sci.*, 30 (1985): 931–41.

185. P. W. L. Lum and P. Lebish, "Identification of Peyote via Major Non-Phenolic Peyote Alkaloids," *J. Forensic Sci. Soc.*, 14 (1974): 63–9.

186. K. Bailey, D. R. Gagne, and R. K. Pike, "Identification of Some Analogs of the Hallucinogen Phencyclidine," *J. Assoc. Off. Anal. Chem.*, 59 (1976): 81–9.

187. D. R. Gagne and R. K. Pike, "Identification of 1-(1-Cyanocycloalkyl) amines, Intermediates in the Synthesis of Phenycyclidine and Its Analogs," *J. Assoc. Off. Anal. Chem.*, 60 (1977): 32–47.

188. K. Bailey, "Identification of a Street Drug as *N*-Ethyl-1-phenylcyclohexylamine, a Phencyclidine Analog," *J. Pharm. Sci.*, 67 (1978): 885–6.

189. K. Bailey and D. Legault, "Identification of Analogs of the Hallucinogen Cyclohexamine," *J. Assoc. Off. Anal. Chem.*, 62 (1979): 1124–37.

190. W. H. Soine, R. L. Balster, K. E. Berglund, C. D. Martin, and D. T. Agee, "Identification of a New Phencyclidine Analog, 1-(1-Phenylcyclohexyl)-4-Methylpiperidine, as a Drug of Abuse," *J. Anal. Toxicol.*, 6 (1982): 41–3.

191. G. F. Phillips and R. J. Mesley, "Examination of the Hallucinogen 2,5-Dimethoxy-4-Methylamphetamine," *J. Pharm. Pharmacol.*, 21 (1969): 9–17.

192. R. C. Shaler and J. J. Padden, "Identification of Hallucinogens in Illicit Seizures I: 2,5-Dimethoxyamphetamine," *J. Pharm. Sci.*, 61 (1972): 1851–5.

193. K. Bailey, H. D. Beckstead, D. Legault, and D. Verner, "Identification of 2-, 3-, and 4-Methyoxyamphetamines and 2-, 3-, and 4-Methylamphetamines," *J. Assoc. Off. Anal. Chem.*, 57 (1974): 1134–43.

194. K. Bailey, A. W. By, D. Legault, and D. Verner, "Identification of the *N*-Methylated Analogs of the Hallucinogenic Amphetamines and Some Isomers," *J. Assoc. Off. Anal. Chem.*, 58 (1975): 62–9.

195. K. Bailey, D. R. Gagne, and R. K. Pike, "Investigation and Identification of the Bromination Products of Dimethoxyamphetamines," *J. Assoc. Off. Anal. Chem.*, 59 (1976): 1162–9.

196. K. Bailey, D. R. Gagne, D. Legault, and R. K. Pike, "Spectroscopic and Chromatographic Identification of Dimethylamphetamines," *J. Assoc. Off. Anal. Chem.*, 60 (1977): 642–53.

197. D. Delliou, "4-Bromo-2,5-Dimethoxyamphetamine: Psychoactivity, Toxic Effects and Analytical Methods," *Forensic Sci. Int.*, 21 (1983): 259–67.

198. W. H. Soine, R. E. Shark, and D. T. Agee, "Differentiation of 2,3-Methylenedioxyamphetamine from 3,4-Methylenedioxyamphetamine," *J. Forensic. Sci.*, 28 (1983): 386–90.

199. C. C. Clark, "The Identification of Methoxy-*N*-Methylamphetamines," *J. Forensic Sci.*, 29 (1984): 1056–71.

200. F. A. Ragan, Jr., S. A. Hite, M. S. Samuels, and R. E. Garey, "4-Bromo-2,5-dimethoxyphenethylamine: Identification of a New Street Drug," *J. Anal. Toxicol.*, 9 (1985): 91–3.

201. F. T. Noggle, Jr., J. DeRuiter, and M. J. Long, "Spectrophotometric and Liquid Chromatographic Identification of 3, 4-Methylenedioxyphenylisopropylamine and Its *N*-Methyl and *N*-Ethyl Homologs," *J. Assoc. Off. Anal. Chem.*, 69 (1986): 681–6.

202. T. A. Dal Cason, "The Characterization of Some 3,4-Methylene-dioxyphenylisopropylamine (MDA) Analogs," *J. Forensic Sci.*, 34 (1989): 928–61.

203. A. W. By, B. A. Dawson, B. A. Lodge, G. A. Neville, W. Sy, and J. Zamecnik, "Synthesis and Spectral Properties of 2,5-Dimethoxy-4-Ethoxyamphetamine and Its Precursors," *J. Forensic Sci.*, 35 (1990): 316–35.

204. A. W. By, R. Duhaime, and B. A. Lodge, "The Synthesis and Spectra of 4-Ethoxyamphetamine and Its

Isomers," *Forensic Sci. Int..* 49 (1991): 159–70.

205. A. W. By, G. A. Neville, and H. F. Shurvell, "Fourier Transform Infrared/Raman Differentiation and Characterization of *cis-* and *trans-*2,5-Dimethoxy-4β-Dimethyl-β-Nitrostyrenes: Precursors to the Street Drug STP," *J. Forensic Sci.*, 37 (1992): 503–12.

206. J. L. da Costa, A. Y. Wang, G. A. Micke, A. O. Maldaner, R. L. Romano, H. A. Martins-Junior, O. N. Neto, and M. F. M. Tavares, "Chemical Identification of 2–5-Dimethoxy-4-bromoamphetamine (DOB)," *Forensic Sci. Int..* 173 (2007): 130–6.

207. J. S. Cowie, A. L. Holtham, and L. V. Jones, "Identification of the Major Impurities in the Illicit Manufacturer of Tryptamines and Related Compounds," *J. Forensic Sci.*, 27 (1982): 527–40.

208. R. J. Mesley and W. H. Evans, "Infrared Identification of Some Hallucinogenic Derivatives of Tryptamine and Amphetamine," *J. Pharm. Pharmacol.*, 22 (1970): 321–2.

209. M. G. Rockley, M. Woodard, II. H. Richardson, D. M. Davis, N. Purdie, and J. M. Bowen, "Determination of Phencyclidine and Phenobarbital in Complex Mixtures by Fourier Transformed Infrared Photoacoustic Spectroscopy," *Anal. Chem.*, 55 (1983): 32–4.

210. T. Mills, III, J. C. Roberson, C. C. Matchett, M. J. Simon, M. D. Burns, and R. J. Ollis, Jr., *Instrumental Data for Drug Analysis*, vols. 1–6, 3rd ed. (Boca Raton: CRC Press, 2005).

211. A. C. Moffat, M. D. Osselton, and B. Widdop, eds., *Clarke's Analysis of Drugs and Poisons,* vol. 2, 3rd ed. (London: Pharmaceutical Press, 2004).

212. F. T. Noggle, Jr., C. R. Clark, T. W. Davenport, and S. T. Coker, "Synthesis, Identification, and Acute Toxicity of α-Benzylphenethylamine and α-Benzyl-*N*-Methylphenethylamine. Contaminants in Clandestine Preparation of Amphetamine and Methamphetamine," *J. Assoc. Off. Anal. Chem.*, 68 (1985): 1213–22.

213. K. Bailey, J. G. Boulanger, D. Legault, and S. L. Taillefer, "Identification and Synthesis of Di-(1-phenylisopropyl) methylamine, an Impurity in Illicit Methamphetamine," *J. Pharm. Sci.*, 63 (1974): 1575–8.

214. R. P. Barron, A. V. Kruegel, J. M. Moore, and T. C. Kram, "Identification of Impurities in Illicit Methamphetamine Samples," *J. Assoc. Off. Anal. Chem.*, 57 (1974): 1147–58.

215. D. Blachut, K. Wojtasiewicz, and Z. Czarnocki, "Identification and Synthesis of Some Contaminants Present in 4-Methoxyamphetamine (PMA) Prepared by the Leuckart Method," *Forensic Sci. Int.*, 127 (2002): 45–62.

216. R. H. Kreft, S. S. Masumoto, and T. V. Caldwell, "Characterization of *N*-Ethyl-1-Phenylcyclohexylamine Reaction Components," *J. Forensic Sci.*, 34 (1989): 1266–79.

217. T. A. Dal Cason, S. A. Angelos, and J. K. Rancy, "A Clandestine Approach to the Synthesis of Phenyl-2-Propanone from Phenylpropenes," *J. Forensic Sci.*, 29 (1984): 1187–1208.

218. T. Lukaszewski, "Spectroscopic and Chromatographic Identification of Precursors, Intermediates, and Impurities of 3,4-Methylenedioxyamphetamine Synthesis," *J. Assoc. Off. Anal. Chem.*, 61 (1978): 951–67.

219. A. W. By, B. A. Lodge, W. Sy, J. Zamecnik, and R. Duhaime, "Chemical and Physical Properties of (Z)- and (E)-Monoethoxy-1-(2-nitro-1-propenyl) benzenes: Important Precursors to the Monoethoxyamphetamines," *Can. Soc. Forensic Sci. J.*, 23 (1990): 91–107.

220. S. A. Angelos and J. A. Meyers, "The Isolation and Identification of Precursors and Reaction Products in the Clandestine Manufacture of Methaqualone and Mecloqualone," *J. Forensic Sci.*, 30 (1985): 1022–47.

221. K. Yu Zhingel, W. Dovensky, A. Crossman, and A. Allen, "Ephedrone: 2-Methylamino-1-Phenylpropan-l-One (Jeff)," *J. Forensic Sci.*, 36 (1991): 915–20.

222. E. C. Person, J. A. Meyer, and J. A. Vyvyan, "Structural Determination of the Principal Byproduct of the Lithium–Ammonia Reduction Method of Methamphetamine Manufacture," *J. Forensic Sci.*, 50 (2005): 87–95.

223. A. C. Allen, M. L. Stevenson, S. M. Nakamura, and R. A. Ely, "Differentiation of Illicit Phenyl-2-Propanone Synthesized from Phenylacetic Acid with Acetic Anhydride versus Lead (II) Acetate," *J. Forensic Sci.*, 37 (1992): 301–22.

224. E. T. Solomans and J. K. Jones, "The Determination of Polydimethylsiloxane, (Silicone Oil) in Biological Materials: A Case Report," *J. Forensic Sci.*, 20 (1975): 191–9.

225. S. Tsunenari, K. Yonemitsu, Y. Uchimura, H. Takaesu, and M. Kamisato, "A Rare Fatal Case of Wood Preservative, Monochlronapthalene (MCN), Poisoning," *Forensic Sci. Int.*, 20 (1982): 173–8.

226. A. Coutselinis, P. Kentarchou, and D. Boukis, "Separation and Identification of the Insecticide 'Endosulfan' from Biological Materials," *Forensic Sci. Int.*, 8 (1976): 251–4.

227. H. I. Dhahir, N. C. Jain, and J. I. Thornton, "The Identification of Ibogaine in Biological Material," *J. Forensic Sci. Soc.*, 12 (1972): 309–13.

228. M. Feldstein, "The Determination of Blood Carbon Monoxide by Infrared Spectrophotometry," *J. Forensic Sci.*, 10 (1965): 43–51.

229. M. Feldstein, "Analysis of Toxic Gases in Blood by Infrared Spectroscopy," *J. Forensic Sci.*, 10 (1965): 207–16.

230. L. J. Luskus, H. J. Kilian, W. W. Lackey, and J. D. Biggs, "Gases Released from Tissue and Analyzed by Infrared and Gas Chromatography/Mass Spectroscopy Techniques," *J. Forensic Sci.*, 22 (1977): 500–7.

231. W. L. Brannon, W. R. Benson, and G. Schwartzman, "Infrared Spectrophotometric Analysis of Medicinal Gases for Trace Impurities," *J. Assoc. Off. Anal. Chem.*, 59 (1976): 1404–8.

232. O. Laakso, M. Haapala, P. Jaakkola, R. Laaksonen, J. Nieminen, M. Pettersson, M. Rasanen, and J-J. Himberg, "The Use of Low-Resolution FT-IR Spectrometry for the Analysis of Alcohols in Breath," *J. Anal. Toxicol.*, 24 (2000): 250–6.

233. O. Laakso, M. Haapala, T. Pennanen, T. Kuitunen, and J-J. Himberg, "Fourier-Transformed Infrared Breath Testing After Ingestion of Technical Alcohol." *J. Forensic Sci.*, 52 (2007): 982–7.

234. M. Deveaus and J. Huvenne, "Toxicological Applications of Gas Chromatography Using Fourier Transform Infrared Spectrometric Detection," *Trends Anal. Chem.*, 4 (1985): 1459–55.

235. K. S. Kalasinsky, B. Levine, M. L. Smith, J. Magluilo, Jr., and T. Schaefer, "Detection of Amphetamine and Methamphetamine in Urine Using Gas Chromatography/Fourier Transform Infrared (GC/FT-IR) Spectroscopy," *J. Anal. Toxicol.*, 17 (1993): 359–64.

236. K. S. Kalasinsky, B. Levine, and M. L. Smith, "Feasibility of Using GC/FT-IR for Drug Analysis in the Forensic Toxicology Laboratory," *J. Anal. Toxicol.*, 16 (1992): 332–6.

237. I. Ojanper, R. Hyppola, and E. Vuori, "Identification of Volatile Organic Compounds in Blood by Purge and Trap PLOT-Capillary Gas Chromatography Coupled with Fourier Transform Infrared Spectroscopy," *Forensic Sci. Int.*, 80 (1996): 201–9.

238. E. G. de Jong, S. Kelzers, and R. A. A. Maes, "Comparison of the GC/MS Ion Trapping Technique with GC-FTIR for

the Identification of Stimulants in Drug Testing," *J. Anal. Toxicol.*, 14 (1990): 127–31.

239. G. E. Platoff, Jr., D. W. Hill, T. R. Koch, and Y. H. Caplan, "Serial Capillary Gas Chromatography/Fouier Transform Infrared Spectrometry/Mass Spectrometry (GC/IR/MS): Qualitative and Quantitative Analysis of Amphetamine, Methamphetamine, and Related Analogues in Human Urine," *J. Anal. Toxicol.*, 16 (1992): 389–97.

240. K. S. Kalsinsky, J. Magluilo, Jr., and T. Schaefer, "Hair Analysis by Infrared Microscopy for Drugs of Abuse," *Forensic Sci. Int.*, 69 (1993): 253–60.

241. K. S. Kalasinsky, J. Magluilo, Jr., and T. Schaefer, "Study of Drug Distribution in Hair by Infrared Microscopy Visualization," *J. Anal. Toxicol.*, 18 (1994): 337–41.

242. D. A. Kodali, D. M. Small, J. Powell, and K. Krishnan, "Infrared Micro-Imaging of Atherosclerotic Arteries," *Appl. Spectrosc.*, 45 (1991): 1310–7.

243. J. A. Centeno, K. G. Ishak, F. G. Mullick, W. A. Gahl, and T. J. O'Leary, "Infrared Microspectroscopy and Laser Raman Microprobe in the Diagnosis of Cystinosis," *Appl. Spectrosc.*, 48 (1994): 569–72.

244. E. Benedetti, L. Teodori, M. L. Trinca, P. Vergamini, F. Salvati, F. Mauro, and G. Spremolla, "A New Approach to the Study of Human Solid Tumor Cells by Means of FT-IR Microspectroscopy," *Appl. Spectrosc.*, 44 (1990): 1276–80.

245. M. Diem, S. Boydston-White, and L. Chiriboga, "Infrared Spectroscopy of Cells and Tissues: Shining Light onto a Novel Subject," *Appl. Spectrosc.*, 53 (1999): 148A–61A.

246. S. G. Ryland, "Infrared Microspectroscopy of Forensic Paint Evidence," in *Practical Guide to Infrared Microspectroscopy*, ed. H. J. Humecki (New York: Marcel Dekker, Inc., 1995), pp. 163–243.

247. E. M. Suzuki, "Infrared Spectra of U.S. Automobile Original Topcoats (1974–1989): I. Differentiation and Identification Based on Acrylonitrile and Ferrocyanide C≡N Stretching Absorptions," *J. Forensic Sci.*, 41 (1996): 393–406.

248. E. M. Suzuki, "Infrared Spectra of U.S. Automobile Original Topcoats (1974–1989). V. Identification of Organic Pigments Used in Red Nonmetallic and Brown Nonmetallic and Metallic Monocoats—DPP Red BO and Thioindigo Bordeaux," *J. Forensic Sci.*, 44 (1999): 297–313.

249. G. Massonnet and W. Stoecklein, "Identification of Organic Pigments in Coatings: Applications to Red Automotive Topcoats. Part III: Raman Spectroscopy (NIR FT-Raman)," *Sci. Justice*, 39 (1999): 181–7.

250. E. M. Suzuki and M. Carrabba, "*In Situ* Identification and Analysis of Automotive Paint Pigments Using Line Segment Excitation Raman Spectroscopy: I. Inorganic Topcoat Pigments," *J. Forensic Sci.*, 46 (2001): 1053–69.

251. P. G. Rodgers, R. Cameron, N. S. Cartwright, W. H. Clark, J. S. Deak, and E. W. W. Norman, "The Classification of Automotive Paint by Diamond Window Infrared Spectrophotometry. Part I: Binders and Pigments," *Can. Soc. Forensic Sci. J.*, 9 (1976): 1–14.

252. J. I. Thornton, "Forensic Paint Examination," in *Forensic Science Handbook*, vol 1, 2nd ed. R. Saferstein (Englewood Cliffs, NJ: Prentice-Hall, Inc., 2002), 429–79.

253. S. Ryland, G. Bishea, L. Brun-Conti, M. Eyring, B. Flanagan, T. Jergovich, D. MacDougall, and E. Suzuki, "Discrimination of 1990s Original Automotive Paint Systems: A Collaborative Study of Black Nonmetallic Base Coat/Clear Coat Finishes Using Infrared Spectroscopy," *J. Forensic Sci.*, 46 (2001): 31–45.

254. J. Zieba and A. Pomianowski, "A Statistical Criterion for the Value of Evidence: Application to the Evaluation of the Results of Paint Spectral Analysis," *Forensic Sci. Int.*, 17 (1981): 101–8.

255. R. F. E. Percy and R. J. Audette, "Automotive Repaints: Just a New Look?" *J. Forensic Sci.*, 25 (1980): 189–239.

256. E. M. Suzuki and W. P. Marshall, "Infrared Spectra of U.S. Automobile Original Topcoats (1974–1989): IV. Identification of Some Organic Pigments Used in Red and Brown Nonmetallic and Metallic Monocoats—Quinacridones," *J. Forensic Sci.*, 43 (1998): 514–42.

257. E. M. Suzuki, "Infrared Spectra of U.S. Automobile Original Topcoats (1974–1989): VI. Identification and Analysis of Yellow Organic Automotive Paint Pigments—Isoindolinone Yellow 3R, Isoindoline Yellow, Anthrapyrimidine Yellow, and Miscellaneous Yellows," *J. Forensic Sci.*, 44 (1999): 1151–75.

258. G. Massonnet and W. Stoecklein, "Identification of Organic Pigments in Coatings: Applications to Red Automotive Topcoats. Part II: Infrared Spectroscopy," *Sci. Justice*, 39 (1999): 135–40.

259. E. W. W. Norman, R. Cameron, L. J. Cartwright, N. S. Cartwright, W. H. Clark, and D. A. MacDougall, "The Classification of Automotive Paint Primers Using Infrared Spectroscopy—A Collaborative Study," *Can. Soc. Forensic Sci. J.*, 16 (1983): 163–73.

260. T. R. Harkins, J. T. Harris, and O. D. Shreve, "Identification of Pigments in Paint Products by Infrared Spectroscopy," *Anal. Chem.*, 31 (1959): 541–5.

261. P. G. Rodgers, R. Cameron, N. S. Cartwright, W. H. Oark, J. S. Deak, and E. W. W. Norman, "The Classification of Automotive Paint by Diamond Window Infrared Spectrophotometry. Part II: Automotive Topcoats and Undercoats," *Can. Soc. Forensic Sci. J.*, 9 (1976): 49–68.

262. P. G. Rodgers, R. Cameron, N. S. Cartwright, W. H. Clark, J. S. Deak, and E. W. W. Norman, "The Classification of Automotive Paint by Diamond Window Infrared Spectrophotometry. Part III: Case Histories," *Can. Soc. Forensic Sci. J.*, 9 (1976): 103–11.

263. D. Deaken, "Automotive Body Primers: Their Application in Vehicle Identification," *J. Forensic Sci.*, 20 (1975): 283–7.

264. N. S. Cartwright and P. G. Rodgers, "A Proposed Data Base for the Identification of Automotive Paint," *Can. Soc. Forensic Sci. J.*, 9 (1976): 145–54.

265. R. J. Audette and R. F. E. Percy, "A Rapid, Systematic, and Comprehensive Classification System for the Identification and Comparison of Motor Vehicle Paint Samples. I: The Nature and Scope of the Classification System," *J. Forensic Sci.*, 24 (1979): 790–807.

266. R. J. Audette and R. F. E. Percy, "A Rapid, Systematic, and Comprehensive Classification System for the Identification and Comparison of Motor Vehicle Paint Samples. II: Paint Data Collected from Chrysler-Manufactured Cars," *J. Forensic Sci.*, 27 (1982): 622–70.

267. N. S. Cartwright, L. J. Cartwright, E. W. W. Norman, R. Cameron, D. A. MacDougall, and W. H. Clark, "A Computerized System for the Identification of Suspect Vehicles Involved in Hit-and-Run Accidents," *Can. Soc. Forensic Sci. J.*, 15 (1982): 105–15.

268. L. J. Cartwright, N. S. Cartwright, E. W. W. Norman, R. Cameron, D. A. MacDougall, and W. H. Clark, "The Classification of Automotive Paint Primers Using the Munsell Color Coordinate System—A Collaborative Study," *Can. Soc. Forensic Sci. J.*, 17 (1984): 14–18.

269. J. L. Buckle, D. A. MacDougall, R. R. Grant, "PDQ Paint Data Queries: The History and Technology Behind the Development of the Royal Mounted Canadian Police Forensic Laboratory Services Automotive Paint Database," *Can. Soc. Forensic Sci. J.*, 30 (1997): 199–212.

270. J. A. Gothard, "Evaluation of Automotive Paint Flakes as Evidence," *J. Forensic Sci.*, 24 (1979): 636–41.

271. S. G. Ryland and R. J. Kopec, "The Evidential Value of Automotive Paint Chips," *J. Forensic Sci.*, 24 (1979): 140–7.

272. S. G. Ryland, R. J. Kopec, and P. N. Somerville, "The Evidential Value of Automotive Paint Chips. Part II: Frequency of Occurrence of Topcoat Colors," *J. Forensic Sci.*, 26 (1981): 64–74.

273. J. Buckle, T. Fung and K. Ohashi, "Automotive Topcoat Colours: Occurrence Frequencies in Canada." *Can. Soc. Forensic Sci. J.*, 20 (1987): 45–56.

274. G. G. Volpe, H. S. Stone, J. M. Rioux, and K. J. Murphy, "Vehicle Topcoat Colour and Manufacturer: Frequency Distribution and Evidential Significance." *Can. Soc. Forensic Sci. J.*, 21 (1988): 11–8.

275. G. Edmondstone, J. Hellman, K. Legate, G. L. Vardy, and E. Lindsay, "An Assessment of the Evidential Value of Automotive Paint Comparisons," *Can. Soc. Forensic Sci. J.*, 37 (2004): 147–53.

276. S. E. J. Bell, L. A. Fido, S. J. Speers, and W. J. Armstrong, "Rapid Forensic Analysis and Identification of "Lilac" Architectural Finishes Using Raman Spectroscopy," *Appl. Spectrosc.*, 59 (2005). 100 0.

277. S. E. J. Bell, L. A. Fido, S. J. Speers, W. J. Armstrong, and S. Spratt, "Forensic Analysis of Architectural Finishes Using Fourier Transform Infrared and Raman Spectroscopy, Part II: White Paint," *Appl. Spectrosc.*, 59 (2005): 1340–6.

278. S. E. J. Bell, L. A. Fido, S. J. Speers, W. J. Armstrong, and S. Spratt, "Forensic Analysis of Architectural Finishes Using Fourier Transform Infrared and Raman Spectroscopy, Part I: The Resin Bases," *Appl. Spectrosc.*, 59 (2005): 1333–9.

279. P. Buzzini and G. Massonnet, "A Market Study of Green Spray Paints by Fourier Transform Infrared (FTIR) and Raman Spectroscopy," *Sci. Justice*, 44 (2004): 123–31.

280. F. Govaert, G. De Roy, B. Decruyenaere, and D. Ziernicki "Analysis of Black Spray Paints by Fourier Transform Infrared Spectrometry, X-Ray Fluorescence and Visible Microscopy," *Problems of Forensic Sciences*, 47 (2001): 333–9.

281. F. Govaert and M. Bernard, "Discriminating Red Spray Paints by Optical Microscopy, Fourier Transform Infrared Spectroscopy and X-Ray Fluorescence," *Forensic Sci. Int.*, 140 (2004): 61–70.

282. Infrared Spectroscopy Committee of the Chicago Society for Coatings Technology, *An Infrared Spectroscopy Atlas for the Coatings Industry* (Philadelphia: Federation of Societies for Coatings Technology, 1980).

283. Infrared Spectroscopy Atlas Working Committee. *An Infrared Spectroscopy Atlas for the Coatings Industry*, 4th ed., vols. I and II (Blue Bell, PA: Federation of Societies for Coatings Technology, 1991).

284. W. R. Heilman, "Nondestructive Infrared and X-Ray Diffraction Analyses of Paints and Plastics," *J. Forensic Sci.*, 5 (1960): 338–45.

285. B. Cleverley, "Comparison of Plastic Materials and Paint Films Using Infrared Spectroscopy," *Med. Sci. Law*, 7 (1967): 148–52.

286. J. A. Gothard, "Evaluation of Automobile Paint Flakes as Evidence," *J. Forensic Sci.*, 21 (1976): 636–41.

287. R. J. Audette and R. F. E. Percy, "A Novel Pyrolysis Technique for Micro Paint Analysis," *J. Forensic Sci.*, 23 (1978): 672–78.

288. H. K. Raaschou Nielson, "Forensic Analysis of Coatings," *J. Coatings Technol.*, 56, No. 718 (1984): 21–32.

289. J. B. Lear, "Analysis of Paint Films," *J. Coatings Technol.*, 53, No. 675 (1981): 63–5.

290. S. G. Ryland and R. J. Kopec, "The Evidential Value of Automobile Paint Chips," *J. Forensic Sci.*, 24 (1979): 140–7.

291. S. Denton, "Attenuated Total Reflection (ATR) Infrared Spectra—Some Applications in Forensic Science," *J. Forensic Sci. Soc.*, 5 (1965): 112–4.

292. S. E. Polchlopek and R. L. Harris, *ATR Spectra of Surface Coatings* (Stamford, CT: Barnes Engineering Co., 1963).

293. D. L. Harms, "Identification of Complex Organic Materials by Infrared Spectra of Their Pyrolysis Products," *Anal. Chem.*, 25 (1953): 1140–55.

294. K. W. Smalldon, "The Identification of Paint Resins and Other Polymeric Materials From the Infra Red Spectra of Their Pyrolysis Products," *J. Forensic Sci. Soc.*, 9 (1969): 135–40.

295. K. Krishnan and J. R. Ferraro, "Techniques Used in Fourier Transform Infrared Spectroscopy," in *Fourier Transform Infrared Spectroscopy*, Vol. 3, eds. J. R. Ferraro and L. J. Basile (New York: Academic Press, 1982), pp. 149–209.

296. D. W. Schiering, "A Beam Condenser/Miniature Diamond Anvil Cell Accessory for the Infrared Microspectrometry of Paint Chips," *Appl. Spectrosc.*, 42 (1988): 903–6.

297. A. R. Cassista and P. M. L. Sandercock, "Comparison and Identification of Automotive Topcoats: Microchemical Spot Tests, Microspectrophotometry, Pyrolysis–Gas Chromatography, and Diamond Anvil Cell FTIR," *Can. Soc. Forensic Sci. J.*, 27 (1994): 209–23.

298. J. W. Wilkinson, J. Locke, and D. K. Laing, "The Examination of Paints as Thin Sections Using Visible Microspectrophotometry and Fourier Transform Infrared Microscopy," *Forensic Sci. Int.*, 38 (1988): 43–52.

299. L J. Cartwright, N. S. Cartwright, and P. G. Rodgers, "A Microtome Technique for Sectioning Multilayer Paint Samples for Microanalysis," *Can. Soc. Forensic Sci. J.*, 10 (1977): 7–12.

300. J. Van der Weerd, H. Brammer, J. J. Boon, and R. M. A. Heeren, "Fourier Transform Infrared Microscopic Imaging of an Embedded Paint Cross-Section," *Appl. Spectrosc.*, 56 (2002): 275–83.

301. K. Flynn, R. O'Leary, C. Lennard, C. Roux, and B. J. Reedy, "Forensic Applications of Infrared Chemical Imaging: Multi-Layered Paint Chip," *J. Forensic Sci.*, 50 (2005): 832–41.

302. H. J. Humecki, "Polymers and Contaminants by Infrared Microspectroscopy," in *Infrared Microspectroscopy*, eds. R. G. Messerschmidt and M. A. Harthcock (New York: Marcel Dekker, Inc., 1988), pp. 51–72.

303. T. J. Allen, "Paint Sample Presentation for Fourier Transform Infrared Microscopy," *Vibrational Spectros.*, 3 (1992): 217–37.

304. J. C. Shearer, D. C. Peters, and T. A. Kubic, "Forensic Microanalysis by Fourier Transform Infrared Spectroscopy," *Trends Anal. Chem.*, 4 (1985): 246–51.

305. E. G. Bartick, M. W. Tungol, and J. A. Reffner, "A New Approach to Forensic Analysis with Infrared Microscopy: Internal Reflection Spectroscopy," *Anal. Chim. Acta*, 288 (1994): 35–42.

306. Y. Giang, S. Wang, L. Cho, C. Yang, and C. Lu, "Identification of Tiny and Thin Smears of Automotive Paint Following a Traffic Accident," *J. Forensic Sci.*, 47 (2002): 625–9.

307. H. Dannenberg, J. W. Forbes, and A. C. Jones, "Infrared Spectroscopy of Surface Coatings in Reflected Light," *Anal. Chem.*, 32 (1960), 365–70.

308. J. A. Reffner and W. T. Wihlborg, "Microanalysis by Reflectance FT-IR Microscopy," *Am. Lab.*, 22 (April 1990): 26–34.

309. S. G. Ryland, T. A. Jergovich, and K. P. Kirkbride, "Current Trends in Forensic Paint Examination," *Forensic Sci. Rev.* 18 (2006): 97–117.

310. J. H. Hartshorn, "Applications of FTIR to Paint Analysis," in *Analysis of Paints and Related Materials: Current Techniques for Solving Coatings Problems*, ed. W. C. Golton (Philadelphia: ASTM, 1992), pp. 127–47.

311. P. Burke, C. J. Curry, L. M. Davies, and D. R. Cousins, "A Comparison of Pyrolysis Mass Spectrometry, Pyrolysis Gas Chromatography and Infra-Red Spectroscopy for the Analysis of Paint Resins," *Forensic Sci. Int.*, 28 (1985): 201–19.

312. L. A. O'Neill, "Analysis of Paint by Infra-Red Spectroscopy," *Med. Sci. Law*, 7 (1967): 145–7.

313. R. W. May and J. Porter, "An Evaluation of Common Methods of Paint Analysis," *J. Forensic Sci.*, 15 (1975): 137–46.

314. E. G. Clair, "Forensic Chemistry in Canada in Review and Retrospect," *Can. Soc. Forensic Sci. J.*, 11 (1978): 167–77.

315. M. W. Tungol, E. G. Bartick, and A. Montaser, "Forensic Examination of Synthetic Textile Fibers by Microscopic Infrared Spectrometry," in *Practical Guide to Infrared Microspectroscopy*, ed. H. J. Humecki (New York: Marcel Dekker, Inc., 1995), pp. 245–86.

316. K. P. Kirkbride and M. W. Tungol, "Infrared Microspectroscopy of Fibres," in *Forensic Examination of Fibres*, 2nd ed.; eds. J. Robertson and M. Grieve (Boca Raton: CRC Press, 1999), 179–222.

317. K. G. Wiggins, "Forensic Textile Fiber Examination across the USA and Europe," *J. Forensic Sci.*, 46 (2001): 1303–8.

318. M. B. Eyring and B. D. Gaudette, "An Introduction to the Forensic Aspects of Textile Fiber Examination," in *Forensic Science Handbook*, vol. II, 2nd ed. R. Saferstein (Englewood Cliffs, N. J.: Prentice-Hall, Inc., 2005), pp. 231–95.

319. M. M. Houck, "Forensic Fiber Examination and Analysis," *Forensic Sci. Rev.*, 17 (2005): 29–49.

320. R. H. Fox and H. I. Schuetzman, "The Infrared Identification of Microscopic Samples of Man-Made Fibers," *J. Forensic Sci.*, 13 (1968): 397–406.

321. R. A. Rouen and V. C. Reeve, "A Comparison and Evaluation of Techniques for Identification of Synthetic Fibers," *J. Forensic Sci.*, 15 (1970): 410–32.

322. K. W. Smalldon, "The Identification of Acrylic Fibers by Polymer Composition as Determined by Infrared Spectroscopy and Physical Characteristics," *J. Forensic Sci.*, 18 (1973): 69–81.

323. R. Cook and M. D. Paterson, "New Techniques for the Identification of Microscopic Samples of Textile Fibres by Infrared Spectroscopy," *Forensic Sci. Int.*, 12 (1978): 237–43.

324. E. F. Garger, "An Improved Technique for Preparing Solvent Cast Films from Acrylic Fibers for the Recording of Infrared Spectra," *J. Forensic Sci.*, 28 (1983): 632–7.

325. M. C. Grieve and L. R. Cabiness, "The Recognition and Identification of Modified Acrylic Fibers," *Forensic Sci. Int.*, 29 (1985): 129–46.

326. M. C. Grieve, J. Dunlop, and T. M. Kotowski, "Bicomponent Acrylic Fibers—Their Characterization in the Forensic Science Laboratory," *J. Forensic Sci. Soc.*, 28 (1988): 25–34.

327. M. C. Grieve and J. A. Keames, "Preparing Samples for the Recording of Infrared Spectra from Synthetic Fibers," *J. Forensic Sci.*, 21 (1976): 307–14.

328. M. C. Grieve and T. M. Kotowski, "The Identification of Polyester Fibers in Forensic Science," *J. Forensic Sci.*, 22 (1977): 390–401.

329. C. Gentilhomme, A. Piguet, J. Rosset, and C. Eyraud, "Infrared Analysis of Acrylonitrile Copolymers," *Bulletin de la Societe Chemique de France* (1960): 901–6.

330. G. A. Tirpak and J. P. Sibilia, "A New Fiber-Sampling Technique for Infrared Spectroscopy as Applied to Nylon 6 and Poly(ethylene terephthalate), *J. Appl. Polym. Sci.*, 17 (1973): 643–8.

331. D. J. Carlsson, F. R. S. Oark, and D. M. Wiles, "Infrared Spectra of Monofilaments," *Textile Res. J.*, 46 (1976): 318–21.

332. D. J. Carlsson, T. Suprunchuk, and D. M. Wiles, "Fiber Identification at the Microgram Level by Infrared Spectroscopy," *Textile Res. J.*, 47 (1977): 456–8.

333. P. A. Wilks, Jr. and M. R. Iszard, "The Identification of Fibers and Fabrics by Internal Reflection Spectroscopy," in *Developments in Applied Spectroscopy*, vol. 4, ed., E. N. Davis (New York: Plenum Press, 1965), pp. 141–9.

334. G. Gillberg and D. Kemp, "Surface Characterization of Polyester Fibers," *J. Appl. Polym. Sci.*, 26 (1981): 2023–51.

335. S. R. Samanta, W. W. Lanier, R. W. Miller, and M. E. Gibson, Jr., "Fiber Structure Study by Polarized Infrared Attenuated Total Reflection Spectroscopy," *Appl. Spectrosc.*, 44 (1990): 286–9.

336. N. J. Harrick, "Nanosampling Via Internal Reflection Spectroscopy," *Appl. Spectrosc.*, 41 (1987): 1–2.

337. F. J. DeBiase, "Nanosampling Internal Reflection Spectroscopy of Solids and Liquids," *Am. Lab.*, 20 (June 1988): 96–107.

338. E. Espinoza, J. Przybyla, and R. Cox, "Analysis of Fiber Blends Using Horizontal Attenuated Total Reflection Fourier Transform Infrared and Discriminant Analysis," *Appl. Spectrosc.*, 60 (2006): 386–91.

339. P. Garside and P. Wyeth, "Use of Polarized Spectroscopy as a Tool for Examining the Microstructure of Cellulosic Texile Fibers," *Appl. Spectrosc.*, 61 (2007): 523–9.

340. L. K. Read and R. J. Kopec, "Analysis of Synthetic Fibers by Diamond Cell and Sapphire Cell Infrared Spectrophotometry," *J. Assoc. Off. Anal. Chem.*, 61 (1978): 526–32.

341. A. W. Hartshorne and D. K. Laing, "The Identification of Polyolefin Fibres by Infrared Spectroscopy and Melting Point Determination," *Forensic Sci. Int.*, 26 (1984): 45–52.

342. J. E. Katon, P. L. Lang, J. F. O'Keefe, and D. W. Schiering, "Instrumental Methods and Sampling Factors in Infrared Microspectroscopy," in *The Design, Sample Handling, and Applications of Infrared Microscopes*, ed. P. B. Roush (Philadelphia: ASTM, 1987), pp. 49–63.

343. P. L. Lang, J. E. Katon, J. F. O'Keefe, and D. W. Schiering, "The Identification of Fibers by Infrared and Raman Microspectroscopy," *Microchem. J.*, 34 (1986): 319–31.

344. G. W. White, "A Simple High-Pressure Anvil and Template Device for the Production of Infrared Spectra from Microfiber Samples," *J. Forensic Sci.*, 37 (1992): 620–31.

345. C. J. Curry, M. J. Whitehouse, and J. M. Chalmers, "Ultramicrosampling in Infrared Spectroscopy Using Small Apertures," *Appl. Spectrosc.*, 39 (1985): 174–80.

346. D. B. Chase, "Infrared Microscopy: A Single-Fiber Technique," in *The Design, Sample Handling, and*

Applications of Infrared Microscopes, ed. P. B. Roush (Philadelphia: ASTM, 1987), pp. 4–11.

347. E. G. Bartick, "Considerations for Fiber Sampling with Infrared Microspectroscopy," in *The Design, Sample Handling, and Applications of Infrared Microscopes,* ed. P. B. Roush (Philadelphia: ASTM, 1987), pp. 64–73.

348. G. C. Pandey, "Fourier Transform Infrared Microscopy for the Determination of the Composition of Copolymer Fibres: Acrylic Fibres," *Analyst,* 114 (1989): 231–2.

349. M. W. Tungol, E. G. Bartick, and A. Montaser, "The Development of a Spectral Data Base for the Identification of Fibers by Infrared Microscopy," *Appl. Spectrosc.,* 44 (1990): 543–9.

350. M. W. Tungol, E. G. Bartick, and A. Montaser, "Analysis of Single Polymer Fibers by Fourier Transform Infrared Microscopy: The Results of Case Studies," *J. Forensic Sci.,* 36 (1991): 1027–43.

351. M. W. Tungol, E. G. Bartick, and A. Montaser, "Forensic Analysis of Acrylic Copolymers by Infrared Microscopy," *Appl. Spectrosc.,* 47 (1993): 1655–8.

352. S. P. Bouffard, A. J. Sommer, J. E. Katon, and S. Godber, "Use of Molecular Microspectroscopy to Characterize Pigment-Loaded Polypropylene Single Fibers," *Appl. Spectrosc.,* 48 (1994): 1387–93.

353. M. C. Grieve, "Another Look at the Classification of Acrylic Fibres, Using FTIR Microscopy," *Sci. Justice,* 35 (1995): 179–90.

354. M. C. Grieve, "New Man-made Fibres Under the Microscope— Lyocell Fibres and Nylon 6 Block Co-polymers," *Sci. Justice,* 36 (1996): 71–80.

355. M. C. Grieve, R. M. E. Griffin, and R. Malone, "Characteristic Dye Absorption Peaks Found in the FTIR Spectra of Coloured Acrylic Fibres," *Sci. Justice,* 38 (1998): 27–37.

356. M. C. Grieve and R. M. E. Griffin, "Is it a Modacrylic Fibre?" *Sci. Justice,* 39 (1997): 151–62.

357. R. Chen and K. A. Jakes, "Effect of Pressing on the Infrared Spectra of Single Cotton Fibers," *Appl. Spectrosc.,* 56 (2002): 646–50.

358. L. K. Peterson, "Characterization of Polylactic Acid (PLA) Fibers," *Microscope,* 50 (2002): 37–43.

359. V. Causin, C. Marega, G. Guzzini, A. Marigo, "Forensic Analysis of Poly(ethylene terephthalate) Fibers by Infrared Spectroscopy," *Appl. Spectrosc.,* 58 (2004): 1272–6.

360. V. Causin, C. Marega, S. Schiavone, and A. Marigo, "A Quantitative Differentiation Method for Acrylic Fibers by Infrared Spectroscopy," *Forensic Sci. Int.,* 26 (2005): 125–31.

361. P. Garside and P. Wyeth, "Use of Polarized Spectroscopy as a Tool for Examining the Microstructure of Cellulosic Textile Fibers," *Appl. Spectrosc.,* 61 (2007): 523–9.

362. L Cho, J. A. Reffner, B. M. Gatewood, and D. L. Wetzel, "Single Fiber Analysis by Internal Reflection Infrared Microspectroscopy," *J. Forensic Sci.,* 46 (2001): 1309–14.

363. J. A. Reffner, "Infrared Microprobe Analysis Using Reflection Methods," *Microscope,* 53 (2005): 33–6.

364. L Cho, J. A. Reffner, B. M. Gatewood, and D. L. Wetzel, "A New Method for Fiber Comparison Using Polarized Infrared Microspectroscopy," *J. Forensic Sci.,* 44 (1999): 275–82.

365. L Cho, J. A. Reffner and D. L. Wetzel, "Forensic Classification of Polyester Fibers by Infrared Dichroic Ratio Pattern Recognition," *J. Forensic Sci.,* 44 (1999): 283–91.

366. K. Flynn, R. O'Leary, C. Roux, and B. J. Reedy, "Forensic Analysis of Bicomponent Fibers Using Infrared

Chemical Imaging," *J. Forensic Sci.*, 51 (2006): 586–96.

367. O. Kirret, P. Koch, and L. Lahe, "Characterization and Identification of Polyacrylonitrile Fibres and Their Modifications and Modacrylic Fibres by Infrared Spectroscopy," *Eesti NSV Tead. Akad. Toim. Keem. Geol.*, 31, No. 3 (1982): 197–203.

368. O. Kirret, M. Pank, and L. Lahe, "Characterization and Identification of Polyester Fibres and Their Modifications by Infrared Spectrometric Methods," *Eesti NSV Tead. Akad. Toim. Keem. Geol.*, 29, No. 2 (1980): 92–6.

369. O. Kirret, P. Koch, and L. Lahe, "Characterization and Identification of Polyamide Fibres by Infrared Spectrophotometric Method," *Eesti NSV Tead. Akad. Toim. Keem. Geol.*, 30, No. 4 (1981): 281–8.

370. O. Kirret, P. Koch, and L. Lahe, "Characterization of Polyvinyl Chloride Fibres by Infrared Spectroscopic Method," *Eesti NSV Tead. Akad. Toim. Keem, Geol.*, 31, No. 1 (1982): 50–3.

371. O. Kirret, P. Koch, and L. Lahe, "The Characterization and Identification of Polyurethane Elastomer Fibers (Thanelast Fibers) with the Aid of Infrared Spectrometry," *Eesti NSV Tead. Akad. Toim. Keem. Geol.*, 33, No. 4 (1984): 2–9.

372. O. Kirret, L. Lahe, and E. Kiljanen, "Characterization and Identification of Nitrogen Containing Chemical Fibres and Wool by Infrared Spectrometric Method," *Eesti NSV Tead. Akad. Toim. Keem, Geol.*, 35, No. 3 (1986): 231–4.

373. J. Was, D. Knittel, and E. Schollmeyer, "The Use of FTIR Microspectroscopy for the Identification of Thermally Changed Fibers," *J. Forensic Sci.*, 41 (1996): 1005–11.

374. V. Causin, C. Marega, G. Guzzini, and A. Marigo, "The Effect of Exposure to the Elements on the Forensic Characterization by Infrared Spectroscopy of Poly(ethylene terephthalate) Fibers," *J. Forensic Sci.*, 50 (2005): 887–93.

375. P. Garside, S. Lahlil, and P. Wyeth, "Characterization of Historic Silk by Polarized Attenuated Total Reflectance Fourier Transform Infrared Spectroscopy for Informed Conservation," *Appl. Spectrosc.*, 59 (2005): 1242–7.

376. C. Q. Yang, R. R. Bresee, and W. G. Fateley, "Studies of Chemically Modified Poly(ethylene terephthalate) Fibers by FT-IR Photoacoustic Spectroscopy and X-Ray Photoelectron Spectroscopy," *Appl. Spectrosc.*, 44 (1990): 1035–9.

377. J. M. Challinor, P. A. Collins, and J. Goulding, "Identification and Discrimination of Trace Quantities of Acrylic and Polyamide Textile Fibres by Pyrolysis Gas Chromatography Compared to Fourier Transform Infrared Spectroscopy," in *Advances in Forensic Sciences*, vol. 4, eds. B. Jacob and W. Bonte (Berlin: Auflage, 1995), pp. 250–4.

378. A. D. Beveridge, S. F. Payton, R. S. Audette, A. J. Lambertus, and R. C. Shaddick, "Systematic Analysis of Explosive Residues," *J. Forensic Sci.*, 20 (1975): 431–54.

379. A. D. Beveridge, W. R. A. Greenley, and R. C. Shaddick, "Identification of Reaction Products in Residues From Explosives," in *Proceedings of the International Symposium on the Analysis and Detection of Explosives* (Washington, D.C.: U.S. Government Printing Office, 1983), pp. 53–8.

380. A. D. Beveridge, "Development in the Detection and Identification of Explosive Residues," *Forensic Sci. Rev.* 4 (1992): 17–49.

381. W. D. Washington and C. R. Midkiff, "Systematic Approach to the Detection of Explosives. I. Basic Techniques," *J. Assoc. Off. Anal. Chem.*, 55 (1972): 811–22.

382. C. M. Hoffman and E. B. Byall, "Identification of Explosive Residues in Bomb Scene Investigations," *J. Forensic Sci.*, 19 (1974): 54–63.

383. H. J. Yallop, "Breaking Offences With Explosives—The Techniques of the Criminal and the Scientist," *J. Forensic Sci. Soc.*, 14 (1974): 99–102.

384. R. G. Parker, M. O. Stephenson, J. M. McOwen, and J. A. Cherolis, "Analysis of Explosives and Explosive Residues. Part 1. Chemical Tests," *J. Forensic Sci.*, 20 (1975): 133–40.

385. M. A. Kaplan and S. Zitrin, "Identification of Post-Explosion Residue," *J. Assoc. Off. Anal. Chem.*, 60 (1977): 619–24.

386. J. Yinon and S. Zitrin, *The Analysis of Explosives* (New York: Pergamon Press, 1981).

387. C. R. Midkiff, "Arson and Explosive Investigation," in *Forensic Science Handbook.*, vol I, 2nd ed. R. Saferstein (Englewood Cliffs, NJ: Prentice-Hall, Inc., 2002), pp. 480–524.

388. W. D. Washington and C. R. Midkiff, Jr., "Explosive Residues in Bombing-Scene Investigations—New Technology Applied to Their Detection and Identification," in *Forensic Science*, 2nd ed. G. Davies (Washington, D.C.: American Chemical Society, 1986), pp. 259–78.

389. C. R. Midkiff, and W. D. Washington, "Systematic Approach to the Detection of Explosive Residues. III. Commercial Dynamite, *J. Assoc. Off. Anal. Chem.*, 57 (1974): 1092–7.

390. W. D. Washington, R. J. Kopec, and C. R. Midkiff, "Systematic Approach to the Detection of Explosive Residues. V. Black Powders," *J. Assoc. Off. Anal. Chem.*, 60 (1977): 1331–40.

391. W. D. Kinard and C. R. Midkiff, Jr., "Developments in Firearms Residue Detection," in *Forensic Science*, 2nd ed. G. Davies (Washington, D.C.: American Chemical Society, 1986), pp. 241–57.

392. T. G. Kee, D. M. Holmes, K. Doolan, J. A. Hamill, and R. M. E. Griffin, "The Identification of Individual Propellant Particles," *J. Forensic Sci. Soc.*, 30 (1990): 285–92.

393. R. E. Peimer, W. D. Washington, and K. B. Snow, "On the Examination of the Military Explosive, C-4," *J. Forensic Sci.*, 25 (1980): 398–400.

394. R. O. Keto, "Improved Method for the Analysis of the Military Explosive Composition C-4," *J. Forensic Sci.*, 31 (1986): 241–9.

395. C. R. Midkiff and W. D. Washington, "Systematic Approach to the Detection of Explosive Residues. IV. Military Explosives," *J. Assoc. Off. Anal. Chem.*, 59 (1976): 1357–74.

396. R. E. Meyers, "A Systematic Approach to the Forensic Examination of Flash Powders," *J. Forensic Sci.*, 23 (1978): 66–73.

397. R. G. Parker, "Analysis of Explosives and Explosive Residues. Part III: Monomethylamine Nitrate," *J. Forensic Sci.*, 20 (1975): 257–60.

398. F. Pristera and M. Halik, "Infrared Method for Determination of *o*-, *rn*-, and *p*-Mononitrotoluene and 2,4-Dinitrotoluene and 2,4-Dinitrotoluene in Mixtures," *Anal Chem.*, 27 (1955): 217–22.

399. F. Pristera, "Infrared Method for the Determination of Alpha (2–4-6) Beta (2–3-4), Gamma (2–4-5), Trinitrotoluene and 2–4 Dinitrotoluene in Admixtures such as Found in TNT Exudates," *Appl. Spectrosc.*, 7 (1953): 115–21.

400. H. K. Evans, F. A. J. Tulleners, B. L. Sanchez, and C. A. Rasmussen, "An Unusual Explosive, Triacetonetriperoxide (TATP)," *J. Forensic Sci.*, 31 (1986): 1119–25.

401. G. M. White, "An Explosive Drug Case," *J. Forensic Sci.*, 37 (1992): 652–6.

402. A. J. Bellamy, "Triacetone Triperoxide: Its Chemical Destruction," *J. Forensic Sci.*, 44 (1999): 603–8.

403. R. N. Holmes and J. E. Chrostowski, "The Identification of Silver Fulminate in the Analysis of Fun Snaps," *Crime Lab. Digest*, 79 (December 1979): 4–6.

404. S. Pinchas, "Determination of Diethylene Glycol Dinitrate and Nitroglycerin by Infrared Spectroscopy," *Anal. Chem.*, 23 (1951): 201–2.

405. F. Pristera, "Analysis of Propellants by Infrared Spectroscopy," *Anal. Chem.*, 25 (1953): 844–56.

406. F. Pristera, M. Halik, A. Castelli, and W. Fredericks, "Analysis of Explosives Using Infrared Spectroscopy," *Anal. Chem.*, 32 (1960): 495–508.

407. J. Carol, "Infrared Analysis of Erythritol Tetranitrate, Penta-erythritol Tetranitrate, and Mannitol Hexanitrate," *J. Assoc. Off. Anal. Chem.*, 43 (1960): 259–61.

408. D. E. Chasan and G. Norwitz, "Quantitative Analysis of Primers, Tracers, Igniters, Incendiaries, Boosters, and Delay Compositions on a Microscale by Use of Infrared Spectroscopy," *Microchem. J.*, 17 (1972): 31–60.

409. T. Fung, "Identification of Two Unusual Pipe Bomb Fillers," *Can. Soc. Forensic Sci. J.*, 18 (1985): 222–6.

410. L. R. Cabiness and R. D. Blackledge, "Trioxane—An Unusual Component in an Improvised Explosive-Actuated Incendiary Device," *J. Forensic Sci.*, 28 (1983): 282–4.

411. W. D. Washington and C. R. Midkiff, "Forensic Applications of Diamond Cell-Infrared Spectroscopy. I: Identification of Blasting Cap Leg Wire Manufacturers," *J. Forensic Sci.*, 21 (1976): 862–7.

412. W. D. Washington, C. R. Midkiff, and K. B. Snow, "Dynamite Contamination of Blasting Cap Leg Wire Insulation," *J. Forensic Sci.*, 22 (1977): 329–31.

413. R. J. Kopec, W. D. Washington, and C. R. Midkiff, "Forensic Applications of Sapphire Cell-Infrared Spectroscopy: Companion to the Diamond Cell in Explosive and Leg Wire Identification," *J. Forensic Sci.*, 23 (1978): 57–65.

414. T. Chen, "Identification and Quantitation of an Unknown Explosive," in *Proceedings of the International Symposium on the Analysis and Detection of Explosives* (Washington, D.C.: U.S. Government Printing Office, 1983), pp. 143–7.

415. D. J. Reutter, E. C. Bender, and T. L. Rudolph, "Analysis of an Unusual Explosive: Methods Used and Conclusions Drawn from Two Cases," in *Proceedings of the International Symposium on the Analysis and Detection of Explosives* (Washington, D.C.: U.S. Government Printing Office, 1983), pp. 149–58.

416. S. Zitrin, S. Kraus, and B. Glattstein, "Identification of Two Rare Explosives," in *Proceedings of the International Symposium on the Analysis and Detection of Explosives* (Washington, D.C.: U.S. Government Printing Office, 1983), pp. 137–41.

417. R. D. Blackledge, "Methenamine—An Unusual Component in an Improvised Incendiary Device," *J. Forensic Sci.*, 36 (1991): 261–3.

418. F. A. Miller and C. H. Wilkins, "Infrared Spectra and Characteristic Frequencies of Inorganic Ions," *Anal. Chem.*, 24 (1952): 1253–94.

419. R. M. Silverstein, F. X. Webster, and D. Kiemle, *Spectrometric Identification of Organic Compounds*, 7th ed. (New York: John Wiley & Sons, 2005).

420. J. F. Brown, Jr., "The Infrared Spectra of Nitro and Other Oxidized Nitrogen Compounds," *J. Am. Chem. Soc.*, 77 (1955): 6341–51.

421. R. H. Riddell and T. Mills, III, "Analysis of Explosives by HPLC-FTIR," in *Proceedings of the International Symposium on the Analysis and Detection of Explosives* (Washington, D.C.: U.S. Government Printing Office, 1983), 289–307.

422. A. A. Cantu, W. D. Washington, R. A. Strobel, and R. E. Tontarski, "Evaluation of FTIR as a Detector for the HPLC Analyses of Explosives," in *Proceedings of the International Symposium on the Analyses and Detection of Explosives* (Washington, D.C.: U.S. Government Printing Office, 1983), pp. 349–63.

423. M. Ashraf-Khorassani and L. T. Taylor, "Qualitative Supercritical Fluid Chromatography/Fourier Transform Infrared Spectroscopy Study of Methylene Chloride and Supercritical Carbon Dioxide Extracts of Double-Base Propellant," *Anal. Chem.*, 61 (1989): 145–8.

424. C. W. Saunders and L. T. Taylor, "Determination of the Degree of Nitration of Cellulose Nitrates via GPC/FT-IR Using an On-Line Flow Cell," *Appl. Spectrosc.*, 45 (1991): 900–5.

425. D. J. Johnson and D. A. C. Compton, "Quantitative Analysis of Nitrocellulose and Pulp in Gunpowder Using TGA-FTIR," *Am. Lab.*, 23 (Jan. 1991): 37–43.

426. K. P. Kirkbride and H. J. Kobus, "The Explosive Reaction Between Swimming Pool Chlorine and Brake Fluid," *J. Forensic Sci.*, 36 (1991): 902–7.

427. R. A. Pesce-Rodriguez and R. A. Fifer, "Applications of Fourier Transform Infrared Photoacoustic Spectroscopy to Solid Propellant Characterization," *Appl. Spectrosc.*, 45 (1991): 417–9.

428. M. A. Harthcock, L. A. Lentz, B. L. Davis, and K. Krishnan, "Applications of Transmittance and Micro/FT IR to Polymeric Materials," *Appl. Spectrosc.*, 40 (1986): 210–4.

429. M. A. Harthcock, "Applications of Recent Developments in Fourier Transform Infrared Spectroscopic Microsampling Techniques to Polymeric Materials," in *The Design, Sample Handling, and Applications of Infrared Microscopes*, ed. P. B. Roush (Philadelphia: ASTM, 1987), pp. 84–96.

430. E. V. Miseo and L. W. Guilmette, "Industrial Problem Solving by Microscopic Fourier Transform Infrared Spectrophotometry," in *The Design, Sample Handling, and Applications of Infrared Microscopes*, ed. P. B. Roush (Philadelphia: ASTM, 1987), pp. 97–107.

431. E. G. Bartick, "Microscopy/Infrared Spectroscopy for Routine Sample Sizes," *Appl. Spectrosc.*, 39 (1985): 885–9.

432. F. M. Mirabella, Jr., "Applications of Microscopic Fourier Transform Infrared Spectrophotometry Sampling Techniques for the Analysis of Polymer Systems," in *The Design, Sample Handling, and Applications of Infrared Microscopes*, ed. P. B. Roush (Philadelphia: ASTM, 1987), pp. 74–83.

433. J. Andrasko, L. Haeger, A. C. Maehly, and L. Svensson, "Comparative Analysis of Synthetic Polymers Using Combinations of Three Analytical Methods," *Forensic Sci. Int.*, 25 (1984): 57–70.

434. J. G. Grasselli, "Analysis of Polymers by Fourier Transform Infrared Spectroscopy," in *Proceedings of the International Symposium on the Analysis and Identification of Polymers* (Washington, D.C.: U.S. Government Printing Office, 1984), pp. 61–6.

435. B. M. Fanconi, "Trends in Polymer Development and Analytical Techniques," in *Proceedings of the International Symposium on the Analysis and Identification of Polymers* (Washington, D.C.: U.S. Government Printing Office, 1984), 87–108.

436. P. Maynard, K. Gates, C. Roux, and C. Lennard, "Adhesive Tape Analysis: Establishing the Evidential Value of Specific Techniques," *J. Forensic Sci.*, 46 (2001): 280–7.

437. R. A. Merrill and E. G. Bartick, "Analysis of Pressure Sensitive Adhesive Tape: I. Evaluation of Infrared ATR Accessory Advances," *J. Forensic Sci.*, 45 (2000): 93–8.

438. A. L. Hobbs, J. Gauntt, R. Keagy, P. C. Lowe, and D. Ward, "A New Approach for the Analysis of Duct Tape Backings," *Forensic Sci. Commun.*, 9 (2007): 1–5.

439. T. G. Kee, "The Characterization of PVC Adhesive Tape," in *Proceedings of the International Symposium on the Analysis and Identification of Polymers* (Washington, D.C.: U.S. Government Printing Office, 1984), pp. 77–85.

440. R. O. Keto, "Forensic Characterization of Black Polyvinyl Chloride Electrical Tape," in *Proceedings of the International Symposium on the Analysis and Identification of Polymers* (Washington, D.C.: U.S. Government Printing Office, 1984), 137–43.

441. I. Kirkwood and M. D. J. Isaacs, "The Analysis of Vehicle Sidelight Plastics," *Forensic Sci. Int.*, 43 (1989): 51–62.

442. R. D. Blackledge, "Examination of Automobile Rubber Bumper Guards by Attenuated Total Reflectance Spectroscopy Using a Fourier Transform Infrared Spectrometer," *J. Forensic Sci.*, 26 (1981): 554–6.

443. E. G. Bartick, M. W. Tungol, and J. A. Reffner, "A New Approach to Forensic Analysis with Infrared Microscopy: Internal Reflection Spectroscopy," *Anal. Chim. Acta.*, 288 (1994): 35–42.

444. A. E. Parybyk and H. J. Kobus, "The Characterization of Plastic Automobile Bumper Bars Using Fourier Transform Infrared Spectroscopy (FTIR), Pyrolysis Gas Chromatography (PGC), and Energy Dispersive X-Ray Microanalysis Combined with a Scanning Electron Microscope (SEM-EDX)," *J. Forensic Sci.*, 35 (1990): 281–92.

445. B. Cleverley, "The Identification of Motor Body Fillers," *J. Forensic Sci. Soc.*, 10 (1970): 73–6.

446. K. A. J. Walsh, B. W. Axon, and J.S. Buckleton, "New Zealand Body Fillers: Discrimination Using IR Spectroscopy, Visible Microspectrophotometry, Density, and SEM-EDAX," *Forensic Sci. Int.*, 32 (1986): 193–204.

447. G. Sarkissian, J. Keegan, E. Du Pasquier, J.-P. Depriester, and P. Rousselot, "The Analysis of Tires and Tire Traces Using FTIR and Py-GC/MS," *Can. Soc. Forensic Sci. J.*, 37 (2004): 19–37.

448. B. Cleverley, "The Comparison and Matching of Low Density Polyethylene Plastic Bags by Infrared Spectroscopy," *J. Forensic Sci.*, 24 (1979): 339–45.

449. T. Hashimoto, D. G. Howitt, D. P. Land, F. A. Tulleners, F. A. Springer, and S. Wang, "Morphological and Spectroscopic Measurements of Plastic Bags for the Purpose of Discrimination." *J. Forensic Sci.*, 52 (2007): 1082–8.

450. J. F. Demers-Kohls, S. L. Ouderkirk, J. L. Buckle, E. W. Norman, N. S. Cartwright, and C. Dagenais, "An Evaluation of Different Evidence Bags Used for Sampling and Storage of Fire Debris," *Can. Soc. Forensic Sci. J.*, 27 (1994): 143–70.

451. R. M. E. Griffin, R. Lewis, J. Bennett, J. Hamell, and T. G. Kee, "Analysis of Cling Films and Coloured Cellophanes and the Application to Casework," *Sci. Justice*, 36 (1996): 219–27.

452. J. Gilburt, J. M. Ingram, M. P. Scott, and M. Underhill, "The Analysis of Clingfilms by Infrared Spectroscopy and Thermal Desorption Capillary Gas Chromatography," *J. Forensic Sci. Soc.*, 31 (1991): 337–47.

453. G. van Dalen, P. C. M. Heussen, R. den Adel, and R. B. J. Hoeve, "Attenuated Total Internal Reflection Infrared Microscopy of Multilayer Plastic

Packaging Foils," *Appl. Spectrosc.*, 61 (2007): 593–602.

454. C. J. Lennard and P. A. Margot, "The Analysis of Synthetic Shoe Soles by FTIR Microspectrometry and Pyrolysis-GC: A Case Example," *J. Forensic Ident.*, 39 (1989): 239–43.

455. E. M. Suzuki and W. R. Gresham, "Forensic Analysis of Polymers Using Diffuse Reflectance Infrared Fourier Transform Infrared Spectroscopy," in *Proceedings of the International Symposium on the Analysis and Identification of Polymers* (Washington, D.C.: U.S. Government Printing Office, 1984), pp. 127–9.

456. M. C. Grieve, "Glitter Particles—An Unusual Source of Trace Evidence?" *J. Forensic Sci. Soc.*, 27 (1987): 405–12.

457. B. B. Coldwell and M. Smith, "The Comparison and Identification of Adhesives on Questioned Documents," *J. Forensic Sci.*, 11 (1966): 28–42.

458. W. Noble, B. B. Wheals, and M. J. Whitehouse, "The Characterization of Adhesives by Pyrolysis Gas Chromatography and Infrared Spectroscopy," *Forensic Sci.*, 3 (1974): 163–74.

459. E. S. Kubik, "Super Glue Analysis by Infrared and Protein Nuclear Magnetic Resonance Spectroscopy," in *Proceedings of the International Symposium on the Analysis and Identification of Polymers* (Washington, D.C.: U.S. Government Printing Office, 1984), 131–3.

460. W. F. Rowe, "A Bizarre Death Caused by a Model Airplane," *J. Forensic Sci.*, 36 (1991): 1262–5.

461. E. M. Enlow, J. L. Kennedy, A. A. Nieuwland, J. E. Hendrix, and S. L. Morgan, "Discrimination of Nylon Polymers Using Attenuated Total Reflection Mid-infrared Spectra and Multivariate Statistical Techniques," *Appl. Spectrosc.*, 59 (2005): 986–92.

462. S. Sugawara, "Passport Examination by Polarized Infrared Spectra," *J. Forensic Sci.*, 52 (2007): 974–7.

463. R. D. Blackledge, "Viscosity Comparisons of Polydimethylsiloxane Lubricants in Latex Condom Brands via Fourier Self-Deconvolution of Their FT-IR Spectra," *J. Forensic Sci.*, 40 (1995): 467–9.

464. R. D. Blackledge and M. Vincenti, "Identification of Polydimethylsiloxane Lubricant Traces from Latex Condoms in Cases of Sexual Assault," *J. Forensic Sci. Soc.*, 34 (1994): 245–56.

465. R. L. Brunelle, "Questioned Document Examination," in *Forensic Science Handbook*, vol I, 2nd ed. R. Saferstein (Englewood Cliffs, NJ: Prentice-Hall, Inc., 2002), pp. 697–744.

466. A. A. Cantu, "Analytical Methods for Detecting Fraudulent Documents," *Anal. Chem.*, 63 (1991): 847A-54A.

467. J. P. Deley, R. J. Gigi, and A. J. Liotti, "Identification of Coatings on Paper by Attenuated Total Reflectance," *J. Tech. Assoc. Pulp Paper Ind.*, 46 (1963): 188A-92A.

468. A. Kher, M. Mulholland, B. Reedy, and P. Maynard, "Classification of Document Papers by Infrared Spectroscopy and Multivariate Statistical Techniques," *Appl. Spectrosc.*, 55 (2001): 1192–8.

469. D. N. S. Hon, "Fourier Transform IR Spectroscopy and Electron Spectroscopy for Chemical Analysis—Use in the Study of Paper Documents," in *Historic and Paper Materials Conservation and Characterization*, eds. H. L. Needles and S. H. Zeronian (Washington, DC: American Chemical Society, 1986), pp. 349–61.

470. A. J. Sommer, P. L. Lang, B. S. Miller, and J. E. Katon, "Applications of Molecular Microspectroscopy to Paper Chemistry," in *Infrared Microspectroscopy*, eds. R. G. Messerschmidt and M. A. Harthcock (New York: Marcel Dekker, Inc., 1988), pp. 245–58.

471. J. Andrasko, "Microreflectance FTIR Techniques Applied to Materials Encountered in Forensic Examination

of Documents," *J. Forensic Sci.*, 41 (1996): 812–23.

472. J. D. Kelly and P. Haville, "Procedure for the Characterization of Zinc Oxide Photocopy Papers," *J. Forensic Sci.*, 25 (1980): 118–31.

473. J. Harris, "A Preliminary Report on the Nondestructive Examination of Ballpoint Pen Ink on Questioned Documents by FT-IR Spectroscopy," *Can. Soc. Forensic Sci. J.*, 24 (1991): 5–21.

474. R. A. Merrill and E. G. Bartick, "Analysis of Ball Point Pen Inks by Diffuse Reflectance Infrared Spectrometry," *J. Forensic Sci.*, 37 (1992): 528–41.

475. B. Trzcinska, "Infrared Spectroscopy of Ballpen Paste," *Forensic Sci. Int.*, 46 (1990): 105–9.

476. P. G. Varlashkin and M. J. D. Low, "FT-IR Photothermal Beam Deflection Spectroscopy of Black Inks on Paper," *Appl. Spectrosc.*, 40 (1986): 507–13.

477. J. Wang, G. Luo, S. Sun, Z. Wang, Y. Wang, "Systematic Analysis of Bulk Blue Ballpoint Pen Ink by FTIR Spectrometry," *J. Forensic Sci.*, 46 (2001): 1093–7.

478. J. Zieba-Palus and M. Kunicki, "Application of the Micro-FTIR Spectroscopy, Raman Spectroscopy and XRF Method Examination of Inks," *Forensic Sci. Int.*, 158 (2006): 164–72.

479. E. Fabianska and B. M. Trzcinska, "Differentiation of Ballpoint and Liquid Inks—A Comparison of Methods in Use," *Problems of Forensic Sciences*, 47 (2001): 383–400.

480. T. J. Wilkinson, D. L. Perry, M. C. Martin, W. R. McKinney, and A. A. Cantu, "Use of Synchrotron Reflectance Infrared Microspectroscopy as a Rapid, Direct, Nondestructive Method for the Study of Inks on Paper," *Appl. Spectrosc.*, 56 (2002): 800–3.

481. H. J. Humecki, "Experiments in Ball Point Ink Aging Using Infrared Spectroscopy," in *Proceedings of the International Symposium on Questioned Documents* (Washington, D.C.: U.S. Government Printing Office, 1985), pp. 131–5.

482. R. L. Brunelle and A. A. Cantu, "A Critical Evaluation of Current Ink Dating Techniques," *J. Forensic Sci.*, 32 (1987): 1522–36.

483. W. C. McCrone, "Vinland Map 1999," *Microscope*, 47 (1999): 71–4.

484. W. C. McCrone, "Authenticity of Medival Document Tested by Small Particle Analysis," *Anal. Chem.*, 48 (1976): 676A-9A.

485. R. N. Totty, "Analysis and Differentiation of Photocopy Toners," *Forensic Sci. Rev.*, 2 (1990): 1–23.

486. G. S. Kemp and R. N. Totty, "The Differentiation of Toners Used in Photocopy Processes by Infrared Spectroscopy," *Forensic Sci. Int.*, 22 (1983): 75–83.

487. R. L. Williams, "Analysis of Photocopying Toners by Infrared Spectroscopy," *Forensic Sci. Int.*, 22 (1983): 85–95.

488. G. Tandon, O. P. Jasuja, and V. N. Sehgal, "The Characterization of Photocopy Toners Using FTIR," *Int. J. Forensic Doc. Examiners*, 3 (1997): 119–26.

489. W. D. Mazzella, C. J. Lennard, and P. A. Margot, "Classification and Identification of Photocopying Toners by Diffuse Reflectance Infrared Fourier Transform Spectroscopy (DRIFTS): I. Preliminary Results," *J. Forensic Sci.*, 36 (1991): 449–65.

490. W. D. Mazzella, C. J. Lennard, and P. A. Margot, "Classification and Identification of Photocopying Toners by Diffuse Reflectance Infrared Fourier Transform Spectroscopy (DRIFTS): II. Final Report," *J. Forensic Sci.*, 36 (1991): 820–37.

491. J. Zimmerman, D. Mooney, and M. J. Kimmett, "Preliminary Examination of Machine Copier Toners by Infrared Spectrophotometry

and Pyrolysis Gas Chromatography," *J. Forensic Sci.*, 31 (1986): 489–93.

492. C. J. Lennard and W. D. Mazzella, "A Simple Combined Technique for the Analysis of Toners and Adhesives," *J. Forensic Sci. Soc.*, 31 (1991): 365–71.

493. J. A. de Koeijer and J. J. M. de Moel, "Identifying Black Toners Using FTIR and Pyrolysis-GC/MS," *Problems of Forensic Sciences*, 47 (2001): 413–27.

494. B. M. Trzcinska, "Classification of Black Powder Toners on the Basis of Integrated Analytical Information Provided by Fourier Transform Infrared Spectrometry and X-Ray Fluorescence Spectrometry," *J. Forensic Sci.*, 51 (2006): 919–24.

495. J. Brandi, B. James, S. J. Gutowski, "Differentiation and Classification of Photocopier Toners," *Int. J. Forensic Doc. Examiners*, 3 (1997): 324–43.

496. J. Andrasko, "A Simple Method for Sampling Photocopy Toners for Examination by Microreflectance Fourier Transform Infrared Spectrophotometry," *J. Forensic Sci.*, 39 (1994): 226–30.

497. R. A. Merrill, E. G. Bartick, and W. D. Mazzella, "Studies of Techniques for Analysis of Photocopy Toners by IR," *J. Forensic Sci.*, 41 (1996): 264–71.

498. R. A. Merrill, E. G. Bartick, and J. H. Taylor III, "Forensic Discrimination of Photocopy and Printer Toners. I. The Development of an Infrared Spectral Library," *Anal. Bioanal. Chem.*, 376 (2003): 1272–8.

499. W. J. Egan, S. L. Morgan, E. G. Bartick, R. A. Merrill, and H. J. Taylor III, "Forensic Discrimination of Photocopy and Printer Toners. II. Discriminant Analysis Applied to Infrared Reflection-Absorption Spectroscopy," *Anal. Bioanal. Chem.*, 376 (2003): 1279–85.

500. C. L. Gilmour, "A Comparison of Laser Printed and Photocopied Documents: Can They Be Distinguished?" *Can. Soc. Forensic Sci. J.*, 27 (1994): 245–59.

501. J. Harris and D. MacDougall, "Characterization and Dating of Correction Fluids on Questioned Documents Using FTIR," *Can. Soc. Forensic Sci. J.*, 22 (1989): 349–76.

502. M. Poslusny and K. E. Daugherty, "Nondestructive Adhesive Analysis on Stamps by Fourier Transform Infrared Spectroscopy," *Appl. Spectrosc.*, 42 (1988): 1466–9.

503. J. H. Wang, "A Versatile Analytical Method of Identifying Adhesive on Stamps by Specular Reflectance Fourier Transform Infrared Spectroscopy," *Appl. Spectrosc.*, 44 (1990): 447–50.

504. B. Cleverley, "The Comparison of Lubricating Greases Using Infra-Red Spectroscopy," *J. Forensic Sci. Soc.*, 8 (1968): 69–70.

505. M. Arredondo, G. M. LaPorte, J. D. Wilson, T. McConnell, D. K. Shaffer, and M. Stam, "Analytical Methods Used for the Discrimination of Substances Suspected to be Bar Soap: A Preliminary Study," *J. Forensic Sci.*, 51 (2006): 1334–43.

506. L. Gardner, "Application of Infrared Spectroscopy to the Examination of Lubricants," *Can. J. Spectrosc.*, 9 (1964): 136–42.

507. H. L. Yip, "The Identification of Lubricating Oils on Clothing by Column Chromatography, Infrared Spectroscopy, and Refractometry," *J. Forensic Sci.*, 18 (1973): 263–70.

508. J. Zieba, "Examination of Lubricating Oils by Infrared Spectroscopy," *Forensic Sci. Int.*, 27 (1985): 31–9.

509. J. Zieba, "Differentiation of Lubricating Oil Stains on Textile by Infrared Spectroscopy," *Forensic Sci. Int.*, 30 (1986): 45–51.

510. L. Gardner, "Infrared Spectroscopic Examination of Used Lubricating Oils," *Can. J. Spectrosc.*, 11 (1966): 98–101.

511. J. Zieba-Palus, P. Koscielniak, and M. Lacki, "Differentiation Between Used Motor Oils on the Basis of Their

IR Spectra with Application of the Correlation Method," *Forensic Sci. Int.*, 122 (2001): 35–42.

512. J. Zieba-Palus, P. Koscielniak, and M. Lacki, "Differentiation of Used Motor Oils on the Basis of Their IR Spectra with Application of Cluster Analysis," *J. Molec. Struct.*, 596 (2001): 221–8.

513. J. Zieba, "Examination of the Rate of Oil Degradation during Car Use by Infrared Spectroscopy," *Forensic Sci. Int.*, 29 (1985): 269–74.

514. J. S. Mattson, "'Fingerprinting' of Oil by Infrared Spectrometry," *Anal. Chem.*, 43 (1971): 1872–73.

515. P. F. Lynch and C. W. Brown, "Identifying the Source of Petroleum by Infrared Spectroscopy," *Environ. Sri. Tech.*, 7 (1973): 1123–7.

516. C. W. Brown, P. F. Lynch, and M. Ahmadjian, "Applications of Infrared Spectroscopy in Petroleum Analysis and Oil Spill Identification," *Appl. Spectrosc. Rev.*, 9 (1975): 223–48.

517. C. D. Baer and C. W. Brown, "Identifying the Source of Weathered Petroleum: Matching Infrared Spectra with Correlation Coefficients," *Appl. Spectrosc.*, 31 (1977): 524–7.

518. Y. Mammo, S. Nagatsuka, and Y. Oba, "Clay Mineralogical Analysis Using the < 0.05 mm Fraction for Forensic Science Investigation—Its Application to Volcanic Ash Soils and Yellow-Brown Forest Soils," *J. Forensic Sci.*, 31 (1986): 92–105.

519. Y. Mammo, S. Nagatsuka, and Y. Oba, "Rapid Clay Mineralogical Analysis for Forensic Science Investigation—Clay Mineralogy Over the Short Distances," *J. Forensic Sci.*, 33 (1988): 1360–8.

520. R. J. Cox, H. L. Peterson, J. Young, C. Cusik, and E. O. Espinoza, "The Forensic Analysis of Soil Organic by FTIR," *Forensic Sci. Int.*, 108 (2000): 107–16.

521. D. Changwen, R. Linker, and A. Shaviv, "Characterization of Soils Using Photoacous---tic Mid-Infrared Spectroscopy," *Appl. Spectrosc.*, 61 (2007): 1063–7.

522. J. Hopkins, L. Brenner, and C. S. Tumosa, "Variation of the Amide I and Amide II Peak Absorbance Ratio in Human Hair as Measured by Fourier Transform Infrared Spectroscopy," *Forensic Sci. Int.*, 50 (1991): 61–5.

523. K. L. A. Chan, S. G. Kazarian, A. Mavraki, and D. R. Williams, "Fourier Transform Infrared Imaging of Human Hair with a High Resolution without the Use of a Synchrotron," *Appl. Spectrosc.*, 59 (2005): 149–55.

524. L. Brenner, P. L. Squires, M. Garry, and C. S. Tumosa, "A Measurement of Human Hair Oxidation by Fourier Transform Infrared Spectroscopy," *J. Forensic Sci.*, 13 (1985): 420–6.

525. C. S. Tumosa and L. Brenner, "The Detection and Occurrence of Human Hair Oxidation by Fourier Transform Infrared Spectroscopy," in *Proceedings of the International Symposium on Forensic Hair Comparisons* (Washington, D.C.: U.S. Government Printing Office, 1985), pp. 153–5.

526. A. Gordon and S. Coulson, "The Evidential Value of Cosmetic Foundation Smears in Forensic Casework," *J. Forensic Sci.*, 49 (2004): 1244–52.

527. K. Kelder and B. Burton, "Examination of a Deployed Airbag for DNA and Cosmetics to Answer the 'Driver Question,'" *Can. Soc. Forensic Sci. J.*, 35 (2002): 165–75.

528. T. J. Wilkinson, D. L. Perry, M. C. Martin, and W. R. McKinney, Abstract Paper, *Am. Chem. Soc.*, 222 (2001).

529. D. K. Williams, R. L. Schwartz, and E. G. Bartick, "Analysis of Latent Fingerprint Deposits by Infrared Microspectroscopy," *Appl. Spectrosc.*, 58 (2004): 313–6.

530. A. Grant, T. J. Wilkinson, D. R. Holman, and M. C. Martin, "Identification of Recently Handled Materials by Analysis of Latent Human Fingerprints Using

Infrared Spectroscopy," *Appl. Spectrosc.*, 59 (2005): 1182–7.

531. N. J. Crane, E. G. Bartick, R. S. Perlman, and S. Huffman, "Infrared Spectroscopic Imaging for Noninvasive Detection of Latent Fingerprints," *J. Forensic Sci.*, 52 (2007): 48–53.

532. C. Ricci, P. P. Phiriyavityopas, N. Curum, K. L. A. Chan, S. Jickells, and S. G. Kazarian, "Chemical Imaging of Latent Fingerprint Residues," *Appl. Spectrosc.*, 61 (2007): 514–22.

533. W. C. McCrone, *Judgment Day for the Shroud of Turin* (Buffalo, NY: Prometheus Books, 1999).

534. M. Lesney, "Analyzing Artistry: Spectroscopy is Indispensable in Examining the Provenance of Artifacts and Paintings," *Today's Chem. Work*, 11 (2002): 22–4.

535. J. Riederer, "The Detection of Art Forgeries with Scientific Methods," in *Forensic Science Progress*, vol. 1, eds. A. Maehly and R. L. Williams (New York: Springer-Verlag, 1986), pp. 153–68.

536. W. C. McCrone, "1500 Forgeries," *Microscope*, 38 (1990): 289–98.

537. W. C. McCrone, "The Microscopical Identification of Artists' Pigments," *J. Int. Inst. Conserv., Can. Grp.*, 7 (1982): 11–34.

538. J. S. Olin, M. E. Salmon, and C. H. Olin, "Investigations of Historical Objects Utilizing Spectroscopy and Other Optical Methods," *Appl. Optics.*, 8 (1969): 29–39.

539. E. H. Van't Hul-Ehrnreich, "Infrared Microspectroscopy for the Analysis of Old Painting Materials," *Stud. Conserv.*, 15 (1970): 175–82.

540. M. J. D. Low and N. S. Baer, "Application of Infrared Fourier Transform Spectroscopy to Problems in Conservation," *Stud. Conserv.*, 22 (1977): 116–28.

541. R. Newman, "Some Applications of Infrared Spectroscopy in the Examination of Painting Materials," *J. Am. Inst. Conserv.*, 19 (1980): 42–62.

542. J. C. Shearer, D. C. Peters, G. Hoepfner, and T. Newton, "FTIR in the Service of Art Conservation," *Anal. Chem.*, 55 (1983): 874A-80A.

543. H. Staat, E. H. Korte, and D. Kolev, "Infrared Reflection Studies of Historical Varnishes," in *Recent Developments in Molecular Spectroscopy*, eds. R. Jordanov, N. Kirov, and P. Simonva (Teaneck, NJ: World Scientific Publishing Co. Inc., 1989), pp. 64–74.

544. M. V. Oma, P. L. Lang, J. E. Katon, T. F. Mathews, and R. S. Nelson, "Applications of Infrared Microspectroscopy to Art Historical Questions About Medieval Manuscripts," in *Archaeological Chemistry IV*, ed, R. O. Allen (Washington, D.C.: American Chemical Society, 1989), pp. 265–88.

545. R. J. Meilunas, J. G. Bentsen, and A. Steinberg, "Analysis of Aged Paint Binders by FTIR Spectroscopy," *Stud. Conserv.*, 35 (1990): 33–51.

546. M. T. Doemenech-Carbo, A. Doemenech-Carbo, J. V. Gimeno-Adelantado, and F. Bosch-Reig, "Identification of Synthetic Resins Used in Works of Art by Fourier Transform Infrared Spectroscopy," *Appl. Spectrosc.*, 55 (2001): 1590–1602.

547. C. Miliani, F. Rosi, I. Borgia, P. Benedetti, B. G. Brunetti, and A. Sgamellotti, "Fiber-Optic Fourier Transform Mid-Infrared Reflectance Spectroscopy: A Suitable Technique for *in Situ* Studies of Mural Paintings," *Appl. Spectrosc.*, 61 (2007): 293–9.

548. M. R. Derrick, D. C. Stulik, and J. M. Landry, *Infrared Spectroscopy in Conservation Science* (Los Angeles: Getty Trust Publications, 2000).

549. S. Litt, "Scientist Raises Possibility Paintings Might Not Be Pollocks," *The Plain Dealer Dealer*, November 30, 2007. http://www.cleveland.com/plaindealer/stories/index.ssf?/base/entertainment-0/1196415851165630.xml=2

550. K. J. Ewing and B. Lerner, "Infrared Detection of the Nerve Agent Sarin (Isopropyl Methylphosphonofluori-date) in Water Using Magnesium Oxide for Preconcentration," *Appl. Spectrosc.*, 55 (2001): 407–11.

551. V. R. Sreenivasan and R. A. Boese, "Identification of Lachrymators," *J. Forensic Sci.*, 15 (1970): 433–42.

552. J. A. Gag and N. F. Merck, "Concise Identifications of Commonly Encountered Tear Gases," *J. Forensic Sci.*, 22 (1977): 358–64.

553. K. E. Ferslew, R. H. Orcutt, and A. N. Hagardom, "Spectral Differentiation and Gas Chromatographic/ Mass Spectrometric Analysis of the Lachcrimators 2-Chloroacetophenone and *O*-Chorobenzylidene Malononitrile," *J. Forensic Sci.*, 31 (1986): 658–65.

554. H. W. Avdovich, A. By, J.-C. Ethier, and G. A. Neville, "Spectral Identification of a Lachrymatory Exhibit as CS," *Can. Soc. Forensic Sci. J.*, 14 (1981): 172–8.

555. T. Fung, W. Jeffrey, and A. D. Beveridge, "The Identification of Capsaicinoids in Tear Gas Spray," *J. Forensic Sci.*, 27 (1982): 812–21.

556. P. M. L. Sandercock, "An Unusual Use for the Herbicide Glyphosate: A Case Report," *Can. Soc. Forensic Sci. J.*, 30 (1977): 191–7.

557. G. K. Lee, "Analytical Chemistry Tracks Poachers," *Anal. Chem.*, 63 (1991): 513A-15A.

558. J. F. Amick and C. W. Beheim, "Screen-Printing Ink Transfer in a Sexual Assault Case," *J. Forensic Sci.*, 47 (2002): 619–24.

559. S. J. Dignan, "The Effects of Moisture on Safe Insulations Containing Portland Cement," *Can. Soc. Forensic Sci. J.*, 19 (1986): 37–48.

560. C. Ricci, K. L. A. Chan, and S. G. Kazarian, "Combining the Tape-Lift Method and Fourier Transform Infrared Spectroscopic Imaging for Forensic Applications," *Appl. Spectrosc.*, 60 (2006): 1013–21.

561. S. Palenik and C. Palenik, "Microscopy and Microchemistry of Physical Evidence," in *Forensic Science Handbook*, vol. II, 2nd ed. R. Saferstein (Englewood Cliffs, NJ: Prentice-Hall, Inc., 2005), pp. 175–230.

562. N. Petraco and P. R. De Forest, "Trajectory Reconstructions I: Trace Evidence in Flight," *J. Forensic Sci.*, 35 (1990): 1284–96.

563. J. J. Benko, "Investigating Coating Defects with Optical Microscopy and FT-IR Microspectroscopy," *Microscope*, 47 (1999): 141–6.

564. C. S. Pappas, P. A. Tarantilis, P. C. Harizanis, and M. G. Polissiou, "New Method for Pollen Identification by FT-IR Spectroscopy," *Appl. Spectrosc.*, 57 (2003): 23–7.

565. J. T. Chen and R. W. Dority, "Contamination Control in Infrared Microanalysis," *J. Assoc. Off. Anal. Chem.*, 53 (1970): 978–86.

566. W. C. McCrone, R. G. Draftz, and J. G. Deily, *The Particle Atlas* (Ann Arbor, MI: Ann Arbor Science Publishers, 1967).

567. P. L. Lang, J. E. Katon, and A. S. Bonanno, "Identification of Dust Particles by Molecular Microspectroscopy," *Appl. Spectrosc.*, 42 (1988): 313–17.

Bibliography

General

Adler, H. H. "Some Basic Considerations in the Application of Infrared Spectroscopy to Mineral Analysis." *Econ. Geol.*, 58 (1963): 558–68.

Allen, R. O. and P. Sanderson. "Characterization of Epoxy Glues with FTIR." *Appl. Spectrosc. Rev.* 24 (1988): 175–87.

Avram, M. and G. D. Mateescu. *Infrared Spectroscopy—Applications in Organic*

Chemistry. New York: John Wiley & Sons, 1972.

Beauchaine, J. P., J. W. Peterman, and R. J. Rosenthal. "Applications of FT-IR/Microscopy in Forensic Analysis." *Mikrochim. Acta* I (1988): 133–8.

Barilaro, D, G. Barone, V. Crupi, and D. Majolino. "Characterization of Archaeological Findings by FT-IR Spectroscopy." *Spectroscopy*, 20, No. 4 (2005): 16–22.

Bhargava, R. and I. Levin. *Spectrochemical Analysis Using Infrared Multichannel Detectors.* Malden, MA: Blackwell Publishing, 2005.

Bell, R. J. *Introductory Fourier Transform Spectroscopy.* New York: Academic Press, Inc., 1972.

Bellamy, L. J. *The Infrared Spectra of Complex Molecules.* London: Chapman and Hall, Ltd., 1975.

Bertie, J. E. "Fourier Transform Infrared Spectroscopy." In *Vibrational Spectra and Structure*, vol. 14, ed. J. R. Durig. New York: Elsevier, 1985, 221–53.

Borman, S. A. "Voyager Infrared Spectrometer." *Anal. Chem.* 53 (1981): 1544A–53A.

Brame, E. G. Jr. and J. G. Grasselli, eds. *Infrared and Raman Spectroscopy.* New York: Marcel Dekker, Inc., Part A, 1976; Part B, 1977; Part C, 1977.

Brown, D. J., L. F. Schneider, and J. A. Howell. "Solving Mysteries Using Infrared Spectrometry and Chromatography." *Anal. Chem.* 60 (1988): 1005A–11A.

Chalmers, J. M., and M. W. Mackenzie. "Solid Sampling Techniques." *In Advances in Applied Fourier Transform Infrared Spectroscopy*, ed. M. W. Mackenzie. New York. John Wiley & Sons, 1988, 105–88.

Chalmers, J. M., and P. R. Griffiths, eds. *Handbook of Vibrational Spectroscopy.* New York: John Wiley & Sons, 2002.

Chamberlain, J. *The Principles of Interferometric Spectroscopy.* New York: John Wiley & Sons, 1979.

Chen, J. T., and R. W. Dority. "Contamination Control in Infrared Microanalysis," *J. Assoc. Off. Anal. Chem.* 53 (1970): 978–86.

Clarke, R. J. H., and R. E. Hester, eds. *Advances in Infrared and Raman Spectroscopy.* Philadelphia: Heyden, Vol. 1, 1975; Vol. 2, 1976; Vol. 3, 1977; Vol. 4, 1978; Vol. 5, 1979; Vol. 6, 1980; Vol. 7, 1980; Vol. 8, 1981; Vol. 9, 1982. New York: John Wiley & Sons, Vol. 10, 1983; Vol. 11, 1984; Vol. 12, 1985.

Coates, J. P. "IR Analysis of Toxic Dusts: Analysis of Collected Samples of Asbestos." *Am. Lab.* 9 (December 1977): 57–65.

Coates, J. P., J. M. D'Agostino, and C. R. Friedman. "Quality Control Analysis by Infrared Spectroscopy, Part 2: Practical Applications." *Am. Lab.* 18 (December 1986): 40–6.

Coleman, M. M., and P. C. Painter. "Fourier Transform Infrared Spectroscopy: Proving the Structure of Multicomponent Polymer Blends." *Appl. Spectrosc. Rev.* 20 (1984): 255–346.

Coleman, P. B. ed. *Practical Sampling Techniques for Infrared Analysis.* Boca Raton: CRC Press, 1995.

Colthup, N. B., L. H. Daly, and S. E. Wiberley. *Introduction to Infrared and Raman Spectroscopy.* New York: Academic Press, 1990.

Compton, S., and J. Powell, "Forensic Applications of IR Microscopy." *Am. Lab.*, 23 (November 1991): 41–51.

Conley, R. T. *Infrared Spectroscopy*, 2nd ed. Boston: Allyn and Bacon, Inc., 1972.

Cooper, J. W. *Spectroscopic Techniques for Organic Chemists.* New York: John Wiley & Sons, 1980.

De Faubert Maunder, M. J. *Practical Hints on Infrared Spectroscopy from a Forensic Analyst.* London: Hilger, 1971.

Derrick, M. R., D. C. Stulik, and J. M. Landry. *Infrared Spectroscopy in Conservation Science.* Los Angeles: Getty Trust Publications, 2000.

Drake, A. "Infrared Spectroscopy." In *Clarke's Analysis of Drugs and Poisons*, 3rd ed. vol. 1, eds. A. C. Moffat, M. D. Osselton, and B. Widdop. London: Pharmaceutical Press, 2004.

Durig, J. R., ed. *Analytical Applications of FT-IR to Molecular and Biological Systems*. Boston: D. Reidel Publishing Co., 1980.

Durig, J. R., ed. *Chemical, Biological and Industrial Applications of Infrared Spectroscopy*. New York: John Wiley & Sons, 1985.

Durig, J. R., ed. *Vibrational Spectra and Structure, Vol. 18-Applications of FT-IR Spectroscopy*. New York: Elsevier, 1990.

Everall, N., ed. *Vibrational Spectroscopy of Polymers: Principles and Practice*. New York: John Wiley & Sons, 2007.

Farmer, V. C. *The Infrared Spectra of Minerals*. London: Mineralogical Society, 1974.

Ferraro, J. R., and L. J. Basile, eds. *Fourier Transform Infrared Spectroscopy*. New York: Academic Press. Vol. 1, 1978; Vol. 2, 1979; Vol. 3, 1983; Vol. 4, 1985.

Ferraro, J. R., and K. Krishnan, eds. *Practical Fourier Transform Infrared Spectroscopy*. New York: Academic Press, Inc., 1990.

Ferrer, N. "Forensic Science, Applications of IR Spectroscopy." In *Encyclopedia of Spectroscopy and Spectrometry*, eds. G. C. Tranter and J. L. Holmes. New York: Academic Press, 1999, 603–21.

Gadsden, J. A. *Infrared Spectra of Minerals and Related Inorganic Compounds*. New York: Butterworths, 1975.

Gauglitz, G. and T.Vo-Dinh, eds. *Handbook of Spectroscopy*. New York: John Wiley & Sons, 1986.

George, W.O., and P. McIntyre. *Infrared Spectroscopy*. New York: John Wiley & Sons, 1987.

Gregoriou, V. G, and M. S. Braiman, eds. *Vibrational Spectroscopy of Biological and Polymeric Materials*. Boca Raton: CRC Press, 2006.

Gremlich, H. and B. Yan. *Infrared and Raman Spectroscopy of Biological Materials*. Boca Raton: CRC Press, 2001.

Griffiths, P. R., ed. *Transform Techniques in Chemistry*. New York: Plenum Press, 1978.

Griffiths, P. R., and J. A. De Haseth. *Fourier Transform Infrared Spectroscopy*, 2nd ed. New York: Wiley InterScience, 2007.

Griffiths, P. R., S. L. Pentoney, Jr., A. Giorgetti, and K. H. Shafer. "The Hyphenation of Chromatography and FT-IR Spectrometry." *Anal. Chem.* 58 (1986): 1349A–66A.

Guelachvili, G., and K. N. Rao. *Handbook of Infrared Standards*. New York: Academic Press, Inc., 1986.

Günzler, H. and H. Gremlich. *IR Spectroscopy: An Introduction*. New York: John Wiley & Sons, 2002.

Holland-Moritz, K., and H. W. Siesler. "Infrared Spectroscopy of Polymers." *Appl. Spectros. Rev.* 11 (1976): 1–55.

Harrick, N. J. *Internal Reflection Spectroscopy*. Ossinning, N.Y.: Harrick Scientific Corp., 1987.

Harrick, N. J. "Optical Spectroscopy: Six Sampling Techniques." *Am. Lab.* 20 (October 1988): 98–105.

Herres, W. HRGC-FTIR: Capillary Gas Chromatography-Fourier Transform Infrared Spectroscopy. New York: Huthig, 1987.

Hollas, M. J. *Modern Spectroscopy*. New York: John Wiley & Sons, 1988.

Humecki, H. J. *Practical Guide to Infrared Microspectroscopy*. New York: Marcel Dekker, 1995.

Hummel, D.O., ed. *Polymer Spectroscopy*. New York: Verlag, 1974.

Hummel, D.O. *Atlas of Polymers and Plastics Analysis*, vol. 2. New York: VCH Publishers, 1988.

Hunt, B. J. and M. I. James. *Polymer Characterisation*. New York: Springer, 1993.

Ishida, H., ed. *Fourier Transform Infrared Characterization of Polymers*. New York: Plenum Press, 1987.

Johnston, S. F. *Fourier Transform Infrared— A Constantly Evolving Technology*. New York: Ellis Horwood, 1991.

Karr, C. *Infrared and Raman Spectroscopy of Lunar and Terrestrial Minerals*. New York: Academic Press, 1975.

Katon, J. E., G. E. Pacey, and J. F. O'Keefe. "Vibrational Molecular Microspectroscopy." *Anal. Chem.* 58 (1986): 465A–81A.

Katon, J. E., and A. J. Sommer. "Infrared Microspectroscopy." *Appl. Spectrosc. Rev.* 25 (1989–1990): 173–211.

Katon, J. E., and A. J. Sommer. "IR Microspectroscopy—Routine IR Sampling Methods Extended to the Microscopic Domain." *Anal. Chem.* 64 (1992): 931A-40A.

Kendall, D. N., ed. *Applied Infrared Spectroscopy*. New York: Reinhold Publishing Corp., 1966.

Koenig, J. L. *Infrared and Raman Spectroscopy of Polymers*. New York: Rapra Technology, 2001.

Kortum, G. *Reflectance Spectroscopy*. New York: Springer-Verlag, 1969.

Kuptsov, A. H., and G. N. Zhizhin. *Handbook of Fourier Transform Raman and Infrared Spectra of Polymers*. Amsterdam: Elsevier, 1998.

Lang, P. L., J. E. Katon, and A. S. Bonanno. "Identification of Dust Particles by Molecular Microspectroscopy." *Appl. Spectrosc.* 42 (1988): 313–7.

Mackenzie, M. W. *Advances in Applied Fourier Transform Infrared Spectroscopy*. New York: John Wiley & Sons, 1988.

Mantsch, H. H., and D. Chapman. *Infrared Spectroscopy of Biomolecules*. New York: Wiley-Liss, 1996.

Marshall, A. G., and F. R. Verdun. *Fourier Transforms in NMR, Optical and Mass Spectrometry—A User's Handbook*. New York: Elsevier, 1989.

Martoglio, P. M., S. P. Bouffard, A. J. Sommer, J. E. Katon, and K. A. Jakes. "Unlocking the Secrets of the Past—The Analysis of Archeological Textiles and Dyes." *Anal. Chem.* 62 (1990): 1123A–28A.

Messerschmidt, R. G. and M. A. Harthcock, eds. *Infrared Microspectroscopy: Theory and Applications*. New York: Marcel Dekker, 1988.

Michaelian, K. H. *Photoacoustic Infrared Spectroscopy*. New York: Wiley Interscience, 2003.

Miller, R. G. J., and B. C. Stare, eds. *Laboratory Methods in Infrared Spectroscopy*, 2nd ed. New York: Heyden and Sons, Ltd., 1972.

Mills III, T. and G. J. Fontis. "Applications of Infrared Spectroscopy in Drug Analysis." In *The Analysis of Drugs of Abuse*, ed. T. A. Gough. New York: John Wiley & Sons, 1991, 225–81.

Mirabella, F. M., ed. *Modern Techniques in Applied Molecular Spectroscopy*. New York: John Wiley & Sons, 1998.

Mirabella, F. M., ed. *Internal Reflection Spectroscopy*. New York: Marcel Dekker, 1993.

Morris, M. D. *Microscopic and Spectroscopic Imaging of the Chemical State*. Boca Raton: CRC Press, 1993.

Mossobam, M. M. ed. *Spectral Methods in Food Analysis: Instrumentation and Applications*. Boca Raton: CRC Press, 1999.

Nakamoto, K. *Infrared and Raman Spectra of Inorganic and Coordination Compounds*. 3rd ed. New York: John Wiley & Sons, 1978.

Nakamoto, K. *Infrared and Raman Spectra of Inorganic and Coordination Compounds, Part A: Theory and Applications in Inorganic Chemistry*, 5th ed. New York: John Wiley & Sons, 1997.

Nakamoto, K. *Infrared and Raman Spectra of Inorganic and Coordination Compounds, Part B: Applications in Coordination, Organometallic, and Bioinorganic Chemistry*. New York: John Wiley & Sons, 1997.

Nichols, G. "FT-IR Microscopy: Microanalysis Using Infrared Spectroscopy," *Proc. Royal Micro. Soc.* 25 (May 1990): 205–11.

Osland, R. C. J., W. J. Price, and A. H. Devenish. "Infrared Techniques in the Analysis of Rubber." *Am. Lab.* 10 (March 1978): 111–20.

Parker, F. S. *Applications of Infrared, Raman, and Resonance Raman Spectroscopy in Biochemistry.* New York: Springer, 1983.

Pattacini, S. C., and T. J. Porro. "Problem Solving Using FTIR Spectroscopy." *Am. Lab.* 20 (August 1988): 24–32.

Rosencwaig, A. *Photoacoustics and Photoacoustic Spectroscopy* (New York: John Wiley & Sons, 1990).

Roush, P. B. *The Design, Sample Handling, and Applications of Infrared Microscopes.* Philadelphia: ASTM, 1987.

Schrader, B. *Infrared and Raman Spectroscopy, Methods and Applications.* Weinheim: VCH, 1995.

Siesler, H. W. and K. Holland-Moritz. *Infrared and Raman Spectroscopy of Polymers.* New York: Marcel Dekker, 1980.

Smith, A. L. *Applied Infrared Spectroscopy: Fundamentals, Techniques, and Analytical Problem-Solving.* New York: John Wiley & Sons, 1975.

Smith, B. C. *Fundamentals of Fourier Transform Infrared Spectroscopy* Boca Raton: CRC Press, 1995.

Sommer, A. J., and J. E. Katon. "Diffraction-Induced Stray Light in Infrared Microspectroscopy and Its Effect on Spatial Resolution." *Appl. Spectrosc.* 45 (1991): 1633–40.

Stuart, B. *Biological Applications of Infrared Spectroscopy.* New York: John Wiley & Sons, 1997.

Stuart, B., B. George, and P. McIntyre. *Modern Infrared Spectroscopy,* New York: John Wiley & Sons, 1998.

Stuart, B. H. *Infrared Spectroscopy: Fundamentals and Applications.* New York: John Wiley & Sons, 2004.

Szymanski, H. A. *IR: Theory and Practice of Infrared Spectroscopy.* New York: Plenum Press, 1964.

van der Maas, J. H. *Basic Infrared Spectroscopy.* New York: Heyden & Sons, 1972.

Weiner, S., and P. Goldberg. "On-Site Fourier Transform-Infrared Spectrometry at an Archaeological Excavation." *Spectroscopy,* 5, No. 2 (1990): 46–50.

Wendlandt, W. W., and H. G. Hecht. *Reflectance Spectroscopy.* New York: John Wiley & Sons, 1966.

White, R. *Chromatography/Fourier Transform Infrared Spectroscopy and Its Applica-tions.* New York: Marcel Dekker, Inc., 1990.

Willis, H. A., J. H. Van Der Maas, and R. G. J. Miller, eds., *Laboratory Methods in Vibrational Spectroscopy,* 3rd ed. New York: John Wiley & Sons, 1988.

Wilson, R. H. "Fourier Transform Mid-Infrared Spectroscopy for Food Analysis" *Trends Anal. Chem.* 9 (1990): 127–31.

Workman, J. Jr. *Applied Spectroscopy: A Compact Reference for Practitioners.* New York: Academic Press, 1998.

Zbinden, R. *Infrared Spectroscopy of High Polymers.* New York: Academic Press, 1964.

Functional Group Analysis and Spectral Data Interpretation

Bellamy, L. J. *Advances in Infrared Group Frequencies.* London: Chapman and Hall, Ltd., 1975.

Bruno, T. J., and P. D. N. Svoronos. *CRC Handbook of Fundamental Spectroscopic Correlation Charts.* Boca Raton: CRC Press, 2006.

Coates, J. P. "Interpretation of Infrared Spectra, A Practical Approach." In *Encyclopedia of Analytical Chemistry,* ed. R. A. Meyers. New York: John Wiley & Sons, 2000.

Coates, J. P. "The Interpretation of Infrared Spectra: Published Reference Sources."

Appl. Spectrosc. Rev. 31 (1996): 179–92.

Degen, I. A. *Tables of Characteristic Group Frequencies for the Interpretation of Infrared and Raman Spectra.* New York: Harrow, 1997.

Dolphin, D., and A. Wick. *Tabulation of Infrared Spectral Data.* New York: John Wiley & Sons, 1977.

Dyer, J. D. *Applications of Absorption Spectroscopy of Organic Compounds.* Englewood Cliffs, NJ: Prentice-Hall, Inc., 1965.

Feinstein, K. *Guide to Spectroscopic Identification of Organic Compounds.* Boca Raton: CRC Press, 1995.

Field, L. et al. *Organic Structures from Spectra,* 3rd ed. New York: John Wiley & Sons, 2002.

Lambert, J. B., H. F. Shurvell, D. A. Lightner, and R. G. Cooks. *Organic Structural Spectroscopy.* Upper Saddle River, NJ: Prentice-Hall, Inc., 1998.

Lin-Vien, D., N. B. Colthup, W. Fateley, and J. G. Grasselli. *The Handbook of Infrared and Raman Characteristic Frequencies of Organic Molecules.* New York: Academic Press, Inc., 1991.

Mayo, D. W., F. A. Miller, and R. W. Hannah, *Course Notes on the Interpretation of Infrared and Raman Spectra.* New York: John Wiley & Sons, 2003.

Mohan, J. *Organic Spectroscopy Principles and Applications,* 2nd ed. Boca Raton: CRC Press, 2005.

Ning, Y. *Structural Identification of Organic Compounds with Spectroscopic Techniques.* New York: John Wiley & Sons, 2005.

Nyquist, R. A. *Interpreting Infrared, Raman, and Nuclear Magnetic Resonance Spectra,* vols. 1 and 2. New York: Academic Press, 2001.

Nyquist, R. A., R. O. Kagel, C. L. Putzig, and M. A. Leugers. *The Handbook of Infrared and Raman Spectra of Inorganic Compounds and Organic Salts.* New York: Academic Press, 1996.

Pavia, D. L., G. M. Lampman, and G. S. Kriz Jr. *Introduction to Spectroscopy: A Guide for Students of Organic Chemistry,* 2nd ed. New York: Harcourt Brace, 1996.

Pretsch, E., and J. Clerc. *Spectra Interpretation of Organic Compounds.* New York: John Wiley & Sons, 1997.

Roeges, J. *A Guide to the Complete Interpretation of Infrared Spectra of Organic Structures.* New York: John Wiley & Sons, 1993.

Shriner, R. L., C. K. F. Hermann, T. C. Morrill, D. Y. Curtin, and R. C. Fuson. *The Systematic Identification of Organic Compounds,* 8th ed. New York: John Wiley & Sons, 2004.

Silverstein, R. M., F. X. Webster, and D. Kiemle. *Spectrometric Identification of Organic Compounds,* 7th ed. New York: John Wiley & Sons, 2005.

Smith, B. C. *Infrared Spectral Interpretation: A Systematic Approach.* Boca Raton: CRC Press, 1999.

Socrates, J. *Infrared Characteristic Group Frequencies, Tables & Charts.* New York: John Wiley & Sons 1994.

Szymanski, H. A. *Interpreted Infrared Spectra.* New York: Plenum Press, 1964.

Whittaker, D. *Interpreting Organic Spectra.* London: Royal Society of Chemistry, 2000.

Theory

Alpert, N. L., W. E. Keiser, and H. A. Szymanski. *IR—Theory and Practice of Infrared Spectroscopy,* 2nd ed. New York: Plenum Press, 1970.

Banwell, C. N. *Fundamentals of Molecular Spectroscopy,* 4th ed. New York: McGrawHill, 1994.

Barrow, G. M. *Introduction to Molecular Spectroscopy.* New York: McGraw-Hill Book Co., Inc., 1962.

Bauman, R. P. *Absorption Spectroscopy.* New York: John Wiley & Sons, Inc., 1962.

Bower, D. I. and W. F. Maddams. *The Vibrational Spectroscopy of Polymers.* Cambridge,UK: Cambridge University Press, 1998.

Brittain, E. F. H., W. O. George, and C. H. J. Wells. *Introduction to Molecular Spectroscopy—Theory and Experiment.* New York: Academic Press, 1970.

Brugel, W. *An Introduction to Infrared Spectroscopy.* New York: John Wiley & Sons, 1962.

Colthup, N. B., L. H. Daly, and S. E. Wiberley. *Introduction to Infrared and Raman Spectroscopy,* 2nd ed. New York: Academic Press, 1975.

Decius, J. C., and R. M. Hexter, *Molecular Vibrations in Crystals.* New York: McGraw-Hill, 1977.

Gans, P. *Vibrating Molecules: An Introduction to the Interpretation of Infrared and Raman Spectra.* London: Chapman and Hall, Ltd., 1971.

Gribov, L. A., and W. J. Orville-Thomas. *Theory and Methods of Calculation of Molecular Spectra.* New York: John Wiley & Sons, 1988.

Harris, D. C., and M. D. Bertolucci. *Symmetry and Spectroscopy: An Introduction to Vibrational and Electronic Spectroscopy.* New York: Dover Publications, 1989.

Herzberg, G. *Molecular Spectra and Structure Volume I: Spectra of Diatomic Molecules,* 2nd ed. New York: Van Nostrand Reinhold Co., 1950.

Herzberg, G. *Molecular Spectra and Molecular Structure, Volume II: Infrared and Raman Spectra of Polyatomic Molecules.* New York: Van Nostrand Reinhold Co., 1945.

McHale, J. L. *Molecular Spectroscopy.* Upper Saddle River, NJ: Prentice-Hall, 1999.

Molloy, K. C. *Group Theory for Chemists: Fundamental Theory and Applications.* New York: Horwood Publishing, 2004.

Painter, P. C., M. M. Coleman, and J. L. Koenig. *The Theory of Vibrational Spectroscopy and Its Applications to Polymeric Materials.* New York: Wiley-Interscience, 1982.

Papousek, D. and M. R. Allev. *Molecular Vibrational–Rotational Spectra.* New York: Elsevier, 1982.

Schutte, C. J. H. *The Theory of Molecular Spectroscopy,* vol.1. New York: Elsevier, 1976.

Steinfeld, J. I. *Molecules and Radiation: An Introduction to Modern Molecular Spectroscopy,* 2nd ed. New York: Dover Publications, 1985.

Straughan, B. P. and S. Walker, eds. *Spectroscopy,* vol. 2. New York: John Wiley & Sons, 1976.

Wilson, E. B., Jr., J. C. Decius, and P. C. Cross. *Molecular Vibrations—The Theory of Infrared and Raman Vibrational Spectra.* New York: McGraw-Hill Book Co., 1955.

Woodward, L. A. *Introduction to the Theory of Molecular Vibrations and Vibrational Spectroscopy.* London: Oxford University Press, 1972.

Zhizhin, G. N., and E. Mukhtarov. *Optical Spectra and Lattice Dynamics of Molecular Crystals.* New York: Elsevier, 1995.

Selected Infrared Spectral Data Collections

The spectral data of a few of the libraries listed (as well as others that are not available in published form) are also available as digital files for use on most FT-IR systems.

Afremow, L. C. and J. T. Vandeberg. "High Resolution Spectra of Inorganic Pigments and Extenders in the Mid-Infrared Region From 1500 cm^{-1} to 200 cm^{-1}," *J. Paint Technol.,* 38 (1966): 169–202.

Association of Official Analytical Chemists. *Infrared and Ultraviolet Spectra of Some Compounds of Pharmaceutical Interest, Revised Edition.* Washington,

D.C.: Association of Official Analytical Chemists, 1975.

Bentley, F. F., L. D. Smithson, and A. L. Rozek. *Infrared Spectra and Characteristic Frequencies ~700–300 cm⁻¹*. New York: Interscience Publishers, Inc., 1968.

British Pharmacopoeia Commission. Infrared Reference Spectra. London: H. M. Stationary Office, 1980; First Supplement, 1981; Second Supplement, 1982; Third Supplement, 1984.

Chasan, D. E., and G. Norwitz. "Qualitative Analysis of Primers, Tracers, Igniters, Incendiaries, Boosters, and Delay Compositions on a Microscale by Use of Infrared Spectroscopy," *J. Microchem.*, 17 (1972): 31–60.

Coates, J. P., and L. C. Setti. *Oils, Lubricants, and Petroleum Products—A Library Containing Spectra from Fuels, Lubricants, Additives, and Related Materials*. Norwalk, CT: The Perkin-Elmer Corp., 1983.

Craver, C. D. *Gases and Vapors Special Collection of Infrared Spectra*. Kirkwood, MO: The Coblentz Society, Inc., 1991.

Craver, C. D. *Halogenated Hydrocarbons: A Special Collection of Infrared Spectra from the Coblentz Society, Inc.* 3rd ed. Kirkwood, MO: The Coblentz Society, Inc., 1984.

Craver, C. D. *Infrared Spectra of Regulated and Major Industrial Chemicals*. Kirkwood, MO: The Coblentz Society, Inc., 1983.

Craver, C. D. *Plasticizers and Other Additives: A Special Collection of Infrared Spectra from the Coblentz Society, Inc.* 2nd ed. Kirkwood, MO: The Coblentz Society, Inc., 1980.

Fazzari, F. R., M. F. Sharkey, C. A. Tuciw, and W. L. Brannon. "Infrared and Ultraviolet Spectra of Some Pharmaceutical Compounds," *J. Assoc. Off. Anal. Chem.*, 51 (1968): 1154–67.

Hansen, D. L., ed. *The Sprouse Collection of Infrared Spectra*. Paoli, PA: Sprouse Scientific Systems, Inc., *Book I:* *Polymers* (1987), *Book II: Solvents by Cylindrical Internal Reflectance* (1987), *Book III: Surface Active Agents* (1988), *Book IV: Solvents—Condensed Phase, Vapor Phase and Mass Spectra* (1990). In addition to these four books, Sprouse has infrared spectral search libraries on disk composed of the following: *The Canada Collection; Coal, Shale and Clay Minerals; Coatings and Resins; Environmental Toxins; Epoxy Resins, Curing Agents and Additives; Fragrances and Essential Oils; Fibers by IR Microscope; Gas Phase IR of Environmental Chemicals; Small Molecule Gases & Environ. Pollutants; General Chemical Compounds; GA State Crime Lab. Forensic Library; GA State Crime Lab. Automotive Paint; Inorganics on KBr Beam Splitter; Inorganics on CsI Beam Splitter; Lubricants, Additives and Raw Materials; Minerals, U.S. Geological Survey Collection; Polymers by Transmission; Polymers by ATR (Attn. Total Reflectance); Polymer Additives; General Organic Compounds; Solvents; Solvents by CIR (Cylindrical Internal Refl.); Solvents, Vapor Phase; and Surface Active Agents.*

Hayden, A. L., W. L. Brannon, and C. A. Yaciw. "Infrared Spectra of Some Compounds of Pharmaceutical Interest," *J. Assoc. Off. Anal. Chem.*, 49 (1966): 1109–53.

Hayden, A. L., O. R. Sammul, G. B. Selzer, and J. Carol. "Infrared, Untraviolet, and Visible Absorption Spectra of Some USP and NF Reference Standards and Their Derivatives," *J. Assoc. Off. Anal. Chem.*, 45 (1962): 797–900.

Holubek, J. *Spectral Data and Physical Constants of Alkaloids.* London: Heyden and Sons, vol. 1 (1965), vol. 2 (1966), vol. 3 (1968), vol. 4 (1969), vol. 5 (1970), vol. 6 (1971), vol. 7 (1972), vol. 8 (1973).

Hummel, D.O. *Atlas of Plastic Additives: Analysis by Spectrometric Methods*. New York: Springer, 2002.

Hummel, D.O. *Atlas of Polymer and Plastics Analysis*. New York: Verlag, vol. 1 (1978), vol. 3 (1981).

Infrared Spectroscopy Committee of the Chicago Society for Coatings Technology. *An Infrared Spectroscopy Atlas for the Coatings Industry*. Philadelphia: Federation of Societies for Coatings Technology, 1980.

Infrared Spectroscopy Atlas Working Committee. *An Infrared Spectroscopy Atlas for the Coatings Industry*, 4th ed., vols. I and II. Blue Bell, PA: Federation of Societies for Coatings Technology, 1991.

Jones, G. C., and B. Jackson. *Infrared Transmission Spectra of Carbonate Minerals*. New York: Springer, 1993.

Karcher, W., R. J. Fordham, J. J. Dubois, P. G. J. M. Glaude, and J. A. M. Ligthart, eds. *Spectra Atlas of Polycyclic Aromatic Compounds*. Boston: Kluwer Academic Publishers, vol. 1 (1983), vol. 2 (1988).

Keller, R. J. *The Sigma Library of FT-IR Spectra*, vols. I and 2. St. Louis: Sigma Chemical Co., 1986.

Lang, L., ed. *Absorption Spectra in the Infrared Region*. New York: Robert E. Krieger Publishing Co., vol. 1 (1974), vol. 2 (1976), vol. 3 (1977), vol. 4 (1978), vol.5 (1980).

Merck, E., ed. *Merck IR Atlas—A Collection of FT-IR Spectra*, Part I. New York: VCH Publishers, 1988.

Miller, F. A. and C. H. Wilkins. "Infrared Spectra and Characteristic Frequencies of Inorganic Ions," *Anal. Chem.*, 24 (1952): 1253–94.

Mills, T. III, J. C. Roberson, C. C. Matchett, M. J. Simon, M. D. Burns, and R. J. Ollis, Jr. *Instrumental Data for Drug Analysis*, vols. 1–6, 3rd ed. Boca Raton: CRC Press, 2005.

Moffat, A. C., M. D. Osselton, and B. Widdop, eds. *Clarke's Analysis of Drugs and Poisons*, vol. 2, 3rd ed. London: Pharmaceutical Press, 2004.

Morris, W. W. "High Resolution Infrared Spectra of Fragrance and Flavor Compounds," J. Assoc. Off. *Anal. Chem.*, 56 (1973): 1037–64.

Nicodom Ltd. *Nicodom FTIR Inorganic Library I. Minerals. Nicodom FTIR Inorganic Library II. Boron Compounds. Nicodom FTIR Library III. Inorganics and Organometallics. Nicodom FTIR Oils and Lubricants Library*. Hlavni, Czech Republic: Nicodom Ltd., 2007. These are the libraries that are sold in book form but there is also a large collection of reference spectra available in digital format at http://www.ir-spectra.com

Nyquist, R. A. and R. O. Kagel. *Infrared Spectra of Inorganic Compounds*. New York: Academic Press, 1971.

Pierson, R. H., A. N. Fletcher, and E. St. Clair Gantz. "Catalog of Infrared Spectra for Qualitative Analysis of Gases," *Anal. Chem.*, 28 (1956): 1218–39.

Pouchert, C. J., ed. *The Aldrich Library of FT-IR Spectra: Vapor Phase*, vol 3. Milwaukee: Aldrich Chemical Co., 1989.

Pristera, F. "Analysis of Propellants by Infrared Spectroscopy," *Anal. Chem.*, 25 (1953): 844–56.

Pristera, F., M. Halik, A. Castelli, and W. Fredericks. "Analysis of Explosives Using Infrared Spectroscopy," *Anal. Chem.*, 32 (1960): 495–508.

Roberts, G., B. S. Gallagher, and R. N. Jones. *Infrared Absorption Spectra of Steroids*, vol. II. New York: Interscience Publishers, Inc., 1958.

Sadtler Research Laboratories. *The Sadtler Collection of Spectra Handbooks*. Philadelphia: Sadtler Research Laboratories. This collection includes handbooks devoted to a number of specialty compounds and products including coating chemicals, monomers and polymers, polymer additives (polymerization materials, protective materials and processing and auxiliary materials), rubber chemicals, surfactants, building blocks of polymers, adhesives and sealants, common organic solvents, inorganic compounds, intermediates, minerals and clays, priority pollutants and toxic chemicals, and vapor phase spectra.

Sammul, O. R., W. L. Brannon, A. L. Hayden. "Infrared Spectra of Some Compounds of Pharmaceutical Interest," *J. Assoc. Off. Anal. Chem.*, 47 (1964): 918–91.

Schrader, B. *Raman/Infrared Atlas of Organic Compounds.* New York: VCH, 1989.

Sigma-Aldrich Chemical Co. *The Aldrich Library of FT-IR Spectra*, 2nd ed. Milwaukee: Sigma-Aldrich Chemical Co., vols. 1–3, 1997.

Sunshine, I., and S. R. Gerber. *Spectrophotometric Analysis of Drugs.* Springfield, IL: Charles C. Thomas, 1963.

Sunshine, I., ed. *CRC Handbook of Spectrophotometric Data of Drugs.* Boca Raton, FL: CRC Press, Inc., 1981.

Thermodynamics Research Center Hydrocarbon Project. *Selected Infrared Spectral Data.* College Station, TX: Texas A&M University, Thermodynamics Research Center, 1990.

Visser, T. *Infrared Spectra of Pesticides.* Boca Raton, FL: CRC Press, Inc., 1993.

Wagland, L., and P. J. Weiss. "Infrared Spectra of Some Antibiotics of Interest," *J. Assoc. Off. Anal. Chem.*, 48 (1965): 965–72.

Welti, D. *Infrared Vapour Spectra.* New York: Heyden & Sons, Inc., 1970.

Wenninger, J. A., R. L. Yates, and M. Dolinsky. "High Resolution Infrared Spectra of Some Naturally Occurring Sesquiterpene Hydrocarbons," *J. Assoc. Off. Anal. Chem.*, 50 (1967):1313–35.

Wenninger, J. A., and R. L. Yates. "High Resolution Infrared Spectra of Some Naturally Occurring Sesquiterpene Hydrocarbons. II. Second Series," *J. Assoc. Off. Anal. Chem.*, 53 (1970): 949–63.

Zeller, M. Y., and M. P. Juszli. *Reference Spectra of Minerals.* Norwalk, CT: The Perkin-Elmer Corp., 1975.

4

■ ■ ■

Infrared Microscopy and Its Forensic Applications

Edward G. Bartick, Ph.D.
Retired, FBI Laboratory, Counterterrorism Forensic Science Research Unit

Current
Director of the Forensic Science Program
Department of Chemistry and Biochemistry
Suffolk University
Boston, Massachusetts

INTRODUCTION

The goal of the forensic scientist is to identify the various constituents in a given sample and compare these constituents to those of another sample. If forced to limit the scope of their laboratory to only one instrument, trace analysts are likely to choose a visual light microscope. Valuable identification features, such as geometry, color, and optical properties, are readily observable with a visual light microscope. If given the option of a second instrument in the laboratory, an excellent choice would be an infrared (IR) spectrometer microscope system. The IR microscope permits the rapid and nondestructive acquisition of molecular spectra for each portion of the specimen observed with the visual light microscope. Thus, the combination of the two instruments nondestructively yields both physical and chemical information for microscopic-size samples.

The development of microscope attachments for infrared spectrometers is the greatest advancement in forensic applications of IR spectroscopy since Fourier transform infrared (FT-IR) spectrometry. At the time of publication of the first edition of this volume in 1993, IR microscopes were just beginning to find their way into forensic trace evidence laboratories. They have since evolved as work-horses for many applications. IR microscopes are extremely useful in the forensic laboratory because of the convenience they provide for sampling microscopic-size specimens. Because the area sampled is so small, less sample preparation is required. Whereas with traditional IR spectrometry lengthy sample preparation is often required to yield a sufficiently uniform sample, with IR microscopy the small area sampled is often sufficiently uniform in itself. The horizontal stage of the IR microscope permits one to easily position a specimen in the beam of the IR, thus eliminating tedious specimen mounting. In addition, standard-size specimens are often more easily prepared and sampled with the IR microscope than by traditional techniques. For example, the thin edge of a polymer specimen might be sampled with the microscope rather than cast into a thin film.[1] The ease of nondestructive sampling made possible with IR microscopes has made FT-IR a more practical tool in the fast-paced setting of the forensic laboratory.

Microscopes are not recent developments to IR analysis. As early as 1949, Barer, Cole and Thompson[2] reported the application of a microscope to infrared analysis. The microscope, developed by Burch,[3] was all reflecting, achromatic, and absent of absorbing materials and, thus, permitted measurements into the mid-infrared region. Good results were obtained on crystals and fibers with diameters of 20 to 50 μm and weight ranges between 10 and 100 ng. Similar results were also reported by Gore in separate work in 1949.[4]

The first commercial IR microscope was the Perkin-Elmer Model 85 produced in 1953 for the P-E Models 12, 112, and 13 single-beam spectrometers. Coates, Offner, and Siegler[5] designed the condenser and objective with Schwarzschild reflecting lenses. Although this microscope produced reasonably good spectra of microscopic-size samples, the lengthy times required to obtain spectra discouraged sales and it was not a commercial success. Approximately twenty-five years later, in 1978 Coates, with his own firm, Nanometrics, renewed the interest in IR microscopy by producing a commercial IR microscope system. This model, the NanoSpec® 20IR, consisted of an IR microscope coupled with a specially designed filter instrument and linked to a computer. This single-beam instrument could store background spectra that were subsequently ratioed to produce a double-beam-like output. With spectra processed in approximately two minutes, IR microscopy became a reality. FT-IR spectrometers, however, offer significant advantages over filter- and dispersive-type spectrometers because of their higher speed, greater energy throughput, greater frequency precision, and increased computational capabilities. In 1982, Muggli[6] reported the successful attachment of a Perkin-Elmer Model 85 microscope to a Digilab FTS20 spectrometer. This was the first step in the evolution of FT-IR microscope systems.

In 1983, a Digilab, Division of Block Engineering, and Analect Instruments, both FT-IR manufacturers, introduced commercial microscopes for their spectrometers. After several buyouts, the Digilab line is under the name of Varian instruments; Analect Instruments, purchased by Laser Precision, Inc., is no longer marketed. Some of the major commercial FT-IR microscopes are currently produced by Thermo Electron Corporation, PerkinElmer Corporation; Bruker Optics, and Varian Instruments. Although all IR spectrometer manufacturers do not make IR microscopes, any FT-IR spectrometer can be fitted with a microscope attachment. With the commercial microscope attachments now available, spectra can be obtained of specimens on the order of 10 μm or less in diameter and quantities in the picogram range.[7]

The objective of this chapter is to review the optical design of FT-IR microscopes, the different features available, sample preparation methods, and forensic applications. When the first edition of this volume was written, there were few existing publications that specifically addressed the forensic applications of IR microscopy. However, this has changed, and the information provided should assist the prospective IR microscope users in their selection and help current users optimize the use of their existing FT-IR microscope system.

OPTICAL DESIGN

Forensic trace evidence analysts are very familiar with the visual light microscope and its use. A great deal of comparative physical information can be obtained from the visual image. For the purposes of this discussion, a visual light microscope is defined as a microscope that operates in the visible frequency range (400 to 800 nm) of the electromagnetic spectrum and uses the human eye to detect images. Spectroscopic light microscopes also utilize electromagnetic radiation, but use detectors that respond to the light to produce electronic signals that generate spectra. These spectra are plots of intensity versus frequency or wavelength. Spectroscopic measurements in the visible range provide information with regard to color. Visible spectroscopic microscopes, typically referred to as *microspectrophotometers,* are frequently used to compare colors. Microspectrophotometry is also done in the ultraviolet range (200 to 400 nm), where absorption yields information about the electronic structure of molecules. Ultraviolet and visible spectroscopic microscopes are frequently combined in one instrument. With a high-energy light source, certain compounds are excited in the ultraviolet range and emit energy by fluorescing in the visible frequency range. Fluorescence microscopes may be used to compare the fluorescent components used in certain materials. Spectroscopic measurements in the mid-infrared region (2.5 to 25 μm) yield bond vibration information that relates directly to chemical structure. As described in Chapter 3, the uniqueness of IR spectra makes them extremely valuable for identification and comparison of chemical composition. Because of the small sample sizes often encountered with physical evidence, IR microscopes have become "a natural" for forensic applications. Raman spectroscopy, with its complementary usefulness along with IR, has reemerged because of recent technical developments and has included the addition of microscopes as well. However, IR microscopy is the sole topic of this chapter.

Components

The components of infrared microscopes compare closely with those of visual microscopes. As depicted in Figure 4-1, both microscopes contain the following: (1) an illumination source, (2) an aperture, (3) a condenser, (4) a specimen stage, (5) an objective, (6) an eyepiece tube, and (7) a detector.

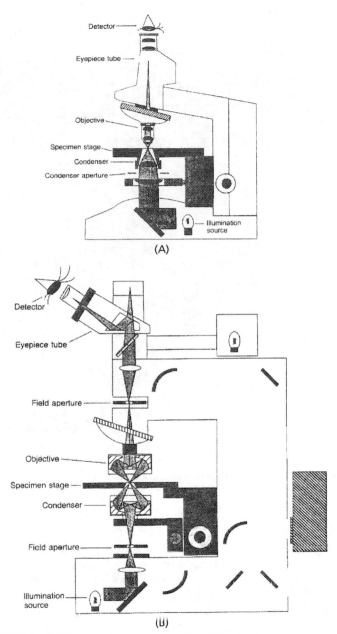

FIGURE 4-1 (A) Visual light microscope. (B) FT-IR microscope in the visual configuration.

Because the electromagnetic radiation (light) properties differ between visible and IR radiation, materials and construction differ between the two types of microscopes. Visual microscopes use glass-refracting lenses because glass is transparent to light in the visible range. Glass absorbs strongly, however, throughout much of the mid-IR range and is thus unsuitable for IR optics. Other IR-transparent materials,

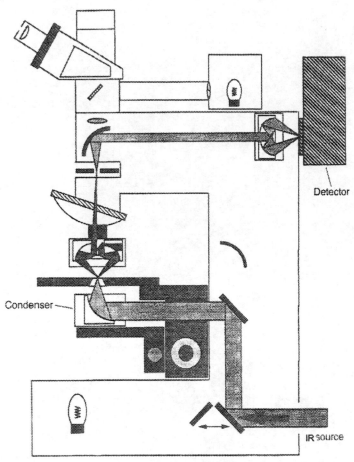

FIGURE 4-2   (A) FT-IR transmission optical configuration of an off-axis condenser.

such as alkali halides, although used in certain instances, present additional problems. Alkali halides are hygroscopic and become cloudy after absorbing water. Optical aberrations are subsequently produced as a result of the non-uniformity of the eroded material. Metallic, reflecting optics, typically aluminum coated, are most commonly used in the IR beam path of these microscopes.

For viewing the specimen, both visual and IR microscopes operate in a similar fashion. The illumination light is directed with transfer mirrors toward the condenser. The condenser aperture diaphragm on a visual microscope is used to adjust the angular aperture of light reaching the specimen for illumination. Field apertures on IR microscopes are located remotely from the sample in the image planes. These apertures are used to isolate the specific area for infrared spectral measurement and to block stray light from outside the specimen area. The condenser focuses the illumination light on the specimen. The objective above the stage magnifies the image with a refracting glass lens on a visual microscope and a reflecting Schwarzschild

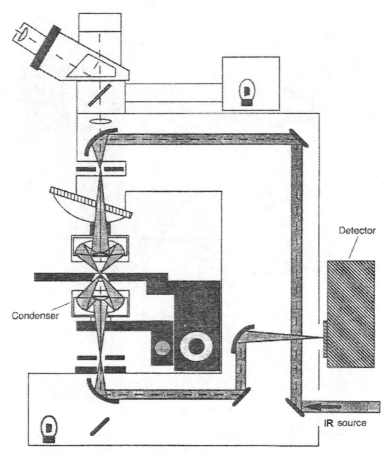

FIGURE 4-2 (B) FT-IR transmission optical configuration with an on-axis condenser.

design on the IR microscope (frequently misnamed as a *Cassegrainian design,* as on a reflecting telescope). In both IR and visual microscopes, the light is then directed through refracting eyepiece lenses to the human eye for detecting images.

With the IR microscope, conversion to the IR spectral measurement configuration is achieved via two movable mirrors. The first mirror directs the incoming IR beam into the visible beam path while displacing the visible beam. The second mirror redirects the beam from the eyepiece to the IR detector. The IR beam may traverse the shared portion of the optics (including the sample) in either the same direction or the opposite direction as the visible beam.

In the IR spectral measurement configuration, the IR beam must be aligned exactly with the visible light through the portion of the optics that the two beams share. Thus, what is seen in the visual mode is what is analyzed in the IR mode.

Figure 4-2 shows two representative optical arrangements for the IR transmission configuration. In Figure 4-2A, the IR beam enters the microscope at the bottom

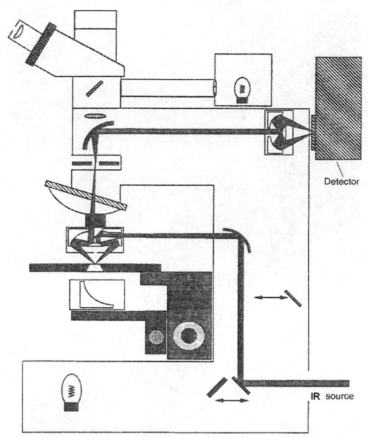

Detector

IR source

FIGURE 4-3 (A) Reflectance optical configurations with the IR source input through the side of the objective.

and is directed to an off-axis ellipsoid mirror that focuses the beam onto the sample. Next, a Schwarzschild objective collects and images the IR radiation at the image plane. At this point, the IR beam passes through an aperture that is adjustable to the area of interest on the specimen. Finally, the beam is refocused onto the IR detector by a Schwarzschild lens.

Figure 4-2B shows an on-axis Schwarzschild design for the condenser as well as the objective. This on-axis design focuses the beam more precisely onto the sample than does the off-axis design, and thus produces a higher-quality visual and infrared image of the specimen while also increasing the intensity of IR radiation passing through the sample area. In this particular example, the IR beam enters the microscope at the top and apertures are present above the objective and below the condenser. Both the objective and condenser are focused to produce a sharp

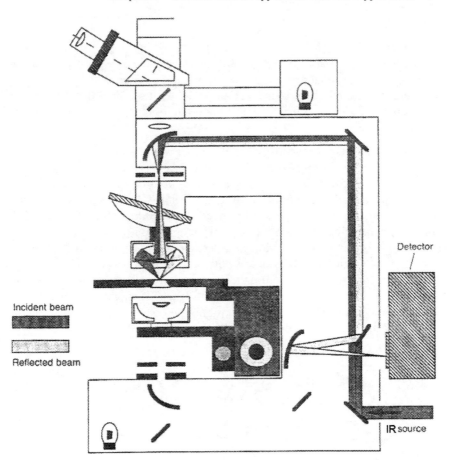

Incident beam

Reflected beam

Detector

IR source

FIGURE 4-3 (B) Reflectance optical configuration with the IR source input through the top of the objective.

image of the sample and are simultaneously image apertured above and below the sample.

FT-IR microscopes can also operate in a reflectance mode similar to that traditionally performed in the sample compartment of a spectrometer bench. Two different optical designs for the reflectance configuration are shown in Figure 4-3. In Figure 4-3A, the IR beam enters the microscope at the bottom. The beam passes a mirror that has been moved out of the transmission configuration position and strikes a mirror that focuses it onto the pick-off mirror located in the Schwarzschild objective. The beam is directed down onto the specimen, where it is reflected back up to the objective and then onto the detector. In the design shown in Figure 4-3B, the IR beam enters the objective at the top, is reflected off the sample, and returns toward the top. A pick-off mirror then directs the returning IR beam to the detector.

FEATURES

When purchasing an FT-IR microscope system, it is important to carefully consider the features available on the instrument under evaluation. Energy levels are low and samples are small; therefore, it is important to retain as much of the original IR energy through the system as possible. In addition, the system must be as carefully optimized as possible. The most important of these features are discussed in more detail next.

SCHWARZSCHILD REFLECTING OPTICS   The heart of an FT-IR microscope is the Schwarzschild optical configuration. This optical design is used for the objectives on all IR microscopes and also for the condenser in on-axis designs. The configuration resembles the originally reported Burch design.[3] Figure 4-4 shows a cutaway view of the two mirrors, aspherical surface arrangement, also known as *Schwarzschild aplanats.* The incoming beam is reflected from the "a" mirror surface to the "b" mirror, which condenses the beam to a focal point where the specimen is placed. The standard objective magnification is $15\times$, whereas objectives of up to $64\times$ are available. The higher magnification does not improve the IR energy throughput, but allows improved observation and easier isolation of smaller objects when viewing the sample.

The light energy collected by the Schwarzschild optics (i.e., the throughput) is a function of the numerical aperture (NA) as shown in Equation 4-1:

$$NA = \eta \sin (AA/2) \qquad (4\text{-}1)$$

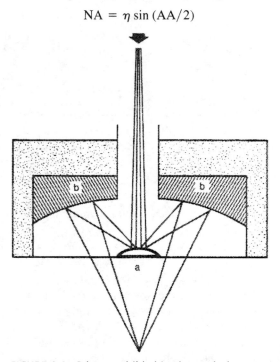

FIGURE 4-4   Schwarzschild objective optical configuration. (a) Secondary mirror; (b) primary mirror.

where η is the refractive index of the medium above the specimen, and AA, the angular aperture, is the maximum angle of light rays that pass through the optical element. The larger the AA, the larger the NA; therefore, the greater the ability to collect light. The numerical aperture of $15\times$ objectives on the market varies from approximately 0.25 to 0.60, resulting in a wide range of performance.

In designs where the IR beam enters at the bottom of the microscope, the objective comes after the specimen in the beam path. In this configuration, it is important to have a large NA so that light scattered by irregularly shaped samples may be collected. In designs where the IR beam enters at the top, a large NA condenser is advantageous to collect and refocus scattered light caused when passing through certain specimens.

Infrared window materials used to support or compress samples during the analysis cause a defocus of the beam as a result of refraction. *Spherical aberration,* an error in the longitudinal focus, is produced. The amount of refraction is dependent on the refractive index of the material and its thickness. Because the specimen is no longer at the focal point of the beam, less energy reaches the specimen, and the signal-to-noise ratio (S/N) is reduced. Compensation adjustments on the Schwarzschild optics are provided on certain IR microscopes to correct for the spherical aberration. By adjusting the position of the Schwarzschild objective and condenser, the sample can be brought into sharp focus. Higher-quality and more reproducible spectra are thus produced.

The spatial resolving power of a microscope increases with the numerical aperture of the objective. The *limit of resolution* is defined as the minimum distance between two points that can still be distinguished in the observed image. In visual microscopy, the resolution is the fineness of detail observable with the microscope. In IR microscopy, *spatial definition,* the ability to define an area for analysis in order to obtain spectral purity, is analogous to spatial resolution in visual microscopy. Because NA is fixed for a given objective, the means with which to define the area for analysis is the positioning of the apertures.

APERTURES   In IR microscopy, the area to be analyzed is isolated from the remainder of the field of view with apertures. As the specimen is viewed, the region to be analyzed is defined or masked with apertures that are located remotely from the specimen. Infrared apertures may be either rectangular or circular. The original designs of apertures consisted of four blackened metal knife edges all separately controlled by the operator and circular apertures of either fixed or variable size. The variable circular aperture is a diaphragm with a single control. Although apertures are opaque in the IR, in certain microscopes the design when using e-glass makes them transparent in the viewing mode, thus allowing the entire field of view to be observed while the apertures are in place. This is helpful for keeping the entire sample in view while isolating a small portion for analysis.

The purpose of the apertures is two-fold: They define an area of the sample for infrared spectral measurement and they block radiation that originates outside the specimen from reaching the detector. When this stray light is allowed to reach the detector, absorption bands, which should absorb totally, may display significant

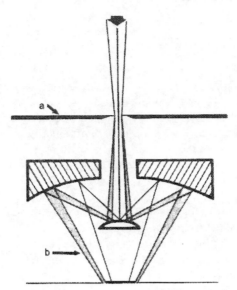

FIGURE 4-5   Diffraction of radiation produced at an aperture. (a) Aperture; (b) Airy disc portion of rays produced by diffraction.

reductions in intensity, or this radiation passes through material outside of the defined area.

Unfortunately, isolating sample areas in order to obtain well-defined spectral purity is not all that simple in the IR region. Light undergoes diffraction when striking a high contrast edge, the magnitude of which increases with wavelength. Thus, diffraction effects are greater in the infrared range than in the visible range. The result of diffraction is *light intensity* (i.e., diffracted light), which appears in the geometric shadow of the high-contrast aperture edge as shown in Figure 4-5. The light forms a diffraction pattern (often referred to as an *Airy disc* for a point source) described in detail by Messerschmidt.[8] The gray area in the ray pattern shown in Figure 4-5 does not define the specimen, and is spurious energy or stray light.

Two situations can occur with the diffraction problem. First, if the entire specimen is isolated by an aperture, the diffracted radiation passes through the air surrounding the specimen, reaches the detector, and dilutes the intensity of absorption bands in the spectrum. A reference spectrum obtained from a large poly(styrene) film is shown in Figure 4-6A. Many bands absorb totally in this spectrum. Figure 4-6B shows the spectrum of a 54-μm-wide strip of the same poly(styrene) film that was obtained with one aperture located after the sample in the beam path. Note that bands that were absorbing totally in Figure 4-6A show a loss of intensity in Figure 4-6B. Figure 4-6C shows the spectrum of the same poly(styrene) strip obtained with one aperture located before the sample in the beam path. A significant loss of photometric accuracy is apparent under these conditions, particularly at longer wavelengths (lower frequency) where diffraction effects are greater. Any quantitative spectral measurements acquired under these conditions result in significant errors.

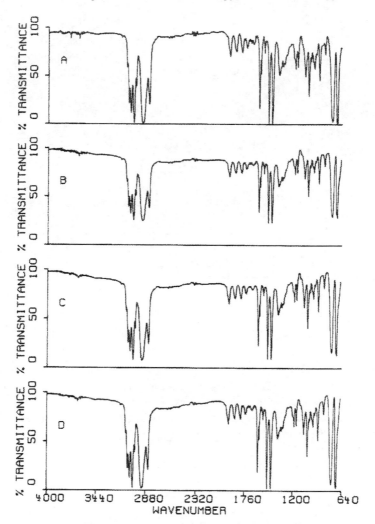

FIGURE 4-6 Infrared spectra of polystyrene film with different sample width and aperture conditions. (A) Wide film, no apertures required. (B–D) 54 μm diameter ribbon. (B) Single aperture, after the sample. (C) Single aperture, before the sample. (D) Double apertures.

Second, the area defined by an aperture may be only a portion of a larger sample. In this situation, the diffracted light passes through the surrounding material, and spectral features of the surrounding material appear in the spectrum of the area visually selected for examination. Figure 4-7 shows a photomicrograph of a five-layer laminate that was microtomed to produce a thin cross-section.[9] Spectra were obtained of all layers with one aperture located after the sample. The spectrum of the first layer, approximately 40-μm wide, is shown in Figure 4-8. The spectrum is primarily that of poly(ethylene), but additional poly(vinyl acetate) bands are present

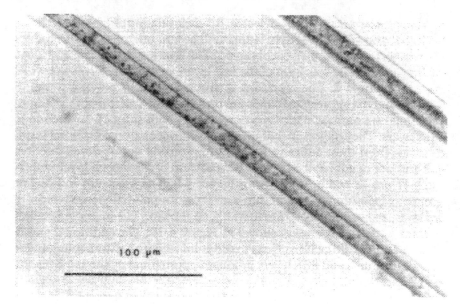

FIGURE 4-7   Photomicrograph of a cross-sectioned five layer laminate.   (*Source:* Reproduced from reference 9 by permission of the American Society for Testing and Materials; copyright 1987.)

that arise from the adjacent layer. Note the narrow, dark layers present on both sides of the second and fourth layers. These layers are adhesive, and were not analyzed. Spectral impurities arising from these adhesive layers were probably not observed because of the small amount of adhesive present. The spectrum of the second layer, approximately 15 μm in width, is shown in Figure 4-9. The spectrum indicates the

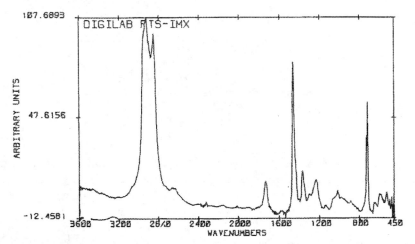

FIGURE 4-8   Infrared spectrum of layer one from Figure 4-7, approximately 40-μm wide.   (*Source:* Reproduced from reference 9 by permission of the American Society of Testing and Materials; copyright 1987.)

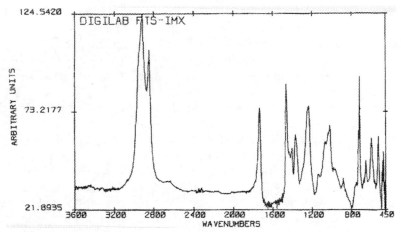

FIGURE 4-9 Infrared spectrum of layer two from Figure 4-7, approximately 15-μm wide. (*Source:* Reproduced from reference 9 by permission of the American Society of Testing and Materials; copyright 1987.)

presence of poly(vinyl acetate), but also includes poly(ethylene) bands. The third layer, approximately 80 μm in width, appears to yield an uncontaminated spectrum of poly(ethylene) as shown in Figure 4-10. The additional width of this layer reduces diffraction effects to the point where no extraneous bands are visible. The fourth and fifth layers produced approximately the same results as the first and second layers.

Although these two phenomena produce inaccuracies in spectra, if one understands the problems that occur, proper qualitative interpretation of the data can be

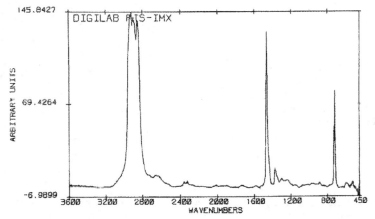

FIGURE 4-10 Infrared spectrum of layer three from Figure 4-7, approximately 80-μm wide. (*Source:* Reproduced from reference 9 by permission of the American Society of Testing and Materials; copyright 1987.)

made. In the first situation, where the spectrum is diluted by diffracted light passing through the surrounding air, qualitative identification of most spectra can be made in spite of the incorrect peak heights. In the second situation, where diffracted light passes through the surrounding sample, qualitative identification of most spectra can still be made, provided the identification of the surrounding material has been made.

Significant improvement, however, can be made by using two image plane apertures, available on certain microscopes, that are located both before and after the sample in the beam path.[10] Figure 4-6D shows the spectrum of the same 54-μm-wide poly(styrene) strip discussed earlier obtained using two apertures. The photometric accuracy is significantly improved. If only one aperture is used, placing the aperture before the sample in the beam path produces better accuracy than placing it after the sample in the beam path. With the aperture located before the sample, only the area of interest on the sample is illuminated by the source image.[11] Because diffraction spreads the light in an infinite pattern, even with two apertures, diffracted radiation has been observed 40 μm from a sample edge.[11] A similar illustration of these effects has been demonstrated using an opaque wire in the sample beam.[12] If photometric accuracy is important and double remote image plane apertures are not available on the system, one can mask the specimen physically with direct contact using pinhole apertures. Because the aperture contacts the sample physically, diffraction effects are eliminated and good photometric accuracy is achieved.[13]

DETECTORS Detectors are normally dedicated to the microscope assemblies; that is, the detector is used solely for the microscope and not shared with the spectrometer bench. Certain lower-cost microscopes, however, are designed to be used in the spectrometer sample compartment, and thus use the detector available with the bench. Typically, high-detectivity (D^*) detectors are used for FT-IR microscopes. However, if a microscope is designed for the sample compartment and the spectrometer bench includes a deuterated triglycine sulfate (DTGS, or simply TGS) detector, the sensitivity limits samples to those specimens greater than 100 μm in diameter. The sensitivity of a TGS detector is three to six times less than that of a wide-range mercury cadmium telluride (MCT) detector. MCT detectors are the most frequently used detectors for IR microscopes and are available in several ranges. The narrow-range MCT offers the greatest sensitivity, but limits the lower end of the frequency range to approximately 750 cm^{-1}, depending on the individual detector. Wide-range MCT detectors are four to eight times less sensitive than the narrow-range detectors, but provide a lower frequency limit of approximately 450 cm^{-1}. The relative D^* values and frequency ranges for the three nominal MCT detectors are shown in Figure 4-11.[14] Because very small samples are being analyzed, the narrow-range detector is usually used. However, the additional information obtainable in the lower-frequency region may warrant sacrificing sensitivity for range. For example, pigments found in paint often have characteristic absorptions at frequencies below 650 cm^{-1}, and specimens are usually large enough, 50–100 μm in diameter, that a wide-range detector provides sufficient sensitivity to obtain a good

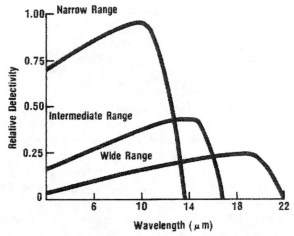

FIGURE 4-11 Relative detectivity (D*) values for the three MCT detector frequency ranges. Approximate low-frequency cutoffs for the narrow, intermediate, and wide range detectors are 750 cm^{-1} (13.3 μm), 600 cm^{-1} (16.7 μm), and 450 cm^{-1} (22.2 μm), respectively. (Reproduced from reference 14 by permission of the American Chemical Society; copyright 1983.)

spectrum. The choice of detector is up to the user, depending on the type of samples examined most frequently.

MULTIELEMENT DETECTORS These detectors, also known as *array detectors*, have recently come into use for the application of spectral imaging. These configurations permit the simultaneous individual recording of spectral intensity over a defined spatial area, with a spatial resolution established by the pixel density of the array. Therefore, images (pictures) can be produced based on the chemical composition. Laboratory application of spectral imaging began with medical diagnostics for chemical histological analysis, and is now being developed for trace evidence analysis. Applications are described later in the chapter.

REFLECTION OPERATION OPTICS Three basic optical designs are available to execute the conversion from the transmittance configuration to the reflectance configuration. All of these designs block a portion of the IR beam in at least one of the configurations. In the first design, a movable beam splitter is located in the beam path before the objective. Movable beam splitters leave the IR beam intact in the transmission mode, but block 75% of the energy in the reflectance mode (50% of the beam on its way to the sample and another 50% of the beam as it returns to the detector). In the second design, a movable pick-off mirror is located in the beam path before the objective that returns only 50% of the beam energy to the detector. The third design contains a fixed pick-off mirror in the Schwarzschild objective that blocks 50% of the beam energy in both transmission and reflectance modes.

GLASS OBJECTIVES   Several IR microscope manufacturers provide nosepiece positions for mounting low-power glass objectives for use in the visual configuration. These glass objectives are useful for locating specimens initially on the sample mounts. A typical magnification for a low-power glass objective is 4×, although 10× and others are available.

VISIBLE POLARIZERS   Visible light polarizers can be used in the visual mode to highlight specimen features. Viewing the sample between crossed polars is extremely useful when analyzing mixtures of similar-appearing components. Particles of different composition may easily be differentiated by their retardation colors and then selected for IR analysis. As an example, drug samples may be analyzed rapidly by selecting the drug and diluent's crystals using crossed polars, followed by IR analysis of the individual crystals. Although quantitative birefringence measurements are not typically made with the FT-IR microscope, all the necessary features can be included in the visual mode for this type of analysis.

INFRARED POLARIZERS   Polarized infrared spectroscopy can be performed with an FT-IR microscope. Whereas polarized light microscopy can be used to measure birefringence, polarized IR microscopy can be used to measure dichroism. *Dichroism,* the difference in IR absorption for different polarization orientation, yields more information than does birefringence. Whereas birefringence gives average values of all the components and phases present, dichroism is specific to particular absorption bands. Thus, dichroism can be applied to different groups on the same molecular chain, different segments in a copolymer, and different components of a polymer blend. Dichroism and its applications are discussed in more detail in the section on fiber analysis.

PHOTOMICROGRAPHY   Most FT-IR microscopes are equipped to accommodate photography equipment ranging from Polaroid™ cameras to digital color video monitors and printers.

MOTORIZED STAGE   Motorized microscope stages offer convenience for the micropositioning of specimens. Mapping and multielement spectral imaging software for obtaining composition profiles of materials is available for certain systems. No application of mapping has been reported in forensic work with IR microscopes; however, spectral imaging with multielement detectors has begun. The end of the applications section describes studies that have been initiated.

SYNCHROTRON SOURCE   IR radiation produced by a synchrotron light source has provided benefit through its high-intensity beam and improved spatial resolution.[15] Although these features are beneficial for trace evidential materials, it is impractical for routine forensic use because of its large size and cost. However, one application is described by Kalasinsky (described later in the chapter) and is reported in the applications of drug analysis.

SPECTRAL MEASUREMENT METHODS
AND SAMPLE PREPARATION

Infrared spectrometry is well known for the many forms of samples to which it can be applied. Solids, liquids, and gases can all be analyzed. Although most trace evidence is in the solid form, occasionally the need arises to analyze liquids and gases. With the development of FT-IR, there has been a proliferation of newly developed optical configurations for spectral measurement methods, such as ATR and old sampling methods have been enhanced with microscopes. Infrared microscopy can incorporate a number of methods, including transmission and all types of reflection.

The various measurement methods involve different sample preparation techniques that may require little or extensive effort in order to obtain good spectra.[16–18] Many analysts have their own "pet" preparation techniques that they have adopted during their practice of IR spectrometry, and many of these techniques have become somewhat of an art form. Regardless of the method used, the important objectives are as follows: (1) Keep the technique simple, (2) make the technique repeatable, and (3) obtain spectra that represent accurately the whole material of which the specimen is a part. Sample preparation is important for any analytical technique, including routine-size IR analysis, but it is of utmost importance for microsampling. Small irregularities such as sample shape and contaminants are accentuated in the process of obtaining a spectrum under these conditions.

Although several techniques are often applicable for a particular sample type, it is important to be consistent in the method and preparation technique used for the sake of spectral comparison. Minor differences can occur in peak intensity, shape, and frequency with different measurement methods. Consistency is particularly important when using computerized spectral libraries for comparison. Computers cannot account for spectral irregularities the way a trained eye can. If one is careful, however, and understands the spectral differences that occur, spectral libraries prepared with different spectral measurement methods can sometimes be used successfully. A general overview of IR spectrometry methods and sample preparation follows. One must consider the needs of the specific laboratory in order to determine which equipment to acquire and which sample preparation techniques to use to obtain the information required.

Transmission

Historically, transmission has been the most commonly used and preferred method not only for IR microscopy, but for IR spectroscopy in general as well. Transmission methods typically require more extensive sample preparation than do reflection methods. In general, however, fewer spectral artifacts occur with transmission methods than with reflection methods. The most important objective in transmission measurements is to get the sample thin enough, typically on the order of 2 to 5 μm. Depending on the specimen, this may be done by slicing with a scalpel, pressing with a high-pressure hydraulic press or hand press, compressing in a diamond anvil cell (DAC) or a compression cell, or by rolling with a roller bearing or the end of a probe. A compression cell uses two IR transparent windows and is configured so the sample can be squeezed flat between the windows. Most materials that appear quite hard on a macro scale are in fact quite malleable on a micro scale. For particularly hard specimens, repeating the combination of slicing and pressing is usually sufficient to make the specimen thin enough. Although it is desirable to have parallel upper and lower faces, it is more important not to have irregularly shaped specimens that cause a large amount of scattering. This can significantly distort the baseline and peak shapes.

When operating in the transmission mode, the specimen must be suspended in air, placed on an IR window, or sandwiched between two IR windows.[19] Although every analyst has his or her own preferred sample-preparation techniques, there are physical phenomena associated with each method that must be considered and adjusted for if necessary. Air offers the least interference of any matrix. IR window materials all refract the beam to some extent and thus defocus the IR beam. Flattening the specimen and mounting it across the aperture of a sample holder, therefore, is the simplest configuration for the IR beam. However, for extremely small or brittle samples, which cannot be mounted across an aperture, or for elastomeric materials, which will not stay flattened, other sample mounting techniques must be used.

Very small or brittle samples can be placed on the surface of an IR window and sampled. The IR beam is defocused on passing through the window material. This defocusing of the beam may be corrected for, and spherical aberration compensation adjustments are available on certain objectives and condensers, as discussed previously.

Certain materials, when measured in air, give rise to interference fringes in the IR spectrum. To reduce the internal reflection which produces this phenomenon, the sample may be sandwiched between two IR windows in a compression cell and a background spectrum acquired from a small crystal of KBr sandwiched adjacent to the sample. Certain very pliable materials may be both flattened and measured between IR windows with the use of a compression cell. In these cases, the IR beam undergoes defocusing spherical aberration in both windows, both before and after passing through the sample. Again, these defocus and spherical aberrations may be corrected with adjustments available with certain microscopes.

Harder-textured samples require a less brittle window material than used in compression cells and may be flattened and measured between diamond windows with the use of a DAC or diamond windows in a compression cell. Some analysts, in fact, prefer a DAC with a beam condenser over the use of microscopes in general. The most frequent reason given for this approach is the additional frequency range available with a TGS detector. Using a standard TGS detector, a lower-frequency limit of 400 cm^{-1} can be obtained with standard KBr optics, although a lower limit of 200 cm^{-1} can be obtained with CsI optics. Although TGS detectors have a lower-frequency limit near 200 cm^{-1}, wide-range MCT detectors sacrifice only a little range with a lower limit of approximately 450 cm^{-1}. If the additional range beyond that of a narrow-range MCT detector is considered important, an IR microscope system with a wide-range MCT detector is certainly more versatile and easier to use than a DAC.

Diamond cells were originally available only as high-pressure anvil cells. The greatest disadvantage of these cells is that the diamond window thickness causes the absorption between 2200 and 1900 cm^{-1} to be too strong, leaving this region of the spectrum blank. The thinner windows of the more recently introduced moderate-pressure, miniature diamond compression cells (MDCs), however, permit compensation in this frequency region. There is enough working distance on most IR microscopes that the miniature diamond cell fits under the objective, and it is often preferred over compression cells with other IR window materials that crack easily under pressure. Care must be also taken that the pressure is applied evenly when tightening individual screws on certain miniature MDC designs. Diamonds can and will crack when uneven pressure is applied. In addition, too much pressure should not be applied to samples, because high pressures can alter their crystalline form and thus produce changes in their spectra.[19]

External Reflection

External reflection sampling is convenient with IR microscopy because of the minimal or no sample preparation required. A comprehensive overview of the subject has been presented by Reffner and Wihlborg.[20] There are three types of external reflection that commonly occur on samples: reflection–absorption (R-A), specular reflection (SR), and diffuse reflection (DR). These three types of reflection are interdependent, and more than one type is always present. Although sample preparation is more convenient for reflectance measurements, the spectra are often more difficult to interpret than transmission spectra.

Reflection–Absorption

Reflection–absorption (R-A) occurs with a thin film coating on a metallic surface. The IR beam passes through the thin-film sample, reflects off the metallic surface, and passes back through the thin film as depicted in Figure 4-12. Absorption occurs when the beam passes through the film in both directions. Spectra of clear coatings,

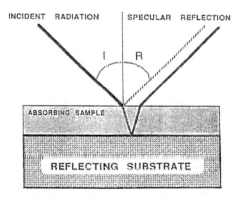

FIGURE 4-12 Reflection–absorption (R-A) sample geometry and beam path. (*Source:* Reproduced from reference 20 by permission of International Scientific Communications, Inc.; copyright 1990.)

certain paints, and smeared films on metal surfaces are commonly obtained by R-A. Because of the two passes the IR beam makes through the sample, this method is also referred to as *double transmission spectroscopy.* Reflection–absorption is the most convenient reflection technique to use provided the specimen is not opaque or too thick. The most common problem with this method is that intense interference fringes may be superimposed on the spectrum. Roughening the surface slightly with fine sandpaper often removes the fringes.

When the angle of incidence exceeds 60°, R-A spectra are termed *grazing angle spectra.* The increased path length and the high angle of incidence provide the ability to obtain spectra of coatings as thin as one monolayer. A specialized IR microscope objective is available that permits the collection of grazing angle spectra. No forensic applications of this objective have been reported as yet.

Specular Reflection

Specular reflection (SR), also known as *Fresnel reflection,* is the reflection from the exterior surface of a material as depicted in Figure 4-13. This type of reflection usually occurs on very shiny surfaces. With pure SR, the absorption bands are inverted and distorted when compared to transmission spectra. Usually, however, there is a combination of specular and diffuse reflection, the result of dispersion because of a rapid change of refractive index that causes some bands to take on a derivative shape. The upper spectrum in Figure 4-14 was acquired by SR of an extruded nylon pellet and displays these derivative-shaped bands. The lower, "normal-appearing" spectrum in Figure 4-14 was produced from the upper spectrum by a Kramers–Kronig (K-K) transformation.[19] Kramers–Kronig transform software is available from FT-IR instrument manufacturers. Because several types of reflectance occur simultaneously and indices of refraction vary between materials, the K-K computation does not always produce a fully transformed spectrum.

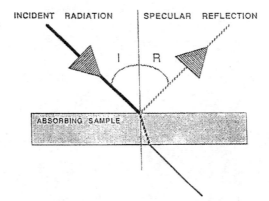

FIGURE 4-13   Specular reflection (SR) sample geometry and beam path.   (*Source:* Reproduced from reference 20 by permission of International Scientific Communications, Inc.; copyright 1990.)

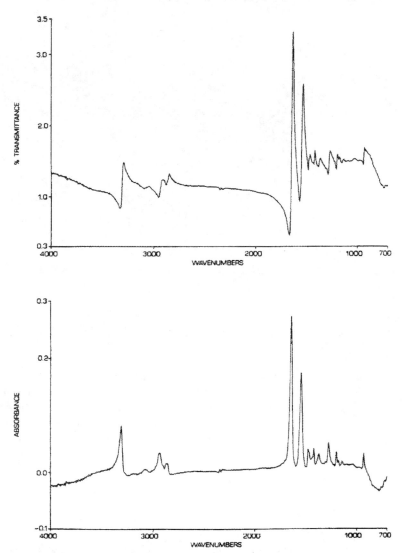

FIGURE 4-14 Specular reflectance spectrum (top) and Kramers–Kronig corrected absorbance spectrum (bottom) of a 200- × 200- × 200-μm extruded nylon pellet. (*Source:* Reproduced from reference 18 by permission of Academic Press, Inc.; copyright 1990.)

Diffuse Reflection

Diffuse reflection (DR) is produced from an irregular surface where the beam is reflected randomly over 180° from a nominally horizontal surface, as depicted in Figure 4-15. Diffuse reflection occurs for incident radiation that has penetrated the sample surface. Reflection, refraction, scattering, and absorption may all occur within the sample. Radiation that then exits from the sample surface is termed *diffuse*

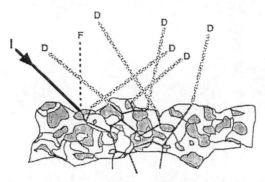

I = Incident radiation   D = Diffuse reflection

F = Fresnel reflection (specular)

FIGURE 4-15 Diffuse reflection (DR) sample geometry and beam path. (*Source:* Reproduced from reference 20 by permission of International Scientific Communications, Inc.; copyright 1990.)

reflectance. For powdered materials or materials with a matte surface, diffuse reflectance may be the preferred method of analysis. The Schwarzschild objective, with its large numeric aperture, is an excellent collecting element for the scattered beam.[21] On routine-size samples, DR has held acclaim for ease of use and this holds for microsamples as well. Diffuse reflectance was sometimes originally perceived as a panacea for sampling devices because of the interest in no sample preparation. It was soon realized, however, that contributions from specular reflectance distorted the spectra. Minimal sample preparation, such as mixing the material in a KBr or KCl matrix or roughing up the surface, helps reduce the specular component and produces a more interpretable spectrum. With this minimal sample preparation, DR is a very convenient method that can be performed with IR microscopy.

Diffuse Transmittance

Diffuse transmittance (DT) is an effect that scattering samples can create when operating in the transmission mode. With macrosample measurement, the results are poor; however, the large collection angle of the Schwarzschild objectives and condensers make this method feasible with IR microscopes.[22,23] Extracted materials can be cast onto KBr powder and kept within a 100-μm diameter spot, thus preventing the spreading that occurs when a solution is cast onto an IR window. This method has an advantage over DR when solvents with boiling points greater than 80°C are used, because the slower evaporation of the solvent causes a greater penetration of the solute into the KBr or KCl matrix. In contrast, DR is more effective when the solute is located near the surface. Diffuse transmittance has been used to analyze high-performance liquid chromatography (HPLC) effluents[22] and could potentially be used with specimens where a small amount of extracted material was removed with a high-boiling solvent.

Internal Reflection

Internal reflection spectroscopy (IRS), also referred to as *attenuated total reflectance (ATR),* is based on the total reflection of radiation in an internal reflection element (IRE), or simply a crystal, at angles that exceed the critical angle.[24,25] A high-refractive index, IR transparent material is used as the medium to reflect the IR beam internally. The specimen must have a considerably lower refractive index and be in close contact with the IRE. This method has been applied extensively on routine-size samples for opaque objects such as polymers. The recent development of an IRS microscope objective, however, has made microscale analysis possible by this method.[26] An optical diagram of the microscope objective is shown in Figure 4-16A. Fourier plane masks located on a slide are used to define the angular aperture ranges needed to separate (1) the survey, (2) the contact, and (3) the analysis (ATR) modes of operation. Figure 4-16A shows the ray path for the ATR mode. A single-reflection, hemispherical ATR crystal, shown in Figure 4-16B, is used to make contact with the specimen. Attenuated total reflectance on a microscale is important

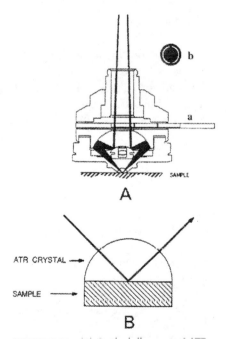

FIGURE 4-16 (A) Optical diagram of ATR objective shown in the analysis (ATR) mode. (a) Slide that positions Fourier masks to control modes of operation. (b) Top view of the mask for the ATR mode. (B) Sample geometry and beam path of the hemispherical IRE. (Figures contributed by Dr. John Reffner of Spectra-Tech, Trace Consulting, Stamford, CT.)

not only for small specimens, but for standard-size evidence that has been contaminated as well. With the ability to analyze an area as small as $100 \ \mu m^2$, one is more likely to find a clean portion of the surface for analysis. With the easy-to-use single-reflection sample compartment ATR accessories, the use of ATR with microscopes is not as required for many samples when the spot size is not critical. The spot size of a typical in-sample-compartment ATR is approximately 0.75 mm with a diamond/KRS-5 versus 0.09 mm for a diamond microscope objective. Several examples in the following applications section illustrate the use of microscopic IRS for forensic use.

APPLICATIONS

The ease of use of FT-IR microscopes makes almost any type of sample that would be analyzed by IR more easily examined on a microscale. Forensic analysts who have an FT-IR microscope available have revealed that indeed, the microscope attachment is used extensively. The forensic applications of IR microscopy are described next.

Synthetic Polymers

Polymers are ubiquitous in our society, and their prevalence at crime scenes causes them to be commonly encountered as forensic evidence. The large variety of polymer types makes it necessary to categorize them by application in order to gain a general understanding of variations within each group. In so doing, the evidence may often be individualized to a greater extent, its significance more clearly understood, and its evidentiary value enhanced.

Fibers

The forensic examination of fibers by visual light microscopy is complemented by IR microscopy. Infrared spectroscopy plays an important role in the systematic approach to the complete characterization of fibers.[27–31] Infrared data provide an unequivocal identification of the generic class, as well as the subclass created by chemical variations within the generic class. In addition, the American Society for Testing and Materials (ASTM) now lists IR spectroscopy as the preferred method of analysis for identifying human-made fibers, stating, "Where the data are consistent and the spectra obtained and interpreted by an experienced spectroscopist, the infrared procedure has no known bias."[32]

Single-fiber analysis using traditional IR methods is well covered in Chapter 3. Forensic IR analysis of fibers has not been extensive, however, because of the difficulty and destructiveness of traditional sampling methods. The introduction of IR microscopes, which provide the capability for simple and rapid analysis of single fibers, quickly made the use of IR in forensic fiber analysis popular.

Infrared microscopy offers several important advantages over other IR methods. These advantages include the following: (1) Virtually *all* fibers can be analyzed; (2) sample preparation is minimal (most fibers can be pressed reasonably flat and sufficiently thin); (3) the method is essentially nondestructive and the fiber is not chemically altered (as may occur with solubility testing); (4) short segments of individual fiber strands can be examined, including areas as small as $10 \times 10 \ \mu m$ (representing sub-nanogram amounts of material); and (5) with rectangular apertures, the area sampled can be adjusted to accommodate the amount of sample available.

Although optimum spectra are produced by flattening the fibers, fibers can often be sampled directly depending upon their diameters and cross-sectional shapes.[33–39] Round and irregular cross-sectional shapes cause lensing and scattering, respectively,[39] but the spectra obtained are usually sufficient to identify at least the generic class. Under these conditions, however, distortions in peak ratios, poor baselines, and low S/N can make it difficult to identify the less-intense but important spectral features required for more detailed chemical structure information. Therefore, it is important to flatten the fibers to obtain optimum spectra.[20,34,38–43] Usually only a very small portion of the fiber must be flattened, so that the physical appearance of the remainder of the fiber need not be altered. A number of methods have been reported for flattening fibers, including the use of a KBr pellet press,[37] a hand-held press,[38,39] a DAC,[20,34,41] or a metal roller.[19] Although most fibers remain flat after pressing and are not required to be kept under pressure during sampling, this is not true for elastomeric fibers such as Spandex or Lycra. For elastomers, the fibers can be pressed in a compression cell or miniature DAC or possibly sliced longitudinally with a scalpel. If a DAC is used for flattening fibers on a general basis, care must be taken not to apply too much pressure. As mentioned previously, the crystalline structure of the polymer can be altered and the resultant IR spectrum distorted to the point where the subclass may not be identified correctly. The ATR microscope objective shows great promise for nondestructive fiber analysis. A summary of fiber sampling techniques for the infrared microscope is given by Tungol, Bartick, and Montaser.[19]

The development of a spectral database for fiber identification has been described.[19] This database was updated and reported in electronic form.[43] The electronic publication includes a copy of all the fiber spectra in JCAMP.DX format, a standard format that can easily be converted into the formats of most IR instrument manufacturers.[44,45] This spectral database was further added to for a total of eighty-four polymeric types of fibers and is made available through the FBI Laboratory called *Version 4*. To assist in the identification of fiber composition especially for the identification of subclasses within a generic class, the database includes IR spectra for twenty-eight subtypes of acrylics including bicomponents. This is an addition of eight named by Grieve.[46] The IR spectra of the acrylics commonly encountered during casework [47] are shown in Figure 4-17. Eleven nylon subclasses are included in the database, and the IR spectra of several are shown in Figure 4-18. The original database was applied to a study of approximately 100 forensic fiber cases to determine

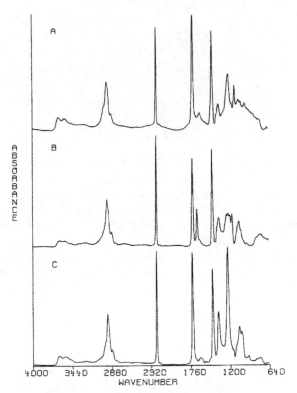

FIGURE 4-17   Infrared spectra of acrylic fibers:
(A) poly(acrylonitrile:methyl methacrylate),
(B) poly(acrylonitrile:methyl acrylate), and
(C) poly(acrylonitrile:vinyl acetate).

the frequency of occurrence for various fiber subclasses.[47] The results are shown in Table 4-1. Frequency data of this type may potentially be used to improve evidential value by utilizing statistical information once a more thorough statistical study has been completed.

Another database approach consists of a combined IR spectra and text information library.[48] The database contains IR spectra of fibers from the Collaborative Testing Services (CTS) collection. [a] Included with the IR spectra is manufacturer information with chemical and physical data. Physical data, such as cross section and diameter, can be used for a pre-search to filter out only those files that contain the parameter(s) of interest prior to the spectral search. When the entire library is searched by IR spectra alone, many fibers with the same chemical composition are often listed as the top hits. By first selecting fiber files with the correct physical properties, the chances are greatly improved that the IR spectral search selects the correct manufacturer as the first hit.

Semi-quantitative analysis has been used to demonstrate the potential for further distinguishing between acrylic fibers within subclass by relative monomer

[a]Collaborative Testing Services, Inc., P.O. Box 1049, Herndon, VA 22070.

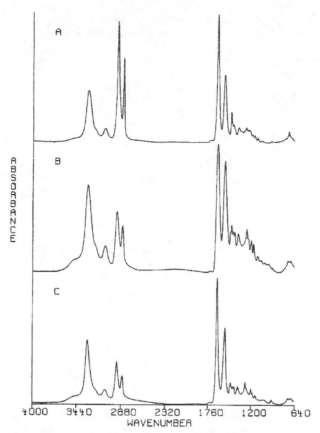

FIGURE 4-18 Infrared spectra of nylon fibers: (A) nylon 12;
(B) nylon 6; (C) nylon 6,6.

ratios.[49] The American Trade Commission defines *acrylics* as consisting of at least 85% acrylonitrile units.[50] Thus up to 15% of the fiber may consist of one or more comonomers. Typically, at least one of the minor comonomers is a carbonyl-containing unit so that variations in the comonomer ratio alter the carbonyl/nitrile peak area ratio. The actual comonomer concentration was not the aim of these studies, but rather (1) the degree of precision with which the carbonyl/nitrile peak area ratio could be measured, (2) whether manufacturers could be differentiated by this ratio, and (3) whether sufficient differences exist in commercial fibers such that this ratio would be a significant point of comparison. The study demonstrated that the potential does exist. The results of carbonyl/nitrile peak area ratio studies on Du Pont and Badische poly(acrylonitrile:methyl acrylate) fibers are shown in Table 4-2. For these particular fiber types, the two manufacturers are clearly distinguishable from each other by this method. Additional acrylic copolymer studies were conducted more recently by Causin et al.[51] Grieve[52] evaluated the interpretation of modacrylic fibers utilizing IR microscopy.

Polarization studies have been performed on single fibers with IR microscopy by Chase,[13,53] Young,[54] and Reffner,[55] who have demonstrated the capability of IR

TABLE 4-1 Fiber Types Identified by IR Spectra for 98 Cases

Fiber Type[a]	Number of Occurrences[b]	Occurrence (%)
Acrylic	33	34.7
AN	1	1.1
AN:MA	12	12.6
AN:MMA	8	8.4
AN:VA	9	9.5
Polyester	25	26.3
PET	25	26.3
Nylon	21	22.1
Nylon 6	7	7.4
Nylon 6,6	14	14.7
Polyolefin	7	7.4
Polypropylene	7	7.4
Acetate	4	4.2
Acetate	2	2.1
Triacetate	2	2.1
Modacrylic	3	3.2
AN:VC	3	3.2
Aramid	1	1.1
Nomex	1	1.1
Rayon	1	1.1

[a]Definitions: AN, acrylonitrile; MA, methyl acrylate; MMA, methyl methacrylate; PET, poly(ethylene terephthalate); VA, vinyl acetate; VC, vinyl chloride.

[b]The total number of occurrences is greater than 98 because of fiber blends and multiple fiber types per case.

microscopy to yield valid polarization data. Polarized IR microscopy has also been studied to demonstrate the forensic potential to differentiate between polyester fibers with differing degrees of crystallinity and molecular orientation.[56] Molecular orientation and crystallinity vary between fiber products of the same chemical composition as a result of different manufacturing processes. Polyester fibers are frequently encountered during case work and are predominantly composed of poly(ethylene terephthalate) (PET). Because PET fibers are so common, if they are undyed, the fibers are usually considered to have little evidential value. Because various producers process PET differently, however, the molecular orientation and degree of crystallinity vary between different types. These differences can be observed by measuring dichroic ratios using polarized IR microscopy. Because only that component of the IR beam which is parallel to the bond transition moment in the molecule can be absorbed, absorption bands display different intensities in IR beams polarized parallel and perpendicular to the fiber axis. The degree of this difference is a function of the degree of orientation in the molecule. A randomly oriented or amorphous polymer displays no difference between parallel and perpendicular

TABLE 4-2 Results for Peak Area Ratio Analysis of AN:MA Copolymer Fibers.[a]

Fiber Type	One Location (10 Times)	Along Length (10 Locations)	10 Fibers
Du Pont	1.066	1.083	1.103
Orlon 42	0.002	0.014	0.067
CTS 81A0012	0.19%	1.3%	6.1%
Du Pont	1.258	1.068	1.138
Orlon TR01	0.004	0.011	0.023
CTS 81A0031	0.32%	1.0%	2.0%
Badische	1.734	1.696	1.688
A201	0.004	0.198	0.093
CTS 81A0105	0.23%	11.7%	5.5%
Badische	1.721	1.658	1.681
A201	0.005	0.025	0.089
CTS 81A0106	0.29%	1.5%	5.3%
Badische	1.540	1.608	1.656
A302	0.004	0.096	0.076
CTS 81F0111	0.26%	6.0%	4.6%

[a]The first number shown in each block is the average carbonyl/nitrile peak area ratio, followed by the standard deviation and the relative standard deviation.

polarized spectra, whereas a highly oriented or crystalline polymer displays significant differences between the two spectra.

The objective of the dichroism research on PET fibers was two-fold: (1) to determine if dichroism information can be obtained with adequate precision by polarized IR microscopy for use in forensic examination of fibers, and (2) to determine if the orientation characteristics of commercial PET fibers differ enough that dichroism information may be used as a significant point of comparison in fiber examinations. Spectra were acquired with the IR polarizer oriented parallel and perpendicular to the fiber axis. Dichroic ratio, R, measurements were calculated by two methods as shown in Equations 4-2 and 4-3.

$$R = A_{\parallel}/A_{\perp} \tag{4-2}$$

$$DR = (A_{\parallel} - A_{\perp})/(A_{\parallel} + A_{\perp}) \tag{4-3}$$

The true dichroic ratios, DR, of several bands were demonstrated to yield adequate precision and sufficient variation such that the potential for forensic application was shown.

A striking example of differences in dichroism among polyester fibers is illustrated in Figure 4-19. The two polarized spectra on the top were obtained from a polyester fiber produced for melt-bonding that was not drawn (stretched) during the manufacturing process. As a result, little orientation was developed in the fiber and

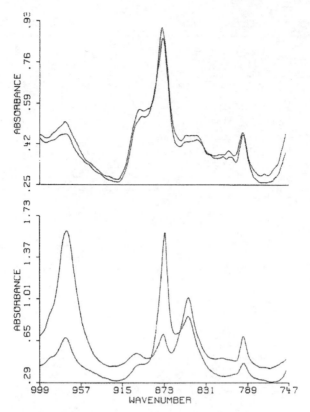

FIGURE 4-19   Polarized infrared spectra of an undrawn poly(ethylene terephthalate) (PET) fiber (top) and a drawn PET fiber (bottom). Note the similarity between the parallel and perpendicularly polarized spectra in the undrawn fiber and the differences in the drawn fiber.

the parallel and perpendicular polarized spectra are very similar. The two polarized spectra on the bottom were obtained from a polyester fiber that was drawn during the manufacturing process. As a result of the stretching, molecular orientation was produced in the fiber and the parallel and perpendicular polarized spectra show considerable differences in band intensity. Additional studies of polarization to polyester fibers have been conducted and reported in the literature.[56–59]

Because very small areas can be analyzed with the IR microscope, it is possible to obtain spectra of the individual lobes of a side-by-side bicomponent fiber.[46,60–61] For example, the IR spectra of both lobes of a DuPont Orlon 21 fiber are shown in Figure 4-20. Although both lobes are acrylic, differences are evident. The IR microscope is also useful for obtaining individual spectra of the two components of sheath-and-core bicomponent fibers.[47] After flattening the fiber, the sheath is identified by acquiring a spectrum near the fiber edge; the core is subsequently identified by acquiring a spectrum from the fiber center and subtracting the spectrum of the sheath.

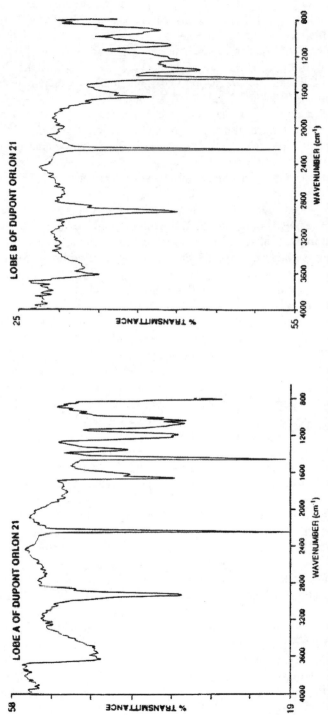

FIGURE 4-20 Infrared spectra of two lobes of a Du Pont Orlon 21 bicomponent fiber obtained using an infrared microscope. (*Source:* Reproduced from reference 60 with permission from San Francisco Press, Inc. 1987.)

For nonwoven fabrics, it is possible to obtain spectra of both the fibers and the binder adhesive by isolating the individual areas to be analyzed with an aperture(s).[61]

A degradation study of buried fibers was performed on rayon and acetate fibers.[62] Rayon showed little change, whereas acetate fibers showed clear evidence of hydrolytic cleavage of the acetate groups. Causin et al.[63] demonstrated the effects of the elements on PET fibers. Fibers having undergone thermal effects have been studied by IR microscopy.[64,65]

The use of ATR microscopy to obtain single fiber spectra is described by Bartick, Tungol, and Reffner.[66] The limited surface penetration of ATR has been utilized to determine finishes on fibers was conducted by Cho et al.[67] Reffner[68] showed the use of an ATR-based IR microscope for Kevlar fibers originating from a bulletproof vest. He also obtained ATR-IR spectra on many other materials of evidential interest.

PAINT   Chapter 3 provides an introduction to IR sampling methods for the analysis of paint composition using sample introduction with diamond cells in beam condensers used in the sample compartment. This section discusses the IR microscopic analysis of automotive topcoats and multilayer paint samples using IR microscopes. Tillman[69] developed a good automotive paint analysis scheme in which IR microscopic analysis plays an important role. A flowchart for the classification of paint binders and interpretation of spectra from this scheme is shown in Figure 4-21. Ryland[70] and Ryland, Jergovich, and Kirkbride[71] also published analytical approaches to paints in general that serve as a basis for the SWGMAT Paint Guidelines.[72]

Tillman and Bartick[73] also made a significant contribution to forensic paint analysis with the development of an IR spectral database of the CTS American automotive topcoat collection. Samples were prepared by thinning with a scalpel and subsequent flattening with a KBr hand press. An evaluation of the database was performed using test specimens from the reference panels, a salvage yard, and actual cases for a total of 23 test specimens. The database was searched with an algorithm that calculated the absolute difference of the first derivatives of the spectra. Nicolet Analytical Instruments' Omni search was used to pre-search (pre-filter) by color and metallic versus nonmetallic. Pre-filtering the IR spectra in a database with text information greatly improves search results, as discussed previously for fibers. Initial results produced 57% correct first hits with no correct hits falling lower than eighth place. All paints were identified as to year, make, and model for the specific paint usage once a visual inspection was made of the reference panels for the top ten hits. An evaluation of incorrect results revealed that most errors were attributable to over-absorption and low S/N in the test spectra. Significant improvements were obtained after additional thinning of test specimens and additional signal averaging to improve S/N. This study illustrates the importance of good sample preparation and data processing.

The CTS collection was terminated in 1989. However, the Royal Canadian Mounted Police (RCMP) Laboratory developed an automotive database that they currently maintain and that is supported through the Paint Subgroup of SWGMAT. The database, called Paint Data Query (PDQ),[74] has been prepared by using diamond cells mounted in beam condensers in the FTIR bench sampling compartment, but is often used when sampling through an IR microscope.

AUTOMOTIVE PAINT BINDER INFRARED CLASSIFICATION FLOW CHART

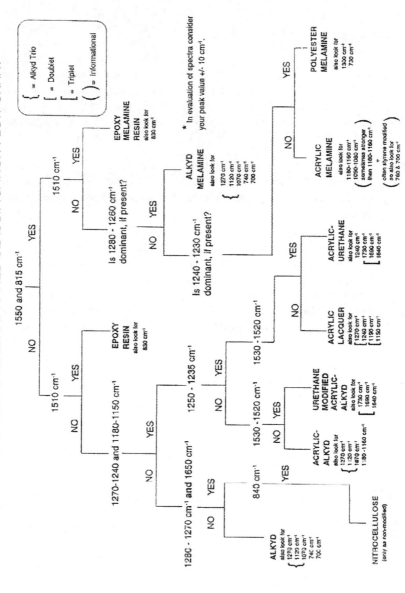

FIGURE 4-21 Flow scheme for the classification of automotive paint binders by their infrared spectra. (*Source*: Contributed by Warren L. Tillman, Georgia Bureau of Investigation.)

FT-IR microscopic analysis of paint layers is also a very powerful comparison technique for paint evidence. Topcoats can be very similar in composition, whereas there is greater diversity among undercoats, as described in Chapter 3. In addition, a match between two multilayer paint samples provides a much greater probability that the questioned specimen originated from a suspect vehicle paint profile than does a match between two single types of paint. Wilkinson, Locke, and Laing[75] describe the acquisition of IR spectra from multilayer paint samples with a microtome and a water-based embedding medium. Cross sections 2- to 5-μm thick were sampled by transmission spectroscopy. Areas of 30×20 and 30×15 μm^2 were sampled from two layers. A method of oblique sectioning has been described[76] that effectively increases the width of the layers and thus provides a larger area from which to obtain spectra. In addition, a wide range of paint analytical techniques and applications have been demonstrated for forensic purposes using IR microscopic analysis.[77–85]

AUTO PARTS Automobile producers currently place a great deal of emphasis on polymeric components. The need for parts that are both lightweight and noncorrosive has become important. Plastic parts are found throughout automobiles, including the outer bodies. Although there has not been extensive reporting of the analysis of these components using IR microscopes, a few papers have appeared.

The part that has gained the most interest, because of the frequency of hit-and-run cases, is the black rubber bumper. Blackledge[86] reported the application of ATR for rubber bumper analysis using a dispersive spectrometer. With sufficient material this would be reasonably convenient, but with small amounts this approach becomes much more difficult. Potential exists for the use of an ATR microscope objective for this type of analysis. The spectrum of a 100 μm^2 area of a Toyota Camry door guard acquired with an ATR microscope objective is shown in Figure 4-22.[66]

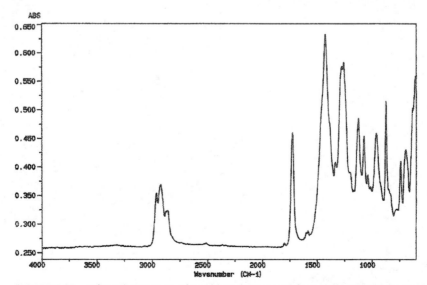

FIGURE 4-22 Infrared spectrum of a rubber door guard from 1989 Toyota Camry obtained with an ATR objective apertured to 100 μm^2. (*Source:* Spectrum contributed by Dr. John Reffner of Spectra-Tech, Trace Consulting, Stamford, CT.)

Similar-quality spectra have also been obtained of rubber automobile bumpers. Smears that originate from auto parts should be analyzed easily without removal from the substrate, thus making this technique extremely useful in the forensic laboratory.

Infrared microscopic analysis has also been performed in combination with other techniques to provide more discrimination among auto parts. Parybyk and Kobus[87] used a KBr die to press slices from bumper bars for IR microscope preparation of specimens. Eight different polymer categories were isolated. When they used the combination of FT-IR, pyrolysis gas chromatography (PGC), and scanning electron microscopy with energy dispersive X-ray (SEM-EDX), twenty-five categories were identified. Rubber bumper and tire particles have been studied by Pavilova et al.[88] using an MDC. This group complemented the FT-IR microscopic analysis with electron spin resonance (ESR) and PGC.

ADHESIVES AND TAPES   Adhesives and tapes are frequently recovered at crime scenes from explosive devices, bound victims, and so forth. Bartick and Merrill[89] reported the application of IRS for the analysis of black plastic tapes. Both the adhesive and backing were sampled with a standard-size IRS accessory. This approach works well unless the tape is contaminated and it is difficult to find a clean portion. Contamination of the adhesive poses the most concern because it is more difficult to clean. Two techniques can be used to obtain a clean spectrum of the adhesive with an IR microscope. First, a small portion of adhesive may be excised from the tape with a probe or scalpel and subsequently compressed between two IR windows with a compression cell for sampling by transmission. A spectrum of adhesive acquired in this manner from a piece of Tuck™ electrical tape is shown in Figure 4-23 (upper spectrum). Second, a small, clean area of the adhesive may be analyzed with an ATR

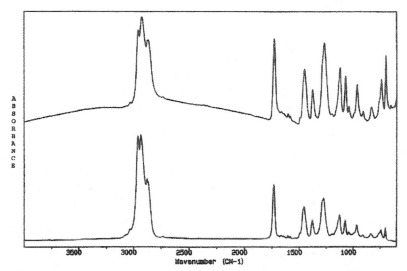

FIGURE 4-23 Transmission infrared spectrum of adhesive from Tuck™ electrical tape obtained by flattening excised adhesive in a compression cell (bottom) and spectrum obtained directly from the same tape using an ATR microscope objective (top). (*Source:* Spectra contributed by Dr. John Reffner of Spectra-Tech, Trace Consulting, Stamford, CT.)

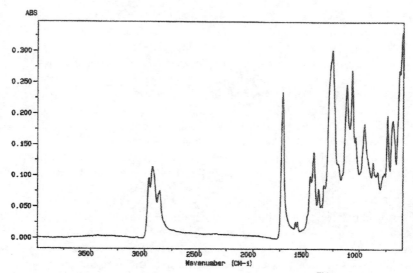

FIGURE 4-24   Infrared spectrum of the backing side of a Tuck™ electrical tape obtained with an ATR objective apertured to 100 μm^2.   (*Source:* Spectrum contributed by Dr. John Reffner of Spectra-Tech, Trace Consulting, Stamford, CT.)

microscope objective.[66] An ATR microscope objective with a 100-μm diameter aperture was used to obtain the lower spectrum in Figure 4-23. Note the greater intensity of the peaks at lower frequencies in the ATR spectrum. The more intense peaks result from greater penetration of the IR beam into the sample at longer wavelengths and can be an asset when interpreting the spectra. A spectrum obtained from the backing side of the Tuck™ electrical tape with the ATR microscope objective is shown in Figure 4-24. A comparison of various ATR configurations from in the sampled compartment to microscope arrangements was studied by Merrill and Bartick.[90]

Adhesives other than from tapes can also be sampled readily. As mentioned previously, Reffner, Messerschmidt, and Coates[61] demonstrated the identification of adhesive in a nonwoven fabric. A transmission spectrum of the binding adhesive was obtained by aperturing between the fibers.

COPY TONERS   IR microscopy has been applied to inks,[91,92] but the greatest amount of applications have been to copy toner analysis.[92–98] The most used method has been by reflection–absorption. Andrasko[92] removes the toner sample from the paper and places it on an SEM sample post. Merrill et al.[94] remove the sample with heat from a soldering iron and smear the toner with its resin onto aluminum foil. The IR beam passes through the toner resin and reflects back to the IR detector via a beam splitter. Toners from more than 800 machines have been measured in to create a successful database.[96,97]

MULTILAYER POLYMERS   The advantage of IR microscopy is that small areas may be isolated within a particular specimen, thus eliminating tedious separation procedures. In the discussion of paint examinations, the analysis of paint layers has been described by cross-sectional microtoming with subsequent isolation of each layer with the aperture(s) on the IR microscope. Several authors have reported the analysis of cross-sectioned layers of several other types of laminated polymer products.[55,99,100] Harthcock[100] describes the analysis of three layers of a food wrapping. A comparison was made between ATR and IR microscopy on the two outer layers. In the lower-frequency region of the spectra, severe band distortions occurred in the spectra obtained by microscopy. A single aperture was used that produced diffraction problems. Reffner, Coates, and Messerschmidt[101] discuss the isolation of five layers of a laminate, producing essentially spectroscopically pure individual spectra with the use of two apertures. One must remember, however, that even with two apertures, extraneous spectral contributions from adjacent layers can occur as far away as 40 μm from the aperture edge.[11] However, when double apertures are used, the contributions are minimal. In a different type of cross-section situation, Reffner[55] showed changes in oxidation as a result of weathering from the surface of a poly(propylene) material into the inner part of the material.

MISCELLANEOUS POLYMERS   Additional polymers are frequently found at crime scenes and can often be useful as physical evidence. In one FBI Laboratory case, a homicide was believed to have occurred on a cruise ship's jogging track by way of a fight and a push overboard. Spectra of rubber particles found deeply embedded in the running suits of both the female victim and male suspect were shown to match spectra acquired of pieces of the jogging track. The spectra were obtained with an IR microscope of the particles squeezed in a compression cell to flatten them. The spectra, shown in Figure 4-25, reveal primarily calcium carbonate, a common filler in rubber. These data contributed strongly, along with additional evidence, to the conviction of the suspect.

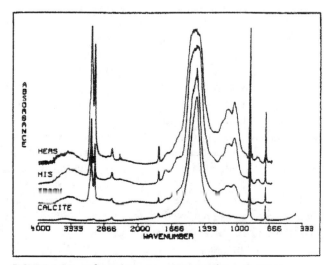

FIGURE 4-25   Infrared spectra obtained from particles removed from the suspect's sweatpants, the victim's sweatpants, the jogging track, and calcite.

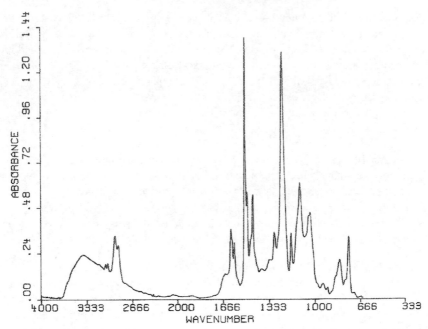

FIGURE 4-26 Infrared spectrum of a thermoset resin prepared by obtaining a thin slice from the bulk of the material.

In another case, it was necessary to determine who had been driving an automobile involved in a crime. A white deposit was found on the sole of the right shoe of one of the suspects and also on the brake pedal of the vehicle. Particles of the white material were scraped off both objects and IR spectra were obtained after the material was smeared on an IR window. Both white materials were identified as stearates, which are used as catalysts for curing rubber and sometimes bloom to the surface. This information was used to determine the driver of the vehicle.

The ease of preparing samples and recording spectra with IR microscopy has resulted in the method becoming widespread, not only for microsamples but also for samples that would usually be considered on a macroscopic scale. The horizontal stage makes a convenient sampling platform. It is not necessary to mount samples in a vertical fashion. Once prepared, often the samples need only be placed on an IR window. A small slice from a standard-size polymer is a simple preparation.[1] A cured polymer is usually considered a difficult type of material to thin sufficiently for IR sampling. Slicing with a scalpel, however, is a quick preparation. Figure 4-26 shows the spectrum obtained from a slice of thermoset epoxy resin. Paper or other materials can often be torn to yield a thin edge where the specimen can be analyzed. When sufficient sample is available, a spectrum can be obtained quickly from a small clump of fibers.[1] This method avoids even the small task of pressing a single fiber and provides greater assurance that all the fiber types in a blend are included in the spectrum. The development of convenient techniques for IR microscopy are limited only by the user's imagination.

Controlled Substances

Several IR analysis approaches for drug analysis by FT-IR microscopy have been reported. First, Suzuki[102] compares the use of a high-pressure DAC coupled with a beam condenser to a MDC used with a microscope. For both diamond-cell techniques, particles are hand-picked from drug mixtures under a stereomicroscope. Suzuki suggests that one can become reasonably skilled at physical separation with some practice. Another advantage of hand-selecting particles is that it avoids the possibility of recrystallization from solvents that can alter the crystalline structure. The high-pressure DAC does not require an IR microscope (it can be used with some microscopes), but it does require a larger sample in order to cover the entire diamond face. A microscope with an MDC can be used for any particle size that can be manipulated. If used with a narrow-range MCT detector, however, the lower-frequency limit of the IR microscope is restricted to approximately 700 cm^{-1}, whereas a beam condenser with a TGS detector has a lower-frequency limit of 400 cm^{-1} and a wideband MCT has a lower limit of about 450 cm^{-1}. Hida and Mitsui[103] demonstrate a means of identifying lysergic acid (LSD). Ways of detecting supermarket tampering is shown by Tomlinson et al.[104] Kalasinsky, both alone[105] and with coworkers,[106,107] has done extensive studies of detecting drugs in hair using an IR microscope. The use of a synchrotron source was applied to improve the spatial resolution of the drugs within the hair.[105] Hair analysis for additional forensic purposes has been conducted by Tagliaro et al.[108] Cosmetics on hair has been studied by Briese and Kijewski,[109] with reference to medicolegal aspects.

Explosives

Explosive analysis by IR microscopy has not been explored significantly because single-reflection IR-ATR with sample compartment accessories work well for samples that can be placed under a probe having a spot size of approximately 0.75mm diameter.[90] Clement and Le Pareux[110] report the identification of smokeless powder traces on wounds and hands of persons who had fired handguns. This work was done using a Nanospec/20 IR, a filter instrument, rather than an FT-IR spectrometer. Diffuse reflectance has been demonstrated as a viable method for sampling explosives and their residues.[111] Figure 4-27 shows a spectrum of Pyrodex^{TM} obtained as a 1% KBr mix in the reflectance operation of an IR microscope. This is a convenient method for sampling explosives that can be ground gently. The infrared spectrum of barium carbonate, a pyrotechnic component, obtained in this manner is shown in Figure 4-28. Plastic explosives have been analyzed by internal reflectance spectroscopy on routine-size samples (200–300 mg).[112] The sample size could be reduced significantly if an ATR microscope objective were used. There is also the potential for the application of IR microscopy to the analysis of explosive residues.

Art Forgeries

IR microscopes have become workhorses as an analytical tool in the area of art conservation.[113] IR microscopy application has also been reported for archaeological studies of art work in which forgeries have been discovered.[114] Very small samples

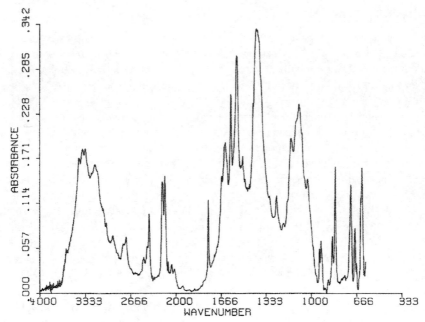

FIGURE 4-27 Infrared spectrum of 1% Pyrodex^TM in KBr powder obtained by DR with an IR microscope.

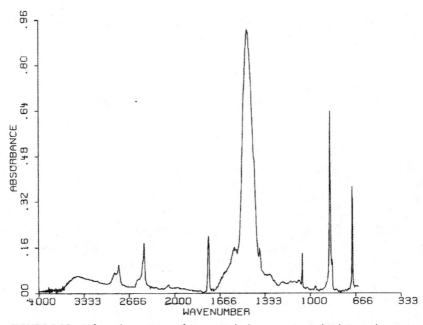

FIGURE 4-28 Infrared spectrum of a pyrotechnic component, barium carbonate, 5% in KBr obtained by DR with an IR microscope.

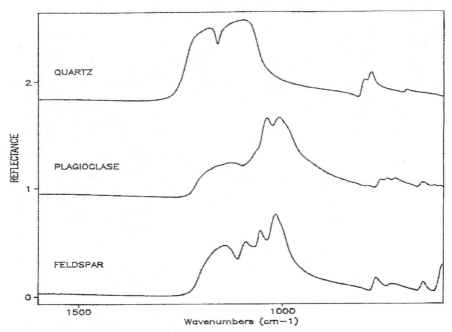

FIGURE 4-29 Specular reflectance spectra of three metamorphic phases of a rock. (*Source:* Reproduced from reference 20 with permission from International Scientific Communications, Inc., copyright 1990.)

were excised using a narrow scalpel and the specimens placed on an IR window. To avoid scattering of the IR radiation, the specimens were mixed with a few grains of KBr and pressed with a probe. Too little material was available to use a micro KBr pellet press. Paints and pigments can be analyzed to determine if modern materials were used, as in a forgery, or materials appropriate for the period in which the questioned painting was created.

Inorganic Samples

Infrared spectrometry is not always considered readily applicable to inorganic materials; however, it can often be a very useful tool for the analysis of many inorganic substances. The acquisition of mineral spectra by both transmission and reflection spectroscopy has been demonstrated by Reffner.[115] A variety of silicate spectra were shown in this report. Another example of mineral analysis was the comparison of several metamorphic phases of a single rock.[21] A cut and polished rock was sampled by reflectance. Spectra of quartz, plagioclase, and feldspar phases were produced as shown in Figure 4-29. These applications show potential for the classification of inorganic materials in forensic analyses.

Dentine and enamel from human teeth were compared to calcium phosphates by reflectance with an FT-IR microscope.[82] A higher degree of calcification of the dentine resulted in less reflectivity compared to the enamel. Infrared analysis does

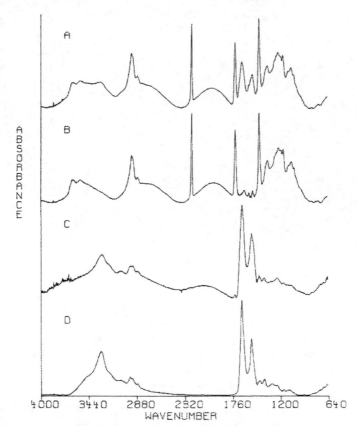

FIGURE 4-30   (A) and (B) Infrared spectra of two acrylic fibers acquired for comparison. Note the additional absorption bands in spectrum A. (C) Difference spectrum of spectra A and B (A–B). (D) Infrared spectrum of blood.

not appear to have the ability to distinguish the ivory of different animal species; however, the method can be used to identify the material as natural ivory or artificially produced material.[83] This work was done using a standard-size specular reflectance accessory, but where sample size is limited, an IR microscope in the reflectance mode would be the sampling method of choice.

Contaminants

Contaminants can contribute to IR spectra and interfere with the interpretation of the data.[47] One must be particularly careful with microsampling, because the relative contaminant contributions can be significantly greater than for routine-size samples. When the only difference between two spectra is the presence of additional bands in one spectrum, the difference might be attributable to a contaminant on the sample producing the additional bands. The spectra of two red acrylic fibers are shown in the upper half of Figure 4-30. The fiber from which the top spectrum was acquired was contaminated

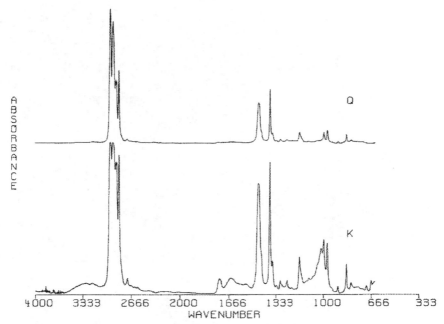

FIGURE 4-31   Infrared spectra of polypropylene fibers. The spectrum of the "K" fiber contains absorption bands in addition to those of polypropylene.

with blood that was not visible because of the color of the fiber. Additional absorption bands are present in the spectrum when compared to the second spectrum. The third spectrum is the difference between the two fiber spectra. The fourth (bottom) spectrum is that of blood. After washing, the two fibers displayed similar spectra.

However, the presence of a contaminant can also increase the evidential value of a fiber match when the contaminant is shown to be present on both the questioned and known samples. Infrared spectra were obtained of fibers Q and K as shown in Figure 4-31. Fibers Q and K were both identified as polypropylene; however, fiber K contained additional absorption peaks near 1730, 1651, 1017, and 669 cm^{-1}. These differences initially precluded a match between fibers Q and K. Spectra shown in Figure 4-32 were obtained after aperture size and sampling locations on the fibers were changed. An increase in aperture size resulted in the appearance of the additional bands in fiber Q, whereas a decrease in aperture size resulted in a reduction in intensity of the additional bands in fiber K. This fluctuation with aperture size revealed that the source of the additional bands was associated with the presence of a contaminant rather than a difference in the composition between fibers Q and K. The increase in aperture size resulted in the inclusion of the contaminant in the sampling field, whereas the reverse process excluded most of the contaminant from the sampling field.

An MDC was used to obtain a spectrum of a black particle found adhering to one of the fiber samples. Figure 4-33 shows the comparison of this spectrum to the difference spectrum obtained by subtracting Q No. 1 from Q No. 2. From the

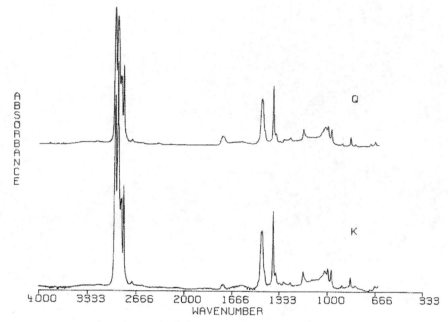

FIGURE 4-32   Infrared spectra of the same polypropylene fibers as in Figure 4-31, but analyzed in different locations with different aperture sizes.

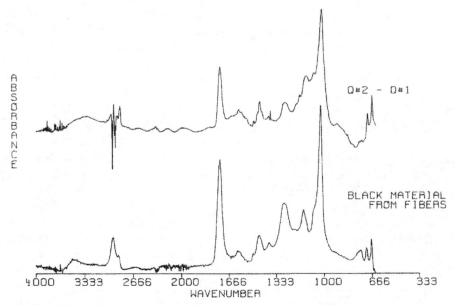

FIGURE 4-33   Difference spectrum of Q (Figure 4-32) minus Q (Figure 4-31) (top) and infrared spectrum of black particle removed from one of the fibers obtained with a MDC (bottom).

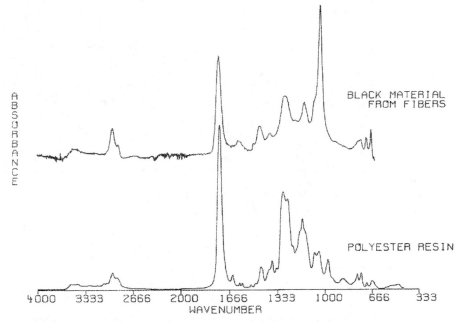

FIGURE 4-34 Infrared spectrum of black material from the polypropylene fibers (top) and reference spectrum of polyester resin from searched spectral library (bottom).

spectral similarities in Figure 4-33, the black particle was concluded to consist of the same material that produced the spectral differences between fibers Q and K shown in Figures 4-31 and 4-32. The spectrum of the black particle is similar to a polyester resin, as shown in Figure 4-34, with additional absorption bands at 1024 and 672 cm^{-1}. These peaks may be accounted for by the presence of talc (or other inorganic filler), as shown in Figure 4-35. The contaminant responsible for the spectral differences was probably an adhesive used in the construction of the automobile trunk liner from which the fibers were subsequently found to have originated.

Spectral Imaging

Spectral imaging is a process where images (pictures) are produced from spectroscopic intensity responses array detectors.[116] This is similar to photographs produced on charge-coupled device (CCD) digital cameras. The visible photographs are produced over a broad range of frequencies (broadband). IR images can be produced with broad band or limited wavenumber range to improve the resolution of the frequency response on mercury cadmium telluride (MCT) and other detectors with high response in the mid-IR. When monitoring wavelengths specific to functional groups, an image is produced that emphasizes particular chemical components of interest. This method has been explored extensively in the area of medical histological diagnostics.[117]

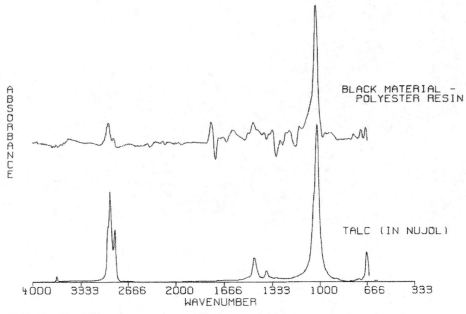

FIGURE 4-35 Difference spectrum of black material (Figure 4-33) minus the reference spectrum of polyester resin (top) and reference spectrum of talc from searched spectral library (bottom).

Forensic applications started appearing with interest in new ways to develop fingerprints. Bartick et al.[118] announced that images of latent fingerprints could be developed using the near-IR and the visible spectroscopic regions. This work was an off-shoot of single point detection using the mid-IR for determining the chemical composition of fingerprints.[119] This work evolved to the imaging of trace evidence located and identified while in the area of latent prints.[120,121] Additional trace evidence materials that have been identified within fingerprints are cocaine, methamphetamine, and single acrylic fibers of two different generic subgroups. Fingerprints have been developed from a wide range of substrates.[122,123]

Additional materials explored are bicomponent fibers where the separate components were imaged and identified.[124] The ability to image these materials by different colors based on chemical composition permits clear visualization of the different polymer structures. This same approach was used in the imaging of multilayered paints.[125] Ricci et al. demonstrated the application of ATR imaging of drugs tapelifted from various surfaces including fingers.[126] To the knowledge of the author, these types of applications have not been used in actual cases. However, since this method does not require chemical developers, it is non-invasive, and therefore, it is possible to conduct subsequent evidence analysis by other methods. Thus, IR spectral imaging should be very important in the near future.

THE FUTURE

The diverse applications demonstrated in this chapter serve to illustrate the workhorse that FT-IR microscopy has become in the forensic laboratory. Forensic users of the IR microscope have found that the microscope becomes used increasingly more often and standard-size sample preparation increasingly less often, regardless of the original sample size. The development of the ATR microscope objective opened a realm of applications and found extensive use. The increased ease of sample preparation, time saved, and nondestructive nature of the technique make it well worth the initial cost.

Fourier transform infrared microscope systems are now standard instrumentation in forensic laboratories. The applications, such as spectral imaging, continue to proliferate in areas where IR spectrometry has traditionally been used and in completely new areas that were impractical in the past. Forensic applications of IR microscopy for a multitude of physical evidence are limited only by the user's imagination.

Acknowledgment

The author wishes to give special thanks to Dr. John Reffner of Trace Consulting, Stamford, Connecticut, for his contribution of figures, assistance in obtaining references, review of the manuscript, and general helpfulness during the preparation of this manuscript.

References

1. E. G. Bartick, "Microscopy/Infrared Spectroscopy of Routine Sample Sizes," *Appl. Spectrosc.*, 39 (1985): 885–89.

2. R. Barer, A. R. H. Cole, and H. W. Thompson, "Infrared Spectroscopy with the Reflecting Microscope in Physics, Chemistry and Biology," *Nature*, 163 (1949): 198–201.

3. C. R. Burch, "Semi-Aplanat Reflecting Microscopes," *Proc. Phys. Soc. (London)*, 59 (1947): 47–49.

4. R. C. Gore, "Infrared Spectrometry of Small Samples with the Reflecting Microscope," *Science*, 110 (1949): 710–11.

5. V. J. Coates, A. Offner, and E. H. Siegler, Jr., "Design and Performance of an Infrared Microscope Attachment," *J. Opt. Soc. Am.*, 43 (1953): 984–89.

6. R. Z. Muggli, "FT-IR Through a Microscope," presented at *Inter/Micro-82*, Chicago. 1982.

7. J. E. Katon, G. E. Pacey, and J. F. O'Keefe, "Vibrational Molecular Microspectroscopy," *Anal. Chem.*, 58 (1986): 465A–81A.

8. R. G. Messerschmidt, "Photometric Considerations in the Design and Use of Infrared Microscope Accessories," in *The Design, Sample Handling, and Applications of Infrared Microscopes, ASTM STP 949*, ed. P. B. Roush (Philadelphia: American Society for Testing and Materials, 1987): 12–26.

9. E. V. Miseo and L. W. Guilmette, "Industrial Problem Solving by Microscopic Fourier Transform Infrared Spectrophotometry," in *The Design,*

Sample Handling, and Applications of Infrared Microscopes, ASTM STP 949, ed. P. B. Roush (Philadelphia: American Society of Testing and Materials, 1987): 97–107.

10. R. G. Messerschmidt, "Minimizing Optical Nonlinearities in Infrared Microspectroscopy," in *Infrared Microspectroscopy: Theory and Applications,* eds. R. G. Messerschmidt and M. A. Harthcock (New York: Marcel Decker, Inc., 1988): 1–19.

11. A. J. Sommer and J. E. Katon, "Diffraction Induced Stray Light in Infrared Microspectroscopy and Its Effect on Spatial Resolution," *Appl. Spectrosc.*, 45 (1991): 1633–40.

12. J. Ryan, J. Kwiatkoski, and J. A. Reffner, "FTIR Microscopy: Diverging Perspectives," *Am. Lab.* (April 1989): 26–31.

13. D. B. Chase, "Infrared Microscopy: A Single-Fiber Technique," in *The Design, Sample Handling, and Applications of Infrared Microscopes, ASTM STP 949,* ed. P. B. Roush (Philadelphia: American Society of Testing and Materials, 1987): 4–11.

14. P. R. Grifiths, J. A. de Haseth, and L. V. Azarraga, "Capillary GC/IR," *Anal. Chem.*, 55 (1983): 1361A–1367A.

15. P. Dumas, "Microanalysis and Imaging Capabilities of Synchrotron Infrared Microscopy," *J. Phys. IV France,* 104 (2003): 359–364.

16. P. B. Roush, ed., *The Design, Sample Handling, and Applications of Infrared Microscopes, ASTM STP 949* (Philadelphia: American Society for Testing and Materials, 1987).

17. R. G. Messerschmidt and M. A. Harthcock, eds., *Infrared Microspectroscopy: Theory and Applications* (New York: Marcel Decker, Inc., 1988).

18. K. Krishnan and S. L. Hill, "FT-IR Microsampling Techniques," in *Practical Fourier Transform Infrared Spectroscopy,* eds. J. R. Ferraro and K. Krishnan (New York: Academic Press, 1990): pp. 103–65.

19. M. W. Tungol, E. G. Bartick, and A. Montaser, "The Development of a Spectral Data Base for the Identification of Fibers by Infrared Microscopy," *Appl. Spectrosc.,* 44 (1990): 543–48.

20. J. A. Reffner and W. T. Wihlborg, "Microanalysis by Reflectance FTIR Microscopy," *Am. Lab.* (April 1990): 26–34.

21. F. J. Bergin, "Some Novel Applications of an Infrared Microscope," *Appl. Spectrosc.,* 43 (1989): 511–15.

22. D. J. J. Fraser, K. L. Norton, and P. R. Griffiths, "HPLC/FT-IR Measurements by Transmission, Reflection-Absorption and Diffuse Reflection Microscopy," in *Infrared Microspectroscopy: Theory and Applications,* eds. R. G. Messerschmidt and M. A. Harthcock (New York: Marcel Dekker, Inc., 1988): pp. 197–210.

23. D. J. J. Fraser, K. L. Norton, and P. R. Griffiths, "Comparison of Diffuse Reflectance and Diffuse Transmittance Spectrometry for Infrared Microsampling," *Anal. Chem.,* 62 (1990): 308–10.

24. N. J. Harrick, *Internal Reflection Spectroscopy* (Ossining, NY: Harrick Scientific Corp., 1967).

25. "Standard Practices for Internal Reflection Spectroscopy," *Annual Book of ASTM Standards,* E573-01(2007) (Philadelphia: American Society of Testing and Materials, 2007).

26. J. A. Reffner, W. T. Wihlborg, and S. W. Strand, "Chemical Microscopy of Surfaces by Grazing Angle and Internal Reflection FTIR Microscopy," *Am. Lab.* (April 1991): 46–50.

27. Scientific Working Group for Materials (SWGMAT), Forensic Fiber Examination Guidelines, *Forensic Sci. Communications,* 1 no. 1 (1999). http://www.fbi.gov/hq/lab/fsc/backissu/april1999/index.htm

28. M. B. Eyring and B. D. Gaudette, "An Introduction to the Forensic Aspects of Fiber Examination," *Forensic Science*

Handbook, Vol. 2, 2nd ed., ed. R. Saferstein (Upper Saddle River, NJ: Pearson/Prentice Hall, 2005): pp. 231–95.

29. M. W. Tungol, E. G. Bartick, and A. Montaser, "Forensic Examination of Synthetic Textile Fibers by Microscopic Infrared Spectrometry," *Practical Guide to Infrared Microspectroscopy,* ed. H. J. Humecki (New York: Marcel Dekker, 1995): pp. 245–85.

30. K. P. Kirkbride and M. W. Tungol, "Infrared Microspectroscopy of Fibres," *Forensic Examination of Fibres—II,* eds., J. Robertson and M. Grieve (Philadelphia: Taylor and Francis, 1999): 179–222.

31. M. M. Houck, "Forensic Fiber Examination and Analysis," *Forensic Sci. Rev.,* 17 (2005): 29–49.

32. "Identification of Textile Materials," *Annual Book of ASTM Standards,* D276-00a (Philadelphia: American Society of Testing and Materials, 2000).

33. S. C. Paticini and T. J. Porro, "Problem Solving Using FTIR Spectroscopy," *Am. Lab.* (August 1988): 24–32.

34. P. L. Lang, J. E. Katon, J. F. O'Keefe, and D. W. Schiering, "Instumental Methods and Sampling Factors in Infrared Microspectroscopy," in *The Design, Sample Handling, and Applications of Infrared Microscopes, ASTM STP 949,* ed. P. B. Roush (Philadelphia: American Society of Testing and Materials, 1987): pp. 49–63.

35. K. Krishnan, "Applications of FT-IR Microsampling Techniques to Some Polymer Systems," *Polym. Preprints,* 25 (1984): 182–83.

36. P. L. Lang, J. E. Katon, A. S. Bonanno, and G. E. Pacey, "The Identification and Characterization of Polymer Contaminants by Infrared Microspectroscopy," in *Infrared Microspectroscopy: Theory and Applications,* eds. R. G. Messerschmidt and M. A. Harthcock (New York: Marcel Dekker, Inc., 1988): pp. 41–50.

37. N. R. Smyrl, R. L. Howell, D. M. Hembree, Jr., and J. C. Oswald, "Industrial Problem Solving Using Microvibrational Spectroscopy," in *Infrared Microspectroscopy: Theory and Applications,* eds. R. G. Messerschmidt and M. A. Harthcock (New York: Marcel Decker, Inc., 1988): pp. 211–28.

38. E. G. Bartick, "Applications of a New High Pressure Anvil Cell for IR Spectroscopy," in *Proceeedings of the International Conference on Fourier and Computerized Infrared Spectroscopy, SPIE 553,* eds. J. G. Grasselli and D. G. Cameron (Bellingham, WA: Society of Photo-Optical Engineers, 1985): pp. 322–23.

39. E. G. Bartick, "Considerations for Fiber Sampling with Infrared Microscpectroscopy," in *The Design, Sample Handling, and Applications of Infrared Microscopes, ASTM STP 949,* ed. P. B. Roush (Philadelphia: American Society of Testing and Materials, 1987): pp. 64–73.

40. J. C. Shearer, D. C. Peters, and T. A. Kubic, "Forensic Microanalysis by Fourier Transform Infrared Spectroscopy," *Trends Anal. Chem.,* 4 (1985): 246–51.

41. J. E. Katon, P. L. Lang, J. F. O'Keefe, and D. W. Schiering, "The Identification of Fibers by Infrared and Raman Microspectroscopy," *Microchem. J.,* 34 (1986): 319–31.

42. A. J. Sommer, P. L. Lang, B. S. Miller, and J. E. Katon, "Applications of Molecular Microspectroscopy to Paper Chemistry," in *Infrared Microspectroscopy: Theory and Applications,* eds. R. G. Messerschmidt and M. A. Harthcock (New York: Marcel Decker, Inc., 1988): pp. 245–58.

43. M. W. Tungol, E. G. Bartick, and A. Montaser, "Spectral Data Base of Fibers by Infrared Microscopy," *Spectrochimica Acta.,* 46B (1991): 1535E–44E.

44. R. S. McDonald and P. A. Wilks, "JCAMP-DX: A Standard Form for

Exchange of Infrared Spectra in Computer Readable Form," *Appl. Spectrosc.,* 42 (1988): 151–62.

45. P. A. Wilks, "Infrared in the Real World: Direct Transmission of Infrared Spectra Is Now Possible, Thanks to JCAMP-DX," *Spectroscopy,* 1, no. 9 (1986): 49–50.

46. M. C. Grieve, "Another Look at the Classification of Acrylic Fibres Using FTIR Microscopy;" *Science & Justice,* 35 (1995): 179–90.

47. M. W. Tungol, E. G. Bartick, and A. Montaser, "Analysis of Single Polymer Fibers by Fourier Transform Infrared Microscopy: The Results of Case Studies," *J. Forensic Sci.,* 36 (1991): 1027–43.

48. E. G. Bartick, M. W. Tungol, G. R. Carroll, E. J. Carnahan, and J. F. Sprouse, "A Combined Infrared Spectroscopic and Text Data Base for Forensic Fiber Identification," presented at the *12th Meeting of the International Association of Forensic Sciences,* Adelaide, S. Australia, Oct. 24–29, 1990, unpublished.

49. M. W. Tungol, E. G. Bartick, and A. Montaser, "Forensic Analysis of Acrylic Copolymer Fibers by Infrared Microscopy," *Appl. Spectosc.* 47, (1993): 1655–58.

50. *Federal Trade Commission Rules and Regulations under the Textile Products Identification Act,* Title 15, U.S. Code section 70, *et seq.* 16 CFR 303.7.

51. V. Causin, C. Marega, S. Schiavone, and A. Marigo, "A Quantitative Differentiation Method for Acrylic Fibers by Infrared Spectoscopy," *Forensic Sci. Int.,* 151, (2005): 125–31.

52. M. C. Grieve, "Is It a Modacrylic Fibre?" *Science & Justice,* 39 (1999): 151–22.

53. B. Chase, "Dichroic Infrared Spectroscopy with a Microscope," *Infrared Microscpectroscopy: Theory and Applications,* eds. R. G. Messerschmidt and M. A. Harthcock (New York: Marcel Decker, Inc., 1988): pp. 93–102.

54. P. H. Young, "The Characterization of High-Performance Fibers Using Infrared Microscopy," *Spectroscopy,* 3, no. 9 (1988): 25–30.

55. J. A. Reffner, "Infrared Spectral Mapping of Polymers by FT-IR Microscopy," *Microbeam Analysis—1989,* ed. P. E. Russell (San Francisco: San Francisco Press, Inc., 1989): pp. 167–70.

56. M. W. Tungol, E. G. Bartick, and A. Montaser, "Polarized Infrared Study of Poly(ethylene Terephthalate) Fibers," *Crime Lab. Dig.,* 22 (1995): 86.

57. D. I. Wetzel and L. Cho, "Single Fiber Characterization by Polarization FT-IR Microspectroscopy," *Microchim. Acta [Suppl.],* 14 (1997): 349–51.

58. L. Cho, J. A. Reffner, B. M. Gatewood, and D. I. Wetzel, "A New Method for Fiber Comparison Using Polarized Infrared Microspectroscopy," *J. Forensic Sci.,* 44 (1999): 275–82.

59. L. Cho, J. A. Reffner, and D. I. Wetzel, "Forensic Classification of Polyester Fibers by Infrared Dichroic Ratio Pattern Recognition," *J. Forensic Sci.,* 44 (1999): 283–91.

60. M. C. Grieve, J. Dunlop, and T. M. Kotowski, "Bicomponent Acrylic Fibers—Their Characterization in the Forensic Science Laboratory," *J. Forensic Sci. Soc.,* 28 (1988): 25–34.

61. J. A. Reffner, R. G. Messerschmidt, and J. P. Coates, "Infrared Microbeam Analysis," *Microbeam Analysis—1987,* ed. R. H. Geiss (San Francisco: San Francisco Press, Inc. 1987): pp. 180–84.

62. S. M. Singer, D. M. Northrup, M. W. Tungol, and W. F. Rowe, "The Infrared Spectra of Buried Acetate and Rayon Fibers," *Biodeteriation Res.,* 3 (1990): 577–78.

63. V. Causin, C. Marega, G. Guzzini, and A. Marigo, "The Effect of Exposure to the Elements on the Forensic Characterization by Infrared Spectroscopy of Poly(ethylene Terephthalate) Fibers," *J. Forensic Sci.,* 50 (2005): 887–93.

64. J. Was, D. Knittel, E. Schollmeyer, "The Use of FTIR Microspectroscopy for the Identification of Thermally Changed Fibers," *J. Forensic Sci.*, 41 (1996): 1005–11.

65. J. Was, "The Identification of Thermally Changed Fibres," *Forensic Sci. Int.*, 85 (1997): 51–63.

66. E. G. Bartick, M. W. Tungol, and J. A. Reffner, "A New Approach to Forensic Analysis with Infrared Microscopy: Internal Reflection Spectroscopy, *Anal. Chim. Acta,* 288 (1994), 35–42.

67. L. Cho, J. A. Reffner, B. M. Gatewood, and D. I. Wetzel, "Single Fiber Analysis by Internal Reflection Infrared Microspectroscopy," *J. Forensic Sci.*, 46 (2001): 1309–1314.

68. J. A. Reffner, "Infrared Microprobe Analysis Using Reflection Methods," *Microscope*, 53 (2005): 33–36.

69. W. Tillman, "Automotive Paint Systems Identification," in *Proc. Internatl. Symp. Forensic Asp. Trace Evid.*, (Washington, DC: U.S. Government Printing Office, 1991): 123–52.

70. S. G. Ryland, "Infrared Microspectroscopy of Forensic Paint Evidence," in *The Practical Guide to Infrared Microspectroscopy,* ed. H.J. Humecki, (New York: Marcel Dekker, 1995): pp. 163–243.

71. S. G. Ryland, T. A. Jergovich, and K. P. Kirkbride, "Current Trends in Paint Examination," *Forensic Sci. Rev.,* 18 (2006): 97–117.

72. Scientific Working Group for Materials (SWGMAT), "Forensic Paint Analysis and Comparison Guidelines," *Forensic Sci. Communications,* 1, no. 2 (July 1999), http://www.fbi.gov/hq/lab/fsc/backissu/july1999/index.htm

73. W. L. Tillman and E. G. Bartick, "The Evaluation of an Infrared Spectroscopic Automobile Paint Data Base," *Crime Lab. Dig.,* 22 (1995): 92.

74. J. L. Buckle, D. A. MacDougall, and R. R. Grant, "PDQ—Paint Data Queries: The History Behind the Royal Canadian Mounted Police Forensic Laboratory Services Automotive Paint Database," *Can. Soc. Forensic Sci. J.,* 30 (1997): 199–212.

75. J. W. Wilkinson, J. Locke, and D. L. Laing, "The Examination of Paints as Thin Sections Using Visible Microspectrophotometry and Fourier Transform Infrared Microscopy," *Forensic Sci. Int.,* 38 (1988): 43–52.

76. J. A. Reffner, "Molecular Microspectral Mapping with the FT-IR Microscope," *Inst. Phys. Conf. Ser. No 98,* (1990): 559–69.

77. J. Zieba-Palus, "Application of Transmittance and Reflectance FT-IR Microscopy to Examination of Paints Transferred onto Fabrics," *Mikrochim. Acta [Suppl.],* 14 (1997): 361–62.

78. J. Zieba-Palus, "The Use of Micro Fourier-Transform Infrared Spectroscopy and Scanning Electron Microscopy with X-ray Microanalysis for the Identification of Automobile Paint Chips," *Mikrochim. Acta [Suppl.],* 14 (1997): 357–59.

79. J. Zieba-Palus, "Selected Cases of Forensic Paint Analysis," *Science & Justice,* 39 (1999): 123–27.

80. J. Nieznanska and J. Zieba-Palus, "Physico-Chemical Study of Car Paints Coats," *Z. Zagadnien Nauk Sadowych, z.* 34, (1999): 77–94.

81. F. Govaert, G. de Roy, B. Decruyenaere, and D. Ziernicki, "Analysis of Black Spray Paints by Fourier Transform Infrared Spectro-metry, X-ray Fluorescence and Visible Microscopy," *Prob. Forensic Sci.,* XLVII (2001): 333–39.

82. F. Govaert and M. Bernard, "Discriminating Red Spray Paints by Optical Microscopy, Fourier Transform Infrared Spectroscopy and X-ray Fluorescence," *Forensic Sci. Int.,* 140 (2004): 61–71.

83. S. E. I. Bell, L. A. Fido, S. J. Speers, "Forensic Analysis of Architectural Finishes Using Fourier Transform

Infrared and Raman Spectroscopy. Part I: The Resin Bases," *Appl. Spectrosc.*, 59 (2005): 1333–39.

84. S. E. I. Bell, L. A. Fido, S. J. Speers, "Forensic Analysis of Architectural Finishes Using Fourier Transform Infrared and Raman Spectroscopy. Part II: White Paint," *Appl. Spectrosc.*, 59 (2005): 1340–46.

85. J. Zieba-Palus and R. Borusiewicz, "Examination of Multilayer Paint Coats by the Use of Infrared, Raman and XRF Spectroscopy for Forensic Purposes," *J. Molec. Struct.*, 792–93 (2006): 286–92.

86. R. D. Blackledge, "Examination of Automobile Rubber Bumper Guards by Attenuated Total Reflectance Spectroscopy Using a Fourier Transform Infrared Spectrometer," *J. Forensic Sci.*, 26 (1981): 554–56.

87. A. E. Parybyk and H. J. Kobus, "The Characterization of Plastic Automobile Bumper Bars Using Fourier Transform Infrared Spectroscopy (FTIR), Pyrolysis Gas Chromatography (PGC), and Energy Dispersive X-ray Microanalysis Combined with a Scanning Electron Microscope (SEM-EDX)," *J. Forensic Sci.*, 35 (1990): 281–92.

88. G. V. Pavilova, G. S. Bezhanishvili, A. Kh. Kuptsov, and G. P. Voskerchian, "Automotive Rubber Microparticle Examination by FT-IR, ESR and PGC Methods," presented at the *12th Meeting of the International Association of Forensic Sciences*, Adelaide, S. Australia, Oct. 24–29, 1990, unpublished.

89. E. G. Bartick and R. A. Merrill, "Forensic Analysis of Black Plastic Tapes," presented at the *Pittsburgh Conference and Exposition*, New Orleans, Feb. 22–25, 1988, unpublished.

90. R. Merrill and E. G. Bartick, "Analysis of Pressure Sensitive Adhesive Tape I: Evaluation of Infrared ATR Accessory Advances," *J. Forensic Sci.*, 45 (2000): 93–98.

91. J. Zieba-Palus and M. Kunicki, "Application of the Micro-FTIR Spectroscopy, Raman Spectroscopy and XRF Method Examination of Inks," *Forensic Sci. Int.*, 158 (2006): 164–72.

92. J. Andrasko, "Microreflectance FTIR Techniques Applied to Materials Encountered in Forensic Examination of Documents," *J. Forensic Sci.*, 41 (1996): 812–23.

93. C. L. Gilmour, "A Comparison of Laser Printed and Photocopied Documents. Can They Be Distinguished?" *Can. Soc. Forens. Sci. J.*, 27 (1994): 245–59.

94. R. A. Merrill, E. G. Bartick, and W. D. Mazzella, "Studies of Techniques for Analysis of Photocopy Toners by IR," *J. Forensic Sci.*, 41 (1996): 264–71.

95. B. M. Trzcinska and Z. Bozek-Much, "The Possibilities of Identifying Photocopy Toners by Means of Infrared Spectroscopy (FT-IR) and Scanning Microscopy (SEM-EDX)," *Mikrochim. Acta [Suppl.]*, 14 (1997): 235–37.

96. R. A. Merrill, E. G. Bartick, and J. H. Taylor III, "Forensic Discrimination of Photocopy and Printer Toners. I. The Development of an Infrared Spectral Library," *Anal. Bioanal. Chem.*, 376 (2003), 1272–78.

97. W. J. Egan, S. L. Morgan, E. G. Bartick, R. A. Merrill, and J. H. Taylor III, "Forensic Discrimination of Photocopy and Printer Toners. II. Discriminant Analysis Applied to Infrared Reflection-Absorption Spectroscopy," *Anal. Bioanal. Chem.*, 376 (2003): 1279–85.

98. B. M. Trzcinska, "Analytical Differentiation of Black Powder Toners of Similar Polymer Composition for Criminalistic Purposes," *Chem. Anal (Warsaw)*, 51 (2006): 147–57.

99. M. A. Harthcock, L. A. Lentz, B. L. Davis, and K. Krishnan, "Applications of Transmittance and Reflectance Micro/FT-IR to Polymeric Materials," *Appl. Spectrosc.*, 40 (1986): 210–14.

100. M. A. Harthcock, "Applications of Recent Developments in Fourier

Transform Infrared Spectroscopic Microsampling Techniques to Polymeric Materials," in *The Design, Sample Handling, and Applications of Infrared Microscopes, ASTM STP 949*, ed. P. B. Roush (Philadelphia: American Society of Testing and Materials, 1987): 84–96.

101. J. A. Reffner, J. P. Coates, and R. G. Messerschmidt, "Chemical Microscopy with FTIR Microspectroscopy," *Am. Lab.* (April 1987): 86–97.

102. E. M. Suzuki, "Fourier Transform Infrared Analysis of Some Particulate Drug Mixtures Using a Diamond Anvil Cell with a Beam Condenser and an Infrared Microscope," *J. Forensic Sci.*, 37 (1992): 467–87.

103. M. Hida and T. Mitsui, "Rapid Identification of Lysergic Acid Diethylamide in Blotter Paper by Microscope FT-IR," *Analyt. Sci.*, 15 (1999): 289–291

104. J. A. Tomlinson, J. B. Crowe, N. Ranieri, J. P. Kindig, and S. F. Platek, "Supermarket Tampering: Cocaine Detected in Syringes and in Fruit," *J. Forensic Sci.*, 46 (2001): 144–46.

105. K. S. Kalasinsky, "Drug Distribution in Human Hair by Infrared Microscopy," *Cell. Molec. Bio.*, 44 (1998): 81–87.

106. K. S. Kalasinsky, J. Magluilo, Jr., and T. Schaefer, "Hair Analysis by Infrared Microscopy for Drugs of Abuse," *Forensic Sci. Int.*, 63 (1993): 253–60.

107. K. S. Kalasinsky, J. Magluilo, Jr., and T. Schaefer, "Study of Drug Distribution in Hair by Infrared Microscopy Visualization," *J. Analyt. Tox.*, 18 (1994): 337–41.

108. F. Tagliaro, F. P. Smith, Z. De Battisti, G. Manetto, and M. Marigo, "Hair Analysis—A Novel Tool in Forensic and Biomedical Sciences: New Chromatographic and Electrophoretic/Electrokinetic Analytical Strategies," *J. Chromatog. B.*, 689, (1997): 261–71.

109. B. H. Briese and J. Kijewski, "Fourier Transform Infrared Microscopy Analysis of Human Hairs after Cosmetic Treatment and Other Influences with Reference to Medico-Legal Aspects," *Rom. J. Leg. Med.*, 8 (2000): 117–27.

110. J. L. Clement and A. Le Pareux, "Identifying Traces of Smokeless Powder by Infrared Microspectrophotometry," *Int. Crim. Police Rev.*, 38, no. 375 (1984): 34–41.

111. A. Miller, "FTIR Analysis of Explosives Residues," Master's thesis (University of Virginia, 1988).

112. E. G. Bartick and R. A. Merrill, "Analysis of Plastic Bonded Explosives II: Bulk Analysis by Infrared Internal Reflection Spectroscopy," in *Proc. Internatl. Symp. Forensic Asp. Trace Evid.* (Washington, DC: U. S. Government Printing Office, 1993): 277–79.

113. M. R. Derrick, D. Stulik, and J. M. Landry, "Infrared Spectroscopy in Conservation Science," (Los Angeles: Getty Conservation Institute, 1999).

114. M. V. Orna, P. L. Lang, J. E. Katon, T. F. Mathews, and R. S. Nelson, "Applications of Infrared Microspectroscopy to Art Historical Questions Regarding Medieval Manuscripts," in *Archaelogical Chemistry—IV*, ed. R. Allen (Washington, DC: American Chemical Society, 1989): 265–88.

115. J. A. Reffner, "Mineral Analysis by FT-IR Microscopy," *Microbeam Analysis—1988*, ed. D. E. Newbury (San Francisco: San Francisco Press, Inc., 1988), pp. 227–29.

116. C. P. Schultz, "Precision Infrared Spectroscopic Imaging: The Future of FT-IR Spectroscopy," *Spectroscopy*, 16 (October 2001): 24–33.

117. R. Bhargava and I. W. Levin, "Recent Developments in Fourier Transform Infrared (FTIR) Microspectroscopic Methods for Biomedical Analysis: From Single-Point Detection to Two Dimensional Imaging," *Biomedical Photonics Handbook*, ed. T. Vo-Dinh, (New York: CRC Press, 2003): 32–1-32–15.

118. E.G. Bartick, and R. Schwartz, "Spectral Imaging of Latent Fingerprints," FACSS, Nashville, Sept. 2000.

119. D. K. Williams, R. L. Schwartz, and E. G. Bartick, "Analysis of Latent Fingerprint Deposits by Infrared Microspectroscopy," *Appl. Spectrosc.,* 58 (2004): 313–16.

120. E. G. Bartick, R. Schwartz, R. Bhargava, M. Schaeberle, D. Fernandez and I. Levin, "Spectrochemical Analysis and Hyperspectral Imaging of Fingerprints," *Proc. 16th Meet. Internatl. Assoc. Forensic Sci.,* Montpellier, France, Sept. 2–7, 2002; E. Baccino, ed., Bologna, Italy: Monduzzi Editore, IPD, (2002) pp. 61–64.

121. E. G. Bartick and R. Schwartz Perlman, "Noninvasive Latent Fingerprint Development and Chemical Identification of Trace Evidence within the Prints," *FBI Laboratory 2005 Report,* (Quantico, VA: Federal Bureau of Investigation, 2005) pp. 39–40.

122. M. Tahtouh, J. R. Kalman, C. Roux, C. Lennard, and B. Reedy, "The Detection and Enhancement of Latent Fingermarks Using Infrared Chemical Imaging," *J. Forensic Sci.,* 50 (2005): 54–72.

123. N. C. Crane, E. G. Bartick, R. Schwartz Perlman, and S. Huffman, "Infrared Spectroscopic Imaging for Noninvasive Detection of Latent Fingerprints," *Forensic Sci.,* 52 (2007): 48–53.

124. K. Flynn, R. O'Leary, C. Roux, and B. J. Reedy, "Forensic Analysis of Bicomponent Fibers Using Infrared Chemical Imaging," *J. Forensic Sci.,* 51 (2006): 586–96.

125. K. Flynn, R. O'Leary, C. Lennard, C. Roux, and B. J. Reedy, "Forensic Applications of Infrared Chemical Imaging: Multi-Layered Paint Chips," *J. Forensic Sci.,* 50 (2005): 832–41.

126. A. Ricci, K. L. A. Chan, and S. G. Kazarian, "Combining the Tape-Lift Method and Fourier Transform Infrared Spectroscopic Imaging for Forensic Applications," *Appl. Spectrosc.,* 60 (2006): 1013–21.

5

■■■

Forensic
Pharmacology

David M. Benjamin, Ph.D.
Clinical Pharmacologist and Toxicologist

Forensic pharmacology is a new expression for an old discipline, coined by forensic scientists in order to describe the application of the principles of pharmacology to the purposes of the law. *Black's Law Dictionary*[1] defines *forensic medicine* as, "That science which teaches the application of every branch of medical knowledge to the purposes of the law," and goes on to state that, "Anatomy, physiology, medicine, surgery, chemistry, physics, and botany lend their aid as necessity arises; and in some cases all these branches of science are required to enable a court of law to arrive at a proper conclusion on a contested question affecting life or property."

In developing the definition of forensic medicine, the editor of *Black's Law Dictionary* must have had the field of pharmacology in mind, because pharmacology, more than any other medical science, relies on the methods and teachings of the other biological and natural sciences in order to exist. Although the science of pharmacology is chiefly concerned with the action of drugs on living systems, its scope ranges from the study of the molecular interaction of drugs with cellular receptors, to the effects of environmental pollutants on entire populations. Because the body of information pharmacologists wish to study is so extensive, few individuals can be trained to work equally well in all areas—therefore, specialization is essential. In general, pharmacology may be thought of as being composed of nine major areas of specialization: clinical pharmacology, molecular pharmacology, biochemical pharmacology, neuropharmacology, cardiovascular pharmacology, chemotherapy, behavioral pharmacology, toxicology, and endocrine pharmacology. All of these subspecialties are interdependent, relying heavily on one another for new methodologies and innovative approaches to the study of drug actions and toxicities. However, with respect to the impact that these disciplines have on humankind, they all find their common denominator in clinical pharmacology.

Clinical pharmacology, as its name implies, is concerned primarily with the study of drugs in humans. This body of knowledge on the actions of drugs, the doses required to produce these effects, their corresponding blood levels, and the toxicities associated with drug administration to patients and healthy individuals alike constitutes the type of information courts and juries rely on in order to resolve legal issues.

BASIC PRINCIPLES OF PHARMACOLOGY

Pharmacology can be defined concisely as the study of drugs. What, then, is a drug? A *drug* is a chemical that affects, or causes a response in, a living organism. Drugs can exist in any physical state—solid, liquid, or gas—and can gain access to the bloodstream following oral ingestion, injection, inhalation, percutaneous absorption, or by application to any of the mucous membranes of the mouth, nose, vagina, or rectum—to name some of the more common routes.

Drug effects can be beneficial (therapeutic) or undesirably toxic. Forensic scientists are frequently faced with the situation of having to analyze body fluids for the presence and concentration of drugs that have caused an adverse reaction or death in an individual, and then are asked (sometimes under oath) to try to relate the presence of the drug to the toxic manifestations observed in the person from whom the sample was obtained.

In order to be able to form such an opinion, the forensic scientist should be familiar with both the pharmacokinetics and the pharmacodynamics of a drug, as well as any correlation(s) between the two. The pharmacokinetics of a drug mathematically define the movement of the drug into and out of the body and can be described as occurring in four different but concurrent stages: *absorption, distribution, metabolism,* and *excretion*—or *ADME,* as they are frequently referred to in jargon. As a result of these four simultaneous processes, a dynamic equilibrium is established in the body and all four processes operate in concert until all the drug has been excreted. When a drug is absorbed into the blood, it is subsequently metabolized to another compound called a *metabolite.* As the concentration of the metabolite increases, it, too, establishes its own dynamic equilibrium separate from that of the "parent" drug from which it was synthesized, and is handled by the body as a completely different drug with pharmacokinetic and pharmacodynamic properties of its own. The dynamic equilibrium of absorption, distribution, metabolism, and excretion is depicted schematically in Figure 5-1.

Figure 5-1 illustrates how drugs travel between different pharmacokinetic "compartments" in the body and serves as an introduction to another tool of pharmacokinetics called *compartmental analysis.* In Figure 5-1, the circulating blood is usually referred to as the *central compartment* and the other tissues of the body represent *peripheral compartments.* When a blood sample is analyzed for its drug concentration, the analyst is measuring the concentration of the drug in the central compartment. Therefore, in the case of a drug whose site of action resides in some peripheral compartment (e.g., narcotics work in the brain, not in the blood), the blood level cannot tell you what the concentration of drug is in the tissue compartment where the drug actually exerts its pharmacologic effect(s). In order for blood level analyses to reflect the activity of the drug accurately, there must be a good correlation among

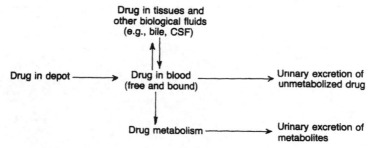

FIGURE 5-1 The dynamics of absorption, distribution, metabolism and excretion in compartmental analysis.

the drug concentration in the central compartment; the drug concentration in the peripheral compartment, where the drug interacts with its receptors; and the expression of the activity of the drug as indicated by the individual's response.

The pharmacokinetics of many common drugs can be described by a model in which the drug is assumed to be distributed to a single peripheral compartment from the central compartment and, after interacting with its receptor, the drug returns to the central compartment for metabolism and excretion. This particular pharmacokinetic model is called a *two-compartment open model*: *two-compartment* because there are two compartments, one central and one peripheral; and *open* because there is elimination (excretion) as opposed to a closed situation, such as in renal failure.

When a drug that follows a two-compartment open model is administered intravenously to a subject, a graph of the plasma concentration on the Y-axis plotted against time on the X-axis looks like the example shown in Figure 5-2.

In Figure 5-2, if we assume that the site of action of the drug is located in the peripheral compartment, then the drug will not begin to exert its pharmacodynamic activity until the concentration of the drug in the peripheral compartment reaches a pharmacologic level, despite declining levels in the blood (i.e., the central compartment).

Furthermore, if monitoring of blood levels of the parent drug is to be effective in determining a therapeutic or toxic level of the drug and thus permit the physician to modify or titrate the dosage according to the response, then there must be a good correlation between the distribution of the drug from the central compartment, where the blood sample comes from, to the peripheral compartment, where the drug actually exerts its effects.

The two-compartment open model can be expressed mathematically by the following formula:

$$P = Ae^{-\alpha t} + Be^{-\beta t} \tag{5-1}$$

where

P = plasma concentration

t = time

α = the distribution rate constant

β = the elimination rate constant

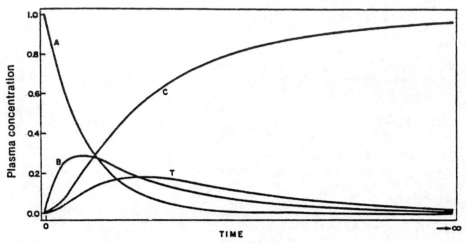

FIGURE 5-2 Disposition of parent drug and metabolite in plasma, tissue, and urine. Curve A represents the blood level–time profile of a typical drug whose pharmacokinetics can be described by a two-compartment open model. In this example, the drug has been administered intravenously (IV). Note that because of the IV route of administration, the blood level of the drug starts out at infinity (curve A) and declines rapidly during the distribution phase. As the injected drug is metabolized, the appearance of the parent drug's principal metabolite in blood can be seen in curve B. The principal metabolite begins to accumulate in plasma, and its elimination from the central compartment and appearance in urine can be seen in curve C, which represents a cumulative urinary excretion pattern for the metabolite. As the processes of distribution continue, the appearance of the parent drug in the tissues or peripheral (second) compartment can be seen in curve T. (*Source:* Reprinted from *Biopharmaceutics and Pharmacokinetics: An Introduction* by R. E. Notari, pp. 114, 1971, by courtesy of Marcel Dekker, Inc., New York, NY.)

and A and B represent the Y-intercepts when α and β are extrapolated to zero. The use of this formula to define the pharmacokinetics of a drug whose pharmacokinetics follow a two-compartment open model can be seen in Figure 5-3. Note that unlike Figure 5-2, this curve begins at zero (rather than at infinity) because this plot represents oral rather than intravenous (IV) administration. With oral administration, the rate of rise of the curve from zero to the *point of maximum concentration* (C_{max}) is representative of the rate of absorption of the drug from the GI tract into the bloodstream (central compartment). Parenteral administration by the intramuscular (IM) and subcutaneous (SC) routes produce a similarly shaped curve; however, the absorption rates from parenteral administration should generally be more rapid than following oral administration, with the exception of benzodiazepines like diazepam (Valium®), which appear to be absorbed more rapidly following oral administration than IM.

Inspection of Figure 5-3 reveals that as absorption proceeds and the drug in the central compartment is distributed to peripheral sites, the peak or maximum plasma concentration, C_{max}, is ultimately reached. The time at which the C_{max} is achieved is called the *time of maximum concentration* (T_{max}). Following the attainment of C_{max}, drug absorption from either the GI tract or the parenteral injection site is generally

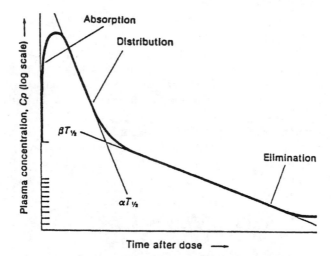

FIGURE 5-3 Graph of two-compartment open pharmacokinetic model for orally administered drug. C_p = plasma concentration, t = time, α = the distribution rate constant, β = the elimination rate constant. (*Source:* Reprinted by permission of the publisher from *Medical Toxicology, Diagnosis and Treatment of Human Poisoning,* by M. J. Eilenhorn and D. G. Barcela, p. 105, copyright 1981 by Elsevier Science Publishing Co., Inc.)

considered to be complete and the drug is now said to be in the post-absorptive stage. At this point, the first downward slope of the curve provides the *distribution half-life,* or the rate of the rapid distribution of the drug into most vascular tissues. The second downward slope of the curve provides the *elimination half-life* ($T_{\frac{1}{2};}$), which represents the speed at which the body rids itself of the drug.

If one determines the area under the curve by integration, one obtains an indication of the bioavailability of the administered dosage form. Because absorption from the GI tract may not be complete for all oral dosage forms, two dosage forms (e.g., tablet vs. capsule, tablet vs. solution) could contain the same amount of drug yet have very dissimilar bioavailabilities. Clinically, this type of problem may arise when an individual is switched from a brand-name product to a generic one, or when a more bioavailable formulation such as a solution is substituted for a tablet.

As pharmacokinetics has matured, many other useful calculations have been derived in order to improve the scientist's ability to describe drug movement in the body. The *apparent volume of distribution* (V_d) of a drug is an indicator of the extent to which a drug is distributed in the body. The calculation of V_d does not correspond to any true physiologic compartment in the body, but does provide an indicator of the distribution properties of the drug. The V_d can be calculated most easily by administering a fixed dose of a drug, say 100 mg, to a subject. Following complete absorption, a blood sample is obtained and the drug concentration determined. For this example, assume that the plasma drug concentration (C_p) is 20 mg/1. The V_d would be calculated as follows:

$$V_d = \frac{\text{Amount of drug administered}}{\text{Plasma concentration}} = \frac{\text{Dose}}{C_p} = \frac{100 \text{ mg}}{20 \text{ mg/1}} = 5 \text{ liters} \quad \textbf{(5-2)}$$

Because the circulating blood volume of a typical 70-kg man is approximately 5 liters, the drug in the foregoing example is not highly distributed and is confined primarily to the central compartment. Some reasons for a low V_d could include a high degree of drug binding to plasma proteins, or a drug with a low lipophilicity or that exists chiefly in its ionized form at physiological pH and cannot pass through the lipid-soluble cell membranes (see the discussion of the Henderson–Hasselbalch equation under "Absorption").

A second common way to express V_d is to normalize the data for body weight. This can be done either by expressing the initial dose in milligrams per kilogram (mg/kg), or by dividing the V_d obtained in the foregoing by the subject's body weight. In the example, using 70 kg as the subject's weight, the V_d expressed in terms of body weight would be

$$V_d = \frac{5 \text{ liters}}{70 \text{ kg}} = 0.07 \text{ l/kg}$$

Another important concept in pharmacokinetics is clearance. Clinically, *clearance* is used to express renal function, with glomerular filtration rate (GFR) calculated clinically by determining creatinine clearance. However, clearance of a drug can be determined across any organ by utilizing the Fick principle which states that if you can measure the concentration of a substance in the blood supply to an organ (e.g., the renal artery), the concentration of a substance in the blood leaving the organ (e.g., the renal vein), and the amount of substance removed by the organ, you can calculate how much blood passed through the organ during a specific time interval. Therefore, clearance is always expressed in units of volume per time (e.g., ml/min, liters/hr) and represents a rate of blood or plasma flow through an organ, rather than an amount of substance "cleared." (For additional information, see the discussions under "Metabolism" and "Excretion.")

Absorption, Distribution, Metabolism, and Excretion

ABSORPTION   With the exception of drugs that are applied locally and exert their primary effects topically (e.g., antidandruff shampoos, sunscreens, local anesthetics, antibiotic creams), most drugs must reach the bloodstream before they can exert an effect. Even in the case of a locally applied drug such as a steroid cream, active drug may be absorbed through intact or abraded skin and produce systemic side effects. The initial site of application or administration of a drug represents a depot or reservoir where the drug resides until it has been disposed of by the body. Following oral administration, the gastrointestinal (GI) tract may be considered the reservoir. IM injection places a bolus of drug into a large muscle such as the deltoid, gluteus maximus, or vastis lateralis. For rapid IV injection, there is no depot; but for slow IV infusions, the IV bag serves as an extracorporeal reservoir.

During passive drug absorption, the rate of appearance of a drug in the bloodstream is proportional to the blood flow through the tissue depot and the surface area of drug exposed to the perfusing blood. These two factors alone explain why gases can produce an effect so quickly when inhaled into the lungs, as well as why topical application of most drugs to the skin has such a long latency period prior to producing systemic effects.

Absorption is the process by which a drug is made available to the fluids of distribution of the body. Thus, drugs must pass through a biological barrier or membrane in order to get from the depot into the systemic circulation. In the case of an oral dosage form, the barrier is the lining of the gastrointestinal tract, whereas the nasal mucosa and the lining of the respiratory tract, the skin, and the mucous membranes of the rectum serve as the barriers to absorption for drugs administered by inhalation, topical application, and suppository, respectively.

Because biological membranes are composed primarily of lipids, absorption is facilitated when drugs exist in a nonpolar lipophilic state; therefore, a drug's intrinsic physicochemical properties are critical in predicting its *bioavailability* (e.g., the rate and extent of its absorption). Because most drugs are either weak acids or weak bases, their lipophilicity is partially determined by each drug's *pKa* and the ambient pH of the surrounding milieu. This relationship is described by the equation for the dissociation of a weak acid HA, which dissociates in water to form H+ and A−. Applying the law of mass action,

$$Ka = \frac{[\text{H}+][\text{A}-]}{[\text{HA}]}$$

and rearranging the terms yields

$$[\text{H}+] = \frac{Ka[\text{HA}]}{[\text{A}-]}$$

where *Ka* is the dissociation constant of the acid, [H+] is the hydrogen ion concentration, and [A−] is the corresponding anion concentration. Taking the negative log of both sides of the equation provides the common form of the Henderson–Hasselbalch equation (5-3)

$$\text{pH} = pKa + \log\frac{[\text{A}-]}{[\text{HA}]} \text{ or } \frac{[Base]}{[Acid]} \text{ or } \frac{\text{Concentration ionized drug } (I)}{\text{Concentration un-ionized drug } (U)} \quad \textbf{(5-3)}$$

However, in the case of the absorption of a solid oral dosage form from the stomach or small intestines, a significant paradox exists. Before the drug in the tablet or capsule can be absorbed, the dosage form must first disintegrate and its active ingredient(s) dissolve. Because the fluids of the entire GI tract (excluding the bile) are aqueous in nature, lipophilic forms of drugs tend to be relatively insoluble in the fluids of the stomach or the small intestines. Therefore, a dynamic equilibrium is established that permits the aqueous form of a drug to dissolve in the intestinal juices and, as it goes into solution, a percentage is converted to the nonpolar form, which is available for absorption.

The ratio of polar (ionized) drug to nonpolar (un-ionized) drug can be calculated from the Henderson–Hasselbalch equation. (Note that when pH = *pK*, the ratio of *I/U* = 1 and each species of molecule is present at 50%). As drug is absorbed from the GI tract, the ratio of *I/U* shifts, providing more un-ionized drug molecules for absorption. Regardless of whether the absorption process takes place in the acid environment of the stomach (pH 1) or the environment of the small intestines (pH 6), the dynamics are the same.

Pharmaceutical scientists are well aware of the relationships described in the foregoing example; therefore, it is not uncommon for oral dosage forms to contain buffers, surfactants, or solubilizers that "promote" an insoluble drug's absorption. Moreover, solid oral dosage forms also frequently contain inert ingredients called *excipients* (e.g., talc, lactose) that may prolong a drug's stability or provide a better matrix for compressibility when the powdered drug mixture is compressed by the dies of the tableting machine.

DISTRIBUTION   Once a drug has been absorbed into the bloodstream, it is circulated, to some degree, to all areas of the body to which there is blood flow. This is the process of distribution. Because nature has already provided the greatest amount of blood flow to the brain, heart, heart, liver, and other vital organs, these organs tend to take up and accumulate drugs more readily than other less-vascular organs. Striated muscle also receives a large percentage of blood flow, especially when the muscle is doing work. Therefore, redistribution of drugs from the general circulation to the large muscle groups is another way certain drugs, such as thiopental, are inactivated without undergoing actual metabolism. This explains why it may be necessary to determine the amount of drug present in various tissues such as liver, muscle, fat, and cerebrospinal fluid (CSF) in addition to blood in order to estimate the *total body load* of drug.

Among the constituents of blood are a variety of plasma proteins. Albumin makes up about 55% of plasma proteins; alpha- and beta-globulins represent approximately 27%; gamma globulins approximately 11%; and fibrinogen 6% to 7%.[2] Most drugs are bound, to some extent, to one or more of these plasma proteins. As drugs enter the systemic circulation, they become bound to the appropriate species of protein. The remainder of the drug is left in the unbound or free state and is available to act on target tissues and exert a pharmacologic effect. As free drug is taken up by various tissues or organs, bound drug dissociates from its carrying sites on proteins and is liberated into the plasma, thus establishing a dynamic equilibrium between bound and free drug. Because only unbound (free) drug is able to interact with receptors (located on target tissues) to produce a pharmacologic effect, the percentage of drug bound to plasma proteins is an important factor to consider during drug distribution.

Some drugs, such as the coumarin class of orally administered anticoagulants (e.g., Warfarin®), are approximately 98% bound to plasma proteins. This leaves only 2% of the absorbed dose free to exert its anticoagulant activity. If a second drug also bound to the same sites on the protein molecule is administered to a patient receiving Warfarin®, the second drug may displace the anticoagulant from its protein binding sites, thus increasing the concentration of free drug in the plasma and greatly enhancing the anticoagulant effect. This drug interaction can precipitate a hemorrhage or make it quite difficult to stop the bleeding from even a minor break in the skin, such as when the patient uses a razor to shave. Because only 2% of the drug is actually producing a pharmacologic effect, an increase of only 1% free drug is tantamount to increasing the anticoagulant activity by 50% (i.e., from 2% to 3% equals a 50% increase). Because of the importance of the amount of free drug available to exert pharmacologic activity, patients with low plasma albumin levels, as a result of insufficient synthesis (i.e., in liver disease) or to loss of protein in the urine (proteinuria) because of renal disease are frequently more sensitive to the effects of drugs than patients with normal hepatic and renal function.

METABOLISM   Circulating drug molecules must be inactivated and excreted from the body. This process is usually initiated by altering the chemical structure of the drug molecule in such a way as to promote its excretion. The biotransformation of a drug to a chemically related compound that is generally more easily excreted from the body is called *metabolism*. The original drug is frequently called the *parent compound*, and the product of the chemical conversion is the *metabolite*.

Drug metabolism is most often carried out by the microsomal enzymes of the liver, although metabolism can also occur during transmural GI absorption or in the kidney, the lungs, or other peripheral sites. Drug metabolism in the liver usually proceeds in two stages or phases. The phase I type of reaction involves conversion of the drug molecule to a molecule with a *reactive handle,* and includes, among others, oxidation to –OH, N–, and O– demethylation, and sulfoxidation, which permit the intermediate metabolites to form more polar ether or ester conjugates with sulfate or glucuronic acid, or, less frequently, N-substituted glycine or acetyl derivatives during the phase II reaction. These metabolites are more water soluble than the parent compounds and are more easily excreted in urine than the more lipophilic compounds from which they were derived.

Some drug metabolizing enzymes can be induced or inhibited by other drugs. These types of drug interactions can dramatically alter the half-life of many drugs and cause clinically significant increases or decreases in a drug's activity, which can lead to toxicity via an exaggerated pharmacodynamic response or an insufficient therapeutic effect.

Drug metabolism has also been called *detoxification* because, in general, the metabolite is less active than the parent compound. However, some drugs must be metabolized to an active form before they can act. These drugs are called *prodrugs* because they are actually precursors of the active drug. An example of a prodrug is azathioprine (Imuran®), which, after metabolism in the body, liberates 6-mercaptopurine, the active immunosuppressive agent. Also, it is not uncommon for metabolites to possess greater toxicities than their corresponding parent drug. For example, the antiarrhythmic agent procainamide is metabolized to the compound N-acetyl procainamide (NAPA) which can produce a lupus-like reaction in some patients; and meperidine (Demerol®) is demethylated to normeperidine, which is about 50% as active as an analgesic but possesses central nervous system (CNS)–stimulating properties that can cause tremors and convulsions in patients who have accumulated high plasma concentrations of normeperidine following extended treatment with meperidine, or have some degree of renal failure. However, regardless of the activity of the metabolite, the one feature all metabolites seem to share is that they are more water soluble than their corresponding parent. This water solubility is nature's way of facilitating the elimination of the metabolites in the urine.

The major organ of drug metabolism is the liver. As drug molecules enter the liver, special cellular components containing enzymes convert drugs to their metabolites, and primary metabolites are converted to secondary metabolites. Metabolism can also occur in the gut wall during absorption, in the lungs, the kidneys, and other body sites. Drugs that undergo extensive uptake and metabolism during transmural GI absorption or during their first pass through the liver are said to be subject to a *first-pass effect* that significantly reduces the quantity of drug available to exert activity when the drug is administered for the first time. Sometimes these types of drugs are described as having a *high hepatic clearance,* which is just another way of saying that the drug is extensively "cleared" from the plasma as it passes through the liver, until the liver enzymes become saturated during subsequent dosing.

Once the water-soluble metabolite is formed, it is released into the systemic circulation. Metabolites are also bound to plasma proteins in an analogous manner as was described for parent compounds. In some instances, accumulated metabolites can compete for binding sites on plasma proteins normally occupied by the parent compound, thus causing displacement of the parent compound from protein binding sites. Other metabolites undergo additional changes in chemical configuration as they pass through the liver; more often, metabolites are conjugated with glucuronic acid or sulfate anions, thus becoming even more polar and water soluble. The formation of a water-soluble metabolite is the first step in the process of excretion, which occurs primarily during the formation of urine by the kidneys.

EXCRETION *Excretion* is the process by which a drug is eliminated from the body. Drugs and metabolites can be excreted in most body secretions, including saliva, sweat, tears, bile (a major route for some drugs that are concentrated in the bile), mother's milk, expired air, fecal material, hair, and urine. Because individuals form between 1,500 to 2,500 ml of urine per day, the urinary route is generally of the greatest importance.

Drugs and metabolites enter the kidney via the renal artery. As the blood is forced through the basement membrane of the glomerulus, blood cells and proteins are filtered out, leaving the plasma and its solutes to form the filtrate. As the filtrate continues through the tubules of the kidney, water, sodium, and glucose are reabsorbed into the circulation. However, the water-soluble metabolites remain dissolved in the filtrate and become concentrated in urine as water is reabsorbed. As blood leaves the kidney through the renal vein, it has been cleared of many drug molecules. The urine formed during filtration contains the metabolites and other salts that escaped reabsorption by the kidney.

Clearance is expressed as a rate of flow in milliliters per minute (ml/min) or liters per hour (l/hr), and generally refers to a hypothetical volume of solution that would have to pass through a certain organ in order to permit the determined quantity of drug to have been extracted from the solution by the organ. Experimentally, this can be determined by intravenously injecting a nonmetabolized and nonreabsorbed substance such as the sugar inulin into a volunteer. The clearance of this compound is equal to the ratio of the urinary concentration to the plasma concentration multiplied by the rate of urine formation. The formula is

$$\text{Renal Clearance} = \frac{\text{Urinary concentration}}{\text{Plasma concentration}} \times \text{Rate of urine formation (ml/min)}$$

Regardless of the units of concentration, they cancel out in the equation, and what is left is a rate of flow.

In normal, healthy people, renal clearance is approximately 130 ml/min. Drugs with renal clearances less than 130 are reabsorbed during urine formation, and drugs with renal clearances greater than 130 are actively secreted into urine. Glucose is an example of a compound that is actively reabsorbed by the kidney, and penicillin is an example of a drug that is actively secreted into urine. Because penicillin is actively secreted, it is commonly administered with the drug probenecid, which competes with penicillin renal secretion and greatly prolongs the duration of time the penicillin stays in the body.

Drugs found in the feces were either not absorbed from the more proximal portions of the GI tract or entered the intestines via the bile. Demeclocycline (Declomycin®), a tetracycline, is concentrated by the liver in the bile, and high concentrations are found in the feces. For patients with impaired renal function, the administration of drugs that are significantly excreted in the bile may provide a safer alternative by reducing the likelihood of drug accumulation and toxicity.

When equal doses of the same drug are given orally and intravenously, and the oral formulation is completely absorbed, a plot of the blood level of the drug versus time looks like the graph shown in Figure 5-4. When new dosage forms of a drug are

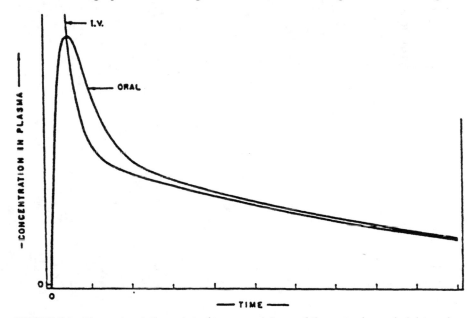

FIGURE 5-4 Plasma level–time plot of two equal doses of the same drug administered orally and intravenously (IV). (*Source:* Reprinted from *Biopharmaceutics and Pharmacokinetics: An Introduction* by R. E. Notari, p. 165, 1971, by courtesy of Marcel Dekker, Inc., New York, NY.)

developed, they are frequently compared to a standard consisting of the same dose of drug administered either intravenously or as an oral aqueous solution in order to determine the bioavailability of the new formulation. If the areas under the blood level–time curves (AUCs) are the same, then the oral formulation is equally available to act within the body as the reference dose. If the IV and oral formulations are metabolized differently, or if the oral dose is subject to a first-pass effect as it passes through the gut wall, then this is apparent from differences in the AUC graphs. Because many oral dosage forms are not absorbed completely, drug effects following oral administration are caused only by the fraction of the dose (FD) that actually arrives in the systemic circulation.

The duration of a drug's effect is proportional to the length of time the drug remains in the body. Because absorption, distribution, metabolism, and excretion all occur contemporaneously, the rate constant that is commonly used to describe the persistence of a drug in the body is half-life ($T_{1/2}$). *Half-life* is defined as the amount of time required to eliminate half of the drug from the body. Naturally, half-life can be determined only after a dose of drug has been absorbed completely into the systemic circulation, in the so-called *post-absorptive phase* of a drug's pharmacokinetic disposition. Once a drug is in the post-absorptive phase, a plot of the log of the blood concentration versus time transforms the logarithmic elimination portion of the curve into a straight line with a slope equal to the half-life. This relationship is shown in Figure 5-5.

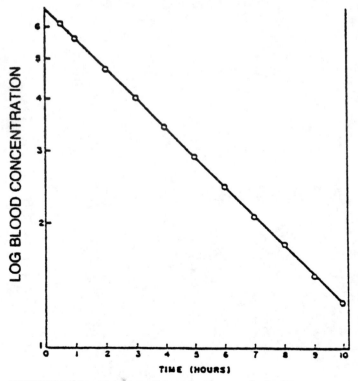

FIGURE 5-5 Semi-log plot of blood level versus time. (*Source:* Reprinted from *Biopharmaceutics and Pharmacokinetics: An Introduction* by R. E. Notari, p. 144, 1971, by courtesy of Marcel Dekker, Inc., New York, NY.)

The half-life of the drug depicted in Figure 5-5 can be determined by observing that the concentration at 1 hour is 6 units. The question you must now ask is, "After how many hours will the concentration be one-half what it is at 1 hour?" Inspection of the graph reveals that the blood concentration falls to 3 units at the fifth hour; thus, 4 hours were required in order to reduce the blood concentration to one-half its peak level. Note that because of the linearity of the relationship, the time required to reduce the blood concentration from 4 units to 2 units is also 4 hours.

Certain drugs are metabolized by a saturable enzyme system. Therefore, when the plasma concentration of the drug exceeds the metabolic capacity of the enzyme, the enzyme becomes saturated and the half-life of the drug increases. Experimentally, this is observed as a increase in the slope of the elimination phase of the drug's pharmacokinetic profile.

Drug Action and Pharmacodynamics

One of the most fascinating things about drugs is that although they are taken in such small quantities, they produce such dramatic effects. For example, a few micrograms of LSD, a few milligrams of cocaine, or a few grams of alcohol taken into the body and dissolved in approximately 5 liters of blood and distributed throughout another 35 to 40 liters of body water produces effects that are perceived by humans within minutes. This phenomenon is produced through what pharmacologists call *receptors,* which are highly specific and specialized areas of target organs activated by a drug molecule. Receptors are frequently located on the target organ's cell membrane and are composed of complex macromolecules. When the drug comes in contact with the receptor, the drug combines with or binds to the receptor. Activation of the receptor causes a cell, tissue, or organ to respond in its prescribed manner. For example, drugs that stimulate receptors on muscle cells cause those cells to contract. The more cells that are stimulated, the more the muscle contracts until it reaches its position of maximal contraction. Drugs that stimulate receptors on glands cause that gland to secrete a substance. In the case of a sweat gland, perspiration is produced, but if the pancreas is stimulated, insulin is released into the bloodstream or amylase is secreted into the GI tract.

Drugs that bind to a receptor and produce a response are called *agonists.* An agonist has affinity for a receptor and produces a response. Drugs that bind to a receptor but do not produce an effect are called antagonists. Antagonists can block or reverse the effects of agonists. For example, an individual who has overdosed on a narcotic can be saved from respiratory failure by an injection of the narcotic antagonist naloxone (Narcan®).

Most drugs act either by enhancing or inhibiting a natural biochemical or physiologic process in the body. Vital functions such as temperature, heart rate, blood pressure, and respiration as well as most functions in the body are under the control of several body systems, some stimulatory and others inhibitory. In this manner, the body can regulate the activity of these systems via feedback mechanisms designed to maintain homeostasis. Therefore, if there is not a specific antagonist to a specific drug (which is the usual case), there is probably a drug that can stimulate an opposing or antagonistic natural body system, the effect of which is to reverse or minimize the action of the first drug. For example, in a man who has ingested an unknown drug that has caused his heart rate to accelerate greatly, use of a beta-blocker or a calcium-channel blocker slows the heart rate.

DOSE–RESPONSE RELATIONSHIPS How does a physician know what dose of a drug to prescribe? At what point is a safe effective dose exceeded and its therapeutic effects superseded by toxic side effects? These are questions that must be answered for all drugs before they can be used with any confidence to benefit humankind. The answers to these questions are determined by specially trained physicians and pharmacologists working in pharmaceutical companies and at large medical centers throughout the world. Starting with evaluations of drugs for toxicity and efficacy first in animals and finally in humans, the long process of drug evaluation begins.

Pharmacologists have known for years that a dose of drug that produces no effect in one animal (or one species) may have a beneficial effect in a second animal (or species) and a toxic effect in a third. The identical principle applies equally to humans. Some people act drunk after ingesting a single martini, whereas others appear sober after ingesting three or four. These observations have led scientists to the inevitable conclusion that some people (species) are more sensitive than others to the effects of certain drugs. Stated another way, each person (and each species) exhibits his or her own sensitivity to the effects of a specific drug (or class of drugs), so that there is a threshold or minimal dose of that drug that causes him or her to begin to exhibit pharmacologic effects characteristic of that drug. This sensitivity is genetically determined and, as such, is present even before birth. It then follows that all humankind represents a population of individuals who display a range of sensitivities to drug effects.

If we want to depict this information graphically, we can plot the range of sensitivities (in terms of dose) on the horizontal axis and the frequency of occurrence in the population on the vertical axis. The result is the bell-shaped curve shown in Figure 5-6.

The bell-shaped curve shown in Figure 5-6 is what statisticians refer to as a normal distribution. The vertical dotted line that divides the graph into two equal and symmetrical halves is called the *median*. The median dose (ED_{50}) is effective in 50%

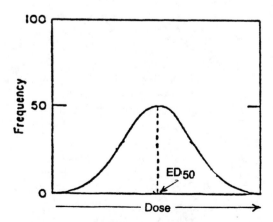

FIGURE 5-6 Normal Distribution of Responses To A Range of Doses.

of the population. Therefore, half of the population responds to a dose below the median and half of the population requires a dose above the median. This graph then represents the variance or range of sensitivities in the population to a fixed dose of drug.

During a drug's investigational phase, clinical pharmacologists conduct dose-ranging studies in human volunteers to determine the typical dose of a drug in order to provide practicing physicians with the data required to treat patients safely and effectively.

How does one go about determining the ED_{50} of a drug experimentally? In the laboratory, the best way is to assemble a group of animals and administer increasing doses of the test drug while measuring the response drug administration has produced. For example, to test a drug that lowers blood pressure, one selects a group of hypertensive animals. Then, after administering a fixed dose of drug to each animal, the animal's blood pressure is measured at an appropriate time. The next day, the dose is increased and the blood pressure measurements repeated at the same time. This procedure continues until enough data are obtained to plot what is known as a *dose–response curve*. This plot is shown in Figure 5-7.

When the dose is too low, there is no response (*A*). This is because the dose is below the threshold dose at which the response is initiated. As the dose is increased, the response begins very slowly (*A – B*), then more quickly (*B*). At this point, the curve begins to straighten and becomes linear. From *B* to *D*, the curve remains straight, as increasing the dose produces a proportional increase in response. As the dose approaches the point where response is almost maximal (*D*), the curve begins to bend again, finally reaching a point (*E*) where response is maximal and a further increase in dose produces no further increase in response. The ED_{50} (*C*) is located in the middle of the S curve and also in the middle of the linear portion of the curve.

When physicians prescribe a drug for a patient, they draw on all of their previous experience, the prescribing information supplied by the manufacturer, and the numerous reports they have read in medical journals in order to supply them with the information required to choose the proper dose of drug for the patient. The doctors begin with a dose that has been found to have been effective in most patients (much like the ED_{50}), then increase or decrease the dose according to the patient's response

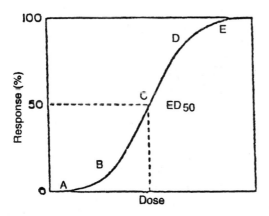

FIGURE 5-7 Dose-Response Curve.

or the emergence of side effects. This process of adjusting the dose of medication as a function of the patient's individualized response is called *titration*. Because doctors are familiar with the dose–response characteristics of each drug, they generally use doses that are found on the linear portion of the dose–response curve. Once the dose exceeds position D on the curve, further increases in dose provide very little additional benefit to the patient.

The previous discussion of dose–response relationships should not be interpreted to mean that titration occurs independently of side effects—this, of course, is not the case. Because all drugs exhibit a variety of effects, including toxicity, every time physicians prescribe a drug, they must consider the benefit-to-risk ratio inherent in the use of that drug. Because different drugs exhibit different relative toxicities, physicians must also be aware of the relationship between the incidence of side effects or death and increasing doses of drug.

The relationship between lethality (toxicity) and dose is determined experimentally in animals in an analogous manner as that described for the determination of dose–response relationships. However, in this series of experiments, several groups of animals are treated with doses of drug high enough to produce death in some percentage of the population. Once again, a dose–response curve is constructed; however, this time the endpoint is lethality rather than response. This type of plot is shown in Figure 5-8.

In Figure 5-8, the dose that causes death in 50% of the population is called *the median lethal dose*, or LD_{50}. The higher the LD_{50}, the safer the drug. Also, the larger the difference between the LD_{50} and the ED_{50}, the higher the benefit-to-risk ratio of the drug. Another indicator of the relative safety of a drug is the *therapeutic index (T.I.)*, which is obtained by dividing the LD_{50} by the ED_{50} according to the following equation:

$$T.I. = \frac{LD_{50}}{ED_{50}} \tag{5-5}$$

The higher the TI, the safer the drug.

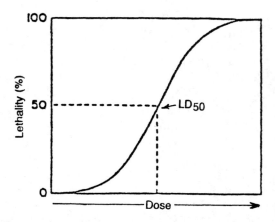

FIGURE 5-8 Determination of Lethality As A Function of Dose. The Median Lethal Dose (LD_{50}) is the dose which kills 50% of the population.

A final comment on the value of these indices of activity on efficacy and toxicity in humans is in order. In the laboratory, it is easy to determine either the ED_{50} or LD_{50} of a drug in animals. Experiments can be done on mice, rabbits, dogs, or monkeys and the drugs can be administered orally, intravenously, rectally, or by any other route that serves the scientist's purpose. However, the results differ depending on the conditions of the experiment. Thus the ED_{50} of a drug administered orally to dogs differs from the ED_{50} of the same drug administered intravenously to the same species of dog; and the LD_{50} of a drug administered intravenously to dogs differs from the LD_{50} of the same drug administered intravenously to monkeys, even when dosage is normalized for weight (i.e., a fixed number of milligrams administered per kilogram of body weight, mg/kg). Thus, when choosing an animal species for subsequent extrapolation of the results to humans, it is important to select an appropriate animal model. Innate differences between certain animal species and humans may not permit valid extrapolation of efficacy or toxicity data to humans. Therefore, results obtained from studies in animals are useful primarily as indicators of what may or may not be expected to occur in humans.

BLOOD LEVEL DATA: SIGNIFICANCE AND USE   Although the use of the therapeutic index and lethality data are very useful tools for determining the relative toxicity of drugs in animal species or by various routes of administration in the same animal species, lethality data cannot be obtained under controlled experimental conditions in humans, thus rendering the calculation of the therapeutic index in humans unattainable by classical methods. Instead, clinical scientists have attempted to determine correlations between a drug's therapeutic (pharmacologic) activity and its corresponding blood levels. This relationship has been referred to as the correlation between a drug's pharmacokinetics (blood level–time profile) and its pharmacodynamics (activity).

With the advent of newer analytical techniques for the quantitative determination of drugs in body fluids, virtually any drug can be identified and followed during its sojourn through the body. Once an assay for a particular drug has been developed, serial blood sampling just prior to the administration of the next dose (trough value) and at the time of maximum blood concentration (peak value) can provide important information on the range of blood concentrations associated with both therapeutic and toxic effects of a drug. An objective of such clinically oriented studies of correlations between a drug's blood levels and its effects is to define a drug's *therapeutic window* or the range of drug blood concentrations throughout which therapeutic activity is manifested without producing intolerable side effects. These principles are shown in Figure 5-9.

In general, blood levels of drugs below the lower limit of the therapeutic window (Figure 5-9, curve 3) are too low to produce therapeutic effects. Blood levels above the upper limit of the therapeutic window (Figure 5-9, curve 1) tend to produce intolerable side effects that most probably outweigh any beneficial effects. Ideally, both the peak and the trough blood levels should reside within the therapeutic window (Figure 5-9, curve 2). When the dose of drug that produces optimal blood levels has been determined, administration of this dose once every half-life produces

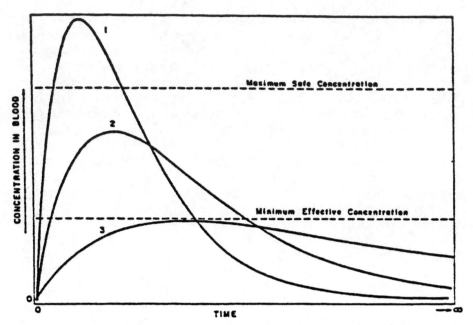

FIGURE 5-9   "Therapeutic Window" and Blood Levels. Curve 1—Peak Blood Levels are in Toxic Range. Curve 2—Peak Blood Levels are in Therapeutic Range. Curve 3—Peak Blood Levels are too low to be effective.   (*Source:* Reprinted from *Biopharmaceutics and Pharmacokinetics: An Introduction* by R. E. Notari, p. 119, 1971, by courtesy of Marcel Dekker, Inc., New York, NY.)

increasing blood levels for five half-lives and then attains steady state after the sixth dosage interval, at which time the amount of drug absorbed into the systemic circulation equals the amount excreted (Figure 5-10).

Unfortunately, all drugs do not show a good correlation between their blood levels and their activities. This is because measurement of blood levels is just that— the concentration in the blood, not the concentration of the drug at its site of action, where the receptors are located. For example, with antiarrhythmic drugs, blood levels are of assistance only in determining the effects on the heart if the concentration of the drug in the peripheral blood is in equilibrium with the concentration of drug in the tissues of the myocardium, where the drug actually acts. Blood levels of drugs that act in the brain on the CNS are of use to clinicians attempting to titrate their patient's dose of antidepressant or antiseizure medication only if peripheral blood levels provide a good indication of drug activity in the area of the brain where the drug acts.

To date, therapeutic and toxic blood concentrations have been determined for hundreds of commonly used drugs including antibiotics, antiarrhythmics, sedatives, hypnotics, narcotics, non-narcotic analgesics, antidepressants, alcohol, and many others. Information on dosage, blood levels, pharmacokinetic data, and effects and toxicity of most drugs can be found in the manufacturer's product labeling (i.e., the

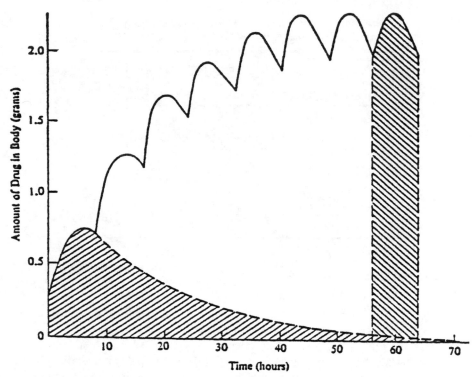

FIGURE 5-10 Steady-state blood levels are achieved when a drug is administered once per half-life for six doses (half-lives). (*Source:* Reprinted from *Clinical Pharmacology, Basic Principles in Therapeutics* by K. L. Melman and H. Morrelli, eds., p. 53, 1972, with permission of McGraw-Hill, Inc., New York, NY.)

package insert), in the *Physician's Desk Reference (PDR)*, in various pharmacology textbooks, or in the published literature.

Half-life and blood-level data can also be used to estimate the amount of time an analyte is likely to be detectable in blood. As body stores are depleted, the drug concentration in blood, plasma, and tissues are decreasing and the rate of appearance of parent drug and metabolites in urine are increasing at a decreasing rate. The elimination of drug from the body as a function of half-life is shown in Table 5-1.

As can be seen from Table 5-1, for a drug that follows *first-order elimination* (i.e., the amount of drug eliminated from the central compartment is proportional to the blood concentration of the drug), more drug is eliminated during the first half life (50% of the absorbed dose) than in subsequent half-lives. In contrast, ethyl alcohol is eliminated by zero-order kinetics (i.e., the amount of alcohol eliminated from the blood is independent of the blood-alcohol concentration). The *burnoff rate* of alcohol is quite variable and ranges from 10 to 60 mg/dl/hr, and is relatively constant over a large range of blood–alcohol concentrations. Depending on the dose(s) of drug ingested, the drug blood levels, the half-life of the parent drug and its metabolites, the

TABLE 5-1 Elimination of drug body stores as a function of drug half-life.

Elapsed Half-Lives	Percentage Body Stores or Total Body Load
0	100
1	50
2	25
3	<12
4	6
5	3
6	1.5
7	<1

amount of urine formed, urine pH, and the sensitivity of the assay procedure, one can estimate the duration of time throughout which the drug and its metabolites will be detectable in both blood and urine (Table 5-2). However, a confirmed positive urine or blood test for a drug indicates only prior exposure, but does not prove current or past impairment. The degree of impairment (i.e., drug effect) is variable and depends, in part, on the situation, tolerance level of the individual, whether the level is rising or falling, and the interaction of the drug with any other drugs to which the individual was exposed.

To function effectively as a forensic toxicologist, one must be familiar with the metabolism of heroin and morphine, cocaine, and marijuana (tetrahydrocannabinol, THC).

Heroin and Morphine

Heroin is also known as *diacetylmorphine*. The metabolism of heroin and morphine are shown in Figure 5-11.

6-Monoacetylmorphine can be found in urine for 2 to8 hours, and some demethylated morphine (normorphine) and morphine sulfates also appears in the urine. Morphine metabolites are secreted in bile and may be subject to enterohepatic recirculation.

```
        Occurs in blood                              Occurs in the liver
        T½ = 2–10 mins                               T½ = 10–15 mins
Heroin———————————>6-monoacetylmorphine (6-MAM)——————————-> morphine
        Occurs in the liver
        T½ = 2–8 hrs
Morphine ——————————->morphine-3-glucuronide and morphine-6-glucuronide.
```

FIGURE 5-11 Metabolism of Heroin and Morphine

TABLE 5-2 Summary of pharmacokinetic and detectability data for drugs of abuse

Substance	Dose (mg)	Route of Administration	Approximate Plasma Concentration	$T^{\frac{1}{2}}$ Range (hrs)	Detectable in Urine[a]
Amphetamine (racemic)	5	Oral	20 ng/ml	7–34	1–2 days
	30	Oral	<111 ng/ml		
d-Amphetamine	160	Intravenous	<590 ng/ml		
Methamphetamine (Desoxyn)	5	Oral	10–50 ng/ml		1–2 days
Barbiturates					
Amobarbital (Amytal)	120	Oral	<1.8 µg/ml	15–40	1–3 days
Butabarbital (Butisol)	200 mg/hr × 3	Oral	7.6–17 µg/ml	34–42	24–30 hr
Pentobarbital (Nembutal)	100	Oral	1–3 µg/ml	20–30	24–30 hr
Phenobarbital (Luminal)	30	Oral	0.7 µg/ml		Days to weeks
	200 mg/day	Oral	16–48 µg/ml		
Secobarbital (Seconal, Tuinal)	231	Oral	2 µg/ml	0.7–1.5	1–2 days
Cocaine	140	Intranasal	161 ng/ml		
	140	Oral	210 ng/ml (at 1 hr)		
	32	Intravenous	308 ng/ml (at 5 mins)		
Narcotics/Opioids[b]					
Morphine	8.75	Intravenous	440 ng/ml (at 30 sec)		2–4 days
	8.75	Intramuscular	70 ng/ml (10–20 min later)		
	7	Epidural	80 ng/ml (at 10 min)		
	20–30	Oral	20 ng/ml (for 4–6 hr)		
Codeine	15	Oral	>30 ng/ml	2–4	Hours to days
	60	Oral	>134 ng/ml		
	65	Intramuscular	195–340 ng/ml		
Heroin (diacetylmorphine)	5	Intravenous	35 ng/ml (at 25 min)	1–5[c]	2–4 days
Hydrocodone (Vicodin)	5	Oral	>11 ng/ml	3.8	Estimate: 12–24 hr
	10	Oral	>24 ng/ml		
Hydromorphone (Dilaudid)	4	Oral	18–22 ng/ml	1.5–3.8	Estimate: 12–24 hr
Levorphanol (Levo-Dromoran)	2	Intravenous	<8 ng/ml	11	Estimate: 1–2 days

Table continued on following page

327

TABLE 5-2 Summary of pharmacokinetic and detectability data for drugs of abuse (*continued*)

Substance	Dose (mg)	Route of Administration	Approximate Plasma Concentration	$T^{1/2}$ Range (hrs)	Detectable in Urine[a]
Meperidine (Demerol)	100	Oral	100–200 ng/ml	2–5	Estimate: 12–24 hr
	100	Intramuscular	160–360 ng/ml		
	50	Intravenous	520 ng/ml (mean level)		
Methadone (Dolophine)	15	Oral	<75 ng/ml[d]	15–55	Estimate: 2–6 days
	10	Intramuscular	34–96 ng/ml		
	10	Intravenous	<500 ng/ml		
Oxycodone (Percodan)	5	Oral	9–37 ng/ml	4–5	Estimate: 12–24 hr
Propoxyphene (Darvon)	65	Oral (as HCl salt)	40–50 ng/ml	6–24	See footnote [e]
Benzodiazepines					See footnote [f]
Alprazolam (Xanax)	0.5–3	Oral	7–40 ng/ml	10–12	
Chlordiazepoxide (Librium)	30	Oral	<1.6 µg/ml	6–27	
	50	Intramuscular	0.5–1.2 µg/ml		
Diazepam (Valium)	10	Oral	148 ng/ml	21–37	
	20	Intravenous	<1.6 µg/ml		
Flurazepam (Dalmane)[g]	15–30	Oral	0.5–4.0 ng/ml	2–3	
Lorazepam (Ativan)	2	Oral	15–25 ng/ml	9–16	
			382 ± 192 ng/ml (at steady state)		
Triazolam (Halcion)	0.25	Oral	2–4 ng/ml	1.5–5.5	
	0.50	Oral	1.7–9.4 ng/ml		
Ncn-Barbiturate, Non-Benzodiazepine Sedative Hypnotics					
Glutethimide (Doriden)	500	Oral	2.9–7.1 µg/ml (at 2 hr) 4–6 µg/ml (4-OH- glutethimide at 24 hr)	5–22	Hours to days
Methaqualone (Quaalude, Sopor)[i]	250	Oral (as HCl salt)	2–5 µg/ml (at 2 hr)	20–60	3–10 days

Hallucinogens

Drug	Dose	Route	Blood/plasma level	Half-life (hr)	Detection time in urine
Cannabinoids[j]	Grams	Smoked or eaten	10–100 ng/ml	20–57	
Occasional users					1–3 days
Use 2–3 times per week					Up to 3 weeks
Daily users					1–2 months
Lysergic acid diethylamide (LSD)	160 µg	Oral	9 ng/ml (within 5 hr)	3–4	30–72 hr
Mescaline, peyote	500	Oral	2–5 µg/ml	6	1–2 days
Phencyclidine (PCP, Angel Dust)[k]			1–240 ng/ml	7–55	At least 7 days

Abbreviations:

µg—microgram (1/1,000,000 of a gram)

mg—milligram (1/1,000 of a gram)

ng—nanogram (1/1,000,000,000 of a gram)

ml—milliliter (1/1,000 of a liter)

[a] Detection of drugs in urine is a function of the sensitivity of the assay used; the amount of urine produced; variability in drug metabolism and half-life; urine pH; fluid intake; and the dose, route, and frequency of drug administration. The values presented here are reasonable estimates only.

[b] The 3-OH group of morphine is phenolic and the 6-OH group is alcoholic, and both are acetylated in heroin. In humans, the 3-OH is de-acetylated rapidly in plasma ($T\frac{1}{2}$ = 40 min) to morphine. 6-MAM and morphine are the active agents through which heroin exerts its pharmacologic activity. Clinical studies have shown that heroin is about twice as potent as morphine on a milligram-for-milligram basis (i.e., 5 mg of heroin exerts the same narcotic effect as 10 mg of morphine). The reason heroin is twice as active as morphine and why it is so easy for heroin abusers to overdose on the drug is because heroin is distributed into the CNS much more rapidly than morphine. These structure–activity relationships (SAR) between morphine and heroin demonstrate how chemical modification of a prototype drug molecule can dramatically alter the pharmacologic activity of a drug by enhancing its lipophilicity, thereby speeding its distribution into the CNS (peripheral compartment, where its receptors are located and where it exerts its activity).

[c] Half-life for conversion of heroin to morphine.

[d] Chronic oral administration of 100–200 mg to tolerant subjects produced plasma levels of 0.57–1.06 µg/ml.

[e] Norpropoxyphene, the primary metabolite, may be detectable 1–3 days.

[f] Benzodiazepines, the shorter-acting triazolobenzodiazepines, like alprazolam and triazolam, and the metabolites of these drugs that have much longer half-lives can all be determine in urine for up to several days.

[g] Major metabolite: N-1-desalkylflurazepam.

[h] Glutethimide toxicity is a serious medical problem complicated by the formation of active metabolites like 4-OH-glutethimide, which accumulates in plasma as the parent drug is metabolized. Intoxicated patients may demonstrate decreasing signs of coma as parent drug levels decrease, only to develop greater CNS depression shortly thereafter, as active metabolites are formed.

[i] During the 1960s, methaqualone developed a reputation among drug users as a "love drug" or an aphrodisiac, and a large street market for the drug ensued. Unfortunately, when methaqualone is taken concomitantly with alcohol the CNS depressant activities of both drugs are markedly potentiated and serious toxicity may develop in individuals who were able to tolerate typical doses of either drug alone.

[j] Delta-9-tetrahydrocannabinol (THC), marijuana, pot, and hashish.

[k] Dose and route not specified.

Cocaine

Cocaine has a mean half-life of approximately 1 hour, plus or minus 15 minutes. Snorting approximately 100 mg of cocaine HCl produces blood levels of 100–200 ng/ml, a sufficient level to produce a pharmacologic effect including tachycardia and euphoria. Approximately 25% to 40% of ingested cocaine is metabolized to benzoylecgonine (BE) and approximately 18% to 22% is excreted as ecgonine methyl ester (EME). Only 1% of ingested cocaine is excreted as intact drug. The remainder of the ingested cocaine is excreted as norcocaine, ecgonine, and lesser known metabolites.[3]

The half-life of BE is approximately 7.5 hours and the half-life of EME is approximately 3.5 hours. Because most urine analyses for cocaine actually test for BE, BE may be found in the urine for up to 3 days. This stems from its half-life of 7.5 hours and the 10 half-lives it takes to eliminate BE from the blood, or to lower its concentration to below the level of sensitivity of the assay in use (usually at or below 50 ng/ml).[4]

Let's look at some potential scenarios involving the presence or absence of parent compound and metabolites in blood and urine, using cocaine as an example.

Scenario 1: Cocaine is present in blood at a level of 100–200 ng/ml. No BE is found in blood or urine.

Scenario 2: Cocaine is present in blood at a level of 100–200 ng/ml. BE is found in blood, but not in urine.

Scenario 3: Cocaine is present in blood at a level of 100–200 ng/ml. BE is found in blood and in urine.

Scenario 4: No cocaine is found in blood. BE is found in blood and urine.

Scenario 5: No cocaine is found in blood. No BE is found in blood. BE is found in urine.

What scientifically valid conclusions can be drawn in each of these scenarios regarding either impairment or time of cocaine ingestion?

Scenario 1: The presence of cocaine in the blood at a level of 100–200 ng/ml with the absence of BE in either the blood or urine indicates very recent use by any of several routes and a high likelihood of impairment at the time the blood sample was collected. The absence of BE in either blood or urine indicates that insufficient time has elapsed to permit metabolism of the cocaine to BE or that the BE is present at a concentration below the limit of detection (LOD) of the analytical procedure.

Scenario 2: The presence of cocaine in the blood at a level of 100–200 ng/ml with the presence of BE in the blood but not in the urine indicates relatively recent use and the likelihood of impairment at the time the blood sample was collected. The presence of BE in blood indicates that sufficient time elapsed to permit metabolism of the cocaine to BE, but insufficient time elapsed to permit excretion of the BE into urine, or that BE is present in urine at a concentration below the LOD of the analytical procedure.

Scenario 3: The presence of cocaine in the blood at a level of 100–200 ng/ml with the presence of BE in the blood and in the urine indicates either prior high dose use or continued or repeated use of cocaine. There is a reasonable probability of impairment at the time the blood sample was collected. The presence of BE in blood indicates that sufficient time elapsed to permit metabolism of the cocaine to BE, and the presence of BE in the urine indicates that sufficient time has passed for the BE to reach a urine concentration above the LOD or cutoff level of the analytical procedure.

Scenario 4: The absence of cocaine in the blood indicates that 6 to 10 hours have elapsed since cocaine was ingested. The presence of BE in blood and urine indicate that sufficient time elapsed to permit the cocaine to have been metabolized to BE and for the BE to have been excreted into urine. An individual with this blood/urine pattern is probably not impaired on cocaine, but may be in the depressive phase that often follows cocaine use.

Scenario 5: The absence of cocaine and BE in blood but the presence of BE in urine indicates that cocaine has not been ingested for approximately 48 to 75 hours. The lower the BE value in urine, the more time that has elapsed.

Another aspect of cocaine use causing major confusion in the federal criminal courts is the difference between "crack" cocaine, "free base," and cocaine HCl. During the 1980s, smoking crack cocaine replaced free basing as the most popular way to smoke cocaine. Part of this was because of the self-immolation of comedian Richard Pryor, who set himself on fire after extracting the free base of cocaine into ether, and then "firing up" his pipe while the ether fumes remained in the room. To avoid similar occurrences, cocaine smokers began eliminating the final extraction procedure and just converted the cocaine HCl into its free base form by "cooking it up" with sodium bicarbonate or another alkali like household ammonia that removed the proton from the quaternary nitrogen and produced a water-insoluble form of cocaine, which, when dried, volatilizes at a temperature of 90–98°C instead of decomposing at 195°C, which is what the HCl salt does. This type of free base became known as *crack,* named for the crackling sound it made when heated in a pipe. Because it could be made so easily and because our legislators believed that crack was more addictive and more dangerous than injecting cocaine HCl, because crack allegedly reached the brain more quickly and was therefore more likely to cause addiction, greater penalties were imposed.[5] A summary of published studies[6] indicates that this perception was false, and that the pharmacokinetics of single-dose self-administration of smoking 50 mg of crack and the intravenous injection of 32 mg of cocaine HCl were similar, with arterial levels being 10 times higher than venous concentrations with a T_{max} of 15 seconds on the arterial side compared to a T_{max} of 3–6 minutes in venous blood. On cumulative dosing, smoking produced greater subjective effects (i.e., euphoria) than IV administration. Both IV cocaine HCl and smoking cocaine base produces a more rapid and more intense effect than nasal insufflation.

However, because of the prevalence of crack throughout the United States, our legislators sought to deter drug abusers from using, distributing or trafficking crack by passing federal sentencing guidelines in 1986 (21 U.S.C. §841(a)(1)) that required first-time offenders in possession of 5 grams of crack to serve a mandatory minimum of five years in prison, while a first-time offender possessing a similar weight of cocaine HCl or free base serves only one year. However, in December of 2007 Kimbrough v US came down from the 4th circuit and set forth fairer sentencing guidelines that put "crack" cocaine and cocaine HCl on a more even level.

The differences in pharmacokinetics, pharmacodynamics, and physical and chemical properties among cocaine HCl, free base, and crack are shown in Table 5-3.

Marijuana (Tetrahydrocannabinol, THC)

The interpretation of urine tests for tetrahydrocannabinol (THC), and more specifically, the determination of whether an individual has been using marijuana recently or is still excreting body stores of the inactive THC metabolite, 11-nor-9-carboxy-tetrahydrocannabolic acid (THC-COOH) in the urine is a frequent question that must be addressed by forensic toxicologists. Although the active THC metabolite, 11-hydroxy-THC (11-OH-THC), may be found in blood for a short time after smoking, it is rarely found in the urine, but THC-COOH is retained in the body fat stores for long periods of time and can be quantitated in urine.

Issues involving the question of "When did this person last use marijuana?" frequently arise in violation of probation (VOP) hearings. Because THC-COOH is very lipophilic, in frequent marijuana users, THC-COOH can remain sequestered in fat stores for weeks or months and can redistribute back into plasma, falsely elevating plasma concentrations and subsequently providing the basis for a positive urine test.

One group of investigators developed two models, one based on the blood THC versus time plot that they claim predicts the elapsed time after THC use for infrequent smokers, and a second model based on the blood THC-COOH/THC ratio versus time for infrequent smokers.[8] However, results from such laboratory controlled studies differ greatly from patterns of random use in the population at large, and the use of these models to infer impairment has not yet gained general acceptance in the forensic toxicology or clinical pharmacology communities.

Urine drug test data, even those confirmed by GC/MS are only useful in estimating a "window of time" during which a specific drug may have been used. Urine drug test data cannot be used to infer impairment.[9,10]

In attempting to determine if a person has been smoking marijuana recently by screening urine for THC-COOH, because there is so much variability in the volume of urine produced in 24 hours from day to day, and from person to person, and the amount of THC-COOH redistributed from deep tissue stores into the blood and subsequently into urine, serial quantitative determinations do not always indicate a decreasing trend. Take the following example, initially presented in reference 10, pp.58–59.

Urine	Day 2	Day 4	Day 6
THC-COOH ng/ml	100	65	127

TABLE 5-3 Comparison of Pharmacokinetic, Pharmacodynamic, and Subjective Properties Among Cocaine Hydrochloride, Free-Base Cocaine, and Crack Cocaine

Route of Administration	Cocaine Hydrochloride Intravenous/Intranasal	Free-Base Cocaine Smoked	Crack Cocaine Smoked
Amount used (mg)	32 96	50	50
Free base equivalent (mg)	28.6 85.7	N/A	N/A
Bioavailability	100% ~58%	60–70%	60–70%
Time of arterial C_{max}	15 sec 15 sec	15 sec	
Time of venous C_{max}	3–6 min. 30–40 min	3–6 min	3–6 min
Peak arterial concentration (ng/ml)	1500–2000	1500–2000	1500–2000
Peak venous concentration (ng/ml)	~170 200	180	180
Time of maximum euphoria	(min) 15–40 min	min	min
Time of maximum euphoria	(min) 10–20 min	min	min
Volatile/sublimes on heating	No, decomposes	Yes	Yes
Melting point	195°C	90°C	90°C
Soluble in water	Yes	No	No
Soluble in ether	No	Yes	Yes
Characteristic metabolite(s)	BE, EME	Anhydroecgonine methyl ester (AEME), BE, EME, and other pyrolysis products[b]	
Characteristic excipients	Many	NaHCO$_3$ may be present	NaHCO$_3$ and impurities
Confirmed identification	GC/MS, IR	No	GC/MS, IR

[b]Until recently, the presence of AEME in the blood or urine of suspects was believed to indicate the prior smoking of cocaine base; however, a recent study[7] indicates that AEME can be formed as a pyrolysis artifact of the GC/MS analytical process for cocaine. Simultaneous analyses for derivatized cocaine and metabolites led investigators to conclude that AEME was formed by pyrolysis of cocaine metabolites at the CG injection port. Moreover, these same authors concluded that "Anhydroecgonine cannot be used as a marker for the abuse of cocaine by smoking because it is also pyrolytically produced from cocaine metabolites on the GC

Because we don't know how much water was consumed or how much urine was produced on the collection days, it is difficult to interpret these data with reasonable scientific certainty (the standard required by the law to distinguish speculation from a reliable opinion), knowing that such a report of recent use to the court is grounds to violate the subject's probation and send him or her back to prison.

However, if the concentration of THC-COOH in urine (ng/ml) is normalized for the creatinine concentration in urine (mg/ml), the data provide greater insight.

Following are the urine creatinine concentrations:

Urine	Day 2	Day 4	Day 6
Creatinine (mg/dl)	120	83	181
Creatinine (mg/ml)	1.2	0.83	1.81

Following are the THC-COOH/Creatinine ratios

	Day 2	Day 4	Day 6
THC-COOH (ng/ml)	100	65	127
Creatinine (mg/dl)	1.2	0.83	1.81

Does this pattern indicate that the subject smoked marijuana on day 5 or 6?

	Day 2	Day 4	Day 6
ng THC-COOH / mg Creatinine	83	78	70

By normalizing the THC-COOH excretion for creatinine excretion, a clear pattern of decreasing THC-COOH excretion per milligram of creatinine is apparent.

Once again, we see that an improper interpretation of the data could easily occur by an untrained expert, and an innocent person could be sent back to prison based on arbitrary and capricious conclusions offered by pseudo-experts who claim to be pharmacologists or toxicologists.[11] Many clinical pharmacologists and forensic toxicologists are of the opinion that the communities are moving toward a time when all urine drug concentrations will be expressed in terms of urinary creatinine excretion.

OTHER FACTORS THAT MUST BE CONSIDERED IN THE INTERPRETATION OF DRUG BLOOD LEVELS

Post-Mortem Redistribution and Sampling Site Issues

Analysis of blood and tissue samples for forensic testing frequently involves obtaining the samples from dead subjects, and sometimes embalmed or buried cadavers that have been exhumed. Before even addressing the reliability of quantitative post-mortem blood concentrations, one must also address the question of whether there are differences in results depending on the post-mortem site of sampling.

Post-mortem redistribution (PMR) is a phenomenon that frequently affects the blood levels of drugs with a large volume of distribution (V_d), causing drug molecules that were sequestered in peripheral tissue sites or vascular organs to redistribute back into the blood after death. PMR usually occurs during the first 24 hours after death, and does so as a result of two major mechanisms: movement of blood from one organ to another through a connecting artery, and redistribution of drugs with high volumes of distribution from peripheral tissue stores back into the central compartment. For example after death, organ-to-organ drug-rich blood from the lungs can drain back into the right ventricle through the pulmonary artery, or drug-rich blood leaving the liver through the hepatic portal vein can be shunted into the inferior vena cava and produce elevated drug levels in blood samples collected from the right atrium.[12] Thus a blood sample labeled *Cardiac Blood* could have been obtained from the cardiac atria or ventricles, and represent not ante-mortem blood levels, but blood levels that were in the lung (pulmonary artery) or the liver (inferior vena cava) just before death.

With regard to the second mechanism involved in post-mortem redistribution, studies in animals[13] and humans[14] involving the post-mortem redistribution of the tricyclic antidepressant amitriptyline have indicated up to ten-fold differences between heart blood and peripheral (femoral) blood. Many other widely distributed drugs that are taken up and bound in peripheral tissue sites are subject to post-mortem redistribution. Post-mortem changes that occur in the body that give rise to PMR include tissue autolysis, changes in pH, ionic strength, and a loss of electrical membrane potential and inhibition of energy-dependent binding processes in peripheral tissues.[15] This leads to diffusion of drug into interstitial fluid, through the capillaries and into larger blood vessels.

The lesson to take away from all of this is that it is not a simple procedure to interpret post-mortem drug levels that have undergone PMR, and attempts at doing so are frequently confounded by submission of blood samples from unspecified sites, the mixing of blood from several sites, and sometimes the submission of blood obtained from small samples found in the abdominal or thoracic cavity. These illegitimate samples cannot be considered reliable, and any drug levels reported from analysis of such samples may bear little resemblance to ante-mortem peripheral blood levels. One author asks the Society of Forensic Toxicologists (SOFT) to "design a standard reporting form" and cautions pathologists to "refuse to interpret results when they come from mystery samples."[16]

Although blood samples taken from the femoral vein are generally considered to provide the most reliable site of sampling for post-mortem drug analysis, there is no guarantee that even such samples are reliable. After death, blood from the inferior vena cava can diffuse into the groin, and large quadriceps muscles rich in drug can release sequestered drug, which can diffuse through vessel walls, artificially elevating femoral blood drug levels. An excellent review of the mechanisms of post-mortem distribution can be found in an article by Pélissier-Alicot et al.[17]

Sample Stability

When blood samples are obtained in an emergency room or hospital, health-care professionals follow accepted practices to ensure aseptic handling of the patient and the vacutainer or syringe used to draw the blood sample. However, many forensic samples are taken from trauma patients and dead bodies, and the potential for bacterial contamination is significant. In addition, there is no standardization of anticoagulant or preservative use in collecting and preserving forensic blood samples. Sometimes whole blood is used for an analysis; sometimes serum is used. Many drugs have different partitioning properties between whole blood and serum. It is important to identify the specimen that was analyzed (e.g., serum vs. whole blood) and interpret quantitative data in relation to their relative concentrations in serum and whole blood.

One group of researchers studied the stability of 46 drugs in post-mortem femoral blood stored for one year at –20°C,[18] Drugs included benzodiazepines, antidepressants, analgesics, and hypnotics. Five substances showed a decrease: ethanol, desmethylmianserin, 7-amino-nitrazepam, THC, and zopiclone; two substances showed an increase: ketobemidone and thioridazine. The effect of potassium fluoride on the stability of the same array of drugs in vitreous humor was also evaluated. Only ethanol and zopiclone showed a significantly lower concentration in the non-fluoridated samples. The authors concluded that the use of a preservative and storage at –20°C was adequate to prevent degradation of most drugs. Addition of 1%–2% sodium fluoride is recommended to prevent bacterial growth.[19]

ETHANOL ABSORPTION, DISTRIBUTION, METABOLISM, AND EXCRETION

Ethanol is subject to the same four pharmacokinetic processes in the body that every drug undergoes: absorption, distribution, metabolism and excretion (see Figure 5-4).

First, ethanol is absorbed from both the stomach and then more quickly from the small intestines. As it is absorbed, ethanol is distributed to all the water-containing tissues in the body according to the degree of vascularization of each tissue. The more vascular the organ and the greater the organ is perfused with blood, the faster the ethanol reaches the tissue or organ. This is why the brain takes up ethanol so readily—high perfusion leads to rapid accumulation.

Absorption

The rate of the absorption of ethanol and its subsequent appearance in the blood[19] depends on the following factors:

1. The rate of consumption (chugging vs. sipping).
2. The concentration or proof of ethanol in the beverage: (e.g., beer = ~4.2%–5.5%; wine = ~12%; vodkas = 40% or 50%; whiskeys = 43%; schnapps = variable percentages, look at the bottle).
3. The volume consumed (e.g., a 1.25- to 1.5-oz. shot vs. a 12-oz. beer vs. 4 oz. of wine).
4. The presence or absence of carbonation (i.e., the ethanol from champagne or sparkling wine is absorbed more quickly than uncarbonated white wine, and the ethanol from scotch and soda is absorbed more quickly than the ethanol from scotch and water).
5. The presence or absence of food in this the stomach. The presence of food in the stomach delays the absorption of ethanol by the increasing the amount of time it takes for the ethanol to move from the stomach to the small intestines, where ethanol is absorbed at its fastest rate. This phenomenon is known as *gastric emptying time,* and can also be influenced by drugs that affect GI motility.

As a rule of thumb, an individual, drinking a 12-ounce beer over 15–20 minutes on an empty stomach achieves a peak blood ethanol concentration within 30 minutes after starting the beer.[20] With food in the stomach, the same person drinking the same 12-ounce beer over the same 15–20 minutes on a full stomach achieves a lower peak blood ethanol concentration approximately 60–90 minutes after starting the beer. This is because the food absorbs some of the ethanol and slows down the gastrointestinal transit (movement) of the ethanol from the stomach to the small intestines.

Distribution

Once reaching the organ, ethanol diffuses from the blood into the organ by passive diffusion. Because ethanol is taken up only by organs with a high water content, the amount of fat on a person's body determines the extent of the tissue uptake, and that ethanol which does not diffuse into tissues and organs remains in the blood. For this reason, determining an individual's volume of distribution (V_d) or an individual's Widmark Distribution Factor, r, is important in calculating blood alcohol concentrations (BAC) by the Widmark formula.

When citizens are taken to the police station for breathalyzer testing, most jurisdictions require law enforcement to wait at least 15 minutes before initiating breathalyzer testing. This accomplishes three things: (1) It minimizes the likelihood that there will be any residual mouth alcohol present from the possible use of breath sprays, asthma inhalers, smokeless tobacco, medications, mouthwash, or any other alcohol-containing material the citizen may have used during the prior 15-minute interval; (2) it allows any belching or hiccoughing by the subject to be observed; and (3) it minimizes the likelihood that the subject is absorbing ethanol from his GI tract, which is known to produce a falsely elevated breathalyzer test because of the differences between venous and arterial blood–ethanol concentrations.

Metabolism

In the liver, ETOH is metabolized by the enzyme alcohol dehydrogenase (ADH) to acetaldehyde and acetaldehyde is metabolized by aldehyde dehydrogenase to acetic acid which re-enters the blood and is distributed to the kidneys for urinary excretion.

In addition to their lower body weights and higher fat-to-lean body masses, an absence of gastric mucosal alcohol dehydrogenase in women predisposes them to a greater sensitivity to ethanol than men. At higher blood-alcohol concentrations and extremely low ethanol concentrations (less than 0.01%), there is additional metabolism from the cytochrome P-450 2E1 (CYP 2E1) system, which used to be called the *microsomal enzyme oxidizing system (MEOS)*. CYP 2E1 is also inducible with repeated ethanol use or concomitant ingestion of certain anticonvulsant drugs like phenobarbital and phenytoin. This provides frequent ethanol users with a higher burn-off rate, and is the body's way of developing metabolic tolerance to ethanol by enhancing its rate of metabolism and excretion.

When large amounts of ethanol (i.e., several drinks or beers) are ingested, the metabolism of ethanol is generally said to follow *zero-order kinetics,* which means that a graph of the blood alcohol concentration (BAC) on the vertical axis and time on the horizontal produces a straight line with a negative slope that describes the burn-off rate (see Figure 5-12). With high BACs and very low BACs (<0.01%), ethanol elimination becomes first order and is now concentration dependent.

In people with normal liver function, large doses of acetaminophen deplete hepatic glutathione, leading to the formation of acetaminophen's hepatotoxic metabolite, *n*-acetyl-*p*-benzoquinone-imine (NAPQI).[21] In individuals who consume a large amount of ethanol each week or take prescription drugs that induce the CYP 2E1 enzyme, there is also an increase in the conversion of acetaminophen to its hepatotoxic metabolite, NAPQI. For this reason, it is a good idea for heavy ethanol users and

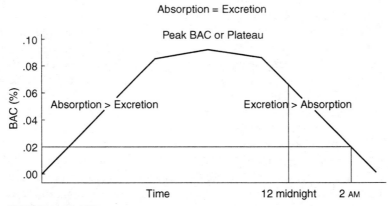

FIGURE 5-12 T/K

those taking phenobarbital and phenytoin to limit their intake of acetaminophen to less than 4–6 grams per day.

Excretion (Burn-Off Rate)

The combination of metabolism and excretion is frequently collectively referred to as the *burn-off rate.* There are major differences in the capacities of various individuals to metabolize ethanol.

Typical burn-off rates for ethanol generally are reported as 10 to 25 mg/dl/hr (0.010 to 0.025%/hr), with an arithmetic mean of 17 mg/dl/hr (0.017%/hr). However, studies have shown that those individuals who drink several times per week have higher average burn-off rates of almost 20 mg/dl/hr or higher.

Ethanol is also excreted in tears, sweat, urine, and expired air. For breath, the ratio of the amount of ethanol in 1 ml or blood to expired air is often cited as 1:2100 and is based on Henry's Law, which states that at 34°C, the amount of ethanol contained in 1 ml of blood is equal to the amount of ethanol contained in 2100 ml of deep lung air. Deep lung air, also called *alveolar air,* is the air in the deep portions of the lung in equilibrium with the blood, which is on the other side of the capillary membrane that lines the deep alveoli in the lungs.

INTERPRETING SERUM ETHANOL CONCENTRATIONS AND POST-MORTEM ETHANOL CONCENTRATIONS

Blood samples for forensic analysis of ethanol may be drawn from living subjects or cadavers. With post-mortem samples, special laboratory methods unavailable at a hospital or coroner's office are required in order to analyze for volatile organic chemicals (VOCs) such as methanol and 2-butanol that may have formed after death. This means that samples must be stored and shipped to remote locations. Whether in the freezer in the laboratory or en route to another location, sample stability and integrity are important. In a forensic case, quantitative results may end up in court, and the reliability of the result depends on the proper handling and storage of the sample.

Serum ethanol levels may be up to 18% higher than whole-blood ethanol values, depending on the subject's hematocrit and degree of hydration at the time of collection. Moreover, if a blood or serum sample has been collected from a decomposed body or stored without a preservative like sodium azide or sodium fluoride, post-mortem ethanol can be produced by bacterial metabolism of glucose. During decomposition, putrefaction products of proteins, amino acids, and fats can also serve as ethanol progenitors.[22]

When ethanol is found in the blood of a deceased automobile driver or a pilot involved in a fatal aircraft accident, determining if the ethanol present was because of ante-mortem ingestion or post-mortem production (either *in vivo* or *in vitro*) is an important issue in the forensic community. Two accepted methods for differentiating between ante- and post-mortem ethanol production involve testing for the presence of other volatiles like methanol, acetaldehyde, acetone, and 2-butanol, which indicate putrefaction and possible post-mortem formation of ethanol. Also, vitreous humor and bladder urine often remain free of bacteria, and generally do not undergo post-mortem ethanol production, so a negative test for ethanol in either vitreous humor (when the subject is deceased and the sample can be collected) or urine may indicate a lack of ante-mortem ethanol ingestion.[23]

Widmark Calculations

The Widmark formula is often used to calculate an individual's BAC based on their height, body weight, and the amount of ethanol they consumed over a specific time period. Widmark calculations begin with the calculation of how much ethanol was ingested, as shown next.

Calculating the Amount of Ethanol in a Beverage

Let's Start with a Beer

A 12-ounce can of Budweiser Light contains 4.2% ethanol volume to volume (v/v). Twelve ounces of beer × 0.042% = 0.50 fluid ounces of pure ethanol in the 12-ounce can or glass. However, if you want to convert a volume of ethanol in ounces to grams, you must multiply that number by 30, the approximate number of milliliters in a fluid ounce, and then multiply that number by the specific gravity (Sp. Gr.) of ethanol, 0.79, because ethanol weighs only 0.79 grams per milliliter. To complete the calculations, 0.5 fluid ounce of ethanol × ~30 ml/oz. = 15 ml × 0.79 = 11.85 grams. These calculations become part of the numerator in the Widmark Formula, presented next.

One Shot of Whiskey

Scotch or rye whiskey is 86 proof, or 43% ethanol. A 1.25-ounce shot of whiskey, either "neat" or mixed, contains a total of 1.25 × 0.43 = 0.54 fluid ounces of pure ethanol.

One Glass of Wine

Wine usually contains 12% ethanol (v/v). A glass of wine usually contains 4 fluid ounces. So, 4 oz. × 0.12 = 0.48 fluid ounces of ethanol in a 4-ounce glass of wine.

As you can see, a 12-ounce can of beer, a 4-ounce glass of wine, and a 1.25-ounce shot of whiskey all contain approximately the same amount of ethanol—one-half ounce.

Calculating an Individual's BAC from His or Her Height, Weight, and the Amount of Ethanol Consumed

To calculate an individual's BAC from the amount of ethanol he or she consumed, one can use the Widmark Formula, the generally accepted method in the forensic toxicology community.

$$BAC = \frac{(SpGr\ Blood)\ (grams\ of\ ETOH)\ (SpGr\ ETOH)}{(Body\ weight\ in\ kg)(Widmark\ r)}$$

$$-(burn\text{-}off\ rate \times number\ of\ hours\ elapsed)$$

$$r = Widmark\ distribution\ coefficient$$

Notice that the Widmark equation is the same as the volume of distribution equation (described earlier), which has been rearranged to solve for BAC instead of V_d,

$$V_d = \frac{\text{Amount of drug in body}}{\text{BAC}}$$

Problem: A 170-pound man consumes a 12-ounce Budweiser Light in 30 minutes, on an empty stomach. What is his BAC 30 minutes later?

Constants: SpGr of Blood = ~1.06; SpGr of ethanol = 0.79; 1 fluid ounce contains ~30 ml; 1 kg = 2.2 lbs.

Substituting into the Widmark equation:

$$\text{BAC} = \frac{(1.06)(0.5 \text{ oz of ETOH in a beer} \times 30)(0.79)}{(170 \text{ lbs.}/2.2 = 77.3 \text{ kg}) \text{ (Widmark } r \text{ for non-fat males} = 0.68)}$$

$$- \ 0.02\% \text{ per hr} \times 0.5 \text{ hr}$$

$$\text{BAC} = \frac{(1.06)(15g)(0.79)}{(77.3 \text{ kg})(0.68)} - 0.01$$

$$\text{BAC} = \frac{12.561g}{52.564 \text{ kg}} - 0.01 = \frac{0.24 \text{ g}}{\text{kg}}$$

However, percent (%) has the units grams per 100 milliliters, so we divide top and bottom by 10 by moving the decimal place one place to the left. So, 0.024 grams/100 ml less what was burnt off in 30 minutes (0.01), and the BAC becomes 0.024 – 0.010 = 0.014%.

This formula is very useful for answering hypothetical questions regarding an individual's BAC following the ingestion of a certain number of alcoholic drinks. All the toxicologist need do is develop a chronology from the depositions, bar receipts, and testimony of the fact witnesses as to how many of what type of drinks were ingested by the individual in question, select an absorption rate based on how much food the subject consumed, determine the ratio of the subject's height and weight so that the appropriate Widmark distribution factor (*r*) can be selected (average for men is 0.68; average for a woman is 0.55, because women have a higher percentage of fat in their bodies), and then select an appropriate burn-off rate (β), based on the individual's drinking habits [for light drinkers, use the Widmark mean of 0.017 (17 mg/dl/hr) or less; for frequent drinkers, use a faster burn-off rate of at least 0.020 (or 20/mg/dl/hr)].

TOLERANCE TO ETHANOL

Tolerance (to ethanol or any drug) is an adaptive response of the body that leads to a diminished response after repeated administration. There are many different types of tolerance, involving changes in a variety of physiological functions. Perhaps the easiest way to describe differences in tolerance is by the amount of time required for tolerance to develop (i.e., acutely vs. chronically).

For ethanol, acute tolerance (also referred to as the *Mellanby Effect*) occurs rapidly during the continuous consumption of several ethanol-containing drinks. Figure 5-12 demonstrates that during the absorptive phase, the BAC increases from

0% to 0.08%; then, after the plateau phase, the BAC descends from its peak and descends through 0.08% during the post-absorptive phase. The basic question is, "Is an individual equally impaired when the BAC is rising through 0.08% during the absorptive phase as he or she is when the BAC is descending through 0.08% in the post-absorptive phase?" The answer is that an individual is more impaired at a BAC of 0.08% during the absorptive phase than at a BAC of 0.08% during the post-absorptive phase. The reason for this is acute tolerance.

The mechanism of acute tolerance is most likely related to changes in sensitivity of the neurons in the CNS to ethanol. This may be referred to as *pharmacodynamic tolerance.* Another mechanism may involve a difference in the permeability of the membranes surrounding the neurons to ethanol because of changes in the composition of the membrane, some of which may be genetically determined.

It is important to appreciate that ethanol is always a CNS depressant. The reason people get "high" or euphoric on ethanol (or other CNS depressants) during the earlier stages of ethanol ingestion is because ethanol (and other CNS depressants) depresses inhibitory neurons preferentially before depressing stimulatory neurons. That is why people get up and dance, sing loudly, and act rowdy, because they lose their sense of inhibition and can then act without normal behavioral restraints that govern good conduct. After this initial phase of pseudo-stimulation, even without additional ethanol intake, people tend to become sleepy, lose their dexterity, and either fall asleep in the corner or, depending on the amount of ethanol ingested, exhibit a continuum of signs of intoxication such as slurred speech, loss of coordination, poor judgment, impaired sensation of pain, vomiting, lethargy, stupor, and general CNS depression up to and including depression of the medullary vasomotor and respiratory centers, which can be lethal and is classically described as occurring at BACs higher than 0.45% in individuals with no tolerance to ethanol.

In addition to the pharmacodynamic form of tolerance, there is also a type of metabolic tolerance and metabolic intolerance. *Metabolic tolerance* refers to the development of an increased rate of ethanol metabolism (elevated burn-off rate), higher than the classical range of 10–25 mg/dl/hr (or 0.10–0.25%/hr) described by Widmark. Two studies[24,25] reported mean burn-off rates of 19 mg/dl/hr for frequent drinkers, and a range of 13–36 mg/dl/hr with a mean of 22 mg/dl/hr for alcoholics undergoing detoxification.[26] Once again, this increased capacity to metabolize ethanol resides in the induction of the CYP 2E1 enzyme, whose presence or activity is auto-induced by repeated ethanol ingestion.[27]

However, an increased rate of metabolism is not sufficient to explain the survival of patients with reported serum ethanol concentrations of 650 mg/dl (BACs of 552 mg/dl) and 780 mg/dl (BACs of 663 mg/dl), and the granddaddy of all reports, serum ethanol of 1510 mg/dl (BAC of 1284 mg/dl).[28] A second brief report[29] summarized published reports of numerous other investigators who also reported 50–100 patients with blood or serum ethanol concentrations in the 300–500+ mg/dl range. Almost all of the patients were chronic heavy alcohol users, and as observation continued, motor coordination improved and EEG tracings became almost normal. The authors concluded that the great degree of tolerance observed was merely a reflection of a "normal CNS adaptive process."[29]

Frequent ethanol drinkers also can develop *learned tolerance* or *behavioral tolerance* which refers to the ability of an intoxicated person to develop coping skills sufficient to mask the effects of intoxication. Usually these coping skills are related to the masking of motor impairment, such as being able to walk a straight line when intoxicated, rather than the ability to compensate for cognitive decrements. It is called *learned tolerance* because it is acquired as people become accustomed to drinking large quantities of ethanol and spend a lot of their time with ethanol in their systems, thus requiring them to develop some degree of compensatory behavior in order to fool people at work or in the world at large that they are not impaired. In its simplest form, *behavioral tolerance* involves just taking greater care in performing certain tasks that require motor coordination. So, more attention is focused on walking, moving, talking, and performing simple actions. If a behaviorally tolerant individual continues to ingest ethanol, learned compensatory behavior is lost because the individual can no longer compensate for the CNS depressant effects of higher BACs. *Reverse tolerance,* or an increased sensitivity to ethanol, can also occur because of a slow metabolic (burn-off) rate, genetic factors, or the prior ingestion of chloral hydrate ("Mickey Finn" or "Knock-Out Drops"), which inhibits alcohol dehydrogenase.

THE ETHICAL DUTIES OF THE FORENSIC TOXICOLOGIST

In most forensic toxicology cases, someone has been injured or has died and drugs are highly suspected as the cause. Moreover, the ultimate facts of the case are going to be tried in a courtroom by members of the legal profession and decided by a group of jurors, all of whom, most likely, have no special training in forensic toxicology. This specific setting imposes two basic duties on the forensic toxicologist: (1) Use your learning, training and experience to determine whether the drugs in question caused or contributed to the injury or death that is the subject of the case, and (2) become an outstanding educator and communicator, and teach the jury what they must know in order to do their job. Under all circumstances, regardless of who retained you, the forensic toxicologist, or is paying for your time, you owe a duty both to science and the law.[30] Your duty to science is to use proper procedures, practices, and methods that are generally accepted as valid by the forensic community, and to know the limitations of your knowledge and training, and not to testify outside of your area(s) of expertise. Your duty to the law is to tell the truth. That means saying, "I don't know" when you do not. In one seminar, the Honorable William Young, Chief Judge of the U.S. District Court in the 1st Circuit in Boston, referred to the application of epistemology to science (i.e., the study of the limitations or validity of knowledge). Forensic scientists, lawyers, and judges all must be cognizant of what cannot be deduced as well as what can be said with "reasonable certainty."

Because lawyers have a duty only to their client and not to the experts they retain, in the courtroom, attorneys try to elicit testimony from witnesses that is favorable to their case. Accordingly, the testifying forensic expert must listen attentively to all questions and provide answers that preserve the truth, regardless of which side is asking the questions.

References

1. H.C. Black, *Black's Law Dictionary*, 5th ed. (Abridged), St. Paul: West Publishing Co., 1983), p. 332.

2. A. White, P. Handler, and E. Smith, eds., *Principles of Biochemistry*, 5th ed., (New York: McGraw-Hill), 1973, p. 804.

3. R.L. Hawks and C.N. Chiang, eds., "Urine Testing for Drugs of Abuse," *Natl. Inst. Drug Abuse Res. Mono.*, 73(1986): 93.

4. J. Ambre, "The Urinary Excretion of Cocaine and Metabolites in Humans: A Kinetic Analysis of Published Data," *J. Analyt. Tox.*, 9(1985): 241–45.

5. S. B. Karch, "Scientific Basis for Cocaine Sentencing Laws Questioned," *Forensic Drug Abuse Advis.*, 9(1987): 17–18.

6. D. K. Hatsukami and M. W. Fischman, "Crack Cocaine and Cocaine Hydrochloride—Are the Differences Myth or Reality?" *JAMA,* 276(1996): 1580–88.

7. P. S. Cardona, A. K. Chaturvedi, J. W. Soper, and D . Canfield, "Simultaneous Analyses of Cocaine, Cocaethylene, and Their Possible Metabolic and Pyrolytic Products," *Forensic Sci. Internat.*, 157(2006): 46–56.

8. E. J. Cone and M.A. Huestis, "Relating Blood Concentrations of Tetrahydrocannabinol and Metabolites to Pharmacologic Effects and Time of Marijuana Usage," *Ther. Drug Monit.*, 15(1993): 527–32.

9. American Society for Clinical Pharmacology and Therapeutics: "Clinical Pharmacologic Implications of Urine Screening for Illicit Substances of Abuse," *Scientific Consensus Conference: Published Consensus Statement* (1988): 2.

10. R.L. Hawks and C.N. Chiang, eds., "Urine Testing for Drugs of Abuse," *Natl. Inst. Drug Abuse Res. Mono.*, 73(1986): 80.

11. D. M. Benjamin, "Are Pharmacologists/ Toxicologists without Medical Degrees or MDs Best Qualified to Testify About Drugs?" *Proc. Am. Acad. Forensic Sci.*, (2001): 150–51.

12. S. B. Karch, MD, ed., *Drug Abuse Handbook,* (Boca Raton: CRC Press, 1998): p. 979.

13. T. Hilberg, A. Ripel, A. J. Smith, L. Slordal, J. Morland, and A. Bjorneboe, "Postmortem Amitriptyline Pharmacokinetics in Pigs after Oral and Intravenous Routes of Administration," *J. Forensic Sci.*, 43(1998): 380–87.

14. A. M. Langford and D. J. Pounder, "Possible Markers for Postmortem Drug Redistribution," *J. Forensic Sci.*, 42(1997): 88–92.

15. R. W. Prouty and W. H. Anderson, "The Forensic Science Implications of Site and Temporal Influences on Postmortem Blood–Drug Concentrations," *J. Forensic Sci.*, 35(1990): 243–70.

16. S. B. Karch, "Postmortem Drug Redistribution Dispute," *Forensic Drug Abuse Advis.*, 12(2000): 38.

17. A.-L. Pélissier-Alicot, J.-M. Gaulier, P. Champsaur, and P. Marquet, "Mechanisms Underlying Postmortem Redistribution of Drugs: A Review," *J. Analyt. Tox.*, 27(2003): 533–44.

18. P. Holmgren, H. Druid, A. Holmgren, and J. Ahlner, "Stability of Drugs in Stored Postmortem Femoral Blood and Vitreous Humor," *J. Forensic Sci.*, 49(2004): 820–25.

19. D. M. Benjamin, "Understanding the Pharmacology of Ethanol," in *Liquor Liability Update 2006—Dram Shop, Social Host and Employer Liability,* Massachusetts Continuing Legal Education, Boston: 2006.

    Parts of this publication on absorption, distribution, metabolism and excretion, including a modification of

Figure 5-12 have been reproduced from Section 5, pp.108–12, and attribution is provided pursuant to agreement with the publisher.

20. *Alcohol and the Impaired Driver,* Chicago: American Medical Association (1968) pp. 15–16.

21. M. Bogusz, M. Guminska, and J. Markiewicz, "Studies of the Formation of Endogenous Ethanol in Blood Putrefying *in Vitro*," *J. Forensic Med.,* 17(1970): 156–68.

22. M. J. Ellenhorn and D. G. Barceloux, *Medical Toxicology* (New York: Elsevier, 1988): pp. 157–58.

23. D. V. Canfield, T. Kupiec, and E. Huffine, "Postmortem Alcohol Production in Fatal Aircraft Accidents," *J. Forensic Sci.,* 38(1993): 914–17.

24. D. F. Brennan, S. Betzelos, R. Reed, and J. L. Falk, "Ethanol Elimination Rates in an ED Population," *Am. J. Emerg. Med.,* 13(1995): 276–80.

25. A. W. Jones and L. Anderson, "Influence of Age, Gender, and Blood-Alcohol Concentration on the Disappearance Rate of Alcohol from Blood in Drinking Drivers," *J. Forensic Sci.,* 41(1996): 922–26.

26. A. W. Jones and B. Sternebring, "Kinetics of Ethanol and Methanol in Alcoholics During Detoxification," *Alcohol and Alcoholism,* 27(1992): 647.

27. S. B. Karch, MD, ed., *Drug Abuse Handbook,* (Boca Raton: CRC Press, 1998): p. 343.

28. R. A. Johnson, E. C. Noll, and W. M. Rodney, "Survival after a Serum Ethanol Concentration of 1½%," *Lancet,* December 18 (1982): 1394.

29. A. R. Davis and A. H. Lipson, "Central Nervous System Depression and High Blood Ethanol Levels," *Lancet,* March 8 (1986): 566.

30. D. M. Benjamin, "Elements of Causation in Toxic Tort Litigation: Science and Law Must Agree," *J. Leg. Med.,* 14(1993): 153–65.

6

▪▪▪

Drug Interactions

Thomas C. Kupiec, Ph.D.
Toxicologist and Pharmaceutical Scientist

Vishnu Raj, BDS, MSFS
Forensic Research Analyst

INTRODUCTION

The use of prescription drugs has seen a drastic increase in recent years, partly as a result of an aging population as well as the development of newer and more effective drugs. In conjunction with this increase in prescription drug use, multidrug regimens have evolved and become common in therapeutic applications. Concomitant use of multiple drugs leads to an increased potential for drug interactions that are responsible for significant morbidity and mortality. A drug interaction occurs when one drug modifies the disposition or physiological effect exerted by another drug. The most common types of drug interactions are observed during coadministration of drugs that are metabolized by the same enzyme. Mechanisms of interaction include enzyme induction or inhibition, interaction at drug targets (e.g., receptors, transporters), and altered drug pharmacokinetics. Additive or synergistic effects may also occur when drugs with the same or similar mechanism of action are coadministered.

Prescription and recreational drugs are often used together because of the enhanced euphoric, hallucinogenic, or depressant properties of these combinations. In forensic toxicology, polydrug combinations are frequently observed and may complicate the interpretation of drug levels, and the effect of the individual drugs. Further clouding this issue is the possibility of interactions with food and nutraceuticals. Factors that should be considered in polydrug fatalities include drug pharmacokinetics, pharmacodynamics, pharmacogenomics, and drug–drug interactions. This chapter provides a succinct outline of the mechanisms of drug interactions with examples of frequently encountered drugs in forensic toxicology.

Drug Interactions

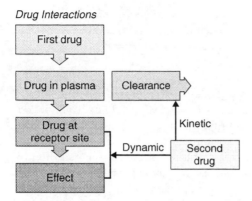

FIGURE 6-1 Types of drug interactions. (*Source:* Adapted from reference 1.)

TYPES OF DRUG INTERACTIONS

Drug interactions (Figure 6-1) may be classified into *pharmacokinetic* interactions, which affect drug concentrations; *pharmacodynamic* interactions, which affect the physiologic response to a drug; and *pharmacogenomic* interactions, which may influence both kinetics and dynamics. Pharmacokinetic interactions may influence drug response indirectly by altering drug concentrations and can occur at any stage (absorption, distribution, metabolism, and excretion). Pharmacodynamic interactions usually occur at the receptor level, and are contingent on the pharmacologic actions of individual drugs.

Stages of Pharmacokinetics

There are four stages of drug pharmacokinetics: absorption, distribution, metabolism, and excretion.

ABSORPTION *Absorption* refers to the uptake of a drug from the site of exposure (stomach, skin, eye, etc.) into systemic circulation. Absorption is primarily mediated via passive diffusion and specialized transport mechanisms. The rate of absorption is affected by the surface area and type of epithelial layer of the exposed site, and the degree of subepithelial circulation, the physiochemical properties of the drug (e.g. pKa, hydrophilicity, molecular weight) and the type of epithelial layer. Active transport mechanisms, which transport endogenous substances such as amino acids and glucose, are also able to transport structurally similar drugs. *Bioavailability*, a term often used to express the relative availability of a drug in the body, refers to the proportion of a given dose of drug that reaches blood plasma compared to the amount that reaches plasma following intravenous (IV) administration. Bioavailability is dependent on the route of administration and the drug's traits. Drugs that are highly hydrophilic or lipophilic have less bioavailability. Following oral administration, a drug may be incompletely absorbed due to lack of absorption from the gut or interference from food or other drugs. Some drugs undergo extensive first-pass metabolism prior to entering systemic circulation, and this leads to a substantial reduction in bioavailability. Drugs administered intravenously are almost completely absorbed.

DISTRIBUTION   Following absorption, drugs may distribute into vascular spaces and tissues as well as interstitial, intracellular, and extracellular fluids. Distribution to these areas is determined by lipid solubility, transmembrane pH gradient, and chemical properties of the drug. Lipid-soluble, non-ionized drugs can generally enter cells through simple diffusion based on concentration gradients, whereas highly ionized or hydrophilic drugs may require special membrane transporters such as albumin and α_1-acid glycoprotein. Albumin is a major carrier for acidic drugs such as salicylates, barbiturates, and penicillins. Basic drugs, such as warfarin, digoxin, and quinine, bind to α_1-acid glycoprotein. Protein binding is dependent on the functional groups present on the drug molecule and can have a significant effect on drug distribution. The fraction of total bound drug is determined by the drug serum concentration and the affinity and availability of binding sites for the drug.

Drug binding to plasma proteins continues until there is an equilibrium established between the bound and unbound fractions of a drug. That fraction of drug which is protein bound is unable to elicit a pharmacological effect. Some drugs are bound extensively (more than 99%), leaving less than 1% available in circulation to exert action. The administration of a second drug capable of displacing the bound drug may cause a dramatic increase in the serum concentration of the now unbound drug. For a highly bound drug, this displacement of 1%–2% could easily double the effective concentration, thereby leading to potentially significant adverse effects. One such example is the administration of chloral hydrate to a patient on warfarin therapy. Chloral hydrate is metabolized to trichloroacetic acid, which has a higher affinity for plasma proteins compared to warfarin, and therefore causes displacement of warfarin. This creates an increase in unbound warfarin, which leads to enhanced anticoagulant effects that can cause clinically significant morbidity and mortality.[2]

The *volume of distribution (V_d)*, an important determinant of drug activity, refers to the volume into which the total amount of drug in the body must be distributed uniformly to provide the concentration of drug actually measured in plasma or blood.[3] It is important to remember that V_d refers to an apparent volume only, and not a physiologically identifiable volume. Drugs with very high volumes of distribution have much higher concentrations in extravascular tissue than in the vascular compartment and are thus not distributed homogeneously. Drugs that are completely retained in intravascular compartments have a minimal volume of distribution equal to the volume of the vascular compartment.[4] A drug's volume of distribution therefore reflects the extent to which it is present in extravascular tissues, and not in the plasma.

METABOLISM   For most drugs, *metabolism* is integral for drug elimination as well as for the cessation of pharmacologic activity. The majority of drugs are hydrophobic, thus facilitating intracellular ingress through the lipid bilayers, where the drugs interact

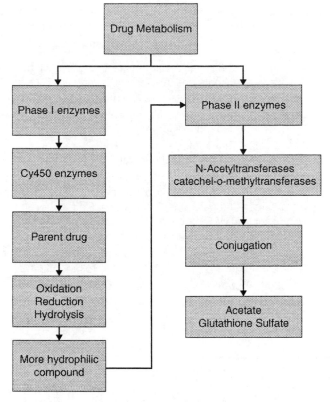

FIGURE 6-2 Stages of drug metabolism.

with their target receptors or proteins. Usually, drug metabolism creates a more water-soluble, ionized, and less pharmacologically active metabolite. However, some drugs (e.g., codeine) are pro-drugs, and their metabolism generates the active drug (e.g., codeine to morphine). Drug metabolism may be classified into phase I and phase II reactions (Figure 6-2).

Phase I reactions include oxidation, reduction, and hydrolysis, which render the drug more polar by introducing or exposing a functional group on the parent compound. The Cytochrome P450 (CYP) enzyme system, which represents a large family of enzymes, is responsible for the phase I metabolism of the majority of drugs. Table 6-1 provides an example of some common CYP enzymes and their substrates.

Phase II reactions usually involve drug conjugation to an endogenous substance, leading to the formation of a covalent linkage between a functional group on the parent compound and endogenously derived glucuronic acid, sulfate, glutathione, acetate, or methyl groups. These highly polar conjugates are generally inactive and are excreted rapidly in the urine. However, some drugs (e.g., morphine) may have metabolites with increased activity after initial phase II conjugation. Examples of phase II enzymes include glutathione-S-transferases (GST), UDP-glucuronosyltransferases (UGT),

TABLE 6-1 List of CYP enzymes and substrates.

CYP Enzyme	Drugs Metabolized
CYP1A2	Amitriptyline, Caffeine, Clomipramine, Clozapine, Erythromycin, Fluvoxamine, Haloperidol, Imipramine, Naproxen, Paracetamol, Propranolol, Theophylline, Verapamil, Warfarin
CYP2C9	Dextromethorphan, Diclofenac, Fluoxetine, Ibuprofen, Naproxen, Phenytoin, S-Warfarin, Tolbutamide
CYP2C19	Aminopyrine, Citalopram, Clomipramine, Diazepam, Imipramine, Mephenytoin, Omeprazole, Phenytoin, Progesterone, Sertraline
CYP2D6	β-Blockers, Chlorpromazine, Debrisoquine, Dextromethorphan, Fentanyl, Flecainide, Haloperidol, Mexiletine, Meperidine, Paroxetine, Procainamide, Propafenone, Risperidone, SSRIs (Fluoxetine), Thioridazine, Tricyclic antidepressants, Trazadone Pro-drug activation of Tramadol, Codeine, Venlafaxine, and Oxycodone
CYP2E1	Acetaminophen, Chlorzoxazone, Ethanol, Halothane, Isoflurane, Pentobarbitone, Propranolol, Rifampicin, Tolbutamide
CYP3A4	Alfentanil, Alprazolam, Ca channel blockers, Carbamazepine, Clonazepam Cacaine, Codeine, Cyclosporin A, Dexamethasone, Diazepam, Erythromycin, Fentanyl, Haloperidol, HIV protease inhibitors, Hydrocortisone, Ketoconazole, Lidocaine, Methadone, Midazolam, Ropivacaine, Sufentanil, Terfenadine, Testosterone, Triazolam

sulfonyltransferases (SULT), *N*-acetyltransferases (NAT), and methyltransferases (MT). Generally, multiple metabolic steps are required to remove a drug from the body. In addition, there are multiple metabolic pathways and intermediates for each drug, and each can play a role in drug interactions.[3,5]

EXCRETION   In the process of elimination from the body, drugs are rendered more hydrophilic to facilitate easier excretion via glomerular filtration in the kidney. As a result of glomerular reabsorption of lipophilic compounds, renal excretion of unchanged drug does not contribute substantially to the overall elimination of most therapeutic agents. A reduced rate of glomerular filtration can result in accumulation of drugs that do not have an alternative route of excretion, thereby predisposing an individual to adverse drug interaction. In addition, interference with renal excretion of drugs can cause drug interactions through competition for renal tubular secretion or altered tubular reabsorption.[6] Agents that alter the pH of the urine significantly may cause an increase or decrease in the rate of excretion of an agent. For example, acidification of urine via administration of ammonium chloride can enhance the excretion of amphetamine.[5]

Pharmacokinetic Drug Interactions

A *pharmacokinetic interaction* is represented by one drug causing a change in the concentrations of another drug. Pharmacokinetic drug interactions occur through various mechanisms, such as alterations in drug absorption, distribution, metabolism, and excretion. Metabolic interactions are the most common, and the magnitude is dependent on the mechanism of interaction between the two drugs, the dose, the duration, the route of administration, the environment, individual social habits (e.g., smoking, diet), and patient genetics.[7] Absorption may be affected by variations in gastric pH, whether environmental or drug-induced. Interactions may occur with the use of some chelating agents, or by a drug affecting gastrointestinal motility. Reduction in gastrointestinal motility may facilitate a delayed excretion, thereby increasing dissolution and absorption.[6] Anticholinergic drugs, opiates, and certain foods may retard gastric emptying, which may in turn delay the time to peak level and reduce the peak concentration of many drugs.

Following absorption, some drugs undergo protein binding, and this is determined by the relative concentration and affinity of each drug for binding sites. As discussed earlier, one drug may compete with another bound drug and displace it. One example is salicylate-induced displacement of coumarins from protein binding sites, which enhances the effects of the anticoagulants and increases the risk of a bleeding event.[8] This type of drug interaction increases the unbound fraction, and thereby increases the pharmacological response and the possibility of toxicity. However, the unbound fraction is also eliminated more easily, thereby establishing a new equilibrium, where the concentration of the unbound drug is the same as before the displacement.[9]

Prominent among the enzymatic systems involved in pharmacokinetic drug interactions are the CYP450 enzymes. Metabolic drug interactions may also be precipitated by drugs that induce or inhibit the activity of CYP enzymes. Enzyme-inducing drugs cause an increase in the production of particular P450 enzymes leading to increased metabolism and decreased blood levels of substrates of those enzymes. Enzyme induction is affected by numerous factors, including pollutants, dietary/nutritional factors, and cigarette smoking. Heavy smokers are known to exhibit a large degree of enzyme induction.[10] CYP inhibitors impair the ability of specific P450 enzymes to metabolize their target substrates, thus producing increased blood levels of those substrates. Drug interactions as a result of CYP inhibition may be stereo-selective, as in the case of the drug enoxacin, which selectively decreases clearance of *R*-Warfarin but not *S*-Warfarin.[11]

ENZYME INDUCTION   The conventional definition of *enzyme induction* is an increase in *de novo* (new) synthesis of enzyme molecules resulting from an increase in transcription of the respective gene following an appropriate stimulus. *Induction* has often been used as a generic term describing the increase in the amount or activity of a drug-metabolizing enzyme as a result of exposure to an inducing agent. Induction is a slow process dependent on the rate of protein synthesis and usually requires several days to two or more weeks to exert a meaningful effect on drug metabolism. Although enzyme induction is usually associated with high doses of a drug, normal therapeutic dosages of certain drugs have also been known to cause an induction response. For example, phenytoin, rifampin, barbiturates, and carbamazepine have

TABLE 6-2 A selected list of CYP inducers and inhibitors.

Inducers	Inhibitors
Barbiturates	Azole antifungals (e.g., ketoconazole)
Carbamazepine	Grapefruit juice
Phenytoin	Macrolide antibiotics (e.g., erythromycin)
Ethanol	Quinidine
Rifampin	SSRIs
	Ritonavir
	Ginseng
	St. John's wort

all been implicated in clinically relevant drug interactions attributable to enzyme induction (Table 6-2).[12,13]

Molecular mechanisms of phase I enzyme induction can be better elucidated using the example of polycyclic environmental pollutants. Naphthalene, phenanthrene, anthracene, and benzanthracene are some polycyclic aromatic hydrocarbons (PAH) found in cigarette smoke and are potent inducers of *CYP1A1* and *1A2*. Alterations in *CYP1A2* activity by smoking, for example, may modify the requirements for theophylline among asthmatics and haloperidol among psychiatric patients. Caffeine metabolism is also induced by smoking, and this may explain the increased tolerance to caffeine among smokers.[14] Induction of *CYP1A1* involves an interaction between the respective chemical, or *ligand,* and a cytosolic receptor, the Ah receptor (AhR). After this interaction, the ligand–receptor complex translocates to the nucleus where it associates with a protein called the Ah receptor nuclear translocator (Arnt). This AhR–Arnt complex acts as a transcription factor and binds to specific xenobiotic response elements that form part of the promoter sequence of the respective gene encoding the enzyme. The de novo synthesis of new protein is then regulated through the transcription of RNA followed by the addition of the heme group, which completes the new CYP enzyme.[14]

A recently proposed mechanism describes the induction of some hepatic CYP enzymes by xenobiotics. Three "orphan" nuclear receptor super-family members designated CAR (constitutive androstane receptor), PXR (pregnane X receptor), and PPAR (peroxisome proliferator-activated receptor) mediate the induction (i.e. transcription) of the hepatic P450 enzymes belonging to families *CYP2, CYP3,* and *CYP4,* respectively.[14] The UDP-glucuronosyltransferases (UGTs) are a family of enzymes responsible for the conjugation of numerous endogenous substances and xenobiotics. Recently, it has been demonstrated that the phase II enzyme UGT can be induced by PAHs found in cigarette smoke. UGTs play an important role in metabolism of analgesics, especially the NSAIDS, which undergo extensive glucuronidation and are susceptible to UGT-mediated drug interactions.[14]

ENZYME INHIBITION *Enzyme inhibition* occurs when the respective enzyme is unable to metabolize its substrate effectively due to interference by another substance. Enzyme inhibition can be reversible or irreversible. Reversible inhibition is further classified into competitive, noncompetitive, or uncompetitive processes.[11] Alternatively, inhibition may result from the metabolite of a substrate causing a negative feedback, thereby causing cessation of enzyme production. Enzymatic inhibition is usually immediate, particularly if the inhibition is competitive in nature. *In vivo,* the degree of enzyme inactivation depends on the dose of the drug, the duration of administration, and drug half-life.[11] In general, CYP enzyme-mediated reactions follow Michaelis–Menten (MM) kinetics with a single enzymatic binding site for the substrate and a saturable reaction rate. The maximum reaction velocity is designated V_{max}. The MM constant (K_m) is the amount of substrate necessary for a 50% optimum reaction between substrate and enzyme. The potency of enzyme inhibitors may be classified according to their affinity for the enzyme. This is based on the concept of inhibitory concentration, or K_i, which refers to the quantity of inhibitor that is required to cause a 50% inhibition of the enzyme.

Drug interactions *in vivo* are determined by the potency of the inhibitor, as reflected by the K_i value, but also on the concentration of the inhibitor at the enzyme. For clinical significance, the fraction of the drug's clearance affected by the metabolic inhibitor needs to represent a major contribution to its overall clearance. The individual's inherent enzyme activity is also of importance for the extent of interaction *in vivo,* because in general, subjects with the highest baseline metabolic activity often display the largest inhibitory effects.[15] Consequences of enzymatic inhibition are substrate dependent. For example, the pro-drug codeine exhibits decreased therapeutic activity when its metabolizing enzyme is inhibited.[16] An active drug like methadone, however, may exhibit a toxic reaction in response to increased plasma levels. Some common examples of enzyme inhibitors include the azole antifungals, protease inhibitors such as ritonavir, macrolide antibiotics such as erythromycin, and selective serotonin reuptake inhibitors (SSRIs) such as fluoxetine (Table 6-3). Cimetidine, an antihistamine, is a potent enzyme inhibitor and contains an imidazole ring that is reported to react with the heme portion of the CYP enzyme leading to its inactivation. Inhibition occurs rapidly and lasts for at least 30 days after discontinuation of cimetidine therapy.

TABLE 6-3 Effect of polymorphic CYP2D6 on drug disposition.

Drug	Effect Due to Polymorphic *CYP2D6*
Nortriptyline	Therapeutic inefficacy (EM) to toxicity (PM)
Codeine	Respiratory depression (EM) to lack of analgesia (PM)
Oxycodone	Respiratory depression (PM)
Fluoxetine	Higher plasma drug concentrations among PM relative to EM
Tramadol	Higher parent-drug : metabolite ratio with increased number of functional alleles

Other pharmacokinetic mechanisms of drug interaction include drug-induced changes in hepatic circulation and interactions due to changes in drug excretion. Genetic variations in CYP enzyme activity are a well-known fact, especially for *CYP2D6, CYP2C9, CYP2C19,* and *CYP3A4. CYP2D6* is believed to be non-inducible, therefore genetic variations in enzyme expression are more relevant to drug interactions with this enzyme.[17] Individuals with differences in the number of genes coding for the enzymes may exhibit differences in metabolism of substrate drugs.

Pharmacodynamic Drug Interactions

Pharmacodynamic interactions occur when one drug modifies the pharmacologic effect of another drug. Pharmacodynamic interactions usually occur at the receptor level and may be any of the following:

1. *Additive,* where the effect of two drugs in combination is equal to the sum of their individual effects. Coadministration of two drugs with the same pharmacologic effect may produce additive effects, as is the case for alcohol and barbiturates.[18]
2. *Potentiating,* where the presence of one drug may prolong the action of another by reducing metabolism or elimination. An example is the coadministration of penicillin derivatives and probenecid.[19]
3. *Synergistic,* where two drugs in combination produce an effect greater than the sum of their individual effects. An example is the combination of alcohol and diazepam, which may cause a greater reaction than the sum of the individual effects of each drug used separately.
4. *Antagonistic,* where two drugs in combination lead to one drug attenuating the effect of the other. For example, oral anticoagulants prolong clotting time by inhibiting effects of dietary vitamin K.

Pharmacogenomics and Drug Interactions

The physiologic response to a given dose of a drug varies among individuals, and this response may range from adverse effects in one individual to an absence of therapeutic effect in another. Pharmacogenomics is the study of the association between an individual's genotype and their response to drugs. Most drug effects are determined by the interaction of several gene products (e.g., drug targets, enzymes, and transporters) that influence the pharmacokinetics and pharmacodynamics of medications (Figure 6-3). Polymorphisms have been identified in genes encoding for drug metabolizing enzymes, drug transport proteins, and drug targets/receptors. Polymorphic gene products can affect drug disposition, thereby increasing the potential for adverse effects. An individual's drug metabolism phenotype is partly determined by the inheritance of alleles that encode enzymes, transporters, and targets.

Based on genetic polymorphisms of *CYP2D6,* three metabolizer types are recognized: ultra-extensive metabolizers (UM), extensive metabolizers (EM), and poor metabolizers (PM).[20,21] Individuals with a UM phenotype generally have multiple copies of a gene leading to rapid metabolism of drugs, which results in subtherapeutic

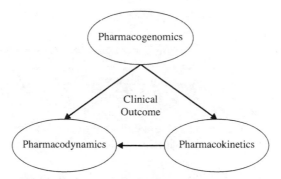

FIGURE 6-3 Determinants of drug disposition.

plasma drug levels at ordinary drug dosages. In contrast, individuals with a PM genotype may require substantial dose reductions to prevent toxicity (Table 6-3). A fourth metabolizer type, the intermediate metabolizer (IM), has been proposed for some drugs. For example, in the metabolism of the tricyclic antidepressant nortriptyline, poor metabolizers have zero copies of the *CYP2D6* enzyme, intermediate metabolizers have one copy, extensive metabolizers have two copies, and ultra-extensive metabolizers have more than two copies.[22] The clinical manifestations of these genetic drug metabolism profiles could range from therapeutic inefficacy to toxicity for the same dose of a drug. *CYP2D6* deficiency can either cause magnified drug effects when *CYP2D6* is the major inactivation pathway (tricyclic antidepressants),[23] or depreciated effects when *CYP2D6* is the activator (codeine).[16,24] Enzyme inhibition in an individual with a PM genotype may not produce a clinically relevant interaction owing to the pre-existing paucity of enzyme. Similarly, individuals with an EM genotype are more susceptible to enzyme induction than PMs because of the larger quantity of enzyme present.

The incidence of drug interactions may exhibit variable rates among different ethnicities. For instance, the extent of inhibitory effect of omeprazole on *S*-mephenytoin and diazepam was reportedly greater in European Caucasians than in Chinese people. The difference was reportedly due to an overrepresentation of the heterozygous genotype of *CYP2C19* among Chinese EMs. Similar to PMs, these heterozygous EMs were evidently less susceptible to enzyme inhibition than homozygous EMs.[11] Although genotyping does not affect the interpretation of the cause of death, it could be of significance in interpreting the manner of death.[25]

DRUG INTERACTIONS IN FORENSIC TOXICOLOGY

Alcohol

Alcohol, when used in combination with other drugs, can lead to significant interactions through alterations in drug pharmacokinetics and pharmacodynamics. Alcohol is metabolized principally by alcohol dehydrogenase and aldehyde dehydrogenase, and to a lesser extent by catalase and *CYP2E1*. According to Weathermon and Crabb, as cited in Tanaka,[26] there are two types of alcohol–drug interactions: pharmacokinetic interactions, where alcohol interferes with drug metabolism, and pharmacodynamic interactions, in which alcohol enhances the effects of the drug, particularly in the central nervous system (CNS).[26] Pharmacokinetic interactions generally occur in the liver, where both alcohol and many drugs are metabolized, frequently by the same enzymes.

One of the most frequently noted interactions with alcohol is the disulfiram or Antabuse reaction. Disulfiram is used as a deterrent to prevent alcohol consumption, and alcohol ingestion concomitant with disulfiram use leads to flushing, tachycardia, breathlessness, and nausea and vomiting. The pharmacologic effects of disulfiram are the result of the inhibition of acetaldehyde dehydrogenase, which converts acetaldehyde to acetate. Disulfiram-like reactions are also observable when ethanol is used with cephalosporin antibiotics, metronidazole, ketoconazole, and certain edible fungi.

Acute or chronic ingestion of alcohol when combined with antipsychotic drugs may lead to several clinically significant interactions, including delayed metabolism of those drugs. Drugs undergoing metabolism may also show increased metabolic clearance with chronic alcohol ingestion. This interaction may be observed with tricyclic antidepressants such as clomipramine, imipramine, and amitriptyline, and SSRIs, including sertraline, citalopram, and paroxetine. The combination of the TCA amitriptyline and ethanol can produce marked sedative effects, which may be additive. Although amitriptyline does not affect the absorption and elimination of ethanol, increased amitriptyline plasma concentrations may occur with ethanol use, because of a reduction in amitriptyline hepatic clearance, resulting in a reduced first-pass extraction.[26]

Sellers and Holloway, as cited by Tanaka,[26] suggest that the probability and mechanism of alcohol–drug interactions can be predicted in part on the extent of plasma protein binding of the drug, the capacity of the liver to extract the drug from the hepatic blood stream and the true distribution space of the drug. Highly bound drugs with low intrinsic hepatic clearance are commonly reported to have their kinetics altered by ethanol (e.g., benzodiazepines, phenytoin, warfarin) and the metabolism of psychiatric drugs is altered by ethanol if they are highly bound. Ethanol increases the absorption and raises the serum levels of some benzodiazepines. Alprazolam and alcohol together may possibly increase behavioral aggressiveness. The metabolism of psychiatric drugs such as imipramine and desipramine is faster in alcoholics, because chronic ethanol use can increase microsomal protein and CYP enzymes, resulting in an increased metabolic ability of the liver.[26]

Ethanol use in conjunction with illicit drugs, such as marijuana, cocaine, opioids, and amphetamines, can lead to myriad interactions. Cannabis is known to alter the bioavailability of ethanol and reduces and delays the peak blood alcohol levels. The effects appear to be additive. The combination of alcohol and cocaine tends to have greater-than-additive effects on heart rate, concomitant with up to 30% increased blood cocaine levels.[27] Coadministration of ethanol and cocaine leads to the formation of the metabolite cocaethylene, which may enhance the cardiotoxic effects of these drugs. The potential for a pharmacokinetic interaction between heroin and ethanol is reported by Polettini et al.[28] Ethanol appeared to inhibit the hydrolysis of 6-AM to morphine, and reduce glucuronidation of morphine. Consequently, there is a decrease in morphine conjugation, and a larger fraction of the free metabolites are present in blood with a decrease in excreted fraction. Antihistamines such as promethazine, chlorpheniramine, and diphenhydramine may increase the depressant effects of alcohol by means of an additive CNS depression. Concomitant use of barbiturates and alcohol can also lead to additive CNS depression, and acute alcohol ingestion may inhibit liver enzymes responsible for barbiturate metabolism.[29]

Cannabinoids

Inhalation is the most common method of marijuana use, and Δ-9-tetrahdrocannabinol (THC) is responsible for the characteristic pharmacological effects of smoked marijuana.[30] THC is highly lipid soluble and is sequestered in the adipose (fat) tissue, and THC is subsequently redistributed from the fatty tissue to blood. THC is metabolized by the Cytochrome enzymes to the active metabolite 11-hydroxy-THC, which is further metabolized to the inactive 11-nor-9-carboxy-Δp-tetrahydrocannabinol (THCCOOH).[31] Smoking cannabis can produce acute physiological effects like increased heart rate, blood pressure, and body temperature.[32] Because of these side effects, it is believed that cannabis has the potential to interact with drugs like beta-blockers, anticholinergics, and cholinesterase inhibitors, all of which may also affect heart rate and blood pressure.[33] Individuals on tricyclic antidepressants (TCA), such as nortriptyline and imipramine, have reported tachycardia after the use of marijuana.[29] Cannabinoids are likely to produce sedation, impaired memory, anxiety, euphoria, dry mouth, tremor, and slurred speech. Impairment of psychomotor and cognitive performance can also been seen. These effects may all be enhanced when cannabis is used with alcohol, benzodiazepines, opiates, and other CNS depressants.[34] Although acute toxicity is low with cannabis use and no deaths have been related directly to it alone, there is evidence that when used in combination with other drugs, death from toxicity increases.[32]

Opioids

Opioid drugs include a variety of naturally occurring and synthetic compounds that are used frequently for analgesia. Opioids exhibit high abuse liability because of their euphorigenic effects. Naturally occurring opioids include morphine, codeine, and their analogs such as oxymorphone, oxycodone, hydrocodone, and the illicit drug heroin. Synthetic derivatives have dissimilar structure, but have similar mechanisms of action to natural opioids, and include meperidine, fentanyl, propoxyphene, butorphanol, pentazocine, methadone, and tramadol. These agents are used widely for the treatment of acute and long-term pain associated with a variety of disease states.

Opioids exert their pharmacologic action through the opioid receptors (i.e. μ, κ, and δ receptors). Activity at the μ1 and κ receptors produces analgesic effects, whereas activity at the μ2 receptors is responsible for respiratory depression and constipation. Metabolism of opioids is mediated through the liver, and generally ends in glucuronidated metabolites that are eliminated renally.[35] Morphine-3-glucuronide (M3G) and morphine-6-glucuronide (M6G), make up 90% of morphine metabolites. Of these metabolites, M6G alone retains considerable pharmacologic activity, having been shown to be significantly more potent and active than morphine.[36] Codeine is metabolized to its active form, morphine, by *CYP2D6*, and oxycodone uses the same pathway to get metabolized to oxymorphone. Individuals lacking functional *CYP2D6* are not able to activate these prodrugs and experience little to no analgesic effect from these medications.[16] The analgesic effects of codeine, dihydrocodeine, and hydrocodone are attenuated or abolished by quinidine as a result of *CYP2D6* inhibition of conversion of these drugs to their active metabolites (i.e., morphine, morphinoid metabolites, and hydromorphone). However, this interaction is likely to occur only in extensive metabolizers who have multiple copies of the *CYP2D6* gene, because poor metabolizers are unlikely to find quinidine effective. Pharmacogenomic inactivity of *CYP2D6* has been known to affect opioid analgesics in different ways—it renders codeine inactive, slightly decreases the clearance of methadone, and slightly reduces the efficacy of tramadol.

Opioid drug interactions are of special significance in forensic toxicology because opioid drugs are a common finding in polydrug-related deaths. The majority of these interactions tend to be pharmacodynamic in nature, and frequently involve other CNS depressants. Drugs known to interact with opioids include benzodiazepines, barbiturates, centrally acting muscle relaxants, ethanol, and other opioids. Some of these combinations may present a greater risk of respiratory depression resulting from synergistic effects on the respiratory center.[37] Severe hypotension has been reported with coadministration of fentanyl and midazolam. The concomitant use of two opioid drugs, for example morphine and alfentanil, can lead to an additive respiratory depression.

Inhibition and induction of enzyme systems also play a role in opioid interactions. Meperidine undergoes an increased conversion to its more toxic metabolite, normeperidine, as a result of phenobarbital-stimulated enzyme induction. In addition, the interaction of *CYP3A4* inducers, such as rifampin or somatostatin, with morphine leads to a loss in morphine efficacy.[39,40] *CYP3A4* inhibition can lead to decreased metabolism of fentanyl, alfentanil, and methadone, resulting in decreased clearance, increased plasma levels, and the potentiation of their activity.[38]

Oxycodone is a pure opioid analgesic with similar actions to morphine. Oxycodone fatalities often include the presence of other drugs, the most frequently reported of which include benzodiazepines, alcohol, cocaine, other opioids, marijuana, and antidepressants. A study by Cone et al.[41] found that mean oxycodone blood levels in deaths including other opioids, benzodiazepines, antidepressants, muscle relaxants, and so on were lower by 50% or more than the oxycodone-only groups, therefore substantiating the hypothesis that lower average oxycodone blood concentrations would be evident in deaths involving oxycodone with multiple drugs, compared to deaths with oxycodone alone.[41] This can be attributed to the additive and synergistic effects evinced by the combination of opioids with other centrally acting drugs. Fluoxetine, a potent *CYP2D6* inhibitor, has been purported to increase oxycodone (a *CYP2D6* substrate) requirement in a poor metabolizer.[42]

Tramadol, a weak opioid, is frequently detected in several multidrug toxicity cases[43,44] and is metabolized by *CYP2D6* to the more potent *O*-desmethyltramadol (ODT) and the pharmacologically inactive *N*-desmethyltramadol (NDT). Concomitant use with amitriptyline, a *CYP2D6* substrate, may result in competitive inhibition of *CYP2D6*, thereby resulting in decreased metabolism and high parent-drug concentrations.[43] Tramadol may also increase the anticoagulant effect of warfarin; however, the rationale behind the interaction is unclear. In a study of 33 autopsy cases where tramadol was found, a distinct correlation was evident between the number of functional *CYP2D6* alleles and the ratios of tramadol to *O*- and *N*-desmethyltramadol, thereby elucidating a potential genetic basis for high tramadol levels.[45]

Fentanyl, an opioid analog, is almost 50 times more potent than morphine and has a narrow therapeutic range. Respiratory depression and hypotension have been reported with concomitant use of fentanyl with the benzodiazepines diazepam or midazolam. Fentanyl is metabolized by *CYP3A4*, and concomitant use of fentanyl with potent *CYP3A4* inhibitors such as ritonavir, ketoconazole, itraconazole, erythromycin, and clarithromycin may lead to a potentially fatal respiratory depression because of an increase in plasma fentanyl concentrations.[38] Conversely, individuals on anticonvulsants such as phenytoin and carbamazepine may potentially need more fentanyl because of enzymatic induction and enhanced fentanyl metabolism.

Methadone is an opioid analog used to treat opioid withdrawal symptoms as a result of the use of heroin and oxycodone. More recently there have been a substantial number of deaths attributable to methadone, and there is a significant overlap between therapeutic methadone concentrations and the concentrations described in fatalities.[46] Methadone is principally metabolized by *CYP2D6* and *CYP3A4*, and changes in the metabolism and elimination of methadone are mainly caused by CYP inhibition or induction, with a consequent increase or decrease of the amount of drug levels in blood and tissues.[47] Some drugs that may interact with methadone include benzodiazepines, antidepressants, anticonvulsants, macrolide antibiotics, and antifungals. These drugs are inhibitors, inducers, or substrates of *CYP3A4* or *CYP2D6*.[47] Chronic alcohol abuse may induce *CYP3A4* activity, thereby leading to decreased serum methadone levels and withdrawal. Serum methadone levels can be reduced by the concurrent use of the enzyme-inducing anticonvulsant drugs phenytoin, carbamazepine, and phenobarbital. The antifungal drug fluconazole causes a moderate increase in the serum levels of methadone, plausibly as a result of the inhibition of *CYP3A4*.[48]

Benzodiazepine abuse is frequently associated with individuals in methadone maintenance treatment, and benzodiazepines are often-encountered co-intoxicants in methadone-related deaths.[49–51] The risk of methadone overdose may also be enhanced by the concurrent administration of inhibitors of *CYP3A4*, such as erythromycin.[52] A significant interaction is evident with concomitant administration of fluvoxamine, which inhibits both *CYP3A4* and *CYP2D6*, leading to a consequent increase in serum methadone levels.

BENZODIAZEPINES Benzodiazepines (BZDs) are a widely used class of drugs and exhibit sedative, hypnotic, anxiolytic, and muscle-relaxant properties. Benzodiazepines are centrally acting drugs, and exert their action on GABA receptors in the brain. Owing to their depressant effects, benzodiazepines are a popular recreational drug, and are often used in combination with alcohol for enhanced effect. In addition, some benzodiazepines, particularly flunitrazepam, have been used to induce sedation in cases of drug-facilitated sexual assault. Based on their duration of action, BZDs may be short (0–6 hours), intermediate (6–24 hours), or long acting (more than 24 hours). The most commonly used BZDs include alprazolam, midazolam, lorazepam, clonazepam, diazepam, and temazepam. BZDs are principally metabolized *by CYP3A4, CYP3A5,* and *CYP2C19. CYP3A* is the primary metabolic route for the three short-acting and structurally similar benzodiazepines alprazolam, midazolam, and triazolam. *CYP2C19* appears to play a role in *N*-demethylation of diazepam, temazepam, and a few others.[53] BZDs are highly protein bound (70%–99%), and are subject to first-pass metabolism.[37] Both pharmacokinetic and pharmacodynamic interactions have been reported with BZDs, and the potential for forensically significant drug interactions is substantial.

Enzyme induction and inhibition are responsible for the majority of pharmacokinetic interactions involving BZDs. The induction of *CYP3A4, 3A5,* and *2C19* leads to decreased plasma concentrations, decreased therapeutic half-life, and decreased clinical effectiveness. Known inducers of these CYP enzymes include carbamazepine[54] and phenytoin.[55] Pretreatment with phenytoin has been purported to increase clonazepam clearance by 46% to 58% and reduce clonazepam half-life by 31%.[56] Clinical studies have shown that carbamazepine and phenytoin may enhance the elimination of diazepam, midazolam, and clobazam.[37] Conversely, the azole antifungals (e.g., ketoconazole, fluconazole, itraconazole), which are known inhibitors of *CYP3A4,*[57] may lead to increased plasma–drug concentrations and prolong the half-life of benzodiazepines, thereby potentially increasing the magnitude and duration of depressant effects. Other CYP inhibitors such as fluoxetine, cimetidine, macrolide antibiotics, sertraline, and isoniazid may also interact through a similar mechanism.

Additive CNS and respiratory depression is the principal mechanism of pharmacodynamic drug interactions with BZDs. The concomitant use of depressant drugs such as opioids, barbiturates, and ethanol can lead to hypotension, profound sedation, and possibly coma. BZD interactions with opioids have been documented for both natural and synthetic opioids. The combination of methadone and diazepam has been reported to produce an additive effect greater than either drug alone. Propoxyphene, an opioid analgesic, has been reported to prolong the half-life of alprazolam; however, it did not significantly alter the pharmacokinetics of diazepam and lorazepam, the metabolism of which depends on non-*CYP3A* pathways.[7] Increased sedative effects have also been reported with midazolam or diazepam in combination when used with the opioid drugs morphine, meperidine, and fentanyl.[37] The combination of alprazolam and dextropropoxyphene may lead to a combined CNS depressant effect because of a possible increase in serum levels of alprazolam.[29] Ethanol appears to cause additive impairment with concomitant benzodiazepine use.[29] In addition, the rate of BZD absorption and peak plasma concentrations are increased in the presence of ethanol.[58]

Drugs like theophylline and caffeine can reduce the effectiveness of benzodiazepines. Both agents are purported to block adenosine receptors in the CNS and antagonize the sedative effects of benzodiazepines.[59] Varying interactions between benzodiazepines and nutraceutical agents such as St. John's wort,[60] kava, dong quai, valerian, bitter orange, passionflower, tan-shen, magnolia, and skullcap[61] are also thought to exist.

ANTIDEPRESSANTS   Antidepressants are possibly one of the most frequently prescribed group of medications and include the TCAs, monoamine oxidase inhibitors (MAOIs), and SSRIs. TCAs such as amitriptyline, imipramine, and clomipramine were popular a few years ago; however, they have since been replaced with newer drugs. TCAs act by altering the reuptake and deactivation of neurotransmitters and by competitive antagonism at muscarinic acetylcholine receptors. TCAs are metabolized to a large extent by *CYP2D6*, which exhibits genetic variability. SSRIs are known to inhibit *CYP2D6*-mediated metabolism with paroxetine exerting the greatest degree of inhibition and fluvoxamine the least.[37] However, the interaction between TCAs and SSRIs is greatest in individuals with UM or EM phenotypes and least in the PM genotypes. This is due to the relatively lower quantity of *CYP2D6* in a PM as compared to UM or EM. The antifungal terbinafine is a highly potent competitive inhibitor of *CYP2D6*, and the concomitant use of terbinafine was reported to cause significantly increased serum concentrations of amitriptyline and nortriptyline. TCA blood concentrations were reportedly decreased by concomitant use of carbamazepine, a potent enzyme inducer.[37]

The MAO inhibitors reduce the activity of the monoamine oxidase enzymes A and B, which degrade the neurotransmitters dopamine, noradrenalin, and serotonin. Combinations of MAOIs, TCAs, and SSRIs have been used for their synergistic effects; however, in some cases, due to the increase in free serotonin, these combinations can lead to a pharmacodynamic interaction characterized by convulsions, coma, and disseminated intravascular coagulation, referred to as *serotonin syndrome*. Meperidine has been reported to inhibit the reuptake of serotonin and can induce serotonin syndrome when coadministered with an MAOI.[37] Moclobemide, a selective MAO-A inhibitor, may interact with some SSRIs and the TCAs imipramine and desipramine, thereby leading to serotonin syndrome.

SSRIs act by blocking the reuptake of serotonin, thus enhancing central serotonergic function.[15] Citalopram, an SSRI, is a frequent finding during autopsy.[25,44] Citalopram is metabolized to the inactive metabolites *N*-desmethylcitalopram and didesmethylcitalopram by *CYP2C19*, *CYP2D6*, and *CYP3A4*.[25] A study found that pretreatment with citalopram attenuated the psychological state produced by 3, 4-methylenedioxymethamphetamine (MDMA) in sixteen healthy volunteers. MDMA has been shown to release serotonin and dopamine, and because citalopram acts by inhibiting serotonin reuptake, this leads to a pharmacodynamic interaction between citalopram and MDMA.[9]

Fluoxetine is metabolized by *CYP2D6*, with *CYP2C9* and *CYP3A4* playing a contributory role.[15] Fluoxetine is a potent inhibitor of *CYP2D6* and norfluoxetine has a moderate inhibitory effect on *CYP3A4*. Fluoxetine used concurrently with alprazolam may lead to a decrease in alprazolam clearance and concomitant increase in plasma levels, plausibly the result of a reduction in alprazolam metabolism. Fluoxetine has also been known to inhibit the metabolism of carbamazepine by the liver, presumably because of *CYP2D6* inhibition. Fluvoxamine has been reported to cause a rise in serum phenytoin concentration, and this may be the result of inhibition of both *CYP2C9* and *2C19*.[62]

SSRIs and antidepressants have been associated with suicides and accidental deaths, leading to a potential conundrum in delineating one from the other based on plasma–drug concentrations alone.[44] Plasma concentrations of fluoxetine and paroxetine were found to correlate significantly with genetic status. The study indicated that individuals with a poor metabolizer genotype for fluoxetine had significantly higher drug–plasma concentrations compared to extensive metabolizers.[63]

ANTICONVULSANTS   Drugs used for the treatment of partial seizures and generalized tonic–clonic seizures are collectively referred to as *anticonvulsants* and include phenytoin, carbamazepine, valproate, and barbiturates. Many of these drugs are not highly protein bound, and absorption is usually very good, with 80% to 100% of the dose reaching circulation.[4] Combination of barbiturates with alcohol can lead to additive CNS depression, and acute alcohol ingestion may inhibit liver enzymes responsible for barbiturate metabolism.[29] Notable exceptions include phenytoin and carbamazepine, which are highly protein bound, therefore exhibiting a potential for interactions with other drugs that displace the bound fraction. Phenytoin is primarily metabolized by *CYP2C9* and *CYP2C19* isozymes. Fluconazole, propoxyphene, and cimetidine, which are also metabolized by *CYP2C9*, have been known to decrease the metabolism of phenytoin, thereby leading to increased phenytoin plasma concentrations.[6]

Isoniazid, propoxyphene, erythromycin, cimetidine, and fluoxetine inhibit liver enzymes responsible for the metabolism and clearance of carbamazepine. The result is a rapid increase in the serum levels of carbamazepine, presumably due to *CYP2D6* inhibition.[29,64] Inducers of *CYP3A4* (phenobarbital, phenytoin, and rifampin) may increase the metabolism of carbamazapine, leading to decreased plasma levels.[29,37,65] Valproic acid (VPA) is metabolized by the liver with two metabolites, 3-oxo-VPA and a glucuronide conjugate, accounting for more than 70% of the administered dose.[66] Through enzyme induction, phenytoin, carbamazepine, primidone, and phenobarbital increase VPA metabolism and decrease plasma levels.[67] Phenobarbital is metabolized by the *CYP450* system primarily by *CYP2C9,* with *CYP2C19* and *2E1* playing minor roles. VPA, an enzyme inhibitor, can inhibit the metabolism of phenobarbital, decreasing the clearance and increasing the likelihood of toxic effects. This interaction is the result of inhibition of *CYP2C9* or *CYP2C19*.[64,68] The combination of barbiturates with alcohol can lead to additive CNS depression, and acute alcohol ingestion may inhibit liver enzymes responsible for barbiturate metabolism.[29]

ANTIMICROBIALS   Antimicrobials include antibiotics, antiviral drugs (including antiretroviral drugs), and antifungal drugs, and are associated with a variety of drug

TABLE 6-4 Antimicrobial drug interactions.

Rifampin	Alprazolam, anticoagulants, diazepam, codeine, ketoconazole, itraconazole, midazolam, morphine, nortriptyline
Erythromycin	Alcohol, alprazolam, carbamazepine, diazepam, fluoxetine, midazolam sodium valproate
Azole antifungals	Anticoagulants, carbamazepine, clozapine, diazepam, midazolam phenytoin, rifampin, triazolam
Tetracycline	Alcohol, anticonvulsants, phenothiazines, rifampin

interactions (Table 6-4). Among the macrolide antibiotics, erythromycin and troleandomycin bind strongly to and inhibit *CYP3A4*. Coadministration of a potent *CYP3A4* inhibitor, such as erythromycin, with fentanyl and alfentanil may cause decreased clearance of these drugs and potentiate the opioid effects.[38] Macrolide antibiotics may also lead to increased plasma concentrations of benzodiazepines through enzymatic inhibition, leading to reduced clearance, prolonged half-life, and increased volume of distribution. Erythromycin has been reported to cause a rapid rise in serum levels of the anticonvulsant drug carbamazepine. The antibiotic rifampin is a strong inducer of most cytochrome enzymes, and is known to increase the metabolism of many drugs that are metabolized by *CYP1A2, 2C9, 2C19,* and *3A4.*

The absorption of the antibiotic tetracycline can be decreased due to action of multivalent cations (Ca^{2+}, Mg^{2+}, Fe^{2+}, and Al^{3+}), dairy products, antacids, or alkaline pH.[4] Alcohol use with antibiotics does not generally induce interaction, with the exception of some cephalosporins, griseofulvin, and possibly doxycycline and erythromycin succinate. Enzyme induction by drugs such as carbamazepine, phenytoin, barbiturates, or chronic alcohol ingestion can shorten the half-life of doxycycline by as much as 50%.[4]

The azole antifungals (i.e., ketoconazole and itraconazole) are substrates of *CYP3A4*, and erythromycin, a *CYP3A4* inhibitor, may lead to increased plasma concentrations of these drugs. Azole antifungals may also precipitate certain interactions due to CYP inhibition. Fluconazole could potentially lead to an increase in phenytoin and warfarin concentrations, presumably because of *CYP2C9* inhibition.[6] Ketoconazole may lead to a decreased clearance of alprazolam and a prolonged half life as a result of *CYP3A4* inhibition.[29]

Interactions with antiretroviral drugs are especially relevant considering that drug abusers may potentially be prescribed HIV medications. Ritonavir is a potent inhibitor of *CYP2D6* and *CYP3A4*, and when used with substrates of those enzymes, could potentially lead to drug toxicity because of an increase in serum drug levels.

SYMPATHOMIMETICS Sympathomimetic amines directly or indirectly mimic the effects of epinephrine or norepinephrine, and include drugs like amphetamines, methylphenidate, and methamphetamine, which are all known to have a high potential for abuse.[32] Interactions of amphetamines with other drugs are not very well documented in the literature. *CYP2D6*, which is responsible for the demethylation of

MDMA, is inhibited by Ritonavir, and there has been one reported fatality owing to a severe serotonergic reaction arising from the concomitant use of MDMA with Ritonavir. This case shows the potential for interactions between illicit and prescribed drugs.[29]

The use of amphetamines with other sympathomimetics could lead to excessive cardiovascular or CNS stimulation.[37] Saito et al.[69] reported a fatality due to a potential interaction between fenoterol and methamphetamine, both of which are β_1 and β_2 agonists, and their concomitant use may lead to an additive pharmacodynamic interaction, and thus may significantly increase cardiac stimulation. Amphetamines are contraindicated during or within 14 days of MAOI use[37] and concurrent use can lead to hypertensive crises, which can be fatal. *Rauwolfia* alkaloids (i.e., reserpine) are used to treat hypertension, and when used with direct-acting sympathomimetic amines, the effects may be increased and may cause a substantial decrease in blood pressure.

Cocaine has peripheral sympathomimetic activity, and exerts an excitatory effect on the CNS, principally due to the inhibition of the reuptake of dopamine.[4] Alcohol and cocaine are a popular combination, and when used together may lead to the formation of cocaethylene, an active metabolite. In case of coingestion of alcohol and cocaine, hepatic synthesis of cocaethylene may even occur post-mortem, therefore lowering cocaine concentration and resulting in an elevated cocaethylene concentration.[70]

HERB–DRUG INTERACTIONS

In recent years, there has been a significant rise in the use of herbal supplements or nutraceuticals, such as ginseng, ginkgo biloba, St. John's wort, and hawthorne root. According to a recent report, approximately 40% of the American population uses complementary and alternative medicines during their lifetime.[71] A survey in 1999 showed that at least 18% of adults in the United States at that time used prescription drugs concurrently with herbal or vitamin products, placing an estimated 15 million individuals at risk of potential drug–supplement interactions.[72] Nutraceuticals are usually complex mixtures of multiple ingredients with potential to cause interactions with various classes of drugs, including induction or inhibition of metabolizing enzymes and drug efflux proteins. However, the consumer is quite unaware of the inherent potential for herb–drug interactions, especially considering the lack of ingredient labels on a number of these non-FDA-mandated nutraceuticals.

Some herbal drugs that are known to interact with CYP enzymes include cat's claw (inhibiting), ginseng, kava, quercetin, and yerba santa. *CYP2C9*-inhibiting herbs include milk thistle, silymarin, and St. John's wort (*Hypericum perforatum*), which is believed to exert more prominent effects on *3A4*. Drugs that inhibit *CYP3A3* or *3A4* may elicit increases in serum levels of yohimbine. St. John's wort appears to inhibit *CYP3A4* acutely, and then to induce the enzyme following repeated administration. *CYP3A*-inhibiting herbs include cannabinoids, ginseng, grapefruit juice, milk thistle, and peppermint oil.[72] St. John's wort is known to interfere with the metabolism of a large number of medicines because of its ability to induce *CYP3A4*.

St. John's wort is known to inhibit monoamine neurotransmitter uptake in several biologic systems, Several *in vitro* studies have shown that St. John's wort and its constituent hyperforin specifically inhibit synaptosomal uptake of serotonin, norepinephrine, and dopamine. This mechanism of action of St. John's wort creates potential for interactions with SSRIs and TCAs, thereby enhancing the possibility of a serotonin syndrome–like reaction as a result of relative increases in levels of neurotransmitters.[73,74] Reports have documented the decreased efficacy of anticoagulants such as warfarin when used with St. John's wort, with the possible mechanism being the induction of *CYP2C9*.[74]

Kava, a popular herbal preparation, has the potential to exhibit both pharmacokinetic and pharmacodynamic reactions. Several kavalactones are potent inhibitors of *CYP1A2, CYP2C9, CYP2C19, CYP2D6, CYP3A4, CYP4A9,* and *CYP4A11*.[75] Kava has been purported to exhibit additive interactions when used with benzodiazepines, because both act on GABA receptors. The most significant interaction between kava and pharmaceutical drugs could potentially occur through CYP inhibition by kavalactones, resulting in pharmacokinetic interactions.[73]

Primary mechanisms of drug–herb interaction involve induction or inhibition of CYP enzymes and intestinal drug efflux proteins such as P-glycoprotein (P-gp). This can cause clinically relevant drug–herbal interactions and alter drug bioavailability. St. John's wort has been implicated in a number of clinically relevant drug interactions and has been known to decrease the therapeutic efficacy of many drugs. Among its various constituents, hyperforin is the main constituent responsible for its purported antidepressant action, which is mediated through inhibition of synaptic reuptake of neurotransmitters. Long-term therapy with *Hypericum* has been known to lower methadone trough concentrations, plausibly due to *CYP3A4* induction, thereby causing a reduction in serum methadone levels and subsequent induction of withdrawal symptoms.[75]

Various clinical studies have indicated that St. John's wort lowered steady-state plasma concentrations of amitriptyline, cyclosporin, digoxin, fexofenadine, indanavir, methadone, midazolam, nevirapine, phenprocoumon, saquinavir, simvastatin, tacrolimus, theophyline, and warfarin.[76] *In vitro* studies indicate that the hyperforin ingredient of St. John's wort is a potent inducer of *CYP2B6* and *3A4*. Ginseng is commonly used to treat fatigue, debility, lack of concentration, impotence, and anxiety. Chinese ginseng has been reported to produce adverse effects with phenelzine, warfarin, and alcohol.

The herb ginkgo (*Ginkgo biloba*), is the largest selling nutraceutical in the United States, and is frequently consumed for the enhancement of memory functions, intermittent claudication, vertigo, and tinnitus. Ginkgo extract contains various flavonoids, biflavonoids, and proanthocyanidins. Ginkgo has well-documented anti-platelet and anti-thrombotic activity, and has been known to produce adverse effects with several drugs such as aspirin, omeprazole, acetaminophen, and warfarin.[75] Other potential interactions of ginkgo include dilantin, depakote, ticlopidine, clopidogrel, and dipyridamole. A recent case study[77] documented a fatal epileptic event potentially caused by an herb–drug interaction between *Ginkgo biloba* and the drugs phenytoin and valproic acid. A recent study by Hu et al.[75] found significant inductive effect of ginkgo on *CYP2C19* activity. Ginkgo leaf and seed contain low levels of a neurotoxin 4′-*O*-methylpyridoxine, which could induce convulsions and reduce GABA and glutamic acid decarboxylase activity, This could potentially lower the seizure threshold by mitigating the effect of coadministered antiepileptic drugs (e.g., carbamazepine, phenytoin, phenobarbital).[75]

Mechanisms of Herb–Drug Interactions

Herb–drug interactions proceed through several different mechanisms.

1. *Competitive Inhibition:* A nutraceutical constituent can be a substrate of a CYP enzyme or efflux transporter, thereby competing with another substrate (the drug) for either metabolism by the CYP enzyme or efflux transporter. This leads to higher plasma concentrations as a result of competitive inhibition.
2. *Enzyme Induction:* Nutraceuticals can act to induce one or more CYP enzymes or efflux transporters, thus leading to subtherapeutic plasma concentrations of coadministered or subsequently administered substrate drug.
3. *Enzyme Inhibition:* Nutraceuticals can cause enzyme inhibition, resulting in decreased enzyme activity, with two potential manifestations; toxicity due to high levels of unmetabolized active parent drug, or therapeutic inefficacy as a result of unmetabolized pro-drug.

Grapefruit juice is a potent enzyme inhibitor and is frequently implicated in drug interactions. In particular, *CYP3A4* is inhibited, leading to altered drug disposition of a number of substances including the antihistamine terfenadine, with the potential to result in fatal cardiac arrhythmia. Grapefruit juice acts through inhibition of intestinal *CYP3A4*, which regulates presystemic metabolism. Simultaneous consumption of grapefruit juice with a number of therapeutic agents that are subject to first-pass intestinal/hepatic metabolism resulted in higher plasma levels with subsequent adverse effect.[78]

CYP3A4 inhibition by grapefruit juice has led to an increase in diazepam concentrations as reported by Ozdemir et al.[79] Peak concentrations of triazolam and midazolam are also increased following consumption of grapefruit juice, with the resultant potential for increased CNS depression.[79] The anticonvulsant carbamazepine also exhibits an increased plasma concentration following grapefruit juice ingestion. In spite of the ubiquitous use of herbal drugs, the documentation of herb–drug interactions is mostly restricted to case reports. Inferential analysis of herb–drug interactions through clinical trials would be very beneficial in establishing the mechanism of specific interactions.

Conclusion

Drug interactions probably play a more integral role in drug-related deaths than is currently understood. Analytical limitations, undefined mechanisms of action, pharmacogenomics, post-mortem redistribution, herbal supplements and environmental factors may all contribute to interactions that go unrecognized. When attributing the cause and manner of death, in drug-related fatalities, it is imperative to investigate all potential contributors and not rely on drug concentrations alone. As discussed in this chapter, the manifestation of a drug's concentration or physiological effect is frequently influenced by other drugs, and cognizance of the various possibilities enhances the accuracy of interpretation. Advances in genomic technologies and predictive research will increase the ability to establish the incidence and prevalence of drug interactions.

References

1. C. B. Nemeroff, S. H. Preskorn, and C. L. Devane, "Antidepressant Drug–Drug Interactions: Clinical Relevance and Risk Management," *CNS Spectr.*, 12, 5 Suppl 7 (2007), 1–13.

2. E. M. Sellers and J. Koch-Weser, "Potentiation of Warfarin-Induced Hypoprothrombinemia by Chloral Hydrate," *N. Engl. J. Med.*, 283 (1970), 827–31.

3. H. C. Ansel, L. V. Allen, and G. P. Nicholas (eds.), *Pharmaceutical Dosage Forms and Drug Delivery Systems,* 7th ed. (Philadelphia: Lippincott Williams & Wilkins, 1999).

4. B. G. Katzung (ed.), *Basic and Clinical Pharmacology,* 9th ed. (New York: Lange Medical Books/McGraw-Hill, 2004).

5. R. Saferstein (ed.), *Forensic Science Handbook—Vol III* (New Jersey: Regents/Prentice Hall, 1993), pp. 253–86.

6. C. R. Gregg, "Drug Interactions and Anti-Infective Therapies," *Am. J. Med.,* 106 (1999), 227–37.

7. R. Yuan, D. A. Flockhart, and J. D Balian, "Pharmacokinetic and Pharmacodynamic Consequences of Metabolism-Based Drug Interactions with Alprazolam, Midazolam, and Triazolam," *J. Clin. Pharmacol.,* 39 (1999), 1109–25.

8. R. G. Hart, O. Benavente, and L. A. Pearce, "Increased Risk of Intracranial Hemorrhage When Aspirin Is Combined with Warfarin: A Meta-Analysis and Hypothesis," *Cerebrovasc. Dis.,* 9 (1999), 215–17.

9. K. Brosen and C. A. Naranjo, "Review of Pharmacokinetic and Pharmacodynamic Interaction Studies with Citalopram," *Eur Neuropsychopharmacol,* 11 (2001), 275–83.

10. S. Zevin and N. L. Benowitz, "Drug Interactions with Tobacco Smoking: An Update," *Clini. Pharmacokinet.,* 36 (1999), 425–38.

11. J. H. Lin and A. Y. Lu, "Inhibition and Induction of Cytochrome P450 and the Clinical Implications," *Clin. Pharmacokin.,* 35 (1998) 361–90.

12. G. A. Gilman, T. W. Rall, A. S. Nies, and P. Taylor (eds.), *The Pharmacological Basis of Therapeutics,* 8th ed. (New York: Pergamon Press, 1991), pp. 436–62.

13. H. H. Zhou, L. B. Anthony, A. J. Wood, and G. R. Wilkinson, "Induction of Polymorphic 4'-Hydroxylation of *S*-Mephenytoin by Rifampicin," *Br. J. Clin. Pharmacol.,* 30 (1990), 471–75.

14. B. P. Sweeney and J. Bromilow, "Liver Enzyme Induction and Inhibition: Implications for Anaesthesia," *Anaesthesia,* 61 (2006), 159–77.

15. A. Hemeryck and F. M. Belpaire, "Selective Serotonin Reuptake Inhibitors and Cytochrome P450 Mediated Drug–Drug Interactions: An Update," *Curr. Drug Metab.,* 3 (2002), 13–37.

16. M. T. Susce, E. Murray-Carmichael, and J. De Leon, "Response to Hydrocodone, Codeine and Oxycodone in A CYP2D6

Poor Metabolizer," *Prog. Neuro-Psychopharmacol. Biol. Psych.*, 30 (2006), 56–58.

17. M. Ingelman-Sundberg, "Genetic Polymorphisms of Cytochrome P450 2D6 (CYP2D6): Clinical Consequences, Evolutionary Aspects and Functional Diversity," *Pharmacogenomics J.,* 5 (2005), 6–13.

18. S. M. MacLeod, H. G. Giles, G. Patzalek, J. J. Thiessen, and E. M. Sellers, "Diazepam Actions and Plasma Concentrations Following Ethanol Ingestion," *Euro. J. Clin. Pharmacol.,* 11 (1977), 345–49.

19. D. Ganes, V. Batra, and R. Faulkner, "Effect of Probenecid on the Pharmacokinetics of Piperacillin and Tazobactam in Healthy Volunteers," *Pharm. Res.*, 8, Suppl 10 (1991), S-299.

20. M. W. Linder, R. A. Prough, and R. Valdes, Jr., "Pharmacogenetics: A Laboratory Tool for Optimizing Therapeutic Efficiency," *Clin. Chem.*, 43 (1997), 254–66.

21. N. Poolsup, A. Li Wan Po, and T. L. Knight, "Pharmacogenetics and Psychopharmacotherapy," *J. Clin. Pharm. Thera.*, 25 (2000), 197–220.

22. D.A. Fishbain, D. Fishbain, J. Lewis, R. B. Cutler, B. Cole, H. L. Rosomoff, and R. S. Rosomoff, "Genetic Testing for Enzymes of Drug Metabolism: Does It Have Clinical Utility for Pain Medicine at the Present Time? A Structured Review," *Pain Med.*, 5 (2004), 81–93.

23. J. Kirchheiner, J.Sasse, I. Meineke, I. Roots, and J. Brockmoller, "Trimipramine Pharmacokinetics after Intravenous and Oral Administration in Carriers of CYP2D6 Genotypes Predicting Poor, Extensive and Ultrahigh Activity," *Pharmacogenetics*, 13 (2003), 721–28.

24. Y. Gasche, Y. Daali, M. Fathi, A. Chiappe, S. Cottini, P. Dayer, and J. Desmeules, "Codeine Intoxication Associated with Ultrarapid CYP2D6 Metabolism," *N. Engl. J. Med.,* 351 (2004), 2827–31.

25. P. Holmgren, B. Carlsson, A. L. Zackrisson, B. Lindblom, M. L. Dahl, M. G. Scordo, H. Druid, and J. Ahlner, "Enantioselective Analysis of Citalopram and Its Metabolites in Postmortem Blood and Genotyping for CYD2D6 and CYP2C19," *J. Analyt. Toxicol.*, 28 (2004), 94–104.

26. E. Tanaka, "Toxicological Interactions Involving Psychiatric Drugs and Alcohol: An Update," *J. Clin. Pharm. Ther.,* 28 (2003), 81–95.

27. E. J. Pennings, A. P. Leccese, and F. A. Wolff, "Effects of Concurrent Use of Alcohol and Cocaine," *Addiction*, 97 (2002), 773–83.

28. A. Polettini, V. Poloni, A. Groppi, C. Stramesi, C. Vignali, L. Politi, and M. Montagna, "The Role of Cocaine in Heroin-Related Deaths. Hypothesis on the Interaction between Heroin and Cocaine," *Forensic Sci. Int.*, 153 (2005), 23–28.

29. I. H. Stockley, *Drug Interactions*, 5th ed. (London: Pharmaceutical Press, 1999).

30. R. A. Hirst, D. G. Lambert, and W. G. Notcutt, "Pharmacology and Potential Therapeutic Uses of Cannabis," *Br. J. Anaesthes.*, 81 (1998), 77–84.

31. M. A. Huestis and E. J. Cone, "Urinary Excretion Half-Life of 11-nor-9-carboxy-delta9-tetrahydrocannabinol in Humans," *Therap. Drug Mon.*, 20 (1998), 570–76.

32. O. H. Drummer and M. Odell, *The Forensic Pharmacology of Drugs of Abuse* (London: Arnold, 2001).

33. W. Hall, N. Solowij, and J. Lemon, "The Health and Psychological Consequences of Cannabis Use," *National Drug Strategy Monograph Series No. 25*, Canberra: Australian Government Publishing Service, 1994.

34. R. N. Kumar, W. A. Chambers, and R. G. Pertwee, "Pharmacological Actions and Therapeutic Uses of Cannabis and Cannabinoids," *Anaesthesia,* 56 (2001), 1059–68.

35. USPDI, *Drug Information for the Health Care Professional: Vol. IB.* 8th ed., United States Pharmacopeial Convention, Inc., 1988.

36. P. A. Glare and T. D. Walsh. Clinical pharmacokinetics of morphine. Therapeutic Drug Monitoring.; 13(1):1–23, 1991.

37. A. Mozayani and L. P. Raymon (eds.), *Handbook of Drug Interactions,* (New Jersey: Humana Press Inc., 2004), pp. 123–48.

38. Micromedex® Healthcare Series (electronic version). Thomson Micromedex, Greenwood Village, CO. Available at: http://www.thomsonhc.com, 2007.

39. M. F. Fromm, K. Eckhardt, S. Li, G. Schänzle, U. Hofmann, G. Mikus, and M. Eichelbaum, "Loss of Analgesic Effect of Morphine Due to Coadministration of Rifampin," *Pain,* 72 (1997), 261–67.

40. C. Ripamonti, F. De Conno, R. Boffi, L. Ascani L and M. Bianchi, "Can Somatostatin Be Administered in Association with Morphine in Advanced Cancer Patients with Pain?" *Ann. Oncol.,* 9 (1998), 921–23.

41. E. J. Cone, R. V. Fant, J. M. Rohay, Y. H. Caplan, M. Ballina, R. F. Reder, and J. D. Haddox, "Oxycodone Involvement in Drug Abuse Deaths. II. Evidence for Toxic Multiple Drug–Drug Interactions," *J. Anal. Toxicol.,* 28 (2004), 616–24.

42. E. Kalso, "Oxycodone," *J. Pain Symp. Manage.,* 29, 5 Suppl (2005), S47–56.

43. N. D. Bynum, J. L. Poklis, M. Gaffney-Kraft, D. Garside, and J. D. Ropero-Miller, "Postmortem Distribution of Tramadol, Amitriptyline, and Their Metabolites in a Suicidal Overdose," *J. Anal. Toxicol.,* 29 (2005), 401–06.

44. A. Jonsson, P. Holmgren, and J. Ahlner, "Fatal Intoxications in Swedish Forensic Autopsy Material During 1992–2002," *Forensic Sci. Int.,* 143 (2004), 53–59.

45. A. Levo, A. Koski, I. Ojanpera, E. Vuori, and A. Sajantila, "A Post-Mortem SNP Analysis of CYP2D6 Gene Reveals Correlation between Genotype and Opioid Drug (Tramadol) Metabolite Ratios in Blood," *Forensic Sci. Int.,* 135 (2003), 9–15.

46. C. M. Milroy and A. R. Forrest, "Methadone Deaths: A Toxicological Analysis," *J. Clin. Pathol.* 53 (2000), 277–81.

47. A. Ferrari, C. P. Coccia, A. Bertolini, and E. Sternieri, "Methadone—Metabolism, Pharmacokinetics and Interactions," *Pharmacol Res.,* 50 (2004), 551–9.

48. Y. Tarumi, J. Pereira, and S. Watanabe, "Methadone and Fluconazole: Respiratory Depression by Drug Interaction," *J. Pain Symp. Manage.,* 23 (2002), 148–53.

49. B. C. Wolf, W. A. Lavezzi, L. M. Sullivan, R. A. Middleberg, and L. M. Flannagan, "Alprazolam-Related Deaths in Palm Beach County," *Am. J. Forensic Med. Pathol.,* 26 (2005), 24–27.

50. I. Mikolaenko, C. A. Robinson, Jr., and G. G. Davis, "A Review of Methadone Deaths in Jefferson County, Alabama," *Am. J. Forensic Med. Pathol.,* 23 (2002), 299–304.

51. T. C. Kupiec and V. Raj, "The Methadone Conundrum," *Tox. Talk* 29 (2005), 7.

52. J. M. White and R. J. Irvine, "Mechanisms of Fatal Opioid Overdose," *Addiction,* 94 (1999), 961–72.

53. L. Bertilsson, T. K. Henthorn, E. Sanz, G. Tybring, J. Sawe, and T. Villen, "Importance of Genetic Factors in the Regulation of Diazepam Metabolism: Relationship to S-Mephenytoin, but Not Debrisoquin, Hydroxylation Phenotype," *Clin. Pharmacol. Therapeu.,* 45 (1989), 348–55.

54. G. W. Arana, S. Epstein, M. Molloy, and D. J. Greenblatt, "Carbamazepine-Induced Reduction of Plasma Alprazolam Concentrations: A Clinical Case Report," *J. Clin. Psych.,* 49 (1988), 448–49.

55. D. R. Abernethy, D. J. Greenblatt, H. R. Ochs, and R. I. Shader, "Benzodiazepine Drug–Drug Interactions Commonly

Occurring in Clinical Practice," *Curr. Med. Res. Opin.*, 8, Suppl 4 (1984), 80–93.

56. E. Tanaka, "Clinically Significant Pharmacokinetic Drug Interactions with Benzodiazepines," *J. Clin. Pharm. Ther.*, 24 (1999), 347–55.

57. K. Venkatakrishnan, L. L. von Moltke, and D. J. Greenblatt, "Effects of the Antifungal Agents on Oxidative Drug Metabolism: Clinical Relevance," *Clin. Pharmacokin.*, 38 (2000), 111–80.

58. U. Laisi, M. Linnoila, T. Seppala, J. J. Himberg, and M. J. Mattila, "Pharmacokinetic and Pharmacodynamics Interactions of Diazepam with Different Alcoholic Beverages," *Eur. J. Clin. Pharmacol.*, 16 (1979), 263.

59. S. A. Henauer, L. E. Hollister, H. K. Gillespie, and F. Moore, "Theophylline Antagonizes Diazepam-Induced Psychomotor Impairment," *Eur. J. Clin. Pharmacol.*, 25 (1983), 743–47.

60. A. Kawaguchi, M. Ohmori, S. Tsuruoka, K. Nishiki, K. Harada, I. Miyamori, R. Yano, T. Nakamura, M. Masada, and A. Fujimura, "Drug Interaction between St John's Wort and Quazepam," *Br. J. Clin. Pharmacol.*, 58 (2004), 403–10.

61. B. J. Gurley, S. F. Gardner, M. A. Hubbard, D. K. Williams, W. B. Gentry, Y. Cui, and C. Y. Ang, "Cytochrome P450 Phenotype Ratios for Predicting Herb–Drug Interactions in Humans," *Clin. Pharmacol. Ther.*, 72 (2002), 276–87.

62. K. Mamiya, K. Kojima, E. Yukawa, S. Higuchi, I. Ieiri, H. Ninomiya, and N. Tashiro, "Phenytoin Intoxication Induced by Fluvoxamine," *Ther. Drug Monit.*, 23 (2001), 75–77.

63. C. Charlier, F. Broly, M. Lhermitte, E. Pinto, M. Ansseau, and G. Plomteux, "Polymorphisms in the CYP 2D6 Gene: Association with Plasma Concentrations of Fluoxetine and Paroxetine," *Ther. Drug Monit.*, 25 (2003), 738–42.

64. G. E. Schumacher (ed.), *Therapeutic Drug Monitoring* (Norwalk, CT: Appleton & Lange, 1995), pp. 345–95.

65. J. G. Hardman, L. E. Limbird, and A. G. Gilman, *Goodman & Gilman: The Pharmacological Basis of Therapeutics,* 10th ed. (New York: McGraw Hill, 2001), pp. 521–47.

66. R. Davis, D. H. Peters, and D. McTavish, "Valproic Acid: A Reappraisal of Its Pharmacological Properties and Clinical Efficacy in Epilepsy," *Drugs,* 47 (1994), 332–72.

67. J. T. DiPiro (ed.), *Pharmacotherapy: A Pathophysiologic Approach*, 5th ed. (New York: McGraw-Hill, 1999), pp. 1031–60.

68. E. Perucca, "Clinically Relevant Drug Interactions with Antiepileptic Drugs," *Br. J. Clin. Pharmacol.*, 61 (2006), 246–55.

69. T. Saito, I. Yamamoto, T. Kusakabe, X. Huang, N. Yukawa, and S. Takeichi, "Determination of Chronic Methamphetamine Abuse by Hair Analysis," *Forensic Sci. Int.*, 112 (2000), 65–71.

70. F. Moriya and Y. Hashimoto, "The Effect of Postmortem Interval on the Concentrations of Cocaine and Cocaethylene in Blood and Tissues: An Experiment Using Rats," *J. Forensic Sci.*, 41 (1996), 129–33.

71. R. C. Kessler, R. B. Davis, D. F. Foster, M. I. Van Rompay, E. E Walters, S. A. Wilkey, T. J. Kaptchuk, and D. M. Eisenberg, "Long-Term Trends in the Use of Complementary and Alternative Medical Therapies in the United States," *Ann. Intern. Med.*, 135 (2001), 262–68.

72. C. Ulbricht, E. Basch, W. Weissner, and D. Hackman, "An Evidence-Based Systematic Review of Herb and Supplement Interactions by the Natural Standard Research Collaboration," *Expert Opin. Drug Saf.*, 5 (2006), 719–28.

73. Y. N. Singh, "Potential for Interaction of Kava and St. John's Wort with Drugs," *J. Ethnopharmacol.*, 100 (2005), 108–13.

74. L. Henderson, Q. Y. Yue, C. Bergquist, B. Gerden, and P. Arlett, "St John's Wort (*Hypericum perforatum*): Drug Interactions and Clinical Outcomes," *Br. J. Clin. Pharmacol.*, 54 (2002), 349–56.

75. Z. Hu, X. Yang, P. C. Ho, S. Y. Chan, P. W. Heng, E. Chan, W. Duan, H. L. Koh, and S. Zhou, "Herb–Drug Interactions: A Literature Review," *Drugs,* 65 (2005), 1239–82.

76. S. Zhou, E. Chan, S. Q. Pan, M. Huang, and E. J. Lee, "Review: Pharmacokinetic Interactions of Drugs with St. John's Wort," *J. Psychophamacol.*, 18 (2004), 262–76.

77. T. Kupiec and V. Raj, "Fatal Seizures Due to Potential Herb–Drug Interactions with Ginkgo Biloba," *J. Anal. Tox.* 29 (2005), 755–58.

78. D. G. Bailey, J. Malcolm, O. Arnold, and J. D. Spence, "Grapefruit Juice–Drug Interactions," *Br J Clin Pharmacol.,* 58 (2004), S831–40.

79. M. Ozdemir, Y. Aktan, B. S. Boydag, M. I. Cingi, and A. Musmul, "Interaction between Grapefruit Juice and Diazepam in Humans," *Eur. J. Drug Metab, Pharmacokinet,* 23 (1998), 55–59.

7

■ ■ ■ ■

Deoxyribonucleic Acid Structure and Function—A Review

Lawrence Kobilinsky, Ph.D.
John Jay College of Criminal Justice, The City University of New York

A revolution in molecular biology has occurred since the mid-1990s as a result of the development of several novel methods for the isolation and subsequent analysis of deoxyribonucleic acid (DNA). Perhaps even more important has been the development of methods that enable scientists to recombine segments of DNA obtained from different species and manipulate the DNA molecule efficiently and at will to produce new and desirable genes in any quantity necessary. DNA carries the genetic information that defines a species as such, that allows an organism to synthesize ribonucleic acid (RNA) and protein molecules, which in turn enable an organism to conduct all of its metabolic requirements. DNA contains the genetic program for the construction of all of the various cells, tissues, and organs that constitute an organism throughout its lifetime, and also provides the information that makes every individual unique. It is because of these qualities that the study of DNA is important to those who specialize in the chemical, physical, and life sciences.

Now that the human genome, consisting of some 3.1 billion nucleotide base pairs, has been sequenced, we have learned that this DNA contains only 20,000 genes yet codes for the synthesis of some 100,000 proteins, which direct the growth and development of the fertilized egg cell (zygote) into the multicellular organism known as *Homo sapiens*. Now that we have a better understanding of the composition of the human genome, scientists can begin to probe the secrets of human life and to understand, detect, and ultimately cure human genetic diseases that number between 3,000 and 4,000. Clinicians have learned how to determine at an early stage whether an individual has the potential to develop a genetically related disease such as cancer, cardiovascular disease, and even behavioral disorders.

Even more exciting is the prospect of gene therapy to prevent or cure these inborn plagues that have caused so much human suffering and misery. Advances in biotechnology and genetic engineering and the knowledge gained from the human genome project will change the way medicine is practiced and will have great impact on people's lives. Genetic screening of individuals for medical purposes promises to have a profound influence on improving health care, but also raises equally profound and troubling ethical questions concerning the availability of this information to interested parties, such as potential employers and insurance companies. These problems must be addressed by scientists, clinicians, lawyers, clergy, and other concerned professionals.

The study of the structure and function of DNA is a very important subject within the biological and chemical sciences. Research on DNA is being performed by scientists in many related disciplines such as molecular biology, genetics, biochemistry, and organic and physical chemistry. The recent development of analytical methods whereby DNA can be utilized for individualization purposes[1-4] makes the subject especially important to forensic scientists.

Prior to the development of research tools to perform DNA analysis for human identification, forensic serologists analyzed polymorphic proteins and antigens found in blood and other physiological fluids and tissues in an effort to individualize biological evidence.[5,6]

Polymorphic proteins and enzymes are useful as genetic markers because multiple forms of the same functional protein exist in the population, and each form can be discriminated by commonly used physicochemical techniques such as electrophoresis, isoelectric focusing, or high-performance liquid chromatography (HPLC). In this way, biological evidence can be evaluated statistically to determine the probability that a substance such as blood or semen was derived from a particular individual. This may be vitally important in exculpating or incriminating an individual suspected to have committed or participated in a violent crime.

Since the mid-1980s, increasing attention has been paid to the use of DNA for individualization purposes in criminal cases, primarily because the molecule is both highly stable in stains and extremely polymorphic, and therefore highly informative for the purpose of establishing strain origin. DNA analysis is also used for paternity determinations and in other matters such as establishing indirect biological relationships.

Because of the increasing importance of DNA analysis in criminal matters, the structure and function of nucleic acids should be understood thoroughly by forensic scientists and other criminal justice personnel. The use of restriction fragment length polymorphism (RFLP) analysis of variable number of tandem repeat (VNTR) markers[7] became an important subject for the medicolegal profession. The development of another procedure capable of amplifying a small specific fragment of DNA, known as the polymerase chain reaction (PCR),[8,22] accompanied by dot-blot hybridization and the subsequently developed amplified fragment length polymorphism (AmpFLP) methodology.[23] further strengthened the capabilities of the forensic analyst to individualize biological evidence when the DNA within the sample is limited in size and relatively poor in quality (e.g., high molecular weight DNA has been degraded to low molecular weight forms). Today, we routinely use PCR to amplify many different areas of the human genome as well as the DNA found within the cellular organelles known as *mitochondria*. For these reasons, a basic understanding of DNA is both desirable and necessary.

Many reviews have been written about the structure of DNA[24–30]; its physical characteristics[31]; properties of DNA-protein complexes[32–34]; chromatin[35]; interaction of DNA with metals,[36,37] drugs,[38] or with water[39]; on topoisomerases[40–42]; and on superhelical DNA.[43,46] The reader is referred to these monographs for a more comprehensive treatment of these subjects.

CHEMICAL COMPOSITION

In 1868, while studying nuclei isolated from white cells present in discarded bandages of wounded soldiers, Johann (Friedrich) Miescher, a Swedish biologist, discovered an unusual substance that contained phosphorus.[47] It differed from all other macromolecules known at the time including proteins, carbohydrates, and lipids. The material, which he named *nuclein,* was found to contain both acidic and basic components. The former was DNA, and the latter, the associated basic proteins known as *histones.* In Miescher's subsequent studies of salmon spermatozoa, a similar nuclein substance was discovered. Thus it soon became clear that DNA was both ubiquitous and universal.

The nucleic acids, deoxyribonucleic acid (DNA) and ribonucleic acid (RNA), consist of subunits known as *nucleotides.* Chemically, DNA consists of phosphoric acid, D-2-deoxyribose (β-D-2'-deoxyribofuranose) and 4 nitrogenous bases, namely, the purines—adenine (6-aminopurine) and guanine (2-amino-6-oxypurine)—and the pyrimidines cytosine (2-oxy-4-amino-pyrimidine) and thymine (5-methyl-2,4-dioxypyrimidine) (Figures 7-1 and 7-2). The related molecule RNA consists of phosphoric acid, D-ribose, and the same four bases with the exception of thymine, which is replaced by the pyrimidine uracil (2,4-dioxypyrimidine). In DNA the bases are abbreviated A, G, C, T; in RNA, the bases are A, G, C, U. Occasionally, unusual bases can be found in DNA that are the result of derivitization of the usual bases by either methylation or glycosylation, depending on the type of DNA. These modifications are used to provide specific recognition signals for restriction enzymes, which have the capability of cleaving covalent bonds linking adjacent nucleotide subunits).

Both purines and pyrimidines are heterocyclic, flat, planar molecules capable of stacking one on the other. Structurally, the purines are arranged as two attached rings, whereas the pyrimidines are single-ring molecules. Both are relatively water insoluble. The free nitrogenous bases exist in tautomeric equilibria. *Tautomers* are compounds whose structures differ significantly in the arrangement of atoms but that are in equilibrium. Adenine and cytosine can exist in either amino or imino

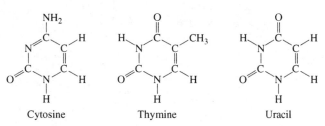

PURINES

Adenine   Guanine

PYRIMIDINES

Cytosine   Thymine   Uracil

FIGURE 7-1 Structures of the major purines and pyrimidines in DNA and RNA. (*Source:* J. D. Rawn, *Biochemistry* (North Carolina: Neil Patterson Publishers, Carolina Biological Supply Co., 1989), p. 629.)

configurations (Figure 7-3); amino configurations are the predominant form. Similarly, guanine and thymine can exist in tautomeric keto or enol forms (Figure 7-4); with the keto structure being the major form. Knowledge of the tautomeric form is important, because each tautomer can form hydrogen bonds with other such bases in different ways, thus altering the overall structure of the molecule.

Each nucleotide subunit of DNA consists of a pentose sugar in the β furanose form, a phosphoric acid group, and a nitrogenous base. A nucleoside, however, is a sugar–nitrogenous base adduct. The nucleotide subunits used in the construction of DNA are known as *deoxyribonucleoside 5'-triphosphates* and are represented as *d*ATP, *d*GTP, *d*CTP, and *d*TTP. Analogously, the nucleotides of RNA are called *ribonucleoside 5'-triphosphates* and are represented as ATP, GTP, CTP, and UTP. The nitrogenous base is joined to the pentose carbon atom #1, thus forming an *N*-glycosyl linkage (Figure 7-5). The phosphoric acid group is esterified to pentose carbon #5. Nucleotides linked end-to-end by covalent phosphodiester bonds form an oligonucleotide, a polynucleotide, or a nucleic acid, depending on the relative number of subunits constituting the molecule.

Erwin Chargaff found that DNA contains equal amounts of purines and pyrimidines. Regardless of the species from which the DNA had been isolated, the ratio (A + G)/(C + T) always approximately equaled 1.0. Chargaff determined that in DNA, for every mole of A, there is a mole of T, and for every mole of G, there is a mole of C. This observation was to be of critical importance in unraveling the structure of DNA. This rule was based on his discovery that the four common bases

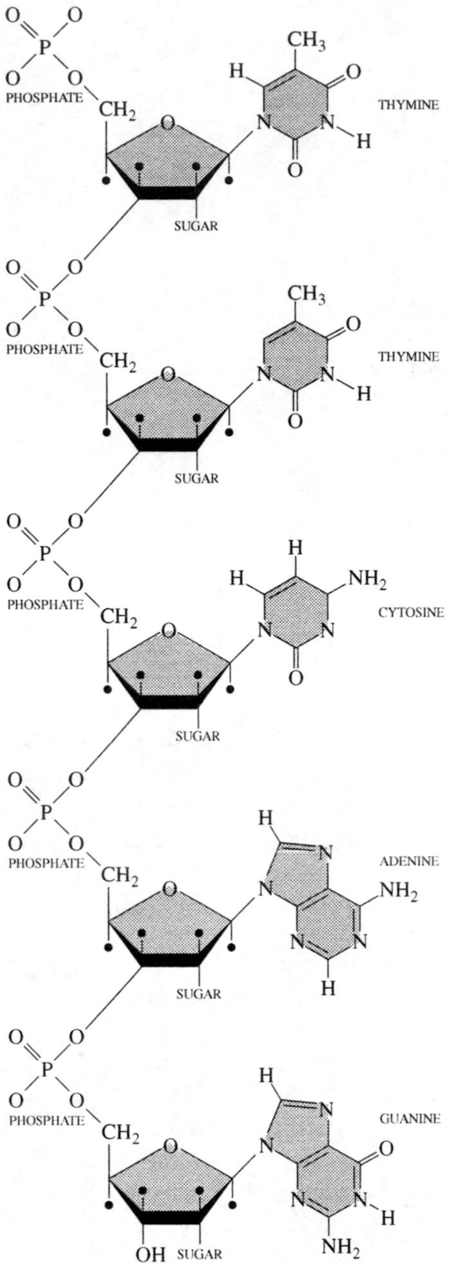

FIGURE 7-2 A single-stranded oligonucleotide sequence of DNA illustrating the pentose–sugar phosphate "backbone" and attached nitrogenous bases. (*Source:* H. Curtis, *Biology* (New York: Worth Publishers, 1968), p. 422.)

found in the DNA isolated from organisms of different species were present in different ratios and that a simple mathematical relationship existed between them.[48] DNA obtained from humans, sheep, turtles, salmon, sea urchins, wheat germ, *E. coli,* yeast, and various phage particles was analyzed for base composition. As illustrated in Table 7-1, the base composition in mol% varies from species to species.

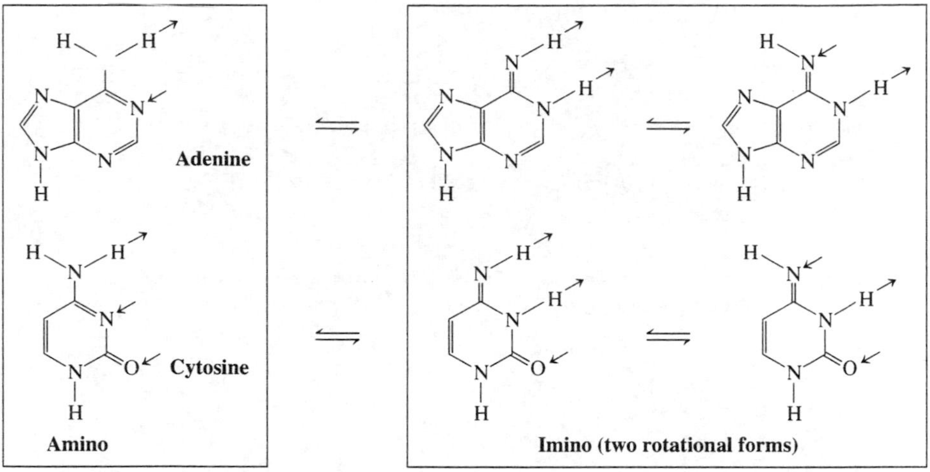

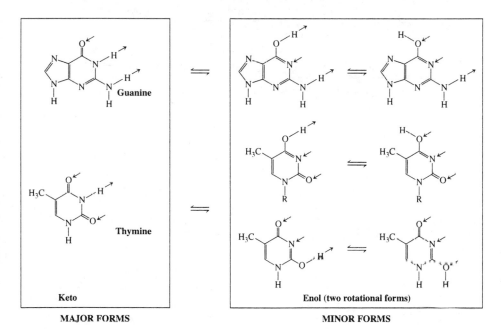

FIGURE 7-3 Adenine and cytosine in amino and imino configurations. The amino forms are the major configurations, whereas the imino forms are found in exceedingly small amounts. (*Source:* C. K. Matthews and K. E. van Holde, *Biochemistry* (California: Addison-Wesley Publishing, 1990), p. 94.)

FIGURE 7-4 Guanine and thymine in keto and enol configurations. The keto forms are the major configurations, whereas the enol forms are found in very small amounts. (*Source:* C. K. Matthews and K. E. van Holde, *Biochemistry,* (California: Addison-Wesley Publshing, 1990), p. 94.)

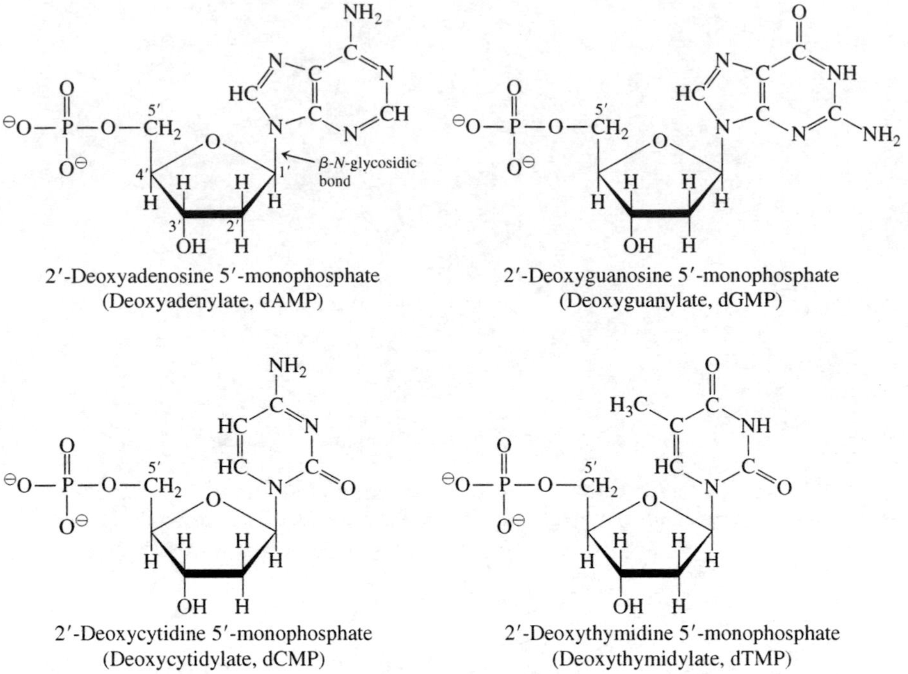

2'-Deoxyadenosine 5'-monophosphate
(Deoxyadenylate, dAMP)

2'-Deoxyguanosine 5'-monophosphate
(Deoxyguanylate, dGMP)

2'-Deoxycytidine 5'-monophosphate
(Deoxycytidylate, dCMP)

2'-Deoxythymidine 5'-monophosphate
(Deoxythymidylate, dTMP)

FIGURE 7-5   Each nitrogenous base is linked to pentose carbon number 1, forming an N-glycosyl linkage.   (*Source:* J. D. Rawn, *Bichemistry* (North Carolina: Neil Patterson Publishers, Carolina Biological Supply Co., 1989), p. 667.)

TABLE 7-1 The base composition of DNA isolated from various organisms.

	Adenine (%)	Thymine (%)	Guanine (%)	Cytosine (%)	$\dfrac{A + G}{C + T}$
Human (sperm)	31.0	31.5	19.1	18.4	1.00
Cattle (sperm)	28.7	27.2	22.2	22.0	1.03
Chicken	28.8	29.2	20.5	21.5	0.97
Salmon	29.7	29.1	20.8	20.4	1.02
Locust	29.3	29.3	20.5	20.7	0.99
Sea urchin	32.8	32.1	17.7	17.7	1.02
Yeast	31.7	32.6	18.8	17.4	1.00
Tubercle bacteria	15.1	14.6	34.9	35.4	1.00
Escherichia coli	26.0	23.9	24.9	25.2	1.04
Vaccinia virus	29.5	29.9	20.6	20.3	1.00
Bacteriophage T_2	32.6	32.6	18.2	16.6[a]	1.03

Source: From Gerald J. Stine, *Biosocial Genetics.* Copyright © 1977 Macmillan Publishing Company. All Rights Reserved

[a]5-Hydroxymethylcytosine

Interestingly, it appears that some distantly related species such as humans and yeast have similar base compositions, whereas some closely related species appear to have markedly different base compositions. However, in all species the ratios of A/T and G/C and the ratio of purines (A + G) to pyrimidines (C + T) is approximately equal to 1.0. Furthermore, Chargaff found that DNA isolated from different organs of the same species had the same base composition, and that this composition is not altered by age or nutritional state of the organism. These observations were most important for the structural studies of DNA that were soon to follow.

THE WATSON–CRICK MODEL OF DNA

In 1953, James Watson, an American geneticist, and Francis H. C. Crick, an English physicist, both of whom were working at the University of Cambridge, published a two-page paper in the journal *Nature* in which they presented a model of the structure of the DNA molecule.[49] Their conclusions were based, in part, on Chargaff's earlier findings (described previously) and also on the x-ray studies of Rosalind Franklin and Maurice Wilkins, which had been performed in 1951. Crystals of DNA had been analyzed by x-ray diffraction, and the resulting patterns indicated the existence of two "periodicities" along the long axis of the fibers. The more frequent repeat unit had dimensions of 3.4 Å (1Å = 10^{-10} meters), and the less common periodicity had dimensions of 34 Å. Along the short axis, the x-ray patterns revealed a molecular width of 20Å. Watson and Crick constructed a three-dimensional model of DNA, taking into account these measurements together with Chargaff's earlier discoveries about base composition (e.g., that A = T and G = C) (Figure 7-6).

The Watson–Crick model consists of two strands of nucleotides, both of which are wound into a right-handed helix rotating around the same axis, thereby forming a right-handed double helix.

Each of the two strands of the DNA molecule is constructed with a repeating backbone of pentose sugar–phosphate–pentose sugar–phosphate. . . . Because these phosphates are fully ionized and negatively charged at physiological pH, the molecule is highly acidic *in vivo*. The phosphate groups are positioned at the surface of the molecule adjacent to surrounding water. The planar, nitrogenous bases (purines and pyrimidines) attached to the sugar are found in the inner central portion of the double helix and are nonpolar and hydrophobic.

Each strand has a sidedness based on the 5'-3' phosphodiester bridges that connect adjacently linked nucleotides. The strands are oriented in opposite directions in that one strand extends in the direction 5' to 3', whereas the other strand extends in the direction 3' to 5'. The two strands of the duplex structure are thus antiparallel to each other. These numbers reflect the fact that it is the 5'-OH group of the sugar from one subunit that is indirectly attached to the 3'-OH group of the sugar from the adjacent subunit (Figure 7-7). A strand of DNA or RNA therefore has polarity in that it has a distinct 5' and 3' end based on the linkages discussed in the foregoing. A base sequence is generally described beginning with the 5' end proceeding toward the 3' end. A simple way to designate a sequence is the following: 5'-pApGpCpT-3', or by omitting the phosphates, (p) it becomes 5'-AGCT-3'.

5′ End   3′ End

5′ End

3′ End

Hydrogen
Bonds

3′ End

5′ End

FIGURE 7-6   Double-stranded DNA molecule illustrating polarity of complementary strands.   (*Source:* D. L. Kirk, *Biology Today,* 3rd ed. (New York: McGraw Hill Publications, 1980), p. 286.)

Within each strand the bases are stacked one on top of the other. The distance between adjacent bases is 3.4Å. It is interesting to note that each of the two heterocyclic base pairs in the double helix do not stack precisely perpendicular to the axis of the helix. Instead, the bases are somewhat twisted in relationship to each other, with a slight roll of the bases relative to the axis of the helix.

The helix turns completely (360°) every 10 bases, resulting in a periodicity of 34 Å. A 1.0-μm length of DNA helix is equivalent to 2×10^6 daltons. A 31-cm length of DNA weighs approximately 1 picogram (10^{-12} g).

Purines and pyrimidines on adjacent strands are held together in the same plane by hydrogen bonding. Two such bonds are formed between adenine and thymine, whereas three hydrogen bonds form between the bases guanine and cytosine (see Figure 7-7). Watson and Crick found that a DNA molecule in which

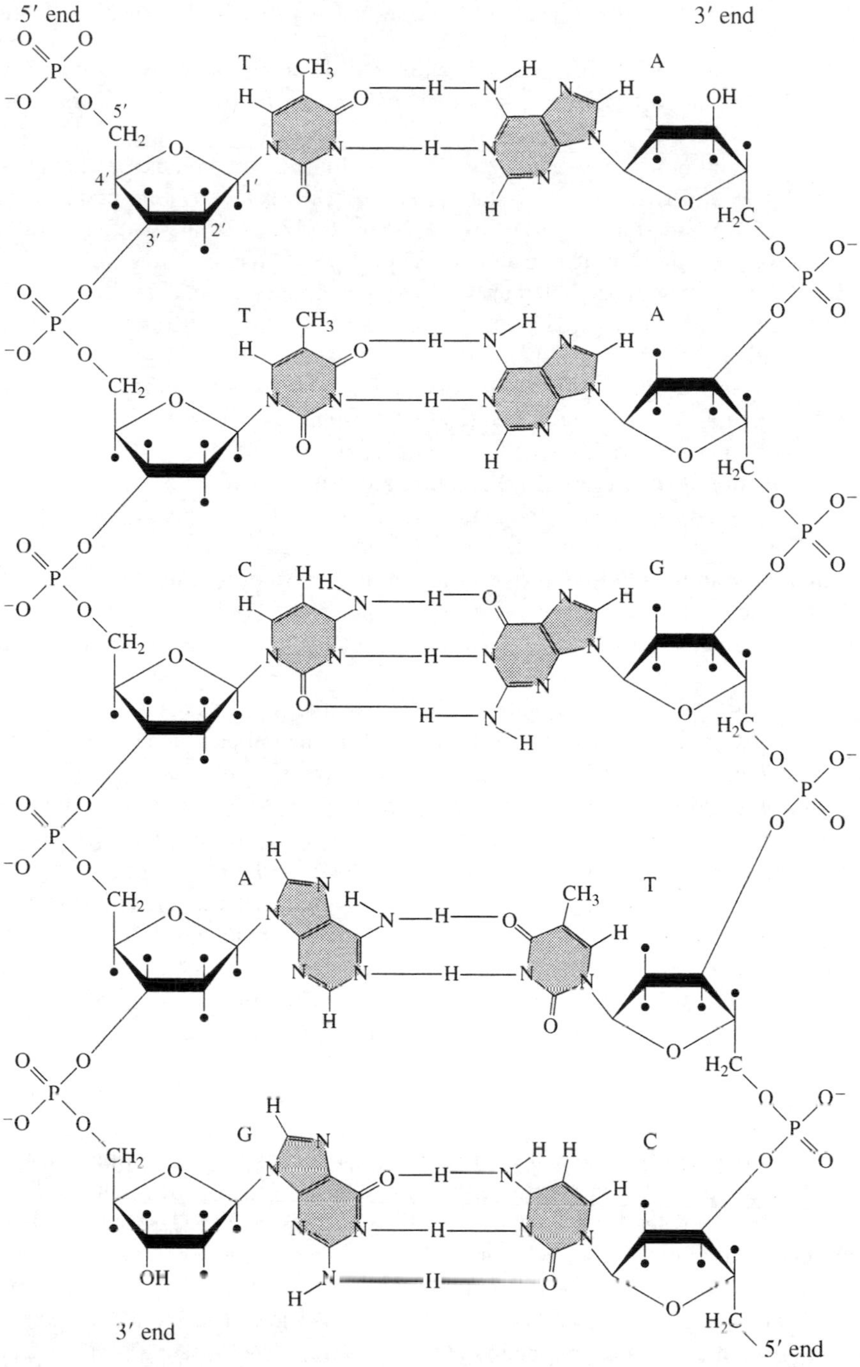

FIGURE 7-7 Antiparallel double-stranded DNA illustrating complementary binding of bases. G–C base-pairs are held together by three hydrogen bonds and A–T base-pairs are held together by two hydrogen bonds. The 5'-OH group of the sugar from one subunit is indirectly attached through a phosphate group to the 3'-OH group of the sugar from an adjacent subunit. (*Source:* H. Curtis, *Biology* (New York: Worth Publishers 1968), p. 422.)

two purine or two pyrimidine bases are chemically bonded is inherently unstable. This explains Chargaff's observations that for every A there is a T, and for every G there is a C.

The overall molecular shape resembles a cylinder with a diameter of approximately 20 Å, and two "grooves" that appear on the surface (i.e., a major, deep groove and a minor, shallow one) (Figure 7-8). The bases of the two antiparallel strands are complementary to one another. Thus, if the sequence of one strand is 5'-AATGCCAT-3', then the complementary hydrogen bonded strand has the sequence 3'-TTACGGTA-5'. For every A on one strand, there is a corresponding T on the opposite strand; and for every G on one strand, there is a corresponding C on the other strand. The association of a purine on one strand with its complementary pyrimidine on the opposite strand is referred to as a *base-pair*. The specificity exhibited by the bases on opposite strands is an important feature for the molecule's function in information storage and transfer. The antiparallel strands are held together primarily by the combined forces of the many hydrogen bonds that link complementary bases. There is also a hydrophobic interaction that excludes water from the inner portion of the molecule and adds to the stability of the double helix. The two strands of the duplex can be separated by heating or by alkali treatment. The separation is referred to as *denaturation*. The strands can be reannealed under the appropriate conditions.

DNA may be linear or circular, depending on the type of organism in which it is found. *Prokaryotes*, organisms that lack a well-defined nuclear membrane and include the unicellular bacteria and *cyanobacteria* (formerly called *blue-green algae*), contain a closed double-stranded circular DNA. *Eukaryotes*, organisms whose cells are more complex and have a defined nuclear membrane and include algae, fungi, plants, and animals, contain linear DNA within their nuclei. These organisms also possess *mitochondria*, organelles responsible for cellular respiration and the generation of chemical energy in the form of ATP (adenosine triphosphate). Mitochondria contain a unique form of circular DNA. Plants and algae, eukaryotes that photosynthesize, contain chloroplasts as well as mitochondria. Chloroplasts contain another unique form of circular DNA.

Stability

DNA is a very stable molecule *in vitro* despite the fact that polynucleotides are thermodynamically unstable and undergo a slow hydrolysis *in vivo*. Fragments of DNA have even been isolated from fossils. Nevertheless, DNA can be degraded rapidly by either chemical hydrolysis or cellular nucleases. These include endonucleases that can cleave two adjacent nucleotides within a strand and exonucleases that can cleave away terminal residues, one at a time, at either the 3' end or the 5' end. Cellular organelles known as *lysosomes* contain both DNAases and RNAases, which are capable of breaking down DNA and RNA, respectively, when appropriate. These degradative enzymes are also synthesized by the pancreas and secreted into the duodenum of the small intestine, where they play an important role in the digestive process.

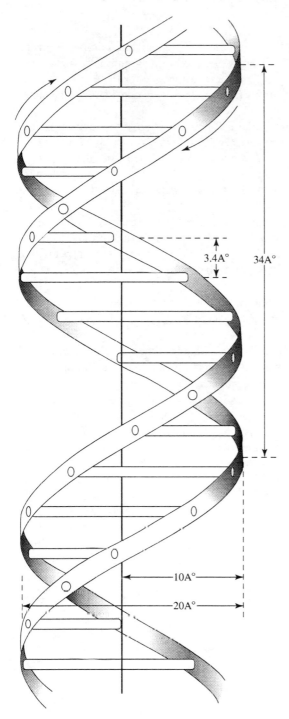

3.4A°   34A°

10A°

20A°

FIGURE 7-8 Schematic diagram of the Watson–Crick DNA double helix, illustrating periodicities observed by x-ray diffraction. (*Source:* H. Curtis and N. S. Barnes, *Biology,* 5th ed. (New York: Worth Publishers, 1989), p. 289.)

CENTRAL DOGMA

The history of genetics began in 1866 with Gregor Mendel's classic paper on the transmission of plant characteristics from generation to generation.[50] Mendel believed that individual pairs of factors (genes) are responsible for the expression of a given characteristic. The observable traits (phenotypes) were considered to be either dominant or recessive.

His theories provided an explanation for the mechanism of evolution that Charles Darwin had described some years earlier in his classic publication, *On the Origin of Species by Means of Natural Selection.*[51] Mendel died without recognition for his profound discoveries and insights. In 1900, his research and writings were rediscovered, and he was rightly credited for his discoveries and named the Father of Genetics.[52–55]

Our current understanding of genes is that they are discrete and fundamental units of heredity responsible for transmission of particular heritable traits to future generations. *Structural genes* are nucleic acid carriers of information that specify the primary structure (amino acid sequence) of both enzymatic and structural proteins. The assembly of amino acid subunits into proteins is known as *translation.* These proteins are directly or indirectly responsible for phenotypic expression. Another class of genes codes for the functional, but nontranslated, types of RNAs (i.e., *t*RNA and *r*RNA) important for the process of protein synthesis. There are also genes that specify regulatory information, *regulatory genes,* that in some way control structural gene function. The complete genetic composition of an individual, including nuclear and mitochondrial DNA, is known as its *genome.*

In 1958, Crick described what is known as the *central dogma of molecular biology*, a concept based on the fact that DNA does not serve as a direct template for protein synthesis but rather, during the process of transcription, the information of DNA is transferred to RNA, which in turn provides the information for the synthesis of the specified protein in the process known as *translation* (Figure 7-9). In order for the cell to produce enzymes and structural proteins, the nucleotide sequence information for their syntheses must first be transcribed from the DNA template into the form of a messenger RNA. The term *messenger RNA* (*m*RNA) was coined by Francois Jacob and Jacques Monod in 1961. The *m*RNA is complementary to the base sequence of the DNA and is produced by the enzyme RNA polymerase. There is a direct linear relationship between the primary structure (amino acid sequence) of

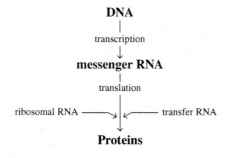

FIGURE 7-9 The flow of information from the informational level of DNA, to the intermediate *m*RNA, and ultimately to the synthesis of specific proteins.

the product protein and the sequence of bases in the DNA of the gene. The vast majority of cellular RNA is *m*RNA. Two other classes of RNA molecules are produced by transcription, both of which are vital to protein synthesis, namely, *ribosomal RNA* (*r*RNA), which is used to construct the *ribosome* (the organelle on which protein synthesis takes place), and *transfer RNA* (*t*RNA), which is the RNA responsible for bringing the appropriate amino acid into position on the ribosome for covalent linkage so that subunit assembly can proceed and a protein can be produced. Transcription of various genes into *m*RNA is a very selective process, because only certain genes within the genome are transcribed at any one time. Indeed, some genes, such as the one that codes for the non-alpha chain of fetal hemoglobin, are transcribed for only a brief period in the life cycle of the organism. The selection of which structural genes are to be transcribed and when transcription is to take place is under the control of various regulatory genes found scattered throughout the genome.

The central dogma of a unidirectional transfer of information from DNA to *m*RNA to protein was accepted faithfully throughout most of the 1960s until the publications of Howard Temin and Satoshi Mizutani[57] and of David Baltimore[58] describing an enzyme in Rous Sarcoma virus (avian virus) capable of transcribing RNA into a strand of complementary DNA. The enzyme, reverse transcriptase, is now known to be present in the class of viruses known as *retroviruses* as well as some cells. Reverse transcriptase is an RNA-directed DNA polymerase, and is present together with double-stranded RNA within the core of retroviruses. The central dogma was modified to indicate that, in some instances, the transcription process is bidirectional.

THE GENETIC CODE

The processes of transcription and translation result in the synthesis of a protein with a specific amino acid sequence, or *primary structure.* The information required to assemble the primary structure is coded within the informational strand of DNA. Each amino acid is specified by a *triplet code,* a sequence of three adjacent nucleotide bases within DNA, which is used in the production of a triplet of nucleotide bases, the *codon,* found in *m*RNA. Of the 64 possible triplets that can be formed from the 4 bases, 61 code for amino acids and 3 are used as translational stop signals.

In 1961, Marshall Nirenberg and Heinrich Matthaei reported that they had deciphered the first codon of the genetic code, namely, UUU coding for phenylalanine.[59] This was done by supplying a synthetic messenger, polyU (polyuridilylic acid), which had been produced by the action of polynucleotide phosphorylase; an *E. coli* extract, GTP; and all 20 common amino acids. All were placed in different test tubes. However, in each of the 20 tubes, a different radiolabeled amino acid was supplied; thus, each tube contained 19 "cold" amino acids and 1 labeled amino acid. The resulting mixtures were incubated for a period of time and the contents of each tube were analyzed. Only one tube contained a radioactive peptide, polyphenylalanine; thus it was concluded that the polyU messenger coded for polyphenylalanine and that the triplet codon UUU specified phenylalanine. Using the same technique it was soon found that polyC (polycytidylic acid) coded for polyproline, thus CCC is the codon for proline; and that polyA (polyadenylic acid) coded for polylysine, so that AAA was the codon for lysine. Nirenberg and Matthaei produced other synthetic messengers using the polynucleotide phosphorylase enzyme with varying amounts of the precursor diphosphates ADP, UDP, CDP, and GDP. Using this approach, they were able to identify all of the bases in each codon triplet. However, the specific sequence of bases in each codon still remained unknown.

In 1964, Nirenbeg and Philip Leder solved this problem.[60] Using a mixture of trinucleotides of known sequence, *E. coli* ribosomes and amino-acyl *t*RNAs, they were able to show that specific *t*RNAs would become bound to the ribosome only if the anticodon (triplet region of a *t*RNA molecule) and codon matched, and so a specific amino acid was incorporated only if the correct triplet codon was available for binding in the initiation complex (Figure 7-10). By 1965, the identification of every codon had been accomplished. The complete genetic code is shown in Figure 7-11.

The genetic code has been found to be universal, with codons representing the same amino acids in all organisms studied thus far, including viruses. The only exceptions found to date consist of the yeast mitochondrial codon AUA, which codes for methionine instead of the expected isoleucine, and the codon UGA, which normally serves as one of the three translation terminators, but in yeast mitochondria codes for tryptophan. There are also some minor differences in the protists and in some bacteria.

The codons UAG, UAA, and UGA are known as *nonsense codons* because they do not specify any amino acid. They are terminator signals found at the end of each *m*RNA molecule to signal the end of translation. The codon for methionine, AUG, also serves as the *initiator codon,* the triplet that signals the starting site on the *m*RNA for translation.

Because the code is read in triplets without punctuation between adjacent codons, the reading frame must be demarcated by specific signals at the beginning and end of the region of DNA to be transcribed. It is obvious that if the reading frame is misread or if a nucleotide is skipped or inserted into the *m*RNA sequence, the product is a *missense protein.* The effect of such a mutation varies depending on the position of the insertion or deletion within the gene.

The code is considered to be *degenerate* because generally more than one codon specifies each amino acid. In fact, only methionine and tryptophan are represented by a single codon. The other amino acids are represented by six codons (leucine and serine), four codons (glycine and alanine) or two codons (glutamic acid, tyrosine, and histidine). Despite the degeneracy of the code, any one codon can specify only a single amino acid. It is significant to note that where a single amino acid is represented by multiple codons, the codons differ primarily in the third base of the codon (3' end). Thus, arginine is represented by the codons CGU, CGC, CGA, and CGG, and alanine is represented by the codons GCU, GCC, GCA, and GCG. It appears that the first two bases of the triplet determine

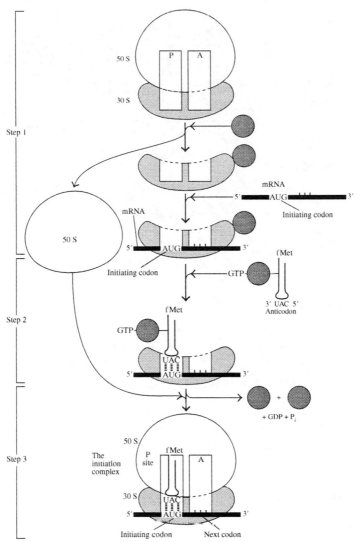

FIGURE 7-10 Initiation complex illustrating the interaction of initiating factors, *t*RNA, and *m*RNA on the prokaryotic ribosome. Protein synthesis requires the two ribosomal subunits (50S and 30S), the initiating *t*RNA (formylmethininyl-*t*RNA), three protein initiation factors (IF), and GTP. In step 1, IF 3 binds to the small ribosomal subunit. The complex now combines with *m*RNA such that the initiator codon AUG is seated properly on the subunit. In step 2, IF2 bound to GTP and to the initiating *t*RNA becomes bound to the complex formed in step 1. The anticodon on the *t*RNA base-pairs with the AUG codon on the messenger. In step 3, the large 50S subunit becomes bound to the complex as GTP is hydrolyzed to GDP and inorganic phosphate. Simultaneously IF2 and IF3 are released. The initiation complex has two sites, the A (aminoacyl) and P (peptidyl) site. The former binds incoming aminoacyl *t*RNAs. The latter is the site of binding of the growing peptidyl-*t*RNA chain. The initiation complex participates in the processes of elongation and termination, resulting in the nascent peptide chain.   (*Source: A. L. Lehninger, Principles of Biochemistry (New York: Worth Publishers, 1982), p. 884.*)

1st position (5′ end) ↓	U	C	A	G	3rd position (3′ end) ↓
U	Phe	Ser	Tyr	Cys	U
	Phe	Ser	Tyr	Cys	C
	Leu	Ser	STOP	STOP	A
	Leu	Ser	STOP	Trp	G
C	Leu	Pro	His	Arg	U
	Leu	Pro	His	Arg	C
	Leu	Pro	Gln	Arg	A
	Leu	Pro	Gln	Arg	G
A	Ile	Thr	Asn	Ser	U
	Ile	Thr	Asn	Ser	C
	Ile	Thr	Lys	Arg	A
	Met	Thr	Lys	Arg	G
G	Val	Ala	Asp	Gly	U
	Val	Ala	Asp	Gly	C
	Val	Ala	Glu	Gly	A
	Val	Ala	Glu	Gly	G

FIGURE 7-11   The genetic code. The triplet codons in *m*RNA are each translated into an amino acid. For example, the codon UAC is translated as tyrosine.   (*Source:* B. Alberts, D. Bray, J. Lewis, M. Raff, K. Roberts, and J. D. Watson, *Molecular Biology of the Cell,* 2nd ed. (New York: Garland Publishing Co., 1989), p. 103.)

coding for an amino acid and that the third base, although important, is somewhat less specific.

A comparative study of the nucleotide base sequence for each codon and the anticodon region of the corresponding *t*RNAs led Crick to develop his "Wobble Hypothesis" in 1966.[61] Crick proposed that the first two nitrogenous bases of each codon form relatively strong and highly specific "Watson–Crick" complementary base pairs by hydrogen bonding with the corresponding bases of the anticodon. However, the first base at the 3′ end of some anticodon triplets allows for the binding of several different codons, despite specifying a single amino acid. Because the anticodon can wobble during base pairing, the result is that the anticodons of many *t*RNAs can form stable base-pairs with more than a single codon. It is believed that the loose pairing of the third base is necessary to allow rapid dissociation of *t*RNAs from their codons in the *m*RNA during translation. Furthermore, for a given amino acid, codons that differ in either of the first two bases require different *t*RNAs. The result of this is that a minimum of 32 *t*RNAs are required to translate all 61 different amino-acid codons.

METHYLATION OF BASES IN DNA

In the mid-1970s, 5-methylcytosine was discovered in calf thymus DNA. Since then, it has been found in numerous species.[62,63] In mammalian DNA, 2% to 7% (depending on the species) of cytosine is converted to 5-methylcytosine by enzymatic methyl transfer from S-adenosylmethionine.[64–68] In vertebrate DNA, 5-methylcytosine is the only modified base found thus far. Therefore, 5-methylcytosine represents a fifth unique nitrogenous base in DNA. In prokaryotes, both cytosine and adenine can be found in the methylated state. Fewer than 1% of these bases are, in fact, methylated. In mammalian systems, the methylating enzymes recognize the sequence CG, and methylate the cytosine on one strand as well as the cytosine on its complementary strand. Thus the DNA sequence appearing as

$$5'.....................C\text{-}G.....................3'$$
$$3'.....................G\text{-}C.....................5'$$

becomes

$$5'.....................*C\text{-}G.....................3'$$
$$3'.....................G\text{-}C*.....................5'$$

where the asterisk (*) indicates a methyl group.

DNA methylation has been implicated in several biological processes including DNA repair (mismatch error correction) and also in gene expression. Inactive genes can be stimulated to undergo transcription by 5-azacytidine, a drug that interferes with cytosine methylation. Methylation at a particular site in DNA appears to be a heritable phenomenon. When eukaryotic DNA is replicated, cellular methylases maintain all daughter-cell DNA in the same methylated condition as the parental DNA. In prokaryotes, methylation serves to protect host cell DNA from cleavage by restriction endonucleases. Methylation of bases can be extremely important to molecular biologists, because certain restriction enzymes are sensitive to methylation. The enzyme HpaII, for example, which normally restricts (cleaves) the sequence CCGG, will not do so if the sequence has been methylated. Other restriction enzymes, such as MspI, remain unaffected by base methylation and cleave the sequence regardless of methylation.

The function of base methylation in eukaryotes is less obvious than in prokaryotes. Because it has been found that in most eukaryotes, DNA is modified after its synthesis by the enzymatic conversion of many cytosine residues to 5-methylcytosine, and because this methylation is often tissue specific, it is possible that methylation plays a role in gene regulation by preventing gene transcription.[69–73]

TRANSCRIPTION AND TRANSLATION

The processes of transcription and translation mentioned earlier refer to the mechanism of the transfer of information from the level of DNA to the level of RNA and the subsequent synthesis of protein based on this information. First, specific genes are selectively transcribed into a form of RNA known as *heterogeneous nuclear RNA (H*nRNA). This *m*RNA precursor is relatively long and generally contains sequences not found in functional *m*RNA. *H*nRNA undergoes several modifications within the nucleus that ultimately transform it into functional *m*RNA. These modifications include (1) attachment of a polyA tail, consisting of some 100 to 200 adenylate residues at the 3′ end of the messenger; (2) attachment of a 5′ cap, consisting of at least a 7-methylguanosine residue linked to the 5′ end of the messenger via a triphosphate linkage; and (3) excision of one or more *introns,* which are extraneous, usually noncoding sequences of nucleotides within the primary (*H*nRNA) transcript. Excision takes place with the assistance of another class of RNA molecules known as *small nuclear RNAs (sn*RNAs) that ensure that cleavage occurs at the precise location between each intron and its surrounding coding DNA (exons). Following excision, the remaining exons are then ligated together, and the resulting *m*RNA molecule migrates out of the nucleus, through the pores of the nuclear membrane, to the cytoplasm, where it then participates in the process of translation (protein synthesis).

Messenger RNA is a single-stranded molecule that carries the information found in DNA to the ribosomes in the cytoplasm. In this way, the DNA remains safely housed within the nucleus of the cell while the information that is required for translation moves out of the nucleus to its target on the ribosome. Messengers vary in length, and in prokaryotes may contain information for only one polypeptide (monogenic or monocistronic) or for two or more polypeptides (polygenic or polycistronic). As described in the foregoing, the *m*RNA contains not only the base sequence required for synthesis of the peptide, but also a "leader" stretch of some 100 to 200 bases attached to its 5′ end. Some polycistronic *m*-RNA may also contain noncoding, intervening sequences between the regions that code for proteins, which serve some regulatory role controlling the translational process.

Both ribosomal RNA and *t*RNA are made from larger precursor RNAs transcribed by RNA polymerase. Ribosomal RNA constitutes about 65% by weight of the ribosome, and is found in three forms in prokaryotes and four forms in eukaryotes. These forms are differentiated by their sedimentation properties and are sized by their sedimentation *(S)*[*] values, as described earlier. Prokaryotic ribosomal RNAs are initially transcribed as a single 30*S* RNA precursor. This precursor is subsequently processed by cleavage and base modifications to yield 16*S* and 23*S* ribosomal RNAs. The 5*S* *r*RNA segment is derived from the 3′ end of the same 30*S* precursor. In eukaryotes, a 45*S* precursor is modified by methylation and cleavage in the nucleolus, an organelle within the nucleus, to produce the 18*S* and

---

*Relatively large molecules and complexes such as ribosomal subunits can be characterized by analytical ultracentrifugation to determine a sedimentation coefficient that is related to the speed of sedimentation in centimeters per second (cm/sec) and the angular rotation of the centrifuge rotor in radians per second (rad/sec). Thus the sedimentation coefficient is given by $dx/dt/\omega^2 x$, where x is the distance from the center of rotation in centimeters. The sedimentation coefficient is described in units of seconds and is expressed as Svedberg units, where $1\ S = 1 \times 10^{-13}$ sec. It provides an indication of relative size (molecular weight) and mass.

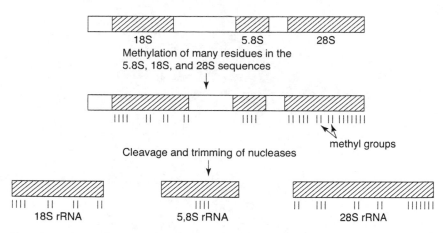

18S   5.8S   28S

Methylation of many residues in the
5.8S, 18S, and 28S sequences

methyl groups

Cleavage and trimming of nucleases

18S rRNA   5,8S rRNA   28S rRNA

The 5S rRNA arises separately.

FIGURE 7-12   The 45S ribosomal RNA precursor molecule is first methylated at approximately 100 sites and then enzymatically cleaved to produce the three rRNA molecules. Adapted from: A. L. Lehninger, *Principles of Biochemistry* (New York: Worth Publishers, 1982), p. 858.

28S rRNA molecules. The 5.8S rRNA molecule is also derived from this precursor. The 5S rRNA is made from a different precursor molecule (Figure 7-12). The 18S ribosomal RNA molecule is used to construct the 40S (small) subunit of the eukaryotic ribosome, whereas the large subunit (60S) is constructed around a 5S, a 5.8S, and a 28S ribosomal RNA. More than 70 proteins can be isolated from the complete ribosome, which measures approximately 21 nm in diameter and has a sedimentation coefficient of 80S.

Transfer RNA molecules are also made from longer precursors. Sequences at the 3' and 5' end are removed, and the trinucleotide sequence of -C-C-A is added at the 3' end (acceptor stem), unless the molecule has already been transcribed with this 3'-OH sequence. Transfer RNA molecules also contain bases modified by methylation, deamination, or reduction.

Transfer RNAs (formerly known as *soluble RNA*) are single stranded, consisting of about 75 to 100 nucleotide bases that are folded into a cloverleaf pattern (Figure 7-13) and then refolded into a more complex three-dimensional shape. For each of the 20 different amino acids found in the cell, there is at least one tRNA available. Each tRNA can become covalently associated at its 3'-OH end with its corresponding amino acid. The tRNA can then bring this amino acid into a position on the ribosome that corresponds to the sequence of nucleotide bases on the mRNA. Thus, the sequence of codons in the mRNA determines the sequence of tRNAs that become associated with the ribosome and ultimately determines the sequence of amino acids that become covalently linked to one another via peptide bonds. The overall process of translation is shown in Figure 7-14.

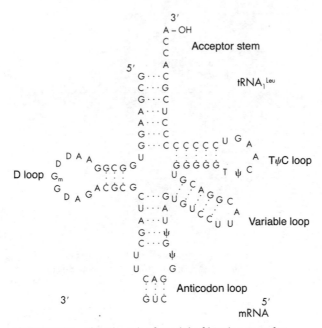

FIGURE 7-13   The Cloverleaf model of leucine transfer RNA. All *t*RNA molecules share a similar shape as a result of base pairing in specific regions of the molecule. Although various *t*RNAs differ in length, they all share a 5′ guanosine on one end and a -C-C-A-3′ sequence at the other end. There are also several loops consisting of unpaired bases including the DHU (dihydrouridine) loop; the anticodon loop, consisting of the triplet of bases complementary to the corresponding codon on *m*RNA; and the TψC loop, which contains pseudouridine. In some *t*RNAs, an extra loop is present that varies in size   (*Source:* C. K. Matthews and K. E. van Holde. *Biochemistry* (California: Addison-Wesley Publishing, 1990), p. 960.)

INTRONS

Unlike prokaryotic genes, most mammalian genes contain intervening, noncoding sequences of nucleotides, referred to as *introns* (short for *intervening sequences*) scattered within the coding regions (exons) of the gene.[74–76] Discovered in 1977, introns interrupt the precise colinear relationship between the nucleotide base sequence in the gene and the amino acid sequence found in the corresponding protein. Both introns and exons are transcribed by RNA polymerase, but only the exons are translated. The introns must be removed and adjacent exons spliced together. Introns were first studied in the vertebrate ovalbumin and *β* globin genes. Many more genes have been studied since then, most of which have been found to contain from 2 to 50 introns. The gene that codes for the protein collagen has been found to contain more than 50 introns.

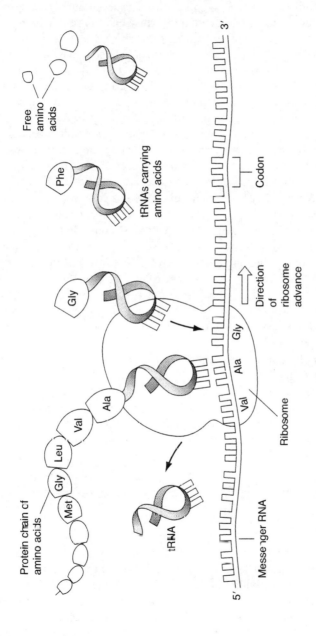

FIGURE 7-14 The overall process of translation, protein synthesis. (*Source:* C. K. Matthews and K. E. van Holde, *Biochemistry.* (California: Addison-Wesley Publishing, 1990), p. 120.)

Protein chain of amino acids

Met Gly Leu Val Ala

tRNA

Messenger RNA

5'

Ala Gly

Val

Ribosome

Direction of ribosome advance

Codon

3'

Gly

Phe

tRNAs carrying amino acids

Free amino acids

With the exception of the genes coding for histones, all informational genes studied to date contain introns in varying numbers and in varying positions. Within mammalian genes, there is usually much more DNA present in the form of introns than that which is found in exons. For example, examination of the egg ovalbumin gene reveals the presence of seven introns and eight coding exons. The seven introns represent more than 85% of the entire length of DNA containing this gene. As described in the previous section, the $HnRNA$ molecule, the primary transcript, which is synthesized and processed within the nucleus, can be 10^1 to 10^2 times as large as the final $mRNA$ molecule that exits the nucleus and enters the cytoplasm to be used for translation.

All introns found to date begin with the nucleotides 5'-GT and end with the nucleotides AG-3'. Thus each intron contains specific signals for its removal by excision enzymes within the nucleus. Excision of introns and splicing of exons appears to be conducted by RNA-protein complexes known as *spliceosomes*. Splicing requires ATP and takes place in a two-step enzymatic reaction. Introns appear to form loops of 80 to 10,000 nucleotides that can be recognized by the spliceosome and removed with great precision.[77–79] Splicing of the remaining exons in various ways can result in several different $mRNA$ molecules, each of which can code for a different protein.

The mechanism by which the spliceosome functions appears to involve small nuclear RNA molecules. These small RNAs ($snRNAs$) consisting of about 100 nucleotide residues are found in the nucleus and are complementary to the sequences at the ends of each intron. By binding of the $snRNA$ to the $HnRNA$, the introns within the $HnRNA$ form loops allowing the adjacent exons to be brought into close contact with each other. Thus, with the assistance of the $snRNAs$, enzymes can splice together adjoining exons to form the final $mRNA$. With the assistance of two proteins the completed messenger can now be transported out of the nucleus via pores situated in the nuclear membrane.

The function of the intron is unknown at this time, but its ubiquitous presence implies an important function. It has been speculated that the presence of introns results in the fragmentation of the gene into recombinable subgene units resulting in the creation of novel gene sequences that are important in evolutionary terms for the survival of the species. Alternately, the cell may produce different $mRNA$ molecules and, therefore, proteins during different stages of development or during different stages of the cell cycle. Some introns have been found to code for specific proteins.

CHROMOSOME STRUCTURE

In 1869, Eduard Strasburger developed improved histochemical staining techniques that allowed him to see and describe rod-like forms within the nucleus at cell division.[80] In 1879, Walther Flemming named the material within the cell nucleus *chromatin*.[81] He noted that during early meiotic division, chromatin took on different configurations and positions within the cell. Waldeyer, a cytologist, coined the term *chromosome* to describe the condensed rodlike chromatin structures within a species. DNA of eukaryotic cells is found in the form of chromosomes, the exact number being dependent on the species; for example, humans have 46 chromosomes, consisting of 22 pairs of autosomes and 2 sex chromosomes—XX in the female and XY in the male. The number is not exclusive to a particular species; for example, both humans and bats have 46 chromosomes in each nucleated cell.

Each chromosome consists of a single double-stranded linear DNA molecule. The total genetic constitution of the cell is referred to as its *genome*. It consists of all the genes found within its chromosomes as well as those found in extranuclear organelles such as mitochondria and chloroplasts in plant cells. The human genome is thought to be composed of approximately 100,000 genes, approximately one third of which are variable from individual to individual. During mitosis and meiosis, when replicated DNA must be parceled out to daughter cells, chromatin is condensed into chromosomes, thereby facilitating the movement of large amounts of DNA, while at the same time preventing loss of portions of the molecule. Chromatin consists of a dispersed, amorphous mixture of DNA, protein, and RNA in the percentage ratio of approximately 35:60:5. Most of the proteins associated with chromatin are basic and are called *histones*. They function in packaging the DNA into structures called *nucleosomes* (*nu bodies*), which resemble beads on a string (Figure 7-15).[35] Chromosomes also contain some nonbasic proteins that are important structural components.

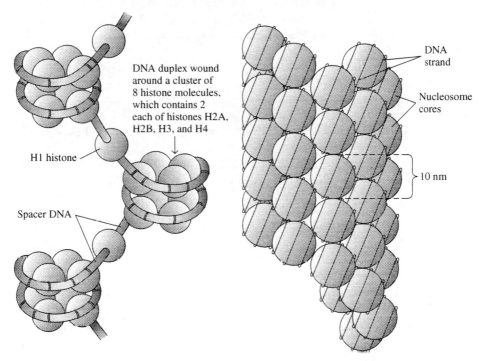

FIGURE 7-15 Nucleosomes, the basis for packaging DNA in the eukaryotic chromosome. The figure on the left illustrates the simple structure of DNA combined with the five classes of histones producing what appears to be an arrangement of "beads on a string." The nucleosomes consist of approximately 200 base-pairs of DNA wound around a grouping of eight histone molecules. The spacer DNA is combined with the H1 histone. The schematic illustration on the right shows that these chromatin fibers are arranged into a tightly packed lattice structure. (*Source:* A. L. Lehninger, *Principles of Biochemistry* (New York: Worth Publishers, 1982), p. 819.)

TABLE 7-2 The five major categories of histone proteins.

Type	Molecular Weight	Residues (No.)	Basic Residues (No.)	Acidic Residues (No.)
H1	21000	213	65	10
H2A	14000	129	30	9
H2B	13800	125	31	10
H3	15300	135	33	11
H4	11300	102	27	7

Source: J. D. Rawn, *Biochemistry* (Burlington, NC: Neil Patterson Publishers, 1990), p. 684.

Histones are small, basic proteins having molecular weights of approximately 11,000 to 21,000 daltons. They are rich in the basic amino acids, lysine and arginine. At pH 7.0, these amino acids are positively charged and can form electrostatic bonds with the negative groups found on the phosphate atoms of DNA. Histones are categorized based on their content of arginine and lysine, into five major classes (Table 7-2). Histone H1 is lysine rich (29% lysine residues); histones H2A and H2B contain both lysine and arginine in high percentages; histones H3 and H4, called *arginine-rich histones,* contain large amounts of arginine (13.5% and 14%, respectively). H3 and H4 have significant sequence homology in many eukaryotic species, so it is probable that they serve similar fundamental functions.

The histones interact with the DNA to form the nucleosomes. These beadlike structures consist of double-stranded DNA (approximately 200 base-pairs) wound around the core of histone proteins. The bead consists of eight histone molecules, including two H2A, two H2B, two H3, and two H4 proteins, and has a diameter of about 10 nm. H1 histone is found associated with linker DNA (double-stranded DNA of varying lengths that connect each nucleosome). In human cells, the linkers extend for approximately 50 bases. These nucleosomes are further arranged in an orderly fashion within the chromosome. Nonhistone proteins play a role in forming and maintaining a superstructure or lattice, thereby allowing a large amount of DNA to be packaged into a rather small volume. Prior to replication, this elaborate packaging must be reversed so that the bases on each strand may become exposed to appropriate enzymes, ions, and precursors. The nature of this reversal remains an important area of research.

DNA SYNTHESIS IN THE CELL CYCLE

The *cell cycle* refers to the events that take place within the cell between one cell division and another. It consists of four phases, including mitosis (M phase), DNA synthesis (S phase) and two "gap" periods (G_1 and G_2). The mitotic phase is itself divided into periods known as prophase, metaphase, anaphase, and telophase. During mitosis, the chromatin becomes condensed into discrete chromosomal units, the nuclear membrane breaks down, duplicate chromosomes move to opposite poles of the

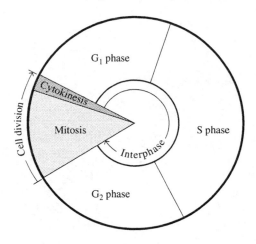

FIGURE 7-16 DNA synthesis takes place during the S phase of the cell cycle and precedes nuclear division. (*Source:* H. Curtis and N. S. Barnes, *Biology,* 5th ed. (New York: Worth Publishers, 1989), p. 146.)

cell with the assistance of the mitotic spindle fibers, two nuclei form at opposite ends of the cell, and the two new daughter cells become separated from each other as a result of cytokinesis in animal cells or plate formation in plant cells. The G_1, S, and G_2 phases are collectively known as *interphase* and represent periods in the cell cycle when the cell is actively metabolizing and growing, and, of course, synthesizing (replicating) DNA in preparation for the next mitotic division (Figure 7-16). Specific factors are important in controlling the cell cycle. Many of these are coded for by the CDC (cell division controlling) genes. Among the most important are CDC 2 (protein p34, a protein kinase), CDC 13 (cyclin, a protein that increases in concentration during the cell cycle and is then destroyed in M—cell division—phase) and CDC 25 (protein p80 or *string,* which coordinates the formation of MPF—maturation promoting factor—at the G2–M boundary from the CDC 2 and CDC 13 gene products). MPF initiates the beginning of M phase. Also important are a series of similar genes that operate during G1 phase to turn on S phase and with it, DNA replication.

Replication of prokaryotic DNA is a complex process involving at least 12 enzymes.[82] *E. coli* has been the organism most often selected for replication studies. Its DNA is double stranded, closed, circular, and supercoiled into a helical shape.

Replication of eukaryotic DNA is somewhat more complex than the same process in the prokaryote. These differences can be explained in part because of the linear nature of the molecule within each chromosome and the presence of histones and other associated molecules that are involved in packaging of the DNA molecule into nucleosomes.

The human diploid cell contains 46 chromosomes with more than 1,000 times as much DNA (2 m in length) as does *E. coli* (1.4 mm in length). This structural difference between eukaryotic and prokaryotic genomes necessitates special mechanisms for eukaryotes to expose the DNA to the replicating enzymes of the cell. Despite this, the same types of enzymes that have been described in prokaryotes are also found in eukaryotes, such as DNA polymerase, ligase, helicase, and other associated proteins. DNA labeling experiments were performed with eukaryotic DNA. These studies led to the conclusion that DNA replication is bidirectional. However, instead of only a single point of origin, as is found in prokaryotes, there

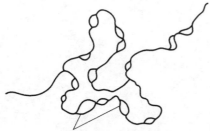

"Bubbles" formed by multiple points of bidirectional replication

(a)

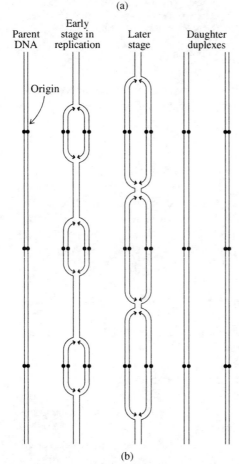

(b)

FIGURE 7-17 Replication of a eukaryotic chromosome. (a) Replicating segment of DNA (of *Drosophila melanogaster* eggs) forms "bubbles" by multiple points of bidirectional replication. (b) Bidirectional replication occurs at thousands of origins and continues until the synthesis of the daughter strands is complete. The two daughter duplex molecules now separate. (*Source:* A. L. Lehninger, *Principles of Biochemistry* (New York: Worth Publishers, 1982), p. 841.)

appear to be approximately 1,000 different origins on each chromosome, and at each origin there is bidirectional replication (Figure 7-17).

DNA Polymerase

In 1956, Arthur Kornberg and his colleagues who were studying DNA replication in *E. coli,* discovered the activity of the enzyme DNA polymerase I.[83–85] The enzyme has a molecular weight of 109,000 and is about 1,000 amino acids in length. It catalyzes the covalent addition of deoxyribonucleotide residues to the end of a DNA strand while releasing inorganic pyrophosphate, PPi, from each precursor deoxyribonucleoside triphosphate. The nucleotides are linked by their α-phosphate groups in a phosphodiester linkage to the 3′—OH end of the preexisting DNA chain, such that the direction of synthesis of the new strand is 5′ to 3′ (Figure 7-18). The energy

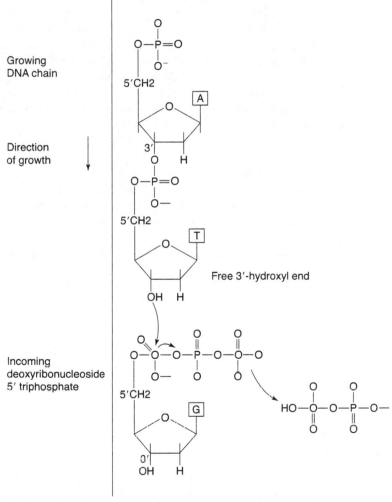

FIGURE 7-18 Elongation of a DNA chain by DNA polymerase. The mechanism uses nucleophilic attack of the free 3′OH group on the α phosphate atom of the incoming deoxyribonucleoside triphosphate. The new internucleotide linkage is formed with the departure of free pyrophosphate (PPi). The template strand is not shown.   (*Source:* A. L. Lehninger, *Principles of Biochemistry* (New York: Worth Publishers, 1982), p. 844.)

required for the process comes from the cleavage of the pyrophosphate (β and γ phosphates) from each nucleoside triphosphate. Its activity requires DNA acting as template and primer, all four deoxyribonucleotides (dATP, dGTP, dCTP, and dTTP) and Mg^{+2}. It also requires Zn^{+2}, which is bound tightly at its active site. The polymerase uses one strand as primer to which the subunits are sequentially added and the other strand as a template on which the complementary bases are laid down. The polymerase cannot synthesize DNA without the presence of a segment of double-stranded DNA; thus the length of the new strand is identical to the length of the template. In addition, the polymerase acts as a 5' to 3' to 5' terminal exonuclease. It can polymerize 600 nucleotides per minute, per molecule, at 37°C.

In the late 1960s, two additional DNA polymerases were found in *E. coli* (i.e., types II and III). Thus, *E.coli* contains three different DNA polymerases: type I (described in the foregoing), type II, and type III. The type II polymerase can also extend a DNA strand in the 5' to 3' direction and can act as an exonuclease in the 3' to 5' direction only. Its molecular weight is 120,000 and has only one-twentieth the activity of the type I enzyme. The most active polymerase, however, is DNA polymerase type III. Like the type I enzyme, it can extend a DNA strand in the 5' to 3' direction and can act as an exonuclease in either direction, but its activity is fifteen times greater than the type I enzyme. In fact, this 400,000-dalton enzyme is the major player in DNA polymerization in *E. coli*. Together with other enzymes, it forms a holoenzyme complex consisting of seven subunits with a combined molecular weight of about 550,000. Like the type I polymerase, it contains Zn^{+2} and requires Mg^{+2}. One of its subunits, copolymerase III, serves to recognize the polymerization initiation site, allowing the remaining portion of the holoenzyme to proceed with polymerization.

The type I polymerase appears to be more concerned with editing errors produced by the base pairing mechanism of replication. If a proper match is in position, this enzyme simply forms the phosphodiester bond between the new base and the 3'—OH group of the neighboring nucleotide. If the match is improper, then the enzyme acts as an exonuclease to remove it.

It has been shown that the type III polymerase begins synthesis of DNA at the end of a short RNA primer and shares some functions with polymerase type I. The type I enzyme functions, not only in repair, but also by removing the RNA primer molecules and replacing them with DNA by extending previously synthesized DNA fragments (known as *Okazaki fragments*—see the following section) to fill in DNA gaps. The type I enzyme may also function as a terminator of type III activity.

The function of type II polymerase has not been completely resolved but it may not be involved in DNA replication. All three enzymes can polymerize DNA and all have 3' to 5' exonuclease activity.

Unlike prokaryotic DNA polymerases, at least four eukaryotic DNA polymerases, α, β, γ, and δ, are known to exist. The δ polymerase is the enzyme responsible for continuous DNA synthesis and in this respect is similar to prokaryotic polymerase III. The β polymerase serves the role of a repair enzyme similar to prokaryotic polymerase I. The γ DNA polymerase is mitochondrial and the γ DNA polymerase's major function is to polymerize the lagging or discontinuous (see later in this chapter) strand. None of the four eukaryotic DNA polymerases exhibits exonuclease activity. Here too, synthesis is bidirectional using replication forks. As described earlier, multiple origin sites are used by each eukaryotic chromosome. Thus each chromosome has multiple replication forks at several sites, all replicating simultaneously. The initiation point or origin of DNA synthesis is called a *replicon.* Thus the major difference between eukaryotic and prokaryotic DNA synthesis aside from initiation is that the latter uses only a single point of origin and results in a single replicon, whereas the former uses multiple initiation points and produces multiple replicons. DNA replication in eukaryotes is relatively slow compared with prokaryotes. Replication fork movement in *E. coli* is about 20 times faster than for eukaryotes (2 to 6 μm/min). *E. coli* can synthesize DNA at a rate of 50 kb/min.

Various forms of DNA polymerase have been used by molecular biologists performing nucleic acid synthesis, sequencing analysis, or amplification of sequences using polymerase chain reactions (PCR). The particular enzymes used in these procedures are chosen because of their thermostability, fidelity, ability to remain on the primer-template duplex without dissociating from it, or because of their enzyme kinetics. They are generally derived from various bacteria or bacteriophages. Among the more commonly used enzymes are the Klenow fragment (large fragment of DNA polymerase I from *E. coli*), the phage T4 and T7 DNA polymerases, and the Taq DNA polymerase isolated from *Thermus aquaticus.*

Okazaki Fragments

Once it had been determined that all known DNA polymerases catalyze the addition of nucleotide units only in the 5' to 3' direction, it became difficult to understand how prokaryotic DNA replication occurred in light of the previous observations that replication takes place bidirectionally and simultaneously, starting at a single point of origin in prokaryotes. How can this occur when the polymerase enzyme synthesizes in only one direction (Figure 7-19)? Reiji Okazaki, studying replication in *E. coli* and other bacteria, found that newly synthesized DNA could be isolated in very small fragments of 1 to 2 kb in length. He correctly hypothesized that one of the newly made strands of DNA is synthesized continuously in the 5' to 3' direction, but that the other strand must be synthesized in small segments, in a discontinuous manner, each one of which is polymerized 5' to 3'.[86] These segments, known as *Okazaki fragments,* are subsequently ligated together enzymatically. It appears that Okazaki fragments are also synthesized during eukaryotic DNA replication, but the fragments are even smaller in length (one tenth the size of those found in prokaryotes).

FIGURE 7-19 Synthesis of the new strand by the polymerase is always in the 5' to 3' direction with incoming nucleotide subunits added to the 3' end of the primer.

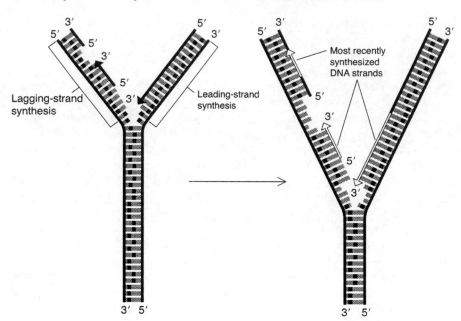

FIGURE 7-20   Generation of Okazaki fragments during DNA replication in *E. coli*. Replication occurs in the 5′ to 3′ direction in both strands. One parental strand is replicated 5′ to 3′ by DNA polymerase III in a continuous fashion. Its complementary strand is also replicated 5′ to 3′ by the polymerase in a direction away from the replication form but in a discontinuous manner. The second strand is called the *lagging strand*. The Okazaki fragment (1–2 kb long) is elongated until the fragment reaches the 3′—OH terminus of the previous Okazaki fragment.   (*Source:* B. Alberts, D. Bray, J. Lewis, M. Raff, K. Roberts, and J. D. Watson, *Molecular Biology of the Cell,* 2nd ed. (New York: Garland Publishing Co., 1989), p. 229.)

The mechanism of DNA replication, which is similar in prokaryotes and eukaryotes, is illustrated in Figure 7-20. Working from the 3′ to 5′ template, the DNA polymerase III moves in the direction of the replication fork, adding each nucleotide triphosphate to the free 3′—OH end of the preceding nucleotide. The newly created complementary DNA strand, which is continuously replicated in the 5′ to 3′ direction, is called the *leading strand* (right side of molecule in Figure 7-20). Replication of the other parental strand (3′ to 5′ template) must also occur in the 5′ to 3′ direction, resulting in a short fragment of DNA. Thus DNA synthesis using this template takes place in the opposite direction from the direction of movement of the replication fork. The fork moves forward another 1 to 2 kb and again, a DNA polymerase III enzyme synthesizes and attaches a new DNA stretch about 1 to 2 kb in length. The 3′ to 5′ replicating strand is called the *lagging strand* because synthesis is discontinuous and smaller fragments must be covalently attached by polymerase I to form complete complementary sequences. Synthesis of the completed strand takes somewhat more time than synthesis of the leading strand.

Surprisingly, it was found that synthesis of Okazaki fragments requires not only the four deoxyribonucleoside triphosphates but also the four ribonucleoside triphosphates for synthesis of RNA as well. A short section of RNA consisting of only approximately ten bases, complementary to the DNA template, is required as a primer for the synthesis of the Okazaki fragments. Essentially, at the replication fork, a DNA primase enzyme synthesizes the small RNA primer in the 5′ to 3′ direction on the DNA template. The RNA primer is then used to support Okazaki fragment synthesis. After the complementary DNA fragment is synthesized by DNA polymerase III, DNA polymerase I catalyzes the removal of the primer RNA sequence one base at a time until they are completely excised from the DNA duplex. At the same time, this polymerase replaces the excised RNA unit with a DNA unit until the nucleotide composition is completely DNA. A DNA ligase then covalently links the 3′OH of the newly made Okazaki fragment to the 5′-phosphate of the previously synthesized Okazaki fragment. Thus DNA synthesis is bidirectional from a single point of origin in prokaryotes.

The covalent linkage of the new Okazaki fragment to the growing DNA strand occurs in an energy requiring reaction and is the function of the enzyme DNA ligase, which forms phosphodiester bonds between the 5′ OH group of the Okazaki fragment and the 3′ phosphate group of the DNA strand that is being extended. The two new strands of DNA form a helix spontaneously without the need for enzymatic activity.

In addition to the DNA polymerases, many other enzymes are required in the process of replication. These enzymes are collectively termed the *DNA replicase system* or *holoenzyme,* and include ligating enzymes[87] and unwinding enzymes (Figure 7-21).

For DNA replication to occur, the antiparallel double helix must first be unwound to expose the bases that lie buried within the backbones of the two strands to the RNA polymerase and other associated molecules. Several enzymes known as

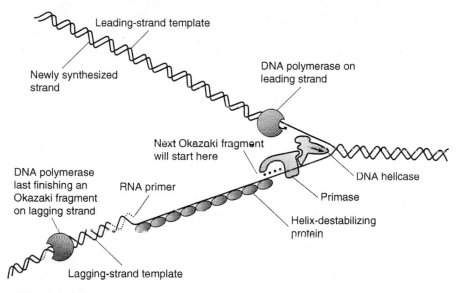

FIGURE 7-21 Summary of the major types of proteins that act at a DNA replication fork. The complex of DNA primase and DNA helicase on the lagging strand is known as the *primosome.* (*Source:* B. Alberts, D. Bray, J. Lewis, M. Raff, K. Roberts. and J. D. Watson, *Molecular Biology of the Cell,* 2nd ed. (New York: Garland Publishing Co.), 1989, p. 233.)

helicases function to catalyze the untwisting of the two strands of the helix just beyond the replication fork. This is an energy-requiring process. As the strands become untwisted, another enzyme termed a *DNA binding protein* combines with each of the two strands, preventing them from coming back together. While the strands are apart, the DNA polymerase can extend one strand 5′ to 3′, and the primase enzyme can synthesize RNA primers for the production of Okazaki pieces on the opposite strand.

Because the replication fork moves so rapidly and because the double helix must be untwisted so rapidly, the entire parent DNA molecule would have to twist at an extraordinarily rapid rate to allow the process to continue. This does not occur. It is thought that a swivel mechanism allows the untwisting to proceed as described, but that it causes no serious problems because the region of DNA beyond the replication fork is acted on by enzymes called *topoisomerases* (or *gyrases* in prokaryotes) that nick one strand of the DNA, allowing a short fragment of DNA to rotate. The enzyme then quickly splices the nicked area. Thus the enzymes topoisomerase I and II nick and splice the strands rapidly in specific locations, allowing the remaining unreplicated molecule to stabilize without the need to rotate rapidly to compensate for the action of the helicase. This unwinding or relaxation precedes further DNA replication. The topoisomerases actually assist the helicase in unwinding the parent strands.

DNA polymerase not only functions to polymerize new strands of DNA and excise nucleotide bases for replication purposes, but it also serves to repair damaged regions of DNA or regions having the incorrect complementary base in position. Genetic studies have shown that the error rate of DNA replication in prokaryotes is exceedingly low (on the order of 1 in 10^9 or 1 in 10^{10} nucleotides). Part of this low error rate is the result of the Watson–Crick base-pairing scheme. However, there is a far more important reason, namely, the ability of the DNA polymerase enzymes to function as exonucleases in either the 5′ to 3′ direction or the 3′ to 5′ direction. Of course the enzyme has polymerase activity in the 5′ to 3′ direction. However, activity in the reverse direction indicates that this enzyme functions in correcting errors brought about by incorrect nucleotide insertion and polymerization. Thus the enzyme excises the incorrect nucleotide and replaces it with a new, correct one as it proceeds with the elongation process. This proofreading function of polymerases I and III is certainly important in maintaining the fidelity of replication and preventing mutation.

REPETITIOUS DNA

In eukaryotes, there are three distinct classes of DNA: (1) unique sequences making up about 70% of the genome and consisting of nonrepeated sequences or segments that are repeated only a few times; (2) moderately repetitive sequences that make up about 20% of the genome and consisting of segments that are repeated at least 1,000 times; and (3) highly repetitive DNA (sometimes called *satellite DNA*) making up about 10% of the genome and consisting of millions of copies of short (less than 10 base-pairs) sequences localized to a limited number of regions throughout the human genome (Table 7-3). When a sequence of bases is repeated numerous times and attached in tandem, it is referred to as a *tandem repeat*. Four classes of tandem repeat sequences exist in the human

TABLE 7-3 Repetitive DNA in the human genome.[123]

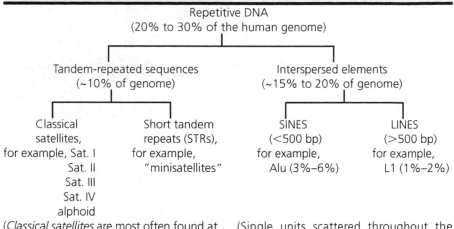

Repetitive DNA (20% to 30% of the human genome)			
Tandem-repeated sequences (~10% of genome)		Interspersed elements (~15% to 20% of genome)	
Classical satellites, for example, Sat. I Sat. II Sat. III Sat. IV alphoid	Short tandem repeats (STRs), for example, "minisatellites"	SINES (<500 bp) for example, Alu (3%–6%)	LINES (>500 bp) for example, L1 (1%–2%)
(*Classical satellites* are most often found at, or near, chromosome centromeres (*heterochromatin*)—likely to be nonmobile. *Minisatellites* are dispersed throughout genome—maybe clustered in some regions.)		(Single units scattered throughout the genome—likely to be mobile genetic elements—may be clustered in some regions.)	

Source: Reference 101.

genome: satellites I, II, III, and IV, which make up 5% of the entire genome. In addition, the human genome contains the alphoid class of repetitive DNA, which is associated with the centromeric region of certain chromosomes. The alphoid satellite consists of tandemly repeated units having a sequence consisting of about 170 nucleotides.

The unique sequence DNA represents coding regions (genes) that carry the information for the synthesis of specific proteins. This DNA also determines the degree of gene expression at various times of development in different tissues. In repetitious DNA, the repeated units are present in tandem arrays and are often localized on the chromosomes adjacent to the centromeric region, but have also been found in telomeres as well.[88–90] The repetitious sequences are noncoding forms of DNA. Because this DNA has no known function, it has often been referred to as *junk DNA*. Many scientists have concluded that this noncoding DNA represents evolutionary "leftovers"; however, it would not be surprising if some important function for much of this material were eventually found.

In addition to satellite DNA, there is a form of DNA known as *mini-satellite DNA*, which consists of short core sequences composed of about 15 to 30 bases arranged in the same order. Although the core sequence can be present as a single copy, it is usually repeated from 2 to 100 times and positioned in tandem. These regions are also known as *VNTR (variable nucleotide tandem repeat) sequences*. A VNTR sequence may be found at only one locus in the genome or at many loci (single- vs. multilocus VNTRs). Each VNTR is present in only a relatively small number of people in the population, but the genome of each person contains many different VNTRs.[82,91–94] A special class of VNTRs known as *short tandem repeats (STRs)* consists of repeated core units, each composed of 4 to 6 bases. STR loci exhibit *genomic variability*—that

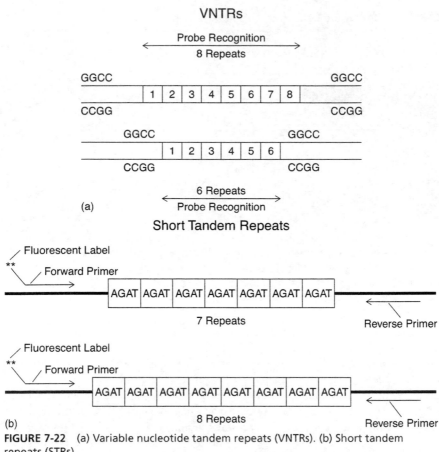

FIGURE 7-22 (a) Variable nucleotide tandem repeats (VNTRs). (b) Short tandem repeats (STRs).

is, there are allelic differences based on the number of repeating subunits. As stated previously, highly repetitious DNA is not translated and does not serve to provide information for protein synthesis. Nevertheless, these highly polymorphic genetic markers are extraordinarily useful for individualization purposes (Figure 7-22).

In addition to satellite and mini-satellite DNA, there is yet another class of DNA known as *interspersed repetitive DNA*. Interspersed elements represent approximately 15% to 20% of the human genome and are characterized as either SINES or LINES depending on the sequence length. This DNA is found scattered throughout the genome hundreds to thousands of times, but not generally situated in tandem arrays. This scattered form of DNA is also noncoding and can be found within introns or in regions adjacent to coding sequences in the genome. Like the other forms of repetitive DNA, its function is unknown. The percentages of the various forms of DNA described in the foregoing vary from species to species.

Some forms of repetitive DNA are transcribed and thus are informational. For example, DNA that codes for the transcription of the four *r*RNA molecules that are required for assembly of eukaryotic ribosomes falls into this category. Another example of transcribed repetitive DNA can be seen in the genes that code for histones, which can occur in the genome in quantities of 1,000 copies or more. The DNA of chickens also contains repetitious DNA that provides information for transcription and translation of feather keratins.

There is an accepted system of nomenclature to describe specific human DNA sequences.[95] In this system, tandem DNA repeat sequences are assigned names bearing information regarding the chromosomal location, if it is found in single- or multiple-copy loci, and the order in which it was detected (i.e., D17S30 is a DNA sequence found on chromosome 17, which is present at a single locus on a pair of homologous chromosomes). Highly repetitive satellite DNA sequences are given the designation Z, as in D17Z1.[96]

PALINDROMIC DNA

Palindromic sequences of DNA are specific regions within the genome that are inverted repetitions of base sequences with twofold symmetry. The result of the inverted sequences and the complementary base-pairing that ensues is a hairpin loop configuration as seen in Figure 7-23. Some palindromic sequences are short, consisting of only a handful of nucleotides, whereas some involve up to 1,000 base-pairs. Both appear to play some role in site recognition and perhaps genetic regulation.

Structural variations of DNA include hairpin loops, single-stranded loops, negative and positive supercoils, bends, left-handed helical sites, and cruciforms.

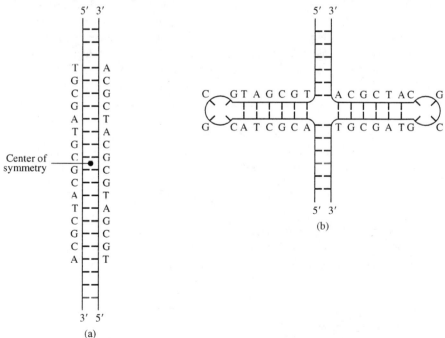

FIGURE 7-23 (a) A *palindrome* of nucleotides showing twofold symmetry about the central point. (b) A *cruciform* structure that forms when the palindrome base pairs within each strand rather than between the strands. Many palindromes exist in eukaryotic DNA. (*Source:* A. L. Lehninger, *Principles of Biochemistry* (New York: Worth Publishers, 1982), p. 826.)

These polymorphic variations in structure may be important as recognition sites by DNA-binding proteins and may be vital in the regulation of gene expression. Information to encode the binding of DNA regulatory proteins is surely contained at the level of the primary DNA sequence, but it may also be contained, in part, at the level of sequence-directed DNA structure. These conformational variations may modulate or even specify the binding of proteins that regulate gene expression.

MITOCHONDRIAL DNA

In addition to nuclear DNA, eukaryotic cells contain a unique mitochondrial form of DNA.[97–101] Mitochondria are the organelles responsible for aerobic cellular respiration and for the generation of ATP through the process of oxidative phosphorylation. The inheritance of mitochondrial genes is exclusively maternal and clearly non-Mendelian. This mitochondrial DNA differs both in shape and base composition from nuclear DNA. Despite the fact that mitochondria contain their own DNA, the genome lacks vital information required for the synthesis of critically important mitochondrial proteins and enzymes. In fact, nuclear DNA contains the information for the construction of most mitochondrial proteins. The assembly of the mitochondrion is therefore dependent on genetic information maintained in both mitochondrial and nuclear DNA.

Human mitochondria contain between two and ten copies of a double-stranded, circular DNA molecule that is about 16.5 kb in length and has a molecular weight of about 10^7. Mitochondrial DNA carries the information for the production of 22 mitochondrial tRNAs and 2 rRNAs and for 13 mitochondrial proteins, all of which are either components of the respiratory chain or of the oxidative phosphorylation system. These proteins are all located within the mitochondrial inner membrane. Each is a component of an oligomeric aggregate, which includes some proteins that are translated on cytoplasmic ribosomes. The human mitochondrial genome has been sequenced and has no known introns; in this way, it resembles the prokaryotic genome.[102] As pointed out previously, the genetic code is somewhat modified, because it has been shown that in the case of yeast mitochondria, the codon AUA codes for methionine instead of the expected isoleucine, and the codon UGA codes for tryptophan rather than serving as a stop signal. The vast majority, perhaps 95%, of all mitochondrial proteins are coded for by nuclear DNA.

The mitochondrial genome contains a highly variable region known as the *D-loop*. Analysis of this region has shown that there are significant differences between unrelated individuals while at the same time the sequence has been shown to be very constant among closely (genetically) related individuals. The D-loop sequence can be amplified by PCR and then analyzed in various ways to determine if there is a match indicating a maternal relationship (Figure 7-24)

It has been estimated that approximately 9000 individuals "disappeared" in Argentina between the years 1975 and 1983. Hundreds of young children and even pregnant women were kidnapped during this time. Newborn children and toddlers were sold on the black market or presented to families unable to bear their own children. Forensic analysis of mtDNA has been used to link many of these kidnapped children to their surviving (maternally related) biological relatives. Despite the

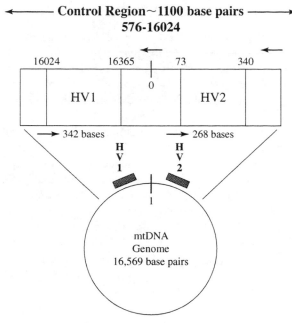

← Control Region~1100 base pairs →
576-16024

FIGURE 7-24 The Control region contains approximately 1100 base-pairs and is divided into two distinct regions known as *hypervariable 1 (HV1)* and *hypervariable 2 (HV2)*. HV1 is found between bases 16024 and 16365. HV2 is found between bases 73 and 340.

absence of information regarding a child's parents, they could still be linked to grandchildren, brothers and sisters, aunts and first cousins.

Because mitochondrial DNA is transmitted exclusively maternally, it is not useful for paternity determinations. Nevertheless, analysis of mitochondrial DNA may, in the future, become important forensically for identification purposes (e.g., to prove a biological link between mother and offspring).

Because of its maternal inheritance and because there appears to be little genetic exchange between mitochondria, RFLP analysis of mitochondrial DNA has been valuable in studying divergent and convergent genetic relationships between apparently closely related species. PCR amplification of the D-loop region followed by sequencing analysis has become a common technique used to establish the origin of biological evidence; however, because of its mode of inheritance, not only do all siblings (brothers and sisters) share the same mitochondrial genome, but all females in a maternal lineage (mother, grandmother, aunt, niece, etc.) also share the same genome.

Study of mitochondrial DNA may have significant medical benefits as well. Several myopathies are associated with mutation of mitochondrial DNA including Leber's hereditary optic neuropathy, a progressive disease that results in blindness.[103,104] The inheritance of this disorder follows a non-Mendelian inheritance pattern, as expected of a disease caused by a mitochondrial genome mutation.

PLASMIDS AS GENE-CLONING VECTORS

Genetic engineering has revolutionized modern biology by allowing for the isolation, manipulation, and controlled recombination of DNA *in vitro*. The techniques by which this is accomplished are relatively easy to perform and take advantage of amplification mechanisms used by cells *in vivo*. One of the most important aspects of genetic engineering is the use of cloning vectors to obtain multiple copies of specific DNA sequences.

A cloning vector is an autonomously replicating DNA molecule that can be linked to a fragment of DNA that is to be cloned, or replicated, in large quantity. The cloning vector containing the desired DNA sequence is inserted into its natural host for replication and amplification. Commonly used vectors include plasmids, cosmids (artificially constructed DNA carriers), and viruses. The vector can then transform *E. coli, Bacillus subtilis,* or even a eukaryote such as *Saccharomyces cerevisiae.* Most genetic engineering is performed with plasmids.

Plasmids that are found in virtually all bacterial species act as endosymbionts.[105] They exist as closed, circular, double-stranded DNA molecules that multiply autonomously within the host cell and are inherited in a regular manner as the host cell divides.[106] Like most other DNA molecules, a plasmid or episome is a double helix, each strand consisting of a linear array of the four nucleotide bases adenine, guanine, thymine, and cytosine. The sequence of bases on one chain is complementary to the sequence on the other chain. They account for only a small fraction of a cell's genome ($< 3\%$). Nevertheless, they alone carry the information for bacterial conjugation and are responsible for several diseases of plants and animals. They confer on their host cells the ability to resist a wide variety of toxic agents, including antibiotics. Genes for resistance to antibiotics are found in (R) plasmids and are transferred from one cell to another by various mechanisms.

By using the same restriction enzyme to cleave plasmid DNA and human DNA and then permitting the fragments to base-pair with each other, a human gene (5 to 10 kb long) can be incorporated into the bacterial plasmid and thus can be cloned by inserting the plasmid into a bacterial cell such as *E. coli,* which replicates the plasmid–human recombinant DNA. In general, transformation is performed in such a way that there is a large excess of bacteria to plasmids so that only one recombinant molecule is incorporated into one bacterium. The plasmid used for transformation also usually contains a gene for antibiotic resistance. After this procedure, all bacteria are grown on solid media containing the antibiotic so that only transformed bacteria grow.

Once large numbers of these plasmids are produced, they can be recovered and restricted by the same enzyme used earlier. In this manner, large quantities of the human gene can be obtained and used for various purposes. For example, amplified genes can be used as probes to search for complementary sequences in the human genome. Such probes can be used to determine whether individuals carry genes for certain genetic diseases such as cystic fibrosis, Duchenne muscular dystrophy, or adult polycystic kidney disease. Similarly, they can be used to seek out mini-satellite regions within the human genome for the purpose of individualization. For a thorough discussion of DNA probes, see Keller and Manak.[107]

POLYMERASE CHAIN REACTION

Polymerase chain reaction (PCR) is a method that has become a fundamental procedure in human identification work.[13,15] PCR is used in laboratories around the world to synthesize billions of copies of a particular nucleotide sequence located within the human genome, a process called *DNA amplification.*[8–12] Some have euphemistically referred to PCR as *molecular Xeroxing.* The PCR technique has found use in virology, microbiology, medical diagnostics, and in many other scientific and clinical applications.[16,17,20,21] DNA amplification by PCR is in widespread use in forensic laboratories because evidentiary biological samples contain DNA that can reveal genetic information about the source of this evidence. Exceedingly small samples or samples that are aged or exposed to a variety of environmental insults can usually still be amplified and typed successfully.

PCR was developed by Kary Mullis in 1985.[10,11] He visualized a way of replicating DNA *in vitro* that resembled the method that cells use to replicate their DNA just prior to cell division. His procedure was labor-intensive and required manually changing the temperature of the reaction by using several water baths to allow various aspects of the process to progress. The polymerase enzyme that he used was temperature sensitive so that it had to be replaced quite often when enzyme activity was lost at elevated temperatures. PCR has advanced in many ways and is now a simple, straightforward, automated procedure. The polymerase enzyme now used is both thermostable and has high fidelity of replication. Furthermore, the temperature control is computerized, and heating and cooling is regulated precisely with an instrument known as a *thermal cycler.*

PCR is one of the most sensitive methods available to the forensic scientist. Although the commercially available test kits in common use are optimized to amplify 1.0 ng of DNA in the reaction mix, results can be obtained from far less DNA. When the amount of template DNA available for copying is less than 100 picograms, another PCR method referred to as *low copy number PCR* can be used. With special techniques, the ability exists to amplify DNA from even a single diploid cell. For this reason, it is essential that when amplifying any quantity of DNA that a sterile technique be used to load PCR reaction microtubes with the needed reagents. Any contamination of any reagent with human DNA or with amplified DNA from previous PCR reactions (*amplicons*) that may accidentally be introduced into the reaction mix can adversely affect the ultimate PCR results. Amplicons are preferentially amplified if present in a subsequent PCR reaction.

PCR requires the use of *primers,* short segments of DNA (18–30 nucleotides long) that specify which region of the human genome is to be copied. To amplify a specific sequence of DNA, the analyst must have two different primers, a forward primer and a reverse primer. Each primer attaches by hydrogen bonding to a complementary region on one of the two DNA strands that compose the region of interest. The primer binding sites flank the region of interest. The primers, based on their specific nucleotide sequences, thereby delineate the boundaries on the template DNA to be copied. Essentially, the polymerase recognizes the site where the primer has become annealed and starts to synthesize the new DNA strand in the 5′ to 3′ direction.

The dNTPs are added one at a time to the 3' end of the primer. The bonding of the incoming dNTP is based on complementary sequence determined by the template DNA. Optimum temperatures and length of time for each step of each cycle depends on the specific primers and template DNA being amplified, and must be determined experimentally.

The sequence of the primers is of the highest importance. The melting temperature of the primers (the point at which the hydrogen bonds between the primer and template start to break) must be in the range of 55°–72°C; the G–C content must be in the range of 40% to 60%; the sequence must be unique, so that it does not bind nonspecifically to other regions of the template DNA; and the primers must not have a sequence that promotes binding to other primers (primer–dimers).

PCR is performed in a small test tube that contains a number of reagents, including the DNA to be amplified (called the *template DNA*); a special type of DNA polymerase that functions at high temperatures (e.g., Taq polymerase, obtained from thermophilic bacteria); the four deoxyribonucleotides (A, T, G and C); $MgCl_2$, which is needed as a cofactor for polymerase activity; and a buffer solution. The PCR procedure mimics what happens during DNA synthesis *in vivo,* but DNA amplification *in vitro* requires changes in temperature to accomplish the doubling process described previously.

PCR consists of three stages that collectively make up a PCR cycle. In the first stage (*denaturation*), the DNA is heated to about 94°C, which causes a breakdown of hydrogen bonding, resulting in separation of the double-stranded DNA segment. At the end of this first step, the DNA molecule has become single stranded. In the next step (*annealing*), the temperature is lowered (usually to about 60°C) so that the each of the two primers can attach to the single-stranded segments of the DNA by complementary base pairing (Figures 7-25, 7-26, and 7-27). In the third and final step

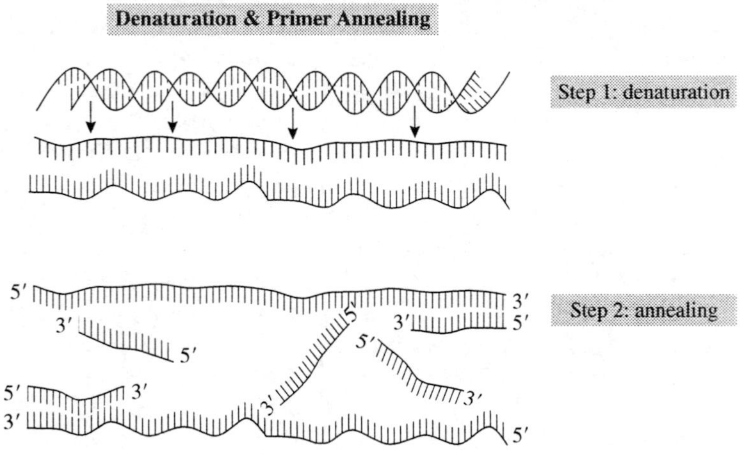

FIGURE 7-25 After the template DNA is denatured as a result of heating, a primer now binds (anneals) to each of the two separated strands based on a complementary base-pairing. (*Source:* Reproduced with the permission of Andy Vierstraete.)

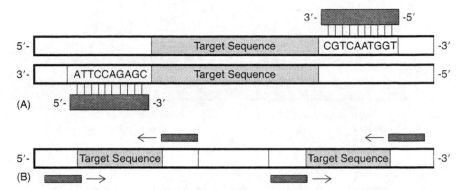

FIGURE 7-26 (A) Primers are synthesized so that they bind to the template by complementary base pairing. (B) Primers set boundaries for portion of DNA molecule that is to be replicated. (*Source:* Reproduced with the permission of Andy

(*extension*), the temperature is raised somewhat (usually to about 72°C) so that the DNA polymerase enzyme can add the appropriate nucleotide bases, one by one (again, by complementary base-pairing). The enzyme can then tie together (*ligate*) these adjacent nucleotides thereby replicating a specific segment of the template DNA (Figure 7-28). The three-step cycle is usually repeated 28 to 30 times. With

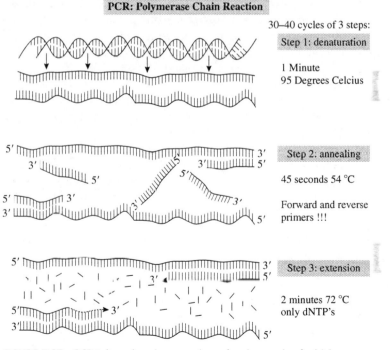

FIGURE 7-27 PCR takes place in a number of cycles, each of which consists of three steps. (*Source:* Reproduced with the permission of Andy Vierstraete.)

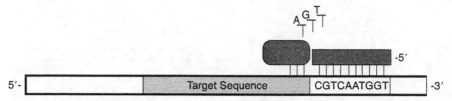

FIGURE 7-28   In extension phase of cycle, the Taq polymerase extends the primer strand one nucleotide at a time (onto the 5′) so that new base corresponds with complementary base on DNA template strand.

each cycle, the amount of DNA is doubled, and the total amount of DNA therefore increases exponentially. The entire thermal cycling procedure is usually completed in less than two hours (Figure 7-29).

PCR Inhibition

Some samples are known to contain substances that interfere with the PCR reaction resulting in poor or no amplification.[108] Successful results often depend on the success in isolating template DNA from the inhibitor. Such substances may interfere with the DNA itself, or with the polymerase enzyme either directly or indirectly by interaction with the enzyme's cofactor, Mg^{+2}. The PCR process of amplification can be partially or completely inhibited. Substances known to act as PCR inhibitors include bile salts in fecal matter, complex polysaccharides, collagen, heme, humic acid, melanin and eumelanin, myoglobin, proteinases, Ca^{+2} ions, urea, hemoglobin, lactoferin, immunoglobulin G, and indigo dye from denim.[109] These substances are usually associated with the evidentiary sample. In addition, high salt (NaCl, KCl, etc.) concentrations, the presence of ionic detergents (sodium dodecyl sulphate, sodium deoxycholate),[110] and ethanol, isopropanol, and phenol results in inhibition of amplification.[111,112] Larger loci are more sensitive to PCR inhibition than shorter loci, which results in a genetic profile that appears similar to that seen for degraded samples. Real-time PCR (see pp. 422–23) can be used to detect the presence of inhibitors because the commercial kits include an internal positive control.[113] Observation of a decrease in amplification efficiency of such a control indicates that the problem is the result of an inhibitor rather than to any degraded DNA in the unknown sample.

PCR of Short Tandem Repeats

Short tandem repeat (STR) technology, the method currently used for most forensic DNA analysis, uses a DNA locus that contains short segments (usually four bases long) of DNA that are repeated one after another. A great deal of variability in the length of the repeated regions in the different STRs is present in the human population (see Figure 7-22). This variability, created by differences in the number of times that the units of four bases are repeated, is used to distinguish one DNA profile from another.

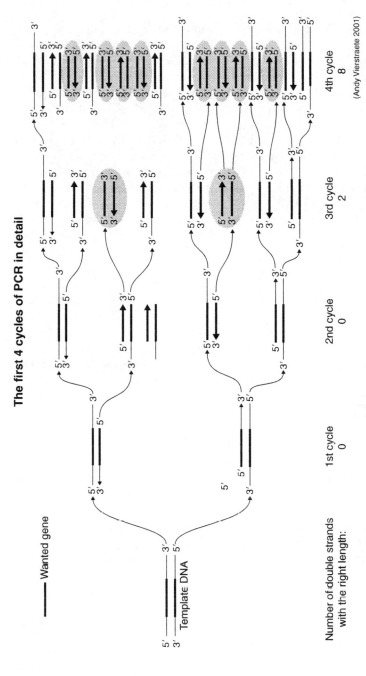

The first 4 cycles of PCR in detail

— Wanted gene

Template DNA

	1st cycle	2nd cycle	3rd cycle	4th cycle
Number of double strands with the right length:	0	0	2	8

(Andy Vierstraete 2001)

FIGURE 7-29 The Taq polymerase processes smaller molecules more efficiently than longer ones. As a result, after third cycle of amplification, virtually all amplified product is identical in size and sequence with their boundaries delimited by primers. (*Source:* Reproduced with the permission of Andy Vierstraete.)

415

Each individual has two alleles (one maternal and one paternal) for each STR locus. The analysis of these autosomal STRs produces the profiles used in courts for DNA identification. The Y chromosome (present only in males) also contains STRs. Although Y-STRs are present in only one copy in each male individual and do not have the power of discrimination of autosomal STRs, they have been used to help distinguish DNA profiles in samples containing mixtures of DNA from multiple individuals (see Chapter 10 in *Forensic Science Handbook,* Volume I, 2nd ed.). The primers used for PCR of STRs are complementary to the regions of the STR locus that lay outside (flank) the area of tandem repeats. In the currently used methods of forensic DNA analysis, one of the two primers (the forward primer) is labeled with a fluorescent dye (fluorochrome). Because the different alleles of the various STR loci must be distinguished by color as well as by size when many STR loci are amplified together (see "Multiplex PCR"), different fluorochromes are used to label loci that overlap in size. The dyes most commonly used to label STR primers are FAM (blue), JOE (green), ROX (red), and TAMRA or NED (yellow). Commercial kits containing appropriate fluorochrome-labeled primers are available for both STR and Y-STR analysis.

At least thirteen STR loci are required for a DNA profile to be uploaded into the Combined DNA Index System (CODIS) operated by the Federal Bureau of Investigation (FBI). In order to conserve the evidence sample and decrease the time and effort expended for DNA analysis, many STR loci are amplified in the same PCR reaction (*multiplex PCR*) and run together in the same capillary. To be distinguishable by capillary electrophoresis CE, the DNA fragments must have different migration times because of differences in their sizes. Because many of the alleles of the thirteen STR loci overlap in size, primers for these overlapping loci are tagged with different dyes so that they may be distinguished by color as well as by size. Many laboratories now use multiplex PCR kits that can amplify sixteen loci at once, with all alleles and loci distinguishable from each other.

MiniSTRs

At times, we must try to amplify samples that have been highly degraded, either as a result of bacterial nucleases or through oxidative or biochemical processes. Commercial STR multiplex kits produce PCR products that range in size from about 100 to 480 base-pairs. When the DNA template is highly degraded, the larger STRs cannot be amplified successfully and, at best, only a partial profile can be obtained. Newer techniques have been developed that can be used to type highly degraded DNA.

MiniSTRs, which produce reduced-size STR amplicons, were developed and used to analyze the degraded DNA from victims of the World Trade Center disaster. The primers for miniSTRs were created by moving the primer binding regions as close as possible to the repeat region of an STR, so that the amplicons produced by PCR can be much smaller than those produced with traditional STR primers (Figure 7-22). Multiplex miniSTRs (*miniplexes*) have been shown to produce full STR profiles with degraded DNA samples that gave only partial profiles with traditional primers, and they have recently been shown to give fuller profiles with LCN DNA samples as well. Because primer positions can be altered to produce miniSTRs for most CODIS loci, most of the information already present in DNA databases would still be usable if STR analysis is eventually changed to a miniplex format.[114-121]

Polymerase Chain Reaction Y-Chromosome STR Analysis

SEXUAL ASSAULT EVIDENCE AND DIFFERENTIAL LYSIS In forensic casework, PCR amplification of STR loci is performed on evidentiary and exemplar specimens to associate a suspect with a crime scene or a suspect with a victim. The analysis is usually conducted to include thirteen autosomal (non–sex chromosome) highly polymorphic loci. Because the national DNA database has been standardized to include these "core" loci, crime laboratories typically perform this analysis in criminal matters. These loci include D3S1358, D16S539, THO1,TPOX, CSF1PO, D7S820, VWA, FGA, D8S1179, D21S11, D18S51, D5S818, and D13S317. In some instances, mixtures of DNA originating from two or more individuals are present in an evidentiary sample. This is usually evident in the appearance of the patterns that are produced by genetic analyzers following separation of amplified DNA fragments using either gel or capillary electrophoresis. In cases of sexual assault, it is important to obtain the genetic profile of the male, because it has been established that the vast majority of such assaults are carried out by males. In cases such as these, a procedure known as *differential lysis* is performed to separate male from female DNA. This is based on the chemical differences in the cell membranes of the two common cell types in such evidence, sperm cells and epithelial cells of the female victim. Although the differential lysis procedure allows for the separation of male from female DNA, it is far less efficient than desired. As a result, male DNA contaminates the isolated female DNA, and DNA originating from the female contaminates the DNA originating from the male component. Interpretation of electrophoretic results must be done carefully.

In cases where the ratio of the female to male DNA contained in the mixture is greater than 1:1, the peak heights can reveal a major and minor component. However, when the ratio is equal to or exceeds 20:1, the smaller component becomes masked and cannot be observed as a distinct pattern of peaks in the electropherogram; thus, autosomal PCR-STR analysis fails to reveal the male genetic profile in the mixture. In cases such as these, analysis of the Y-chromosome STR loci can reveal significant information about the male component. Because females lack the Y-chromosome and cannot contribute to the pattern of peaks on the electropherogram, only male DNA is apparent. Of course, because genetically normal males have only a single Y chromosome, only one allele is seen at each locus. Many polymorphic loci have been identified on the Y chromosome and can be analyzed in the same way as autosomal STR loci are tested. The Y chromosome is inherited paternally, from father to son. As a result, all male relatives share the same genes on their Y chromosomes. These STR loci distributed along the Y-chromosome are all linked to one another and are not inherited independently from one another. Therefore, the calculations usually performed on autosomal STR loci to determine the rarity of the genetic profile using the product rule cannot be used in this case. The genetic profile of linked loci is referred to as a *haplotype,* and these can be studied in large populations resulting in a haplotype frequency database of various patterns. Y-STR analysis is performed in a variety of other situations, including paternity, missing persons, and in cases where the differential lysis procedure cannot be used to separate cell types in a mixed sample (mixture of epithelial cells from two individuals, one male and one female).

For a complete overview of Y-chromosome STR analysis, see Chapter 8.

Low Copy Number DNA Analysis

Amplification of sample DNA present in a very small amount (less than 100 pg) is known as *low copy number (LCN) DNA.* Because there are about 6 pg of DNA in a typical human diploid cell, an LCN sample therefore contains less than 17 cells. In order to analyze samples containing LCN amounts of DNA, the sensitivity of the assay must be increased. This is usually done by increasing the number of PCR cycles from the 28 or 30 that are suggested for commercial kits to about 34 cycles. With increased cycles of PCR, very small starting amounts of DNA may be analyzed.[122–128]

Numerous problems can arise with LCN DNA analysis, and many of these may interfere with the interpretation of LCN DNA profiles. Because so little DNA is present in a LCN DNA sample, less than a full complement of the genome may be available for amplification. In addition, because only the loci amplified in the first rounds of PCR probably show up in the final DNA profile, repeated amplifications of the same LCN sample may give different results. This phenomenon is known as *stochastic variation,* and it frequently occurs with LCN DNA analysis. Sometimes only one of the two alleles of a heterozygous STR locus are amplified (*allele dropout*) and the locus mistakenly appears in the profile as homozygous. Other times, an entire STR locus may fail to amplify (*locus dropout*) or extra alleles may appear (*allele drop in*) that are not relevant to the case at hand. Because of the stochastic variation of these amplification artifacts, the amplification of LCN DNA samples is usually done three times, and the only alleles reported are those present in at least two of the three profiles produced from the same sample.

Additional complications occur with LCN DNA because the smaller amount of input DNA and the increased sensitivity of the PCR amplification make contamination artifacts (allele drop in) more likely. It is also possible that the DNA present in the original LCN DNA sample is not connected to the crime that is under investigation; for example, it may have come into the evidence sample by *secondary transfer* (i.e., from individuals with whom the offender had contact before touching the evidence), or from other individuals who may have touched the item before the evidence was collected.

It has been shown that without increasing PCR cycle number, purification of amplified PCR product prior to electrophoretic separation can increase the sensitivity of allele detection of fluorescently labeled LCN DNA specimens.[129] Despite this improvement, allelic dropout, increased stutter artifact, and sporadic contamination were still observed in resulting electropherograms.

Although LCN DNA analysis is seldom used in courts in the United States, many laboratories are beginning to analyze material with less DNA for leads in burglary and robbery cases.[130] In England, where LCN DNA analysis was pioneered, DNA profiles have also been generated successfully from items such as discarded tools, matchsticks, and weapon handles.

Single Nucleotide Polymorphisms

STR typing of autosomal loci will probably continue to be the preferred method of DNA profiling for many years; however, additional DNA markers are frequently used to obtain more information about a particular sample.

Another type of DNA analysis that has been developed for both autosomes and Y-chromosomes involves the typing of *single nucleotide polymorphisms (SNPs),*[131–137] defined as a single base difference between individuals at a particular point in the genome. There are millions of SNPs in the human genome, some of which have been used as markers in medical studies to track genetic diseases. In forensics, SNPs are being used together with STR analysis, especially in cases where a complete STR profile cannot be obtained from a DNA sample, a phenomenon common when DNA is highly degraded. (Both SNP and miniSTR analysis were used to help identify World Trade Center disaster victims.)

Although most of the variable regions of STRs used for DNA profiling are composed of multiples of a four-nucleotide repeat, an SNP involves only one differing nucleotide. PCR products from SNPs can therefore be much smaller than those of STRs. SNPs are not as informative as STRs because there are usually only two possible nucleotides for a SNP, whereas more than five variations in the number of repeated tetranucleotides can be found at most STR loci. Because of this, many more SNP markers would have to be analyzed to get the same power of discrimination provided by the thirteen CODIS STRs. However, because SNPs have a lower mutation rate than STRs and are thus more likely to become fixed in a population, SNPs may be potentially useful in predicting the ethnic origin of an offender.

SNP analysis is frequently done by minisequencing to identify the nucleotide that has been changed. *Minisequencing* is a variation of the typical DNA sequencing method that is used for mitochondrial DNA analysis. In minisequencing, the SNP and the DNA region immediately surrounding it are amplified; this PCR product is then used in a PCR reaction where only one new nucleotide, the one that defines the SNP, is added after the primer binds. This is accomplished by using only the type of nucleotide (ddNTP) that stops amplification once it is added. The four different ddNTPs are each labeled with a different fluorescent dye so that the nucleotide present in the SNP can be identified. Fortunately, SNP analysis can also be performed as a multiplex such that many SNPs can be identified simultaneously.

Other assays being developed and used to detect SNPs involve variations of techniques used in DNA microarrays. These arrays contain a large number of single-stranded DNA fragments (probes) that represent the SNPs (or other markers or genes of interest), and these are attached to a matrix or membrane in a known position in a tightly spaced grid (*microarray*) or linear fashion (*linear arrays*). The regions of interest are labeled with biotin during amplification of the DNA sample (many SNPs can be amplified at once), and the labeled PCR product is then hybridized to the array. Only DNA complementary to the probe binds to the array and is detectable after washing. By examining which positions on the array are labeled, the sequences (or SNPs) present in the original DNA sample can be determined. A commercial typing kit that permits detection of eighteen SNPs within the HV1 and HV2 regions of mtDNA is available from Roche Applied Sciences.

Real-Time PCR

Prior to performing PCR, it is important to know how much DNA is contained in a sample because commercial human identification typing kits and typing equipment are optimized to work within a specific range of DNA quantities. There are a number of ways to determine the amount of DNA accurately in a sample through PCR thermal cycling, including the use of molecular beacons, SYBR® Green fluorescent dyes, or with a fluorescently labeled TaqMan probe. The TaqMan-based target sequence specific assays are less subject to background "noise" than SYBR Green based assays because the latter can sometimes produce unwanted fluorescence signal because of dye binding to primer dimers. All of these quantitative assays can be performed using the technique known as *real-time PCR*. In the TaqMan probe method, also known as the *5' nuclease assay*, DNA of known quantities, ranging from nanogram to single-digit picogram amounts, are added to a PCR reaction mixture together with primers that are specific for an autosomal, single-copy target located in a nontranslated region at 5p15.33, and a short oligonucleotide probe specific to the target region, containing a different fluorochrome dye at each end. One dye serves as a reporter dye (R) whereas the other serves as a non-fluorescent quencher dye (Q). The reporter fluorochrome is usually green (FAM) and positioned at the 5' end of the probe; the quencher dye serves as an energy transfer acceptor. It does not emit any detectable fluorescence and is located at the 3' end. This quencher dye is attached to a minor groove binder that allows it to fit into the minor groove of duplex DNA. This minor groove binder stabilizes the binding of the probe to the double-stranded DNA. At the same time, it enhances the melting temperature of the probe so that a shorter probe can be used. The former label acts as a fluorescent indicator or reporter, whereas the latter acts as its quencher (Figure 7-30).

While these dyes sit on the probe, no fluorescence is observed from the reporter because of the proximity of the quencher dye. This phenomenon is known as

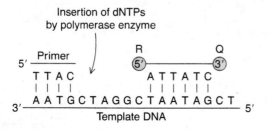

FIGURE 7-30   As the polymerase inserts new dNTPs at the 3' end of the primer it also removes the reporter dye at the 5' end of the probe, thereby resulting in an increase in fluorescence as the extension proceeds.

fluorescence resonance energy transfer. Energy from the reporter dye is transferred to the quencher dye, and when excitatory light hits the reporter dye, no light is emitted. The DNA is then allowed to undergo cycling amplification. The process of amplification can be observed in real time—that is, one can observe the process as it is occurring using these fluorescently labeled probes. Reporter fluorescence that the instrument detects increases as each segment of the targeted region of human DNA is copied. During each cycle of amplification, when the template DNA is denatured and the temperature is then lowered, the primers anneal to the DNA at flanking regions adjacent to the area to be amplified. The double-labeled probe also becomes bound to a specific sequence on the template DNA. On raising the temperature, as the Taq polymerase adds dNTPs to the primer, it also removes the reporter dye as well as nucleotides from the 5′ side of the probe. Now relieved of inhibition by the quencher dye, the reporter can emit a fluorescence signal that can be picked up by the recording instrument. The real-time PCR instrument holds a 96-well plate, and fluorescence in each well is monitored by a CCD camera as amplification proceeds.

Typically, the pattern of fluorescence exhibits three phases. The first phase results from logarithmic increase in copy number; thus, for each cycle, the DNA is doubled. Of course, this assumes that amplification is working at 100% efficiency. The second phase is a linear increase in copy number. During this time, one (or more) component(s) of the reaction mixture has become limiting and the amplified product accumulates arithmetically. The third phase is entered as the increasing degree of fluorescence reaches a plateau.[138] At this time, the reaction has stopped and no additional DNA product is forming. The most precise time to monitor amplification is during the first phase. The overall pattern appears as a sigmoidal curve when plotted.

The graph is plotted in a linear–logarithmic format. The *x*-axis is cycle number and the *y*-axis represents the change in fluorescence. This value is normalized by comparing fluorescence to a passive fluorescent reference dye (ROX). Use of this dye allows for a more precise (normalized) reading by accounting for minor hardware or slight pipetting differences. The larger the amount of DNA added to the reaction mixture, the more rapidly the fluorescence starts its increase in value. Ultimately, the reaction slows down regardless of the quantity of DNA added and the fluorescence levels off with no further increase seen. At a crucial time during the exponential growth of amplification product, when the increase in fluorescence emission has not as yet become linear, the threshold cycle value (C_T) is noted. A plot of C_T value relative to logarithm of the quantity of DNA added to the reaction mix is linear and can be used as a standard calibration curve to determine the quantities of unknown DNA samples. The calibration curve is constructed from standard DNA concentrations ranging from 50ng/μl to 23pg/μl. The fewer cycles needed to see any detectable fluorescence in a sample, the larger the amount of DNA present in that sample. Scientists at the National Institute of Science and Technology (NIST) are providing reference quantification standards of human DNA so that all work in this field can be traced back to these reference specimens.

Real-time PCR can also be used to determine stain identity as blood or semen based on an analysis of mRNA. RNA is isolated from the stain and subjected to reverse transcription followed by real-time PCR using TaqMan gene expression assays.[139]

DNA SEQUENCING

Sequencing analysis of DNA has become an extremely important area of genetics and molecular biology. This exciting technology, which determines the linear sequence of nucleotides A, G, C, and T in a given length of DNA, has great potential for advancing the fields of diagnostic and clinical medicine and forensic science. Advances in sequencing technology in recent years have allowed for the rapid analysis of fairly large stretches of DNA. For example, the entire 170-kb genome of the Epstein–Barr virus has been completely sequenced. Similarly, the entire human mitochondrial chromosome has also been successfully sequenced.

Sequencing technology has advanced dramatically over the past few years, and what was once considered to be an almost impossible goal of sequencing the human genome is now not only a reality, but it is expected in the near future that molecular biologists will be able to accurately sequence the 3.1 billion basepairs[140] of the genome of virtually any person rapidly and economically.[141] In 2007, this was accomplished for James Watson, a fitting accomplishment for one of the two scientists responsible for our understanding of the structure of DNA. The ability to unravel the human genome enables scientists to probe the secrets of life and human disease.

The knowledge of the human genome enables molecular biologists to treat genetic diseases by somatic gene therapy. The ambitious project was first sponsored in the United States by the Department of Energy and later by the National Institutes of Health. Britain's Medical Research Council has also established a major new computerized database for storing and distributing data on the structure and function of the human genome. Japan initiated its genome project in 1981 when its Science and Technology Agency selected A. Wada to conceptualize and direct this effort. In Japan, the emphasis has been to automate the decoding process.

The discovery of restriction enzymes in 1970 and the development of recombinant DNA technology throughout the 1970s, as well as the progress in developing better methods to isolate and analyze DNA, led the way for the production of two different sequencing methods.[142,143] The first is an enzymatic method developed by Sanger and Coulson[144] in 1975, and the second, a chemical method developed by Maxam and Gilbert[145] in 1977. In 1980, the Nobel Committee awarded Gilbert and Sanger the Nobel Prize for their efforts in DNA sequencing.

Enzymatic Sequencing

The method used by Sanger, Nicklen, and Coulson[146] uses dideoxynucleotide elongation terminators to sequence DNA. In this method, an oligonucleotide primer is hybridized to a template strand of DNA, and a DNA polymerase is used to synthesize a complementary strand from the information provided by the template. Synthesis occurs at only one location on the duplex molecule. Cloning methods permit the *in vivo* amplification of a DNA sequence. Single-stranded templates cloned into single-stranded M13 bacteriophage vectors provide easily sequenced pure molecules of DNA for analysis. Double-stranded templates are far more difficult to sequence. The enzymatic method allows one to read more than 500 bp of DNA sequence in a single reaction. Although sequencing can be performed with the large Klenow fragment of DNA polymerase I of

E. coli, or the AMV reverse transcriptase, the DNA polymerase obtained from bacterio-phage T7 appears to provide best the results when sequencing double-stranded DNA.

In one method, the sample of DNA to be sequenced is obtained by harvesting bacteria *(E. coli)* that had previously been infected with M13 bacteriophage. The M13 phage infects only *E. coli* that contain the *F* episome (F^+), an extrachromoso-mal element of DNA capable of independent or integrated existence within the prokaryote genome. It is, in fact, a plasmid. Bacteria that contain the *F* episome can produce pili (conjugation tubes) on their surfaces and thereby can engage in transfer of genetic information with F^- bacteria. As a result of infection, numerous phage particles are extruded from the cultured bacteria. The bacteria and phage can be sep-arated easily by centrifugation using polyethylene glycol (PEG 6,000). In this way, the bacteriophage are harvested and viral DNA can be collected by phenol extraction and alcohol precipitation. Single-stranded DNA can be isolated from clones within M13 vectors and hybrid plasmid–phage vectors (Figure 7-31).

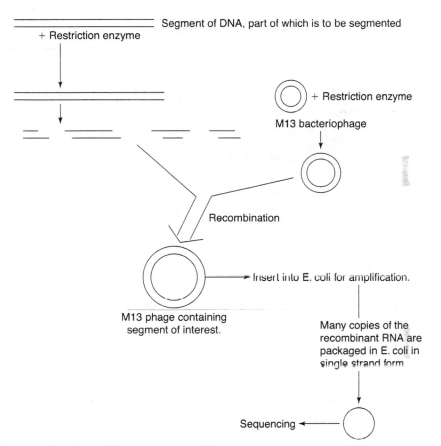

FIGURE 7-31 Procedure for cloning a segment of DNA to be sequenced. (*Source:* B. Alberts, D. Bray, J. Lewis, M. Raff, K. Roberts. and J. D. Watson, *Molecular Biology of the Cell,* 2nd ed. (New York: Garland Publishing Co.), 1989.)

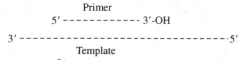

Primer
5' ----------- 3'-OH

3' ------------------------------·5'
Template

In presence of Mg^{2+}, NaCl, temperature shift from 65 °C to 30 °C, the primer will anneal to the template

Primer
5'   -------- XXXXXXXX§

3' -----------------------------·5'
Template

The polymerase adds complementary bases to the 3-OH end of the primer until a ddNTP is incorporated. This effectively terminates extension.

FIGURE 7-32   Incorporation of a 2′,3′-dideoxynucleoside triphosphate effectively terminates DNA synthesis.

In the *Sanger dideoxy sequencing method* (also known as the *chain termination method*), the target DNA is denatured, and a short primer (15–30 bases) is annealed to the template DNA in a molar ratio of at least 5:1. Annealing takes place through hydrogen bonding at a position adjacent to the target region to be sequenced. A minimum of 0.6 μg of single-stranded DNA and 2 to 4 μg of double-stranded DNA are required. The DNA polymerase is added to the primer template. The polymerase extends the primer from the 3′—OH side using 2′deoxyribonucleoside triphosphates (*d*NTPs) as monomers, producing a new strand complementary to the template.

The sample DNA is split into four tubes. All tubes contain ^{32}P or ^{35}S *d*ATP. The following is added to the first tube: dithiothreitol, buffered salts, *d*GTP, *d*CTP, *d*TTP, and *dd*ATP. The second tube is treated similarly, except that dithiothreitol, buffered salts, *d*GTP, *d*CTP, *d*ATP, and *dd*TTP are present. Similarly, the third and fourth tubes contain all of the unlabeled nucleotide precursors and necessary buffered salts, plus the *dd*GTP and the *dd*CTP, respectively. The tubes are allowed to incubate at room temperature for approximately 10 minutes. After this labeling reaction, further polymerization is prevented by addition of the four *d*NTPs. Incorporation of a 2′,3′-dideoxynucleoside triphosphate effectively terminates DNA synthesis because it lacks a free 3′—OH group and cannot be extended (Figure 7-32). The termination reaction lasts about 15 minutes at 37°C.

The result of the foregoing is a population of newly synthesized DNA molecules, each having the same 5′ ends but different 3′ ends, depending on the exact position where the dideoxy-analog was incorporated. The size of each fragment is directly related to the precise sequence of bases in the template. Each sample is then run on a denaturing (6% polyacrylamide) sizing gel and the ^{32}P labeled fragments detected by autoradiography or some other, preferably more rapid, form of detection. If autoradiography is used, then the DNA sequence of the target is determined from the order of the bands in the lanes of the gel (Figure 7-33). The polymerase adds complementary bases to the 3′—OH end of the primer until a *dd*NTP is incorporated. This effectively terminates extension.

Initiation
reference

$\downarrow$ 2   8   10   14
5′ C A C T G G C A T A T G C A T 3′   Deduced Sequence

5′ C A

5′ C A C T G G C A

5′ C A C T G G C A T A

5′ C A C T G G C A T A T G C A

FIGURE 7-33 When terminating newly synthesized copies of cDNA with 2′,3′-dideoxyadenosine triphosphate, four fragments in this example are produced. Each of the fragments shares a common 5′ nucleotide that serves as a reference point. Similarly, each of the fragments ends in the adenine nucleotide. Adenine can be found at positions 2, 8, 10, and 14 in the original sequence. Analysis of the electrophoretic results of all four termination reactions provides the necessary information to deduce the original sequence.

Advances in gel technology made it easier to sequence the sizing gel efficiently and to generate a large amount of data accurately and rapidly. The PCR technology has made it easier to prepare large quantities of specific template for sequencing. There are also improved methods for studying cloned double-stranded DNA without having to subclone the target into single-stranded vectors such as M13. These factors, taken together with the trend toward automation, make this procedure extremely important for future forensic applications.[147–150]

Chemical Sequencing

The method used by Maxam and Gilbert utilizes gel electrophoresis on thin denaturing polyacrylamide gels to separate fragments of DNA based on their relative sizes (weights). Sample DNA is first isolated and purified and then fragmented by cleavage at specific nucleotide sequence sites by restriction enzymes, resulting in an array of *restriction fragments* that differ in number of nucleotide bases. Smaller restriction fragments have greater gel mobility than do larger fragments, but all migrate anodally. The high-resolution electrophoretic technique employed is extremely sensitive and can resolve two fragments differing by as little as one nucleotide. Ethidium bromide, which intercalates within the DNA double helix, can be used as a DNA-specific stain that fluoresces orange on exposure to ultraviolet illumination. By using a calibrated gel (containing known molecular weight markers), the size of each restriction fragment can be determined either by manual calculation or by computer analysis. The migration rate of a fragment of DNA is inversely proportional to the logarithm of its molecular weight. The fragment of interest can be excised from this gel, eluted from the gel matrix, and then subjected to sequence analysis by either the Sanger–Coulson or Maxam–Gilbert method.

In the Maxam–Gilbert procedure, the bases A, A + G, C + T, and C can be cleaved from a DNA fragment. The process is especially useful for analysis of fragments smaller than 50 kb in length, although the Epstein–Barr virus genome consisting of 172,282 bases has been sequenced using this method.

In this sequence analysis, a double-stranded DNA fragment is ^{32}P radiolabeled at the 5′ end of each strand.

$$5′ \quad ^{32}P................ \quad 3′$$
$$3′ \quad ....^{32}P \quad 5′$$

The strands are then separated, and one strand is retained for sequencing. The strands of the duplex molecule that are held together by hydrogen bonds are easily separated (denatured) by heating, use of low-ionic-strength buffers, treatment with a chaotropic agent such as formamide, or treatment with alkali. Following denaturation, four sample tubes are set up, each of which is supplied with a fraction of the single-stranded DNA to be sequenced. Specific bases within the DNA strand are modified in each tube. Subsequently, the modified bases are removed. Chemical reagents then cleave the strand at one or two specific sites that lack bases. In each tube, only a single nucleotide susceptible to the reagent will react (Figure 7-29). It should also be noted that the nucleotide found at the 3′—OH terminus is the nucleotide immediately adjacent to the nucleotide that had been chemically destroyed. Also, the base modifying reactions are controlled so that all the possible fragments do, in fact, appear on the gels. Figure 7-34 illustrates that in tubes 2 and 3, the reactions are specific for purines and pyrimidines, respectively.

Thus the original labeled fragment is denatured and the single-stranded ^{32}P labeled strand is broken into sub-fragments of different lengths within each sample reaction tube. These sub-fragments can then be separated by polyacrylamide gel electrophoresis under denaturing conditions, in the presence of 8M urea, and their band positions can then be visualized by autoradiography and identified. The sequence is then determined by reading the fragments from smallest to largest across all four lanes of the gel.

Several aspects of the sequencing technology have been optimized since the mid-1990s, including the preparation of the target DNA, the conditions of electrophoresis, automation of the electrophoretic separation and detection of banding patterns, use of fluorescent labels and detectors in place of isotopic labels and autoradiography, and improvements in the analysis of the obtained sequences.[149]

Regardless of which method of sequencing is utilized, before a consensus sequence is accepted as correct, the DNA segment is generally sequenced several times and the information developed for one strand is compared with that developed for the second strand. This serves virtually to eliminate any errors in sequence determination.

The development of relatively inexpensive automated DNA sequencers and further advances in PCR technology has made sequencing of the human genome a reality and opened the path for treating and ultimately curing genetically related disease.[150]

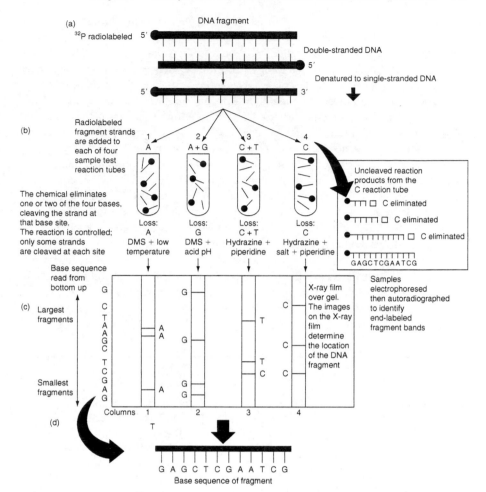

FIGURE 7-34 Maxam–Gilbert method of sequence analysis of DNA fragments. Four reactions are run simultaneously side by side. Specific bases are eliminated at specific sites by treatment with different reagents. (a) Both strands are ^{32}P labeled at the 5′ ends and are separated for sequencing of one strand. (b) Copies of the strand to be sequenced are placed into four different test tubes and a different eliminating reagent is added to each tube. These reagents nick the strand at one or two specific sites. In each tube, a single nucleotide reacts, and as a result, each tube contains a set of fragments, each ^{32}P labeled at the 5′ end. (c) The fragments produced in each of the four tubes are electrophoresed and subjected to autoradiography. Large fragments migrate slowly and shorter fragments move rapidly. (d) The sequence of nucleotides in each lane of the gel is read from bottom to top. Reading from left to right, the first base is G, lane 2; followed by A, lane 1; then G, lane 2; then C, lanes 3 and 4; then T, lane 3; and so on up the gel columns.   (*Source:* G. J. Stine, *The New Human Genetic* (Dubuque, IA: Wm. C. Brown Publishers, 1989), p. 187.)

Today, DNA sequencing is performed using highly efficient automated genetic analyzers and a modification of the Sanger method. Rather than using radioisotope-labeled taggants, each of the four dideoxyribonucleotides (*dd*NTPs) are labeled with a different fluorochrome. The technology is used to sequence DNA fragments up to 800 base-pairs in length. The template DNA to be sequenced is first amplified by PCR. The cloned copies are then denatured into single strands and incubated together with a primer complementary to the 3′ end region of the template strands. In addition, the reaction mixture contains the Taq DNA polymerase, the four deoxyribonucleotide triphosphates (*d*NTPs), and the four differently labeled *dd*NTPs. As the new strands are synthesized off the template, the *d*NTPs are incorporated one by one until a *dd*NTP comes into position in place of the expected *d*NTP. As a result, chain termination occurs and the newly made strand no longer grows. Thus this process produces a large number of newly made DNA fragments with lengths differing by only a single base and with their 3′ ends labeled with a fluorescently labeled *dd*NTP. The fragments are then electrophoresed by either gel or capillary electrophoresis, and as each DNA fragment crosses a window at a specific position in the capillary or gel, an argon laser excites each fluorochrome; the resultant emitted light is detected with a CCD camera. The findings are printed out in an electropherogram as a series of different-colored peaks (blue, green, yellow, red) in sequence. This sequence is complementary to the template strand and is read in the 5′ to 3′ direction.

References

1. A. J. Jeffreys, V. Wilson, and S. L. Thein, "Individual Specific 'Fingerprints' of Human DNA," *Nature* 316 (1985), 76–79.
2. A. J. Jeffreys, "Highly Variable Minisatellites and DNA Fingerprints," *Biochem. Soc. Trans.* 15 (1987), 309–17.
3. B. E. Dodd, "DNA Fingerprinting in Matters of Family and Crime," *Nature* 318 (1985), 506–07.
4. P. Gill, A. J. Jeffreys, and D. J. Werrett, "Forensic Applications of DNA 'Fingerprints,'" *Nature* 318 (1985), 577–79.
5. H. C. Lee, "Identification and Grouping of Bloodstains," in *Forensic Science Handbook,* ed. R. Saferstein (Englewood Cliffs NJ: Prentice-Hall, Inc., 1982), pp. 267–337.
6. G. F. Sensabaugh, "Biochemical Markers of Individuality," in *Forensic Science Handbook,* ed. R. Saferstein (Englewood Cliffs NJ: Prentice-Hall, Inc., 1982), pp. 338–415.
7. Y. Nakamura, M. Leppert, P. O'Connell, R. Wolff, T. Holm, M. Culver, C. Martin, E. Fujimoto, M. Hoff, E. Kumlin, and R. White, "Variable Number of Tandem Repeat (VNTR) Markers for Human Gene Mapping," *Science,* 235 (1987), 1616–22.
8. H. A. Erlich, D. H. Gelfand, and R. K. Saiki, "Specific DNA Amplification," *Nature* 331 (1988), 461–62.
9. R. Higuchi and S. Kwok, "Avoiding False Positives with PCR," *Nature* 339 (1989), 237–38.
10. K. B. Mullis and F. A. Faloona, "Specific Synthesis of DNA *in Vitro* via a Polymerase-Catalyzed Chain Reaction," *Methods Enzymol.* 155 (1987), 335–50.
11. K. B. Mullis, F. Faloona, S. J. Scharf, R. K. Saiki, G. Horn, and H. A. Erlich, "Specific Enzymatic Amplification of DNA *in Vitro*—The Polymerase Chain Reaction," *Cold Spring Harb. Symp. Quant. Biol.,* 51. Part 1 (1986), 263–73.

12. R. A. Gibbs, "DNA Amplification by the Polymerase Chain Reaction," *Anal. Chem,* 62, No. 13 (1990), 1202–14.

13. R. Reynolds, and G. F. Sensabaugh, "Analysis of Genetic Markers in Forensic DNA Samples Using the Polymerase Chain Reaction," *Anal. Chem.,* 63, No. 1 (1991), 2–15.

14. R. K. Saiki, D. H. Gelfand, S. Stoffel, S. J. Scharf, R. Higuchi, G. T. Horn, K. B. Mullis, and H. A. Erlich, "Primer-Directed Enzymatic Amplification of DNA with a Thermostable DNA Polymerase," *Science,* 239 (1988), 487–91.

15. G. F. Sensabaugh and C. von Beroldingen, "The Polymerase Chain Reaction: Application to the Analysis of Biological Evidence," in *Forensic DNA Technology,* eds. M. Farley and J. Harrington, (Washington, DC: ACS Symposium Series, American Chemical Society, 1990), pp. 63–82.

16. H. H. Kazazian, Jr., "Use of PCR in the Diagnosis of Monogenic Disease," in *PCR Technology: Principles and Applications for DNA Amplification,* ed. H. A. Erlich (New York: Stockton Press, 1989), pp. 153–69.

17. S. Kwok and J. J. Sninsky, "Application of PCR to the Detection of Human Infectious Diseases," in *PCR Technology: Principles and Applications for DNA Amplification,* ed. H. A. Erlich (New York: Stockton Press, 1989), pp. 235–44.

18. R. Higuchi, "Simple and Rapid Preparation of Samples for PCR," in *PCR Technology: Principles and Applications for DNA Amplification,* ed. H. A. Erlich (New York: Stockton Press, 1989), pp. 61–70.

19. J.-S. Tung, B. L. Daughtery, L. O'Neil, S. W. Law, J. Han, and G. E. Mark, "PCR Amplification of Specific Sequences From a CDNA Library," in *PCR Technology: Principles and Applications for DNA Amplification,* ed. H. A. Erlich (New York: Stockton Press, 1989), pp. 99–104.

20. R. A. Gibbs, J. S. Chamberlain, and T. C. Caskey, "Diagnosis of New Mutation Diseases Using the Polymerase Chain Reaction," in *PCR Technology: Principles and Applications for DNA Amplification,* ed. H. A. Erlich (New York: Stockton Press, 1989), pp. 171–91.

21. R. K. Saiki, S. J. Scharf, F. Faloona, K. B. Mullis, G. T. Horn, H. A. Erlich, and N. Arnheim, "Enzymatic Amplification of Beta-Globin Genomic Sequences and Restriction Site Analysis for Diagnosis of Sickle Cell Anemia," *Science,* 230 (1985), 1350–54.

22. R. J. White, N. Arnheim, and H. A. Erlich, "The Polymerase Chain Reaction," *Trends Gen.,* 5 (1989), 185–89.

23. A. J. Jeffreys, V. Wilson, R. Neumann, and J. Keyte, "Amplification of Human Minisatellites by the Polymerase Chain Reaction, Towards DNA Fingerprinting of a Single Cell," *Nucleic Acids Res.,* 16 (1988), 10953–71.

24. T. M. Jovin, "Recognition Mechanisms of DNA-Specific Enzymes," *Ann. Rev. Biochem.,* 45 (1976), 889–920.

25. M. Sundaralingam, "Nucleic Acid Principles and Transfer RNA," in *Symposium on Biomolecular Structure, Conformation, Function, and Evolution,* ed. R. Srinivasan (New York: Pergamon Press, 1979), pp. 259–83.

26. R. D. Wells, T. C. Goodman, W. Hillen, G. T. Horn, R. D. Klein, J. E. Larson, U. R Muller, S. K. Neuendorf, N. Panayotatos, and S. M. Stirdivant, "DNA Structure and Gene Regulation," *Prog. Nucleic Acid Res. Mol. Biol.,* 24 (1980), 167–267.

27. R. D. Wells, R. W. Blakesley, S. C. Hardies, G. T. Horn, J. E. Larson, E. Selsing, J. F. Burd, H. W. Chan, J. B. Dodgson, K. F. Jensen, I. F. Nes, and R. M. Wartell, "The Role of DNA Structure in Genetic Regulation," *Crit. Rev. Biochem.,* 4 (1977), 305–40.

28. A. G. Leslie, S. Arnott, R. Chandrasekaran, and R. L. Ratliff, "Polymorphism of DNA Double

Helices," *J. Mol. Biol.* 143 (1980), 49–72.

29. R. Chandrasekaran, S. Arnott, A. Banerjee, S. Campbell-Smith, A. G. W. Leslie, and L. Puigjaner, "Some New Polynucleotide Structures and Some New Thoughts about Old Structures," *ACS Symp. Ser.,* 141 (1980), 483–502.

30. A. Klug, A. Jack, M. A. Viswamitra, O. Kennard, Z. Shakked, and T. A. Steitz, "A Hypothesis on a Specific Sequence-Dependent Conformation of DNA and its Relation to the Binding of the Lac-Repressor Protein," *J. Mol. Biol.* 131 (1979), 669–80.

31. M. T. Record, S. J. Mazur, P. Melancon, J.-H Roe, S. L. Shaner, and L. Unger, "Double Helical DNA: Conformations, Physical Properties and Interactions with Ligands," *Ann. Rev. Biochem.,*50 (1981), 997–1024.

32. J. J. Champoux, "Proteins That Affect DNA Conformation," *Ann. Rev. Biochem.,* 47 (1978), 449–79.

33. P. H. von Hippel and J. D. McGhee, "DNA-Protein Interactions," *Ann. Rev. Biochem.,* 41 (172), 231–300.

34. P. H. von Hippel, "On the Molecular Bases of the Specificity of Interaction of Transcriptional Proteins with Genome DNA," *Biol. Reg. Dev.,* 1 (1979), 279–347.

35. J. D. McGhee and G. Felsenfeld, "Nucleosome Structure," *Ann. Rev. Biochem.,* 49 (1980), 1115–56.

36. V. Swaminathan and M. Sundaralingam, "The Crystal Structures of Metal Complexes of Nucleic Acids and Their Constituents," *Crit. Rev. Biochem.,* 6 (1979), 245–336.

37. S. J. Lippard, "Platinum Complexes— Probes of Polynucleotide Structure and Anti-Tumor Drugs," *Acc. Chem. Res.,* 11 (No. 5) (1978), 211–17.

38. D. J. Patel, "Nuclear Magnetic-Resonance Studies of Drug–Nucleic Acid Interactions at the Synthetic DNA Level in Solution," *Acc. Chem. Res.,* 12 no. 4 (1979), 118–25.

39. J. Texter, "Nucleic Acid–Water Interactions," *Prog. Biophys. Mol. Biol.,* 33 (1978), 83–97.

40. N. R. Cozzarelli, "DNA Topoisomerases," *Cell,* 22 (1980), 327–28.

41. N. R. Cozzarelli, "DNA Gyrase and the Supercoiling of DNA," *Science,* 207 (1980), 953–60.

42. M. Gellert, "DNA Topoisomerases," *Ann. Rev. Biochem.,* 50 (1981), 879–910.

43. W. R. Bauer, "Structure and Reactions of Closed Duplex DNA," *Ann. Rev. Biophys. Bioeng.,* 7 (1978), 287–313.

44. F. H. C. Crick, "Linking Numbers and Nucleosomes," *Proc. Nat'l. Acad. Sci. (USA),* 73 no. 8 (1976), 2639–43.

45. J. C. Wang, "Superhelical DNA," *Trends Biochem. Sci.,* 5 (1980), 219–21.

46. W. R. Bauer, F. H. C. Crick, and J. H. White, "Supercoiled DNA," *Sci. Am.,* 243 (1980), 100–13.

47. F. Miescher, "On the Chemical Composition of Pus Cells," *Hoppe-Seyler Med. Chem. Untersuch,* 4 (1871), 441–60. Translation in "Great Experiments in Biology," M. Gabriel and S. Fogel, eds. (Englewood Cliffs, NJ: Prentice-Hall, 1955) pp. 233–39.

48. E. Chargaff, "Chemical Specificity of Nucleic Acids and the Mechanisms of Their Enzymatic Degradations," *Experientia,* 6 (1950), 201–09.

49. J. D. Watson and F. H. C. Crick, "Molecular Structure of Nucleic Acids. A Structure for Deoxyribose Nucleic Acid," *Nature* 171 no. 4356 (1953), 737–38.

50. G. Mendel, "Versuche uber Pflanzen-hybriden," *Verh. Naturf. Verein Brunn,* 4 (1866), 3–47.

51. C. Darwin, *On the Origin of Species: A Facsimile of the First Edition,* (Cambridge, MA: Harvard Univ. Press, 1975).

52. L. C. Dunn, *A Short History of Genetics.* (New York: McGraw-Hill, 1965).

53. C. Stern (ed.), "The Birth of Genetics." Issued as a supplement to *Genetics,* Vol. 35, 1950. (Contains English

translations of the papers of DeVries, Correns, and Tschermak, in which they first announced their discovery of the laws of genetics that Mendel had previously discovered).

54. C. Stern and E. R. Sherwood eds., *The Origin of Genetics: A Mendel Source Book* (San Francisco: W. H. Freeman, 1966). (Contains English translations of some of Mendel's classic papers and letters).

55. G. H. Hardy, "Mendelian Proportions in Mixed Populations," *Science*, 28 (1908), 49–50.

56. W. S. Sutton, "On the Morphology of the Chromosome Group in *Brachystola magna*," *Biol. Bull.*, 4 (1902), 24–39.

57. H. M. Temin and S. Mizutani, "RNA-Dependent DNA Polymerase in Virions of Rous Sarcoma Virus," *Nature* 226 (1970), 1211–13.

58. D. Baltimore, "Viral RNA–Dependent DNA Polymerase," *Nature*, 226 (1970), 1209–11.

59. M. W. Nirenberg and J. W. Matthaei, "The Dependence of Cell-Free Protein Synthesis in *E. Coli* upon Naturally Occurring or Synthetic Polyribonucleotides," *Proc. Nat'l. Acad. Sci. (USA)*, 47 (1961), 1588–1602.

60. M. Nirenberg and P. Leder, "RNA Codewords and Protein Synthesis," *Science*, 145 (1964), 1399–1407.

61. F. H. C. Crick, "Codon–Anticodon Pairing. The Wobble Hypothesis," *J. Mol. Biol.* 19 (1966), 548–55.

62. R. D. Hotchkiss, "The Quantitative Separation of Purines, Pyrimidines and Nucleosides by Paper Chromatography," *J. Biol. Chem.*, 175 (1948), 315–32.

63. R. H. Hall, "The Modified Nucleosides in Nucleic Acids," in *Handbook of Biochemistry* (New York: Columbia Univ. Press, 1971) H. A. Sober ed. (Chemical Rubber Company, Cleveland, OH, 1970).

64. T. W. Sneider and V. R. Potter, "Methylation of Mammalian DNA: Studies on Novikoff Hepatoma Cells in Tissue Culture," *J. Mol. Biol.*, 42 (1969), 271–84.

65. R. H. Burdon and R. L. P. Adams, "The *in Vivo* Methylation of DNA in Mouse Fibroblasts," *Biochim. Biophys. Acta*, 174 (1969), 322–29.

66. F. Kalousek and N. R. Morris, "The Purification and Properties of Deoxyribonucleic Acid Methylase from Rat Spleen," *J. Biol. Chem.*, 244 (1969), 1157–63.

67. B. F. Vanyushin, S. G. Tkacheva, and A. N. Belozersky, "Rare Bases in Animal DNA," *Nature* (London), 225 (1970), 948–49.

68. B. Sheid, P. R. Srinivasan, and E. Borek, "Deoxyribonucleic Acid Methylase of Mammalian Tissues," *Biochemistry*, 7 (1968), 280–85.

69. E. Scarano, "The Control of Gene Function in Cell Differentiation and in Embryogenesis," *Adv. Cytopharmacol.*, 1 (1971), 13–24.

70. A. D. Riggs, "X Inactivation, Differentiation and DNA Methylation," *Cytogen. Cell Gen.*, 14 (1975), 9–25.

71. R. Holliday and J. E. Pugh, "DNA Modification Mechanisms and Gene Activity during Development," *Science*, 187 (1975), 226–32.

72. R. Sager and R. Kitchin, "Selective Silencing of Eukaryotic DNA," *Science*, 189 (1975), 426–33.

73. R. Holliday, "The Inheritance of Epigenetic Defects," *Science*, 238 (1987), 163–70.

74. P. Chambon, "Split Genes," *Sci. Am.*, 244, no. 5 (1981), 60–71.

75. J. A. Steitz, "Snurps," *Sci. Am.*, 258, no. 6 (1988) 56–63.

76. J. A. Witkowski, "The Discovery of 'Split' Genes: A Scientific Revolution," *Trends Biochem. Sci.*, 13 (1988), 110–13.

77. G. Dreyfuss, M. S. Swanson, and S. Pinol-Roma, "Heterogeneous Nuclear Ribonucleoprotein Particles and the Pathway of *m*RNA Formation," *Trends Biochem. Sci.* 13 (1988), 86–91.

78. C. Guthrie, and B. Patterson, "Splice-ossomal *sn*RNAs," *Ann. Rev. Gen.,* 22 (1988), 387–419.

79. Y. N. Osheim, O. L. Miller, and A. L. Beyer, "RNP Particles at Splice Junction Sequences on Drosophila Chorion Transcripts," *Cell,* 43 (1985), 143–51.

80. E. Strasburger, *Lehrbuch der Botanik* (1875). Translated from the 30th German Ed. by Peter Bell, David Coombe. London: Longman, 1976.

81. W. Flemming, "Contributions to the Knowledge of the Cell and Its Life Phenomena," *Archiv. Mikroskopische Anatomie,* 16 (1879), 302–406. Translation in *Great Experiments in Biology* (M. Gabriel and S. Fogel, eds.) (Englewood Cliffs, NJ: Prentice-Hall, 1955) 240–45.

82. A. R. Wyman and R. White, "A Highly Polymorphic Locus in Human DNA," *Proc. Nat'l. Acad. Sci. (USA),* 77 (1980), 6754–58.

83. A. Kornberg, "The Synthesis of DNA," *Sci. Am.,* 219, no. 4 (1968), 64–78.

84. A. Klein and F. Bonhoeffer, "DNA Replication," *Ann. Rev. Biochem.,* 41 (1972), 301–32.

85. A. Kornberg, I. R. Lehman, and E. S. Simms, "Polydeoxyribonucleotide Synthesis by Enzymes from *Escherichia coli,*" *Fed. Proc.,* 15 (1956) 291–92.

86. R. Okazaki, T. Okazaki, K. Sakabe, K. Sugimoto, and A. Sugino, 1968. "Mechanism of DNA Chain Growth: I. Possible Discontinuity and Unusual Secondary Structure of Newly Synthesized Chains," *Proc. Nat'l. Acad. Sci. (USA),* 59 (1968), 598–605.

87. J. Y. H. Chan, F. F. Becker, J. German, and J. H. Ray, "Altered DNA Ligase I Activity in Bloom's Syndrome Cells," *Nature,* 325 (1987), 357–59.

88. R. K. Moyzis, J. M. Buckingham, L. S. Cram, M. Dani, L. L. Deaven, M. D. Jones, J. Meyne, R. L. Ratliff, and J. R. Wu, "A Highly Conserved Repetitive DNA Sequence, (TTAGGG)n, Present at the Telomeres of Human Chromosomes," *Proc. Nat'l. Acad. Sci. (USA),* 85 (1988), 6622–26.

89. H. J. Cooke, R. A. Brown, and G. A. Rappold, "Hypervariable Telomeric Sequences from the Human Sex Chromosomes are Pseudoautosomal," *Nature,* 317 (1985), 687–92.

90. N. J. Royle, R. E. Clarkson, Z. Wong, and A. J. Jeffreys, "Clustering of Hypervariable Minisatellites in the Proterminal Regions of Human Autosomes," *Genomics,* 3 (1988), 352–60.

91. G. I. Bell, M. J. Selby, and W. J. Rutter, "The Highly Polymorphic Region Near the Human Insulin Gene Is Composed of Simple Tandemly Repeating Sequences," *Nature* 295 (1982), 31–35.

92. J. C. S. Fowler, L. A. Burgoyne, A. C. Scott, and H. W. J. Harding, "Repetitive Deoxyribonucleic Acid (DNA) and Human Genome Variation—A Concise Review Relevant to Forensic Biology," *J. Forensic Sci.,* 33, no. 5 (1988), 1111–16.

93. R. Miesfeild, M. Krystal, and N. Arnheim, "A Member of a New Repeated Family Which Is Conserved Throughout Eukaryotic Evolution," *Nuc. Acids Res.,* 9 (1981), 5931–47.

94. H. Hamada, M. G. Petrino, and T. Kukangu, "A Novel Repeated Element with Z-DNA-Forming Potential Is Widely Found in Evolutionarily Diverse Eukaryotic Genomes," *Proc. Nat'l. Acad. Sci. (USA),* 79 (1982), 6465–69.

95. Human Gene Mapping 9. *Cytoge. Cell Gen.,* 46 (1987), 1–762.

96. J. S. Waye, "Discussion of 'Repetitive Deoxyribonucleic Acid (DNA) and Human Genome Variation—A Concise Review Relevant to Forensic Biology,' (Letter to the Editor)," *J. Forensic Sci.,* 34 (1989), 1296–99.

97. G. Attardi, P. Costantino, and D. Ojala, "Molecular Approaches to the

Dissection of the Mitochondrial Genome in HeLa Cells," in *The Biogenesis of Mitochondria,* A. M. Kroon and C. Saccone eds. (New York: Academic Press, 1974), pp. 9–29.

98. A. W. Linnane, N. Howell, and H. B. Lukins, "Mitochondrial Genetics," in *The Biogenesis of Mitochondria,* A. M. Kroon and C. Saccone eds. (New York: Academic Press, 1974), pp. 193–213.

99. M. C. King, "An Application of DNA Sequencing to a Human Rights Problem," in *Molecular Genetic Medicine,* Vol. 1, T. Friedmann ed. (New York: Academic Press, 1991), pp. 117–32.

100. P. Borst, "Mitochondrial Nucleic Acids," *Ann. Rev. Biochem.,* 41 (1972), 333–76.

101. P. Borst, and L. A. Grivell, "Small Is Beautiful—Portrait of a Mitochondrial Genome," *Nature,* 290 (1981), 443–44.

102. G. Attardi, "The Elucidation of the Human Mitochondrial Genome: A Historical Perspective," *Bioessays,* 5 (1987), 34–39.

103. R. K. H. Petty, A. E. Harding, and J. A. Morgan-Hughes, "The Clinical Features of Mitochondrial Myopathy," *Brain,* 109 (1986), 915–38.

104. S. DiMauro, E. Bonilla, M. Zeviani, M. Nakagawa, and D. C. DeVivo, "Mitochondrial Myopathies," *Ann. Neurol.* 17 (1985), 521–38.

105. R. P. Novick, "Plasmids," *Sci. Am.,* 243 (1980), 102–110.

106. E. A. Adelberg and J. Pittard, "Chromosome Transfer in Bacterial Conjugation," *Bacteriol Rev.,* 29 (1965), 161–72.

107. G. H. Keller, and M. M. Manak, *DNA Probes* (New York: Stockton Press, 1989), 1–259.

108. J. Bessetti, "An Inroduction to PCR Inhibitors," *Prof. DNA* 10, No. 1, (2007) 9–10.

109. P. Rådström, Rickard Knutsson, Petra Wolffs, Maria Lövenklev, and Charlotta Löfström, "Pre-PCR Processing: Strategies to Generate PCR-Compatible Samples," *Mol. Biotechnol.* 26 (2004) 133–46.

110. R. S. Weyant, P. Edmonds, and B. Swaminathan, "Effect of Ionic and Nonionic Detergents on the Taq Polymerase," *BioTechniques* 9 (1990) 308–09.

111. D. Loffert, S. Stump, N. Schaffrath, M. Berkenkopf, and J. Kang, "PCR: Effects of Template Quality," *Qiagen News* 1 (1997) 8–10.

112. L. Katcher and I. Schwartz, "A Distinctive Property of Tth DNA Polymerase: Enzymatic Amplification in the Presence of Phenol," *BioTechniques* 16 (1994) 84–92.

113. E. J. Kontanis and F.A. Reed, "Evaluation of Real-Time PCR Amplification Efficiencies to Detect PCR Inhibitors," *J. Forensic Sci.,* 51 (2006), 795–804.

114. E. Krenke, A. Tereba, S. J. Anderson, E. Buel, S. Culhane, C. J. Finis, C.S. Tomsey, J.M. Zachetti, A. Masibay, D.R. Rabbach, E.A. Amiott, and C. J. Sprecher, "Validation of a 16-Locus Fluorescent Multiplex System," *J. Forensic Sci.,* 47 (2002) 773–85.

115. M. Butler, Y. Shen, and B. R. McCord, "The Development of Reduced Size STR Amplicons as Tools for Analysis of Degraded DNA," *J. Forensic Sci.,* 48, No. 5 (2003) 1054–64.

116. A. Hellmann, U. Rohleder, H. Schmitter, and M Wittig, "STR Typing of Human Telogen Hairs: A New Approach," *Intern'l J. Leg. Med.,* 114 (2001), 269–73.

117. K. Tsukada, K. Takayanagi, H. Asamura, M. Ota, and H. Fukushima, "Multiplex Short Tandem Repeat Typing in Degraded Samples Using Newly Designed Primers for the THO1, TPOX, CSF1PO, and vWA Loci," *Leg. Med.,* 4 (2002) 239–45.

118. T. Chung, J. Drabek, K. L. Opel, J.M. Butler, and B.R. McCord, "A Study on the Effects of Degradation and Temple

Concentration on the Efficiency of the STR Miniplex Primer Sets," *J. Forensic Sci.,* 49 (2004), 733–40.

119. H. Ohtaki, T. Yamamoto, T. Yoshimoto, R. Uchihi, C. Ooshima, Y. Katsumata, and K. Tokunaga, "A Powerful, Novel, Multiplex Typing System for Six Short Tandem Repeat Loci and the Allele Frequency Distributions in Two Japanese Regional Populations," *Electrophoresis,* 23 (2002), 3332–40.

120. D. Cobble and J. M. Butler, "Characterization of New MiniSTR Loci to Aid Analysis of Degraded DNA," *J. Forensic Sci.* 50 (2005)

121. P. Gill, L. Fereday, N. Morling, and P. M. Schneider, "The Evolution of DNA Databases: Recommendations for New European STR Loci," *Forensic Sci. Int'l.,* 156 (2006) 242–44.

122. A. Meyerhans, J.P. Vartanian, and S. Wain-Hobson, "Strand Specific PCR Amplification of Low Copy Number DNA," *Nuc. Acids Res.,* 20, No. 3 (1992) 521–23.

123. Findlay, A. Taylor, P. Quirke, R. Frazier, and A. Urquhart, "DNA Fingerprinting from Single Cells," *Nature,* 389 (1997) 555–56.

124. P. Gill, J. Whitaker, C. Flaxman, N. Brown, and J. Buckleton "An Investigation of the Rigor of Interpretation Rules for STRs Derived from Less Than 100 pg of DNA," *Forensic Sci. Int'l.,* 112 (2000) 17–40.

125. R. A. H. van Oorschot, and M.K. Jones, "DNA Fingerprinting from Fingerprints," *Nature,* 387 (1997), 767.

126. J. P. Whitaker, T. M. Clayton, A. J. Urquhart, E.S. Millican, T. J. Downes, C.P. Kimpton, and P. Gill, "Short Tandem Repeat Typing of Bodies from a Mass Disaster: High Success Rate and Characteristic Amplification Patterns in Highly Degraded Samples," *BioTechniques* 18 (2001), 670–77.

127. J. Abaz, S. J. Walsh, J. M. Curran, D. S. Moss, J. Cullen, J.A. Bright, G.A. Crowe, S. L. Cockerton, and T.E.

Power, "Comparison of the Variables Affecting the Recovery of DNA from Common Drinking Containers," *Forensic Sci. Int'l.,* 126 (2002) 233–40.

128. R. A. Wichenheiser, "Trace DNA: A Review, Discussion of Theory, and Application of the Transfer of Trace Quantities of DNA through Skin Contact," *J. Forensic Sci.,* 47 (2002) 442–50.

129. F. Alessandrini, M. Cecati, M. Pesaresi, C. Turchi, F. Carle, and A. Tagliabracci, "Fingerprints as Evidence for a Genetic Profile: Morphological Study on Fingerprints and Analysis of Exogenous and Individual Factors Affecting DNA Typing," *J. Forensic Sci.,* 48 (2003) 586–92.

130. P. J. Smith and J. Ballantyne, "Simplified Low-Copy-Number DNA Analysis by Post-PCR Purification," *J. Forensic Sci.,* 52, No. 4 (2007) 820–29.

131. L. Li, C.T. Li, R. Y. Li, Y Liu, Y. Lin, T.Z Que, M.Q. Sun, and Y. Li. "SNP Genotyping by Multiplex Amplification and Microarrays Assay for Forensic Application," *Forensic Sci. Int'l.,* 162, Issues 1–3 (2006),74–79.

132. H. Oberacher, H. Niederstatter, F. Pitteri, and W. Parson, "Profiling 627 Mitochondrial Nucleotides via the Analysis ofa 23-Plex Polymerase Chain Reaction by Liquid Chromatography–Electrospray Ionization Time-of-Flight Mass Spectrometry," *Anal. Chem,* 78 (2006), 7816–27.

133. M. F. Hammer, V. F. Chamberlain, V. F. Kearney, D. Stover, G. Zhang, T. Karafet, B. Walsh, and A. J. Redd, "Population Structure of Y Chromosome SNP Haplogroups in the United States and Forensic Implications for Constructing Y Chromosome STR Databases," *Forensic Sci. Int'l.,* 164 (2006), 45–55.

134. D. G. Wang, J. B. Fan, C. J.Siao, A. Berno,P. Young, R. Sapolsky, G. Ghandour, N. Perkins, E. Winchester,

J. Spencer, L. Kruglyak, L. Stein, L. Hsie, T. Topaloglou, E. Hubbell, E. Robinson, M. Mittmann, M. S. Morris, N. Shen, D. Kilburn, J. Rioux, C. Nusbaum, S. Rozen, T. J. Hudson, R. Lipshutz, M. Chee, and E. S. Lander, "Large-Scale Identification, Mapping, and Genotyping of Single-Nucleotide Polymorphisms in the Human Genome," *Science* 280, (1998), 1077–82.

135. M. Krawczak, "Informativity Assessment for Biallelic Single Nucleotide Polymorphisms," *Electrophoresis,* 20 (1999), 1676–81.

136. J. L. Weber and C. Wolng, "Mutation of Human Short Tandem Repeats," *Hum. Mol. Genet.* 2 (1993) 1123–28.

137. J. Huang, W. Wei, J. Zhang, J. Huang, W. Wei, J. Zhang, G. Liu, G. R. Bignell, M. R. Stratton, P. A. Futreal, R. Wooster, K. W. Jones, and M. H. Shapero, "Whole Genome DNA Copy Number Changes Identified by High Density Oligonucleotide Arrays," *Hum. Genomics* 1 No. 4 (2004), 287–99.

138. W. Bloch, "A Biochemical Perspective of the Polymerase Chain Reaction," *Biochemistry,* 30 (1991) 2735–47.

139. T. L. Noreault-Conti and E. Buel, "The Use of Real-Time PCR for Forensic Stain Identification" *Prof. DNA* 10, No. 1 (2007) 3–5.

140. G. L. Trainor, "DNA Sequencing, Automation, and the Human Genomes," *Anal. Chem.* 62 (1990), 418–26.

141. D. Dickson, "Britain Launches Genome Program," *Science,* 243 (1989), 1656–57.

142. L. M. Smith, "DNA Sequence Analysis: Past, Present, and Future," *Am. Biotechnol. Lab.,* 7 (1989), 10–25.

143. C. L. Smith, M. T. Mellon, and R. G. L. Shorr, "Rapid Sequencing of DNA," *Am. Biotechnol. Lab.,* 8 (1990), 48–54.

144. F. Sanger and A. R. Coulson, "A Rapid Method for Determining the Sequence in DNA by Primed Synthesis with DNA Polymerase," *J. Molec. Biol.,* 94 (1975), 444–48.

145. A. M. Maxam and W. Gilbert, "A New Method for Sequencing DNA," *Proc. Nat'l. Acad. Sci. (USA),* 74 (1977), 560–64.

146. F. Sanger, S. Nicklen, and A. R. Coulson, "DNA Sequencing with Chain-Terminating Inhibitors." *Proc. Nat'l. Acad. Sci. (USA),* 74 (1977), 5463–67.

147. J. Zimmerman, H. Voss, C. Schwager, J. Stegemann, and W. Ansorge, "Automated Sanger Dideoxy Sequencing Reaction Protocol," *FEBS Letters,* 233 (1988), 432–36.

148. E. R. Mardis and B. A. Roe, "Automated Methods for Single-Stranded DNA Isolation and Dideoxynucleotide DNA Sequencing Reactions on a Robotic Workstation," *BioTechniques,* 7 (1989), 840–50.

149. R. Lewin, "DNA Sequencing Goes Automatic," *Science,* 233 (1986), 24.

150. R. Lewin, "Japanese Super-Sequencer Poised to Roll," *Science,* 234 (1987), 31.

8

■ ■ ■

The Forensic Application of Y-Chromosome Short-Tandem Repeats

Erin K. Hanson and Jack Ballantyne
National Center for Forensic Science, University of Central Florida, Orlando, FL

INTRODUCTION

Males commit most of the reported violent crime. In the United States, for example, according to the 2005 U.S. Bureau of Justice Statistics, males committed 79% of violent crimes, including approximately 98% of all sexual assaults (http://www.ojp.usdoj. gov/bjs). Therefore, a significant amount of the samples processed in an operational forensic DNA laboratory involve an analysis of male DNA. Currently, autosomal short-tandem repeats (STRs) are the "gold standard" used for the analysis of biological evidence, and in most cases a DNA profile is obtained that is fully able to discriminate all unrelated individuals. However, there are instances in which autosomal STR analysis may fail altogether or produces only limited DNA profile information. In those cases where the failure to obtain the male donor profile is the result of the presence of large quantities of female-derived DNA, probative investigative information may still be obtainable by the judicious use of Y chromosome markers. Such markers are essentially blind to the contaminating female derived DNA in male/female DNA admixtures. Analytical techniques for the examination of short-tandem repeat polymorphisms on the Y-Chromosome have been developed and are proving to be a useful addition to the forensic scientist's armamentarium. This chapter provides an overview of Y-STR analysis applications in forensic genetics and emphasizes, by reference to the unique biology of the Y chromosome, the type of genetic information that is currently obtainable only by this method.

436

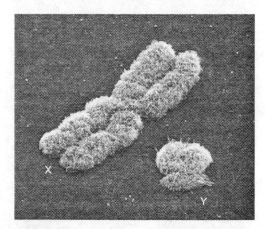

FIGURE 8-1 Human X and Y chromosomes, magnified ~10,000×. (http://news.bbc.co.uk/1/hi/sci/tech/3000742.stm)

BIOLOGY OF THE Y CHROMOSOME

The Y chromosome (Figure 8-1) has often been referred to as a *genetic wasteland,* an evolutionary relic of its X chromosome homologue, that houses few functional genes.[1] However, the Y chromosome contains the gene for gender determination (SRY) and a number of other genes, some of which are necessary for normal male fertility (Table 8-1).

TABLE 8-1 Classification of Human Y-Chromosome Genes

Gene Category	Genes	Functions	Multiple Copies on Y?	Active X Homologue?	X Homologue Inactivated in Females?
Pseudo-autosomal	Many	Equivalently diverse as autosomal genes	No	Yes	Yes[+]
NRY Class I	RSP4Y, ZFY, USP9Y. DBY, UTY, TB4Y, SMCY, EIFIAY	House-keeping	No	Yes	No
NRY Class 2	TTY1, TSPY, PRY, TTY2, CDY, XKRY, DAZ, BPY2	Spermatogenesis	Yes	No	NA
NRY Class 3	SRY	Male determination	No[*]	Yes	Yes
	RDMY	Spermatogenesis	Yes	Yes	Yes
	AMELY	Tooth development	No	Yes	Maybe
	VCY	Unknown	Yes	Yes	NA
	PCDHY	Unknown	No	Yes	No

[*],yes. in some rodents

[+],except for SYBL1, HSPRY3

NA, not applicable

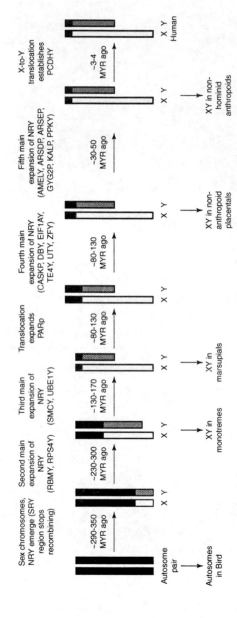

FIGURE 8-2 Evolution of the Human Y-Chromosome. Modified from Reference 2.

Throughout its evolutionary history, the Y chromosome has undergone genetic decay, which is revealed as a significant and progressive reduction in its size (Figure 8-2).[1,2] The Y chromosome uniquely displays an absence of recombination with the X chromosome, rendering it genetically isolated from other nuclear chromosomes.[1,2]

The Y chromosome can be classified into three distinct regions: the euchromatic region, the heterochromatic region, and the *pseudoautosomal regions (PARs)*. The PARs, representing only approximately 5% of the sequence and located at the telomeric ends of the chromosome, are the only portion to undergo meiotic recombination with the X chromosome. The *euchromatin* (which houses all of the functional genes) and the inactive heterochromatin together comprise the remaining approximately 95% of the Y chromosome, referred to as the *non-recombining region (NRY)*. Sequence analysis of the euchromatin has revealed a mosaic of three different sequence classes (Figure 8-3): X-transposed sequences ($\sim$15%), X-degenerate sequences ($\sim$39%), and ampliconic sequences ($\sim$46%).[3]

The X-degenerate sequences are those sequence motifs remaining from the autosomes from which the X and Y chromosomes originated. Sequence similarity between the X and Y chromosomes has been reported to range from 60% to 96%.[3] The X-transposed sequences comprise two blocks that are 99% identical to sequences on the X chromosome (Xq21).[3] This represents an ancient X to Y transposition event that occurred 3 million to 4 million years ago, after the human and chimpanzee lineages diverged.[3] Ampliconic sequences occur in seven segments within the euchromatin that have as much as 99.9% similarity to other sequences in the euchromatin.[3] They are characterized by eight palindromic sequences, and their conservation has been attributed to intra-chromosomal gene conversion events.[3] As can be seen from the brief description of the Y chromosome provided above, there is sufficient homology between the X and Y chromosomes to warrant careful consideration when designing Y-chromosome-specific assays so as not to detect the X chromosome.

The NRY region of the Y chromosome does not undergo genetic recombination with the X chromosome, and is therefore passed unchanged from father to son as a physical block of linked haplotype markers, except for rare mutation events

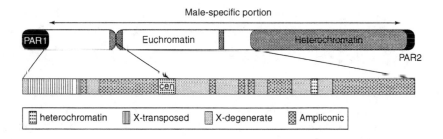

FIGURE 8-3 Sequence classes of the human Y chromosome. Modified from Reference 3.

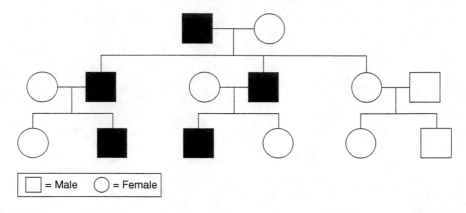

FIGURE 8-4 Patrilineal inheritance of the Y chromosome through three generations.

that may occur (Figure 8-4).[4] The non-independent segregation of Y-chromosome markers in the NRY region results in a reduction in genetic variability compared to autosomal markers. Thus, substantially larger numbers of Y chromosome markers need be used in order to obtain a high discriminatory potential akin to that afforded by autosomal markers. Despite the lower discriminatory capacity of Y-chromosome markers, there are many forensic casework situations in which their use could be beneficial.

Y-CHROMOSOME MARKERS

Several classes of Y-chromosome polymorphisms have been identified, including short-tandem repeats (STRs), single nucleotide polymorphisms (SNPs), and a highly variable minisatellite locus. MSY1, a hypervariable minisatellite, is the most polymorphic single locus present on the Y chromosome, with variation existing in both its sequence and length.[5–8] Challenges associated with minisatellite variant repeat PCR (MVR-PCR), used to analyze MSY1 variation, have resulted in an inability to utilize this highly discriminating minisatellite in routine forensic casework.[9–11] Y-chromosome single nucleotide polymorphisms have also not yet gained widespread use in forensic casework.[12,13] Even though numerous Y-SNP loci have been identified, the discrimination afforded by these loci is not equal to other Y-chromosome markers, thus requiring the need for additional loci to be developed. In addition, there is some uncertainty as to the most suitable analytical platform for multiplex SNP analysis, and any novel instrumentation would require extensive validation.[14] Nevertheless, the use of Y-SNPs for the prediction of ethnogeographic ancestry is likely to increase.

Y-STR loci offer several advantages that make their analysis suitable for routine casework use. Most crime laboratories analyze their autosomal STRs using capillary electrophoresis systems, and hence Y-STR analysis would require no additional equipment. The amplified Y-STR loci alleles typically range in size from 100 bp to

300bp, which allows for their use with partially degraded samples that are frequently encountered in forensic casework. In addition, more than 400 Y-STR loci have been identified, which permit the selection of highly discriminating loci to be incorporated into multiplex systems.[15,16]

FORENSIC USEFULNESS OF Y-STR ANALYSIS

Y-chromosome specific systems can be particularly useful in forensic casework when attempting to determine the genetic profile of the male donor in a male/female DNA admixture that contains the female DNA component in vast excess (e.g., $\geq 100 \times$) and when traditional autosomal STR analysis fails or is not possible.[17–19] Autosomal STR analysis may not be possible if the sample contains a mixture of body fluids other than semen, such as in saliva/saliva mixtures, saliva/vaginal secretion mixtures in cases of oral sodomy, or fingernail scrapings with cells from the perpetrator. In these types of samples a differential extraction to separate the male and female cells is not possible (unlike sperm-containing samples), and the male component is not detectable with the PCR-based autosomal STR systems routinely used. This is due to the kinetics of the PCR process itself, which does not permit minor components to be detected at low levels (i.e., $\leq 1/20$) because of titration of critical reagents by the major DNA component.[20] Autosomal STR analysis may also fail with some semen-containing samples in which the sperm are present in very low copy number, or are present in an extremely fragile state, such as in extended interval (i.e., > 48 h) post-coital samples. Differential extraction of these particular samples may yield no profile from the male donor due to a combination of premature lysis of the sperm's cellular constituents into the non-sperm fraction and to sperm loss during the physical manipulations required of the DNA isolation process. Therefore, the use of Y-STR systems could eliminate the need for separation of the male and female fractions, thus reducing the potential to lose the small amount of male DNA that may be present.

CASE EXAMPLE

The Innocence Project (www.innocenceproject.org)

On the night of June 6, 1998, Clarence Elkin's six-year-old niece was at her grandmother's house when she woke up to hear her grandmother screaming in the other room. She saw her grandmother fighting with an unknown man. She went back to her bedroom thinking the man had not seen her. The next morning she woke up, physically and sexually assaulted, to find her grandmother dead from stab wounds. When questioned by police, she said the intruder looked like her uncle, Clarence Elkins.

Clarence Elkins

Year of incident: 1998
Jurisdiction: OH
Charge: Murder, Attempted Aggravated Murder, Rape, Felonious Assault
Conviction: Murder, Attempted Aggravated Murder, Rape (3cts.)
Sentence: Life

Numerous pieces of biological evidence were collected from the crime scene, including pubic hairs taken from the bodies of both victims. Mitochondrial DNA testing of these hairs, conducted before trial, excluded Elkins as the donor but was not presented to the jury. Elkins had an alibi (drinking at a local bar with friends until 2:30 AM), and there was no other evidence linking him to the crime other than his niece's eyewitness testimony. The jury convicted him of murder and rape based on the eyewitness testimony and sentenced him to life in prison.

In 2002, Elkins' niece recanted her testimony about seeing her uncle that night. That same year, a request was made for DNA testing on the biological evidence collected from the scene. A judge denied his request, stating that the jury would have reached the same decision, even with DNA evidence, because of the eyewitness testimony from his niece. Elkins was able to pay for Y-STR testing, conducted by Orchid Cellmark, a private forensic laboratory. Y-STR analysis of male skin cells taken from a vaginal swab from the deceased grandmother and from the niece's underwear revealed that Elkins was not the donor of either of these samples. Despite these findings, a judge denied Elkins request for a new trial.

Throughout his incarceration, Elkin's wife maintained that her husband was innocent and did some investigating of her own. The investigation led them to believe that a man living near the grandmother's home could be responsible for the crime. This man was in prison, coincidentally in the same cell block as Elkins, and a cigarette butt was taken from the man and was analyzed. His DNA matched that found on the vaginal swab and on the underwear. Elkins was finally released from prison in 2005.

Y-STRs are also useful in determining the number of male contributors in a sample.[21–24] Mixture analysis using autosomal analysis becomes quite complex when the number of donors exceeds two. However, Y-STRs are hemizygous in nature, with one allele being found at each single-copy locus. Therefore, the presence of multiple alleles at each locus can give an indication of the number of male contributors. For example, the profile shown in Figure 8-5A demonstrates the presence of three male individuals in one admixed sample. Three alleles are present at DYS390 and Y-GATA-A7.1. The same three-male mixture was analyzed using standard autosomal STR analysis (Figure 8-5B). Although the presence of multiple donors can be identified (minimum of two), the precise number of donors is less clear.

Y-chromosome polymorphisms could also be used in criminal paternity cases, missing persons cases, and in identification of victims involved in mass disasters.[25–31] In these instances, a reference sample from the (male) victim may not be available. However, Y-chromosome markers are inherited unchanged from one generation to the next (barring any random mutation events). Therefore, a Y-STR profile of the victim may be deduced by typing a male relative in the same lineage. In addition, Y-STR analysis may provide additional discrimination in situations,

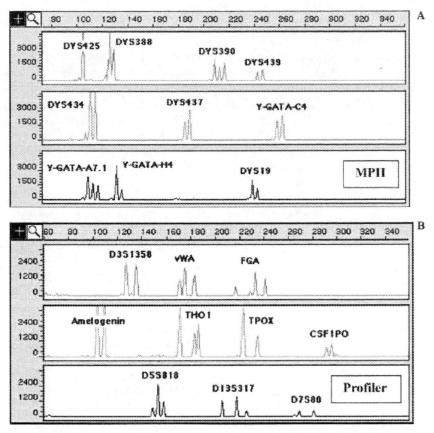

FIGURE 8-5 Male/male admixtures. A mixed DNA sample derived from three male individuals. (A) Y-STR analysis; (B) autosomal STR analysis.

such as mixture interpretation or degraded samples, where a complete autosomal profile is not obtained.[20,32–36]

In the future, Y-STR analysis may aid in *familial searches,* which refers to the use of low-stringency autosomal STR matching of a crime scene profile with an offender database to identify the donor as a possible biological relative of an offender whose profile is in the database.[37,38] With large databases, several individuals from different candidate families arise as possibly being related to the donor of the crime scene profile. Subsequent Y-STR analysis of the crime scene profile and the offenders in the database who might be related to the donor should eliminate most of the adventitious candidates. This not only facilitates the efficiency of the investigative process but also precludes unnecessary invasion of the privacy of non-involved families.

Extending the Post-Coital Interval

Much of the evidence examined by forensic DNA casework analysts is collected by cervico-vaginal sampling of sexual assault victims. Normally, the genetic profile of the perpetrator's semen is determined using standard autosomal STR analysis. However, the ability to obtain an autosomal STR profile of the semen donor diminishes as the post-coital interval is extended. Although an autosomal STR profile can be obtained from samples taken 0–48 hours after intercourse in most cases, it becomes increasingly difficult to obtain such a profile from samples taken more than 48 hours after intercourse. For various reasons, many victims may not report sexual assaults for several days after the incident. During this time, semen evidence may be lost due to drainage from the vaginal canal during normal daily activities performed by the victim, or may be degraded metabolically by constituents of the female reproductive tract. Autosomal STR analysis of extended interval post-coital samples proceeds via the separation of the sperm and non-sperm DNA fractions in order to preclude the necessity to interpret admixed profiles from the semen donor and the female victim. Due to loss or degradation of the semen evidence, however, it is likely that a male profile will not be recovered from such extended interval post-coital samples. As described previously, Y-STRs are particularly useful for the recovery of a male profile in a male/female DNA admixture when the female DNA is present in overwhelming quantities and, if desired, without the need for a differential extraction (separation of sperm and non-sperm fractions). Thus, it is possible that Y-STR analysis could permit extension of the post-coital interval from which a genetic profile of the semen donor can be obtained. Several studies have demonstrated the difficulty in recovering male profiles from post-coital swabs taken 48 to 72 hours after intercourse.[21–23,39,40] However Y-STR based strategies have been developed to recover male DNA donor profiles from samples taken more than 72 hours after intercourse. For example, a commercially available Y-STR multiplex kit (Promega PowerPlex® Y) was able to recover partial profiles from samples taken 4 and 5 days after intercourse (Figures 8-6A and 8-7A). Nine of eleven alleles were obtained from the four-day sample, and seven of eleven alleles were obtained from the five-day sample. Even more of the male DNA profile can be teased out by the use of simple post-PCR purification methods. Subsequent to sample amplification, there is often an excess of non-analyte anionic reactants (e.g., dNTPs, primers, buffer anions) that compete with analyte (DNA alleles) during the electrokinetic injection process necessary for loading the capillary electrophoresis column. Removal of these competing non-analytes can result in a significant enhancement of allelic signals (Figures 8-6B and 8-7B) and the recovery of more profile information.

In many sexual assault investigations, post-coital samples may not be collected from victims if the incident occurred more than three days prior to the medical examination. However the ability to recover male profiles from extended interval samples using Y-STR analysis strategies should have a significant impact on the collection of evidence from, and the resolution of, sexual assault investigations.

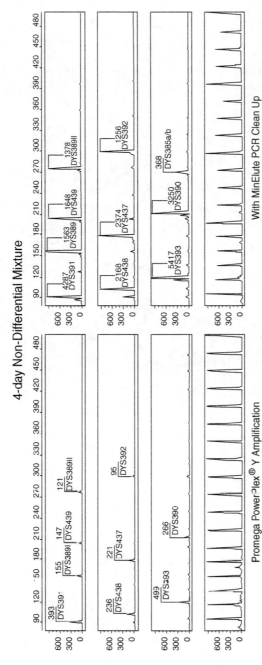

FIGURE 8-6 A) Y-STR profile recovered from a post-coital swab taken four days after intercourse. (B) Improvement in profile recovery after the use of post-PCR purification. (Qiagen MinElute silica gel membrane column; http://www1.qiagen.com/ Products/DnaCleanup/GelPcrSiCleanupSystems/MinElutePCRPurificationKit.aspx)

446

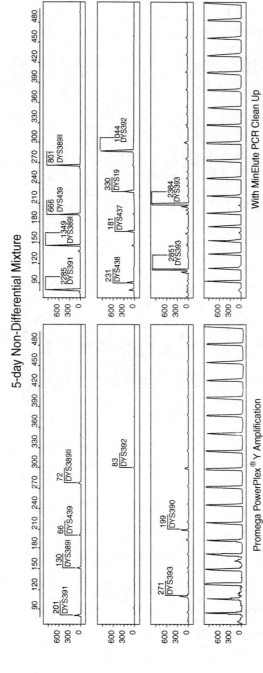

FIGURE 8-7 (A) Y-STR profile recovered from a post-coital swab taken five days after intercourse. (B) Improvement in profile recovery after the use of post-PCR purification. (Qiagen MinElute silica gel membrane column; http://www1.qiagen.com/Products/DnaCleanup/GelPcrSiCleanupSystems/MinElutePCRPurificationKit.aspx)

CHARACTERIZATION OF Y-STR LOCI

More than 400 loci have been identified on the Y chromosome. Figure 8-8 shows a comprehensive annotated physical map of the human Y chromosome that identifies and sequentially positions all currently known Y-STR loci.[15] A majority of loci are located within the Yq11.221 (25.3%), Yq11.222 (16.6%), and the Yq11.223 (18.4%) segments on the long arm of the chromosome, and in the Yp11.2 (22.1%) segment on the short arm. Very few loci are located in the centromeric region, and no loci are present in the telomeric regions of the chromosome. Although several loci are located within functional genes or transcription units, they are confined to the introns or untranslated regions.

The repeat size of most Y-STR loci ranges from 2 bp to 4bp. Knowledge of the repeat size of STR loci is useful in assay development, since stutter products (one

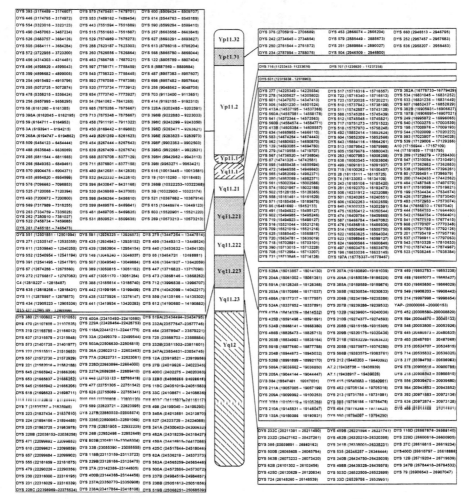

FIGURE 8-8 Annotated physical map of the human Y chromosome.[15]

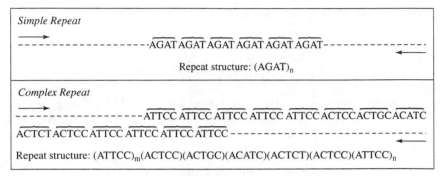

FIGURE 8-9 Simple and complex Y-STR repeat structures.

repeat unit less than the parent allele occurring in true allele positions) are less pronounced with longer core repeat unit sizes, making them more desirable in forensic casework. The known STR loci on the Y chromosome consist of approximately 6% dinucleotide repeats, 39% trinucleotide repeats, 45% tetranucleotide repeats, 9% pentanucleotide repeats, and 1% hexanucleotide repeats.[15] Individual repeat structures can be classified as simple or complex. Simple repeat structures are those with an uninterrupted stretch of the same repeat sequence [e.g., $(AGAT)_n$]. Complex repeat structures contain interruptions in the main repeat array or contain changes in repeat sequence due to mutation events (Figure 8-9).

Single and Multi-Copy Loci

A majority of Y-STR loci are *single copy*, meaning one allele is found at each locus. However, there are a number of loci in which one or both primer sites and associated tandem repeat sequences are duplicated elsewhere on the chromosome. For these so-called bi-local loci, one or two alleles may be present in an individual. Two types of bi-local loci are routinely used in forensic analysis of Y-STRs. The first type involves a single set of primers that will co-amplify two separate loci that are positioned a large distance away from one another along the chromosome (e.g., DYS385, Figure 8-10A). Determination of which locus the individual alleles arose from is not possible, although in some cases unconventional typing strategies can distinguish between them.[41–43] In the second type of bi-local locus, two alleles are also obtained, but in this case the forward amplification primer hybridizes to two loci located relatively close to one another (e.g. DYS389, Figure 8-10B). In the latter situation, the two alleles can be distinguished due to the differences in the size ranges of the obtained alleles.

Although bi-local loci are the most frequently encountered multi-local markers in forensics, several other multi-copy loci have been identified including tri-, tetra-, penta-, and nona-local loci.[15,23,45–49] Only one possible tri-local locus (DYS27), penta-local locus (DYS228), and nona-local locus (DYS398) have been identified *in silico*, but their molecular structure has not been confirmed experimentally.[15] Eight potential tetra-local loci have been identified, two of which (DYS464

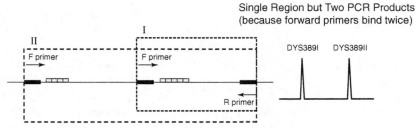

(A) DYS385 a/b

Duplicated regions are
40,775 bp apart and facing
away from each other

Multi-Copy (Duplicated) Marker

a = b   a ≠ b

(B) DYS389 I/II

Single Region but Two PCR Products
(because forward primers bind twice)

DYS389I   DYS389II

FIGURE 8-10   Structure of the two types of bi-local Y-STR loci.[44]

and DYS503) have been further characterized.[15,22,23,45,46,48,49] The presence of one, two, three, or four alleles has been observed for individual samples at these loci. Although the individual gene diversity value of these tetra-local loci is significantly higher than most single-copy loci, determination of the precise genotype can be difficult. A so-called conservative or expanded genotype can be reported (Figure 8-11).

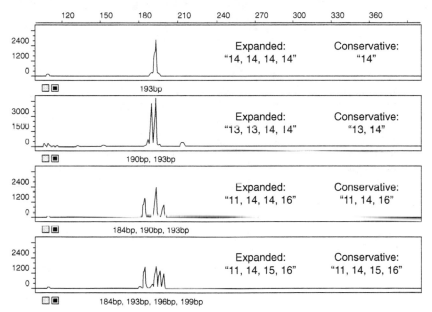

FIGURE 8-11   Conservative and expanded genotyping of a tetra-local Y-STR locus (DYS 503).

The conservative genotype includes only the observed alleles. The expanded genotype includes a determination of all four alleles, even if four distinct alleles are not observed. This relies on an examination of the peak height ratios to determine if multiple copies of the same allele are present. One of the benefits of Y-STR analysis is a more facile determination of the number of male contributors in a mixed sample. The presence of multi-copy loci, particularly tetra-local loci, can confound mixture analysis because of the presence of numerous alleles and a varying number of copies of each allele from an individual donor. Therefore, despite their high discriminatory ability, their use in routine analysis is not recommended.

Nomenclature

The nomenclature of Y-STR loci with simple repeat structures is relatively straightforward, with the repeat structure clearly defined and the allele number determined by the number of repeat units present (Figure 8-9). However, loci with complex repeat structures present the opportunity for designating the same alleles in several different ways. In an attempt to standardize the manner in which repeat structures are determined, in 2006, the DNA Commission of the International Society for Forensic Genetics (ISFG) issued revised guidelines regarding Y-STR locus nomenclature.[50] The repeat structures for a large number of loci were previously determined and are listed in the ISFG publication using their original designations to ensure a universal nomenclature for those loci already in use. Some of these "grandfathered-in" loci would receive different allelic designations if the ISFG rules were to be strictly applied. However, for novel as yet unreported loci, ISFG provides detailed recommendations for the designation of complex repeat structures to assist in nomenclature standardization

Mutation Rates

Since Y-STRs may be useful in paternity testing of deficiency cases (a deceased or otherwise unavailable father) or missing persons investigations, it is important to know the mutation rate to prevent false exclusions. Mutation rate estimates for Y-STRs and autosomal STRs are similar, approximately $1–3 \geq 10^{-3}$ per locus per generation. This is much higher than the single nucleotide mutation rate at any locus of $\sim 10^{-8}$ per nucleotide per generation. The similarity in autosomal and Y-chromosome STR rates indicates that the mutational mechanism is independent of meiotic recombination. Mutations usually result in the gain or loss of one repeat unit, with some evidence of a bias in favor of expansion, which is consistent with the stepwise mutation model of microsatellite evolution.[51] Thus the prevailing hypothesis for the cause of the elevated rate of mutation in microsatellites is one of DNA chain slippage during replication, although sister chromatid recombination subsequent to replication cannot be formally ruled out.[52,53]

The mutation rate at any locus is sufficiently high that one would expect to encounter, albeit rarely, another mutation in the same individual at a second locus, and such double mutations have indeed been observed.[54] This needs to be taken into account when using Y-STRs to infer common ancestry in multigenerational analyses such as paternity and missing person cases.

The high mutation rate is also responsible for the occasional multiple alleles observed at the DYS19, DYS390, DYS391, and DYS385 loci, although all loci are expected to demonstrate the same phenomenon. These multiple alleles arise from a chromosomal duplication or triplication of the region containing the minisatellite, followed by the gain or loss of a repeat unit by replication slippage. Again, this phenomenon needs to be recognized and understood in order to distinguish between rare duplicate (or triplicate) alleles and DNA admixtures of two or more males in casework samples.

COMMONLY USED Y-STR LOCI

A major international multicenter study of thirteen candidate Y-STR markers resulted in recommendations for the use of nine core loci for standard forensic haplotyping,[55] referred to as the *minimal haplotype loci (MHL)*. The nine MHL loci include DYS19, DYS385 (a) and (b), DYS389 (I and II), DYS390, DYS391, DYS392, and DYS393. The MHL loci have proved to be a particularly robust set of genetic markers and have been employed successfully in casework analysis. Despite the initial utility of this set of markers, there was a need for additional Y-STR loci to be used in conjunction with these markers in order to improve the discriminatory capacity of Y-STR testing. For example, in 2002, MHL analysis of 1,705 individuals (599 African Americans, 628 European Americans, and 478 Hispanics) by the custodians of an online MHL U.S. database demonstrated that these individuals collectively possessed 1,116 different haplotypes, a discriminatory capacity of approximately only 65%. The Scientific Working Group on DNA Analysis Methods (SWGDAM) recommended the use of two additional loci, DYS438 and DYS439, to improve discriminatory capacity.[56] The MHL loci plus the two additional loci are referred to as the *SWGDAM core loci*.

Commercial Y-STR Multiplex Systems

The limited quantity of DNA typically recovered from forensic specimens requires simultaneous analysis of Y-STR loci by their incorporation into a multiplex PCR system. The development and optimization of such a system is complicated by primer interactions and homologous sequences on the X chromosome. Several commercial companies have incorporated various combinations of commonly used Y-STR loci into Y-STR multiplex systems (Table 8-2).[57–61] Two of the most commonly used commercial Y-STR multiplex kits are the Promega PowerPlex® Y kit, which contains the SWDGAM core loci plus DYS437; and the Applied Biosystems AmpFlSTR® Yfiler™ kit, which also contains the SWGDAM core loci plus several additional markers [DYS437, DYS448, DYS456, DYS458, C4 (DYS635), and H4].[57,58] The three previously used multiplex kits from Reliagene Technologies (Y-Plex™ 5, Y-Plex™ 6, and Y-Plex™ 12) are no longer commercially

TABLE 8-2 Description of Commercially Available Y-STR Multiplex Amplification Kits

Commercially Available Kit	Manufacturer	Incorporated Loci
Routinely Used in the United States		
PowerPlex® Y	Promega	DYS19, DYS385a/b, DYS389I, DYS389II, DYS390, DYS391, DYS392, DYS393, DYS437, DYS438, DYS439
AmpFlSTR® Yfiler™	Applied Biosystems	DYS19, DYS385a/b, DYS389I, DYS389II, DYS390, DYS391, DYS392, DYS393, DYS437, DYS438, DYS439, DYS456, DYS458, DYS448, DYS635(C4), H4
Used Outside of the United States		
genRES® DYSplex-1	Serac	DYS385a/b, DYS389I, DYS389II, DYS390, DYS391, Amelogenin
genRES® DYSplex-2	Serac	DYS19, DYS389I, DYS389II, DYS392, DYS393
MenPlex® Argus Y-MH	Biotype	DYS19, DYS385a/b, DYS389I, DYS389II; DYS390, DYS391, DYS392, DYS393
Discontinued Commercial Availability		
Y-Plex™ 5	Reliagene	DYS19, DYS385a/b, DYS389II, DYS390, DYS391, DYS393
Y-Plex™ 6	Reliagene	DYS389I, DYS389II, DYS392, DYS393, DYS438, DYS439
Y-Plex™ 12	Reliagene	DYS19, DYS385a/b, DYS389I, DYS389II; DYS390, DYS391, DYS392, DYS393, DYS437, DYS438, DYS439

available.[59–61] All of these kits have been fully validated for forensic use as required by U.S. national DNA standards and in accordance with SWGDAM validation guidelines.[62] They have been optimized to exhibit a high degree of sensitivity and specificity for male DNA, even in the presence of a vast excess of female DNA.

Sequences of the primer sets used to amplify individual loci differ between amplification kits based on the manufacturers' developmental requirements. Since haplotypes obtained in forensic casework are searched against profiles contained in DNA databases, it is essential that laboratories obtain concordant results regardless of the amplification system they utilize.[63] Allelic ladders, which contain frequently occurring alleles for each locus in the multiplex system, are provided with each amplification kit in order to provide consistent results within and between laboratories (Figure 8-12).

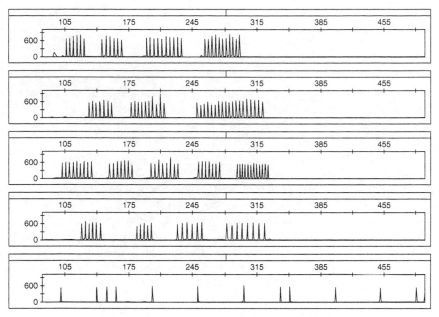

FIGURE 8-12 Example of an Allelic Ladder: Applied Biosytems Yfiler Kit.

STATISTICAL INTERPRETATION OF A Y-STR MATCH

Since the loci in the NRY region of the Y chromosome are inherited as a physical block of physically linked haplotypes, independent assortment does not occur and the loci are in linkage disequilibrium with each other. This non-independence means that the product rule cannot be used to determine multi-locus Y-STR frequencies. As a result a counting method, similar to that used to estimate mtDNA haplotype frequencies, must be employed in order to estimate the frequency of occurrence of a particular Y-STR haplotype. With the counting method, the number of times a particular multi-locus haplotype is observed in a particular database is determined. The frequency of the haplotype is then simply the number of times the haplotype is observed divided by the number of samples in the database. Alternative methods for Y-STR haplotype frequency estimates have been suggested including one based upon a mismatch distribution approach that allows the evaluation of the proportion of pairs of Y-STR haplotypes that are prone to become identical by state (IBS), in one generation, by recurrent mutation.[64]

The application of confidence intervals around the haplotype frequency estimate has been recommended to correct for possible sampling effects when using databases of limited size. Reporting a haplotype frequency without associated confidence intervals may still be acceptable as a factual statement regarding observations in a particular database. If a confidence interval is applied and the haplotype has been observed in the database, the upper 95% confidence limit is calculated using the following formula:

$$p + 1.96 \sqrt{\frac{(p)(1 - p)}{n}}$$

where p is x/n (n = database size, x = number of times observed in the database). If the haplotype has not been observed previously in the database, the formula used to calculate the upper 95% confidence limit is as follows:

$$1 - (0.05)^{1/n}$$

where n is the size of the database. A simplified alternative formulation can also be used in this instance; $3/n$ (n = size of the database). This value will be close to the formula, and 95% of the time the real frequency will be less than that estimate. Due to population differentiation between subpopulations within the broader ethnic groups, an appropriate θ (or F_{ST}) correction, akin to the situation with autosomal STRs, may be applicable.[65,66]

Empirical studies have confirmed the non-linkage of Y-STR haplotypes and autosomal STR profiles.[65] Therefore, in cases where both autosomal and Y-STR analysis is performed, it is possible to multiply the autosomal STR profile frequency with the upper confidence limit bounded Y-STR haplotype frequency to produce an overall frequency estimate for the combined profiles.

Databases

The reliability of haplotype frequency estimates is dependent on the nature of the database being used, which must be relevant and reliable for the forensic purposes intended. Specifically, the database should comprise multi-locus haplotype data from sufficient samples from different populations representing the major ethnic groups.

Allele frequency distributions from diverse population groups have been made available through forensic databases on the worldwide web (Table 8-3).[67–71] A Y-STR haplotype reference database (YHRD) was established by the Institute of Legal

TABLE 8-3 Web-Accessible Y-STR Haplotype Databases (as of January 2008)

Database	No. of Samples	No. of Loci	Web Address
Y Chromosome Haplotype Reference Database (YHRD)	50,867 23,981	9 11	http://www.yhrd.org
Y-STR Haplotype Reference Database (ReliaGene)	4,623 3,406	7 11	http://www.reliagene.com
PowerPlex Y Haplotype Database (Promega)	4,004	12	http://www.promega.com
Yfiler Haplotype Database	3,561	17	http://www.appliedbiosystems.com
Consolidated U.S. YSTR Database	13,906 10,865 4,163	11 12 17	http://www.usystrdatabase.org

Medicine, Berlin in 2000, and contains more than 40,000 samples.[68] Although initially containing MHL data from European populations, this database has now been extended to included United States and Asian populations and the SWGDAM core loci. The commercial manufacturers of Y-STR multiplex kits have also created Y-STR databases accessible to the public that allow for searching using the particular set of Y-STR markers contained within their respective multiplex system. Recently, the diverse U.S. databases have been combined into one consolidated database.[72] A large number of data exist in genealogical databases,[73] but are not generally used in forensics due to uncertainties about data quality.

FUTURE DIRECTIONS

Novel Y-STR Markers

Two commercially available Y-chromosome STR multiplex amplification kits, the Promega PowerPlex® Y kit and the Applied Biosystems AmpF*l*STR® Yfiler® kit, are currently used worldwide for casework.[57,58] These commercial kits employ 12 and 17 markers, respectively, and both include the SWGDAM core loci. Although the kits have adequate discrimination for most cases, the occurrence of coincidental matches between two unrelated individuals can still occur with both systems, and there is a need for the occasional deployment of additional loci. As stated previously, more than 400 Y-STR loci have been identified on the Y chromosome.[15] These loci have been deposited into various public databases, including the Human Genome Database (www. gdb.org), where limited genetic data such as primer sequences, general chromosomal location, and repeat unit size is provided for each locus. The annotated physical map described previously has allowed for the identification of numerous duplicated loci.[15] Twenty-eight pairs of loci were identified that had received separate *DYS* designations but amplified the same sequence. This type of information is of particular interest to those research groups designing novel Y-STR multiplex systems to ensure the presence of non-synonymous loci within in an individual system.

The physical map and associated references present to the forensic community the number and location of all available Y-STR loci; however, most of the loci have not been evaluated empirically for their use in forensic casework. Such evaluation criteria include amplification efficiency, homology with the X chromosome, and the degree of variation afforded when combined with the loci already in use. Presumably, some of these novel Y-STR loci could, upon appropriate validation, prove useful in forensic casework analysis by providing additional discriminatory power whenever needed. However, most studies involving novel Y-STR loci simply report allele frequencies and diversity values in various populations.[48,49,74-86] Significantly, an important study published in 2004 describes the results of an extensive survey of STR loci on the Y chromosome including an overview of repeat structures and variability.[16] It also provides a list of twenty-six markers demonstrating the highest variability of those evaluated in the study. However, these values were determined for a population size of eight samples and may therefore not be accurate estimates. Other highly discriminating loci have also been identified. Individual gene diversity values for ninety-eight non-SWGDAM core Y-STR loci and one Y chromosome InDel are provided in Table 8-4, and range

TABLE 8-4 Individual Gene Diversity Values for 98 Non-Core Y-STR Loci and One Y InDel

	Diversity Values			Diversity Values	
Locus	Caucasian (n = 100)	African American (n = 100)	Locus	Caucasian (n = 100)	African American (n = 100)
DYS464	0.92	0.93	DYS543	0.65	0.65
DYS503	0.92	0.75	DYS444	0.65	0.64
DYS657	0.85	0.91	DYS452	0.62	0.65
DYS688	0.88	0.90	DYS707	0.55	0.65
DYS449	0.77	0.87	DYS505	0.57	0.64
DYS591	0.70	0.87	A7.2	0.54	0.64
DYS685	0.79	0.86	DYS484	0.39	0.64
DYS481	0.72	0.86	DYS556	0.44	0.64
DYS535	0.86	0.85	DYS622	0.68	0.64
DYS527	0.84	0.79	DYS463	0.60	0.63
DYS630	0.72	0.84	DYS522	0.63	0.60
DYS576	0.79	0.82	DYS533	0.59	0.62
DYS570	0.79	0.81	DYS510	0.57	0.62
DYS643	0.56	0.81	DYS495	0.62	0.55
DYS557	0.66	0.79	H4	0.61	0.60
DYS458	0.78	0.77	DYS443	0.49	0.61
DYS447	0.64	0.77	DYS490	0.10	0.61
DYS534	0.77	0.75	DYS441	0.58	0.60
DYS508	0.47	0.76	DYS442	0.51	0.58
DYS627	0.75	0.72	DYS485	0.51	0.58
DYS660	0.75	0.72	DYS437	0.58	0.43
DYS459	0.68	0.75	DYS598	0.55	0.54
C4	0.67	0.75	A7.1	0.55	0.54
DYS446	0.62	0.75	DYS596	0.46	0.55
DYS551	0.62	0.73	DYS634	0.13	0.55
DYS521	0.32	0.73	DYS703	0.54	0.45
DYS607	0.63	0.72	DYS468	0.40	0.54
DYS456	0.72	0.53	DYS572	0.38	0.54
DYS562	0.71	0.71	DYS578	0.53	0.34
DYS448	0.56	0.71	DYS561	0.49	0.52
A10	0.48	0.71	DYS513	0.47	0.51
DYS520	0.48	0.70	DYS445	0.51	0.30
DYS549	0.68	0.64	DYS594	0.30	0.50
DYS552	0.68	0.53	DYS494	0.13	0.50
DYS439	0.64	0.66	DYS540	0.49	0.43

TABLE 8-4 continued

	Diversity Values			Diversity Values	
		African			African
	Caucasian	American		Caucasian	American
Locus	(n = 100)	(n = 100)	Locus	(n = 100)	(n = 100)
DYS588	0.48	0.40	DYS638	0.30	0.13
DYS511	0.48	0.33	DYS488	0.28	0.13
DYS617	0.48	0.33	DYS455	0.28	0.12
DYS636	0.48	0.39	DYS454	0.12	0.21
DYS525	0.30	0.47	DYS593	0.08	0.20
DYS388	0.46	0.22	DYS476	0.20	0.06
DYS462	0.44	0.41	DYS425	0.08	0.16
DYS426	0.44	0.35	DYS641	0.14	0.15
DYS453	0.18	0.44	DYS435	0.15	0.02
DYS450	0.22	0.44	DYS434	0.06	0.12
DYS698	0.44	0.36	DYS436	0.10	0.10
DYS531	0.25	0.43	DYS590	0.06	0.08
YAP	0.04	0.42	DYS575	0.00	0.04
DYS631	0.41	0.25	DYS467	0.00	0.04
DYS497	0.39	0.33			

from 0.04 to 0.93, with the two tetra-local loci (DYS464 and DYS503) having the highest values.[23,48,49] Thus a number of highly discriminating non-core loci are available for possible incorporation into novel multiplex kits.

Although several novel Y-STR multiplex systems containing a combination of non-SWGDAM core and core loci have been reported,[22,23,82,87–89] surprisingly few of the non-core have undergone the full developmental validation studies required by U.S. national standards.[62] Thus it is not sufficient that a locus has a high discriminatory potential (high gene diversity) when combined with other loci in the multiplex. It must also be robust and sensitive enough to work in concert with other loci under the restricted set of reaction conditions imposed by the multiplex format and with the types of compromised samples encountered in forensic casework.

Y-Chromosome Markers and Bio-Geographic Ancestry

Single nucleotide polymorphisms (SNPs) are the smallest and most abundant type of human DNA polymorphisms. It is unlikely that SNPs will replace STRs as the primary method of choice in the forensic field, but their use in evolutionary genetics for defining Y-chromosome and mtDNA haplogroups for population of origin analysis is growing.[12,14,90–100] As a result of unique mutations within the non-recombining region of the Y chromosome (NRY), paternal lineages have arisen and remained throughout human history creating population specific lineages, commonly called *haplogroups*.[12,90–92,95] These haplogroups have been placed within large-scale phylogenetic trees representing worldwide Y-chromosomal variation, mostly SNPs within the NRY, forming haplogroups A–R.[101] Many of these polymorphisms have proved highly informative in tracing human prehistoric migrations and are generating new hypotheses on human colonizations and migrations. It is suspected that migration restrictions and population expansions following the Last Glacial Maximum (LGM) have resulted in the survival of a limited number of particular European haplogroups.[102–106] Thus it may be possible in the future to determine the putative ethnogeographic ancestry of an unknown DNA donor and also provide, through hierarchical, multiplex haplogroup typing of known and as-yet-to-be-discovered markers, the ability to discriminate subpopulations within these broader groups. An example of the population differentiation afforded by Y chromosome haplogroup typing is illustrated in Figure 8-13, which shows frequency clines in some of the European-specific haplogroups across Europe. As can be seen, some haplogroups are more commonly found in individuals from Eastern Europe (R1a), Western Europe (R1b), Scandinavia (I1a), and the Balkans (I1b).

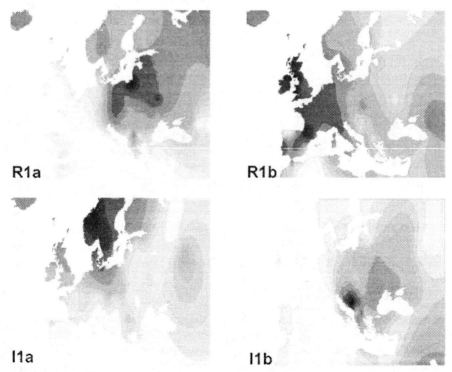

FIGURE 8-13 Variation in Y-chromosome haplogroup frequencies across Europe. European populations can be differentiated according to geographic origin as evidenced by clines in the R1a, R1b, I1a, and I1b haplogroup frequencies. The degree of shading within each contour is directly proportional to the haplogroup frequency. (*From www.relativegenetics.com*).

References

1. B. T. Lahn and D. C. Page, "Functional Coherence of the Human Y Chromosome," *Science* 278 (1997) 675–80.

2. B. T. Lahn, N. M. Pearson, and K. Jegalian, "The Human Y Chromosome, in the Light of Evolution," *Nat. Rev. Genet.* 2 (2001) 207–16.

3. M. E. Hurles and M. A. Jobling, "A Singular Chromosome," *Nat. Genet.* 34 (2003) 246–47.

4. C. A. Tilford, T. Kuroda-Kawaguchi, H. Skaletsky, S. Rozen, L. G. Brown, M. Rosenberg, J. D. McPherson, K. Wylie, M. Sekhon, T. A. Kucaba, R. H. Waterston, and D. C. Page, "A Physical Map of the Human Y Chromosome," *Nature* 409 (2001) 943–45.

5. N. Bouzekri, P. G. Taylor, M. F. Hammer, and M. A. Jobling, "Novel Mutation Processes in the Evolution of a Haploid Minisatellite, MSY1: Array Homogenization without Homogenization," *Hum. Mol. Genet.* 7 (1998) 655–59.

6. M. Brion, R. Cao, A. Salas, M. V. Lareu, and A. Carracedo, "New Method to Measure Minisatellite Variant Repeat Variation in Population Genetic Studies," *Am. J. Hum. Biol.* 14 (2002) 421–28.

7. M. A. Jobling, N. Bouzekri, and P. G. Taylor, "Hypervariable Digital DNA Codes for Human Paternal Lineages: MVR-PCR at the Y-Specific Minisatellite, MSY1 (DYF155S1)," *Hum. Mol. Genet.* 7 (1998) 643–53

8. M. A. Jobling, E. Heyer, P. Dieltjes, and K. P. de, "Y-chromosome-Specific Microsatellite Mutation Rates Re-Examined Using a Minisatellite, MSY1," *Hum. Mol. Genet.* 8 (1999) 2117–20.

9. M. Brion, R. Cao, A. Salas, M. V. Lareu, and A. Carracedo, "A New Method for Analysing Variation from PCR-MVR Data: Analysis of the MSY1 Minisatellite," *Prog. Forensic Gen.* 8 (2000) 284–86.

10. J. L. Soto, S. Bellas, M. Brion, M. V. Lareu, A. Carracedo, C. Pestoni, and M. S. Rodriguez-Calvo, "MVR Analysis of the MSY1 Minisatellite," *Prog. Forensic Gen.* 7 (1998) 413–15.

11. J. Q. Wang, M. Ding, and Z. Sun, [MVR-PCR and forensic medicine], *Fa.Yi.Xue.Za Zhi.* 20 (2004) 40–43.

12. M. A. Jobling, "Y-Chromosomal SNP Haplotype Diversity in Forensic Analysis," *Forensic Sci. Int.* 118 (2001) 158–62.

13. M. A. Jobling and T. E. King, "The Distribution of Y-chromosomal Haplotypes: Forensic Implications," *Prog. Forensic Gen.* 10 (2004) 70–72.

14. B. Sobrino, M. Brion, and A. Carracedo, SNPs in forensic genetics: a review on SNP typing methodologies, *Forensic Sci. Int.* 154 (2005) 181–194.

15. E. K. Hanson and J. Ballantyne, Comprehensive annotated STR physical map of the human Y chromosome: Forensic implications, Leg.Med.(Tokyo) (2005).

16. M. Kayser, R. Kittler, A. Erler, M. Hedman, A. C. Lee, A. Mohyuddin, S. Q. Mehdi, Z. Rosser, M. Stoneking, M. A. Jobling, A. Sajantila, and C. Tyler-Smith, "A Comprehensive Survey of Human Y-Chromosomal Microsatellites," *Am. J Hum. Genet.* 74 (2004) 1183–97.

17. A. Betz, G. Bassler, G. Dietl, X. Steil, G. Weyermann, and W. Pflug, "DYS STR Analysis with Epithelial Cells in a Rape Case," *Forensic Sci. Int.* 118 (2001) 126–30.

18. A. F. Dekairelle and B. Hoste, "Application of a Y-STR-Pentaplex PCR (DYS19, DYS389I and II, DYS390 and DYS393) to Sexual Assault Cases," *Forensic Sci. Int.* 118 (2001) 122–25.

19. P. Martin, C. Albarran, O. Garcia, P. Garcia, M. Sancho, and A. Alonso, "Application of Y-STR Analysis to Rape Cases That Cannot Be Solved by

Autosomal STR Analysis," *Prog. Forensic Gen.* 8 (2000) 526–28.

20. M. Prinz, K. Boll, H. Baum, and B. Shaler, Multiplexing of Y Chromosome Specific STRs and Performance for Mixed Samples," *Forensic Sci. Int.* 85 (1997) 209–18.

21. D. L. Daniels, A. M. Hall, and J. Ballantyne, "SWGDAM Developmental Validation of a 19-Locus Y-STR System for Forensic Casework," *J. Forensic Sci.* 49 (2004) 668–83.

22. E. K. Hanson and J. Ballantyne, "A Highly Discriminating 21 Locus Y-STR 'megaplex' System Designed to Augment the Minimal Haplotype Loci for Forensic Casework," *J. Forensic Sci.* 49 (2004) 40–51.

23. E. K. Hanson, P. N. Berdos, and J. Ballantyne, "Testing and evaluation Of 43 'Noncore' Y Chromosome Markers for Forensic Casework Applications," *J. Forensic Sci.* 51 (2006) 1298–1314.

24. M. Prinz and M. Sansone, "Y chromosome-Specific Short Tandem Repeats in Forensic Casework," *Croat. Med. J.* 42 (2001) 288–91.

25. F. Alshamali, A. Qader Alkhayat, B. Budowle, and N. Watson, "Y Chromosome in Forensic Casework and Paternity Testing," *Prog. Forensic Gen.* 10 (2004) 353–56.

26. S. Andelinovic, D. Sutlovic, I. Erceg, I, V. Skaro, A. Ivkosic, F. Paic, B. Rezic, M. finis-Gojanovic, and D. Primorac, "Twelve-Year Experience in Identification of Skeletal Remains from Mass Graves," *Croat. Med. J.* 46 (2005) 530–39.

27. M. J. Anjos, M. Carvalho, L. Andrade, V. Lopes, A. Serra, L. Batista, C. Oliveira, C. Tavares, F. Balsa, F. Corte-Real, D. N. Vieira, and M. C. Vide, "Individual Genetic Identification of Biological Samples: A Case of an Aircraft Accident," *Forensic Sci. Int.* 146 Suppl (2004) S115–S117.

28. M. A. Jobling, A. Pandya, and C. Tyler-Smith, "The Y Chromosome in Forensic Analysis and Paternity Testing," *Int. J. Leg. Med.* 110 (1997) 118–24.

29. M. Kayser, C. Kruger, M. Nagy, G. Geserick, P. de Knijff, and L. Roewer, "Y-Chromosomal DNA-Analysis in Paternity Testing: Experiences and Recommendations," *Prog. Forensic Gen.* 7 (1998) 494–96.

30. J. Li, [Chromosome STR genetic markers in paternity identification], *Zhong. Nan. Da. Xue. Xue. Bao. Yi. Xue. Ban.* 29 (2004) 432–34.

31. B. Rolf, W. Keil, B. Brinkmann, L. Roewer, and R. Fimmers, "Paternity Testing Using Y-STR Haplotypes: Assigning a Probability for Paternity in Cases of Mutations," Int. J. Leg. Med. 115 (2001) 12–15.

32. B. Berger, H. Niederstätter, S. Köchl, M. Steinlechner, and W. Parson, "Male/Female DNA Mixtures: A Challenge for Y-STR Analysis," *Prog. Forensic Gen.* 9 (2003) 295–99.

33. N. Cerri, U. Ricci, I. Sani, A. Verzeletti, and F. F. De, "Mixed Stains from Sexual Assault Cases: Autosomal or Y-Chromosome Short Tandem Repeats?" *Croat. Med. J.* 44 (2003) 289–92.

34. W. Parson, H. Niederstatter, A. Brandstatter, and B. Berger, "Improved Specificity of Y-STR Typing in DNA Mixture Samples," *Int. J. Leg. Med.* 117 (2003) 109–14.

35. A. Tsuji, A. Ishiko, N. Ikeda, and H. Yamaguchi, "Personal Identification Using Y-Chromosomal Short Tandem Repeats from Bodily Fluids Mixed with Semen," *Am. J. Forensic Med. Pathol.* 22 (2001) 288–91.

36. Y. Yoshida, Y. Fujita, and S. Kubo, "Forensic Casework of Personal Identification Using a Mixture of Body Fluids from More Than One Person by Y-STRs Analysis," *J. Med. Invest.* 51 (2004) 238–42.

37. F. R. Bieber, C. H. Brenner, and D. Lazer, "Human Genetics. Finding

Criminals Through DNA of Their Relatives," *Science* 312 (2006) 1315–16.

38. H. T. Greely, D. P. Riordan, N. A. Garrison, and J. L. Mountain, "Family Ties: The Use of DNA Offender Databases to Catch Offenders' Kin," *J. Law Med. Ethics* 34 (2006) 248–262.

39. A. Hall and J. Ballantyne, "Novel Y-STR Typing Strategies Reveal the Genetic Profile of the Semen Donor in Extended Interval Post-Coital Cervicovaginal Samples," *Forensic Sci. Int.* 136 (2003) 58–72.

40. A. Hall and J. Ballantyne, "The Development of an 18-Locus Y-STR System for Forensic Casework," *Anal. Bioanal. Chem.* 376 (2003) 1234–46.

41. H. Niederstatter, B. Berger, H. Oberacher, A. Brandstatter, C. G. Huber, and W. Parson, "Separate Analysis of DYS385a and b versus Conventional DYS385 Typing: Is There Forensic Relevance?" *Int. J. Leg. Med.* 119 (2005) 1–9.

42. Y. Seo, Y. Takami, K. Takahama, M. Yoshizawa, T. Nakayama, and N. Yukawa, "A Method for Genotyping Y Chromosome-Linked DYS385a and DYS385b Loci," *Leg. Med.* (Tokyo) 5 (2003) 228–32.

43. S. B. Tang, J. Y. Guo, and Z. H. Li, [New improved approaches for DYS385 detection], *Fa. Yi. Xue. Za Zhi.* 19 (2003) 27–29.

44. J. Butler, *Forensic DNA Typing: Biology, Technology and Genetics of STR Markers,* 2nd ed., (Burlington, MA: Academic Press, 2005).

45. B. Berger, H. Niederstatter, A. Brandstatter, and W. Parson, "The Highly Discriminating Y-STR SYS464: A Reasonable Extension of the Minimal Y-STR Haplotype?" *Prog. Forensic Gen.* 10 (2004) 82–84.

46. J. M. Butler and R. Schoske, "Forensic Value of the Multicopy Y-STR Marker DYS464," *Prog. Forensic Gen.* 10 (2004) 278–80.

47. J. M. Butler and R. Schoske, "U.S. Population Data for the Multi-Copy Y-STR Locus DYS464," *J. Forensic Sci.* 50 (2005) 975–77.

48. E. K. Hanson and J. Ballantyne, "Population Data for a Novel, Highly Discriminating Tetra-Local Y-Chromosome Short Tandem Repeat: DYS503," *J. Forensic Sci.* 52 (2007) 498–99.

49. E. K. Hanson and J. Ballantyne, "Population Data for 48 'Non-Core' Y Chromosome STR Loci," *Leg. Med.* (Tokyo) (2007).

50. L. Gusmao, J. M. Butler, A. Carracedo, P. Gill, M. Kayser, W. R. Mayr, N. Morling, M. Prinz, L. Roewer, C. Tyler-Smith, and P. M. Schneider, "DNA Commission of the International Society of Forensic Genetics (ISFG): An Update of the Recommendations on the Use of Y-STRs in Forensic Analysis," *Forensic Sci. Int.* 157 (2006) 187–97.

51. M. Kimura and T. Ohta, "Stepwise Mutation Model and Distribution of Allelic Frequencies in a Finite Population," *Proc. Natl. Acad. Sci (USA)* 75 (1978) 2868–72.

52. C. Schlotterer and D. Tautz, "Slippage Synthesis of Simple Sequence DNA," *Nucleic Acids Res.* 20 (1992) 211–15.

53. P. S. Walsh, N. J. Fildes, and R. Reynolds, "Sequence Analysis and Characterization of Stutter Products at the Tetranucleotide Repeat Locus vWA," *Nucleic Acids Res.* 24 (1996) 2807–12.

54. M. Kayser, L. Roewer, M. Hedman, L. Henke, J. Henke, S. Brauer, C. Kruger, M. Krawczak, M. Nagy, T. Dobosz, R. Szibor, K. P. de, M. Stoneking, and A. Sajantila, "Characteristics and Frequency of Germline Mutations at Microsatellite Loci from the Human Y Chromosome, as Revealed by Direct Observation in Father/Son Pairs," *Am. J. Hum. Genet.* 66 (2000) 1580–88.

55. M. Kayser, A. Caglia, D. Corach, N. Fretwell, C. Gehrig, G. Graziosi,

F. Heidorn, S. Herrmann, B. Herzog, M. Hidding, K. Honda, M. Jobling, M. Krawczak, K. Leim, S. Meuser, E. Meyer, W. Oesterreich, A. Pandya, W. Parson, G. Penacino, A. Perez-Lezaun, A. Piccinini, M. Prinz, C. Schmitt, and L. Roewer, "Evaluation of Y-Chromosomal STRs: A Multicenter Study," *Int. J. Leg. Med.* 110 (1997) 125–129.

56. SWGDAM Y-STR Subcommittee, "Report on the Current Activities of the Scientific Working Group on DNA Analysis Methods Y-STR Subcommittee," Forensic Sci. Commun. 6 (2004).

57. B. E. Krenke, L. Viculis, M. L. Richard, M. Prinz, S. C. Milne, C. Ladd, A. M. Gross, T. Gornall, J. R. Frappier, A. J. Eisenberg, C. Barna, X. G. Aranda, M. S. Adamowicz, and B. Budowle, "Validation of a Male-Specific, 12-Locus Fluorescent Short Tandem Repeat (STR) Multiplex," *Forensic Sci. Int.* 148 (2005) 1–14.

58. J. J. Mulero, C. W. Chang, L. M. Calandro, R. L. Green, Y. Li, C. L. Johnson, and L. K. Hennessy, "Development and Validation of the AmpFlSTR Yfiler PCR Amplification Kit: A Male Specific, Single Amplification 17 Y-STR Multiplex System," *J. Forensic Sci.* 51 (2006) 64–75.

59. J. G. Shewale, H. Nasir, E. Schneida, A. M. Gross, B. Budowle, and S. K. Sinha, "Y-Chromosome STR System, Y-PLEX 12, for Forensic Casework: Development and Validation," *J. Forensic Sci.* 49 (2004) 1278–90.

60. S. K. Sinha, H. Nasir, A. M. Gross, B. Budowle, and J. G. Shewale, "Development and Validation of the Y-PLEX 5, a Y-Chromosome STR Genotyping System, for Forensic Casework," *J. Forensic Sci.* 48 (2003) 985–1000.

61. S. K. Sinha, B. Budowle, S. S. Arcot, S. L. Richey, R. Chakrabor, M. D. Jones, P. W. Wojtkiewicz, D. A. Schoenbauer, A. M. Gross, S. K. Sinha, and J. G. Shewale, "Development and Validation of a Multi-plexed Y-Chromosome STR Genotyping System, Y-PLEX 6, for Forensic Casework," *J. Forensic Sci.* 48 (2003) 93–103.

62. SWGDAM, "Revised Validation Guidelines," *Forensic Sci. Comm.* 6 (2004) 1–4.

63. A. M. Gross, P. Berdos, and J. Ballantyne, "Y-STR Concordance Study between Y-Plex5, Y-Plex6, Y-Plex12, PowerplexY, Y-Filer, MPI, and MPII," *J. Forensic Sci.* 51 (2006) 1423–28.

64. L. Pereira, M. J. Prata, and A. Amorim, "Mismatch Distribution Analysis of Y-STR Haplotypes as a Tool for theEvalu-ation of Identity-by-State Proportions and Significance of Matches—The European Picture," *Forensic Sci. Int.* 130 (2002) 147–55.

65. B. Budowle, M. Adamowicz, X. G. Aranda, C. Barna, R. Chakraborty, D. Cheswick, B. Dafoe, A. Eisenberg, R. Frappier, A. M. Gross, C. Ladd, H. S. Lee, S. C. Milne, C. Meyers, M. Prinz, M. L. Richard, G. Saldanha, A. A. Tierney, L. Viculis, and B. E. Krenke, "Twelve Short Tandem Repeat Loci Y Chromosome Haplotypes: Genetic Analysis on Populations Residing in North America," *Forensic Sci. Int.* 150 (2005) 1–15.

66. National Research Council, *The Evaluation of Forensic DNA Evidence* (Washington, DC: National Academy Press, 1996).

67. "The PowerPlex Y Haplotype Database," *Prof. DNA* 7 (2004) 15.

68. M. Kayser, S. Brauer, S. Willuweit, H. Schadlich, M. A. Batzer, J. Zawacki, M. Prinz, L. Roewer, and M. Stoneking, "Online Y-Chromosomal Short-Tandem Repeat Haplotype Reference Database (YHRD) for U.S. Populations," *J. Forensic Sci.* 47 (2002) 513–19.

69. R. Lessig, S. Willuweit, M. Krawczak, F. C. Wu, C. E. Pu, W. Kim, L. Henke, J. Henke, J. Miranda, M. Hidding, M. Benecke, C. Schmitt, M. Magno, G. Calacal, F. C. Delfin, M. C. de Ungria, S. Elias, C. Augustin, Z. Tun, K. Honda, M. Kayser, L. Gusmao, A. Amorim, C. Alves, Y. Hou, C. Keyser, B. Ludes, M. Klintschar, U. D. Immel, B. Reichenpfader, B. Zaharova, and L. Roewer, "Asian online Y-STR Haplotype Reference Database," *Leg. Med.* (Tokyo) 5 Suppl 1 (2003) S160–S163.

70. L. Roewer, M. Kayser, C. Augustin, A. Caglia, D. Corach, S. Furedi, G. Geserick, L. Henke, M. Hidding, H. J. Kargel, P. de Kniff, R. Lessig, V. Pascali, W. Parson, M. Prinz, B. Rolf, C. Schmitt, P. M. Schneider, R. Szibor, J. Teifel-Greding, and M. Krawczak, "Caucasian Y-STR Haplotype Reference Database for Forensic Application," Prog. Forensic Gen. 8 (2000) 613–15.

71. L. Roewer, M. Krawczak, S. Willuweit, M. Nagy, C. Alves, A. Amorim, K. Anslinger, C. Augustin, A. Betz, E. Bosch, A. Caglia, A. Carracedo, D. Corach, A. F. Dekairelle, T. Dobosz, B. M. Dupuy, S. Furedi, C. Gehrig, L. Gusmao, J. Henke, L. Henke, M. Hidding, C. Hohoff, B. Hoste, M. A. Jobling, H. J. Kargel, K. P. de, R. Lessig, E. Liebeherr, M. Lorente, B. Martinez-Jarreta, P. Nievas, M. Nowak, W. Parson, V. L. Pascali, G. Penacino, R. Ploski, B. Rolf, A. Sala, U. Schmidt, C. Schmitt, P. M. Schneider, R. Szibor, J. Teifel-Greding, and M. Kayser, "Online Reference Database Of European Y-Chromosomal Short Tandem Repeat (STR) Haplotypes," *Forensic Sci.Int.* 118 (2001) 106–13.

72. J. Ballantyne, L. Fatolitis, and L. Roewer, "Creating and Managing Effective Y-STR Databases," *Prof. DNA* 9 (2006) 10–11.

73. K. Brown, "Tangled Roots? Genetics Meets Genealogy," *Science* 295 (2002) 1634–35.

74. H. L. Dai, X. D. Wang, Y. B. Li, J. Wu, J. Zhang, H. J. Zhang, J. G. Dong, and Y. P. Hou, "Characterization and Haplotype Analysis of 10 Novel Y-STR loci in Chinese Han Population," *Forensic Sci. Int.* 145 (2004) 47–55.

75. Y. Gao, Z. Zhang, Y. He, and S. Bian, "Haplotype Distribution of Four New Y-STRs: DYS630, DYS63, DYS634 and DYS635 in a Chinese Population," *Prog. Forensic Gen,* 11 (2006) 186–88.

76. Y. Z. Gao, S. Z. Bian, Z. X. Zhang, and Z. F. Wang, "Haplotype Distributions of Four New Y-STRs: DYS588, DYS622, DYS623 and DYS630 in a Chinese Population," *J. Forensic Sci.* 50 (2005) 708–09.

77. Y. P. Hou, J. Zhang, H. Tang, J. Zhang, J. Wu, Y. B. Li, and J. Yan, "Polymorphism of Two New Y-STR Loci in a Chinese Population," *Prog. Forensic Gen,* 9 (2003) 383–87.

78. Y. M. Huang, Y. J. Qi, J. Q. Xu, Y. L. Zhu, and X. Y. Wu, [Sequence analysis of DYS522 and DYS527 loci and their genetic polymorphism among Guangdong Han population], *Yi. Chuan* 28 (2006) 1355–60.

79. R. Iida, E. Tsubota, K. Sawazaki, M. Masuyama, T. Matsuki, T. Yasuda, and K. Kishi, "Characterization and Haplotype Analysis of the Polymorphic Y-STRs DYS443, DYS444 and DYS445 in a Japanese Population," *Int. J. Leg. Med.* 116 (2002) 191–94.

80. J. Lee, S. E. Kotliarova, A. A. Ewis, A. Hida, T. Shinka, Y. Kuroki, K. Tokunaga, and Y. Nakahori, "Y Chromosome Compound Haplotypes with the Microsatellite Markers DXYS265, DXYS266, and DXYS241," *J. Hum. Genet.* 46 (2001) 80–84.

81. A. J. Redd, A. B. Agellon, V. A. Kearney, V. A. Contreras, T. Karafet, H. Park, K. P. de, J. M. Butler, and M. F. Hammer, "Forensic Value of 14 Novel STRs on the Human Y Chromosome," *Forensic Sci. Int.* 130 (2002) 97–111.

82. R. Schoske, P. M. Vallone, M. C. Kline, J. W. Redman, and J. M. Butler, "High-Throughput Y-STR Typing of U.S. Populations with 27 Regions of the Y Chromosome Using Two Multiplex PCR Assays," *Forensic Sci. Int.* 139 (2004) 107–21.

83. J. P. Tang, Y. P. Hou, H. J. Zhang, Q. F. Zhu, X. D. Wang, Y. B. Li, J. Wu, and L. C. Liao, "Allele Frequencies of Two Y-STRs in a Chinese Population," *J. Forensic Sci.* 48 (2003) 1186.

84. J. P. Tang, Y. P. Hou, Y. B. Li, J. Wu, J. Zhang, and H. J. Zhang, "Characterization of Eight Y-STR Loci and Haplotypes in a Chinese Han Population," *Int. J. Leg. Med.* 117 (2003) 263–70.

85. G. Q. Zhang, Y. Wang, Y. X. Zhang, X. L. Xu, X. P. Xing, Y. Y. Wang, and K. M. Yun, [Study of polymorphism at new Y-STR DYS605 in a Chinese Han population of Shanxi.], *Yi. Chuan* 26 (2004) 295–97.

86. Z. X. Zhang, Y. Z. Gao, Y. He, and S. X. Xia, "Genetic Characteristics of Three New Y-STRs: DYS631, DYS634 and DYS635 in a Chinese Population," *J. Forensic Sci.* 50 (2005) 1492–93.

87. J. M. Butler, R. Schoske, P. M. Vallone, M. C. Kline, A. J. Redd, and M. F. Hammer, "A Novel Multiplex for Simultaneous Amplification of 20 Y Chromosome STR Markers," *Forensic Sci. Int.* 129 (2002) 10–24.

88. E. Ehler, R. Marvan, and I. Mazura, [PCR-multiplex system for analysis of Y-chromosomal microsatellite polymorphisms DYS449, DYS456, DYS458, and DYS464], *Soud. Lek.* 51 (2006) 30–34.

89. R. Iida, K. Sawazaki, H. Ikeda, T. Miyamoto, E. Tsubota, H. Takatsuka, M. Masuyama, T. Matsuki, T. Yasuda, and K. Kishi, "A Novel Multiplex PCR System Consisting of Y-STRs DYS441, DYS442, DYS443, DYS444, and DYS445," *J. Forensic Sci.* 48 (2003) 1088–90.

90. M. F. Hammer, A. B. Spurdle, T. Karafet, M. R. Bonner, E. T. Wood, A. Novelletto, P. Malaspina, R. J. Mitchell, S. Horai, T. Jenkins, and S. L. Zegura, "The Geographic Distribution of Human Y Chromosome Variation," *Genetics* 145 (1997) 787–805.

91. M. F. Hammer, T. Karafet, A. Rasanayagam, E. T. Wood, T. K. Altheide, T. Jenkins, R. C. Griffiths, A. R. Templeton, and S. L. Zegura, "Out of Africa and Back Again: Nested Cladistic Analysis of Human Y Chromosome Variation," *Mol. Biol. Evol.* 15 (1998) 427–41.

92. M. F. Hammer, T. M. Karafet, A. J. Redd, H. Jarjanazi, S. Santachiara-Benerecetti, H. Soodyall, and S. L. Zegura, "Hierarchical Patterns of Global Human Y-Chromosome Diversity," *Mol. Biol. Evol.* 18 (2001) 1189–1203.

93. M. F. Hammer, V. F. Chamberlain, V. F. Kearney, D. Stover, G. Zhang, T. Karafet, B. Walsh, and A. J. Redd, "Population Structure of Y Chromosome SNP Haplogroups in the United States and Forensic Implications for Constructing Y Chromosome STR Databases," *Forensic Sci. Int.* 164 (2006) 45–55.

94. R. S. Just, J. A. Irwin, J. E. O'Callaghan, J. L. Saunier, M. D. Coble, P. M. Vallone, J. M. Butler, S. M. Barritt, and T. J. Parsons, "Toward Increased Utility of mtDNA in Forensic Identifications," *Forensic Sci. Int.* 146 Suppl (2004) S147–S149.

95. R. Lessig, M. Zoledziewska, K. Fahr, J. Edelmann, M. Kostrzewa, T. Dobosz, and W. J. Kleemann, "Y-SNP-Genotyping—A New Approach in Forensic Analysis," *Forensic Sci. Int.* 154 (2005) 128–36.

96. T. J. Parsons and M. D. Coble, "Increasing the Forensic Discrimination

of Mitochondrial DNA Testing Through Analysis of the Entire Mitochondrial DNA Genome," *Croat. Med. J.* 42 (2001) 304–09.

97. L. M. Sims, D. Garvey, and J. Ballantyne, "Sub-populations within the Major European and African Derived Haplogroups R1b3 and E3a Are Differentiated by Previously Phylogenetically Undefined Y-SNPs," *Hum. Mutat.* 28 (2007) 97.

98. B. Sobrino and A. Carracedo, "SNP Typing in Forensic Genetics: A Review," *Methods Mol. Biol.* 297 (2005) 107–26.

99. P. A. Underhill, G. Passarino, A. A. Lin, P. Shen, L. M. Mirazon, R. A. Foley, P. J. Oefner, and L. L. Cavalli-Sforza, "The Phylogeography of Y Chromosome Binary Haplotypes and the Origins of Modern Human Populations," *Ann. Hum. Genet.* 65 (2001) 43–62.

100. J. H. Wetton, K. W. Tsang, and H. Khan, "Inferring the Population of Origin of DNA Evidence within the UK by Allele-Specific Hybridization of Y-SNPs," Forensic Sci. Int. 152 (2005) 45–53.

101. "A nomenclature system for the tree of human Y-chromosomal binary haplogroups," *Genome Res.* 12 (2002) 339–48.

102. M. Richards, V. Macaulay, E. Hickey, E. Vega, B. Sykes, V. Guida, C. Rengo, D. Sellitto, F. Cruciani, T. Kivisild, R. Villems, M. Thomas, S. Rychkov, O. Rychkov, Y. Rychkov, M. Golge, D. Dimitrov, E. Hill, D. Bradley, V. Romano, F. Cali, G. Vona, A. Demaine, S. Papiha, C. Triantaphyllidis, G. Stefanescu, J. Hatina, M. Belledi, R. A. Di, A. Novelletto, A. Oppenheim, S. Norby, N. Al-Zaheri, S. Santachiara-Benerecetti, R. Scozari, A. Torroni, and H. J. Bandelt, "Tracing European Founder Lineages in the Near Eastern mtDNA Pool," *Am. J. Hum. Genet.* 67 (2000) 1251–76.

103. S. Rootsi, C. Magri, T. Kivisild, G. Benuzzi, H. Help, M. Bermisheva, I. Kutuev, L. Barac, M. Pericic, O. Balanovsky, A. Pshenichnov, D. Dion, M. Grobei, L. A. Zhivotovsky, V. Battaglia, A. Achilli, N. Al-Zahery, J. Parik, R. King, C. Cinnioglu, E. Khusnutdinova, P. Rudan, E. Balanovska, W. Scheffrahn, M. Simonescu, A. Brehm, R. Goncalves, A. Rosa, J. P. Moisan, A. Chaventre, V. Ferak, S. Furedi, P. J. Oefner, P. Shen, L. Beckman, I. Mikerezi, R. Terzic, D. Primorac, A. Cambon-Thomsen, A. Krumina, A. Torroni, P. A. Underhill, A. S. Santachiara-Benerecetti, R. Villems, and O. Semino, "Phylogeography of Y-Chromosome Haplogroup I Reveals Distinct Domains of Prehistoric Gene Flow in Europe," *Am. J. Hum. Genet.* 75 (2004) 128–37.

104 A. Torroni, H. J. Bandelt, L. D'Urbano, P. Lahermo, P. Moral, D. Sellitto, C. Rengo, P. Forster, M. L. Savontaus, B. Bonne-Tamir, and R. Scozzari, "mtDNA Analysis Reveals a Major Late Paleolithic Population Expansion from Southwestern to Northeastern Europe," *Am. J. Hum. Genet.* 62 (1998) 1137–52.

105. A. Torroni, H. J. Bandelt, V. Macaulay, M. Richards, F. Cruciani, C. Rengo, V. Martinez-Cabrera, R. Villems, T. Kivisild, E. Metspalu, J. Parik, H. V. Tolk, K. Tambets, P. Forster, B. Karger, P. Francalacci, P. Rudan, B. Janicijevic, O. Rickards, M. L. Savontaus, K. Huoponen, V. Laitinen, S. Koivumaki, B. Sykes, E. Hickey, A. Novelletto, P. Moral, D. Sellitto, A. Coppa, N. Al-Zaheri, A. S. Santachiara-Benerecetti, O. Semino, and R. Scozzari, "A Signal, from Human mtDNA, of Postglacial Recolonization in Europe," *Am. J. Hum. Genet.* 69 (2001) 844–52.

106. Z. H. Rosser, T. Zerjal, M. E. Hurles, M. Adojaan, D. Alavantic, A.Amorim, W. Amos, M. Armenteros, E. Arroyo, G.

Barbujani, G. Beckman, L. Beckman, J. Bertranpetit, E. Bosch, D. G. Bradley, G. Brede, G. Cooper, H. B. Corte-Real, K. P. de, R. Decorte, Y. E. Dubrova, O. Evgrafov, A. Gilissen, S. Glisic, M. Golge, E. W. Hill, A. Jeziorowska, L. Kalaydjieva, M. Kayser, T. Kivisild, S. A. Kravchenko, A. Krumina, V. Kucinskas, J. Lavinha, L. A. Livshits, P. Malaspina, S. Maria, K. McElreavey, T. A. Meitinger, A. V. Mikelsaar, R. J. Mitchell, K. Nafa, J. Nicholson, S. Norby, A. Pandya, J. Parik, P. C. Patsalis, L. Pereira, B. Peterlin, G. Pielberg, M. J. Prata, C. Previdere, L. Roewer, S. Rootsi, D. C. Rubinsztein, J. Saillard, F. R. Santos, G. Stefanescu, B. C. Sykes, A. Tolun, R. Villems, C. Tyler-Smith, and M. A. Jobling, "Y-Chromosomal Diversity in Europe Is Clinal and Influenced Primarily by Geography, Rather Than by Language," *Am. J. Hum. Genet.* 67 (2000) 1526–43.

9

■■■

Forensic Aspects of Firearms Discharge Residue (FDR) Analysis

Arie Zeichner, Ph.D.
Senior Research Fellow
Casali Institute of Applied Chemistry
The Hebrew University of Jerusalem
Jerusalem 91904, Israel

Former Assistant Director for R&D,
Division of Identification and Forensic Science (DIFS),
Israel Police National Headquarters

INTRODUCTION

Numerous serious crimes involve the use of firearms. During discharge of a firearm, a variety of materials are emitted by the muzzle (accompanying the bullet) and other possible openings in the firearm (Figure 9-1). Throughout this chapter, the term *firearms discharge residues (FDR)* is used for all these materials. Analysis of FDR on relevant exhibits can assist in reconstruction of a crime and might provide evidence against suspects involved. For instance, detection and quantification of FDR on a shot target can be used for estimation of a shooting distance, and detection of FDR on a suspect or his clothing may link him or her to a firearm-related crime.

FDR may originate from primer, gunpowder (propellant), lubricant and metals of the bullet, cartridge case, or the gun barrel. The term *gunshot residues (GSR)* is used in this text for primer residues only, although in the relevant literature, GSR or cartridge discharge residues (CDR) are sometimes used instead of FDR, whereas the term *inorganic GSR* refers to primer residues and the term *organic GSR* refers to propellant residues.

467

FIGURE 9-1 High-speed photograph of a firearm discharge. *(Source: Courtesy of the FBI Laboratory.)*

The following topics are discussed in this chapter:

1. Detection and analysis of primer residues (GSR)
2. Detection and analysis of gunpowder (propellant) residues
3. Estimation of shooting distance
4. Associating firearms and ammunition with gunshot entries
5. Estimation of the time since shooting

The emphasis here is on recent developments rather than on historical review. The interested reader may refer to several comprehensive publications[1-9] on some of these topics. Detection of firearm imprints on the hands of a suspect may be useful in linking him or her to a firearm related event. This topic is not in the scope of this text and is discussed elsewhere.[8]

As a background for the subsequent discussion, a short introduction on the construction and the chemical composition of firearms ammunition[4,10,11] is presented next.

THE CHEMISTRY OF FIREARMS AMMUNITION

Cartridge Cases

The cartridge case is designed to house the primer, propellant, and to retain the bullet (projectile) securely in the neck. The vast majority of cartridge cases are made of brass (approximately 70% copper and 30% zinc), but other materials such as steel, which may be coated with zinc, brass, gilding metal (approximately 90% copper and 10% zinc), or copper; nickel-plated brass; cupro-nickel (approximately 80% copper and 20% nickel); gilding metal; aluminum; Teflon-coated aluminum; and plastic are also encountered. Shotgun cartridges are usually plastic with a brass or coated steel base.

When a round of ammunition is discharged in a firearm, the internal gas a pressure causes the cartridge case to expand tightly against the chamber walls. This is a very important function of the cartridge case, because it prevents the rearward escape of gas.

Projectiles

Conventional projectiles for firearms are bullets, whereas pellets and slugs are used for shotguns. There is a very wide range of bullet types based on differences in composition and the geometric design of the bullet core and bullet jacket. Bullets are un-jacketed, jacketed, or partially jacketed (semi-jacketed). When firearms had relatively low muzzle velocities, bullets were made of almost pure lead. However, when the introduction of smokeless gunpowder led to higher muzzle velocities, soft lead bullets were largely superseded by lead-alloy and jacketed bullets to reduce the leading of rifled barrels. Commercial lead-alloy bullets are hardened by alloying with antimony or, less commonly, with tin. The concentration of antimony may vary considerably, from 0.5% to 12%. Unjacketed bullets may have their surfaces coated with a very thin layer of copper or brass. This is referred to as a *wash* or *coat,* and is not a bullet jacket in the conventional sense of the word. Unjacketed bullets are frequently lubricated with some form of wax or grease to prevent or reduce fouling in the barrel of the firearm. Jacketed bullets consist of a lead core surrounded by a jacket of harder material. Usually, the core is left exposed at the base of the bullet; however, the bases of total metal jacket (TMJ) bullets are completely covered by the jacket. Jackets are commonly made of copper, brass, copper–nickel alloy, or mild steel.

Primers

Primers for center fire ammunition are housed in small metal cups which fit into a recess (primer pocket) in the center of the base of the cartridge case. In rimfire ammunition, the priming composition is housed inside the cartridge case in the hollow perimeter of the base. Primer cups are usually made of brass. There are two types of primers used in center fire ammunition that differ only in physical design. In European countries the Berdan primer design is preferred, whereas in Canada and the United States, the Boxer type is used. The Berdan primer does not have an integral anvil, the anvil being a part of the cartridge case, whereas the boxer primer has its own anvil that is inserted into the primer cup.

Priming compositions are mixtures that when subjected to percussion provide a sudden burst of flame that serves to ignite the propellant within the cartridge case. The weight of primer in small-arm ammunition can range from tens to hundreds of milligrams depending on the caliber and type of ammunition.

In general, small-arms primers consist of the following components: an initiating explosive (initiator), an oxidizer, a fuel, a sensitizer, a friction material, and a binder.[3,4,10] Some examples of those types of compounds are

Initiators: lead or silver azide, mercury fulminate, lead styphnate, diazodinitrophenol

Oxidizers: barium nitrate, barium peroxide, potassium chlorate, lead dioxide

Fuels: antimony sulphide, gum arabic, calcium silicide, aluminum powder

Sensitizers: tetracene, TNT, PETN, tetryl

Friction materials: ground glass, aluminum powder

Binders: gum arabic, dextrin, glue

Sometimes in the priming composition more than one compound from any of the previously mentioned classes may be used. Obviously, the composition of primers has changed with time. Mercury fulminate produces a mercury residue that causes deterioration of both gun bores and cartridge cases. It also was found that using potassium chlorate in the primer causes corrosion of the barrel because of formation of potassium chloride residue. Therefore, modern primers are mostly non-corrosive and non-mercuric (NCNM). A typical centerfire primer cap produced today contains lead styphnate, antimony sulphide, barium nitrate, and tetracene.[11] Not all primers, however, contain compounds of antimony and barium. Some .22-caliber rimfire cartridges contain either lead and barium or only lead compounds.

In 1980, Dynamit Nobel AG commercialized a new ammunition called Sintox™, developed to minimize airborne lead levels and possibly other metallic residues such as barium and antimony.[6] In this ammunition lead styphnate is replaced by diazodinitrophenol, and barium nitrate and antimony sulphide are replaced by a mixture of zinc peroxide and titanium metal powder, respectively.[10,11] This primer also contains tetracene and nitrocellulose. The use of this primer coupled with a TMJ bullet eliminates the health hazard problem. Since then, several other ammunition manufacturers have started introducing lead-free ammunition.[6,11–13]

Propellants

Propellants are frequently referred as *gunpowder*. The first propellant used in firearms was black powder. Since the introduction of smokeless powders, the use of black powder as a small-arms ammunition propellant has diminished substantially. However, black powder is still used as a propellant for some special purposes.

Modern smokeless gunpowder for small-arms ammunition almost exclusively contains cellulose nitrate (nitrocellulose, NC) as the main explosive component (single-based). Other explosive ingredients may also be present—for example, glycerol trinitrate (nitroglycerine, NG) (double-based) and nitroguanidine (triple-based, unlikely to be encountered in small-arms ammunition). Double-based powders vary in composition from 60% to 80% NC and 40% to 20% NG. Propellants also contain stabilizers such as diphenylamine (DPA) or ethyl centralite (EC), flash inhibitors such as 2,4-dinitrotoluene (2,4-DNT) and 2,6-dinitrotoluene (2,6-DNT), and plasticizers such as diethyl phthalate and dibutyl phthalate. Some inorganic materials such as chalk, graphite, potassium sulphate, potassium nitrate, and barium nitrate are added to improve ignitability, facilitate handling, and minimize muzzle flash.

The amount of propellant in small-arms ammunition can vary from hundreds of milligrams to several grams. Smokeless powders leave relatively little solid residue on combustion. Combustion of smokeless powder produces primarily nitrogen, carbon monoxide, carbon dioxide, hydrogen, and water.

The Mechanism of FDR Formation

When the firing pin strikes the primer of a cartridge, it provides a burst of flame without the development of a detonating wave.[10] The pressure and temperature go from ambient to about 10^4 kPa and 1500°C to 2000°C in a tenth of a millisecond.[3] The flame causes the propellant to ignite. It burns fast (*deflagration*) but does not detonate. The gunpowder ignites about 0.5 ms after crushing of the primer, with increase in temperature to about 3600°C and in pressure to about 3×10^5 kPa. The pressure and temperature reach peak values between 0.5 and 0.75 ms, and then begin to subside. When the bullet leaves the muzzle of a firearm, the pressure is vented to the atmosphere. This typically occurs before all the propellant is consumed, causing fragments of unburned gunpowder to be emitted from the firearm. Other particulates originate from the decomposition of the primer and from the metals of the cartridge and the firearm. The process of their formation may be described in the following manner[14]: The expanding gases from the propellant deflagration initially compress the bullet axially, so that it expands radially. The enlarged bullet is then *swaged* through the barrel by the rapidly increasing gas pressure, resulting in strong frictional heating. Also, the rifling rips small fragments from the bullet, and these particles are in part melted and in part vaporized. The metal vapors from the projectile mix with the vapors of the decomposition products of the primer and are ejected from all possible openings in the firearm, and may be deposited on surfaces in close proximity to the firer. In flight, the vapors condense into liquid phase and then solidify to particles. Unless modified in the liquid state by impact, they appear as spheroids in the size range from less than 1 micron up to tens of microns,[3,15] (Figure 9-2). Thus the composition of the formed particles may have contributions from the primer, the bullet, the cartridge case, the gun barrel, and the propellant, although the term *primer residue* is occasionally used. More details on the compositions of GSR are presented in the next section.

DETECTION AND ANALYSIS OF GSR (PRIMER RESIDUES)

This section discusses various aspects of detection and characterization of primer residues mainly on suspects, their clothing, and their belongings. The focus of the discussion is on GSR particle analysis by scanning electron microscopy (SEM) combined with energy dispersive x-ray analysis (SEM/EDX), because this is currently the method of choice in advanced crime laboratories.

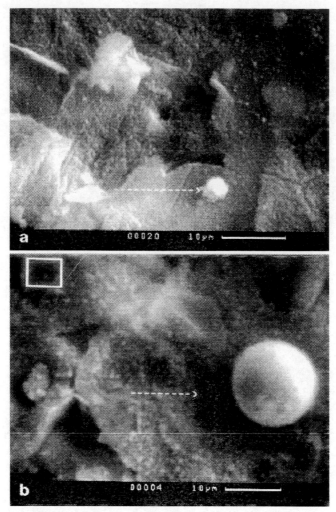

FIGURE 9-2 Examples of GSR particles on skin debris sampled on the double-sided adhesive. Arrows point to the GSR particle in each SEM micrograph.

Color Tests

The earliest method to detect FDR on shooters' hands, known as a *dermal nitrate test* or paraffin test, was introduced in 1933 by Teodoro Gonzales of the Mexico City Police Laboratory. Molten paraffin was poured on the hands of the subject and allowed to solidify to form a cast on the hands. When the paraffin froze, it was peeled off and sprayed with a 0.2% solution of diphenylamine in concentrated sulphuric acid. The reagent gives a deep blue coloration with nitrates and nitrites that may originate from gunpowder and primer residues[16] However, even though nitrates and nitrites may come from other sources (e.g., fertilizers, urine), this test is not specific to nitrates and nitrites only. Other oxidizers like chlorates, iodates, permanganates and others may give positive reaction; false-negative results were also common. In spite of these drawbacks, the test was used for many years before being abandoned by most forensic laboratories. However, the test is still employed in a number of laboratories throughout the world.[3] Recently, the U.S. Department of Energy's Sandia National Laboratories, working with Law Enforcement Technologies, Inc., announced the development of the ISID[TM]-1 (Instant shooter ID Kit). It appears that it is an updated version of the dermal nitrate or paraffin test. As in the case of the dermal nitrate test, it was argued that "The concerns of non-specificity of the ISID[TM]-1 kit need to be critically evaluated in light of its potential usefulness in the field and any legal issues associated with its documented "false positives."[17]

The Griess reagent used to detect nitrites is discussed in the next section dealing with gunpowder residue detection.

In 1959, Harrison and Gillroy[18] developed a test for detection of lead, barium, and antimony that may be found in modern ammunition primer residues. In this method, swabs moistened with dilute hydrochloric acid were used to collect FDR on hands. The swabs were dried and treated with triphenylmethylarsonium iodide, producing orange color with antimony. After drying again, a solution of sodium rhodizonate was applied, giving red coloration with lead or barium. After the addition of dilute hydrochloric acid, the color turned purple if lead was present. The method did not gain wide acceptance because of a lack of specificity of the color reactions, insufficient sensitivity, interference of the color reactions among the three elements, and the instability of the colors developed.

Steffen and Niewhoner[19] conducted a study to visualize zinc containing GSR particles from Sintox[TM] ammunition (lifted from various surfaces by Filmolux® transparent adhesive film) using modified dithizone and xylenolorange tests.

Bulk Analytical Methods

Lead, antimony, and barium may be found on the hands of persons who were not involved with firearms but generally in smaller quantities compared to those who have fired a weapon. Thus, developing a quantitative sensitive method for those elements could assist in differentiating between an innocent person and those involved in a shooting. The term *bulk analytical methods* applies to those methods that determine bulk concentration of the constituents in the analyzed sample. With regard to GSR analysis, the analyzed sample is a collection of many particles. Contrary to the bulk method, a method for particle analysis, such as SEM/EDX, can analyze specific particles in the sample.

In the early 1960s, neutron activation analysis (NAA) was applied for detection of trace elements with high sensitivity.[2,6] Although this method was not applicable for lead, it was used to determine minute quantities of antimony and barium. In 1971, atomic absorption spectrophotometry (AAS) was developed for GSR analysis. Conventional flame AAS had sufficient sensitivity for detection of the lead quantities on firers' hands, but it was not sensitive enough for detection of antimony and barium. Development of graphite furnace AAS (GFAAS) solved this problem. GFAAS is relatively time consuming and subject to some interferences resulting from the presence of high concentrations of non-analyte constituents. Many forensic science laboratories have used NAA or GFAAS for GSR analysis in casework.

Other bulk analytical methods have been studied for GSR analysis in hand samples.[6] Among these, two methods have been implemented in casework: inductively coupled plasma atomic emission spectroscopy (ICP/AES)[20] and ICP mass spectrometry (ICP/MS).[21,22] ICP/AES is a rapid, multi-element technique relatively free of matrix interferences, but commercial instruments lack the sensitivity required for accurate determination of antimony at relevant levels.[21] ICP/MS is now a widely accepted method for trace and ultra-trace analysis of a variety of liquid, gaseous, and solid samples in many applications. Analytical benefits of the method are low detection limits, wide linear dynamic range, relative freedom from interferences, and good precision and accuracy.[21] Nonetheless, the latest survey[23] showed that the most popular bulk analytical method for GSR analysis was GFAAS.

The technique to collect GSR from the subjects' hands must be simple and easy to use in the field, because the samples are usually collected by investigators or trained technicians.[2] The materials used for collection must be free from contamination, because the amount of trace elements detected in GSR from hand samples shortly after the firearm discharge is usually in micrograms or nanograms (the persistence of GSR on various surfaces is discussed later). Obviously, the method should collect possibly all the GSR deposit from the hands and must be compatible with the bulk analytical method to be implemented. Two methods have been used—swabbing with moistened cotton swabs and washing with dilute nitric acid. The first method employs kits that may be prepared in the laboratory or are available commercially. They are practically cotton swabs moistened with 1 M nitric acid and applied to the back and palm areas of the hands. The second method employs kits that contain two plastic containers with 50 ml of 1 M nitric acid and cleaned plastic bags. The hand to be washed is introduced into a plastic bag, the solution is poured in, the hand is shaken in the bag for about 30 seconds, and then the acid is poured back into the plastic container. Recently Reis, Souza Sarkis, Neto et al.[22] reported a new method for collection of GSR from the hands of shooters for the analysis by ICP/MS. The sampling procedure is based on EDTA solution as a complexing agent on moistened swabs. They found that this solution was superior to nitric acid solution or deionized water as a collecting technique for GSR.

Lead, antimony, and barium are not uncommon in the environment and are present singly in a number of materials. For instance, lead is found in batteries, plumbing materials, and in solder and paint. Antimony is found in several alloys, often with lead, and its oxide is used as a fire retardant in cotton-and-polyester-blend fibers. Barium is found in paint, automobile grease, and in paper as barium sulphate. The occurrence of the three elements in one substance is not common. The presence of these elements together and in amounts significantly higher than those normally found on the hands of general population (hand blanks) may indicate the presence of GSR. A number of studies have reported on hand blank levels. The measured levels depend on the area of the hands sampled and, to some extent, on the sampling method used. The average values obtained for various hand blanks were as follows[2]:

20 μg for lead, 0.08 μg for antimony, and 0.8 μg for barium. To indicate the presence of GSR using a bulk analytical method, the three elements should be in amounts of three standard deviations above the average hand blanks levels, that is, 49 μg for lead, 0.22 μg for antimony, and 1.8 μg for barium.

GSR Particle Analysis by SEM/EDX

Until to the mid-1970s, the accepted methods for GSR analysis in casework were bulk analytical techniques as described previously. In the second half of 1970s several studies reported that much higher evidential value could be obtained by examining the composition and morphology of discrete particles formed during a firearm discharge with the aid of scanning electron microscope combined with energy dispersive x-ray analysis (SEM/EDX) (Figure 9-3). A comprehensive treatise on the method may be found elsewhere.[23] The increase in the use of SEM/EDX for GSR

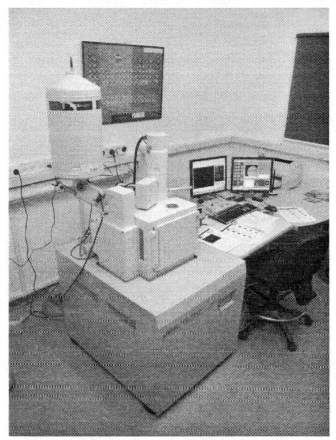

FIGURE 9-3 The new SEM/EDX system operated at the Toolmarks and Materials Laboratory of the Division of Identification and Forensic Science (DIFS), Israel Police National Headquarters. *(Source: Courtesy of DIFS, Israel Police.)*

analysis in casework is shown by comparing two surveys.[24,25] Continuous improvements in the SEM and the EDX technologies are also reflected in the GSR analysis by SEM/EDX. Currently, most manufacturers of SEM/EDX equipment offer automated search systems for GSR particles, which makes the analysis much easier as compared to a very tedious manual search. The principle of the automated search is similar to the manual search, namely detection of a suspected particle by the backscatter electron (BSE) signal and its analysis by EDX. Nevertheless, even with automated search systems the analysis may be quite long, amounting to several hours per square centimeter of a sample, depending on the surface density of particles having high average atomic number. Schwoeble, Lentz, and Lee[26] demonstrated the use of a variable pressure SEM (VPSEM), and Mastruko[27] demonstrated an environmental SEM (ESEM) for the detection and analysis of GSR.

SAMPLING OF GSR AND ITS PERSISTENCE ON VARIOUS SURFACES To collect GSR samples for SEM/EDX, most of the crime labs use 25-mm or 13-mm diameter SEM aluminum stubs coated with adhesive tape (tape-lift method).[23] The coated stubs are kept in the GSR collection kits, which are commercially available or may be prepared in the lab (Figure 9-4). To collect particles from a surface (e.g., a hand), the stub is pressed repeatedly against the surface (see subsequent discussion) (Figure 9-5).

The tapelift method was shown to be the most efficient method of collection among three examined methods (i.e., tapelift, glue-lift, and concentration methods).[28] It was shown that the tapelift surface (non-conductive double-sided adhesive 3M, #465) demonstrated the highest particle collection ability, and it remained stable for all

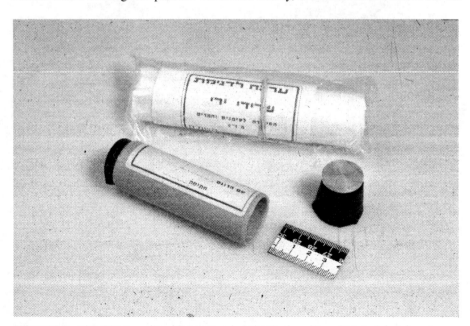

FIGURE 9-4 The GSR sampling kit prepared at the Toolmarks and Materials Laboratory of the Division of Identification and Forensic Science (DIFS), Israel Police National Headquarters. *(Source: Courtesy of DIFS, Israel Police.)*

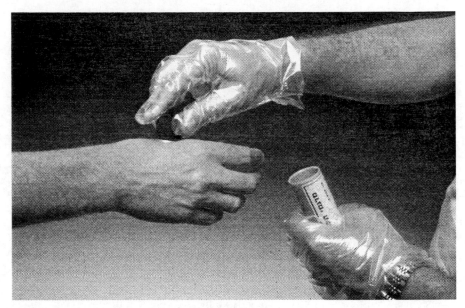

FIGURE 9-5 Sampling hands for GSR using the kit shown in Figure 9-4. *(Source: Courtesy of DIFS, Israel Police.)*

conditions tested. Glue-lift was the least efficient method under all conditions tested. Collection followed by concentration gave highly variable results.

It was reported that in practice there might be an intrinsic difficulty in concentrating GSR on a small area because of pile-up and clogging of the filters used.[29] In another study,[30] a number of adhesives were examined for their suitability for sampling GSR particles with respect to the elemental composition, adhesive properties, and adhesive stability under vacuum and electron beam. This study did not include the double-sided adhesive 3M, #465, but in addition to several non-conductive adhesives, it also included conductive carbon adhesives. The conclusion was that the best overall performance was of the Sellotape 404 double-sided adhesive tape.

In the United Kingdom, swabs have been used to recover GSR and gunpowder residues from skin surfaces of a suspect. The propellant residues are extracted from swabs by organic solvents and filtered through membrane filters on which the GSR particles are collected and examined by SEM/EDX.[31]

A comprehensive study was conducted on collection efficiency of GSR particles from hair and hands using double-sided adhesive tape.[32] Tapelift was found to be a suitable method for collecting GSR from hair, contrary to the previous claim.[33] No significant difference was found between collection efficiency for this technique and the more complicated method of swabbing the hair by use of a comb with a solvent-dampened cloth and filtration proposed elsewhere.[33] It was found that 200 to 300 dabbings are necessary to achieve maximum collection efficiency from hair with the double-side adhesive, although it was observed by subjective assessment that the stub had lost its stickiness after about 100 dabbings. Figure 9-6 shows the decrease

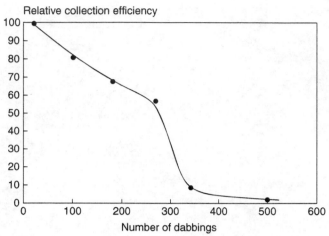

FIGURE 9-6 Collection efficiency of a double-sided adhesive tape as a function of the number of dabbings from hair.

in the collection efficiency of a double-sided adhesive tape as a function of the number of dabbings from hair. A possible explanation for a rather sudden drop in the collection efficiency after a certain number of dabbings instead of the expected linear decrease may be that a certain density of hair fragments on the adhesive surface prevents the effective contact between other particles and the unoccupied adhesive area.

In several studies, the recommended collection procedure from hands by tapelift method is to press the stub repeatedly against the hand until it has lost its stickiness per subjective assessment.[1,34,35] The concern regarding continual dabbing was that skin debris might conceal GSR particles from view.[30,36,37] Nonetheless, it was found that 50 to 100 dabbings are necessary to achieve maximum collection efficiency from hands,[32] whereas stickiness appeared to be lost after about 20 to 30 dabbings, and after about 50 dabbings the stubs appear to be practically covered completely by skin debris (Figure 9-7), although their sampling capability is not considerably reduced. Many of the sampled GSR particles on stubs that were used for about 100 dabbings were on skin debris (see Figure 9-2).

A subsequent study[38] demonstrated that there is no substantial danger of concealing GSR particles by continuous dabbings of hands up to 50 times. This was shown for discrete particles in the size range of 8–30 microns that were mounted in a controlled manner on stubs prior to dabbing. Although a few of them were covered completely by skin debris and could not be detected by secondary electron image (SEI), they were detected without any problem by backscatter electron image (BEI) (Figure 9-8) and identified by the EDX (Figure 9-9). The elements K, Cl, and S in the spectrum originate from the skin (Figure 9-10).

Pukkila and Guranatnam[39] studied the analysis of primer GSR and gunpowder residues from the same sample. In the proposed method, the adhesive tape mounted on the stub is first examined by SEM/EDX for the primer residues and after removing the tape from a stub, it is used for the detection of propellant residues by supercritical fluid extraction/gas chromatography (SFE/GC) analysis (see next section).

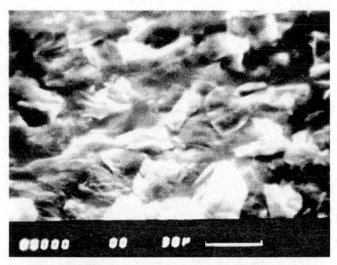

FIGURE 9-7 SEM micrograph of skin debris on a stub that was used to dab hands 50 times.

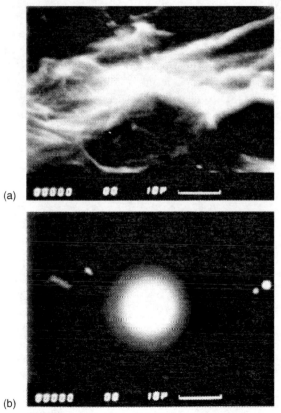

FIGURE 9-8 SEM micrograph of GSR particle completely covered by skin debris: (a) SEI, (b) BEI.

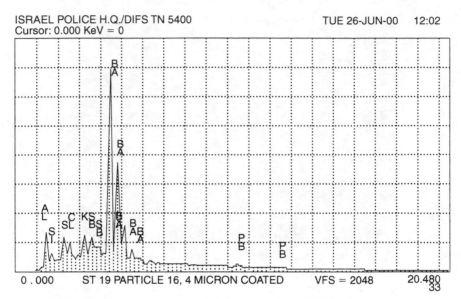

FIGURE 9-9   EDX spectrum of the particle shown in Figure 9-8.

An extraction/concentration technique has been developed to recover GSR retained in human nasal mucus.[40] It was reported that the technique recovered abundant GSR successfully from post-firing sample collection times of 48 hours. This author is not aware of any forensic lab that currently implements an operational method for collecting GSR from nasal mucous. In the past, the Forensic Science Service in London, United Kingdom, used a method for collecting GSR from the

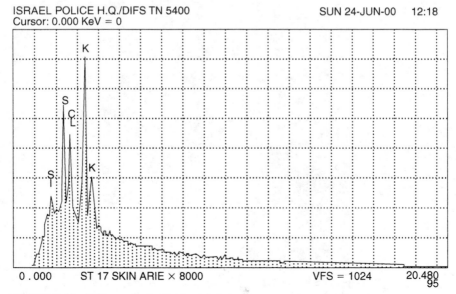

FIGURE 9-10   EDX spectrum of skin debris.

nose. The method was discontinued as it was found that it did not provide any extra information in casework (personal communication with Dr. Geoffrey Warman, the Forensic Science Service in London, United Kingdom, 1996).

Clothing and other surfaces may be sampled for GSR by tape-lift or by vacuum filtration.[31,41]

Once GSR particles are deposited on the hands, they are continuously lost as a result of the normal activities of a living person.[2] It is difficult to generalize as to how long GSR could be retained, because it depends on the type of activity.[2,42] Although laboratory tests using bulk analytical methods have indicated that GSR remain on the hands for only a short time (perhaps one or two hours) in actual cases, detectable amounts have been found several hours later, perhaps because of higher initial amounts of GSR.[2] Using particle analysis, it was reported that the probability of finding GSR on hands more than three hours after firing is very low.[33] In a study conducted by Jalanti, Henchoz, Galluser, et al.[43] on the persistence of GSR on shooters' hands, it was confirmed that there is a rapid drop in GSR particle count as a function of post-firing collection time, with the largest loss occurring in the first two to four hours. Laboratory experiments showed that thirty minutes after firing, no significant difference was observed between samples collected from the right and left hands with regard to the number of GSR particles found, although the shooter used one hand for firing.[33] The accumulated casework experience of about twelve years in Israel has shown that in only a very few cases a large number of particles was found in hand samples, and in a significantly lower number of these cases, considerably more particles were found on one hand as compared to the other one, so that some inference could be made concerning the firing hand.[44] The practical conclusion from these observations is that there is no significance in sampling the suspect's hands separately as a result of redistribution of particles within quite a short period of time. Even more so, there is no value in collecting separate samples from the back and the palm surfaces of the hand because it is more misleading than informative.[45]

A much longer persistence of GSR was found on hair and clothing.[33] Persistence of twenty-four hours was observed in laboratory experiments when the hair had not been washed.[32] Thus, in order not to increase the number of samples collected from a suspect, it was decided in the Israel Police (since the beginning of 1991 onward) to use one stub for sampling both hands and the other one for sampling the hair.[44] Before this change, two stubs were used per suspect—one for the right hand and one for the left hand. Since the beginning of sampling hair, four years' casework experience showed a slightly higher success rate of finding GSR in hand samples than in hair. However, the results showed that it is important to sample both sites, because there were cases where a suspect was positive for GSR on the hand sample and negative on the hair sample, and vice versa. No significant difference was found between the average time lapse between firing and sampling for positive hands samples (2.7 hours) and the positive hair samples (3.3 hours). These results are somehow in contrast to laboratory observations discussed previously. For some reason, so far very few crime labs have introduced sampling hair for GSR, and it was not among the topics for discussion in the recent meeting on GSR.[45]

The overall success rate of finding GSR particles in casework-related samples for the period of six years (1989–1994) in Israel was 13%. The fraction of samples with only one detected GSR particle was 39%; with two to five particles, 44%; and with more than five particles, 17%. It should be remembered that the statistics of success rate in casework is strongly dependent on several unknown variables (in contrast to controlled experiments), such as how many suspects sampled were actually involved in shooting, which environmental conditions the suspects had been in between the incident and sampling, and how many of them washed their hands. The conclusion from these results is that the amount of GSR particles that may be detected on suspects in a realistic scenario (sampling several hours after a shooting) is in the picogram range, and not in the nanogram or microgram range (probably shortly after discharge), as was elucidated by bulk analytical methods.[2]

It was shown that laundering clothing does not always completely remove GSR.[46] Some law enforcement agencies used to put hands of a suspect into paper bags immediately after arrest to prevent losing GSR from the suspect's hands and at the same time prevent their contamination prior to collection of the samples. Kimmett[47] conducted a study on the incidence of GSR transferred to paper-bag hand covers and showed that immediately after firing, a considerable number of particles transfer from the hand to the bag's interior. However, if the hand is bagged half an hour or more after firing, there is small chance to find GSR particles on the bag interior, although the hand is positive for GSR. A plausible explanation for this phenomenon is that as time passes, there is greater chance that all GSR that is going to come off easily has in fact come off, and therefore no transfer occurs.

COMPOSITIONS, CLASSIFICATION AND INTERPRETATION   As discussed earlier, the composition of GSR particles may have contribution from several sources. It was shown that when using lead bullets in ammunition 70% to 100% of GSR particles are lead.[14] If the bullet is coated with copper or brass, the result is the same, except that a substantial portion of all the particles contains some copper. If jacketed or partially jacketed bullets are used, the fraction of lead particles in the total collection is greatly reduced. Only a small portion of the particles contains copper, and the total number of particles is smaller as well. It could be concluded from these observations that most of the lead in GSR comes from the projectile rather than the primer. In another study using X-ray diffraction (XRD),[48] it was found that lead in the metallic form is found to be the main constituent of all GSR tested. Metallic copper appears only in ammunition incorporating copper-rich jackets or plating on the bullet. Because copper does not generally occur in primer residues, it could be concluded that the main source of copper in GSR is the bullet itself, and not the cartridge case. The significant difference found between the GSR compounds' composition formed by ordinary shots (involving bullets) and primer shots can be explained by the far higher temperature and pressure of the former, resulting in almost total combustion of primer components as well as involvement of the projectile.[48]

In their pioneering extensive study, Wolten et al.[1,49,50] proposed a classification scheme for GSR. They divided GSR into two categories: (a) unique or characteristic, and (b) consistent. The compositions that they considered to be unique are as follows:

1. Pb, Sb, Ba (Figures 9-11 and 9-12)
2. Ba, Ca, Si, with traces of S
3. Ba, Ca, Si, with Traces of Pb if Cu and Zn are absent
4. Sb, Ba

The compositions they considered consistent are as follows:

1. Pb, Sb
2. Pb, Ba
3. Pb
4. Ba if S is absent or present only as a trace
5. Sb (rare)

In both categories, one or several of the following elements could also be present: Si, Ca, Al, Cu, Fe, S, P (rare), Zn (only if Cu is also present), Ni (rare and only with Cu and Zn), K, and Cl.

It should be emphasized that the concentrations of the elements in the GSR particles are highly variable because of the very fast process of their formation. This variability is demonstrated in Figures 9-11 and 9-12.

The modifications proposed by Wallace and McQuillan[51] resulted only in two alleged "unique" compositions for GSR: (a1) Pb, Sb, and Ba and (a2) Sb and Ba.

The definition of *unique* for those compositions was based on the experimental fact that they had thus far (at the time of definition) been observed only in GSR.

The problem of classification of various compositions of GSR particles has continued to be a source of concern in casework and of interest for research, in particular the alleged unique compositions to GSR. Currently, most of the experts prefer to use the term *characteristic* instead of *unique*.[45] These compositions were found among particles

ISRAEL POLICE H.Q./DIFS TN 5400   MON 23-JUL-00   13:29
Cursor: 0.000 KeV = 0

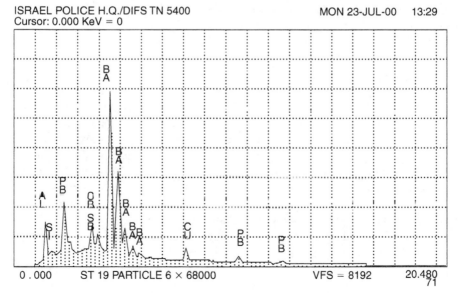

0.000   ST 19 PARTICLE 6 × 68000   VFS = 8192   20.480

FIGURE 9-11 An example of EDX spectrum of the unique composition GSR particle.

TN-5500 POLICE HEADQUARTER SIGNS LAB   THU 17-MAR-94   11:34
Cursor: 0.000 KeV = 0

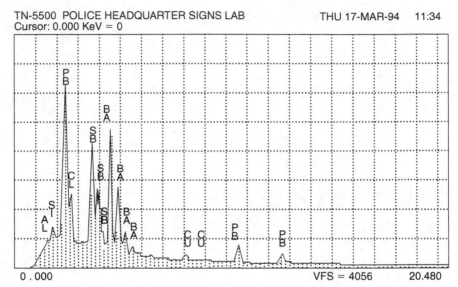

0 . 000   VFS = 4056   20.480

FIGURE 9-12 Another example of EDX spectrum of the unique composition GSR particle.

produced by fireworks[52] and particles collected from various parts of cars and individuals involved in various automobile-related jobs.[53] It was observed, in particular, that particles of composition (a2) might be found, although in very small amounts, in residues from fireworks and among particles collected from automobiles. Very few particles of composition (a1) were found in the residues of one of the types of the tested fireworks. However, an additional element of magnesium (unusual to GSR) was present in those particles. In another study, Torre, Mattutino, Vasino, et al.[54] reported that some types of brake linings contain lead, antimony, and barium, and they can represent a source of particles showing GSR-like elemental profiles. Most of these particles could be discriminated from GSR easily by means of the high levels of iron or the presence of "prohibited" elements in the EDX spectrum. However, particles with iron at minor or trace levels and lacking prohibited elements were also found, but did not have spherical morphology. In view of these findings, the morphological criterion becomes more important for identification of GSR than was suggested by the ASTM committee.[55]

Zeichner, and Levin,[56] proposed including the characteristic particle composition of Pb, Ba, Ca, Si, and Sn (Figure 9-13) formed in discharge of Sellier Bellot (SBP) ammunition in the category of unique or characteristic compositions. This proposition was based on the extensive computerized casework experience of the authors that can lead to a statement that such a composition has thus far been observed only in GSR associated with the SBP ammunition.

Stoney[57] pointed out that it is not possible to reach uniqueness through statistics. Nevertheless, with the advent of autosearch systems for GSR in numerous crime labs, it may be much easier than before (using a manual search) to assess the rarity of various GSR compositions experimentally in a similar manner as the contribution of automated systems for fingerprint and firearms identification.

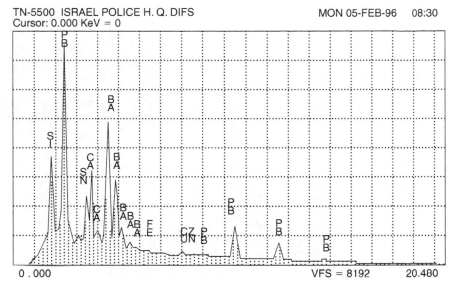

0 . 000   VFS = 8192   20.480

FIGURE 9-13   EDX spectrum of a characteristic GSR particle from 9-mm SBP
ammunition.

In any case, it is very important to compare the GSR compositions found on a
suspect to the GSR compositions of the spent cartridge cases (if found) at the scene
of a crime as well as to the GSR compositions in the suspected firearm (if apprehended). Sometimes the evidential value of such comparisons may be much higher
than the degree of uniqueness of the GSR particles found on the suspect—for instance, if the GSR particles found on a suspect are consistent with the GSR in the
spent cartridge cases of a rare ammunition.

Several studies[58–60] report the formation of mixed composition GSR particles
when firing different ammunitions from the same firearm (Figures 9-14 and 9-15).
Gunaratnam and Himberg[59] found mixed composition particles containing Pb and
Ba in addition to Ti and Zn after firing Sintox lead-free ammunition, even though the
revolver used in the study was thoroughly cleaned before test firing, Ti and Zn being
characteristic elements of the Sintox lead-free ammunition primer. This result is consistent with the previous studies[14,51] that claimed that conventional thorough cleaning of a handgun does not remove all GSR particles. Similar results were reported by
Harris[12] in her study on primer residues from CCI Blazer lead-free ammunition. In
this study, not only mixed composition but three-element (Pb, Ba and Sb) particles
were found as well, and often in a greater number than Sr particles, Sr being the
characteristic element of the CCI Blazer lead-free ammunition primer. In an extensive study, Levin, Tsach, Bergman, et al.[60] showed that the composition (mainly Ti
and Zn) of GSR particles from Sintox lead-free ammunition is characteristic enough
to be included in the consistent category for classification of GSR. It seems that results of the mentioned recent studies concerning GSR compositions and similar
compositions that may be found in particles not related to GSR are not reflected in
the up-to-date ASTM standard guide for GSR analysis.[55]

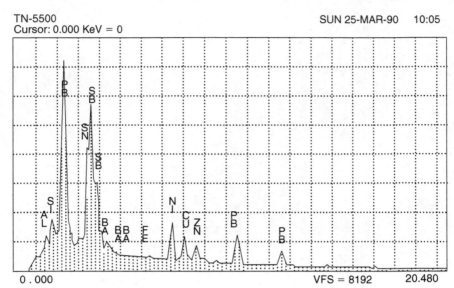

FIGURE 9-14   EDX spectrum of a GSR particle from a shooting test in which 9-mm SBP and 9-mm Geco ammunitions were fired in succession, in the sample from the shooter's hand.

Zeichner, Levin, and Dvorachek[61] and Wallace[62] showed that when firing mercury fulminate–based primer ammunition, the amount of mercury in the GSR particles found on the shooter is considerably less than the amount found in the cartridge cases. This is explained by the fact that mercury would be expected to vaporize more

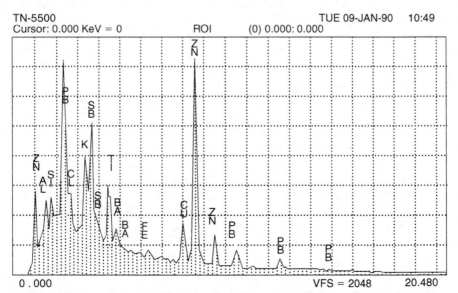

FIGURE 9-15   EDX spectrum of a GSR particle from a shooting test in which 9-mm Sintox and 9-mm TZZ ammunitions were fired in succession, in the sample from the shooter's hand.

from GSR particles moving with the burning propellant (experiencing higher temperatures) and ejected onto the firer than particles remaining in the cartridge case. It was shown that there is a small probability of finding GSR containing a considerable concentration of antimony if the primer of the fired ammunition is antimony-free, even when the surface of the bullet is highly enriched by this element.[63] Miayauchi, Kumihashi, and Shibayama[64] demonstrated contribution of trace elements from smokeless powder to primer residues. Lebiedzik and Johnson[65] reported that indicators of the type of weapon and ammunition used in firing can be obtained from the distribution of GSR shapes and compositions. Coumbaros, Kirkbride, Kobus, et al.[66] studied the distribution of lead and barium in GSR derived from .22-caliber rimfire ammunition. The study confirmed the non-homogeneous nature of GSR.[6] Collins, Coumbaros, Horsley, et al.[67] reported for the first time about glass-containing GSR particles in .22-caliber ammunition using SEM/EDX and time of flight secondary ionization mass spectrometry (TOF/SIMS) for the analysis.

There is no consensus among the forensic science laboratories regarding the number of particles needed to confirm the presence of GSR. In the first survey conducted among the labs (primarily in the United States), there was no difficulty in getting a response to that question, with 50% of the respondents requiring only one particle for confirmation and answers ranging from one particle to as many as ten particles[25]; in the subsequent survey conducted two years later,[23] only two labs out of fifty were willing to provide a concrete answer—one lab responded with "1" and the other answered "2." The controversy among the experts on this question is still unresolved (personal communication, 8th Firearms Working Group Meeting, Bruges, Belgium, 2001, and 11th Firearms Working Group Meeting, Madrid, Spain, 2004). The FBI Laboratory has established a threshold for the number of confirmed GSR particles before it can be concluded that an item has been exposed to gunshot residue. The number of particles used to confirm a GSR population is a minimum of three PbBaSb particles. In addition, other particles consistent with a GSR-type environment also must be present (i.e., SbBa, BaPb, PbSb, or other elements or element composites routinely found in GSR particle populations). However, most experts attending the FBI GSR symposium held in 2005 believed that even one PBBaSb spheroid particle is enough for a "positive" result[45]

There is much more agreement regarding the wording of reports when a lab decides that there is a positive result. In such a case, the statement "The sample is consistent with the suspect having discharged a firearm, having been in the vicinity of a firearm when it was discharged, or having handled an item with GSR on it" resembles the phrasing of most of the labs.[23,45] Speaking about the vicinity of a discharged firearm, two recent studies dealing with this issue should be mentioned.[68,69] It was found that maximum number of GSR could be found in the right front quadrant at a distance of 2 m to 4 m with respect to the shooting firearm position and shooting direction. GSR particles were even found in distance 10 m from the shooting firearm.[68] It was observed that there is an imminent danger of contamination of people who appear at the scene several minutes following shooting. When using a pistol, the possibility of contamination exists within about 8 minutes after the discharge. With a revolver the possibility of contamination takes even longer, up to about 10 minutes.[69]

It was argued that bystanders (i.e., a person present at the time of the shooting who does not come into direct physical contact with the shooter, firearm, or any other surface potentially contaminated with GSR) can test positive for GSR.[45] Lindsay and McVicar[70] concluded that the high degree of variability that exists in the deposition of GSR as a result of the ammunition–firearm combination and the number of shots fired produces an overlap between the GSR concentrations obtained from sampling either a shooter or a bystander as quickly as 15 minutes post-firing. Therefore, the number of particles cannot be used as a basis for determining if someone fired or was merely in the vicinity of a recently discharged firearm.

The possibility of GSR contamination of the law enforcement personnel or of the law enforcement premises should be taken into account when interpreting results in any particular case. Gialamas, Rhodes, and Sugarman[71] conducted a study for the presence of GSR on non-shooting patrol officers' hands. They found that 3 of the 43 examined officers had unique GSR particles. In several other studies it was reported that various extents of GSR contamination may occur in the law enforcement environment.[45] Many GSR experts agree that armed law enforcement officers can transfer GSR particles to a subject through contact, and that it is possible for a handcuffed person's hands to be contaminated by the prior presence of GSR in the backseat of a police vehicle. It was recommended that GSR sampling should be done at the scene, where permissible, and as expeditiously as possible; if the subject's hands cannot be sampled before placing the subject in a police vehicle, the subject's hands should be bagged in order to prevent possible contamination. It was suggested that in order to better distinguish between GSR from contact with law enforcement versus a civilian shooting event, a policy such as that set forth in some European Union countries (e.g., Germany) should be set that mandates that all domestic law enforcement use ammunition with taggants detectable by SEM/EDX.[45]

PROFICIENCY TESTS FOR GSR ANALYSIS BY SEM/EDX Recently, proficiency tests for GSR particles examination have been designed. For example, the tests prepared by Collaborative Testing Services, Inc. (CTS) were based on GSR suspensions in organic solvents. Small volumes of these containing 10 to 20 GSR particles were dropped on the SEM stubs. Because of the large variation among the samples, it was impossible to assess and compare precisely the proficiency of the various labs participating in the test. Lately, a major advance was achieved in the European Network of Forensic Science Institutes (ENFSI) proficiency tests on identification of GSR by SEM/EDX. In these tests developed by Niewohner et al.,[72,73] for the first time, "synthetic GSR particles" (pseudo-particles) were prepared by microelectronics technology on the stubs. All the participating laboratories received the same samples, namely stubs having a flat surface with the same number of pseudo (two-dimensional) particles, in the same locations on the stub and with the same size distribution. In the GSR2003 test,[73] the pseudo-particles were of Pb, Sb, and Ba composition and having sizes of 2.4, 1.2, 0.8, and 0.5 microns. The results show that 75% of the laboratories that participated in the test meet the proficiency criteria for detection of GSR particles having a size of 1.2 microns or larger. However, the capability of detecting submicron particles must be improved. Although these samples differ from real-life samples of GSR, it seems that at present, they are the best to evaluate the proficiency of the procedures used and the SEM/EDX equipment for GSR detection and analysis.

Other Instrumental Methods

In recent years several other instrumental methods have been studied for GSR analysis. Most are still in the research phase and cannot be used in casework. Helmiss, Lichtenberg, and Weiss[74] used SEM equipped with Auger electron spectroscopy analyzer instead of EDX. This method permitted the analysis of elements with low atomic number and elements whose peaks overlap in EDX. Using simultaneous Auger spectroscopy and ion sputtering etching, a profile of the in-depth composition variations of GSR was studied.

Micro-x-ray fluorescence (XRF) has been used recently in a growing number of crime labs for elemental analysis of trace evidence, sometimes instead of SEM/EDX and sometimes in combination with SEM/EDX. Micro-XRF has also been studied for GSR analysis.[75,76] However, it cannot be used for single particle examinations because of the problems of spatial resolution. Nonetheless, it has been implemented operationally for GSR deposit analysis around the bullet holes.

Kage, Kudo, Kaizoji, et al.[77] demonstrated the application of SEM combined with wavelength dispersive x-ray spectroscopy SEM/WDX for detection and analysis of GSR particles from hands, hair, and clothing of a shooter. The authors reported that the method has been implemented in casework.

As mentioned previously, time-of-flight secondary ion mass spectrometry (TOF-SIMS) was studied recently for the analysis of GSR.[67] The method may be used as a complementary technique to SEM/EDX, because it has the capability of depth and trace elements profiling.

Trombka, Schweittzer, Selavka, et al.[78] constructed a breadboard model of a portable XRF system using room-temperature silicon and cadmium–zinc telluride (CZT) detector. This system is similar to those being developed for planetary exploration programs and was aimed to be used in the crime scene for the examination of GSR, blood, and semen. Preliminary experiments were conducted; however, it appears that additional research is needed before the system may be implemented in casework.

Additional techniques that have been studied for GSR analysis are focused ion beam (FIB),[79] Raman microscopy,[80] and laser-induced breakdown spectroscopy (LIBS).[81]

DETECTION AND ANALYSIS OF GUNPOWDER RESIDUES

As discussed in the previous section, SEM/EDX is a well-established method for detection and analysis of GSR (primer residues) on double-sided adhesive-coated aluminum stubs used to sample a suspect, his or her clothing or belongings, and is used by most of the forensic labs in the world. The method, however, has some drawbacks:

1. It is quite slow, even when using an autosearch system.
2. It has a relatively low success rate of detection (about 10%).[31,44]
3. Not all primer residues are considered unique to discharge of firearms.
4. There is a low variability in compositions of primers.

Thus, detection of gunpowder residues on suspects may have an additional evidential value to link them to a firearm-related offence.

Analytical methods for the detection and identification of propellants or their residues are similar to those employed for the analysis of explosives or explosive residues in post-blast samples—for example, gas chromatography/mass spectrometry (GC/MS), gas chromatography/thermal energy analyzer (GC/TEA), or liquid chromatography/mass spectrometry (LC/MS). Numerous studies have been published on the analysis of propellant residues; however, only a few[31,82–84] proposed operational methods (which have also been implemented in casework) for sampling, detection, and identification of these residues on shooters or their clothing.

The amounts of propellant residues that may be left on the shooter's hands several hours after shooting may be very small (usually in the nanogram levels).[31] Thus, the sensitivity of the analytical technique is a crucial factor in its applicability for the detection and identification of the gunpowder residues on suspects of shooting and their clothing.

To the best of the author's knowledge, only two methods have been used operationally for detection and identification of propellant residues on shooters' hands: high performance liquid chromatography with a pendant mercury drop electrode detector (HPLC/PMDE) and GC/TEA because of their high sensitivities (i.e., between tens to hundreds of picograms for NG, 2,4-DNT, and 2,6-DNT). The Forensic Science Service in the United Kingdom employs the same method for sampling and analysis of traces of explosives and gunpowder residues on suspects and their clothing.[31] These residues are recovered from the skin by a swabbing kit (non-woven cotton cloth pre-wetted with a mixed solvent of 80% isopropanol and 20% water). The swabs are used to sample hands, face, and neck of a suspect. In addition, there is a nail scraper and a swab threaded through a comb to sample the hair. Clothing and other items are sampled by vacuum filtration on 1-micron membrane filters. Sample extracts are filtered for GSR (primer) particles and cleaned-up by solid phase extraction (SPE) in a micro-column procedure using Chromosorb 104 as adsorbent. The samples are then analyzed by HPLC/PMDE. In order to properly confirm the identity of a peak from HPLC, it is trapped from the chromatography effluent onto a micro-column of porous polymer using a four-way valve. The trapped HPLC peak is washed from the micro-column and then injected into GC/TEA. The sensitivity of the combined methods corresponds to about 1 nanogram of NG or DNT. In general, the question of which and how many techniques are required for confirmation of identification of an explosives trace is complicated, and there is no single answer.[85] Although comprehensive identification by MS would be a method of choice, it is not sensitive enough in many real-life cases. There seems to be a consensus among experts that at least two orthogonal methods are necessary for this purpose, which is the case for HPLC/PMDE and GC/TEA. A 33% success rate was reported for detection and identification of propellant residues in the United Kingdom during 1991.

It was reported that GC/MS may be sensitive enough for the examination of shooters' clothing.[82]

The swab method to collect primer and gunpowder residues has not been adopted worldwide, in spite of its potentially higher evidential value, and as was pointed out, most forensic labs examine only GSR on double-sided adhesive-coated stubs used for sampling suspects of shooting. It is reasonable to assume that development of an operational method to analyze propellant residues in combination with primer residues on the stubs would encourage at least some of the labs to adopt analysis of both types of residues.

Micellar electrokinetic capillary electrophoresis (MECE) with a diode array UV detector was studied to analyze propellant residues on adhesives. Despite the high discrimination power of the technique, it appears that it is not sensitive enough to be implemented in casework.[86,87] Another disadvantage of the MECE method lies in the fact that the adhesive must undergo preliminary pretreatment (extraction of components that may interfere in the analysis of propellant residues) before its application for collection of GSR and gunpowder residues.

As mentioned in the previous section, a study was conducted[39] to analyze GSR and gunpowder residues from the same sample. In the proposed method, the adhesive tape mounted on the stub is first examined by SEM/EDX for GSR, and after removing the tape from a stub, it is used for the detection of propellant residues by supercritical fluid extraction/gas chromatography (SFE/GC) analysis. The authors claim that several adhesive tapes were studied for that purpose and a tape type was found that made a good compromise between the required properties for SEM/EDX and SFE/GC analyses. Because the study was presented only in the meeting and has not been reported in a peer review publication, it is not clear whether the method was mature enough to be implemented in casework.

In recent years, ion mobility spectrometry (IMS) technology gained a widespread use for the detection of trace explosive evidence because of its portability, good sensitivity (comparable to GC/TEA), reasonable selectivity, and high speed of analysis.[88] The selectivity may be increased by combination of the GC and IMS methods.[89] A method in which the clothing is first sampled by double-sided adhesive for GSR analysis by SEM/EDX, followed by vacuum collection for propellant residue examination by GC/TEA, IMS, and GC/MS was introduced recently into casework in the Israel Police.[84]

More recently, a novel method was reported for extraction and analysis of gunpowder residues on double-sided adhesive-coated stubs after they were examined for GSR by SEM/EDX.[90] Conductive and non-conductive double-sided adhesives were examined and the analysis was carried out by GC/TEA and by IMS. The optimal procedure for the extraction, as was developed in the study, employs two stages:

1. extraction of the stubs with a mixture of 80% v/v aqueous solution of 0.1% w/v of sodium azide and 20% v/v of ethanol employing sonication at 80°C for 15 minutes.
2. The residues from the obtained extract were further extracted with methylene chloride.

The methylene chloride phase was concentrated by evaporation prior to analysis. Extraction efficiencies of 30% to 90% for nitroglycerine (NG) and for 2,4-dinitro toluene (2,4-DNT) were found. No significant interferences in the analysis were observed from the adhesives or skin. Interferences were observed in the analysis by the GC/TEA of the samples collected from hair. When using a high-vacuum SEM, it is imperative to use conductive double-sided adhesives for sampling to avoid carbon coating, which impairs the extraction efficiency tremendously.

Wu, Tong, Yu, et al.[91] reported a novel method for detection and analysis of methyl centralite (MC), one of the possible components in gunpowder, in swabs collected from shooters. The authors claimed that they could detect MC on hands (without washing them) up to eight hours after firing, and after washing them with water up to three hours.

ESTIMATION OF SHOOTING DISTANCE

The range from which a weapon has been fired is an important component in the reconstruction of firearm-related cases (i.e., murder, suicide, or accident). The firing-distance estimation is based on the examination of the appearance of the bullet entrance hole and the examination of FDR patterns around the hole using various techniques. In casework, the patterns obtained in a case are compared to those obtained in test firings. Although many authors in the field use the term *shooting distance determination,* the forensic examiners in the Israel Police prefer to use the term *shooting distance estimation* instead, because of the intrinsic inaccuracy of the examination. The reason for this is a high variability of the FDR patterns from shot to shot when using the same weapon and ammunition. To increase accuracy of the examination, the forensic examiner should use the weapon and ammunition used in the case for test firings whenever possible.

In most of the shooting cases in which there is a need for a firing distance estimation, the victim or the victim's clothing must be examined. In many cases, bullets hit surfaces of various parts of the human body directly without passing through any intermediate medium. In some instances other exhibits such as cars, walls, doors, windows, or furniture that happened to be targets of shooting must be examined. Many of these cannot be processed in the laboratory.

FDR is projected from the muzzle of a firearm in a roughly conical pattern: the larger particles travel higher distances than the smaller particles before they are stopped by the air resistance.[11] Four ranges for shooting distance as described in the literature [92–94] are based on the appearance of the bullet holes on the human body: contact, near contact, intermediate, and distant. In contact wounds, the muzzle of the firearm is held against the surface of the body at the time of discharge. The appearance of tearing, scorching, soot, or the imprint of muzzle characterizes contact wounds. Virtually no FDR is seen around the bullet hole. In near contact wounds, the muzzle of the weapon is few centimeters away from the body. In this case, a wide zone of powder soot overlaying seared blackened skin surrounds the wound. An intermediate range gunshot wound is one in which the muzzle of the firearm is held tens of centimeters away from the body, producing *powder tattooing* of the skin. In distant range gunshot wounds, no damage effects or FDR particle patterns are observed around the gunshot wound. With most handguns, visually detectable FDR is not found in the case of shots fired at ranges greater than 30 cm to 45 cm.[11]

We next review the methods for visual/microscopic, color tests, and instrumental analysis of the entrance bullet holes and FDR patterns around them for shooting distance estimation. Comprehensive treatises on the subject have been published.[92–95] The aspect of shooting distance estimation for targets shot by pellet loads from shotguns may be found elsewhere,[11,92,95] and are not discussed here.

Visual/Microscopic and Color Tests

CLOTHING TARGETS   FDR patterns around the entrance bullet holes consist of propellant and metallic residues from the bullet (e.g., lead and copper) as well as GSR (primer residues). These residues may be detected visually/microscopically if color of the target cloth is bright enough. However, in most cases, there is need for color chemical tests or instrumental analysis to assess the FDR patterns around the entrance bullet holes.

Walker[96] proposed using the Griess reaction to visualize free nitrite ions (on the shot target) originating from the combustion of ester nitrates (i.e., nitrocellulose and nitroglycerine) in the gunpowder. In this test, the Griess reagent, which consists of sulphanilic acid and α-naphthyl amine in acetic acid aqueous solution, is used. The detection of nitrite ions is based on the formation of diazonium ion from sulphanilic acid and nitrite. The diazonium ion couples with α-naphthyl amine to form an orange azo dye. In a series of three papers,[97–99] Dillon reports on the modified Griess test (MGT) as a color test for nitrites and recommends a protocol for FDR examinations in muzzle-to-target distance estimations. In the modified test, Dillon proposes to use α-naphthol instead of α-naphthyl amine (the Walker test) or N-(1-naphthyl)-ethylenediamine dihydrochloride. According to Dillon, both of the replaced reagents are carcinogenic. However, in the literature on chemical safety data,[100] N-(1-naphthyl)-ethylenediamine dihydrochloride is not reported as being carcinogenic. In fact, in Israel, this reagent is used with sulphanilamide routinely for the local MGT.[101] The term *MGT* does not refer to one specific defined test; in fact, it appears that every author who introduces any modification to the original Griess test calls it MGT. The proposed protocol[99] includes visual, microscopic, and chemical (lead and nitrites) tests. It recommends conducting first the MGT and then the sodium rhodizonate test (SRT) for lead, because the rhodizonate is applied directly on the target. Dillon contends that particulate lead is a random non-reproducible phenomenon, whereas the presence of vaporous lead is quite significant in that it is found principally at closer ranges.

Glattstein, Vinokurov, Levin, et al.[101] reported on an improved method for shooting distance estimation on clothing. The novel part of the method includes transfer of total nitrite (nitrite ions and unburned smokeless powder residues) from the target to an adhesive lifter. After the transfer, lead deposits around the bullet entrance hole are partially extracted consecutively to the Benchkote (Whatman) filter papers moistened with dilute acetic acid, and copper deposits around the bullet entrance hole are partially extracted consecutively to the Benchkote (Whatman) filter papers moistened with ammonia solutions. Their patterns are visualized by rhodizonate for lead (red color) and rubeanic acid for copper (dark green color). The MGT

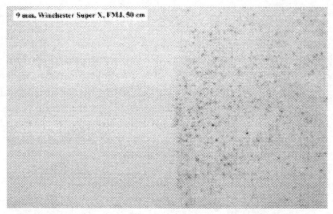

9 mm. Winchester Super X, FMJ, 50 cm

FIGURE 9-16 A test shot on a white cotton cloth; ammunition: 9-mm Winchester super-X FMJ; distance: 50-cm. A color photograph of the target after application of MGT: left half without the hydrolysis prior to MGT; right half with the hydrolysis prior to MGT.

is carried out after alkaline hydrolysis of the smokeless powder residues on the adhesive lifter. The purpose of lifting gunpowder residues from the shot cloth target is to eliminate interferences caused by conducting MGT directly on the target, with or without the hydrolysis step. It was found that an almost complete transfer of gunpowder residues to the adhesive lifter was obtained, and the vaporous lead and copper are not transferred to the adhesive lifter. The widely used MGT detects only free nitrite ions formed from the combustion of smokeless powder; the unburned smokeless powder particles cannot be detected by this method. Alkaline hydrolysis prior to the MGT has been proposed to increase the sensitivity of the test for gunpowder residues. The purpose of the alkaline hydrolysis is to cause a disproportionation of the unburned nitrocellulose and nitroglycerine (the main components of the smokeless powder) to carbonyl compounds and free nitrite ion, thus increasing the available amount of nitrite ions for MGT. The importance of the hydrolysis step in the gunpowder residue visualization is demonstrated in Figure 9-16. As may be seen in this type of ammunition (Winchester Super-X), there is a great difference in the patterns obtained with and without hydrolysis. However, not all ammunition types demonstrate such a difference.

Before beginning the estimation of the shooting distance, it is desirable to determine that the hole is a bullet entrance hole. This can be done by applying methods for chemical visualization of lead (rhodizonate) and copper (rubeanic acid) at the perimeter of the hole[102] (Figures 9-17 and 9-18). From the accumulated experience in the Israel Police, it has been observed that the color tests did not give positive results on all bullet holes in clothing, although it was known that a lead bullet or a full metal jacket (FMJ, brass) bullet was used. Figure 9-19 shows the bullet test kit used by the Israel Police.

A modified sheet printing method for the detection of lead patterns was reported by Stahling.[103] Instead of cellulose hydrate foil, a plastic-based photo-

FIGURE 9-17 Red color obtained with lead deposit at the bullet-hole perimeter by applying sodium rhodizonate test. *(Source: Courtesy of DIFS, Israel Police.)*

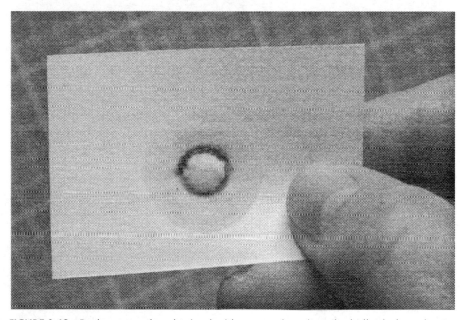

FIGURE 9-18 Dark green color obtained with copper deposit at the bullet-hole perimeter by applying rubeanic acid test. (*Source: Courtesy of DIFS, Israel Police.*)

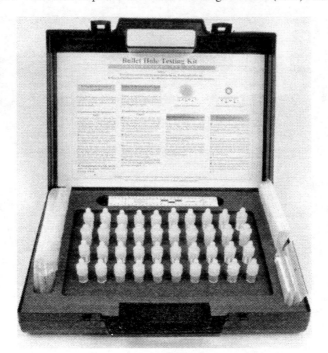

FIGURE 9-19   Bullet Test Kit (BTK) used by DIFS, Israel
Police.   (Source: *Courtesy of DIFS, Israel Police.*)

graphic paper was used as a substrate for transfer of metallic gunshot elements
from cloth.

PERSISTENCE OF FDR ON CLOTHING TARGETS   Several studies dealt with possible
effects of various factors on clothing items after shooting with regard to the shooting
distance estimation,[99,104–108] most of which found that mechanical handling of
clothing or soaking them in blood or in still or running water considerably decreases
the amount of FDR around the bullet entrance holes. Emonet, Bonfanti, and
Gallusser[107] reported that the medical manipulations of clothing lead to an increase
of the loss of visible and nitrated FDR of about 30% to 40%. Even, Bergman,
Springer, et al.,[104] however, did not find a significant effect of soaking in still water
on the obtained FDR patterns. Furthermore, Haag[105] found that a static extraction
procedure utilizing a 12- to 24-hour immersion in an aqueous blood removal solution does not alter the FDR patterns on the shot cloth targets significantly.

Sometimes in casework requests are received to estimate shooting distance on
clothing items that have undergone machine washing. Vinokurov, Zeichner,
Glattstein, et al.[108] conducted a study to assess the effect of machine washing or
brushing of clothing items on FDR patterns around bullet entrance holes. Results
show that those treatments considerably decrease the amount and density of FDR
(machine washing so more than brushing). However, for close shooting distances,
not all of the FDR deposits are removed. Remaining patterns may be visualized by
specific color reactions and used for shooting distance estimation.

EXHIBITS THAT CANNOT BE PROCESSED IN THE LABORATORY   Glattstein, Zeichner, Vinokurov, et al.[109] examined the feasibility of the method developed for clothing[100] described previously for additional materials such as galvanized steel, glass, plywood, and high-pressure laminated plastic sheets of melamine and phenolic materials (Formica™). It was found that for all tested target materials and shooting distances, the amounts and densities of the FDR detected visually (without any treatment) were considerably smaller than those obtained after chemical treatments. Total nitrite patterns visualized on the lifters applied on the various targets were similar to those obtained on the lifters from the cotton cloth at relatively short shooting distances (i.e., up to about 25 cm). As shooting distances become greater, the number and density of nitrite spots on the lifters from all the tested materials targets decreases considerably in comparison to the lifters from the cotton cloth for the same distance; the plywood target showed the most similar results to the cotton cloth.

To improve the accuracy of the shooting distance estimation, test firings should be carried out on target materials as similar as possible to the materials of the examined evidence. If there is no possibility of conducting test firings on a material similar to the evidence, then test firings may be carried out on cotton cloth. In such a case, the visualized pattern of the total nitrite is sufficient to state that the shooting distance on the evidence was equal or below the shooting distance at which similar visualized patterns of the total nitrite are obtained on the cotton cloth.

THE HUMAN BODY AS A TARGET   In many shooting cases, bullets hit surfaces of various parts of the human body (mostly the head) directly, without passage through any intermediate medium. For the purpose of assessing the shooting distance, most of the forensic literature describes only visual/microscopic methods for the examination of appearance of the wound and FDR patterns around it.[92,94,110] Although sodium rhodizonate and rubeanic acid reagents were proposed for the visualization of lead and copper patterns around the gunshot wounds,[111,112] in practice, the author is not aware of any chemical tests conducted on cadavers for the estimation of shooting distance.

As in cases of clothing and other objects, many problems can be encountered when the assessment of shooting distance on cadavers is based merely on visual and microscopic examinations.[92,94,110] The typical problems are as follows:

1. When small-caliber ammunition (short .22 or .32 S&W) is used, the characteristic features of contact gunshot wounds may be absent.
2. Gunpowder tattooing may not be produced on the skin in parts of a body with considerable amounts of hair, and gunpowder particles are difficult to discern.
3. When shots are inflicted through glass panes, glass particles may produce visual patterns similar to the gunpowder tattooing around a gunshot wound.[95,111]
4. The discoloration characteristic of a decomposed body can be similar to the color of soot, and may also mask tattoo marks.
5. In rare instances, insects may produce patterns that resemble gunpowder tattooing on cadavers.

An additional unique problem pertaining only to the human body is that there is no possibility of conducting test firing on the same material, as in the case of other exhibits. The proposed solution for test firings was to use various simulant materials.

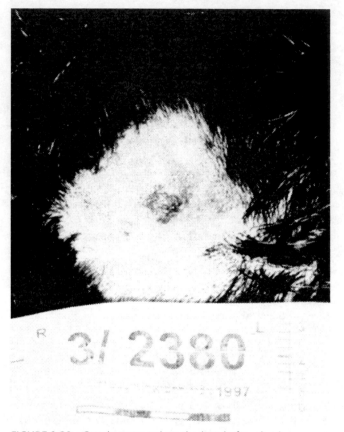

FIGURE 9-20 Gunshot wound on the head after shaving.

Recommendations for those materials were based on the studies comparing those materials to the skin of some animals, such as rabbits or pigs. In a quite exceptional study, Haag and Wolberg[113] conducted experiments on various simulant materials in comparison to a live human skin. The comparison was based on various visual and microscopic characteristics (without chemical treatment) of the FDR on the targets.

Glattstein, Zeichner, Vinokurov, et al.[114] examined the feasibility of applying an adhesive lifter to the entrance bullet wound in human body surfaces to visualize the total nitrite patterns, as was reported for clothing and other exhibits previously. Figures 9-20 and 9-21 demonstrate the applicability of the method in casework: an entrance gunshot wound was found to the left parietal of the cadaver. No gunpowder particles were observed visually on hair before shaving, and no gunpowder tattooing was observed visually after shaving. The total nitrite pattern (Figure 9-20) that was visualized on the adhesive lifter (applied before shaving) indicated a close-shot range.

Stahling and Karlsson[115] reported a similar method for lifting and visualizing gunpowder residues from skin.

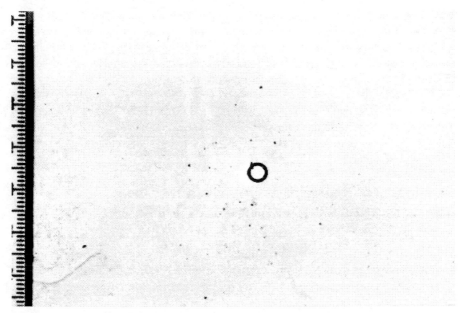

FIGURE 9-21 Visualized total nitrite pattern on the adhesive lifter applied on the hairy area of the wound (before shaving) of the victim in Figure 9-21. The location of the bullet entrance hole is marked with a circle.

INSTRUMENTAL METHODS   FDR patterns around the bullet hole may be visualized by infrared (IR) photography[117] and IR imaging devices[118] because of the considerably higher absorbance of IR radiation by the soot than by other materials, such as fabric. X-ray radiography may also be used for that purpose because of the much higher absorbance of x-radiation by metallic deposits of the FDR than by clothing. X-ray fluorescence (XRF), atomic absorption spectroscopy (AAS), and neutron activation analysis (NAA) have also been used by some laboratories to estimate the range of shooting.[93]

In the past few years, with the advent of the Micro-XRF technology and its increasing use in forensic science for the elemental analysis of trace evidence, some laboratories examined its feasibility for shooting distance estimation.[75,76] Flynn, Stoilovic, Lennard, et al.[75] evaluated the technique for the elemental analysis of GSR and found that micro-XRF can detect GSR particles on the target substrate if the shooting distance is less than 30 cm; they could not detect GSR particles using this technique around the bullet wipe at greater distances. Charpentier and Desrochers[76] used this method to analyze GSR from lead-free ammunition in which the lead in the primer was replaced by strontium and the bullet was plated with copper (TMJ). They found that the technique allows the detection and quantification of strontium residues on the target up to a distance of 45 cm.

Brown et al.[119,120] studied the feasibility of an automated image analysis (IA) technique for shooting distance estimation. In the first study,[119] they developed an IA procedure to measure the amount (number and area) of GSR particles around a gunshot wound. Measurements of GSR from test firings into goat hide were enhanced by using Alizarin Red S to stain the barium and lead components. A comparison was made between the amount of GSR detected on the stained skin sections and backscatter electron micrographs of the same sections, but no significant differences were found between the two. Preliminary results indicated that there was a non-linear decreasing relationship between the firing range and the amount of deposited GSR, and that there was significant variation in the amount of GSR from shot to shot for firing ranges up to 20 cm. The second study[120] was conducted on pig skin with a Ruger .22 semi-automatic rifle with a CCI solid point for shooting ranges between contact and 45 cm.

CHEMICAL ANALYSIS FOR ASSOCIATING FIREARMS AND AMMUNITION WITH GUNSHOT ENTRIES

The most conclusive way to link a fired projectile to a firearm is by identification of the unique markings of the barrel on the projectile. However, quite often in casework, the recovered projectiles are so damaged or disintegrated that the quality of marks (if still identifiable) is not sufficient for comparison. In such cases, it is impossible to achieve a definite linkage. Some level of association may be obtained by comparison of class characteristics such as the caliber or the width of lands and grooves, if this may be assessed from the damaged projectile or its fragments.

There is no method to associate a firearm or ammunition conclusively to a gunshot entry. A class characteristic linkage may be obtained by measuring the diameter of the gunshot entry and by comparing chemical compositions of FDR in the bullet-hole perimeter and around it, FDR in the barrel of the weapon, FDR in the spent cartridge case, and the composition of the fired projectile. Also, unfired ammunition, if apprehended with the suspect, may be analyzed for this purpose. The level of association depends on the rarity of the examined compositions. Analysis of all the components of the FDR (i.e., GSR, propellant residues, and metal particles from a projectile) may serve this purpose.

GSR ANALYSIS   There is little variability in primer compositions used currently for manufacturing various types of ammunition.[4,6,10] Thus, the characteristic GSR composition of the most popular 9-mm caliber ammunitions in Israel is Pb, Sb, and Ba. There are, however, much less frequently encountered ammunitions in Israel, such as SBP (the characteristic GSR composition: Pb, Ca, Ba, Si, and Sn)[56] and Sintox lead-free ammunition (Ti and Zn). If such ammunitions are involved in a shooting case, a higher degree of association may be obtained. The extent of association may be increased further if mixed GSR compositions[58–60] may be found in the compared exhibits.

Samples may be collected from gunshot entries by double-sided adhesive tapes on stubs (used to collect samples from suspects or their clothing), examined by SEM/EDX, and compared to samples collected from the barrel of the suspected firearm and the spent cartridge cases found at the crime scene. Alternatively, the gunshot entry may be cut (if it is in clothing or skin), mounted on a stub, and examined after coating with carbon in the high-vacuum SEM/EDX or without any coating in VPSEM[26] or in ESEM.[27] Micro-XRF may be also used for the analysis,[75,76] but with less accuracy, because its spatial resolution is not sufficient for single particle analysis.

If spent cartridge cases are not found at the scene and no suspected firearm is apprehended, evidence may be obtained from the shooting tests of unfired ammunition, if found in the possession of the suspect.

GUNPOWDER RESIDUE ANALYSIS   Several studies have been conducted for analysis and comparison of unfired and fired propellants. Andrasko[121] used a GC-equipped with a flame ionization detector (FID) and an HPLC equipped with a variable wavelength detector. He reported that the amount of propellant flakes recoverable from clothing (shot from distances shorter than ~50 cm) around the bullet hole was sufficient for the analytical techniques used. A similarity in composition was observed between the propellant particles recovered from the spent cartridges or those recovered from the clothing and the unfired propellant from the same ammunition box. GC and HPLC analyses could distinguish between the gunpowders from different manufacturers; moreover, HPLC analysis was successful in distinguishing between different production lots from the same manufacturer. A similar result was obtained by Wissinger and McCord.[122] Andrasko[121] showed that the composition of subsequent shootings with the same weapon using ammunition from various manufacturers did not indicate any contamination from the propellant flakes from previous shootings.

Several studies [86,87,123–127] used (MECE) for analysis and comparison of fired and unfired propellants. Protocols for the recovery of gunpowder residue components under a variety of sampling conditions were evaluated and improved for MECE analysis. The collection of residue samples where external contaminants such as grease or blood were present on the residue substrate was examined using both tapelifts and solvent–swab protocols.[123] It was found that most common environmental contaminants did not prevent the successful detection of gunpowder residues by MECE. However, the presence of blood was found to be detrimental to MECE analysis, particularly if decomposition had occurred.

Similar to Andrasko,[121] Reardon et al.[124,125] and MacCrehan et al.[126,127] found that compositional analysis of the propellant provides information that can associate residue samples with unfired gunpowder. It was reported that qualitatively identifying and quantitatively determining the additives in gunpowder to calculate a numerical propellant (NG) to stabilizer ratio (P/S) may be a useful index in associating handgun-fired gunpowder residues with unfired powder. In some cases, residues could be differentiated reliably based on P/S and additive identity. Using ammunition loaded with known smokeless powders containing different stabilizers, a sequence of shots was fired from a .357 Magnum revolver and the muzzle exit residues were collected.[126] Compositional analysis of the residues, both in bulk and as single particles, showed only a trace of the previously fired powder in the first shot and none in subsequent shots. These results are similar to those reported by Andrasko.[121] Furthermore, Andrasko[128] reported an attempt to compare the composition of smokeless powder residue collected from inside firearm barrels and that collected from clothing targets. Propellant particles were extracted by methanol and analyzed by HPLC (quantitative comparison) and by GC/MS (qualitative comparison). In most of the test shootings with pistols of 7.65-mm and 9-mm caliber, gunpowder residues suitable for analysis were found inside the barrels. Test shooting with a revolver of .22 caliber only occasionally gave residues suitable for analysis. Similarity was obtained between the composition of gunpowder residues found in the barrel and the composition of the residues on the shot cloth target.

It is apparent that the behavior of gunpowder residues is different from that of GSR (primer residues). As mentioned previously, GSR of mixed compositions are formed when firing different ammunitions from the same firearm.[58–60] Examined propellant residues might, therefore, be more useful than GSR for associating firearms and ammunition with gunshot entries.

ANALYSIS OF PROJECTILES   Elemental composition is a well-established point of comparison for source discrimination for many types of materials that cannot be distinguished based on their physical properties.[129] One application where elemental analysis has been used is the compositional analysis of bullet lead (CABL). In the past, neutron activation analysis (NAA) enabled good discrimination between various lots of bullets.[130] ICP/MS has been used successfully for this purpose, because it is one of the most sensitive methods for elemental analysis.[131–133]

It was shown that there is considerable variability among lead sources despite manufacturers' efforts to control the concentrations of selected elements[129]; therefore, there is a high probability to find different lead compositions from different manufacturers of ammunition. However, in a considerable number of cases very different elemental signatures may be found, even within a single box of bullets in particular regarding trace elements.[133] Randich, Duerfeldt, McLendon, et al.[134] have shown that data for lead alloys supplied to two major ammunition manufacturers confirm that multiple indistinguishable shipments of lead alloys from secondary lead refiners to the ammunition manufacturers are made each year over a period of many years, and that distinguishable compositions can come from the same melt or source of lead alloy. Therefore, they argued that "there is no scientific validity to any conclusions more positive than attributing the possible association as to molten source among bullets from different samples." A similar view was expressed in the report on the subject by the U.S National Academy of Sciences.[135]

In examination of very small bullet fragments found in victim's clothing, the risk of contamination from various sources increases, making the trace element analysis less suitable. In such circumstances, a more suitable method for comparison of small quantities of lead is the determination of lead isotope composition, measured as lead isotope ratio.[136] Lead occurs in nature as a mixture of four stable isotopes. Three of these isotopes, having atomic masses of 206, 207, and 208, are the products of three natural radioactive-decay series. The fourth isotope of atomic mass 204 occurs naturally as a non-radiogenic isotope. There is a relatively large variation in the lead isotopic composition in nature. This fact may be useful for discrimination of various sources of lead in ammunitions. Several technologies were used to measure lead isotope ratio in research and casework for discrimination between ammunitions: thermal ionization mass spectrometry (TIMS), sector field-ICP/MS (SF-ICP/MS), and secondary ionization mass spectrometry (SIMS).[131–133,136–139] A more recent technology of multi-collector ICP/MS (MC-ICP/MS) has been introduced in the field, resulting in better performance, sample throughput, precision, and accuracy with respect to the isotope ratio as compared to the technologies mentioned previously.[140–142] The relative standard deviation (RSD) values obtained by MC-ICP/MS (0.005%–0.02%) are about an order of magnitude better than those for a high-resolution magnetic sector field instrument with a single detector (HR-ICP/MS) (0.05%–0.2%), and up to twenty times better than those for quadrupole ICP/MS (0.1%–0.5%).[143] The levels of analytical precision and accuracy achieved by MC-ICP/MS were comparable to those exhibited by the well-established TIMS technique, which is the traditional method for precise isotope ratio measurements. However, compared to the TIMS technique, the use of MC-ICP/MS for isotope ratio analysis has simplified the analytical procedures considerably for a number of isotopic systems by eliminating tedious sample preparation and reducing the time of the analyses. The use of thallium as an internal standard in lead analysis and subsequent simultaneous measurement of the thallium and lead isotopes enables correction for instrumental isotope fractionation (mass discrimination) in the ICP ion source and takes care of drift, further improving data precision.

It has been shown[144] that various mechanical or chemical methods of cleaning do not completely remove lead deposits (*lead memory*) from barrels of firearms. The implication of this effect is that the lead isotope composition of an FDR deposit collected from a barrel at a certain time is a combination of the lead deposits produced by various firings prior to the sampling. Consequently, this phenomenon lowers the level of association that may be obtained by comparative analysis of lead among a firearm, the fired ammunition, and the gunshot entry in a particular shooting. This is contrary to what was reported for gunpowder residues as discussed in the previous paragraph; nonetheless, it has been shown[144] that analysis of lead isotopic composition may provide valuable evidence in specific scenarios of shooting incidents. For instance, in a shoot-out, where several firearms and ammunitions were involved, it may be necessary to point out which ammunition or firearm caused a particular gunshot entry. This objective may be achieved if the ammunitions involved (bullets and primers) differ considerably in their lead isotopic composition. To obtain the best evidence in casework, all possible involved ammunitions and firearms should be examined in relation to the shot targets, including control test firings.

ESTIMATION OF TIME SINCE DISCHARGE

In a series of papers, Andrasko, Norberg, and Stahling,[145] Andersson and Andrasko,[146] and Andrasko and Stahling[147-149] present a novel method for estimation of time since discharge for some types of weapons and spent cartridge cases. Using solid phase micro-extraction (SPME), samples are taken from the atmosphere inside the barrel of the weapon or the cartridge case and analyzed by GC/TEA, GC/FID, or GC/MS, all of which can detect a variety of combustion products.

Estimation of time since last discharge is based on the escape rate of the volatile discharge residues from the barrel or the cartridge case as a function of time. The method was studied for shotguns, rifles, pistols, revolvers, and spent cartridge cases. The type of ammunition used, the temperature of storage, cleaning of the barrel after shooting, and the number of shots fired can influence the results. Nevertheless, for shotguns, the method could give an indication whether a weapon was fired after a time of, for example, 2 to 3 days, 1 to 2 weeks, or more than 3 weeks previously.[145] In the case of rifles, the produced amount of volatile discharge residues is much smaller than for shotguns, resulting in a reduced accuracy of the results.[148] The volatile compounds escape rapidly from spent cartridge cases, and therefore in these cases an estimation of the time since discharge is generally possible only for a short time after shooting. For shotgun shells and cartridges from sporting rifles, the method can be used for a time period up to about 2 to 3 weeks after shooting. In cartridges from pistols and revolvers, an estimation of the time after discharge was only possible for longer cartridges (magnum type) or small caliber cartridges (.22 inch), and only for a short time after firing (~1-2 weeks).[147] The escape of volatile compounds from pistol and revolver barrels with time is rapid and can generally be measured for only a few days after the latest discharge.[149] Wilson, Tebow, and Moline[150] adopted the SPME method for sampling the volatile product, naphthalene in shotgun shells, and analyzing it by GC/MS. They found that the escape of naphthalene can be measured several weeks after the cartridge has been fired.

References

1. G. M. Wolten, R. S. Nesbitt, A. R. Calloway, G. L. Loper, and P. F. Jones, "Final Report on Particle Analysis for Gunshot Residue Detection," *ATR* 77(7915) 3. (El Segundo, CA: The Aerospace Corporation, 1977).

2. S. S. Krishnan, "Detection of Gunshot Residues: Present Status" in R. Saferstein (ed.) *Forensic Science Handbook* (Upper Saddle River NJ: Prentice-Hall, Inc., 1982).

3. J. I. Thornton, "The Chemistry of Death by Gunshot," *Anal. Chim. Acta.* 288 (1994): 71–81.

4. H. H. Meng and B. Caddy, "Gunshot Residue Analysis-Review," *J. Forensic Sci.* 42 (1997): 553–70.

5. A. J. Schwoeble and D. Exline, *Current Methods in Forensic Gunshot Residue Analysis* (Boca Raton: CRC Press, 2000).

6. F. S. Romolo and P. Margot, "Identification of Gunshot Residue: A Critical Review," *Forensic Sci. Int.* 119 (2001); 195–211.

7. A. Zeichner and B. Glattstein, "Recent Developments in the Methods of Estimating Shooting Distance," *Sci. World J.* (2) 2002: 573–85.

8. A. Zeichner, "Recent Developments in Methods of Chemical Analysis in Investigations of Firearm-Related Events," *Anal. Bional. Chem.* 376 (2003): 1178–91.

9. E. Zadok, G. Hocherman, A. Zeichner, and T. Kahana, *Firearms Report—Speaking Paper 2001–2004.* The 14th Interpol Forensic Science Symposium: Lyon, France 2004.

10. J. S. Wallace, "Chemical Aspects of Firearms Amminition," *AFTE J.* 22 (1990): 364–89.

11. W. F. Rowe, "Firearms Identification" in R. Saferstein (ed). *Forensic Science Handbook* Vol. 2, 2nd ed. (Upper

Saddle River, NJ: Pearson Prentice Hall, 2005).

12. A. Harris, "Analysis of Primer Residue from CCI Blazer Lead Free Ammunition by Scanning Electron Microscopy/Energy Dispersive X-ray," *J. Forensic Sci.* 40 (1995): 27–30.

13. Z. Oomen and S. M. Pierce, "Lead-Free Primer Residues: A Qualitative Characterization of Winchester WinClean, Remington/UMC Leadless, Federal BallisticClean, and Speer Lawman CleanFire Handgun Ammunition," *J. Forensic Sci.* 51 (2006): 509–19.

14. G. M. Wolten and R. S. Nesbitt, "On the Mechanism of Gunshot Residue Particle Formation," *J. Forensic Sci.* 25 (1980): 533–45.

15. S. Basu, "Formation of Gunshot Residues," *J. Forensic Sci.* 27 (1982): 72–91.

16. M. E. Cowan and P. L. Purdon, "A Study of the Paraffin Test," *J. Forensic Sci.* 12 (1967): 19–36.

17. L. Martini and A. DeMaria,"Evaluation of Law enforcement Technologies Inc. ISID01 Instant Shooter ID Kit," *AFTE J.* 34 (2002): 404–06.

18. H. C. Harrison and R. Gilroy, "Firearms Discharge Residues," *J. Forensic Sci.* 4 (1959): 184–99.

19. S. Steffen and L. Niewhoner, "Improved Methods for the Collection of Gunshot Residues (GSR) and for Chemographic Testing of Lead-Free Sintox Ammunition," *AFTE J.* 35 (2003): 152–56

20. R. D. Koons, D. G. Havekost and C. A. Peters, "Determination of Barium in Gunshot Residue Collection Swabs Using Inductively Coupled Plasma-Atomic Emission Spectrometry," *J. Forensic Sci.* 33 (1988): 35–41.

21. R. D. Koons, "Analysis of Gunshot Primer Residue Collection Swabs by Inductively Coupled Plasma–Mass Spectrometry," *J. Forensic Sci.* 43 (1998): 748–54.

22. E. L. T. Reis, J. E. Souza Sarkis, O. N. Neto, C. Rodrigues, M. H. Kakazu, and S.Viebig, "A New Method for Collection and Identification of Gunshot Residues from the Hands of Shooters," *J. Forensic Sci.* 48 (2003): 1269–74.

23. R. L. Singer, D. Davis, and M. M. Houck, "A Survey of Gunshot Residue Analysis Methods," *J. Forensic Sci.* 41 (1996): 195–98.

24. J. I. Goldstein, D. E. Newbury, P. Echlin, D. C. Joy, C. Fiori, and E. Lifshin, *Scanning Electron Microscopy and X-Ray Microanalysis* (New York: Plenum Press, 1984).

25. D. De Gaetano and J. A. Siegel, "Survey of Gunshot Residue Analyses in Forensic Science Laboratories," *J. Forensic Sci.* 35 (1990): 1087–95.

26. A. J. Schwoeble, H. P. Lentz, and K. R. Lee, "Analysis of Gunshot Residue Using Variable Pressure Scanning Electron Microscopy on Samples Collected from Skin, Clothing and Vehicle Interiors," *ICEM* 14, Cancun, Mexico, 1998.

27. V. Mastruko, "Forensic Applications of an ESEM," 8th ENFSI–Firearms Working Group Meeting, Bruges, Belgium, 2001.

28. D. De Gaetano, J. A. Siegel, and K. L. Klomparens, "A Comparison of Three Techniques Developed for Sampling and Analysis of Gunshot Residues by Scanning Electron Microscopy/Energy Dispersive X-Ray Analysis (SEM-EDX)," *J. Forensic Sci.* 37 (1992): 281–300.

29. A. Zeichner, H. A. Foner, M. Dvorachek, P. Bergma, and N. Levin, "Concentration Techniques for the Detection of Gunshot Residues by Scanning Electron Microscopy/Energy Dispersive X-Ray Analysis (SEM/EDX)," *J. Forensic Sci.* 34 (1989): 312–20.

30. H. A. Wrobel, J. J. Millar, and M. Kijek, "Comparison of Properties of Adhesive Tapes, Tabs and Liquids Used for the Collection of Gunshot Residue and Other Trace Materials for SEM Analysis," *J. Forensic Sci.* 43 (1998): 178–81.

31. R. M. King, "The Work of Explosives and Gunshot Residues Unit of the Forensic Science Service (UK)," in J. Yinon (Ed.), *Advances in the Analysis and Detection of Explosives*. Proceedings of the 4th International Symposium on the Analysis and Detection of Explosives, 1992 (Jerusalem, Israel: Kluwer Academic Publishers, 1993), pp. 91–100.

32. A. Zeichner and N. Levin, "Collection Efficiency of Gunshot Residue (GSR) Particles from Hair and Hands Using Double-Side Adhesive Tape," *J. Forensic Sci.* 38 (1993): 571–84.

33. *SEM/MPA Firearms Discharge Residues*, Vols. 1 and 2 (Metropolitan Police Forensic Science Laboratory, London: UK, Nov. 1980).

34. W. L. Tillman, "Automated Gunshot Residue Particle Search and Characterization," *J. Forensic Sci.* 32 (1987): 62–71.

35. D. C. Ward, "Gunshot Residue Collection for Scanning Electron Microscopy," *Scan. Elect. Microsc.*, (1982) part 3: 1031–36.

36. J. S. Wallace and R. H. Keeley, "A Method for Preparing Firearms Residue Samples for Scanning Electron Microscopy," *Scan. Elect. Microsc.*, (1979) part 2: 179–84.

37. E. H. Sild and S. Pausak, "Forensic Applications of SEM/EDX," *Scan. Elect. Microsc.*, (1979) part 2: 185–92.

38. A. Zeichner, "Is There a Real Danger of Concealing Gunshot Residue (GSR) Particles by Skin Debris Using the Tape-Lift Method for Sampling GSR from Hands?" *J. Forensic Sci.* 46 (2001): 1447–55.

39. J. Pukkila and L. Gunaratnam, "The Analysis of Inorganic and Organic GSR's from the Same Sample," IAFS Meeting, LA, 1999.

40. R. H. Schwartz and C. A. Zona, "A Recovery Method for Airborne Gunshot Residue Retained in Human Nasal Mucus," *J. Forensic Sci.* 40 (1995): 659–61.

41. J. Andrasko and S. Petterson, "A Simple Method for Collection of Gunshot Residues from Clothing," *J. Forensic Sci. Soc.* 31 (1991): 321–30.

42. J. W. Kilty, "Activity after Shooting and Its Effect on the Retention of Primer Residues," *J. Forensic Sci.* 20 (1975): 219–30.

43. T. Jalanti, P. Henchoz, A. Galluser, and M. S. Bonfanti, "The Persistence of Gunshot Residue on Shooters' Hands," *Sci. Just.* 39 (1999): 48–52.

44. A. Zeichner and N. Levin, "Casework Experience of GSR Detection in Israel, on Samples from Hands, Hair and Clothing, Using an Autosearch SEM/EDX System," *J. Forensic Sci.* 40 (1995): 1082–85.

45. "Summary of the FBI Laboratory's Gunshot Residue Symposium," May 31–June 3, 2005, *Forensic Sci. Comm.*, Vol. 8, July 2006.

46. D. Chavez, C. Crowe, and L. Franco, "The Retention of Gunshot Residues on Clothing after Laundering," *Int. Assoc. Micro. Anal. (IAMA)*, Vol.2, Issue 1.

47. M. J. Kimmet, "Incidence of Gunshot Residues Transferred to Paper Bag Hand Covers," *Int. Assoc. Micro. Anal. (IAMA)*, Vol. 1, Issue 3.

48. M. Tassa, Y. Leist, and M. Steinberg, "Characterization of Gunshot Residues by X-Ray Diffraction," *J. Forensic Sci.* 27 (1982): 677–83.

49. G. M. Wolten, R. S. Nesbitt, A. R. Calloway, G. L Loper, and P. F. Jones, "Particle Analysis for the Detection of Gunshot Residue. I: Scanning Electron Microscopy/Energy Dispersive X-Ray Characterization of Hard Deposits from Firing," *J. Forensic Sci.* 24 (1979): 409–22.

50. G. M. Wolten, R. S. Nesbitt, A. R. Calloway, and G. L Loper, "Particle Analysis for the Detection of Gunshot Residue. II: Occupational and Environmental Particles," *J. Forensic Sci.* 24 (1979): 423–30.

51. J. S. Wallace and J. McQuillan, "Discharge Residues from Cartridge-Operated Industrial Tools," *J. Forensic Sci. Soc.* 24 (1984): 495–508.

52. P. V. Mosher, M. J. McVicar, E. D. Randall, and E. H. Sild, "Gunshot Similar Particles Produced by Fireworks," *Can. Soc. Forensic Sci.* 31 (1998): 157–68.

53. L. Garofano, M. Capra, F. Ferrari, G. P. Bizzaro, D. DiTullio, M. Dell'Olio, and A. Ghitti, "Gunshot Residue—Further Studies on Particles of Environmental and Occupational Origin," *Forensic Sci. Int.* 103 (1999): 1–21.

54. C. Torre, G. Mattutino, V. Vasino, and C. Robino, "Brake Linings: A Source of Non-GSR Particles Containing Lead, Barium and Antimony," *J. Forensic Sci.* 47 (2002): 494–504.

55. ASTM Committee E-30 on Forensic Sciences. ASTM E 1588–95 (Reapproved 2001), "Standard Guide for Gunshot Residue Analysis by Scanning Electron Microscopy/Energy-Dispersive Spectroscopy," in *Annual Book of ASTM Standards* July (2002);Vol. 14.02.

56. A. Zeichner and N. Levin, "More on the Uniqueness of Gunshot Residue (GSR) Particles," *J. Forensic Sci.* 42 (1997): 1027–28.

57. D. A. Stoney, "What Made Us Ever Think We Could Individualize Using Statistics?" *J. Forensic Sci. Soc.* 31 (1991): 197–99.

58. A. Zeichner, N. Levin, and E. Springer, "GSR Particles Formed by Using Different Types of Ammunition in the Same Firearm," *J. Forensic Sci.* 36 (1991): 1020–26.

59. L. Gunaratnam and K. Himberg, "The Identification of Gunshot Residues Particles from Lead-Free Sintox Ammunition," *J. Forensic Sci.* 39 (1994): 532–36.

60. N. Levin, T. Tsach, P. Bergman, and E. Springer, "A Survey of Titanium and Zinc Particles in Samples Collected from Suspects," Proceedings of the 2nd EAFS Meeting, Cracow, Poland, 2000.

61. A. Zeichner, N. Levin, and M. Dvorachek, "GSR Particles Formed by Using Ammunition Which Has Mercury Fulminate Based Primers," *J. Forensic Sci.* 37 (1992): 1567–73.

62. J. S. Wallace, "Discharge Residue from Mercury Fulminate-Primed Ammunition," *Sci. Just.* 38 (1998): 7–14.

63. A. Zeichner, B. Schecter, and R. Brener, "Antimony Enrichment on the Bullets' Surfaces and the Possibility of Finding It in Gunshot Residue (GSR) of the Ammunition Having Antimony-Free Primers," *J. Forensic Sci.* 43 (1998): 493–501.

64. H. Miyauchi, M. Kumihashi, and T Shibayama, "The Contribution of Trace Elements from Smokeless Powder to Post Firing Residues," *J. Forensic Sci.* 43 (1998): 90–96.

65. J. Lebiedzik and D. L. Johnson, "Handguns and Ammunition Indicators Extracted from the GSR Analysis," *J. Forensic Sci.* 47 (2002): 483–93.

66. J. Coumbaros, K. P. Kirkbride, H. Kobus, and I. Sarvas, "Distribution of Lead and Barium in Gunshot Residue Particles Derived from 0.22 Caliber Rimfire Ammunition," *J. Forensic Sci.* 46 (2001): 1352–57.

67. P. Collins, J. Coumbaros, G. Horsley, B. Lynch, K. P. Kirkbride, W. Skinner, and G. Klass, "Glass-Containing Gunshot Residue Particles: A New Type of Highly Characteristic Particle?" *J. Forensic Sci.* 48 (2003): 538–53.

68. L. Fojtasek, J. Vacinova, P. Kolar, and M. Kotrly, "Distribution of GSR Particles in the Surroundings of Shooting Pistol," *Forensic Sci. Int.* (132) 2003: 99–105.

69. L. Fojtasek and T. Kmjec, "Time Periods of GSR Particles Deposition after Discharge—Final Results," *Forensic Sci. Int.* 153 (2005): 132–35.

70. E. Lindsay and M. J. McVicar, "Passive Exposure and Persistence of Gunshot

Residue on Bystanders to a Shooting: Can a Bystander Be Differentiated from a Shooter Based on GSR?" Joint meeting of the Canadian Society of Forensic Science and the Southern Association of Forensic Science, Mid-Atlantic Association of Forensic Science, and Midwestern Association of Forensic Science, Orlando, Florida, 2004.

71. D. M. Gialamas, E. F Rhodes, and L. A. Sugarman, "Officers, Their Weapons and Their Hands: An Empirical Study of GSR (Gunshot Residue) on the Hands of Non-Shooting Police Officers," *J. Forensic. Sci.* 40 (1995): 1086–89.

72. L. Niewoehner, H. W. Wenz, J. Andrasko, R. Beijer, and L. Gunaratnam, "ENFSI Proficiency Test Program on Identification of GSR by SEM/EDX," *J. Forensic Sci.* 48 (2003): 786–93.

73. L. Niewoehner, J. Andrasko, J. Biegstraaten, L. Gunaratnam, S. Steffen, and S. Uhlig, "Maintenance of the ENFSI Proficiency Test Program on Identification of GSR by SEM/EDX (GSR2003)," *J. Forensic Sci.* 50 (2005).

74. G. Hellmiss, W. Lichtenberg, and M. Weiss, "Investigation of Gunshot Residues by Means of Auger Electron Spectroscopy," *J. Forensic Sci.* 32 (1987): 747–60.

75. J. Flynn, M. Stoilovic, C. Lennard, I. Prior, and H. Kobus, "Evaluation of X-Ray Microfluorescence Spectrometry for the Elemental Analysis of Firearm Discharge Residues," *Forensic Sci. Int.* 97 (1998): 21–36.

76. B. Charpentier and C. Desrochers, "Analysis of Primer Residue from Lead Free Ammunition by X-Ray Microfluorescence," *J. Forensic Sci.* 45 (2000): 447–52.

77. S. Kage, K. Kudo, A. Kaizoji, J. Ryumoto, H. Ikeda, and N. Ikeda, "A Simple Method for Detection of Gunshot Residue Particles from Hands, Hair, Face and Clothing Using Scanning Electron Microscopy/Wavelength Dispersive X-Ray (SEM/WDX)," *J. Forensic Sci.* 46 (2001): 830–34.

78. J. I. Trombka, J. Schweittzer, C. Selavka, M. Dale, N. Gahn, S. Floyd, J. Marie, M. Hobson, J. Zeosky, K. Martin, T. McClannahan, P. Solomon, and E. Gottschang, "Crime Scene Investigations Using Portable, Non-Destructive Space Exploration Technology," *Forensic Sci. Int.* 129 (2002): 1–9.

79. L. Niewoehner and H. W. Wenz, "Applications of Focused Ion Beam Systems in Gunshot Residue Investigation," *J. Forensic Sci.* 44 (1999): 105–09.

80. S Stich, D. Bard, L. Gross, H. W. Wenz, J. Yarwood, and K. Williams, "Raman Microscopic Identification of Gunshot Residues, " *J. Raman Spec.* 29 (1998): 787–90.

81. C. R. Dockery and S. R. Goode, "Laser-Induced Breakdown Spectroscopy for the Detection of Gunshot Residues on Hands of a Shooter," *Appl. Opt.* 42 (2003): 6153–58.

82. S. J. Speers, J. Doolan, J. McQuillan, and J. S. Wallace, "Evaluation of Improved Methods for Recovery and Detection of Organic and Inorganic Cartridge Discharge Residues," *J. Chromatog. A* 674 (1994): 319–27.

83. J. B. F. Lloyd and R. M. King, "One-Pot Processing of Swabs for Organic Explosives and Firearms Residue Traces," *J. Forensic Sci.* 35 (1990): 956–59.

84. A. Zeichner, B. Eldar, B. Glattstein, A. Koffman, T. Tamiri, and D. Muller, "Vacuum Collection of Gunpowder Residues from Clothing Worn by Shooting Suspects, and Their Analysis by GC/TEA, IMS and GC/MS," *J. Forensic Sci,* 48 (2003): 961–72.

85. S. Zitrin, "Recommendations for Combining Techniques to Confirm Identifications," in Proceedings of the Workshop on Explosives Trace Analysis Methods, DERA, UK, April 1999 (S.A. Phillips and R. Hiley, Eds.), *Sci. Just.* (34) 1999: 261–68.

86. D. M. Northrop and W. A. MacCrehan, "Sample Collection, Preparation, and Quantitation in the Micellar Electrokinetic Capillary Eectrophoresis of Gunshot Residues," *J. Liq. Chromatog.* 15 (1992): 1041–63.

87. D. M. Northrop, "Gunshot Residue Analysis by Micellar Electrokinetic Capillary Electrophoresis: Assessment for Application in Casework. Parts I and II," *J. Forensic Sci.* 46 (2001): 549–72.

88. D. D. Fetterolf and T. D. Clark, "Detection of Trace Explosive Evidence by Ion Mobility Spectrometry," *J. Forensic Sci.* 38 (1993): 28–39.

89. F. Kuja, A. Grigoriev, R. Loveless, R. Jackson, and J. S. Nacson, "Applications of GC-IONSCAN M400B for the Determination and Identification of Explosives an Post-Blast Samples," in *Proceedings of the 7th International Symposium on the Analysis and Detection of Explosives, 2001* (A. Cumming, Ed.), Edinburgh, Scotland, 2001; 127–34.

90. A. Zeichner and B. Eldar, "A Novel Method for Extraction and Analysis of Gunpowder Residues on Double-Side Adhesive Coated Stubs," *J. Forensic Sci.* 49 (2004): 1194–1206.

91. Z. Wu, Y. Tong, J. Yu, X. Zhang, C. Yang, C. Pan, X. Deng, Y. Wen, and Y. Xu, "The Utilization of MS–MS Method in Detection of GSRs," *J. Forensic Sci.* 46 (2001): 495–501.

92. K. Sellier, *Shot Range Determination,* Forensic Sci. Prog. 6 (Berlin, Heidelberg: Springer-Verlag, 1991).

93. W. Lichtenberg, "Method for the Determination of Shooting Distance," *Forensic Sci. Rev.* 2 (1990): 38–62.

94. A. Zeichner and D. Glattotoin, "Recent Developments in Methods of Estimating Shooting Distance," *Sci. World J.,* 2 (2002): 573–85.

95. V. G. M. Di Maio, *Gunshot Wounds: Practical Aspects of Firearms, Ballistics and Forensic Techniques* (Boca Raton: CRC Press. 1999).

96. J. T. Walker, "Bullet Holes and Chemical residues in Shooting Cases," *J. Crim. Law and Criminology,* (31) 1940: 497.

97. J. H. Dillon, "The Modified Griess Test: A Chemically Specific Chromophoric Test for Nitrite Compounds in Gunshot Residues," *AFTE J.* (22) 1990: 243–50.

98. J. H. Dillon, "The Sodium Rhodizonate Test: a Chemically Specific Chromophoric Test for Lead in Gunshot Residues," *AFTE J.* 22 (1990): 251–56.

99. J. H. Dillon, "A Protocol for Gunshot Examination in Muzzle to Target Distance Determination," *AFTE J.* 22 (1990): 257–74.

100. R. E. Lenga (ed.), *The Sigma-Aldrich Library of Chemical Safety Data.* (St. Louis: The Aldrich Chemical Co., 1985).

101. B. Glattstein, A. Vinokurov, N. Levin, and A. Zeichner, "Improved Method for Shooting Distance Estimation. Part I. Bullet Holes in Clothing Items," *J. Forensic Sci.* 45 (2000): 801–06.

102. M. Steinberg, Y. Leyst, and M. Tassa, "A New Field Kit for Bullet Hole Identification," *J. Forensic Sci.* 29 (1984): 169–76.

103. S. Stahling, "Modified Sheet Printing Method for the Detection of Lead in Shooting Distance," *J. Forensic Sci.* 44 (1999): 179–81.

104. H. Even, P. Bergman, E. Springer, and A. Klein, "The Effects of Water-Soaking on Firing Distance Estimations," *J. Forensic Sci.* 32 (1988): 319–27.

105. L. C. Haag, (1991) "A Method for Improving the Griess and Sodium Rhodizonate Tests for GSR Patterns on Bloody Garments," *AFTE J.* 23 (1991): 808–15.

106. M. Bonfanti and A. Gallusser, "Problems Encountered in the Detection of Gunshot Residues," *AFTE J.* 27 (1995): 105–22.

107. F. Emonet, M. Bonfanti, and A. Gallusser, "Etude des Phenomes Physique Affectant les Residues de tir et Engenders lors de la Manipulation des Habits par le Personnel Medical," *Can. Soc. Forens. Sci. J.* 32 (1999): 1–13.

108. A. Vinokurov, A. Zeichner, B. Glattstein, N. Levin, A. Koffman, and A. Rozengaten, "Machine Washing or Brushing of Clothing and the Influence on Shooting Distance Estimation," *J. Forensic Sci.* 46 (2001): 928–33.

109. B. Glattstein, A. Zeichner, A. Vinokurov, and E. Shoshani, "Improved Method for Shooting Distance Estimation. Part II. Bullet Holes in Objects That Cannot Be Processed in the Laboratory," *J. Forensic. Sci.* 45 (2000): 1000–08.

110. B. J. Heard, *Handbook of Firearms and Ballistics: Examining and Interpreting Forensic Evidence* (Chicester, West Sussex, England: John Wiley & Sons. 1997).

111. I. C. Stone and C. S. Petty, "Interpretation of Unusual Wounds Caused by Firearms," *J. Forensic Sci.* 36 (1991): 736–40.

112. V. I. Molchanov, V. L. Popov, and K. N. Kalmykov, "Gunshot Wounds and Their Forensic Medicine Examination" (in Russian), (Leningrad: *Meditzina,* 1990).

113. M. Haag and G. Wolberg, "Scientific Examination and Comparison of Skin Simulants for Distance Determination," *AFTE J.* 32 (2000): 136–42.

114. B. Glattstein, A. Zeichner, A. Vinokurov, N. Levin, C. Kugel, and Y. Hiss, "Improved Method for Shooting Distance Estimation. Part III. Bullet Holes in Cadavers," *J. Forensic. Sci.* 45 (2000): 1243–49.

115. S. Stahling, and T. Karlsson, "A Method for Collection of Gunshot Residues from Skin and Other Surfaces," *J. Forensic Sci.* 45 (2000): 1299–1302.

116. Eastman Kodak Company, *Applied Infrared Photography,* Kodak Publication No. M-28 (Rochester, NY: Eastman Kodak Co., 1972).

117. A. Abrink, C. Andersson and A. C. Maehly, "A Video System for the Visualization of Gunpowder Patterns," *J. Forensic Sci.* 29 (1984): 1223–24.

118. I. C. Stone and C. S. Petty, "Examination of Gunshot Residues," *J. Forensic Sci.* 19 (1974): 784–88.

119. H. Brown, D. M. Cauchi, J. L. Holden, H. Wrobel, and S. Cordner, "Image Analysis of Gunshot Residue on Entry Wounds I—The Technique and Preliminary Study," *Forensic Sci. Int.* 100 (1999): 163–77.

120. H. Brown, D. M. Cauchi, J. L. Holden, F. C. L. Allen, S. Cordner, and P. Thatcher, "Image Analysis of Gunshot Residue on Entry Wounds. II—A Statistical Estimation of Firing Range," *Forensic Sci. Int.* 100 (1999): 179–86.

121. J. Andrasko, "Characterization of Smokeless Powder Flakes from Fired Cartridge Cases and from Discharge Patterns on Clothing," *J. Forensic Sci.* 37 (1992): 1030–47.

122. C. E. Wissinger and B. R. McCord, "A Gradient Reversed Phase HPLC Procedure for Smokeless Powder Comparison," *J. Forensic Sci.* 47 (2002): 168–74.

123. W. A. MacCrehan, D. M. Kelly, and W. F. Rowe, "Sampling Protocols for the Detection of Smokeless Powder Residues Using Capillary Electrophoresis," *J. Forensic Sci.* 43 (1998):119–24.

124. M. R. Reardon, W. A. MacCrehan, and W. F. Rowe, "Comparing the Additive Composition of Smokeless Gunpowder and Its Hand-Gun Fired Residues," *J. Forensic Sci.* 45 (2000): 1232–38.

125. M. R. Reardon, and W. A. MacCrehan, "Developing a Quantitative Extraction Technique for Determining the Organic Additives in Smokeless Handgun Powder," *J. Forensic Sci.* 46 (2001): 802–07.

126. W. A. MacCrehan, E. R. Patierno, D. L. Duewer, and M. R. Reardon, "Investigating the Effect of Changing Ammunition on the Composition of Organic Additives in Gunshot Residue (OGSR)," *J. Forensic Sci.* 46 (2001): 57–62.

127. W. A. MacCrehan, M. R. Reardon, and D. L Duewer, "Associating Gunpowder and Residues from Commercial Ammunition Using Compositional Analysis," *J. Forensic Sci.* 47 (2002): 260–66.

128. J. Andrasko, "Analysis of Smokeless Powder from Inside of Firearm Barrels and a Comparison with Grains of Smokeless Powder from Clothing," ENFSI Proficiency Test Meeting, Copenhagen, Denmark, 2006.

129. R. D. Koons, and D. M. Grant, "Compositional Variation in Bullet Lead Manufacture," *J. Forensic Sci.* 47 (2002): 950–58.

130. H. R. Lukens, H. L. Schlesinger, V. P. Guinn, and R. P. Hackelman, "Forensic Neutron Activation Analysis of Bullet-Lead Specimens," USAEC Report GA-10141, Gulf General Atomic Incorporated, San Diego, 1970.

131. Y. Suzuki, and Y. Marumo, "Determination of Trace Impurities in Lead Shotgun Pellets by ICP-MS," *Anal. Sci.* 12 (1996): 129–32.

132. T. Dufosse and P. Touron, "Comparison of Bullet Alloys by Chemical Analysis: Use of ICP-MS Method," *Forensic Sci. Int.* 91 (1998): 197–206.

133. R. O. Keto, "Analysis and Comparison of Bullet Leads by Inductively-Coupled Plasma Mass Spectrometry," *J. Forensic Sci.* 44 (1999): 1020–26.

134. E. Randich, W. Duerfeldt, W. McLendon, and W. Tobin,"A Metallurgical Review of the Interpretation of Bullet Lead Compositional Analysis," *Forensic Sci. Int.* 127 (2002): 174–91.

135. The U.S. National Academy of Sciences Report *Forensic Analysis; Weighing Bullet Lead Evidence* (Washington DC: The Naval Academies Press, 2004).

136. J. Andrasko, I. Kopp, A. Abrink, and T. Skiold, "Measurement of Lead Isotope Ratio in Lead Smears and Bullet Fragments and Its Application to Firearm Investigations," *J. Forensic Sci.* 38 (1993): 1161–17.

137. G. W. Stupian, N. A. Ives, N. Marquez, and B. A. Morgan, "The Application of Lead Isotope Analysis to Bullet Individualization in Two Homicides," *J. Forensic Sci.* 46 (2001): 1342–51.

138. P. Cheylan, A. M. Dobney, W. Wiarda, R. Beijer, and G. J. Q. Peijl, "Fundamental Processes in GSR Formation as Deduced from ICP-AES and SF-ICPMS Experiments," AAFS Meeting, Atlanta, Georgia, 2002

139. B. I. Gulson, J. C. Eames, and J. D. Davis, "Evaluation of Exhibits from a Murder Case Using the Lead Isotope Method and Scanning Electron Microscopy," *J. Forensic Sci.* 47 (2002): 1015–21.

140. A. J. Walder and P. A. Freedman, "Isotope Ratio Measurements Using a Double Focusing Magnetic Sector Mass Analyzer with ICP as Ion Source," *J. Anal. At. Spectrom.* 7 (1992): 571–75.

141. J. Hoogerwerff, "Nite-Crime Thematic Network: Natural Isotopes and Trace Elements in Criminalistics and Environmental Forensics," Proceedings of the 2nd Meeting of the EAFS, Cracow, Poland, 2000.

142. I. Plazner, S. Ehrlich, and L. Halicz, "Isotope-Ratio Measurements of Lead in NIST Standard Reference Materials by Multiple-Collector Inductively Coupled Plasma Mass Spectrometry," *Fresenius J. Anal. Chem.* 370 (2001): 624–28.

143. K. G. Heumann, "Precision and Accuracy in Isotope Ratio Measurements by Plasma Source Mass Spectrometry," *J. Anal. At. Spectrom.* 13 (1998): 1001–08.

144. A. Zeichner, S. Ehrlich, E. Shoshani, and L. Halich, "Application of Lead Isotope Analysis in Shooting Incident Investigations," *Forensic Sci. Int.* 158 (2006): 52–64.

145. J. Andrasko, T. Norberg, and S. Stahling, "Time Since Discharge of Shotguns," *J. Forensic Sci.* 43 (1998): 1005–15

146. C. Andersson and J. Andrasko, "A Novel Application of Time Since the Latest Discharge of a Shotgun in a Suspect Murder," *J. Forensic Sci.* 44 (1999):179–81.

147. J. Andrasko and S. Stahling, "Time Since Discharge of Spent Cartridges," *J. Forensic Sci.* 44 (1999): 487–95.

148. J. Andrasko and S. Stahling, "Time Since Discharge of Rifles," *J. Forensic Sci.* 45 (2000): 1250–55

149. J. Andrasko and S. Stahling, "Time Since Discharge of Pistols and Revolvers," *J. Forensic Sci.* 48 (2003): 307–11.

150. J. D. Wilson, D. Tebow, and K. W. Moline, "Time Since Discharge of Shotgun Shells," *J. Forensic Sci.* 48 (2003): 1298–1301.

Index

■ ■ ■

Note: Page numbers in italics indicate figures or tables.

4-methylenedixoxymethamphetamine (MDMA), 361